10 0295953 8

UNIVERSITY OF NOTTINGHAM
WITHDRAWN
FROM THE LIBRARY

DATE DUE FOR RETURN

UNIVERSITY LIBRARY

 3 0 JUN 2014 A

OWL HALL 13

The loan period may be shortened if the

D1512906

BATMAN (1989).

HISTORY OF THE AMERICAN CINEMA

CHARLES HARPOLE, GENERAL EDITOR

10
A NEW POT OF GOLD: HOLLYWOOD UNDER THE ELECTRONIC RAINBOW, 1980-1989

Stephen Prince

NOTTINGHAM UNIVERSITY LIBRARY

UNIVERSITY OF CALIFORNIA PRESS

Berkeley · Los Angeles · London

University of California Press
Berkeley and Los Angeles, California

University of California Press, Ltd.
London, England

Credits and permissions can be found on pp. 489–490 and should
be considered an extension of the copyright page.

Copyright © 2000 by Stephen Prince

All rights reserved. No part of this book may be reproduced or transmitted in
any form or by any means, electronic or mechanical, including photocopying,
recording, or any information storage and retrieval system, without permission
in writing from the Publisher.

Published by arrangement with Charles Scribner's Sons
An Imprint of the Gale Group

First Paperback Printing 2002

Library of Congress Cataloging-in-Publication Data

Prince, Stephen, 1955–   100 2959538
    A new pot of gold : Hollywood under the electronic rainbow, 1980–1989 /
Stephen Prince.
        p.   cm. — (History of the American cinema v. 10)
    Originally published: New York : C. Scribner's, 2000.
    Includes bibliographical references and index.
    ISBN 0-520-23266-6 (pbk. : alk. paper)
    1. Motion picture industry—United States—History. 2. Motion picture industry—
Economic aspects—United States. 3. Motion pictures—United States—Distribution.
I. Title. II. Series.

PN1993.5.U6 H55 1994 vol. 10
384'.83'0973—dc21   2001053491

Printed in the United States of America

09 08   07   06   05   04   03   02
    9   8   7   6   5   4   3   2   1

The paper used in this publication meets the minimum
requirements of ANSI/NISO Z39.48-1992 (R 1997)
(*Permanence of Paper*). ⊗

Advisory Board

Coordinator
IAN JARVIE
York University

JOSEPH L. ANDERSON
WGBH, Boston

EILEEN BOWSER
Museum of Modern Art

HENRY S. BREITROSE
Stanford University

PETER J. BUKALSKI
Southern Illinois University at Edwardsville

DONALD CRAFTON
University of Notre Dame

JACK C. ELLIS
Northwestern University

RAYMOND FIELDING
Florida State University

DONALD FREDERICKSEN
Cornell University

RONALD GOTTESMAN
University of Southern California

JOHN G. HANHARDT
Whitney Museum of American Art

LEWIS JACOBS†

RICHARD KOSZARSKI
American Museum of the Moving Image

JOHN B. KUIPER
University of North Texas

DANIEL J. LEAB
Seton Hall University

JAY LEYDA†
New York University

JOHN MERCER
Southern Illinois University at Carbondale

JEAN MITRY†

PETER MORRIS
York University

CHARLES MUSSER
Yale University

JOHN E. O'CONNOR
New Jersey Institute of Technology

EDWARD S. PERRY
Middlebury College

VLADA PETRIC
Harvard University

ROBERT ROSEN
University of California, Los Angeles

THOMAS SCHATZ
University of Texas at Austin

DONALD E. STAPLES
University of North Texas

ALAN WILLIAMS
Rutgers University

The Cinema History Project and the
History of the American Cinema
have been supported by grants from the
National Endowment for the Humanities and the
John and Mary R. Markle Foundation.

For Tami and My Parents

Contributors

SCOTT MACDONALD is Professor of Film Studies and American Literature at Utica College. He has published widely on avant-garde film; his books include *Avant-Garde Film: Motion Studies; Screen Writings: Scripts and Texts by Independent Filmmakers;* and *A Critical Cinema: Interviews with Independent Filmmakers* (3 volumes).

CARL PLANTINGA is Professor of Film at Calvin College. His books are *Rhetoric and Representation in Nonfiction Film* and, as co-editor, *Passionate Views: Film, Cognition, and Emotion.*

STEPHEN PRINCE is Professor of Communication Studies at Virginia Tech. He has written many articles on film theory and criticism, and his books include *Savage Cinema: Sam Peckinpah and the Rise of Ultraviolent Movies; The Warrior's Camera: An Introduction to Film; Visions of Empire: Political Imagery in Contemporary American Film; Sam Peckinpah's* The Wild Bunch; and *Screening Violence.*

JUSTIN WYATT is a Senior Research Analyst at Frank N. Magid Associates, an entertainment marketing and consulting firm. He has taught at the University of Arizona and the University of North Texas. Wyatt is the series editor for *Commerce and Mass Culture* at the University of Minnesota Press and the author of *High Concept: Movies and Marketing in Hollywood* and *Poison.*

Contents

Acknowledgments

Writing a book of this scope is a lengthy undertaking, and the following people were especially helpful in supporting my efforts. At Scribner's, John Fitzpatrick, Jeff Chen, and Mark Gallagher were the best of editors, offering extremely useful suggestions for improving the manuscript and being dedicated to producing the best book possible. They were a delight to work with and took exceptionally good care of this author. I must also thank Charles Harpole for inviting me to undertake this project and helping guide it to completion. For some great conversations along the way, I am indebted to David Cook.

Robert Everett provided invaluable research assistance, doggedly pursuing sources and maintaining a keen interest in the project. At Cineplex-Odeon, Lynette Fernandes kindly extended her help by furnishing photographic skills. David Robert Celletti shared his wealth of historical information about the advent of the laserdisc format.

Theresa Darvalics provided critical manuscript support. The late Mr. Fu was a constant companion while I wrote these chapters, occasionally adding his own input by walking on top of the keyboard. And, finally, thanks to Tami Tomasello, who makes this, and all else, so worthwhile.

Introduction

André Bazin famously queried, What is cinema? Until the 1980s, this was a fairly easy question to answer. A second question—Where is cinema?—was even easier to answer, again until the 1980s. Cinema was what one saw in a theater or, when watching movies in the home, on broadcast television. Cinema was celluloid, and movies were consumed in a restrictive set of locations.

Hollywood was in the movie business. Everyone knew this. Hollywood *was* movies. It was an industry that produced a readily identifiable product. One could study the industry by studying this product and the companies—studios—that produced it. Such study entailed no conceptual ambiguity regarding its object or the parameters that defined the object and the study.

But as of the 1980s, this was no longer true. In that decade the film industry and its product underwent a substantial and far-reaching transformation whose implications are still being worked out a decade later, but whose impetus and whose basic alteration of the industry had become clear by decade's end. As a result of these transformations, Hollywood ceased operating as a film industry, and film stopped being its primary product. Instead of making films, the industry shifted to the production of filmed entertainment, a quite different enterprise that encompassed production and distribution of entertainment in a variety of markets and media. Film both was and was not "filmed entertainment." In the sense that it still was, a viewer might watch RAIDERS OF THE LOST ARK (1981), E.T.: THE EXTRA-TERRESTRIAL (1982), or BACK TO THE FUTURE (1985) in a theater or at home on television. But in the sense that film was not "filmed entertainment," that viewer might also play a "Raiders" video game or enjoy the "E.T." and "Back to the Future" rides at Universal Studios. These latter incarnations of film-derived characters and props generated substantial revenues to the studio from alternative, nontheatrical markets. "Filmed entertainment"—not film—encompassed all such markets and formats.

The studios had product-licensing operations before the 1980s, and home video was introduced in the late 1970s. For decades, broadcast television had been a vital nontheatrical market for Hollywood, and the industry produced television shows. The issue is not whether Hollywood had diversified its operations beyond theatrical productions prior to the 1980s. Clearly, it had. The striking fact about the 1980s, instead, is the proliferation of nontheatrical markets and their effect on the industry and its operations. Before the eighties, home video was a minuscule market. During the eighties, it exploded in size and in the revenues that it generated. Cable television, pay cable, and pay-per-view all joined home video in broadening the venues and formats for production and distribution of filmed entertainment. Given these markets, film could no longer exist as film. Celluloid was confined to the area and arena of theatrical exhibition, and it vanished from the other markets, to be replaced by video. Thus, the industry soon found itself in an odd and ironic position, namely, the business of producing films for expanding video markets. As the markets for film were changing, the production process was transformed. Video and film were interfaced during all of the critical phases of filmmaking, most especially in post-production.

The business of film changed, as did the act and art of filmmaking. So, too, did the viewer's understanding of the question, What is cinema? For viewers in the latter 1980s, the move to video was well established and had altered the aesthetics of the medium. Most people by that time were watching their movies at home on television sets in the form of rented videotapes. In this context they were not exposed to cinema at all, as it had been traditionally understood. The transfer of film from a photographic medium to an electronic signal housed on videotape greatly changed its aesthetic properties. The two media are not interchangeable. The film image and the video image have very different characteristics, but these amounted to subliminal differences—and created subliminal effects—for the home viewer of filmed entertainment. The casual viewer either did not notice the differences or considered them acceptable trade-offs for the comforts of home viewing. Videotape was a low-grade medium that substituted for the luminous beauty of correctly projected film images, but millions of viewers happily accepted these limitations and consented to the reduction of cinema to television that video transfer represented. And for new generations of viewers born or reared in the eighties, film *was* video.

Despite the changes that they posed for its traditional product, the Hollywood industry rushed to exploit the new, alternative venues for film distribution and exhibition. And why not? The industry was in deep crisis as the decade began, and the new distribution and exhibition technologies promised a partial solution in the form of a potentially giant pot of gold that the industry could seize and claim, provided it successfully assimilated and adapted to the challenge of taking film away from its celluloid base and out of the theaters. The story of Hollywood in the 1980s is the story of this adaptation and assimilation and the alteration of its product. These were threshold events that fundamentally altered the nature of the industry.

In light of this transformation, the 1980s stand as a seminal decade. The scale and the legacy of the industry's changes make this decade comparable in significance to the other two transforming events in the history of American film, the coming of sound in the late 1920s and the industry's loss of its theaters in the late 1940s. Each of these earlier events defined a before and an after for the film industry, marked a line of historical transition that differentiated the business in hard and clear terms on either side of the marker. The eighties branded the industry in a comparable fashion, taking it away from film and toward filmed entertainment, changing the corporate structure and affiliations of the companies producing filmed entertainment, and setting the industry on a course toward globalization and a new oligarchy of planetary media titans.

Before the 1980s, the film studios had affiliated with large parent corporations, but these tended to be a diverse group of companies operating diverse business segments. Gulf and Western Industries, which owned Paramount, was the prototype of this old-line conglomeration, with business segments in such far-flung areas as automobile replacement parts, sugar harvesting, and motion pictures. As with the industry's nontheatrical operations, what counts here again is the signal shift of emphasis and scale. The industry remained a subsidiary of parent corporations, but these corporations were no longer the traditional conglomerates. After the completion of a wave of mergers and acquisitions that affected virtually every major studio, the film industry was in the hands of global media and communications giants.

The legacy of the 1980s for the film industry is everywhere visible today. The consolidation of the media and communications industry continued through the 1990s with a series of spectacular mergers that joined media programmers (and the film studios should henceforth be understood in those terms) with strategic distribution venues. To illustrate these continuities, it will be helpful to mention briefly several of their more recent manifestations. Although this book treats the 1980s as a unit of history bounded by a span of ten years, the forces examined herein had not been exhausted or concluded by 1989. The eighties thus cast their shadow across the next decade. In 1994, Sumner Redstone's Viacom bought Paramount Communications for $10 billion and then purchased Blockbuster Entertainment, the national video rental chain of three thousand stores. Michael Wolf, a partner with the entertainment industry consulting firm of Booz, Allen, and Hamilton, stressed that the principle guiding such large-scale mergers is the need to control and exploit the hybrid markets for entertainment programming. "It's more a question of, do you have a whole set of assets that you can use to exploit a product? This is really what's going to differentiate whether or not these mergers are going to succeed: their ability to use scale to get a whole broader set of revenues out of any one brand or product." As a result of Viacom's purchases, it can take a property, such as a popular comic book or film character, and generate revenue streams by marketing it as a movie (Paramount), a cable presentation (Showtime, The Movie Channel), a book (Simon and Schuster), a video rental (Blockbuster), and a theme park ride (Paramount).[2]

Two other strategic mergers in the media industry followed Viacom's acquisitions. In July 1995, the Walt Disney Co. agreed to purchase Capital Cities/ABC for $18.5 billion, merging a huge content provider with a national television network. At the time, this was the second-largest merger in U.S. history. Disney's purchase gained it access to 80 percent of the sports network ESPN, twenty radio stations, eight television stations, a radio network, foreign television operations, seven daily newspapers, thirty-four weekly newspapers, and various special-interest publications (*Women's Wear Daily, Institutional Investor*, the Chilton auto books). Network television represented a scarce mass distribution system. Not counting Fox, owned by Rupert Murdoch's News Corp., which also owned 20th Century–Fox film studio, only three national television networks existed that were unaffiliated with Hollywood studios. Thus, Disney's acquisition of ABC gave it a powerful distribution system for its programming. Warren Buffet, an investor who helped broker the deal, described it as "a merger of the No. 1 content company with the No. 1 distribution company."[3] Access to ESPN was also highly valued by Disney because it would enhance its global reach (70 million homes in 130 countries). So strategic, in fact, was the ESPN acquisition that it was valued at half the Cap Cities/ABC deal's total price.[4]

In September 1995, Time Warner and Turner Broadcasting agreed to combine their operations. Time Warner was already a huge media empire, with operations in film and television production (Warner Bros., HBO) and publishing, and it now gained the Turner assets in film and television production (Castle Rock Entertainment, New Line

Cinema) and television and cable systems (Cable News Network, CNN International, Headline News, TNT, WTBS, and Turner Classic Movies).

In the industry's rush to acquire television and cable distribution systems, not all of the studios were winners. Its Japanese owner, Matsushita, hobbled MCA/Universal's plans for expansion. Matsushita, uninterested in augmenting its media acquisitions, squelched MCA/Universal's proposal to acquire CBS in partnership with ITT. Thus, when Matsushita sold MCA/Universal to Seagram's in 1995, the studio came as a content provider without a national television distribution system. As the media industry redefined itself from the 1980s on, content providers that did not also control distribution systems were at a competitive disadvantage. MCA/Universal was thus in a relatively weakened position, especially in comparison with an empire like Murdoch's News Corp., a combined film, television, and publishing colossus. With its 1996 acquisition of New World Communications, Murdoch's Fox network owned and operated twenty-two stations (nine in top-ten markets), making it the biggest TV station owner in the United States.

These recent developments are latter-day symptoms of the transformational process commenced in the 1980s. Thus, our earlier question—Where is cinema?—has become far more difficult to answer. Filmed entertainment now encompasses multiple modalities, and the traditional format for cinema—the theater—has become a small subset of these interlocking, auxiliary markets. Furthermore, these markets, though subtending film, extend far beyond it. Film production feeds these markets and is a key means of rationalizing their revenue-generating potential. As Booz, Allen, and Hamilton's Michael Wolf noted, "The entertainment business is impacting so many other parts of our economy today. It's driving traffic in fast food chains, it's selling toys, it's selling cars, it's selling sneakers. Consumers are making choices on everything from french fries to pajamas based on entertainment properties."[5] These properties are now also a key means of driving revenues in interactive markets, the newest ones to come into the equation. Since the early 1990s, the major studios have been pushing their filmed entertainment properties into the areas of on-line, Web-based promotional services, CD-ROMs, interactive television, and electronic publishing.[6] This development, too, is a legacy of the eighties, when the majors began their large-scale push to extend film properties beyond theatrical markets and to reorganize their corporate structure and affiliations in order to gain access to and a significant measure of control over multiple distribution systems.

The 1980s thereby set in motion a dynamic that has yet to be arrested and a marketing logic that aimed to produce synergies between film entertainment content across a broad range of product formats and through a diverse set of distribution media. That the industry was successful in achieving these goals, and in reinventing itself, is apparent in the continuing consolidations of the 1990s. To write a history of film in the 1980s is thus to pay witness to the disappearance of the industry that had remained relatively stable for so long, stable both in terms of its product (celluloid film) and its distribution formats (theaters and broadcast television). It requires writing about much that can no longer be construed as theatrical motion pictures. It means tracing the assimilation of the Hollywood industry into the larger media and communications industry of which it is now so irrevocably a part.

The most spectacular changes in eighties Hollywood occurred within the business structure of the industry. But important developments also occurred in the films that the industry produced and in the filmmakers who made them and in their place in the production process. The 1980s were a vital decade for American cinema but a paradoxical one, and one that has given rise to some critical misapprehension. As is generally known, the films of Steven Spielberg, George Lucas, and the filmmakers who worked under their production supervision assumed a commercially dominant position within the industry and in the popular culture that the movies spawned. Lucas's second two install-ments of his STAR WARS series were released during the decade, as were Spielberg's sec-ond two Indiana Jones films and E.T.: THE EXTRA-TERRESTRIAL. These pictures had a major effect on the industry because of the huge revenues they generated and the ways in which these returns validated an effects-driven, fast-paced, and emotionally uncom-plicated style of blockbuster filmmaking. Furthermore, Spielberg and Lucas extended the influence of this filmic model through the extensive production supervision they exerted on the works and careers of other filmmakers.

One cannot discount their influence, but it tends to be overstated. Critics frequently dismiss the films of the 1980s as being symptoms of (a) the Spielberg-Lucas model of filmmaking or (b) Reaganesque political culture, and critical commentary frequently intertwines the two sets of symptoms. Discussing Spielberg-Lucas films, for example, Peter Biskind remarks, "By attacking irony, critical thinking, self-consciousness, by pit-ting heart against head, they did their share in helping to reduce an entire culture to childishness, and in so doing helped prepare the ground for the growth of the right."[7]

This is a tall order for movies to fill, especially when one considers that Ronald Reagan's 1980 presidential victory represented the outcome of successful conservative political organizing that had been gaining momentum for the previous fifteen years. It was this organizing and a general cultural turn away from the liberalism of the 1960s, not the films of Spielberg-Lucas, that gave President Reagan the opportunity for a two-term presidency. That presidency helped to set a moral and ideological temper for the eighties; films participated in that process, but not in a unidimensional fashion. Much writing about the era's films, though, has tended to reduce them to a set of ideological symptoms. William Palmer, for example, claims, "The victory of the Reagan agenda changed everything in America and by as early as 1982 had also changed the very nature of Hollywood films."[8] This kind of sweeping statement holds great temptation for schol-ars and critics. It is rhetorically dramatic and claims to explain a great deal. It proposes a model of history that is orderly and tidy—a decade's worth of filmmaking becomes a symptom of some underlying condition, like Reaganism or blockbusters. By contrast, I suggest that a properly nuanced history of American filmmaking in the period is less tidy and less orderly. It is not so easy to find a core set of characteristics unifying the hun-dreds of productions in a range of genres that appealed to greatly differing audiences. These chapters, therefore, address a paradox. From an economic standpoint, a relative-ly clear history of the medium can be assembled, with a chronology of factors, some of which can be assigned causative roles, others reactive ones. From a cultural and aes- thetic standpoint, however, heterodoxy is the norm—a profusion of styles and subjects— tied to the medium's conditions of popularity, its need to appeal to diverse audiences. While some of these films are reducible to a deductive framework (e.g., RAMBO [1985] as a symptom of Reagan-era politics, or the high-concept formula of TOP GUN [1986] as a symptom of its box-office aspirations), many others are not.

In contrast to Biskind, Palmer, and others, therefore, my description and analysis of 1980s filmmaking is much less apocalyptic. The danger in writing about the films of Spielberg-Lucas, and about the connections between film and eighties society, lies in over-stating their effects. This is an understandable temptation, given the frenetic publicity that surrounded their films and the media discourse that a popular president helped generate. As I show in these chapters, neither tendency—of identifying eighties production primarily with Spielberg-Lucas or with Reagan or Reaganism—is appropriate. My analysis thus eschews several ideas that have become part of the "received wisdom" of eighties Hollywood. Blockbuster films did not take over the industry. Bad films (however one conceives them—as blockbusters, special effects showcases, teen comedies) did not drive out good films. Special effects extravaganzas did not vitiate good writing. While there is much irrationality, crassness, and timidity in the business, the market did what it does best—it insured that a wide range of films were available for the nation's moviegoers. Film is a popular medium—that has always been its great strength—and the vitality of eighties filmmaking generated pictures for mass market audiences (TOP GUN) as well as niche audiences (MATEWAN [1987], DINER [1982]), films calculated for a maximum box-office gross as well as those with little commercial potential (MISHIMA [1985], THE LAST TEMPTATION OF CHRIST [1988]).

This diversity was a function of old and new factors. The old factors were inherent in the eclectic audiences that Hollywood aimed to reach and that could not be reliably found through any single category of film or ideological formula. The new factors were the alternative distribution media that matured during the decade. These gave rise to a huge boom by mid-decade in the production and distribution of feature films, and with the consequent upturn in production came a broadening range of film styles and directorial voices. Any decade that sees filmmakers as diverse as Spike Lee, Oliver Stone, Tim Burton, Joe Dante, Barry Levinson, and Lawrence Kasdan establish major careers cannot be under the sway of a single style or prescription for filmmaking. It just ain't so.

Furthermore, to contend that Hollywood production was symptomatic in any fundamental way of Reaganism (however that is construed) is to miss one of the most remarkable facets of the industry's cultural history during the period. Rather than placidly churning out films that manifested some dominant ideology, Hollywood itself was attacked by a range of critics and special interest groups that deemed the industry's products to be unacceptably lewd, bigoted, or sacrilegious. The controversies that erupted over such pictures as CRUISING (1980), DRESSED TO KILL (1980), SCARFACE (1983), THE LAST TEMPTATION OF CHRIST, and slasher horror pictures were intense, bitterly fought contests that showed how volatile the era's cultural politics were and how troubled and problematic was the connection between these politics and Hollywood film. An important characteristic of these culture wars is that they are not reducible to any single political agenda. The political Right as well as the Left attacked the industry and its films, and this phenomenon attests to the industry's troubled connections with American society. The conflicts pitted Hollywood, as the perceived enemy, against a variety of groups united in their hostility to its products.

I raise these issues in order to question the presumption that 1980s Hollywood and its films can be defined in terms of some fundamental schema, like blockbuster production or Reagan-era conservative politics. Obviously, Spielberg and Lucas are of tremendous significance for the period's film, and they get extended treatment in Chapter 6. Equally important are the ways in which Hollywood cinema adjusted itself to the rightward drift of national politics. Productions like RAMBO, TOP GUN, and RED DAWN (1984) are explicit manifestations of the Reagan administration's political tropes and fixations. The industry understood that the Reagan election presaged a more conservative era. Jack Valenti, president of the Motion Picture Association of America

(MPAA), was an essential intermediary between the industry, its public, and official Washington. His rhetoric about the political and moral orientation of the industry and its films shifted from the late 1960s to the 1980s in order to stay in harmony with changing sociopolitical mores. In the late 1960s, for example, the MPAA spearheaded new freedoms for filmmakers and the easing of content restrictions governing sex, violence, and profanity.[9] Valenti defended the new and explicit sex and violence of late-sixties films. Testifying on 19 December 1968, before the National Commission on the Causes and Prevention of Violence, which had been convened in part because of the new levels of violence in film, he informed the commission's members:

> There is a new breed of filmmaker. And mark you well this new filmmaker, because he's an extraordinary fellow. He's young. He's sensitive. He's dedicated. He's reaching out for new dimensions of expression. And he is not bound—not bound—by the conventions of a conformist past. I happen to think that's good.[10]

By 1980 Valenti had changed his outlook. Responding to a ratings controversy in which the MPAA required that Brian De Palma delete some of the violence from DRESSED TO KILL in order to win an R rating, rather than an X, Valenti justified the MPAA's action as being responsive to the times. He now repudiated the type of filmmaker he had earlier defended. "The political climate in this country is shifting to the right, and that means more conservative attitudes toward sex and violence. But a lot of creative people are still living in the world of revolution."[11]

As Valenti's remarks indicated, and as the foregoing discussion has tried to show, the Hollywood industry has never assumed a single or simple relationship with its public. It has made films of varied political stripes and social outlooks, and I have tried to capture this richness in the chapters that are devoted to the films and filmmakers of the period. If we move past the received critical wisdom on eighties Hollywood, we see instead a volatile era, volatile in terms of the industry's restructuring and reorganization and in terms of the connections and relationships between its products and the society that alternately assimilated and attacked them.

This volume proceeds from an economic and industrial analysis to an aesthetic one. I first cover the business of film in the 1980s before proceeding to a discussion of the films that were produced and the people who made them. The initial chapters examine the industry's restructuring, the factors that motivated it, and the outcome of this process by decade's end. Chapter 1 provides the baseline for measurement. It profiles the major studios as they were structured at the dawn of the decade, just before the big changes that lay ahead. It will be essential for the reader to grasp this profile because it illuminates how substantive were the subsequent corporate changes of ownership and operation. The industry in 1980 certainly did not represent an old, classical Hollywood, but in many key respects it did represent a manner of doing business that was even then being superseded. The chapter closes by examining two events that were symptomatic of the emerging new alignments of power in the industry. These were the cable wars between HBO and the studios and the crisis of funding and production control represented by UA's HEAVEN'S GATE (1980) disaster.

In chapter 2, I examine the most striking development in the industry's business history during the decade, the extended program of mergers and acquisitions that saw nearly every major studio change its corporate owner and, in the process, become absorbed in the global communications industry. The merger mania that redefined the studios was itself a subset of larger structural changes in the U.S. economy. This merger-and-acquisitions activity was not unique to the Hollywood industry. Hollywood was participating in a national economic trend that affected a large range of American businesses, not just film. But a series of industry-specific factors combined to make the studios attractive targets for acquisitions; the chapter explores the importance of these factors. The merger wave that hit Hollywood in the 1980s, then, was simultaneously a subset of national economic forces and the result of efforts to exploit new revenue streams offered by emerging nontheatrical distribution technologies. Contrary to predictions at the time, these technologies did not kill or harm the theatrical venue for film exhibition, and the chapter examines the continuing vitality of the nation's movie theaters during the period.

In chapter 3, I explore the place and significance of the auxiliary distribution technologies and their ancillary markets in the new Hollywood. These included cable television, pay cable, pay-per-view, and home video; the last of these, home video, would prove to be the most important for altering the public's viewing habits and general relationship with film and the size and nature of the revenue streams returned to the studios. In some respects, this was not the industry's preferred course of events. The studios were keen on the potential of pay-per-view for becoming the dominant nontheatrical revenue source. Pay-per-view enabled the studios to charge a fee based on each viewing of a film. Viewers would not own the film but merely pay for the privilege of seeing it, much as they had always done with theatrical screenings. Under these terms, the studios would retain control over their product and could generate revenue from every viewing of that product.

But pay-per-view never caught on in a big way, and the studios instead confronted the disturbing prospects represented by home video. Once they sold a tape to a national wholesaler (who in turn would sell to retailers), the studios derived no further revenue from the rental of that tape by consumers. Furthermore, the studios lost a large measure of control over their films because viewers could watch films multiple times (by re-renting them) without paying additional revenues to the studios. Viewers could even tape their own copies of favorite films, a prospect that gave Hollywood executives nightmares. Thus, the studios regarded the home video phenomenon with great ambivalence. The rental market wasn't a bonanza for them. Even as they struggled to come to terms with video, it made substantial inroads into the production process, affecting filmmaking in each of the three critical phases of pre-production, production, and post-production.

An important development in eighties Hollywood, and one much related to the ancillary markets, was the enhanced opportunities for independent film production and distribution. Some independents operated as small-scale funders and distributors of film, but others aspired to mini-major status, undertaking slates of expensively budgeted pictures and negotiating distribution arrangements with major studios. These mini-major aspirants included Carolco Pictures, the Cannon Group, and De Laurentiis Entertainment Group. Chapter 4 (by Justin Wyatt) examines the growth of these companies, the pictures they produced and distributed, and the inflationary problems in the industry that they (like the majors) confronted and that frequently foredoomed their ambitious plans for company expansion.

In American cinema's classical period, from the 1930s to the 1950s, the Hollywood studios maintained repositories of in-house talent—directors, writers, stars—as well as technical departments, such as costuming and art direction. They thus commanded the requisite talent and resources for film production. By contrast, no studio in the 1980s maintained such an array of production personnel and resources. The tradition of placing talent under long-term studio contract had been eroded in previous decades. The studios functioned as funding agencies, producers and distributors of films, and to carry out these operations they required, as ever, talent. But to get the talent, they had to deal with powerful agencies that had assembled the creative personnel under their aegis. The most powerful of these talent agencies were Creative Artists Agency, William Morris, and International Creative Management. In chapter 5, I explore the role of these firms as talent brokers, fostering film production and maintaining a close relationship with the major studios while simultaneously defending and safeguarding their niche on the industry landscape. CAA's head, Michael Ovitz, became one of Hollywood's mythic figures, and the saga of CAA's rise to prominence was one of the industry's legendary success stories.

Chapter 6 shifts the volume's coverage from issues of business to those of aesthetics. In this chapter I examine the careers and output of the decade's major filmmakers and producers and stress the wide range of styles and sensibilities evident in their films. The 1980s were a very good decade for American film. The pictures produced have an invigorating energy and ambition, and the industry was able to negotiate the talents of a highly disparate group of filmmakers. Enduring alliances of individual directors with specific cinematographers, production designers, editors, and composers sustained clear creative profiles throughout the decade's filmmaking as well as a high level of cinematic accomplishment. While a number of prominent seventies auteurs (Martin Scorsese, Robert Altman, Arthur Penn) had a difficult time sustaining their careers in the eighties, other fine filmmakers worked regularly and steadily throughout the period, and a group of important new filmmakers established major careers.

Because the industry produces a relatively large number of films in a given year and because what many people enjoy about the medium is the repetition of character and story situations, much film production occurs within genres or as part of a cycle of films addressing a given topic. In chapter 7, I examine the era's significant genres and production cycles. The status of the industry's enduring genres—fantasy and science fiction, horror, Westerns, musicals, and comedy—is profiled through a discussion of the key films produced in these genres and their evolution in the period. Some of the decade's most important technological developments—in the areas of sound and special effects—occurred in conjunction with the fantasy/science fiction genre, and I assess those in this context. The industry's continued investment in traditional genres helped stabilize relations with the public, and toward this end, traditional American film genres enjoyed great vitality and popularity during the period. Outside the boundaries of genre, American film responded to the ideological and sociocultural issues of the period. Cycles of production—interrelated films clustered about particular issues—coalesced around the era's new cold war, the revolutionary conflicts in Central America, the Vietnam War and its legacy, and the ailing urban infrastructure. A variety of political perspectives, from Left to Right, informed these productions, a feature that demonstrates the ideological flexibility of eighties cinema. In these cycles of topical production, American film alternately endorsed and criticized the White House's domestic and foreign policies.

The political volatility of the 1980s was nowhere more apparent than in the protracted culture wars among competing groups on the political Right and the Left, with agendas about how the nation should conduct itself in such areas as religion, the arts, and morality. Inevitably, film became entangled in these controversies, and Hollywood's products antagonized various groups across the political spectrum. These groups found the content of many of the industry's films to be morally objectionable, and they waged campaigns of vigorous protest against individual films or entire production cycles. In chapter 8, I examine these controversies. The protests centered on depictions of violence, sexuality, and religion in Hollywood film as well as the burgeoning adult film industry, which had modeled itself on Hollywood and whose products came to influence mainstream filmmaking. These culture wars were extremely costly for Hollywood. They helped erode the film industry's moral capital, and they alienated substantial segments of the public from the Hollywood community and its products. As with the industry's economic restructuring, their effects would continue to be felt throughout the next decade. Thus the discussion of production cycles in chapter 7 examines how Hollywood responded to its period, while chapter 9 examines how the period responded to Hollywood and its films.

Chapters 9 and 10 extend the volume's coverage of American film to essential areas outside of mainstream commercial production. Chapter 9 (by Carl Plantinga) profiles the developments in documentary film made possible by changes in its mechanisms of funding and distribution and by the readiness of many documentary filmmakers to formulate responses to the conservative politics of the Reagan presidency. Chapter 10 (by Scott MacDonald) offers a detailed survey of avant-garde filmmaking during the period. MacDonald covers the careers of established filmmakers as well as important new talents debuting during the decade. Viewers and critics have tended to equate American film with the commercial narrative cinema. These chapters demonstrate how partial is that view and how vital are these noncommercial, nonnarrative forms.

Examining the transformation of the American film industry and its products in the 1980s raises a fundamental question. Was the industry better off at decade's end, and into the 1990s, as a result of its consolidation and redefinition? Had the changes improved its fiscal health? For reasons that I explain in the text, assessing the economic health of the industry is difficult. Determining the profitability of a given film can be an elusive undertaking because so many revenue sources figure into this determination and because films are long-lived assets. The studios amortize their production expenses over many years, and a popular film's earnings potential can last as long. (Amortization is a process of gradual debt reduction through regular payments of a portion of the principal plus interest.) These factors make it difficult to find the breakeven point on a production, especially given the presence of gross profit participants (directors, stars, or producers who take a percentage of the box-office return) and the extraction by the distributor of a hefty fee for service. These factors greatly impede a film's earnings potential.

On the one hand, during the 1980s the industry found new revenue sources that were capable of generating more monies across interlocking markets than ever before. On the other hand, the costs of producing and marketing a film exploded in the 1980s, rising to an average of $32 million in 1989. (These costs had reached $76 million in 1998.)[12] The industry's operating margins throughout the 1980s were below those of 1974–79, and its compound annual growth rate from 1984–88 was only 14 percent.[13] Many of the mergers and acquisitions traced in chapter 2 left as their legacy a mountain of long-term corporate debt. Jonathan Dolgen, of Viacom's Paramount studio, pointed to the daunting fiscal realities faced by a company in the business of funding film production: "The fundamentals of the content business are high overhead, high risk, and low margins."[14]

Booz, Allen, and Hamilton's Michael Wolf stressed, "It's no longer sufficient to make a great movie and have it do well at the box office. You've got to be able to exploit every piece of revenue that you possibly can because the cost of creating and marketing the product is so great."[15]

The story of Hollywood in the 1980s, then, is not a story of how the ancillary markets and new distribution technologies saved the industry. If anything, it is a story of delayed and deferred crisis. The new markets and technologies helped the industry stave off the insoluble economic contradictions that it faced then and that it continues to face now. The costs of doing business were soaring; revenue returns were diminished at multiple points by profit participants and by the support personnel required for distribution, marketing, and exhibition; and the business was chronically hit-driven. Only a few pictures made the money, while the rest faced, at best, a long-term and often partial recovery of production costs in the ancillaries. The Hollywood industry bought time in the 1980s, but the economics of its operation remained wasteful and counterproductive to its long-term health. The industry found refuge under its electronic rainbow at decade's end, but the storm clouds of ruinous costs and low margins remained ominously overhead.

1

The Industry at the Dawn of the Decade

As the 1980s began, the Hollywood industry was poised for five straight years of record box-office returns. Industry grosses climbed steadily, from $2.8 billion in 1980 to $4 billion in 1984, before dipping 7 percent to $3.8 billion in 1985.[1] While the studios celebrated this record-setting influx of money as the sign of a robust industry capable of generating ever-increasing business, the grosses provided an incomplete portrait of the industry's performance. Gross data made for compelling publicity and little else. Despite each year's inflated figures, national ticket sales had remained relatively flat, at the 1 billion mark, since 1969.[2] Furthermore, the box-office records of 1980–84 accompanied a steady rise in ticket prices from a national average of $2.69 in 1980 to $3.36 in 1984. With relatively flat sales, the rise in ticket prices helped fuel the box-office records. Table 1.1 summarizes these trends, showing the decade's domestic box-office performance. Chart 1.1 visualizes the disparity between ticket sales and yearly grosses.

Box-office grosses are epiphenomena of the industry, unreliable measures of its health, despite the hoopla they receive in popular media, which track film performance like a horse race to see which title is "winning," that is, which has the biggest gross. National box office might be booming, but Hollywood faced a decade of extraordinary challenge in which the conduct of business as usual would entail certain ruin. Any major that ignored the signposts of change that were everywhere apparent in 1980 would not stay in the game. Change was the watchword in 1980, and the CEOs of the major studios understood that the next several years would be crucial determinants of their firms' abilities to prosper in what would be a new industry with new markets and new products. Yearly box-office grosses, therefore, provided at best a snapshot portrait of the industry, freezing its extraordinary fluidity and openness to change into one moment in time epitomized by a dollar figure that was itself a poor summary of industry performance.

The keys to understanding the industry at the dawn of the decade lie in recognizing this readiness for change and the economic problems and challenges that elicited it. The industry embraced change because it had to. Serious impediments to its continued well-being mandated swift, sweeping, and flexible responses. The welfare of the Hollywood industry would be tested by its ability to survive, and indeed to master, a complex set of institutional, economic, and technological factors that would transform the business as

Table 1.1
Domestic Box-Office Performance

Year	Gross ($billions)	Ticket Sales (billions)	Average Ticket Price
1980	2.8	1.02	$2.69
1981	3.0	1.07	$2.78
1982	3.5	1.17	$2.94
1983	3.8	1.19	$3.15
1984	4.0	1.19	$3.36
1985	3.8	1.06	$3.55
1986	3.8	1.02	$3.71
1987	4.3	1.09	$3.90
1988	4.5	1.08	$4.11
1989	5.0	1.26	$3.99

Source: MPAA, *1996 U.S. Economic Review.*

Chart 1.1
Box-Office Performance

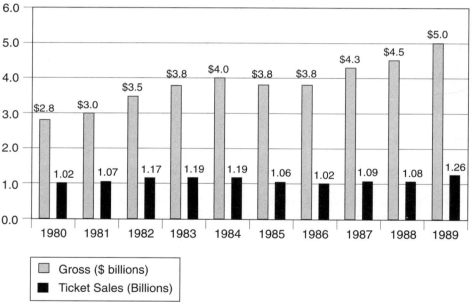

Source: MPAA, *1996 U.S. Economic Review.*

nothing had since the 1947 consent decrees and the appearance of television. From an industry standpoint, the story of the 1980s is the exciting chronicle of a business reinventing itself to accommodate new delivery systems for its products. As a result of these changes, the industry's corporate structure was vastly different by decade's end, as was its definition of the product it produced. Film ceased to be primarily a theatrical medium, based in celluloid. It assumed a variety of alternative and more potentially profitable storage and retrieval formats, including videotape, laserdisc, and satellite transmission to the homes of prepaid cable subscribers. In this new context, movies took their place as one "software" stream among others (e.g., books, magazines, recorded music, television programming) merchandised by global media companies who viewed their marketplace as the planet itself. Thus, on a variety of measures Hollywood entered a period of tumult in which the roiling changes were like a fermentation process, producing a more refined and powerful industry once it subsided.

Outwardly, though, to its theatergoing public, the industry gave few signs that anything was changing. Certainly, the films that Hollywood made in the initial years of the decade held few clues to the industry's mutation. Surveying the big moneymakers, a casual observer might conclude that Hollywood was engaged in business as usual. (Appendix 2 shows the decade's top box-office films.) The biggest moneymaker in 1980 was the second installment of George Lucas's STAR WARS trilogy, THE EMPIRE STRIKES BACK, which returned $120 million to its distributor, Universal, helping to ensure that Universal would have the year's top studio market share. (Revenues returned to a major studio distributor are known as rentals. These are distinct from the box-office gross, which designates the total monies collected from ticket sales. As I will explain later, grosses are subject to deductions taken by several parties. The gross, minus these deductions, yields the rental.) EMPIRE was such a stand-out box-office leader that year that its closest competitor, KRAMER VS. KRAMER, a drama about a marital breakup starring Dustin Hoffman, returned just half as much ($60 million) to its distributor, Columbia Pictures. Both of these films offer normative, highly conventional narratives and emotional rewards, giving moviegoers the kind of excitement and sentiment they had come to look for in Hollywood products.

The other pictures in the top ten that year were from solidly traditional genres, primarily comedy (THE JERK, AIRPLANE, SMOKEY AND THE BANDIT, PRIVATE BENJAMIN, THE BLUES BROTHERS) but including also horror (THE SHINING) and the biopic (COAL MINER'S DAUGHTER). Another George Lucas production, RAIDERS OF THE LOST ARK, dominated the box office in 1981, returning $90 million to its distributor. Fantasy-adventure held a strong appeal for the nation's moviegoers that year. Along with RAIDERS, the top ten included SUPERMAN II and the James Bond thriller FOR YOUR EYES ONLY, both of which were sequels and entries in highly popular franchise series. As in the previous year, though, comedy was the primary genre represented in the top ten films of 1981 (and RAIDERS and SUPERMAN II both have strong comic elements). STIR CRAZY, 9 TO 5, STRIPES, ANY WHICH WAY YOU CAN, ARTHUR, THE CANNONBALL RUN, and FOUR SEASONS were showcase comic vehicles for such popular personalities as Richard Pryor, Gene Wilder, Dolly Parton, Lily Tomlin, Bill Murray, Clint Eastwood, Dudley Moore, Burt Reynolds, and Alan Alda.

In 1982, Steven Spielberg's E.T.: THE EXTRA-TERRESTRIAL was the number one hit, returning $187 million to its euphoric distributor, Universal Pictures. Filling out the top ten that year were sequels (ROCKY III, STAR TREK II: THE WRATH OF KHAN, fantasy-horror (POLTERGEIST), comedies (PORKY'S, THE BEST LITTLE WHOREHOUSE IN TEXAS), melodramas (ON GOLDEN POND, AN OFFICER AND A GENTLEMAN), a musical (ANNIE), and a dark horse candidate (CHARIOTS OF FIRE). Nothing much was different the next year. In 1983, the top ten were nearly all either fantasies (RETURN OF THE JEDI, the year's leader with $165 million in rentals, WARGAMES, SUPERMAN III, OCTOPUSSY) or comedies (TOOTSIE, TRADING PLACES, MR. MOM). The remainder were musicals (FLASHDANCE, STAYIN' ALIVE) and comedy-dramas (48 HRS.).

*The enduring popularity of characters like James Bond
helped the industry maintain the continuity of its product
lines during a period of change and evolution. Roger Moore
returned as Agent 007 in FOR YOUR EYES ONLY, one of the
best of the Bond pictures in which he starred.*

The industry's top theatrical products in the early years of the decade make the business seem essentially unchanged. The product lines are very traditional. Hollywood's moneymakers fall cleanly into established genres whose story lines offer viewers the pleasures of repetition and familiarity. Moreover, the top films tended to be showcases for such popular stars as Harrison Ford, Dustin Hoffman, John Travolta, Clint Eastwood, and Roger Moore, or for such filmmaker stars as Steven Spielberg and George Lucas. Furthermore, the studio distributors of these pictures were old, familiar names (Columbia, Universal, Warners). Some of these were subsidiaries of parent corporations, but the ownership patterns that persisted until the 1980s were relatively stable ones. Thus, to a casual viewer, Hollywood seemed to show few signs of what was to come.

Before I detail the problems and the challenges that the industry faced, it will be helpful to see where the studios were as business enterprises when the decade began, because the corporate playing field and the players would change drastically and at an accelerating pace. Across the 1980s few majors maintained a continuity of corporate identity and business portfolio. What follows, therefore, is a brief profile of the

Hollywood majors at the dawn of the decade. The reader will wish to keep this profile in mind as the zero point against which the changes discussed in the next two chapters should be measured. This profile shows (a) that the majors had already achieved a significant degree of entertainment market integration (e.g., activities in film, music, and video) by 1980; (b) that this integration was accompanied by a maladaptive, old-fashioned style of conglomerated business structure; and (c) that the majors were cognizant that a sweeping technological revolution lay just ahead, though they could not yet envision its shape, outcome, or effects.

20TH CENTURY–FOX

Fox was a stand-alone company in 1980. It was unaffiliated with a parent corporation, and its corporate structure was somewhat less complicated as a result. Its operations fell into two major business segments, Fox Entertainment and Fox Enterprises. Fox Entertainment included (a) production and distribution of movies and television; (b) telecommunications, focusing on the home video market; (c) lab processing of film by Deluxe General, Inc., a Fox subsidiary; and (d) record and music publishing. Fox Enterprises consisted of (a) soft drink bottling through its operation of a territorial franchise, Coca-Cola Bottling Midwest, Inc.; (b) television broadcasting via three VHF stations in Minneapolis/St. Paul, Salt Lake City, and San Antonio; and (c) luxury resort operations through the Aspen Skiing and Pebble Beach Corporations. In addition to Fox Entertainment and Fox Enterprises, the company also had overseas theater operations (seventy-six theaters in Australia and twenty-eight in New Zealand).

This portfolio of operations is significant in several respects. First, it shows that Fox, although a relatively small enterprise, had already begun to diversify its filmed entertainment operations into key areas that would be crucial to industry expansion in the 1980s, namely, those alternatives to theatrical exhibition represented by home video. Second, although Fox stayed out of the mid-decade rush into theater ownership by the majors, it already had exhibition operations when the decade began. Fox's broadcast television operations produced relatively small revenues in comparison to its filmed-entertainment segment, which generated the lion's share of company revenues. (Table 1.2 shows Fox's 1980 revenues by industry segment.) Its recorded-music operations were folded within the filmed-entertainment segment, which also included Fox's production of television programming. (In 1980 Fox produced four primetime network series: "M°A°S°H," "Trapper John, M.D.," "Breaking Away," and "Ladies Man.")

TABLE 1.2
20th Century–Fox Business Segment Revenues

	($THOUSANDS)
Filmed Entertainment	581,913
Soft Drink Bottling	106,136
International Theatres	71,563
Resort and Recreation	48,663
Television Broadcasting	38,983

SOURCE: Fox Annual Report 1980.

*Bob Fosse's ALL THAT JAZZ, with Roy Scheider as a worka-
holic choreographer, was an early success for 20th
Century–Fox in the new market of home video.*

Fox recognized the future trend lines. Its fastest-growing segment was the Telecommunications Division, focused on home video; company CEO Alan J. Hirschfield
foresaw markets in this area "entering a period of unique and extraordinary change and
growth."[3] Fox had moved quickly to gain leverage here. In 1979, Fox acquired
Magnetic Video Corp. to generate earnings from the newly developing home video
market. In 1980, Fox's ALIEN and ALL THAT JAZZ videocassettes set million-dollar
sales records, and Magnetic Video Corp. released 9 TO 5 and THE STUNT MAN only
ninety days after completion of their first-run theatrical engagements. Shrewdly anticipating events in the course of the decade, Fox noted the burgeoning growth of the
home video market, predicting that demands for "software" here would only increase.
This area would thus remain of key importance for the company. CEO Hirschfield concluded, "It is expected that consumer demand will continue to increase and that this
ancillary market for filmed entertainment will generate a significant portion of future
revenues."[4]

Fox distributed fifteen films in the theatrical market during 1980, the most significant of which, THE EMPIRE STRIKES BACK, provided the single biggest chunk of the

$474 million revenue earned by Fox motion pictures in 1980.[5] Other Fox pictures that year included BRUBAKER, MY BODYGUARD, ALL THAT JAZZ, THE ROSE, and 9 TO 5. Film entertainment revenue alone accounted for a 23 percent increase in the company's operating revenue over 1979, a dramatic illustration of the importance for a studio of having a year's leading blockbuster as well as robust videotape sales.

Fox, therefore, was fairly well positioned to maneuver in relation to developments in the home video market. But in other respects, the company was maladapted for the challenges of the 1980s. Revenues from soft drink bottling operations were the company's second largest by industry segment, but these operations represented unnecessary diversification. Most critically, unlike the operations in recorded music and home video, which could be synergistic with theatrical film, soft drink bottling would not enhance film entertainment revenues. Thus it was an area of operation fundamentally unrelated to Fox's main enterprise, film. The same problem was apparent in Fox's resort operations. The Pebble Beach Corp., operating a luxury resort and golf courses, and Aspen Skiing Corp., with four ski areas in Colorado, were leisure-time businesses, but they offered no synergies for filmed entertainment. Taken in the context of 1980s industry developments, they represented an unproductive scattering of Fox's resources, and they gave the company an unattractively diffuse corporate portfolio. Thus, they were quick to go on the auction block, along with the soft drink bottling operations, following Marvin Davis's purchase of Fox in 1981. In sum, Fox, like the other majors, was uncertainly poised for new directions on the threshold of the eighties. The company was an ambiguous mix of forward-looking film entertainment businesses and diffuse nonfilm operations housed within an old-line conglomerate structure.

COLUMBIA

Columbia was a stand-alone company at the beginning of the decade, and its subsequent corporate history, with acquisitions first by Coke and then by Sony, was among the liveliest of the majors in this period. As a stand-alone company, it saw somewhat smaller revenues from its operations than did either Warners or Universal. Columbia's total 1980 revenues were $692 million, whereas their filmed-entertainment and music operations alone generated $1.5 billion for Warners and $953 million for Universal. But Columbia's theatrical film business looked good in 1980, producing record levels of income ($314 million worldwide, a 29 percent increase over 1979).[6] Much of this was attributable to the performance of its hit film, KRAMER VS. KRAMER ($94 million worldwide and the number two film in the domestic market). Other pictures released by Columbia that year included THE ELECTRIC HORSEMAN, a Robert Redford vehicle, and the Neil Simon comedy CHAPTER TWO.

As an independent company, Columbia was modestly diversified, especially in comparison to Warner Bros.' place in Warner Communications' array of product lines or Universal's in MCA's portfolio of activities. Columbia's main business was the production and distribution of theatrical films, but it was also heavily involved in television production and syndication. Columbia Pictures Television saw 1980 revenues of $182 million, up 30 percent over 1979. Among the shows it produced were "Fantasy Island," "Police Story," and the popular soaps "Days of Our Lives" and "The Young and the Restless." Columbia Pictures Television Distribution placed in syndication "The Flintstones," "WKRP in Cincinnati," "Charlie's Angels," and "Bewitched." Through its subsidiary

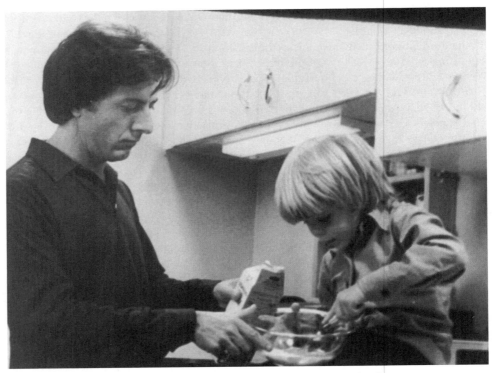

The robust box office of KRAMER VS. KRAMER *in 1981 helped Columbia Pictures secure a record level or revenue from its theatrical film business, even though the scale of its earnings was small compared with Paramount and other majors.*

EUE/Screen Gems, Columbia produced television commercials for clients including Ford, Sears, General Motors, NBC, and Chevrolet.

Like the other majors, Columbia was beginning to explore the market for home video. Columbia Pictures Home Entertainment completed its first year of operation in 1980, releasing twenty-four pictures on video, with another sixty scheduled for release in 1981, including CLOSE ENCOUNTERS OF THE THIRD KIND: THE SPECIAL EDITION and THE CHINA SYNDROME. Columbia had also moved to exploit the pay-cable market, creating Columbia Pictures Pay Television, which in 1980 released THE CHINA SYNDROME, CALIFORNIA SUITE and MIDNIGHT EXPRESS. To realize subsidiary film-related profits, Columbia Pictures Merchandising generated revenue through the licensing of characters from film and television. In addition, Columbia operated an assortment of other businesses, including a pinball game company, five radio stations, and a music publishing company. These areas, however, contributed much smaller revenues than the film and television segments.

Columbia, therefore, was modestly diversified and in sensible directions, with its major operations concentrated in the important markets of film, video and television. These would be the growth areas in the years to come. In contrast with Warner Communications Inc., however, Columbia owned no cable television systems nor any cable programmers like the Movie Channel. In 1980, it attempted to rectify the lack of

of a communications revolution which will bring to consumers an unprecedented variety of relatively inexpensive information and entertainment in the convenience of the home.[9]

In the years to come, WCI would move aggressively to maximize its involvement with these new revenue streams. This required, and produced, a major revamping of WCI's corporate structure and operations, a shift away from consumer electronics and toys and toward filmed entertainment as the key engine driving corporate growth.

UNIVERSAL PICTURES

Universal Theatrical Motion Pictures was a subsidiary of parent corporation MCA, Inc., whose operations were grouped into five business segments.[10] Even more than WCI, MCA's corporate structure exhibited the agglomeration of disparate, loosely related business areas that would make synergy difficult and that the firm's restructuring activities throughout the decade would seek to overcome. In addition to filmed entertainment, MCA's business segments included records and music publishing (primarily on the MCA label and an area of great potential synergy with film), retail and mail order (via Spencer Gifts retail outlets nationwide), financial services (conducted through subsidiaries Columbia Savings and Loan Association and Mid-Continent Computer Services), and other operations. These latter were mostly nonfilm operations, comprising of such disparate enterprises as MCA New Ventures, a minority enterprise small-business investment company; Yosemite Park and Curry Co., providing visitor services in the national park; Womphopper Wagon Works restaurants; Universal Studios Tour and Amphitheatre; MCA Publishing (Putnam); and DiscoVision Assoc., a joint venture with Phillips and IBM to explore an optical videodisc system. MCA's film, book publishing, recorded music, and theme park ventures (in 1981, MCA purchased 423 acres of land in Orlando to be the site for its planned Universal Studios Florida park) were the mutually reinforcing business areas that would become the hubs of the company's restructuring, at the expense of the other, disparate operations.

The filmed-entertainment business sector consisted of the theatrical division, which commanded a 20 percent market share in 1980.[11] MCA was also active in the key areas of pay and cable television. In 1981, MCA joined Time, Inc., and Paramount Pictures as equal partners in a joint venture, USA Cable Network, with over 9 million cable television viewers. USA Cable was designed as an advertiser-supported network carrying sports and entertainment programming, and the partners retained their independent privileges to license films to pay-cable services. For MCA and Paramount, this venture followed their earlier unsuccessful attempt to create Premiere, a national pay-cable competitor with HBO. MCA was also active in production for broadcast television (series production of "Quincy, M.E.," "Magnum, P.I.," "Simon and Simon," and others), in the licensing of characters and logos from films and television for product merchandising via MCA Merchandising, and exploitation of the developing home video market. MCA Videocassette placed eighty titles in release by the end of 1981.

In the early years of the decade, Universal saw year-to-year fluctuations in its theatrical film revenue of amounts approaching $100 million, but this was typical of all the majors, whose theatrical fortunes depended on the number of hits they produced in a given year. Revenue for 1980 of $397 million was up $92 million over 1979 because Universal's product was well represented among the year's biggest-renting films (four

Universal's theatrical earnings soared in 1982 with the release of E.T.: The Extra-Terrestrial.

out of the top ten), though it did not have the year's number one film. In 1981, revenues dropped $84 million, but in 1982, the year of E.T.: The Extra-Terrestrial, they jumped to $608 million, nearly double those of the previous year, giving Universal 30 percent of the domestic film market. Like Warners, Universal was a major contender for theatrical market dominance throughout the 1980s, and its home video and cable television operations positioned it strategically for competition in the ancillary markets. The MCA corporate structure, however, was an awkward mix of unrelated business operations. Filmed entertainment generated the great bulk of corporate revenues, and MCA, like other film company parents, would evolve in that direction during the decade.

Paramount

Paramount Pictures was a subsidiary of Gulf and Western Industries, Inc., which in 1980 was the epitome of a corporate conglomerate. G&W was a diversified, multi-industry company whose operations fell into seven unrelated business segments: a leisure-time group, financial services, manufacturing, apparel and home furnishings, consumer and agricultural products, automotive replacement parts, and natural resources and building products. G&W had sales in 1980 of $5 billion. Revenue from the leisure-time group stood at $1 billion, with theatrical film rentals generating $330 million.[12]

Paramount (housed in the leisure-time segment) released fifteen films domestically in fiscal 1980, including Star Trek, Starting Over, Friday the 13th, and Urban

COWBOY. Paramount Television produced such popular series as "Happy Days," "Laverne and Shirley," "Mork and Mindy," and "Taxi." "Happy Days" went into syndication and helped generate Paramount Television's record 1980 revenue of $224 million. Paramount Home Video, Inc., was formed in 1980 to sell videocassettes to the home video market.

In addition to Paramount Pictures, G&W's leisure-time group also included music publishing (Famous Music Corp.), book publishing (Simon and Schuster), theater operation (the Famous Players circuit in Canada, 386 screens in 266 theaters), and sports entertainment (Madison Square Garden and several horse-racing facilities). Moving into the expanding area of cable programming, G&W, through Madison Square Garden, created a national cable network (USA Network) to carry sports events. Thus, with some exceptions such as the horse-racing operations, the leisure-time group was sensibly diversified along the lines that would be critical for a major's success in the 1980s. Its operations anticipated the mutually reinforcing entertainment synergies (movies, books,

Paramount's URBAN COWBOY, *starring John Travolta, was one of the studio's high-profile releases in 1980.*

music, television programming, home video, cable, and theatrical exhibition) that would
be so important throughout the decade and guide the industry's development.

G&W's other operations, though, ranging among manufacturing, mining, sugar harvesting, and financial services, offered little or no overlap with its leisure-time segment.
Many of these required the maintenance of a heavy-industry infrastructure that the
company was increasingly unwilling to fund, and G&W soon came to regard them as
antiquated operations, as yesterday's businesses, not tomorrow's. The future was in
leisure time, and G&W knew it. Outside the leisure-time segment, G&W was a sprawling entity, with little essential connection among its components. To keep pace with the
evolving communications and entertainment industries, therefore, G&W embarked on
the decade's most striking corporate makeover. It willingly cannibalized itself and permitted the leisure-time group to swallow the corporation.

Metro-Goldwyn-Mayer Film Co.

Among all the major studios, by far the saddest fate befell MGM. It grew sicklier and
more impoverished with each year. By decade's end it was a shell of its former self, so
poor that nobody wanted to buy it, while the other majors were enjoying the fruits of the
industry's reconfiguration. By contrast with this ultimate fate, MGM commenced the
1980s full of hope, as a newly restructured company and one with aggressive ambitions
to expand its share of the film market.

Before January 1980, Metro-Goldwyn-Mayer, Inc. (as it was then called), operated in
two dissimilar business segments, filmed entertainment and hotel and gambling operations. The company produced motion pictures and television programs and also operated
two luxury hotels. These were the MGM Grand Hotel–Las Vegas, a twenty-five-story,
2,076-room hotel and casino, and the MGM Grand Hotel–Reno, a 1,015-room hotel and
casino. Since the mid-1970s, hotel and gambling operations consistently generated
greater revenues for MGM than filmed entertainment. In 1979, for example, film operations saw revenues of $193 million as compared with hotel and gambling's $298 million.[13]
The poor showing of its film operations, relative to hotel and gambling, was a direct result
of the company's decision in the 1970s to withdraw from the film business. Beginning in
1973, MGM had reduced its film production activities. It eliminated its worldwide distribution organization and produced films only on an occasional basis. These two developments were related. By releasing its product through another major, United Artists,
MGM did not need to produce a yearly quota of pictures to feed an in-house distribution
organization. Throughout the 1970s it was an intermittent producer of motion pictures,
and its status as a film major had become degraded.

Because of the disparities between its business segments and its perception that film
production in the 1980s held new opportunities for revenue growth, MGM in 1979
began to study the possibility of divorcing the segments from one another, and the following year it spun off its filmed-entertainment activities. In effect, the company split in
two. In January 1980, the spun-off film operations were incorporated as Metro-
Goldwyn-Mayer Film Co., and on 30 May Metro-Goldwyn-Mayer, Inc., became MGM
Grand Hotels, Inc.

The former MGM had two principal reasons for splitting apart. One was to enable it
to concentrate on its hotel and gambling operations, which had been the company's revenue horse. But the other reason was that new pot of gold which the industry as a whole
was gearing up to secure. MGM planned to expand film production with the goal of pro-

ducing ten to fifteen pictures per year in the 1980s, in comparison to the three to six pictures that it had been producing in the 1970s. Its plans for expanded production were directly tied to the rise of the ancillary markets and to the increasing revenues that top theatrical pictures were earning. MGM saw new opportunities here for reviving its moribund film operations. As management explained in its annual report:

> Among the factors which were considered by MGM when it decided to increase film production were the increased theatrical rentals which have been received on successful pictures in the industry, the improved license fees obtained for both network telecasting and syndication of films to local television stations, and the development of new sources of revenue for film products, including pay television, video cassettes and videodiscs.[14]

To launch its plans for expanded production, however, and to rejuvenate the company as a major studio, MGM confronted some serious problems. One was a problem the entire industry faced—inflation. Because of a substantial industry-wide rise in production costs, MGM implemented a budgetary policy that restricted its production funding to a ceiling of $15 million per picture, with a preferred average in the area of $10 million. These production costs would be competitive with industry averages in the early years of the 1980s. This was, therefore, a sensible and effective policy. Two other problems, though, had more serious consequences: a severe shortage of production capital and the lack of a distribution organization.

MGM "solved" these problems in a manner that placed the company under a crushing debt load for the remainder of the decade and that was a major factor in the repeated attempts of its majority shareholder, Kirk Kerkorian, to dismantle and sell off its assets. MGM increased its revolving line of bank credit to $200 million to finance its expansion of film production. (Studios that have a revolving line of credit may borrow up to a fixed amount within a specified time period, usually a year. As the studio makes payments on principal and interest, it may borrow amounts equal to its repayment.) MGM also borrowed heavily to finance its purchase of a distribution organization. In 1981, MGM purchased United Artists, a major distributor, from its parent company, Transamerica, for $380 million. Transamerica's motive for selling UA was tied to UA's ruinous production of HEAVEN'S GATE; this saga is profiled later in the chapter. Of note is MGM's desperation to regain a distribution organization. MGM's cost for acquiring UA exceeded the net book value of UA's assets by over $243 million, a sum that MGM was willing to amortize over forty years.[15] MGM wanted a distributor badly, so badly that it debt-financed the entire transaction. Under a bank credit agreement, it borrowed $250 million in cash to buy UA and offered a promissory note for the remaining $130 million. MGM was paying a lot and in some ways getting a very bad deal. UA was itself heavily indebted, $200 million worth.

As a result of these activities, tied to its plans to renew itself as a film major, MGM in 1981 had assumed an aggregate long-term debt of $685 million. What is especially striking about this huge figure is its instantaneous appearance. In 1980, MGM's long-term debt was a mere $60 million.[16] In very real terms, MGM was mortgaging its future on a highly speculative plan, namely, that its film production activities would be sufficiently successful to keep it afloat on this ocean of red. Unfortunately, its slate of films scheduled for release in the early 1980s included a line-up of box-office duds: RICH AND FAMOUS; WHOSE LIFE IS IT ANYWAY?; . . . ALL THE MARBLES; CANNERY ROW;

MGM struggled throughout the eighties, and its assets proved to lie not in its contemporary releases but in its vast library of classic films, like GONE WITH THE WIND.

PENNIES FROM HEAVEN; BUDDY, BUDDY; and YES, GIORGIO. MGM's only real asset would prove to be its film library, which included 1,600 of its own features (and what features they were—GONE WITH THE WIND, THE WIZARD OF OZ, BEN-HUR, SINGIN' IN THE RAIN) plus 2,500 pictures for which UA owned distribution rights. These included twelve James Bond features and the Rocky and Pink Panther series. The UA library also included 550 pre-1950 Warner Bros. titles (including CASABLANCA, THE MALTESE FALCON, and THE TREASURE OF THE SIERRA MADRE) and 700 RKO features (including KING KONG and CITIZEN KANE).

Here was the money. The rise of pay cable and home video markets would turn this library into a gold mine, but it would not be enough to salvage MGM. The company's debt-financed plan of expansion was a daring and foolhardy venture. The company could not stay afloat, and even in the merger-and-acquisitions frenzy of the period, MGM had great difficulty attracting buyers. Hardly a prized purchase, MGM's fate in the 1980s was to be cannibalized and dismembered, its assets scattered and sold. From its ambitious start at the beginning of the decade, the company quickly became the industry pauper, passed unwanted from buyer to buyer. Among the majors, MGM was the big loser in the high-stakes game that the industry had entered.

WALT DISNEY PRODUCTIONS

In contrast with MGM, Disney in the 1980s was one of the industry's great success stories. During the latter half of the decade, Disney reemerged as a major force in motion picture entertainment, but at the top of the decade, it seemed directionless and its family films increasingly anachronistic. Disney's share of the theatrical film market in 1980 was a paltry 4 percent, and it saw worldwide film rentals of $161 million, only about half of what the other majors were experiencing.[17] Its 1981 animated feature THE FOX AND THE HOUND generated $28 million in rentals, this during the blockbuster era, when the biggest films could approach or surpass $100 million. In development were several projects that would perform dismally at the box office upon release: TEX (1982), TRON (1982), and SOMETHING WICKED THIS WAY COMES (1983). Disney's film revenues were especially small in comparison with its Disney World and Disneyland theme park revenues ($640 million) and were not much more than the company realized through its Character Merchandising, Records and Music Publishing, and Educational Media divisions ($109 million).

A corporate image study demonstrated that, despite its theme park operations, most people thought of Disney as a producer of motion picture and television programming, yet the income generated by these activities was out of balance with the company's other sectors. Upcoming films would not help much: THE DEVIL AND MAX DEVLON ($6 million in 1981 rentals), DRAGONSLAYER ($6 million in 1981 rentals), and CONDORMAN ($2.5 million in 1981 rentals). POPEYE (1980) earned $24 million, but this was a coproduction with Paramount and incurred a split in rentals between the two distributors. Worse yet, Disney was heavily extended in 1980–82, having committed $800 million to Epcot Center, scheduled to open in 1982. In addition, Tokyo Disneyland was in development for a 1983 opening, and Disney was preparing to launch a pay-cable programming service, the Disney Channel, that same year. The Disney Channel suffered a $28 million operating loss its first year and did not become profitable until the second quarter of 1985.[18]

Disney, therefore, had committed major capital reserves to these theme park and cable ventures, and it could not look to its filmed-entertainment segment for compensatory returns. Film entertainment was failing Disney. It had become a chronic underperformer, and the Disney studio label was synonymous with poor to mediocre box-office performance. In a blockbuster era, when other majors were winning 15–20 percent of the annual market, Disney's films were out of the competition. The company had to increase film revenues, especially given its expensive ventures into cable television and new theme parks. Disney achieved this goal with spectacular success, and it did so, virtually alone among the majors, on its own, without seeking to merge with a giant power in the communications industry. Disney's remarkable success is chronicled in the next chapter. In 1980, though, Disney was barely alive as a major studio.

ORION PICTURES CORP.

Orion was one of the smallest of the industry's major producer-distributors and has sometimes been called a "mini-major." Since it was not a key player in the events covered in the next chapters, it will be helpful to profile Orion in a broader time frame than has been allotted the other majors thus far. The company originated in 1982 from a program of corporate and financial restructuring that was then underway at Filmways, Inc. Filmways had been experiencing severe financial constraints. Its operating loses were substantial, and it could not raise enough capital to finance its production and distribution operations. On 8 February 1982, the company installed new senior management. Arthur Krim, Eric Pleskow, William Bernstein, and Mike Medavoy assumed responsibility for the company's operation. These four had been executives at United Artists. They left UA in 1978 and formed Orion Pictures Company. With their installation as chairman of the board (Krim), president and CEO (Pleskow) and executive vice presidents (Bernstein and Medavoy), Filmways changed its name to Orion Pictures Corp.

Also in February, the company restructured its finances by negotiating a capital infusion of $26 million. The Warburg Pincus Capital Corp. and HBO provided the capital in exchange for newly issued debt and equity securities. Orion also received a new revolving credit line of up to $55 million and formed an extensive pre-sale arrangement with HBO. Orion pledged to license exclusively to HBO all films for which it had the cable and pay-television rights, from February 1982 until January 1985. Just before its restructuring, the company discontinued subsidiary operations so it could concentrate on entertainment programming. Discontinued operations included its publishing business (Grosset and Dunlap), a broadcast equipment manufacturing business, and a paperboard slide mount manufacturing business.

Orion planned to release fourteen to sixteen theatrical films per year. Releases for 1982 included Woody Allen's Broadway Danny Rose; Under Fire, with Nick Nolte and Gene Hackman; and Easy Money, with Rodney Dangerfield. Orion's film library in 1982 included six hundred theatrical and television movies. Recognizing that video and cable markets increased the library's value, Orion engaged independent investment bankers to reassess the library and the company's film distribution operations. As a result, these inventories increased in value by $18 million. Orion, though, moved relatively slowly into these markets. Unlike the other majors, who released films to the video market through their own subsidiaries, Orion licensed home video rights to outside companies, who duplicated and distributed the videos. In 1986, Orion created Orion Home Video to distribute its product to the home markets. Orion also syndicated television programming, some of which had been produced by other companies (e.g., NBC's "Saturday Night Live" episodes from 1975–80).

Compared with other majors, then, Orion was a smaller-scale operation. It remained active in film production and distribution but saw smaller revenues from these in proportion to the other majors. In 1985, for example, Gulf and Western (Paramount) reported revenues from film and television of $916 million, as compared to Orion's $223 million. Unlike the other majors, however, it never claimed the largest share of the theatrical market in any year (see ch. 2, table 2.1). Orion saw its best year in 1987 (thanks to the December 1986 release of Platoon), when its films garnered 10 percent of the domestic market, but this was substantially behind the 20 percent commanded by Paramount as the market leader. In all other years, Orion's share ranged between 1 and 7 percent. Furthermore, Orion escaped the mergers and acquisitions that reshaped the other majors, though it did see substantial stock ownership by Viacom and Metromedia Co. Orion thus remained somewhat on the periphery of those events that were remaking the industry.

Problems and Challenges
Compelling Reorganization

As the preceding survey shows, at the top of the decade many of the major film studios operated as part of a traditionally conglomerated corporate sector that included key, interrelated components (film and television, book publishing, recorded music) as well as unrelated operations (direct-mail marketing, retail gift stores, restaurants, catering services in a national park). By decade's end, this diffuse structure of business activities had been replaced by a tight focus on entertainment and communications operations in which theatrical film was a small but vital component. What changed things? Why did the Hollywood industry, and its parent corporations, shift from an old-line pattern of conglomeration to a tightly focused range of mutually reinforcing entertainment operations?

The majors confronted twin dilemmas. Runaway inflation was devouring their operating capital at the moment when new markets for filmed entertainment were becoming viable. The industry worried over a seemingly uncontrollable rise in film production and marketing costs in the face of a theatrical market that was stagnant, while wrestling with the challenges posed by the new, nontheatrical delivery systems of cable and pay television and home video (cassette and disc), whose precise effect on the industry was as yet unknowable, though everyone realized its scope would be huge. At a minimum, the new delivery systems would change the production, distribution, and consumption of filmed entertainment, and the majors were determined to maintain their accustomed prerogative to control film products and their revenues, whatever the new shapes and formats these might assume.

In 1980, theatrical motion pictures were apparently making more money than anyone dreamed possible just ten years previously. Blockbuster films like THE EMPIRE STRIKES BACK were returning over $100 million in a single year to their distributors. At the same time, though, as I noted at the beginning of the chapter, the theatrical market, measured by ticket sales rather than rental returns, had topped out. Annual ticket sales had remained relatively constant, at around 1 billion, for the past twenty years.[19] Measured in terms of the number of individuals going to the movies, the theatrical market was no longer growing. As Warner Communications, Inc., acknowledged in its 1981 shareholders report, "Although U.S. box office reached a record total of nearly $3 billion, the gain was entirely due to ticket price increases."[20]

The flat theatrical market was especially worrisome and dangerous in the context of the wildly escalating production and marketing costs. These were frightening because they eroded profit taking. Hollywood was not the only industry to face this problem. In the late seventies and early eighties, the U.S. economy as a whole was gripped by recession and inflation. In early 1980, the Consumer Price Index had climbed by nearly 9 percent above its 1975 level, and the economy had seen price increases of almost 40 percent in energy, 16 percent in home prices, and 27 percent in the cost of home financing.[21] By fall of 1982, the national unemployment rate stood at 9.8 percent, and throughout 1981, real disposable income grew less than 2 percent.[22]

The inflationary crisis in Hollywood was a subset of this larger national problem, though it also had its own industry-specific causes. Chief among these was the role assumed by the talent agent and agency in negotiating star and director salaries and offering packages of talent to studios or other funding agencies. The exorbitant salaries paid the industry's top stars were a function of the institutional presence and power of talent agencies and of the willingness of studios to embrace high-cost filmmaking out of a belief that these monies ensured the production values necessary to generate big box office. (Ch. 5, examines the talent agent and the evolution of this industry segment during the decade.)

The price tags attached to big stars and the talent packages marketed by agents were not the only factors driving up production costs. National economic forces also intervened to make production more expensive. In 1980, the Hunt brothers of Texas tried to gain control of the silver market and nearly succeeded. As a result, the price of silver exploded through the roof. In early 1979, silver was priced at $5.40 an ounce; it shot up to $42 an ounce by 14 January 1980. The impact on the film industry was immediate and powerful. Silver halides in color and black-and-white stock register light and form the image on a strip of film. Because it contained these silver halides, the price of raw film stock was responsive to the fluctuations of the silver market. In early January 1980, Eastman Kodak announced large hikes in the price of raw stock, a 45 percent increase for color and a 70 percent increase for black-and-white, which contains a higher concentration of silver.[23] The price hike added approximately $250 to the cost of a release print. For a studio spending $16 million on its theatrical prints, this entailed an additional $4 million to that cost. The release costs of a thousand-print national saturation campaign for a prominent film like STAR TREK would jump a quarter of a million dollars. Peter Myers, senior vice president of domestic distribution for Fox, noted, "Up to now, our only consideration was whether we could afford to go on with the national tv buys required in a mass saturation, assuming that was the only factor because it's so costly. Now, we'd probably have to start taking print costs into consideration as well."[24] Thus, as talent prices were escalating, the studios also faced an unwelcome rise in basic print costs.

These inflationary forces, coupled with the studios' willingness to fund expensive, effects-driven pictures, helped produce the steady escalation in production costs. This ugly trend was one of the decade's most striking features, and it generated considerable anxiety throughout the industry. Chart 1.2 shows the dramatic increase in production costs (known in industry terminology as "negative cost") and the accompanying rise in print and publicity costs. ("Negative cost" designates all of the expenses incurred in a film production prior to release and distribution. These would include the costs of securing the literary property on which the film is based, hiring the talent, constructing sets, operating the camera, etc. "Print cost" designates the expense of manufacturing prints for release to theaters. If a single print costs $2,000, a national saturation release of one thousand prints could cost a studio $2 million in lab fees alone. Publicity for the film would be an additional expense.) In 1979, the average negative cost of a feature was $5 million.[25] In 1980 it jumped to $9 million. In 1981, it reached $11 million, and in 1982 it climbed to $12 million. By 1989, it had soared to $23 million.[26] Advertising and print costs in 1989 averaged $9 million per feature, bringing production and marketing expenses per feature to $32 million, as compared to $13 million in 1980. In its 1980 annual report, 20th Century–Fox observed ominously, "The costs of production and distribution of theatrical motion pictures continue to escalate tremendously," and the studio acknowledged that "the high rates of inflation experienced in recent years have significantly affected the Company's earnings."[27] If adjusted for inflation on a constant-dollar basis, Fox's net earnings for 1980 of $54 million reduced to $33 million. In a similarly sobering tone, Warners explained to its shareholders, "Part of the explanation for the reduction in industry profits in 1980 on essentially flat volume lies in the cost side of the equation. More movies were released in 1980, the average cost of production rose substantially, more money was spent to advertise and promote each picture and thus the industry's profits and return on investment fell sharply."[28]

From December 1980 to September 1981, the majors released 114 films, costing $1.08 billion and returning $1.07 billion in rentals.[29] Thus, returns from domestic box office barely matched production costs. (As we will see, industry financing and distribution practices are considerably more complex than the matching of box-office returns

CHART 1.2

Production, Print, and Publicity Costs ($ millions)

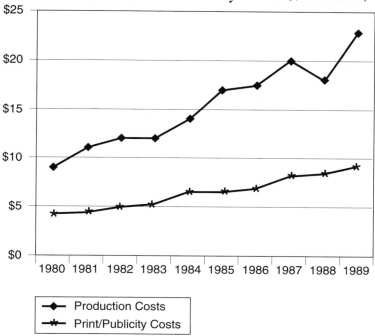

SOURCE: MPAA, *1996 U.S. Economic Review*.

with production costs would imply.) Warner Bros. released 21 pictures, returning $235 million in rentals, but the production costs for this slate of pictures totaled $230 million. Universal released 21 films generating rentals of $155 million, but they cost $210 million. In the worst shape was MGM-UA, releasing 18 films that cost $210 million but that returned only $115 million. The following year, industry-wide domestic rentals increased by 17 percent but the accompanying production costs rose by 19 percent.[30]

Production costs were outpacing the industry's revenues from theatrical exhibition. Returns to the distributor from theatrical exhibition, however, do not in themselves determine a picture's profitability, and it will be helpful here to demonstrate the complexity of industry financing. This complexity makes it difficult to assess the profitability of a given picture and indicates that box-office returns do not map directly onto production costs, though they are, of course, very relevant to those costs. A tangled network of additional factors, beyond box office and production costs, comes into play when assessing profitability, and these are important for the reader to grasp. They include the financing arrangements on a given production, the presence of profit participants, and the multiple points at which the revenue stream from box office is diverted. To minimize their expenses, the major studio-distributors often sought outside investors in production, and the majors were contractually bound to honor the outside or joint investors' claims on exhibition revenues. Such investors, who claim a share of revenue returns based on their initial investments in the production, are one of the two common types of profit participants; the other is the industry talent (a major star or director) who claims a percentage of box-office gross based on the marquee value of his or her name. The rising inflationary costs of the 1980s compelled the studios to look to outside investors as a means of reducing risk and spreading studio capital among a greater range of productions, few of which would be totally funded by studio monies. Financing arrangements often stipulated that outside investors recover their funds as gross profit participants before the distributor would take its cut of returns. In this sense, the gross profit participant is to be distinguished from the net profit participant. The majors are notoriously skilled at claiming losses on popular films when it is in their interest to do so and when the affected party is a net profit participant. Net profit participation (i.e., returns based on revenues left after the distributor, exhibitors, gross profit participants, and the production company take their cuts) is typically a losing bet because net partic- ipants are often last in line. When Art Buchwald filed suit against Paramount Pictures, charging that the film Coming to America (1988) was based on a treatment he wrote but for which he was uncompensated as a net profit participant, the studio demon- strated, through its byzantine bookkeeping practices, that the picture lost money despite its having been the second biggest film of 1988! (The Buchwald case is covered in more detail in Ch. 5.)

In addition to these factors complicating assessments of a film's profitability, which has to be evaluated in relation to gross versus net proceeds and the negotiated splits among the production company, distributor, exhibitor, investors, and profit participants, films are long-lived assets and continue to generate revenue from other, or ancillary, markets after the theatrical distribution window has closed. These ancillary markets grew tremendously in importance during the decade until their revenues outpaced those generated at the theatrical box office. Thus, at a time when production costs were outstripping revenues and when the revenues themselves were hostage to the claims of multiple parties, the ancillaries offered the studios an irresistible opportunity for aug- menting their income. In the ancillaries the studios perceived a significant potential solution to the problem of how to generate sufficient revenues from film production and distribution in a climate of rising costs and increasing profit participation by a range of parties. With uncontrolled inflation in the industry, and with production costs growing at an alarming rate and flattened ticket sales placing a roof on the monies that could be earned from theaters, the industry needed new markets, new venues in which films could be distributed and from which additional revenue streams could be derived.

Hollywood is a business that finds it difficult to make a profit from production under the best of circumstances. Merrill Lynch analyst Harold Vogel has stressed how tough the numbers are.[31] If a major funds twenty productions in a year, budgeted at an aver- age of $15 million with $6 million allocated for print and advertising costs per picture, that studio would have to amortize $420 million in debt over the release cycles of those pictures. If half that cost is allocated for the theatrical release cycle, the distributor must see a return of $210 million. To receive that (assuming the distributor receives 42 per- cent of box office), the box-office gross would need to be $500 million. In 1989, domes- tic box office was $5 billion. Thus, the studio would need a 10 percent market share to *break even* on its production outlay. During the 1980s, only Paramount and Warner Bros. achieved this minimum mark each year. Market share among minor studios rarely hit 10 percent. Chart 1.3 shows how little remains from the box-office dollar to cover print costs and profit. (It will be helpful to explain the terminology used in the chart. The "distribution fee" is a sum levied by the distributor to cover its operating expenses and the maintenance of its home and branch offices. Typically, this ranges between 15

CHART 1.3
How the Box-Office Dollar Is Split

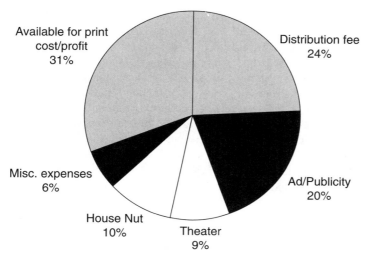

Available for print cost/profit 31%

Distribution fee 24%

Misc. expenses 6%

Ad/Publicity 20%

House Nut 10%

Theater 9%

SOURCE: Harold L. Vogel, *Entertainment Industry Economics*, 2d ed. (New York: Cambridge University Press, 1990).

and 40 percent of gross receipts, less what the exhibitor claims per contract specifications. The "house nut" is a fixed amount of the box-office gross that the exhibitor keeps to cover its operational costs. The chart segment designated "theater" is the remaining amount of the gross kept by the exhibitor [after deducting the nut], as per the contractual terms of the distributor/exhibitor split.)

The picture is even bleaker than the chart indicates. Vogel's display of the data lumps print costs and profit as a single category. In effect, though, "print cost" as Vogel uses it conceals several different categories of expense. Along with the lab costs of duplicating prints and the expense of an advertising campaign, these include the negative cost (i.e., the expense that the production itself has incurred). As I explained earlier, negative cost includes the salaries for everyone from stars to grips and gaffers, as well as the costs of the film stock and all of the resources involved in the production (set design, costuming, etc.). Negative costs can vary wildly depending on the type of production (period films and special effects films are often among the most expensive) and the talent involved. Thus, in Vogel's presentation, the thirty-one cents of the box-office dollar left for this category must be assessed in terms of the negative cost and the claimants to any "profit." It will take much longer for this residual revenue to cover the cost of expensive productions than it will for modestly budgeted pictures. The addition of profit participants further erodes the remaining revenue available for print cost amortization and profit taking by the studio. Participants (e.g., big-name stars) with "points" taken on gross receipts will receive a specified percentage of these off the top. The financing arrangements for a given production may also have stipulated that outside investors, as limited partners, are due a portion of these gross receipts. Thus, the box-office dollar is split into an aggregate of smaller units by the complex nature of film financing and distribution. The remunerative opportunities represented by the ancillaries must be seen in this highly qualified context, one marked by many claimants to the revenue stream produced by film distribution.

As the decade began, the majors had already taken initial steps into video and cable distribution, but important segments of the industry failed to see some of the long-term benefits of these delivery systems. As we will see, they made some foolish decisions. Nevertheless, the new delivery systems would in time rejuvenate film production and strengthen the importance of theatrical exhibition at precisely the moment when it was contributing a diminishing portion of the revenue pie. As WCI explained to its shareholders in 1981, "There is an almost exponential growth in ancillary markets for current feature films and film libraries as well. This growth is the basis for an optimistic view of the long-term prospects for feature films."[32] Other sectors of the industry were also cognizant of the strategic value of these new markets, including the critically important financiers upon whom the studios depended for their capital loans. John Fisher, vice president of the Entertainment Industries Center of Wells Fargo Bank, an important source of industry financing, identified the relevance of new distribution methods for the long-term health of the industry: "A major factor contributing to the growth of entertainment industries in the 1980s will be the revolution in distribution methods which has already begun as a result of the proliferation of television channels made possible by cable, pay TV and advanced electronic systems such as satellite communications."[33] These technologies and distribution venues, he predicted, could be expected to have a favorable effect on the industry by creating an expansion of demand for film product in the 1980s. "This, combined with the maturity and continued profitability of the industry, will be accompanied by increased support from traditional business financing sources."

The promise of new revenue sources for the industry, and increased demand for film production that could result from these, placed Hollywood in a critical phase of its history as the decade began. The majors were embarking on a race for these revenues, and the results could be costly for the losers. MPAA president Jack Valenti foresaw "a pot of gold" for Hollywood at the end of the decade, but he warned that not all would reach it. Quoting Alfred North Whitehead, Valenti remarked that "those events most benefitting mankind almost wrecked the society in which they occurred."[34] Twentieth Century–Fox president Dennis Stanfill concurred, predicting a shake-out in the industry that would eliminate the weaker players as production and marketing costs soared and competitors vied for control of the markets promised by cable and home video. Stanfill said, "We may go through a valley of discontent for a few years before we are able to take advantage of the growing new markets."[35] The shake-out period was accompanied by the wave of mergers and acquisitions as the major studios jockeyed for position. Some majors welcomed buyouts by powerful parent corporations that facilitated control of an integrated stream of revenue from related leisure-time markets. Others tried to fend off hostile takeover attempts, but by decade's end almost no Hollywood major emerged unchanged from the protracted process of shake-out and adaptation. Paramount's president Michael Eisner called the early 1980s "the survival years" and predicted that those film companies "without a strong financial structure will fold."[36] The fiscal and corporate challenges triggered conceptual shifts in the way the industry thought about its medium. In a web of interconnected distribution venues, film would no longer be a celluloid-based medium tied to theaters. Film would be conceived as a form of software needed by an array of technologies servicing the rapidly increasing distribution venues. Smart companies would seek to keep all of those revenue streams in house.

In 1981, studio chief Michael Eisner spoke in detail with *Variety*, the industry's trade paper, about Paramount's corporate philosophy regarding the important role the new markets would play in the company's plans for the 1980s and about the changing role of film in relation to the new technologies. Eisner explained that the company's goal was to obtain "a wholly owned stream of rights that will expand our ability to make software for every entertainment medium." Filmmaking was a kind of software programming, and the most successful such programming would be that capable of running on several different media platforms. "It's all tied to one purpose," Eisner explained, "creating a stream of rights that may start off in motion picture theaters, then move to cable, network, off-network and foreign; or might start in the legitimate theater, or may go directly to cable. It doesn't matter where it ends up. The point is that we will own the software every one of those media needs." Paramount would aim to produce programming for every entertainment medium and to simultaneously control the rights to all media uses of that programming. Furthermore, this philosophy would guide the studio's decisions about which proposed film projects it would back. Eisner cautioned, "We do not make motion pictures for which we don't have the full stream of rights."[37] Eisner's predictions for Paramount would come dramatically true. Gulf and Western, Paramount's parent corporation, would redesign its company structure to more effectively become an all-rights software corporation. (G&W's redesign is detailed in ch. 2.)

Paramount clearly recognized the extent to which control of the ancillary markets was crucial to a firm's success and to its ability to survive the shake-out years. As the president of International Film Investors, Inc., warned, "When you lose control of a film's ancillary rights, you're in trouble. Today that's the core of the movie business."[38] The risk of losing control was real, and it was strikingly illustrated by the pay-cable war waged between Time, Inc.'s HBO and the major studios at the beginning of the decade. This was a battle about the revenues generated by pay-cable transmission of studio films and who would control those revenues. The conflict was significant because it illuminated the new configurations of power in the eighties industry and the extent to which the pursuit of new markets was forcing change. It also demonstrated how the redefinition of films as software necessarily brought new corporate players (sometimes unwelcome ones like HBO) into the industry and forced into being new economic alliances. The most dramatic result of these alliances in the cable war was the overnight creation of a major film studio.

The HBO War and Tri-Star

The majors made a number of miscalculations and errors in their attempts to implement strategies for dealing with the new markets. MCA/Universal, for example, strongly backed the laserdisc format and spent lavishly to develop it in joint ventures with Pioneer and Magnavox, only to withdraw after a few years when that market failed to show much growth. Sometimes the majors were simply slow to act, with perceptions encased by traditional business paradigms that were becoming outmoded. The cable war was an example of the latter problem.

The Hollywood majors nearly lost a substantial amount of control over the production and distribution of films for pay cable. The industry slept unaware while HBO, an industry outsider, maneuvered into a position in the early 1980s from which it could dictate, by virtue of its size and the absence of an effective competitor, the terms of its payments to studios for cable distribution of their films. The industry's slow response to cable facilitated HBO's dominance. The majors' vested interest in theaters and broadcast television as the main delivery systems for its product made it difficult for them to reorient their distribution practices to accommodate a new television medium. According to Time, Inc.'s vice president for video, Gerald Levine, "The movies grew out of the nickelodeon. It's a little hard to transfer allegiance to a new system of distribution when you look at the world in a certain way. HBO happened to find the formula early."[39]

Since 1975, when HBO booked space on RCA's Satcom 1 satellite, it grew to become the number one pay-cable service, locking up more than 60 percent of the nation's pay-cable subscribers (12 million according to HBO, 18 million according to A. C. Neilson Co).[40] By 1983, that had become a $2.4 billion market, of which HBO had the lion's share. Furthermore, Time, Inc., through HBO, had become in the early 1980s one of the nation's largest financiers of movies. In 1983, HBO allocated $250 million for theatrical production and licensing fees (not including funds for production of made-for-cable movies), an amount comparable to the production budget of a Hollywood major.[41] HBO's competitors, Showtime (owned by Viacom before its merger with The Movie Channel) and The Movie Channel (a joint venture of Warners and American Express), had together less than half of HBO's subscribers. By any measure, cable was a significant market. Revenues of $2.4 billion from pay cable were comparable to the domestic box-office gross of $3.4 billion in 1982 and $3.7 billion in 1983.

The Hollywood majors belatedly discovered that they were effectively shut out of this business because HBO was an outside player (owner Time, Inc., was then unaffiliated with any of the majors). Whereas the majors typically received 45–50 percent of revenues generated at the theatrical box office, they complained that HBO's commanding presence in pay cable permitted it to pay the majors less than their films were worth and to retaliate when a studio turned down an HBO bid as being too low. When Fox rejected HBO's bid for its hit film BREAKING AWAY (1979) and sold television rights to NBC instead, HBO bought no films from Fox for a year.[42] Furthermore, HBO's extraordinary capital reserves and its dominance of the market permitted it to pre-buy the cable rights to a film, which incensed the studios. In a pre-buy, HBO would secure exclusive cable rights before a film production was complete and its hit potential could be assessed, effectively shutting studios out of a critical source of ancillary revenue on pictures they agreed to distribute. HBO, for example, paid Universal $3.5 million for exclusive cable rights to ON GOLDEN POND, starring Henry Fonda and Katharine Hepburn. The picture was the third biggest box-office film of 1982, earning a rental of $118 million.[43] Had Universal waited to sell the cable rights, the picture would have commanded a better price. Escalating production costs compelled the majors to seek outside financing for their pictures, and pre-buys were a strategic source of such financing. But the majors grumbled while taking HBO's money. They regarded HBO's pre-buys as an end run, cutting them off from more favorable licensing fees that might otherwise be obtained.

Further antagonizing the majors, HBO in 1983 established Silver Screen Partners (through E. F. Hutton), a limited-partnership financing arrangement seeking to raise $75 million for production of twelve films. HBO guaranteed investors a return of production costs and claimed full rights to exclusive pay-cable showings and television syndication of the completed films.[44] As noted previously, the studios had been compelled to decrease their financial outlay for productions by seeking outside lines of financing (e.g., selling some ancillary rights up front or offering limited partnerships) or by distributing an increasing number of "pickups," finished films that did not require a major to assume

ON GOLDEN POND, *starring Jane Fonda and Henry Fonda (appearing in his last film), was one of the most popular pictures of 1982, but HBO's prebuy of cable rights prevented Universal from basing these ancillary rights on the picture's box-office performance.*

production costs. By investing in production and by providing a guarantee for outside investors, HBO was playing the industry's own game. Thus, as the majors faced curtailed abilities to invest in production, HBO's participation in the financing and production of independent pictures threatened their economic dominance of the industry. When HBO provided over a third of the $12 million production budget of SOPHIE'S CHOICE (1982), starring Meryl Streep, a project in danger of failing for lack of funding, the film's producer, Keith Barish, appreciatively noted, "Financing has become very difficult, and when someone like HBO is willing to step forward—particularly on a difficult project like this—it can have a revolutionary effect on the producing of motion pictures."[45] As far as the majors were concerned, though, HBO represented an enormous and dangerous revenue drain. Fox chair Alan Hirschfield said, "They [HBO] are a tremendous threat to the structure of the industry as we know it today and ultimately to the viability of the creative process."[46] In a fit of hyperbole that demonstrated the industry's anxieties, the chair of Gulf and Western's entertainment and communications sector, Barry Diller, said, "If HBO and Time, Inc. go on unchecked, the motion picture industry, without exception, will be under the total control of one company in less than five years."[47]

Hollywood struck back against HBO on two fronts. Studio executives appealed to the Justice Department for an investigation of HBO's cable practices, which they regarded as monopolistic. To prove monopoly, the executives ironically cited Hollywood's own history, specifically the divestiture ruling of 1948 that directed the studios to relinquish their theater operations because these, in tandem with a studio's production and distribution activities, constituted an unfair restraint of trade. The major studios drew an analogy between the industry's pre-1948 corporate organization (thereby tacitly acknowledging its

A major film in the careers of actor Meryl Streep and director Alan Pakula, SOPHIE'S CHOICE ran into financing problems, and an investment by HBO helped the production to completion. The finished picture was then distributed by Universal Pictures.

monopolistic character) and HBO's current practice of financing and producing films that it then exhibited on its cable service, another production-distribution-exhibition combination, they alleged, operating in restraint of trade.

To the studios' disappointment, Justice failed to launch a prompt investigation. It did, however, quickly scrutinize, and then file suit against, Hollywood's attempt to launch its own pay-cable service, called Premiere, to compete with HBO. Worse yet, Justice seemed to be acting in response to an HBO charge that the studios were combining to restrict competition (e.g., by trying to squelch HBO and by forming Premiere) and were in violation of antitrust statutes. The majors loudly cried foul. Fox's Alan Hirschfield said, "We petitioned the Justice Department a year ago to take action against the dominance of Home Box Office. The Government dragged their feet for a year, but within 90 days of the announcement of the formation of Premiere they filed against us. The timing of this filing . . . is suspicious. Is it motivated by legal considerations or by political considerations?"[48] MCA president Sidney Sheinberg retorted, "I have stated before that failure on the part of the Department of Justice to challenge activities and practices, including acquisitions, of Time Inc. and its subsidiary Home Box Office, raises in my mind the most serious questions of propriety and/or competence imaginable. The recent aggressive filing by the Department of Justice against the companies comprising the Premiere entity, while, to the best of our knowledge, not filing any actions against Home Box Office, significantly increases my earlier fears."[49]

The Premiere cable network was scheduled to begin operating 1 January 1980 and was to have offered twelve to fifteen films a month to cable subscribers. Four Hollywood majors—Paramount, Universal, 20th Century–Fox, and Columbia—combined as partners with Getty Oil, which owned a satellite, to form the network. In going ahead with Premiere, the industry was signaling its determination to compete with HBO and to seize a large, even commanding, portion of pay-cable film revenues. By licensing films to Premiere, the majors could bypass HBO. But the partners made serious blunders in their effort to best HBO. They agreed to set film license fees according to a formula they would work out among themselves, prompting Justice to charge them with price fixing. The partners also agreed to withhold the four participating majors' films from all other cable networks for a nine-month window while the films played on Premiere. This policy would prevent other cable services from playing the high-profile films that were offered to Premiere subscribers. These films included ALL THAT JAZZ, AMERICAN GIGOLO, THE JERK, COAL MINER'S DAUGHTER, and URBAN COWBOY. Since the four majors in the Premiere partnership distributed in 1979 nearly half of all films earning over $1 million in rentals, 34 percent of all films licensed by HBO, and 44 percent of those licensed by Showtime, Justice charged the Premiere partners with a violation of the Sherman Antitrust Act.[50] (This was a federal statute designed to prevent monopolies and restraint of trade.) HBO's lawyer said, "It's simply illegal for companies to get together to set up a mechanism of pricing and to boycott competitors."[51]

A court injunction prevented Premiere from starting up, as planned, on 1 January 1980. Anticipating that they would lose the antitrust suit filed by Justice, the partners formally abandoned Premiere. As a result, the four Hollywood majors still lacked a cable distribution network of their own. The failure of Premiere, therefore, produced a flurry of strategic maneuvering among the majors to correct this deficit and led to new alliances with HBO. Late in 1981, for example, Columbia broke ranks with the other majors and signed a deal with HBO giving the cable service exclusive rights to its films in return for investments by HBO in its film production activities plus an agreement to accept film license fees based on box-office returns. The deal gave Columbia an additional source of outside funding for production and a more favorable return on the cable licensing of its films. But HBO also won in this deal. It had an extensive pre-buy arrangement with a Hollywood major.

In November 1982, Columbia, 20th Century–Fox, and ABC planned to buy a majority interest in Showtime, a smaller-scale competitor with HBO, from its owner Viacom. Columbia withdrew from the deal at the last moment, and another combination of majors—Paramount and Universal—attempted to buy Showtime and merge it with Warner-Amex's The Movie Channel. The Justice Department also blocked this plan, contending that the involvement of Paramount and Universal would produce substantial vertical integration. (*Vertical integration* designates a business structure in which a company controls multiple levels of production and distribution within a single industry and which enables it to affect other competitors adversely. In the film industry, vertical control of production, distribution, and exhibition could be manifest in single-company ownership of a theater chain, a film studio, and a distribution organization. As we will see, these ownership patterns were fraught with ambiguities regarding their likely market impact, and rulings by the Justice Department reflected these ambiguities. If Justice took a tough line against the majors in 1980, it exhibited greater tolerance later in the decade when the majors reentered theatrical exhibition.) The two majors withdrew, and Warner-Amex and Viacom then merged Showtime with The Movie Channel to create a more substantial competitor with HBO.

The Justice Department had blocked attempts by the Hollywood majors to act in concert with one another to create a cable distribution service, or gain control of one, in

Paul Schrader's intensely stylized American Gigolo, *starring Richard Gere, was among the package of initial offerings planned for Premiere before the studio partners abandoned their fledgling cable venture in the face of opposition by the Justice Department.*

order to compete with HBO. In the meantime, Columbia, which withdrew from the Fox-ABC plan to buy Showtime, had been busy forging its new alliances. In 1983, Columbia, CBS, and HBO unveiled their plans for Tri-Star motion pictures (formerly called Nova while in the planning stages), an entirely new and eighth major film studio. Victor Kaufmann, the new studio's chair, described Tri-Star, launched fully funded with enormous start-up capital, as "an instant major." He said, "We think we have the ability to compete effectively against the seven major established studios."[52] Tri-Star's initial plans called for the release of thirty-five films in 1984 and 1985, but its initial performance was shaky and proved disappointing for partners CBS and HBO. By the end of 1984, it had released only twelve films. These included three solid hits, THE NATURAL, THE MUPPETS TAKE MANHATTAN, and PLACES IN THE HEART, but in its first year of operation Tri-Star gained only a 5 percent share of the domestic theatrical market.[53] Many Tri-Star films did poorly at the box office (poor performers in 1984 included SUPERGIRL, MEATBALLS PART II, FLASHPOINT, RUNAWAY, and SILENT NIGHT, DEADLY NIGHT), diminishing their value in the television markets. In response, CBS sold its shares in the company to Columbia in 1985, and the next year, Time, Inc., sold Columbia half of its interest in Tri-Star.

Despite the short-lived partnership among Columbia, HBO, and CBS, the Tri-Star venture had a special, emblematic importance in the developing Hollywood of the 1980s. To grasp this, we first need to look at the tangled business transactions on which Tri-Star rested. An intricate set of financing arrangements enabled Tri-Star to start up with over $400 million in available financing.[54] The three partners contributed $200 million, with an additional $200 million line of credit obtained through several banks. HBO's investments were the largest among the partners, with the cable service pledged to cover 25 percent of the production cost of each Tri-Star film to a total investment of $50 million (in addition to the $67 million HBO pledged as its partner's share in the venture). HBO would then pay license fees for exclusive cable presentation of Tri-Star films. CBS would pay $2 million for each film it licensed for broadcast from Tri-Star, with a commitment to take fifteen films. CBS would be able to show each film twice over a forty-four-month period after the HBO distribution window closed. Furthermore, home video affiliates of the partners (RCA/Columbia and CBS/Fox Video) contributed $5 million for worldwide distribution of Tri-Star pictures in this format.

These intricate financing arrangements provide a striking illustration of the partnerships and players emerging as a result of growing ancillary markets and the evolving status of film as software for a variety of media outlets. Hollywood's new major was a joint venture between established firms specializing in pay cable, broadcast television, and theatrical film production and distribution. As such, Tri-Star could guarantee that its product would derive revenue from these three vital distribution venues, all now contained in-house. Furthermore, Tri-Star could raise production capital through the prebuys engineered with HBO, CBS, and the home video affiliates. Most significantly, Tri-Star represented an undeniable vertical integration of resources and markets, with the production of feature films by the company for distribution across theatrical, pay-cable, and broadcast television outlets that its partners owned.

In this regard, the formation of Tri-Star heralds the inexorable movement throughout the decade toward greater concentrations of media ownership and control of interlocking markets. By the time Tri-Star was formed, other high-profile mergers and acquisitions had occurred (Marvin Davis's 1981 purchase of Fox, TransAmerica's 1981 sale of UA to MGM, Coca-Cola's 1982 purchase of Columbia). But Tri-Star's heteroge-

Barry Levinson's paean to baseball, The Natural, *was among the few hits in the initial batch of Tri-Star releases.*

neous makeup was the most explicit demonstration thus far in the decade (and many more were yet to come) of the industry's growing concentration as it pursued synergies in filmed entertainment markets. Lastly, with its integration of film production and exhibition (on cable and broadcast television), the formation of Tri-Star anticipated the tsunami of production-exhibition combinations that occurred in mid-decade as the majors went on a theater-buying spree. Tri-Star was a significant break with the decades-old split of production from exhibition in the film industry.

In light of this and especially because HBO was such a commanding presence in pay cable, it is notable that the Justice Department saw no potential in the arrangement for the parties involved to act in restraint of trade. On the contrary, Justice reasoned that Tri-Star "may increase competition among motion picture producers and distributors by creating a new competitor in the industry."[55] Justice pointed out that the Universal-Paramount plan to buy ownership of Showtime and The Movie Channel had been nixed because of the potential dangers of collusion in production and distribution if three Hollywood majors (Universal, Paramount, and Warners, the co-owners of The Movie Channel) owned two pay-cable services. By contrast, Tri-Star involved only one major and one pay-cable programmer and therefore according to Justice, represented fewer opportunities for collusion. With Tri-Star, the ancillary, nontheatrical markets (i.e., cable and broadcast television) had combined with a Hollywood major to create a new studio and earned Justice's blessing in the bargain.

In addition to the industry's efforts to gain hegemony over the cable distribution of Hollywood film, a second benchmark event emblemized the emerging new Hollywood of the 1980s. Whereas the creation of Tri-Star added to the industry in a way that showed the arrival of new interests and markets in the film business, this event was more negative and involved the destruction of a venerable Hollywood name, United Artists, a film company of historic significance. The fate of United Artists, sold by its parent company Transamerica in 1981 to MGM, demonstrated how deadly the inflationary climate could be for film companies that did not control their production costs, and it was the official kick-off in the frenzy of film studio mergers and acquisitions. Tri-Star represents the positive components of industry transformation in the early eighties, demonstrating what could be created by the new forces at play. The extinction of United Artists, by contrast, showed the costs of that transformation, what could be lost if management foolishly supported a prohibitively expensive film that possessed little potential for marketing across the ancillary outlets.

The Death of United Artists

Despite long-simmering tensions between United Artists and its parent Transamerica (tensions that led a group of UA executives to leave the company and form Orion Pictures in 1978), the end for United Artists came largely from its ruinous production of HEAVEN'S GATE (1980). This Western swelled from its originally projected cost of $7.5 million to $35 million, and it grossed just $1.3 million in its first weekend of national release.[56] Production of HEAVEN'S GATE was a chronicle of studio waste and of failure to control a runaway production. The film's escalating budget was symptomatic of this inflationary period in Hollywood history and of the industry's willingness to chase big-budget dreams of blockbuster success right to and over the edge of the precipice, as UA did. It also showed the danger of what can happen when a studio assumes great financial risk for a production, and it was the endgame for unrestrained auteurism. But, despite all of this and UA's fate, it would not bring down the curtain on high-stakes production gambles by the industry.

In 1978, director Michael Cimino was flush with the anticipated success of THE DEER HUNTER, which, prior to its release, the Hollywood grapevine had already pegged as a big and important film. The picture dealt with the experiences of three friends from a Pennsylvania steel town who fought in the Vietnam War, and the industry's high expectations for the film were rewarded. It won five Academy Awards, for best director and best picture as well as sound, editing and supporting actor awards. Before THE DEER HUNTER, Cimino was a relative unknown, with limited experience as a filmmaker. He had directed only one other film, THUNDERBOLT AND LIGHTFOOT (1974), a Clint Eastwood vehicle, and he had coscripted a few pictures. Before that, he was directing TV commercials in New York.

Despite this relative lack of experience, Cimino's potential success with THE DEER HUNTER was enough to attract the attention of United Artists, which feared that he might become unapproachable once DEER HUNTER opened to the expected acclaim. Cimino's sudden cachet demonstrates a fundamental irrationality in the film business. Then as now, the industry has willingly courted ambitious filmmakers and financed their expensive visions. But filmmakers with a proven track record offer some collateral. By contrast, when the industry throws money at previously unknown directors who have an

Flush with the success of THE DEER
HUNTER, *Michael Cimino proved irresistible to United Artists in its hopes for
a prestige blockbuster.*

overnight success, it is trusting that this success is a sure-fire sign of a director's blockbuster potential. A more rational alternative would be to avoid the heady romanticism of lavishly courting relatively unproven filmmakers. But UA was not about to be cautious. Blockbuster filmmaking was not about caution, and UA wanted an epic blockbuster of its own and a picture that would win it some Academy Awards. Cimino seemed like a good bet despite the battles he was then having with Universal over the length at which THE DEER HUNTER would be released. Universal wanted a two-hour picture. Cimino fought for and got his 183-minute cut. The resolution of this conflict with Universal augured poorly for UA's relations with the director, and UA quickly found itself pulled in opposing directions by Cimino's artistic demands and by sound fiscal policy. As he did with Universal, Cimino would prevail in his battles with UA, to UA's lasting detriment.

The project Cimino proposed to UA hardly seemed like the stuff from which blockbusters are made. His script was based on the Johnson County War in 1892, a range war between the Wyoming Stock Growers' Association of large cattle ranchers and the settlers and small ranchers who flocked to Wyoming after passage of the Homestead Act, which promised land to any who lived on it and worked it for seven years. This conflict had been the basis for George Stevens's classic SHANE (1953), but Westerns were no longer popular. In fact, they were box-office poison. Science fiction and horror were in vogue, leaving the Western behind in its own dust. Belonging to a genre moviegoers now regarded as passé, HEAVEN'S GATE would have to compete the year of its release with such popular science fiction films as THE EMPIRE STRIKES BACK and potential horror winners like THE SHINING, FRIDAY THE 13TH, and DRESSED TO KILL. These were terrible odds. Furthermore, Cimino's tale was resoundingly downbeat. The script climaxed with a bloody massacre of settlers by killers hired by the Stock Growers' Association. By story's end, all of its protagonists were dead. In light of this, UA's story department wisely advised caution: "If it is a project we want to do because of Mike Cimino's involvement, we should approach it with expectations of a major rewrite. If it were not for Cimino, I would pass."[57]

But UA forged ahead, despite already having one runaway production in APOCALYPSE NOW (1979), helmed by Francis Ford Coppola, a director having difficulties with his material and his locations. Cimino would revise the story, sparing one of its protagonists (Averill, played by Kris Kristofferson) and adding a prologue showing Averill as an idealistic, spirited young man at the 1870 Harvard commencement. An epilogue showed him as a melancholy old man in 1900 ruminating on the past, on those events that made up the body of the film. The revisions, especially the prologue and epilogue, made the film seem less like a Western (to the delight of UA executives) and more like the ambitious, arty picture they wanted.

As the start of production drew near, terrible frictions began to develop between Cimino and his UA producers. In the draft agreement for his first contract, Cimino asked that, should the picture go overbudget and the production fail to meet its scheduled release date, none of the additional expenditures be held against his production company.[58] In effect, he was asking for an unlimited budget and for UA to surrender its power to veto budget expenditures. He also asked for $2,000 in weekly allowances, irrespective of where he was living or working at the time, said expense to be retroactive to the picture's original deal date. These expenditures would be in addition to the $500,000 UA was paying him to direct the picture. Cimino's draft agreement also announced, to the surprise of UA executives, that he expected the film to be no shorter than two and a half hours. He also demanded that his name appear as part of the film's title: "Mr. Cimino's presentation credit shall be in the form 'Michael Cimino's "Heaven's Gate"' (or in such other form as [Cimino] may designate); Mr. Cimino's name in such credit shall be presented in the same size as the title, including all artwork titles, and on a separate line above the title, and shall appear in the form just indicated on theater marquees (United Artists to require such treatment in its agreements with exhibitors)."[59] Cimino made these demands on the basis of having directed only two films, one of which had involved Clint Eastwood, a star who typically exerted the controlling authority on the productions in which he appeared. Thus it was THE DEER HUNTER that gave Cimino the artistic clout to cow UA with these outsized demands. Believing that Cimino, more than the picture or its players, was their star, UA acceded to his remarkable terms. The novice director had won the dangerous privilege of working without budgetary restraint, and UA handed over to Cimino its most fundamental authority as funding agent to supervise production and to hold a filmmaker within a contractually limited schedule and budget. It was auteurism run amok and a recipe for disaster.

On location in Kalispell, Montana, Cimino immediately fell behind schedule while exposing incredible amounts of film. During the first six days of shooting, Cimino fell five days behind. To get a minute and a half of usable footage, he shot nearly sixty thousand feet, processing all of it and incurring nearly $1 million in lab expenses. Filming less than a page of script per day, by week two he shot another sixty thousand feet of film. In twelve days of production, Cimino fell ten days behind. He shot an average of ten thousand feet per day (nearly the length of a two-hour movie) and spent almost $200,000 a day to do it. At this rate, the picture would wind up costing, with marketing expenses, $50 million, a staggering sum at that time for a single production. Cimino ultimately shot 1.5 million feet of film and printed 1.3 million feet, nearly 220 hours of footage, or the equivalent of over one hundred feature films.[60] Steven Bach, a UA senior vice president who has chronicled the HEAVEN'S GATE disaster, placed that $50 million in context:

> It was not merely that the figure represented half of 1979's total production budget but that in consequence, other pictures would not be made, their financing diverted instead to Montana; distribution would, as a further consequence, have fewer pictures to distribute in 1980 and 1981; and finally, UA's overall odds at the box office would be dramatically reduced with fewer dice to roll. HEAVEN'S GATE could consume the company.[61]

Filming HEAVEN'S GATE *as an epic period piece in a remote Montana location required that huge amounts of material and studio resources be committed to the production, even as UA ceded its administrative control over the enterprise.*

Where was the money going, and what was Cimino filming so obsessively? The answer: period detail. HEAVEN'S GATE is a film of breathtaking pictorial beauty, achieved by master cinematographer Vilmos Zsigmond using meticulously detailed period locations, costumes, and props, that is yoked to a slender yet opaque narrative line. The accumulated weight of the period detail overburdened the narrative, which was poorly plotted, erratically developed, and full of confusion. Despite all of this, UA supported Cimino's expensive vision. Francis Coppola had not yet taken his post–APOCALYPSE NOW career fall, and the director-as-superstar still possessed considerable vogue. This cachet is strikingly illustrated by an Eastman Kodak advertisement in *Variety* profiling Cimino during the Kalispell, Montana, shoot and suggesting that a director is justified in expending huge resources to pursue his artistic vision.

Cimino presented UA executives with an early cut of the picture on 26 June 1980. Incredibly, this was their first opportunity to see what the company had paid for, and the picture ran an unreleasable five hours and twenty-five minutes. Prior to the screening, Cimino promised to trim it by fifteen minutes. After pressure from UA to shorten the film, his initial fine cut ran three hours and thirty-nine minutes, and the picture opened in New York on 21 November at this length. The review in the *New York Times* was savage. Vincent Canby proclaimed, "'Heaven's Gate' is something quite rare in movies these days—an unqualified disaster."[62] In its review of the picture, *Variety* sounded a distinct anti-auteur note and publicly questioned UA's management of the production. "The balance of director Michael Cimino's newest film is so confusing, so overlong at three and a half hours and so ponderous that it fails to work at almost every level, all credit to the stunning photography notwithstanding. The trade must marvel that directors now have such power that no one, in the endless months since work on the picture began, was able to impose some structure and sense."[63]

By 1983, for UA's $35 million production cost and $6 million advertising campaign, HEAVEN'S GATE had returned only $1.5 million.[64] This disastrous return, augmented by UA's decision to withdraw the film on 25 November 1981 from distribution in order to prepare a shorter version, accompanied and contributed to a sharp downturn in UA's revenues for 1980. This decline precipitated owner Transamerica's harsh actions. In the first nine months of 1980, a period preceding the HEAVEN'S GATE release, UA's domestic rentals dropped 32 percent from the comparable period in 1979.[65] UA's year-end revenues (derived from television, video, product licensing, and music-publishing activities in addition to its distribution of theatrical films) were $425 million ($306 million from film distribution), down from $469 million in 1979, a loss that resulted from the company's write-off of Cimino's film. As Transamerica Corp. explained to its shareholders, "United Artists' earnings decline was due primarily to a fourth-quarter loss resulting from the establishment of a reserve against the company's investment in the motion picture HEAVEN'S GATE."[66]

Reaction from parent Transamerica was swift. Film distribution provided a tiny share of Transamerica's revenues. Its entire entertainment sector contributed only 10 percent of the company's overall 1980 revenue of $4 billion. With only a small investment in film operations and the ensuing damage to these already faltering operations by HEAVEN'S GATE, Transamerica decided to discontinue its entertainment sector, concluding that its investments in the film industry were not cost effective. As Transamerica explained to its shareholders, "The decision to sell United Artists was an outgrowth of our increased focus in 1981 on long-range strategic planning. United Artists is an excellent company, but given the changes taking place and the major investments required to stay competitive in the entertainment business we felt we should concentrate on growth opportunities in our other businesses."[67]

As noted earlier, UA's decision coincided with MGM's plans for a major expansion in the 1980s. Noting the explosion of box-office revenues that blockbuster films could generate—"grosses the industry never thought possible a decade ago," according to MGM president Frank Rosenfelt—the studio planned to increase film production levels throughout 1980 and 1981, releasing a new film every two months.[68] As part of this expansion, and realizing that Transamerica wanted out of the picture business, MGM and owner Kirk Kerkorian bought UA from Transamerica for $380 million. (MGM had a decade-old relationship with UA wherein the latter company acted as distributor for MGM pictures. MGM would now get its own distribution arm.) This was the opening act in the decade's lengthy MGM/UA saga (covered in ch. 2), which saw the once-mighty MGM progressively stripped of its assets as it was promiscuously passed from owner to owner. *Variety* noted the historic significance of the UA sale: "The traditional structure of the major companies has been dented. For all intents and purposes, United Artists has disappeared as a major, self-contained production and distribution company."[69]

The HEAVEN'S GATE debacle pointed to the absolute need for the majors, in an inflationary climate, to institute tight production controls, especially over ambitious directors who did not have proven box-office track records and who were not working in solidly profitable genres, such as science fiction. Filmmakers like Steven Spielberg, John Landis, or Sydney Pollack would be entrusted with major production budgets because

In the end, and for its millions, United Artists got three hours of lavish period detail amid a bewildering narrative. The critics were savage, and the audience stayed home.

of their flair for handling popular material, but such highly regarded auteurs of the 1970s as Martin Scorsese, Robert Altman, and Arthur Penn would experience a difficult period marked by chronic funding problems. Moreover, UA's fate showed how important it was for studios to seek outside funding for expensive films rather than risk Transamerica's error in betting the house on a single, internally funded production. Thus, production financing shifted by mid-decade toward greater emphasis on limited partnerships and equity offerings.[70] Columbia, for example, relied on Delphi Film Associates II and III to secure funding for itself and Tri-Star. Delphi III committed to fund through public stock offerings a maximum of $4.5 million of the production cost of each Tri-Star film.[71]

Despite these consequences, HEAVEN'S GATE did not prompt the industry to reign in production costs, which continued to spiral upward. As we have seen, many of the factors contributing to this situation were difficult for the industry to control or influence. But, granting this point, the majors showed little inclination to scale production at lower cost points. In September 1982, shortly after the failure of HEAVEN'S GATE and the sell-off of UA, Hollywood embarked on what Variety termed a "spending spree," with twenty films in production or about to be released, each costing over $20 million.[72] Indicative of the shift in mode of financing that was underway, each of these pictures used sources of outside funding or was an independent production picked up by a major for distribution. In 1981, Columbia's ten domestic releases had an average budget of $7.5 million. By contrast, Columbia's upcoming releases through February 1983 included six pictures (out of fourteen) costing $25 million or more; these included TOOTSIE at $30 million and THE TOY at $25 million. MGM/UA had the James Bond thriller OCTOPUSSY ready (at $30 million), and Fox had HIGH ROAD TO CHINA (a $20 million bomb) and REVENGE OF THE JEDI (fully financed at $32 million by Lucas Film, Ltd.).

Making this an ominous trend, expensive pictures were tepid box-office performers in the early 1980s. In 1980 and 1981, the domestic rentals from big-budget films declined, on average, making these problematic investments without substantial returns from ancillary markets. Between 1976 and 1982, only 30 percent of films costing over $15 million earned back their negative cost from the domestic theatrical market.[73] By mid-decade, nearly half of such pictures were earning rentals approaching their negative cost.[74] This was not a good rate of return (because of all the claimants to gross receipts), and it indicated that studios faced great difficulties in realizing profits from the productions they funded. The industry, though, would not or could not change its ways. Other big-budget bombs for the business lay ahead, such as ISHTAR (1987) and THE BONFIRE OF THE VANITIES (1990). Hollywood continued to chase expensive blockbusters, even though the theatrical market was insufficient to cover expenses for high-budget filmmaking. In this context, the ancillaries were very seductive. By mid-decade the industry was earning more from the ancillary markets than from theatrical, and it counted on these to augment revenue shortfalls from theatrical.

These factors point to the crux of UA's quandary with HEAVEN'S GATE. The production was inconsistent with the direction in which the industry was now moving. The film was funded with internal UA capital, and the dreary Western saga possessed little appeal in alternative, nontheatrical outlets, even had they been available in a significant way. But they weren't. The explosion of ancillary markets, and their full potential for exploitation, had not yet occurred when the film was released. As a result, the film's box-office failure was unrecuperable, and it wiped out United Artists. Henceforth, it would be corporate suicide to fund an expensive production that lacked the potential for generating multiple revenue streams across the range of entertainment markets. The death of United Artists certified this principle.

By withdrawing from its theatrical film operations, Transamerica decided to concentrate on its financial services segment, its big moneymaking area. Its decision made Transamerica a definite outlier among the industry's parent corporations. Transamerica moved out of the entertainment sector at a time when existing industry parents were salivating over the new markets and when other, outside companies were looking to get in. The UA sell-off was an opening act in the industry's prolonged process of corporate reconfiguration. In a game of corporate musical chairs, everyone swapped partners and parents, and new players gained entry to the business. The nontheatrical distribution venues promised a huge pot of gold by decade's end. The race was on.

2

Merger Mania

Early on, the industry's key executives knew that big changes were underway. Shortly after its 1982 purchase of Columbia Pictures, the Coca-Cola Co. stated:

> The entertainment business in general and the motion picture business in particular are undergoing significant changes, primarily due to technological developments which have resulted in the availability of alternative forms of leisure time entertainment, including expanded pay and cable television, video cassettes, video discs and video games. During the last several years, revenues from licensing of motion pictures to network television have decreased, while revenues from pay television, video cassettes and video discs have increased. However, the level of theatrical success remains a critical factor in generating revenues in these ancillary markets.[1]

Coke's interest in the revenue potential of alternative leisure markets led to its acquisition of Columbia and motivated its willingness to invest significantly in filmed entertainment as an area complementary to its soft drink operations.

Alan J. Hirschfield, former head of Columbia and 20th Century–Fox, emphasized the importance of the 1980s for the Hollywood industry. Speaking in 1990, after the industry had negotiated the absorption of the new delivery systems, seen the restructuring of its relationship with the exhibition sector, fought a series of format wars, and been married to a variety of new corporate partners, he noted, "It's been a period of the most dramatic change in the history of the industry. It's a totally different business from what it was five years ago."[2] It is not difficult to understand why Hollywood was a tempting target of opportunity for the large entertainment and communications conglomerates that moved in to buy the studios. As table 1.1 has shown, domestic box-office revenue remained robust. The $2.8 billion earned in 1980 had climbed by 1988 to $4.38 billion. In 1989, domestic box office hit $5 billion. But the data on ticket sales showed a somewhat different picture. As explained in the last chapter, national annual ticket sales remained remarkably consistent from year to year, at just above 1 billion.

How one resolves the ambiguities presented by the two sets of data will produce very different portraits of the industry's overall health. On the one hand, the theatrical moviegoing market seemed fully exploited. It had topped out, despite the yearly advances in box-office revenue. The national audience for theatrical motion pictures was no longer expanding. It was stagnant. On the other hand, the robust box office demonstrated that the industry's appeal was stable. Theatrical exhibition continued to perform quite respectably, despite the alternative viewing venues represented by home video and pay cable. Furthermore, to the extent that the economic performance of the major studios was an indicator of the industry's health, nearly all of the studios had one or more outstanding years during the decade. With MGM/UA being a prominent exception because of its debt load and its turbulent history, most of the majors achieved a dominant market share during one or more years of the decade. Table 2.1 shows market share performance by each major over the course of the decade, and chart 2.1 shows each year's market share leader. The most successful majors were Warner Bros. (market share

TABLE 2.1
Majors' Share (%) of Domestic Theatrical Market

Year	Col	Fox	MGM/UA	Par	Univ	WB	Disney	Orion	Tri-Star
1980	14	16	7	16	*20*	14	4	2	
1981	13	13	9	15	14	*18*	3	1	
1982	10	14	11	14	*30*	10	4	3	
1983	14	*21*	10	14	13	17	3	4	
1984	16	10	7	*21*	8	19	4	5	5
1985	10	11	9	10	16	*18*	3	5	10
1986	9	8	4	*22*	9	12	10	7	7
1987	4	9	4	*20*	8	13	14	10	5
1988	3	11	10	16	10	11	20	7	6
1989	8	6	6	14	17	*19*	14	4	7

SOURCE: *Variety*, Jan. 17, 1990, p. 15.

CHART 2.1
Market Share Leaders

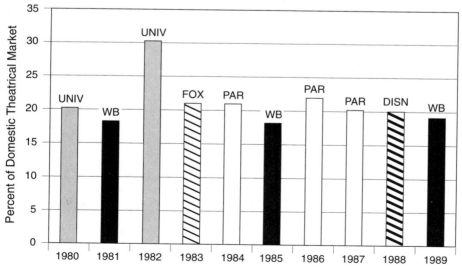

SOURCE: *Variety*, 17 January 1990.

leader in 1981, 1985, 1989), Paramount (market leader in 1984 and 1986–87), and
Disney, by virtue of its spectacular return from the brink of theatrical market extinction
(compare its performance in the first and second halves of the decade).

Blockbuster films were generating whopping returns (table 2.2). THE EMPIRE
STRIKES BACK (1980), E.T.: THE EXTRA-TERRESTRIAL (1982), RETURN OF THE JEDI
(1983), GHOSTBUSTERS (1984), and BATMAN (1989) all passed the $190 million mark in
theatrical rentals. This set a new benchmark for success, and *Variety* would remark upon
the failure, in other years, for a top film to cross the $100 million line. Of chief impor-
tance in understanding why the majors were such attractive buys for larger corporations,
then, is this factor: each of the majors (excepting MGM/UA) produced or distributed at
least one of the decade's blockbusters.

Each of the majors, therefore, was a proven maker and distributor of the industry's
top film in any given year and had the capability of dominating the national moviegoing
market. These are similar but separate attributes, because a blockbuster's success did
not always guarantee market dominance for its studio distributor. One major might have
the year's top film while another had more productions scoring high on the revenue
charts and thus secured market dominance. Furthermore, the terms under which the
majors secured distribution of big pictures were not always as favorable to the distributor as they might have been. Fox, for example, felt that the distributor/production company splits on revenues from THE EMPIRE STRIKES BACK and RETURN OF THE JEDI
lessened the profits it might otherwise have secured from distribution of these films.

These factors made it possible for a major to "fail" to have the top film in a given year
yet emerge as that year's market share leader. In 1980, Fox had the top film, but
Universal had the biggest market share, in part because it distributed four other titles in
the top ten (THE JERK, SMOKEY AND THE BANDIT, COAL MINER'S DAUGHTER, and
THE BLUES BROTHERS). In 1984, Columbia had the top film, but Paramount was the
market leader, in part because it had three titles in the top five (INDIANA JONES AND
THE TEMPLE OF DOOM, BEVERLY HILLS COP, and TERMS OF ENDEARMENT). On several measures, then, all of the majors were associated with the decade's top films, and
these films, along with the studios that produced or distributed them, were giant revenue machines that could drive the ancillary markets to produce additional returns. This

TABLE 2.2
Blockbuster Film Revenues
(Rentals Returned to Distributor)

		($MILLIONS)	STUDIO
1980	THE EMPIRE STRIKES BACK	120	Fox
1981	RAIDERS OF THE LOST ARK	90	Paramount
1982	E.T.: THE EXTRA-TERRESTRIAL	187	Universal
1983	RETURN OF THE JEDI	166	Fox
1984	GHOSTBUSTERS	127	Columbia
1985	BACK TO THE FUTURE	94	Universal
1986	TOP GUN	82	Paramount
1987	BEVERLY HILLS COP II	81	Paramount
1988	WHO FRAMED ROGER RABBIT	78	Buena Vista (Disney)
1989	BATMAN	151	Warner Bros.

SOURCE: *Variety,* 1980–1989.

The high-profile success of blockbuster pictures helped make the studios attractive buys for parent corporations shopping for media subsidiaries. BATMAN (1989) proved to be one of the decade's biggest pictures. Blockbusters, though, presented a rather skewed portrait of the industry's economic health, and not all of the industry's new owners would remain happy with their purchases.

is a principal reason why the Hollywood industry became an attractive buy for the multinational communications firms that shopped and purchased with such alacrity during the era. Get a major studio and you got a company that every few years would produce one of these cash monsters. (MGM/UA released very few films during the decade, none of which were top earners. But the company's value would prove to be enormous because of the studio's library of classic films.)

Other measures of the industry's robust operations are found in the explosion of new theater screens; 1984 was the second year in a row for the biggest expansion increase in any year since 1948, a remarkable boom in exhibition considered later in this chapter. The expansion of screens was, in significant respect, the result of an increase in film production in the early 1980s and a consequent rise in the total number of titles in distribution. Film production climbed from 1983 to 1987 because of its potential to continue generating revenue downstream in the ancillary markets. More films in distribution required more screens on which to play, even as the window of release into the theatrical market tightened for many titles. As an executive for the General Cinema theater circuit explained, "We need more screens to service the supply from the companies and respond to the public's demand. In part because of home viewing, the [theatrical] runs are shorter, and you go through an awful lot of product because of free and pay tv."[3] This expansion of production and distribution was due almost entirely to the proliferation of independent films, that is, films financed or distributed outside the auspices of a major studio. The majors could not underwrite additional production because they had a fixed amount of working capital in any given year, and this was fully committed. The expansion of production and distibution in mid-decade, therefore, occurred largely outside the majors. As chart 2.2 shows, from 1983 to 1987, the number of in-house productions by the studios (Buena Vista [Disney's distribution arm], Columbia, Tri-Star, MGM/UA, Orion, Paramount, 20th Century–Fox, Universal, Warner Bros.) remained relatively constant while the number of independent productions soared. Many of these independent productions, though, failed to secure distribution (table 2.3). Despite this, the number of independent films in release climbed significantly in mid-decade. Thus, a major production boom, fed by the take-off of the ancillary markets, was occurring by the mid-1980s. If the industry was not attracting significantly larger numbers of patrons to its movie theaters, it was putting more product into domestic release as a way of feeding the ancillaries and expanding the total number of venues in which consumers might watch their movies.

These measures indicate why the Hollywood majors were attractive to potential buyers in the communications industry. These buyers understood that big revenues lay in expanding entertainment markets and that the newest growth sectors would be the

CHART 2.2
U.S. Feature Production

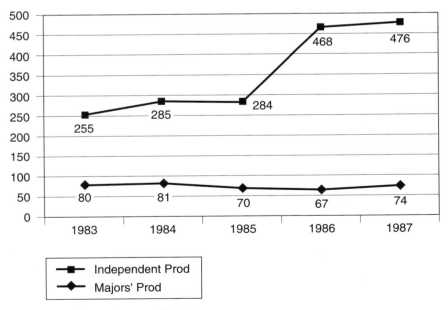

SOURCE: *Variety*, 24 February 1988, p. 66.

Table 2.3

Production and Distribution of U.S. Feature Films

	1983	1984	1985	1986	1987
Total Majors' In-House Productions	80	81	70	67	74
Indie Productions Released by Majors	49	56	36	53	64
Indie Productions Released by Indies	125	127	143	242	203
Indie Productions with No Distributor	81	102	105	173	209
Total U.S. Productions	335	366	354	535	550

SOURCE: *Variety*, 24 February 1988, p. 66.

information industries. In this regard, what happened in Hollywood in the 1980s was a snapshot of a much larger picture. The energetic merger-and-acquisitions activity that swept through Hollywood was a subset of a bigger wave hitting U.S. industries. In the 1980s, the U.S. economy saw the most sustained period of merger-and-acquisitions activity in history, reaching a total of 31,105 transactions carrying a dollar value of $1.34 trillion. Merger-and-acquisitions activity has always characterized the U.S. economy, but what changed in the eighties was a new corporate willingness to use that activity strategically, to implement long-range business plans, rather than as a tool for use in occasional and exceptional circumstances. As one business analyst summed up this development,

> Mergers and acquisitions no longer would be cavalierly handled as hit-or-miss propositions or temporary phenomena cued by short-run economic and financial influences that ultimately fizzled out. The rewards were too lucrative, the techniques too strategically viable, the advantages too compelling for the modern deal-maker to let the ball drop.[4]

To facilitate this strategy and drive merger-and-acquisition activity, a new market infrastructure emerged, consisting of investment bankers, law firms, valuation companies, accountants, and strategic planners whose time and resources were devoted to m&a analysis and forecasting. These substantial new resources encouraged m&a operations, conducted throughout the economy during the eighties, from megafirms down to small businesses.

In this mix, media industries stood out. Measured by the number of merger-and-acquisitions transactions, media was the third most active industry segment from 1980 to 1989 (table 2.4). Measured again by number of transactions, media was the second most attractive U.S. industry for foreign buyers (table 2.5), an attraction that would play out with spectacular results for the Hollywood studios. Furthermore, approximately 30 percent of all m&a transactions involved corporate divestiture of business divisions or subsidiaries.[5] As we will see, one of the most striking components of Hollywood's transformation was its participation in the general deconglomeration of U.S. industry that these divestitures indicated.

The m&a activity of the 1980s was tied as well to the emergence and pursuit by corporate powers of global markets. As already mentioned, one sign of this was the high number of foreign buyers for U.S. industries. Since the film industry has historically been a manufacturer whose goods are among leading U.S. exports, the studios who made and

TABLE 2.4

Most Active Industries For Merger/Acquisitions
by Number of Transactions, 1980–89

	NUMBER OF DEALS	VALUE ($BILLION)
Banking	3,214	77.4
Business Services	2,996	47.7
Media	2,031	89.2
Wholesale	1,674	19.4
Health Care	1,507	84.1
Machinery	1,366	35.8
Retailing	1,324	87.7
Nonbank Financial	1,278	49.4
Energy	1,219	153.2
Computer & Data Processing	1,169	15.3

SOURCE: M&A Database, *Mergers and Acquisitions* (March/April 1990), p. 119.

TABLE 2.5

Most Attractive U.S. Industries for Foreign Buyers, 1980–89

	NUMBER OF DEALS	VALUE ($BILLION)
Business Services	267	7.25
Media	190	17.22
Machinery	182	6.92
Health Care	160	14.34
Food & Tobacco	150	21.53
Wholesale	139	4.18
Energy	131	29.63
Chemicals	130	17.58
Retailing	125	16.72
Electrical & Electronic	115	5.84

SOURCE: M&A Database, *Mergers and Acquisitions* (March/April 1990), p. 99.

distributed those films would be exquisitely attractive buys for globally ambitious companies. Furthermore, the emerging interface between communications and entertainment added to this allure. Rupert Murdoch, whose Australian-based News Corp. Ltd. bought 20th Century–Fox in 1985, described this strategic shift from businesses geared toward the extraction of raw materials to those that processed information:

> We are witnessing the beginning of the transition from the industrial society, in which wealth was created by processing raw materials, to an information society, in which wealth creation will depend on the processing of information. . . . A golden age will come to those countries which turn this wealth of information into knowledge effectively.

In building such an empire, Murdoch stressed the challenges of mastering a fast-paced information environment in which change occurs overnight and it is possible "to store, transmit and process vast quantities of complicated information cheaply, and in seconds." He continued, "Movies are global media. Our U.S.-based Fox Film Corp. operates in almost 50 countries through either its own offices or local agents and distributors. The development of private television channels as a result of deregulation in many markets is likely to widen the basis for international sales. The same is true for the world-wide market for videocassettes." Because the flow of information is transnational, the planet itself is the market. Accordingly, the real players in the communications industry will be global giants. According to Murdoch, "I am sure that the global top league will basically consist of five or six very large media companies."[6]

Indeed, by decade's end, the News Corp. Ltd., Time, Inc., and Japan's Sony and Matsushita were the giants who swallowed whole film studios and integrated film production and distribution with their other information-based operations. The next portion of this chapter chronicles the wave of mergers and buyouts that transformed the industry. I then consider the boom in theatrical exhibition that accompanied this wave and, in significant part, resulted from it. Finally, I close by briefly considering the media synergies that the new corporate alliances aimed to produce.

The Opening Salvo

Notice was served early on that the Hollywood studios were up for grabs. Flush with cash from his wildcat oil operations, Denver oil executive Marvin Davis bought 20th Century–Fox in 1981 for $725 million. It was a highly leveraged buy (leverage being a function of long-term corporate debt), with Davis paying only $50 million in cash, the remainder coming in the form of bank loans and borrowings from Davis's company TCF Holdings, Inc. Unlike subsequent studio purchases, the Davis buy of Fox did not serve to create an expanded corporate ability to operate in multiple leisure-time markets, and the failure of Davis's efforts to diversify into show business is instructive in this respect.

Davis's primary business was oil. His firm specialized in wildcat wells (i.e., wells in unexplored regions) and had been very successful at finding them and exploiting them. As a result, Davis was constantly looking for ways to use and shelter the flood of dollars produced by his oil operations. Shortly before the Fox purchase, for example, he sold $600 million of oil and gas properties, and he had a history of diverting oil revenues into other, ambitious business operations. Davis purchased a majority share of Denver's ninth largest bank, with assets of $190 million, and he invested millions in various Denver real estate projects, including office and shopping complexes.[7] The Fox buy was part of this strategy of sheltering oil revenue.

As a corporate move, it was consistent with traditional policies of diversification that American businesses had been pursuing for decades. Efforts to diversify through acquisitions in unrelated markets historically held more failures than successes, however, and Davis's subsequent history with Fox was consistent with this trend. A study of the two hundred largest U.S. industrial firms by McKinsey and Co., a management consulting firm, examined their efforts to diversify from 1972 to 1983. The study found that, of those firms that attempted to change their business portfolios through diversification, most failed (measured by the failure of returns on investment to exceed acquisition costs).[8] Furthermore, failure was greatest when firms attempted to diversify by means of large, unrelated acquisitions. The trends toward deconglomeration that I examine later in the chapter resulted from the efforts of business to reverse the negative effects of conglomeration and the impulse buying on which it rested. The Davis buy of Fox exemplified the pitfalls of traditional diversification. This is a major point of differentiation with the subsequent marriage of Fox with Rupert Murdoch's News Corp. The Davis effort failed, in part, because the deal carried a huge debt load. It failed as well because there were no synergies between film and the oil industries. Film and oil were fundamentally unrelated and thus made a poor corporate portfolio.

By buying Fox, Davis inherited $426 million in liabilities (Fox profits were down 40 percent in the first half of 1981)[9], and he sold some of the studio's properties and subsidiaries (a midwestern Coca-Cola bottling company and half interest in the resort operations) to cover some $270 million of this liability. Davis brought former Paramount Pictures chair Barry Diller to head the studio, but despite being the market share leader in 1983, Fox's hit films were infrequent, and in 1984 the studio posted a net loss of $90 million.[10] In this context of debt and sub-par performance, the Fox acquisition was a troubled one for Davis.

His purchase of Fox coincided with the aggressive efforts of Rupert Murdoch's News Corp. to expand its operations and holdings in the United States. In 1982, the News Corp. acquired the Boston Herald, in 1984 the *Chicago Sun-Times* and *New Woman* magazine, and in 1985 a slew of aviation and travel magazines. Murdoch and Davis had long known each other, and in April 1985, the News Corp. bought half of Davis's interest in Fox and then bought the remaining half in December. The acquisition of Fox cost Murdoch $575 million. Davis was resigned to the sale in light of Fox's inability to perform at a consistently profitable level during the four years in which he owned the studio. "Our Fox investment was an extremely successful one," he maintained. "While it was not our intention to sell the balance of our interest at this time, we concluded that it made good business sense to accept Rupert Murdoch's offer."[11]

Beyond Fox's performance problems, another factor prompting Davis's decision to sell may have been his reluctance to expand into diversified media operations, and these would be critical for the success of the new Hollywood. Oil was Davis's primary business, and Fox was, at present, unaffiliated with a parent media company. Like the other studios, it was active in film production and in the licensing of films for broadcast television, cable television, and video markets. But its recorded-music operations were modest, and it had no affiliation with a cable television service provider. It had a nonexclusive arrangement with HBO at a time when Paramount, Universal, and Warner Bros. were angling to merge with Showtime and The Movie Channel. (The Justice Department blocked this deal in 1983.) When Fox subsequently tried to partner with Columbia and ABC-TV to buy 75 percent of Showtime, Columbia backed out and partnered instead with HBO and CBS to start Tri-Star.

In light of the forces affecting the industry, Davis's sole ownership of a stand-alone movie studio was backward looking and out of synch. Murdoch discussed with Davis the prospect of jointly purchasing six Metromedia television stations, but Davis decided not to participate in this historic venture. Murdoch's plans for an expansion into U.S. operations included obtaining an umbrella group of communications companies, while Davis seemed uninterested in expanding media operations beyond Fox. Although Fox's recent performance was disappointing, the studio would be a valuable property at sale to an empire builder like Rupert Murdoch, who understood the linchpin role a movie studio could play in international media markets. Accordingly, Davis decided to sell. Explaining Davis's decision, an entertainment industry analyst with Merrill Lynch pointed to the value of movie studios for burgeoning communications empires: "This might not have been a good deal for him, as little as six months ago, but the integration of media empires has changed the nature of the broadcasting and movie connections."[12] He added that this integration had made the movie companies more valuable.

The Fox buy was merely one piece in Murdoch's furiously expanding U.S. operations. In the year before his purchase of Fox, Murdoch tried to win control of Warner Communications, Inc., but WCI successfully blocked the attempt and repurchased Murdoch's stock shares. Murdoch walked away from the defeat with a profit of $40 million.[13] Three months after completing its Fox buy, the News Corp. spent $1.8 billion to acquire the six Metromedia television stations, located in New York, Los Angeles, Chicago, Dallas, Washington, D.C., and Houston, six of the ten largest media markets in the country. This was the twenty-second-largest foreign acquisition of U.S. businesses in the eighties.[14] (The News Corp.'s 1988 purchase of Triangle Publications, Inc., publisher of *TV Guide* and other magazines, was the tenth-biggest foreign buy of the decade.) The News Corp. promptly launched Fox, a fourth broadcast television network, as an alternative to ABC, NBC, and CBS.

By mid-decade, its rapid series of newspaper, magazine, filmed-entertainment, and broadcast television purchases established the News Corp. as a model for the information industries. Rather than pursuing the erratic programs of old-line diversification that had resulted in unwieldy behemoths like Gulf and Western, Murdoch targeted key media markets and programming in order to build a focused corporate structure. By mid-decade, the News Corp. operated in five primary business segments: newspaper publishing (in 1986, three major metropolitan newspapers), magazine publishing (fourteen business and six consumer magazines, *Elle* and *New York* among them), filmed-entertainment operations, and television broadcasting. In 1986, the year after the purchase of Fox Film, the filmed-entertainment segment was the second-biggest revenue generator (after newspapers, which the News Corp. also owned in Europe). The buys of Fox Film and the Metromedia Television stations helped push revenues in the United States ($1.9 billion) far ahead of those generated in the company's other areas of operation, the United Kingdom ($1.1 billion) and Australia ($814 million).[15] The importance of the ancillary markets is dramatically illustrated by a breakdown of News Corp. profits for fiscal 1986. Home video ($46 million) and television ($50 million) generated greater profits than did production and distribution of theatrical film ($43 million).[16]

By 1986, then, 20th Century–Fox had been subsumed within the Murdoch media empire. At decade's end, looking back on the growth of his empire, Rupert Murdoch summarized the business strategy that guided his media purchases:

> If ten years or so ago we had attempted to chart on paper the destiny of our company, we would never have anticipated the 30 very diverse acquisitions we made on four continents, almost all of which arose from unique and unanticipated events. . . . However, I think a very moderate kind of strategy is emerging. It is building up an international company of record that is able to adapt to new technologies.[17]

Coca-Cola and the Pursuit of Synergy

Whereas the initial sale of Fox to Marvin Davis did not position the studio within a leisure-time industry (this not until the Murdoch buy four years later), the purchase of Columbia Pictures by the Coca-Cola Co. on 21 June 1982 for $692 million promptly launched that studio (and Coke) in pursuit of synergies among leisure-time markets and operations. Coke's conviction that synergies could be obtained between movies and soft drinks was problematic from the outset, and its failure to realize the revenue growth it sought from the Columbia purchase demonstrated how elusive the much-vaunted market synergies could be. Coke's experiment at owning a movie studio exemplied the wrong kind of synergies, or, more correctly, it exemplified what happens when a business tries to invent synergies where none really prevail. In their absence, Coke's ill-fated experiment with Columbia stands as another example of old-line corporate diversification. It was clothed in the sexy new garb of strategic synergy. Stripped of this, though, the union of soft drinks and movies was a bad match, an effort to marry dissimilar market segments and products. As Coke would come to realize, and despite its initial enthusiasm, the marriage made for an unsatisfying corporate portfolio.

It also would produce one of the oddest chapters in Hollywood corporate history, namely, the bizarre tenure of David Puttnam as head of Columbia Pictures. Puttnam was appointed president of Columbia with Coke's blessing, and he quickly became the soft drink giant's nemesis. In short order, Puttnam managed to antagonize nearly all of the major Hollywood power brokers and to defy the prevailing norms of Hollywood production. This resulted quickly in his very public ousting from Columbia, and his fate clarified the kinds of films that would and would not be made by Coke's new ward.

The Columbia purchase was an outgrowth of Coke's efforts to reposition itself in the decade and to alter the nature of its business portfolio. In March 1981, the Coca-Cola Co. approved a strategic plan for the 1980s that would guide the firm's decisions about the direction and conduct of its business. Deciding to embark on an aggressive program of business expansion, it sought to pursue growth opportunities beyond its traditional soft drink operations. On 4 March 1981, Coke chairman Roberto C. Goizueta presented "The Strategy for the 1980s" to Coke's board of directors, a document that defined "the future self-definition of The Coca-Cola Company." Goizueta promised that the company would not stray from its traditional areas of strength but would aim through expansion to maximize the returns on shareholder investments. "In choosing new areas of business, each market we enter must have sufficient inherent real growth potential to make entry desirable. It is not our desire to battle continually for share in a stagnant market in these new areas of business."[18] Coke was proud of its global soft drink markets and was committed to enhancing its international marketing prowess. It proclaimed, "The world is our arena in which to win marketing victories as we must." Movies might provide a powerful new means of winning these victories.

Coca-Cola was the world's largest manufacturer and distributor of soft drink syrups and concentrates, and soft drink products produced the overwhelming majority of Coke's revenues in 1982 (85 percent). The company also operated a food-and-wine business segment (Minute Maid juices, Hi-C, Taylor wines, coffee, and pasta products). Soft drink sales, however, were not growing faster than 10 percent a year, and by entering other business areas, Coke believed it could increase its earnings substantially. "We could have had a happy life without doing it, but it's not very exciting to grow at 10%,"

Goizueta remarked. Like other conglomerates who bought movie studios in the 1980s, Coke believed that the growth potential of the new distribution media was substantial and that the movie studios were the engines necessary to drive these new media and markets. Without Hollywood, no firm could be a global force in entertainment, and this became Coke's new vision and ambition. Goizueta explained, "You can't be a national force in soft drinks without a syrup plant, and in entertainment, you need a movie company—that's the turbine, the locomotive."[19]

But there was a major problem here, and in hindsight it is surprising no one saw it. The link between movies and soft drinks is neither strong nor persuasive. How, except in mainly peripheral and transient ways, could movie production and promotion enhance soft drink sales and vice versa? By contrast, the synergies between publishing, recorded music, and broadcast and cable television that are inherent in a marriage like Time Warner or that between Fox and the News Corp. are more compelling and certainly easier to conceive. These mergers brought together groups of information and entertainment media that could be used to cross-promote each other's products (e.g., BATMAN as book, record, movie, and comic strip). Soft drinks, by contrast, are not a form of media. Thus, it would prove difficult to establish synergies between Coke's soft drink operations and its entertainment business sector. From the start, though, Coke believed that its addition of an entertainment business sector to the company's other segments was a good fit. As it informed its stockholders,

> Of all the actions taken in 1982, we view as among the most significant our entry into an exciting new area of inherent profitable growth—entertainment. The acquisition of Columbia emerged from our careful search for a high-growth business that was compatible with the central strengths of the Company. . . . In Columbia we have an excellent complement to our traditional businesses—an almost ideal fit with what we are—and a perfect partner to join with us in becoming what we want to be.[20]

Pushing the analogies between movies and soft drinks, Goizueta announced, "We believe that the thirst we quench (with soft drinks) is no greater than the thirst for entertainment."[21] This, though, was synergy through metaphor and not through market. Continuing, Coke assured its shareholders that its soft drinks have "a commanding position in the home refrigerator. You can also see that Columbia now offers us the potential for an equally commanding position in that other key household center—the television set."[22]

Coke moved quickly to define a long range strategy for growth in its entertainment business sector. Film production would be increased beyond the eight pictures Columbia made in 1982 (the studio distributed domestically a total of twenty-one films that year), but risks would be managed by expanding outside financing of production costs. In this respect, Columbia was employing a funding strategy—offering limited partnerships and tax-sheltered investments in production— that was widely used by the majors in the eighties to augment their available production capital and generate resources to invest in a range of productions.

Escalating production costs and existing provisions in the tax code made this an attractive strategy, at least until the Tax Reform Act of 1986 repealed the investment tax credit that entertainment companies had used to attract investors. ANNIE (1982), POLTERGEIST (1982), ROCKY III (1982), FLASHDANCE (1983), and WHO FRAMED

ROGER RABBIT (1988) were funded through limited-partnership packages.[23] Disney had great success with its Silver Screen Partners, and Columbia financed a series of pictures with Delphi Film Associates. Outside the majors' orbits, the production, distribution, or both of such prominent independent films as THE TRIP TO BOUNTIFUL (1985), CHOOSE ME (1984), and KISS OF THE SPIDER WOMAN (1985) were funded by FilmDallas, an agency offering limited partnerships for productions occurring in the Dallas, Texas, area (see ch. 6).

With respect to Columbia, its 1982 joint venture with Delphi Film Associates had Delphi pledging $80 million to be raised through public stock offerings. In 1983 and 1984, Columbia again offered limited partnerships through Delphi on terms that would be favorable to investors. Delphi III (1984), for example, offered minimum investment units of $5,000, up to a total of $60 million. All distribution fees (17.5 percent of gross receipts) would be deferred until the limited partners had recovered 100 percent of their share of a film's production costs. In addition, Delphi III partners were to receive 8 percent of gross receipts. Columbia's use of partnership packages was a key means for achieving its goal of an expansion in production. Columbia's president, Frank Vincent, said that the boost in production would increase the film properties over which Columbia/Coke retained complete ownership so as to maximize ancillary profits.[24] Moreover, the studio was aggressively targeting these nontheatrical markets. Columbia and RCA had a joint venture—RCA Columbia International Video—for worldwide home video distribution. Columbia had an existing agreement with HBO for the cable presentation of its pictures, and Coke and Columbia moved quickly to strengthen the HBO alliance and to maximize the studio's ability to place more pictures into distribution. In November 1982, five months after Coca-Cola acquired Columbia, the formation of Tri-Star, the new major studio, was announced, created from a partnership among film production (Columbia), pay cable (HBO) and broadcast television (CBS). The new studio would aim to produce and distribute fifteen to twenty films per year, and these would be in addition to the normal load of pictures produced and distributed by Columbia.

Tri-Star is a perfect example of the synergies Coke wished to explore in filmed entertainment because it provided for shared funding of production (and shared risks) and integrated production with exhibition through the provisions for pay-TV and broadcast television screening of its product. Furthermore, the alliance with Coke gave Columbia (and Tri-Star) access to greater levels of funding for the expanded production schedule, this being one of the chief attractions inherent in acquisition by a large parent corporation. Coke's assets were also beneficial to Columbia in marketing and promoting its films. Coke's ability to buy large chunks of air time at volume discounts helped produce an increase of 5 percent in network TV time for Columbia's ads, and the studio and soft drink giant were able to swap air time for each other's products within the blocks they purchased in advance. When ABC aired THE DAY AFTER, for example, a 1983 TV movie about a nuclear war that destroys the United States, Coke backed out of advertising on the program, and Columbia aired a promo for one of its horror films instead. These benefits and arrangements exemplified Coke's movie business philosophy. According to Coca-Cola president Donald Keough, theatrical film "is a commodity business for the rest of the industry."[25] In other words, investment in theatrical film production was a multimarket venture. Columbia's joint projects with RCA, HBO, and CBS provided the pipelines for distributing this commodity (filmed entertainment) through these overlapping markets.

Like other conglomerates attracted to the movie business, though, Coke soon discovered that the business's "inherent growth potential" was erratic and unpredictable. The studio's performance was chronically disappointing for Coke. Throughout the 1980s, Columbia never attained a leading market share position. Its best year was 1984, when it had 16 percent of the market, behind market leader Paramount's 21 percent. Coke acknowledged in its stockholders report that Columbia's performance for 1983, the first full year of performance under its new owner, was "below expectations" and that the majority of profits in the entertainment business sector had been generated by Columbia Pictures Television, mainly through program syndication.[26] In subsequent years, too, Columbia Pictures' performance continued to be softer than Coke executives hoped. (Paramount, Warners, and Universal were the best-performing studios through the decade, having the largest theatrical market shares.[27]) Compounding Coke's dissatisfaction, the studio suffered one of the decade's biggest production and marketing disasters with ISHTAR (1987), a Dustin Hoffman–Warren Beatty comedy that nobody wanted to see. It was wastefully expensive to produce, was trashed by critics, and died in theaters. Like HEAVEN'S GATE earlier in the decade, ISHTAR's awfulness was widely interpreted as a symptom of poor management by the studio and its executives, though unlike HEAVEN'S GATE it did not lead to a major's demise. Columbia had to place $25 million in reserve to cover ISHTAR's losses.

ISHTAR *became one of the decade's most notorious pictures. Its high production budget and box-office failure emblemized for Coca-Cola the disappointing vagaries of the film business.*

Following the ISHTAR debacle, the continuing soft performance of Columbia and Tri-Star, and a year-long crisis of management within Columbia, Coke decided to reorganize its entertainment business sector to produce a leaner and more efficient operation. In December 1987, it merged Tri-Star into the entertainment business sector and renamed it Columbia Pictures Entertainment (CPE). Each studio would continue to operate separately with its own executive staff, but they would now be housed under the CPE umbrella. This reorganization was Coke's answer to a horrendous year at Columbia during which studio management veered far from Coke's visions for the new decade. Columbia's troubled internal operations and its disappointing box-office performance were given stark visibility by the fallout from the CPE reorganization—the ouster of Columbia's chair/CEO David Puttnam. Puttnam's reign had been a disaster for the studio. In his brief, one-year tenure as Columbia head, Puttnam's brash statements that most American films and filmmakers were no good had alienated top executives at Coke and a wide array of movie industry producers, directors, and actors. The Puttnam saga is significant and striking because his production policies and attitudes were glaringly out of synch with the performance Coke wanted to see from Columbia. Puttnam took the studio down a road that neither Coke nor the industry as a whole wished to travel. Puttnam's fate dramatically illuminated the constraints operating on film production when it occurs as part of a diversified leisure industry and when a studio chief brazenly ignores some of the industry's fundamental principles.

The David Puttnam Debacle

Puttnam came to Columbia as the British producer of such highly regarded but modestly performing films as CHARIOTS OF FIRE (1981), LOCAL HERO (1983), and THE KILLING FIELDS (1984), and he was deeply ambivalent about working for the Hollywood industry. Worse yet, he publicly projected this ambivalence. He accepted a multimillion-dollar contract but insisted on a three-year cap because he felt that he had sold out to the system by coming to Hollywood. By limiting his involvement, he said, he could salvage his dignity.

In his speeches Puttnam proclaimed high-minded ideals and a commitment to using film to elevate the moral and social sensibilities of the audience. "Artists and those who work with them have a moral responsibility to the audience" was an idea he frequently repeated in speeches. Motion picture artists should "seriously consider restating our commitment to what benefits the rest of the human race."[28] Puttnam's idealism accompanied a disdain for the commerce of movies. Incredibly, for a man selected as CEO of a major studio, Puttnam disparaged the commercial context in which filmmaking operates, especially its need to turn a profit. Worse yet, from the standpoint of his employers, Puttnam explicitly declared his hostility to film as a profit-making enterprise. RAMBO (1985) had been one of the top, and few, big money-earners for Tri-Star, and Puttnam informed Coke that, had the decision been his, he never would have made the picture. Puttnam quickly put Coke president Donald Keough and chair Roberto Goizueta on notice that seeking big box-office returns would not be his objective as Columbia head (this to Goizueta, who had formulated Coke's 1980s mission statement about investing in business sectors that had major growth potential!). Upon his hire, Puttnam wrote them, "The medium is too powerful and too important an influence on the way we live, the way we see ourselves, to be left solely to the tyranny of the box-office or reduced to the sum of the lowest common denominator of public taste."[29] It

David Puttnam's tenure as head of Columbia Pictures was turbulent and caused dissension within the ranks of Hollywood's power brokers.

would be difficult to imagine Coke having a bigger nightmare than to hear this from the head of the most important sector of its entertainment business segment.

Instead of making blockbusters, Puttnam wished to pursue smaller-scale filmmaking. In pursuit of this plan, he alienated the industry's powerful talent agencies by proclaiming that henceforth Columbia would develop its productions in-house and would turn down "packages," expensive director-star-script combinations brought to studios by the agencies. This was an impossible policy. No major was equipped in the 1980s to operate as studios of the classical period did, funding all of their own productions and staffing them from a vast array of in-house talent. Studios sought outside investors precisely because production had become too expensive and risky to fund through existing house capital revenues and lines of credit, and no studio had a stable of talent on long-term contract. Puttnam's plan, therefore, displayed a basic ignorance of the contemporary industry. Furthermore, he committed Columbia's $300 million production and distribution budget to an ill-considered series of low-budget projects (at their worst, these included THE BEAST [1988], a violence-laden picture about the Afghan-Soviet war, and ME AND HIM [1989], about a talking penis) and such badly chosen big-budget pictures as THE ADVENTURES OF BARON MUNCHAUSEN (1989), which went well over budget. For this film about a nineteenth-century character who was poorly known outside Germany, Columbia failed to secure distribution rights in the vitally important German market!

Puttnam loudly opposed paying the large salaries commanded by the industry's top actors and directors, and his comments in this respect alienated powerhouses Warren Beatty and Dustin Hofman. Accordingly, Columbia's slate of upcoming Puttnam-chosen films lacked the celebrity name recognition that successful marketing generally requires. Worse, Puttnam turned down projects by such top industry figures as producer Ray Stark and director Norman Jewison. One such project became the hit MOONSTRUCK (1987) when Jewison took it to MGM. And worst of all, Puttnam refused to put into production any sequels to Columbia's cash cows, GHOSTBUSTERS (1984), the KARATE KID series (1984, 1986, 1989), and JAGGED EDGE (1985).

Puttnam apparently expected that Coke would acquiesce in these policies. If, on the other hand, Puttnam did not believe that Coke would support him, he was being reckless. "What I was trying to do was a different type of business. Smaller films, smaller risks. Smaller profits but regular profits," he said.[30] The risks, though, were not small, and it was Coke that was taking them. Author Charles Kipps, who as a reporter for

David Puttnam's failure to make a deal with director Norman Jewison (pictured here directing Cher) for Moonstruck *cost Columbia a big hit and gave* MGM, *where Jewison took the project, one of its few solid successes of the decade.*

Variety provided the most penetrating analysis of Puttnam's tenure at Columbia, placed Coke's risk in context:

> At twenty-five cents a pop on the wholesale market—about twelve cents profit—the soft drink maker would have to sell over *two billion* bottles of Coke to offset $270,000,000 should the new lineup of pictures fail at the box office. Add a requisite couple of hundred million for prints and advertising, and Coke might have to ship out four billion units of fizzy caramel-colored liquid to pay for David Puttnam's slate.[31]

To his credit, Puttnam was against making what turned into two of Columbia's biggest embarassments and money-losers, Ishtar and Bill Cosby's Leonard, Part 6 (1987). (He did, however, make decisions that seemed to foredoom Leonard. In a move that prompted cries of cronyism, he assigned the picture to Paul Weiland, a young British director who had little feel for American culture and for the ways Cosby's humor connected with this culture.) On the other hand, the pictures that Puttnam inherited and approved for production and those he brought to the studio proved to have a dismal track record. *Variety* calculated that the thirty-three pictures associated with Puttnam had negative and advertising costs of $432 million and by midyear 1988 had grossed only $112 million at the box office.[32] These pictures included such underperformers as Little Nikita (1988), Old Gringo (1989), and True Believer (1989) as well as such highly regarded films as John Boorman's Hope and Glory (1987) and Bernardo Bertolucci's high-grossing (in relation to production costs) The Last Emperor (1987). Puttnam's

most expensive film, THE ADVENTURES OF BARON MUNCHAUSEN ($33 million in pro-
duction and advertising costs), had earned barely $3 million one month into its release.
Columbia's losses from the Puttnam slate of pictures approached $300 million.

Puttnam's program of small-scale, inexpensive filmmaking, then, was terribly costly
for Columbia. In theory, Puttnam's objectives may have been laudable, but his production choices and the economics of the industry worked against their success. A production
cost of under $10 million generally denotes the absence of prominent stars, name direc-
tors, and complex post-production work (e.g., special effects), all of which studios view
as box-office assets (and all of which Puttnam disdained). In the contemporary industry,
the high costs of advertising and distribution, paradoxically, warrant a high production
cost if it contains these box-office assets. Furthermore, stars and effects are vital for a
film's lifetime earning potential. Stars and effects will continue to generate revenue in
ancillary markets while "little" films without these attention-getting features have a
harder time. The industry's economics, therefore, gear it toward more expensively budgeted productions than Puttnam preferred to undertake. To make a lot of money, you
have to spend a lot of money. Frank Price, Columbia's chair from 1978 to 1983,
explained the logic of these factors: "A $20,000,000 picture with names has less risk than
a $10,000,000 picture without names. You have tangible aspects—video, foreign, and so
on—with major actors and directors. Without them there is a huge risk and you can lose
all the money. In fact, you probably will." Producer Martin Ransohoff pointed out, "If
you elect to go out and make a seven-to-eight-million dollar movie, which in all likelihood means no major stars or major directors, you could be looking at drastically

Columbia's distribution of Bernardo Bertolucci's THE LAST EMPEROR *was one of the
bright spots of David Puttnam's ill-fated tenure as studio head.*

reduced cable and cassette income."[33] Puttnam's preference for small pictures, then, tended to produce exactly those kinds of films that the studio would be ill equipped to market and sell and that would have a short ancillary life, product that would fail to excite the executives to whom its fate was entrusted. In this way, Puttnam's anti-box-office philosophies proved to be self-fulfilling. Columbia could not easily market such low-cost, low-concept films as THE BIG PICTURE (1989), EARTH GIRLS ARE EASY (1989), ROCKET GIBRALTAR (1988), and THINGS CHANGE (1988). The accumulated losses on these "small" pictures put the studio deeper into the red.

Thus, Puttnam's ouster, and his replacement by Hollywood insider Dawn Steel, was inevitable. His performance was antithetical to the system he had been hired to administer. Significantly for Coke, his tenure at Columbia served to demonstrate the inherent uncertainties of film production, particularly when it flies against the dynamics of industry economics, and Coke had failed to recognize these uncertainties when it acquired Columbia. Even expensive productions with stars and effects may suffer a disappointing fate. In 1988, Columbia Pictures Entertainment found all of its expensive (over $14 million) productions performing poorly at the domestic box office.[34] These included RAMBO III, RED HEAT, SWITCHING CHANNELS, LITTLE NIKITA, THE SEVENTH SIGN, SUNSET, SHORT CIRCUIT 2, THE BLOB, and VIBES. (RED HEAT and RAMBO III, however, starred Arnold Schwarzenegger and Sylvester Stallone respectively, performers with a huge international popularity. Overseas rentals on these pictures were especially strong, ensuring that they would be wins for their distributor, Tri-Star.)

In 1988, after Puttnam's tenure had ended, the erratic nature of the film business continued to plague Coke. Columbia and Tri-Star had not become the strong and growing revenue generators Coke had hoped for. Coke always knew that it was primarily a soft drink company, and at decade's end it renounced its pursuit of filmed entertainment gold and re-embraced its core markets. In November 1989 it sold Columbia Pictures Entertainment to Japan's Sony Corp. for $3.4 billion. For Coke, CPE would henceforth be recorded as a discontinued operation, and in its 1989 10-K report profiling the achievements of "an extraordinary decade," the aborted venture into filmed entertainment received no mention. Instead, Coke announced that its achievements for the 1980s lay in the growth of Coke's market share of global soft drink sales from 38 to 45 percent, and its agenda for the 1990s, more modest than that for the 1980s, was phrased, simply, "to increase our global soft drink leadership."[35]

ENTER SONY

The synergies Coke had hoped to obtain in its buy of Columbia Pictures were more startlingly apparent in the Sony-Columbia marriage. Indeed, Sony's expressed intent was to own software-producing companies that would complement its manufacture of audio and video hardware. The cover of Sony's annual report for 1991 pictured a scene from Columbia's film AWAKENINGS (1990) displayed on a Sony Trinitron HDTV and captioned, "Sony seeks to create synergies between its hardware and software businesses."[36] Sony's purchase of Columbia was a vivid example of the era's foreign acquisition of U.S. business giants. This deal was the eighth-largest foreign buy of the decade, and it coincided with an acceleration in the latter 1980s of deals involving offshore buyers. The dollar value of such deals increased 66 percent between 1986 and 1987, from $25 billion to $42 billion. Seeking to expand, foreign firms sought to overcome the limitations of their indigenous European, Australian, or Japanese markets by buying into U.S. industries, and a key factor propelling the growing wave of such deals was the willingness of foreign firms to pay higher prices for targeted businesses than earlier in the decade.[37] Sony and Matsushita (which bought MCA/Universal) were criticized by U.S. analysts for paying inflated prices for the studios, but their behavior was consistent with the parameters of offshore buying in those years.

One of the world's largest manufacturers of audio and video equipment, Sony aimed in the late 1980s to become a global hardware-software company. Accordingly, it made a pair of purchases to gain strategic entry into the U.S. entertainment market. Sony became the world's largest record producer when it bought CBS Records, Inc., in January 1988 for $2 billion. With the November 1989 purchase of Columbia Pictures Entertainment, Sony had the music- and image-based operations it believed were essential for the growth of its hardware business, and in 1991 Sony changed the name of CPE to Sony Pictures Entertainment, Inc. As chart 2.3 shows, Sony's global market ambitions were decisively augmented by its Columbia and CBS purchases. In 1991, the U.S. market provided the leading revenue segment of Sony's global businesses.

Sony's entry into the U.S. film market gained it some unexpected alliances with industry giant Time Warner. Because Sony wanted producers Peter Guber and Jon Peters to head Columbia, Sony bought their Guber-Peters Entertainment Co. for $200 million. Guber and Peters, though, were under exclusive contract with Warner Bros., which promptly sued Sony for $1 billion. Under the settlement, Sony and Time Warner became partners in several joint ventures, which symbolized the increasingly interlocking nature of the business. Warners got a 50 percent interest in Columbia House, a unit of CBS Records that produced a huge volume of mail order recorded-music products. Sony and Warners swapped studio properties in Burbank and Culver City, and Warners got cable distribution rights for all Columbia theatrical and TV films.[38]

By 1991, then, Columbia was tied to a powerful communications industry parent. Sony's filmed entertainment operations (comprising Columbia Pictures, Tri-Star,

CHART 2.3
Globalization: Sony, Net Sales in Major Markets, 1991

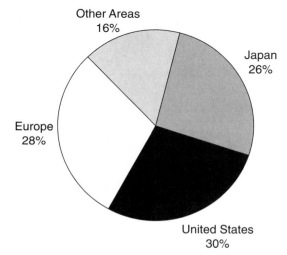

SOURCE: Sony Corp., Form 10-K, 1991, p. 12.

Columbia Pictures Television, Merv Griffin Enterprises, and Loews Theatre Management Corp.) generated $1.8 billion in sales, 7 percent of Sony's total. Sony proudly announced that SPE was "well positioned to become a premiere force in global entertainment through the 1990s and beyond."[39] Columbia had successfully ridden out the industry transformations of the 1980s to become part of the emerging information industry oligopoly.

Deconglomeration in Hollywood

For most of the majors, the industry's reorganization brought new corporate owners, some of the biggest from overseas, while for others it entailed massive programs of divestiture that set them on a course of deconglomeration. In both cases—foreign acquisition and programs of divestiture—the Hollywood industry participated in the larger patterns of corporate restructuring that were shaping U.S. businesses in the 1980s. In this respect, the forces affecting the Hollywood industry were of a macroeconomic order and were influencing multiple U.S. industry segments. Foreign acquisition of U.S. businesses included the major studios as well as Standard Oil Co. and Shell Oil, Pillsbury Co. (food), Firestone Tire and Rubber (tires), SmithKline Beecham Corp. (pharmaceuticals), Chesebrough-Pond (cosmetics), Farmers Group, Inc. (insurance), Texasgulf, Inc. (minerals), Hilton International Co. (hotels), Ogilvy Group (advertising), First Jersey National Corp. (banking), Telex Corp. (communications equipment), and many others. Similarly, the deconglomeration of Hollywood majors or their parent companies accorded with a general trend throughout large U.S. businesses of divesting unrelated market segments in order to concentrate on related areas of operation and to facilitate ongoing merger-and-acquisition activities. As table 2.6 and chart 2.4 show, corporate divestiture in the U.S. economy climbed sharply from 104 transactions in 1980 to a decade high of 1,419 transactions by 1986. Within the Hollywood industry, the most striking cases of deconglomeration were undertaken by Gulf and Western (Paramount) and Warner Communications, Inc. (Warner Bros.).

TABLE 2.6
U.S. Corporate Divestitures 1980–89

	Number of Deals	Value ($billion)
1980	104	5.1
1981	476	10.2
1982	562	8.4
1983	661	12.9
1984	793	30.6
1985	1,039	43.5
1986	1,419	72.4
1987	1,219	57.7
1988	1,273	83.2
1989	1,119	60.8

Source: *Mergers and Acquisitions* 24, no. 5 (1990), p. 95.

CHART 2.4
U.S. Corporate Divestitutes, 1980–89

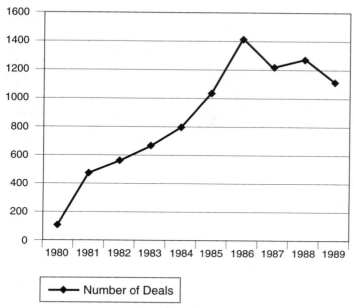

SOURCE: *Mergers and Acquisitions* 24, no. 5 (1990): p. 95.

Beginning in 1983, Gulf and Western embarked on a major process of corporate streamlining. This completely transformed G&W from an old-line conglomerate, with far-flung businesses, to a powerful communications firm ready and willing to risk a hostile takeover of giant Time, Inc., in an ambitious bid to achieve synergies in the home entertainment arena. The precipitating event was the sudden, unexpected death of Charles Bluhdorn, G&W's founder, chairman, and CEO. Bluhdorn, fifty, died 19 February 1983 on a company jet flying to New York from the Dominican Republic, where the company operated a sugar business. Under Bluhdorn, G&W had consisted of a scattered collection of business segments: leisure time, financial services, manufacturing, apparel and home furnishings, consumer and agricultural products, automotive replacement parts, and natural resource and building products. These were nonoverlapping operations, and their disparity held little potential for synergy. Prior to Bluhdorn's passing, G&W recognized that its sprawling corporate structure was disadvantageous and dispersed its resources. Its antiquated structure provided no competitive advantage in the synergistic eighties. Accordingly, from 1980 to 1982, G&W began to redeploy its resources by trimming its corporate structure, strengthening its financial position, and divesting operations that did not fit its evolving corporate profile. With the high inflation of the early eighties, G&W was anxious to shift away from capital-intensive operations, such as zinc mining and paper production, and toward others, such as financial services and leisure-time markets, where it would not have to maintain a heavy-industry infrastructure as a condition for doing business and where the capital invested would ideally generate bigger returns. Before Bluhdorn's death, G&W had defined its long-range strategy thusly:

The death of Charles Bluhdorn (right) accelerated the dramatic corporate transformation of Gulf and Western Industries and its subsidiary Paramount Pictures.

> Gulf & Western has embarked upon a program designed to streamline the Company's overall scope of activities through the disposition of operations that no longer meet G&W's criteria for growth and return on investment. These streamlining efforts also involve the sale of capital-intensive businesses that would require a continuing high level of expenditures for new plants, machinery and equipment without producing a satisfactory return on the capital invested.[40]

Bluhdorn's death accelerated these trends, taking the transformation farther and faster than it may have gone under his continued stewardship. In March 1983, G&W reduced its operating divisions from seven to three. Those remaining were an enlarged leisure-time group (which had Paramount chair Barry Diller as its head), the financial services group, and the consumer and industrial products group.[41] G&W next carried through some major divestitures. It sold its sugar-growing operations in Florida and the Dominican Republic in January 1985. As new CEO Martin S. Davis explained, "Sugar no longer fits in with the company's longterm strategic plan to concentrate principally on higher return consumer-oriented products, financial service and leisure time businesses."[42] In September 1985, G&W sold its entire consumer and industrial products group, leaving it, at mid-decade, operating in three newly-defined core areas: financial services, publishing and information services, and entertainment.

The financial services group was the next to go, but this did not occur until 1989. G&W delayed divesting this unit because it was generating huge revenues. In 1985, financial produced $1.4 billion, far ahead of the $916 million contributed by entertainment and the $664 million contributed by publishing and information services.[43] G&W's decision to sell the financial group, despite its contributions to the company's coffers, underscores the significance of its decision to become a communications firm and its determination to implement this plan. Despite financial's performance, it no longer fit with G&W's evolving design, and its presence in the company confused Wall Street analysts, who believed that it lacked synergy with the entertainment and publishing operations. Wall Street's reaction encouraged the eventual divestiture of financial: the stock was chronically devalued.[44]

In this respect, Wall Street played a major role in helping choreograph and direct the pattern and direction of the period's acquisition and divestiture transactions, penalizing the stock prices of firms that it believed were overly diversified. Merrill Lynch entertainment analyst Harold Vogel explained, "This [selling the financial unit] has been urged upon Davis by the professional investment community. It was an inevitable choice that had to be made." For his part, Davis remarked that the financial operations were "incompatible" with G&W's new communications orientation.[45] Davis called G&W's transformation a process of deconglomeration. He noted, "This restructuring has resulted in a 'deconglomeration' of Gulf & Western into a more rational and focused enterprise, with a clearer sense of purpose and direction."[46] Chart 2.5 shows the striking effects of this process by picturing the company's organization before and after the transformation.

G&W offered the most dramatic symbol it could devise of its new identity. It ceased to exist. In June 1989, its official corporate name became Paramount Communications,

CHART 2.5
Deconglomeration: From G&W to Paramount Communications, Inc.

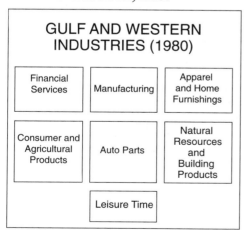

Inc. (PCI). Gulf and Western, as a corporate moniker, to say nothing of its once far-flung business segments, was no more. PCI's annual report for 1989 listed its business operations as, simply, entertainment and publishing. Within each of these areas, though, the holdings were extensive. Publishing operations were aimed at the textbook, trade, and professional information markets and were conducted by such houses as Simon and Schuster, Prentice Hall, Pocket Books, and Allyn and Bacon. Entertainment included Paramount Pictures, Paramount Home Video, Paramount Television (seven independent broadcast television stations), Famous Players theaters (a 472-screen circuit throughout Canada), Cineamerica (a joint venture with Warner Communications, Inc., operating 466 theaters in the western United States), the USA Network (a joint venture with MCA in ownership of this basic cable television network), and Madison Square Garden (activities included presentation of live events as well as cable television programming).

Through its entertainment division, PCI was producing films and television programs, distributing these throughout the world on film and videotape, and operating exhibition showcases (motion picture theaters, broadcast television stations, and a cable network). Through its purposeful, decade-long transformation, in other words, G&W had converted itself into a global, vertically integrated communications company. With revenues from the entertainment sector in 1989 at $2 billion, it prepared to focus its energies and resources on worldwide expansion. Flush with cash from the sale of its financial group, PCI looked about at its communication competitors. Time was about to execute a merger with Warner Communications that would make it the world's biggest producer of information and home entertainment products. But not if PCI succeeded in taking over Time. Intent on becoming an unrivaled global giant, PCI locked, loaded, and put Time, Inc., in its sights.

The Time Warner Saga

The planned merger of Time and Warner Communications was the outgrowth of a reorganization at WCI during which the company redefined itself as a media-only operation in ways that strengthened its ability to conduct business in synergistically related markets. As with Gulf and Western, an immediate crisis did much to trigger the rapid reinvention of WCI. In mid-decade Warner Communications, Inc., cut its operations and corporate holdings in the wake of tremendous and sudden revenue losses incurred by its Atari video games and home computer division. Several factors had contributed to Atari's slide. In its years of peak earnings, Atari faced little significant competition in the video game business. A WCI executive noted in 1982 that "we've never had very deep, meaningful cartridge competition before."[47] Atari and Activision were the major game producers in 1981, but by 1982 as many as fifteen companies had entered the field and flooded the market with product. In addition to Atari's loss of its serendipitous market position, the film-related games ("Raiders of the Lost Ark," "E.T.")that it had counted on to be big sellers failed to perform, and a subsequent shift away from production of film-related games failed to correct Atari's slide.

WCI had acquired Atari in 1975 for a mere $28 million, and at the time Atari's revenues were only $39 million. WCI was jubilant when Atari's earnings skyrocketed, doubling in 1980 and again in 1981. WCI's overall revenues rose more than 50 percent in 1981, to $3.2 billion, and Atari, which earned over $1 billion that year, was the big engine behind this increase. In 1981, the operating income of the consumer electronics division (where Atari was housed) exceeded WCI's entire operating income of 1979. Pleased beyond belief, WCI crowed about Atari's "leadership in the cultural revolution that is video games" and predicted that "Atari's leading position in coin-operated games and the exciting prospects for Atari's home computers indicate that Atari will be a source of significant growth well into the future."[48]

Then the bottom fell out. In December 1982, WCI stunned the investment community with its announcement that Atari's fourth-quarter earnings were projected to be "substantially below expectations." The news triggered a 37 percent drop in Atari's stock in a single week. Things only got worse from there. The news about Atari's 1982 performance was devastating. WCI's Consumer Electronics Division registered a near-complete collapse of its operating income, from $136.5 million in 1981 to $1.2 million in 1982. In the first quarter of 1983, Atari's losses pulled WCI's company-wide revenue down $19 million. Faced with pretax operating losses of $879 million over the previous six quarters, WCI dumped Atari in July 1984. Chair Steve Ross announced, "We have concluded . . . that we must constructively channel our energies and resources to the balance of WCI's businesses."[49] (Counterbalancing the Atari debacle for WCI in 1984 was the remarkable good news about the performance of its feature films. Because of the success of GREMLINS, SUDDEN IMPACT [1983], POLICE ACADEMY, and PURPLE RAIN, film revenue passed $300 million for the first time in Warner history.)

WCI moved quickly to stop the financial hemorrhage. In August 1984, one month after selling Atari, it fired 250 employees, cutting its corporate staff in half. Facing its huge mountain of debt, in December 1984 WCI renegotiated its line of bank credit and, in the words of one Wall Street analyst, "pledged the company" to secure the new agreement.[50] As collateral for a $550 million credit line, WCI pledged the stock from its motion picture, recorded-music, and publishing operations. Under provisions of the agreement, WCI could borrow against its credit line in diminishing amounts through January 1987, depending on the size of its outstanding short-term debt. To raise cash and reduce its debt load, WCI commenced a dramatic program of corporate downsizing and reshaping. It sold its peripheral nonmedia businesses in order to concentrate on entertainment and information operations. Jettisoned operations included the Knickerboker Toy Co., the Malibu Grand Prix Corp., the Franklin Mint, Warner/Lauren Cosmetics, Warner Theatre Productions, the Pittsburgh Pirates baseball team, Gadgets restaurant chain, and the New York Cosmos soccer team. By 1987, WCI had eliminated the vestiges of its old-line conglomeration and had become a strict communication and entertainment business with operations in four areas: filmed entertainment, recorded music, cable and broadcasting, and publishing. Its evolved structure would facilitate combination with other media businesses, and WCI and Time, Inc., were soon courting each other as marriage partners.

Each company stood to gain from their proposed union. Since its founding in 1922, Time had become a strangely bifurcated company. Its main line of business was publication of magazines (*Time, Fortune, Sports Illustrated, People,* and others) and books (Time-Life Books, Book-of-the-Month Club). Time, though, was also heavily involved in cable television operations, through its subsidiary American Television and Communications Corp. (ATC) with 4.4 million subscribers, and in cable programming through its wholly owned subsidiary Home Box Office, Inc. (HBO), with 17 million subscribers. These two areas of operation were roughly equivalent revenue generators for Time. But Time was in a weak strategic position relative to the other communications empires. It owned no copyrighted feature film programming outside of its HBO productions and no recorded-music programming. Thus it was in a poor position to generate products for ancillary film markets.

HBO, as we have seen, had become a powerful force in funding production of Hollywood films, and it had considerable clout in setting the prices that majors would pay for distribution on its premium pay-cable service. But HBO was vulnerable, in turn, to the majors because it did not originate programming for the theatrical market that drove the ancillaries. The attempt to launch Premiere by several of the majors demonstrated HBO's vulnerability to a product cutoff. Time, Inc., therefore, had two areas of operation that, as presently constituted, were non-synergistic and would be poorly competitive with the emerging communications giants. By joining with WCI, however, the new entity would be positioned to operate in the areas of film and television programming (Warner Bros., Warner Bros. Television, Warner Home Video), broadcasting (Warner subsidiary BHC, Inc., operated seven major-market television stations), expanded cable operations (Warner Cable served 1.7 million subscribers), recorded music and music publishing (a host of WCI labels), product licensing of popular film and television characters (WCI's Licensing Corp. of America), and expanded publishing operations (WCI's Warner Books, D.C. Comics, and *Mad* magazine). The marriage with Warner would help insulate Time from hostile takeover and would make it extraordinarily competitive. But the marriage as planned was not to occur.

A dramatic, three-way battle of media titans began 6 June 1989, when Paramount Communications, Inc., threw a bomb into the cash-free, debt-free merger that Time and Warner Communications had planned for their firms. The merger was to have proceeded on the basis of a stock swap between shareholders of the two companies, and it would have created a media giant unburdened by the heavy debt load that corporate acquisitions typically produce. Merging on a debt-free basis was extremely important for Time and WCI, but Paramount's hostile intervention quickly scuttled this possibility. On 6 June, two weeks before Time and Warner shareholders were to vote on the deal, PCI announced its bid to buy Time for $175 a share, or $10.7 billion. (Time's stock had been selling for $125 before this. Paramount's extraordinary bid illustrates the general willingness of firms in the late eighties to pay inflated prices for mergers and acquisitions.) Using a brilliant strategy, PCI argued that Time had put itself into play as a company for sale when it agreed to merge with Warner. Paramount's reasoning was based on the terms of the proposed stock swap, which would have given Warner shareholders 62 percent of Time's shares. PCI argued that this amounted to a "change of control" of Time, and legal precedent had established that, under such conditions, management is obligated to get the highest price for its shareholders.[51] Paramount's inflated bid for Time's shares was a maneuver to compel Time's board of directors to honor this principle, that is, to proceed in the way that would best benefit its shareholders. A buyout rather than a merger would bring a better price.

PCI's bid for Time, and the legal strategy on which it was based, raised ominous issues for corporate administration. If a company planned to merge, did it thereby become vulnerable to a hostile takeover? Would planned mergers henceforth carry this risk? According to many corporate lawyers, a win by Paramount would introduce "an era in which any company that announces a merger also announces that it is up for sale."[52] Furthermore, with all of the merger activity then ongoing in the Hollywood industry and nationwide, and the emergence of ever-bigger combines, PCI's grab for Time threatened everyone. As *Variety* noted, "PCI's preemptive blow against Time/Warner served notice that any one of them could be the next target for domestic predators, or be forced into defensive alliances out of mutual convenience or for self-protection. All of show business is now in play."[53]

Time rejected Paramount's offer and filed suit to block its takeover ploy. On 16 June, Time and Warner took defensive steps by completing a stock swap under which Time got 9 percent of Warner stock and Warner shareholders got 11 percent of Time. Furthermore, Time announced a major revision of the planned merger. It would now buy WCI outright. PCI's move had changed the terms of the deal, killing the merger and forcing Time to pay for an acquisition. Paramount then commenced a bidding war by raising its offer to $200 a share ($12.2 billion), and, joined by dissident Time shareholders who wanted the best price, it filed suit to stop Time's buy of Warners.

Time's board had opened itself to legal attack because it did not ask for shareholder approval to pursue its revised deal (the buy) of Warners. It acted unilaterally and, by rejecting Paramount's offer, it was arguably failing to obtain the best deal for its shareholders. In respect of its action, the behavior of Time's board raised an important legal question about the management of a company's assets. Who runs the firm, the managers or the shareholders? If it is the shareholders, then Time's board was accountable to them and would be constrained from acting in ways that would alter corporate structure or assets without getting shareholder approval. Writing in *Barron's*, lawyer Benjamin J. Stein suggested that, in the Time-Paramount battle, "the real fight is far more basic. It is between the managers of Time and the shareholders of Time," and he noted ironically that "Martin Davis of Paramount got a 50% better deal for the stockholders of Time than their own directors did."[54]

These issues were resolved by the Delaware Chancery Court's 14 July ruling blocking Paramount's bid for Time and backing Time's board in its decision to acquire Warner without shareholder approval. The judge's ruling effectively said that the board of directors runs the company: "The corporation law does not operate on the theory that directors, in exercising their power to manage the firm, are obligated to follow the wishes of a majority of shares. In fact, directors, not shareholders, are charged with the duty to manage the firm."[55] The court found that because Time's directors were pursuing a long-range strategic goal, they were managing the firm in accordance with their perception of its best interest. This decision accorded with the decade's accelerating merger-and-acquisition activities, and it granted corporate managers considerable latitude to pursue m&a ventures unemcumbered by shareholder constraints.

The Time-Warner union now proceeded unhindered to produce an impressive media colossus. In answer to criticism of the new firm's size, Time and Warner justified the combination as a counterthrust to foreign control of American media companies. Besides the buys by Sony, Matsushita, and the News Corp. of Hollywood studios, broadcasting, and record companies, West Germany's Bertelsmann AG had purchased RCA Records and book publisher Doubleday, Inc., in 1986. France's Hachette bought Grollier, Inc., in 1988, the world's biggest publisher of encyclopedias, and the News Corp.'s 50 percent ownership of *Elle* magazine to make it sole owner of *Elle*. And in 1990, Italy's Giancarlo Parretti would maneuver to buy MGM/UA. In this era of foreign entry into U.S. communications and entertainment industries, the Time-Warner combination had a built-in patriotic appeal. Time and Warner chairmen J. Richard Munro and Steven J. Ross said that their plan would "create a combined American entity with the resources to compete globally with anyone in our industry." A major WCI stockholder concurred, emphasizing the importance of keeping the ownership of American communications companies in America and the need for the federal government to back mergers of U.S. firms to provide a hedge against acquisitions by foreign owners: "U.S. companies need megamergers to create critical mass. Congress has got to wake up and allow U.S. companies to accomplish that. We've already made it easier for foreigners by debasing our currency. You can't stop Americans from buying American under rules that don't work anymore." The sheer size of Time Warner, in this context, was an asset because it promised an invulnerability to foreign acquisition. An executive with the Capital Group, an investor in both Time and WCI, said approvingly, "I think the [Time Warner] merger is brilliant because it creates the biggest, best-positioned, most powerful entertainment media company in the world. The way the industry is trending is toward large, global, vertically integrated companies."[56]

How did Time Warner look as a result of the merger? In 1989, the company reported revenues of $10.8 billion.[57] The company's principal lines of business were book and magazine publishing, production and distribution of filmed entertainment and television programming, production and distribution of recorded music and music publishing, operation of cable television systems, and the distribution of cable TV programming. The company published D.C. Comics, *Time, Fortune, Sports Illustrated, People, Money, Life,* and *Sports Illustrated for Kids,* as well as numerous regional magazines. Book-publishing operations included Time-Life Books, Book-of-the-Month Club with over 3 million members, Warner Books, and Little, Brown and Company. The recorded-Music and music-publishing area included the record labels held by WCI (see ch. 1); and its music-publishing business operated worldwide, with most of its revenues derived from overseas.

The filmed-entertainment area, which generated revenues of $2.7 billion for 1989, consisted of the production and distribution operations of Warner Bros., Inc., and Lorimar Telepictures Corp. In 1989, Warners distributed nineteen films worldwide, including BATMAN, 1989's biggest domestic winner and the highest-grossing film in Warners' history. Warners also had the number three film that year, LETHAL WEAPON 2, and it was the major with the biggest share of the domestic market in 1989. Like all the majors, Warners licensed its films to broadcast and pay-cable television, and it had licensing deals in place to total $977 million by year's end. Warner Home Video had a library of over 1,800 pictures available on videocassette and over 350 on videodisc. Eleven Warner Home Video releases in 1989 sold over 150,000 copies each. Warner Bros. also had extensive holdings in exhibition. In a joint venture with Paramount Communications, Warners held a 50 percent interest in 373 theaters in the eastern and western United States. Warners opened three multiplex cinemas in England and planned to construct others in Germany, Denmark, Australia, and the Soviet Union, the first in that country. In addition, it planned to open a movie theme park in Brisbane, Australia.

Time Warner had extensive cable television operations. Its cable systems consisted of the ATC Corp., serving 4 million subscribers in thirty-three states, and Warner Cable, serving 1.7 million subscribers in twenty-two states. Time Warner also offered cable programming via HBO (17 million subscribers) and Cinemax (6 million subscribers). HBO also owned a videocassette distribution subsidiary, HBO Video. In 1988, HBO formed a limited partnership with Cinema Plus to finance feature films, for which HBO would then control exclusive home video and pay television rights. Time Warner also held an 18 percent interest in Turner Broadcasting System, Inc., which included CNN, TNT, Headline News, and a broadcast television station (WTBS) carried on many cable systems; a 17 percent interest in Hasbro Toys; and, through WCI, a 25 percent interest in Atari, which had generated spectacular earnings for WCI before crashing.

The corporate philosophy behind this array of enterprises is instructive. By combining, Time and Warner achieved market synergies far beyond what either possessed alone. In its documentation for shareholders, Time Warner emphasized that the overriding factor behind the decision to unite was the need to compete in international markets and to participate in the globalization of media industries. Time Warner explicitly cited this factor as the fundamental rationale for the corporate marriage: "Time Inc. and Warner Communications Inc. came independently to the same fundamental conclusion: globalization was rapidly evolving from a prophecy to a fact of life. No serious competitor could hope for any long-term success unless, building on a secure home base, it achieved a major presence in all of the world's important markets." The stakes of media competition were now planetary, and the new entity would be good for America's participation in the these markets. "For America, Time Warner ensures a powerful presence among the international giants competing against each other across the planet." Time Warner's rhetoric went even farther by attaching political ideals to its marriage of businesses. It tied the globalization of media markets to the political transformation of Eastern Europe and the Soviet Union. Greater political freedoms, it claimed, would coincide with newly opened markets, and Time Warner, through its products, would thereby contribute to the spread of freedom and democracy:

> The concrete certainties that seemed permanently to imprison that part of the planet have cracked and crumbled. We are witnessing a deep stirring in the world, an aching to share in the democratic freedoms that America enjoys in such abundance, in the options we have in small matters as well as great, and in the diversity of choices we have about what we view or listen to or read. Time-Warner welcomes the role it can play in helping to offer people all over the world a new diversity of thought and expression.

Time Warner closed its discussion of globalization by announcing, none too modestly, that "a new era in human history has begun," one in which "the world is our audience."[58] The new era, it said, would be defined by a concurrent evolution of political and media systems; through Time Warner, America had taken a commanding lead in the race to divide planetary markets, despite the incursions of foreign capital into homegrown industries.

Another Big Buy from the East

The Time Warner union, and its patriotic appeal to the ideal of American ownership of American industries, did not stop foreign buyers from knocking on the doors of U.S. corporate suites. Japan, in particular, had been a steady buyer of American businesses, a development that seemed to cause more anxieties for domestic observers than did the larger number of purchases carried out by European firms. Among countries whose companies were leading buyers of U.S. firms in the 1980s, Japan was actually in tenth place (England and Canada were the top two foreign buyers).[59] But continuing Japanese buys of U.S. firms had triggered a xenophobic reaction that corresponding buys from Canadian and European firms had not. In addition to Columbia and CBS Records, Japan had acquired Firestone Tire and Rubber, the Intercontinental Hotel Group, CIT

Group Holdings, Inc., Gould, Inc., PACE Industries, Westin Hotels and Resorts, Tiffany's, Citicorp, and Pebble Beach. In addition to these, a Japanese firm was poised to make another inroad into Hollywood.

As the eighties ended, MCA, Universal's parent corporation, was a relatively small player in what had emerged by then as a transnational media business. Relative to the industry's evolution in the eighties, MCA stood in a weakened and diminished state. Time Warner was larger, and PCI had greater capital reserves (so much, in fact, that it took an $80 million loss in its bid to acquire Time, Inc.).[60] Columbia was allied with Sony, and Fox was a subsidiary of the News Corp. MCA needed access to more capital to compete in the higher-stakes game that the business had become, and MCA chair Lew Wasserman was convinced that the company could not prosper unless it was allied with a larger enterprise.

In September 1990, MCA began talks with Matsushita Electric Industrial Co., the world's largest television manufacturer (under the brand names Panasonic, Technics, and Quasar) and the world's twelfth-largest corporation. Sony was only one-quarter the size of Matsushita, whose nickname in Japan was "Maneshita," or copycat. The nickname derived from Matsushita's reputation for introducing new products only after competitors had tested the market, as Sony had in the case of buying an American film studio. Matsushita's major product lines included VCRs and television receivers as well as consumer audio products (CD players, DAT recorders). But it also manufactured a wide array of information and communications equipment (personal computers, CRT display devices, plain-paper copiers, mobile telephones, pagers, CATV systems, optical-fiber LAN information systems), home appliances (refrigerators, air conditioners, microwave ovens), electronic components (microcomputer chips, integrated circuits, capacitors, resistors), a range of batteries (manganese, alkaline, lithium, solar, etc.), and assorted other products (bicycles, cameras, water purifiers, prerecorded tapes and discs). Matsushita operated 127 companies in thirty-eight countries, and its overseas markets represented nearly half of its net sales income in 1990 and 1991. Matsushita's expansion into the North American (as well as European and Southeast Asian markets) was part of its plan to "to promote sound and well-balanced global business development."[61] MCA was an attractive buy and would help Matsushita advance its plans for global expansion because of the strategic importance of Hollywood films in world entertainment markets. In 1989, MCA reported the highest revenues, operating income, and earnings per share in the company's history (1989 revenues were $3.4 billion).[62] Besides, now that Fox, Columbia, Warners, and MGM (covered later in the chapter) had been snapped up by other buyers, there were few Hollywood majors left for the pickings.

Like the Sony-Columbia buy, the Matsushita-MCA alliance represented a marriage of hardware and software, and it would give Matsushita a new presence in the arena of entertainment programming. Manufacture of video equipment contributed 27 percent of Matsushita's 1990 revenue of $44 billion. Revenues from movies and television programming were 51 percent of MCA's 1989 revenue of $3.4 billion.[63] Thus, the film-related hardware and software components contributed large segments of each company's annual revenues, and in November 1990, Matsushita and MCA agreed to a deal under which the Japanese colossus purchased MCA for $6 billion, making it the most expensive foreign acquisition ever of a Hollywood major and another example of the willingness of foreign buyers to pay inflated prices for their acquisitions.

Outliers: MGM/UA and Disney

Relative to the major studios, the position of MGM/UA in the industry during the 1980s was a marginal one. Its film production and distribution activities and corresponding market share were minimal, and its corporate history during this period was exceptionally turbulent. Despite these factors, MGM/UA eventually attracted a foreign buyer, and the studio joined the other majors who found overseas parents. But until this point and for most of the period the company's fate was uncertain, as majority shareholder Kirk Kerkorian sought repeatedly to sell portions of the firm. As a result, MGM/UA and its executives operated under a continuing threat of dismemberment. Because of these anxieties, the company had difficulty retaining top executive personnel.

MGM/UA had a few hits during the decade, such as MOONSTRUCK and RAIN MAN (1988), but many of its releases were given only limited distribution, harming the revenues they might otherwise have generated. MGM/UA domestic market shares consistently ranked near the bottom among the majors (table 2.1). Buoyed by the success of ROCKY III in 1982 and by WAR GAMES and OCTOPUSSY in 1983, MGM/UA had a 10–11 percent market share during those years, but in 1986 and 1987, it dropped to a dismal 4 percent of the domestic market.[64] Furthermore, unlike Columbia, Warners, or Paramount during the decade, MGM/UA made little effort to gain leverage within the ancillary markets. It did not aggressively expand into the new technologies of cable and pay TV or diversify into other leisure-time markets. Beset by crippling internal troubles, MGM/UA remained a minor player in the industry and stayed largely outside the sweeping changes in the film business.

As noted in the previous chapter, things had looked different for a brief period at the beginning of the decade. MGM planned for a major expansion of film production that would signal a comeback for the company, but after its 1981–82 pictures performed poorly, the company cut back on production and tended mostly to distribute pickups (i.e., films that had been funded and produced elsewhere and would therefore require little capital investment). However, although its diminished production activities made MGM/UA more of a mini-major, the studio had an extremely alluring asset—its vast library of classic films, including not just MGM product but also films from Warner Bros., UA, and RKO. At a time when the ancillary markets were creating an insatiable demand for film product, the MGM/UA library was a gold mine of material. As MGM/UA was progressively dismembered in the 1980s, the film library remained the prize that investors sought. Because it had not expanded into new distribution technologies and because its production activities were curtailed, MGM/UA offered investors little promise of future corporate potential. However, its past glories, existing in the film library, were a great treasure.

As noted, owner Kirk Kerkorian tried relentlessly to sell portions of MGM/UA to various investors. Until the 1990 purchase by Pathé, the major deal, and the one that had the biggest impact on the company, was the purchase negotiated with Ted Turner in 1985 whereby Turner bought MGM/UA for $1.4 billion, with an immediate sell-back to Kerkorian of UA for $480 million. Turner's broadcasting system was strapped for product. His superstation, WTBS, was running sports shows and old movies and television shows. The majors had hiked the licensing fees on film product (those generated hefty revenues for the studios), and the increase was expected to slash into the station's profits.

Ted Turner's bold plan to purchase MGM/UA netted him a gold mine in the studio's film library, instant programming for Turner's cable operations.

Turner noted the imperative to protect WTBS. "It's an extremely valuable asset, but its future is clouded." Owning a library of classic films would offer just the protection Turner wanted. MGM/UA's library would provide an outstanding bank of programming in perpetuity. As Turner exclaimed after the deal, "We've got 35% of the great films of all time. We've got Spencer Tracy and Jimmy Cagney working for us from the grave."[65]

Turner financed the deal through the accumulation of junk bonds sold by Drexel Burnham Lambert, whose point man in Los Angeles was Michael Milken. (Milken was a financier specializing in such bonds, and he helped fund many of the decade's corporate raiders. His activities came to symbolize the Wall Street excesses of the period, and in 1990 he was convicted of six felony charges involving fradulent junk bond activities. Sentenced to ten years, he served only two, and his ties to Turner endured. Although banned for life from stock market activities, he advised Turner on his 1996 merger of Turner Broadcasting System with Time Warner. Milken earned $50 million for his advice.)[66] When the deal appeared to be threatened by Turner's difficulties raising the requisite funds, MGM/UA willingly accepted a series of scaled-down offers. It was a remarkable demonstration of the studio's difficulty in attracting buyers. Turner's initial offer, made 7 August 1985, had been $1.45 billion, or $29 a share for the company. Drexel couldn't raise the money, so on 2 October MGM/UA accepted $25 a share ($200 million less). Again Drexel was unable to raise the money, and in January 1986 MGM/UA accepted Turner's third offer of $20 per share ($450 million below the original asking price).[67] On 25 March 1986, Turner Broadcasting Systems got MGM/UA, with a concurrent sell-back of UA (a theatrical-distribution arm of little use to Turner) to Kerkorian.

But Turner didn't keep MGM for long. He acquired a mountain of debt totaling $1.75 billion, and he'd paid a much higher price for MGM than many industry observers felt it was worth. As a condition of the financing, he had promised to reduce his debt by $600 million by September 1986. He therefore sold back to Kerkorian for $300 million MGM's movie, television, and videocassette production and distribution operations. For $190 million, Lorimar Telepictures, a subsidiary of Warner Bros., bought the MGM studio lot in Culver City and MGM's film processing lab.[68] MGM had now been broken apart into its various components.

Turner sold all of the studio operations he had purchased, but he kept 3,650 films from the MGM/UA library, which had been his real target from the start. (An unintended effect of the deal bolstered a Turner competitor, American Movie Classics, a cable television showcase for commercial-free old Hollywood films. Just before the Kerkorian-Turner deal was finalized, AMC bought cable rights to 1,450 MGM and UA films. Kerkorian and Turner had to repurchase these rights for $50 million, money that AMC used to expand its service by adding more titles to its programming library. AMC grew from 300,000 subscribers in 1984, when it was still marketing itself to users at two dollars per subscriber, to 7 million homes by the end of 1987, when AMC was wholesaling its service to cable system operators at twenty cents per system subscriber.)[69]

Following the Turner deal, MGM/UA, now shorn of substantial assets, languished on a series of auction blocks, attracting occasional investor interest but no successful deals. On 11 July 1988, MGM/UA announced that Kerkorian would sell a 25 percent interest in the company to a production firm headed by Jon Peters and Peter Guber and industrialist Burt Sugarman and would entertain bids for United Artists. But Guber-Peters-Barris, as the firm was called, withdrew from the $100 million deal. Determined to make MGM/UA a more attractive buy, in January 1989 Kerkorian spent $180 million from his Tracinda Corp. to pay off MGM/UA's bank debt, announcing that he would now entertain bids only for United Artists. One was quickly forthcoming from Australia's Qintex Entertainment, a division of the Qintex Group, which promised to buy UA for $800 million. Qintex, though, failed to secure financing, and the deal fell through. Talks with other potential buyers—the News Corp., Sony, Warners, cable operator Tele-Communications, Inc., and the theater chain United Artists Communications—came to naught.

Then, in November 1990, after protracted attempts to obtain financing, Italy's Pathé Communications Corp. (chaired by Italian investor Giancarlo Parretti) succeeded in a $1.3 billion acquisition of MGM/UA. Pathé was primarily a film producer and exhibitor of low-budget films aimed at the home video market. Beginning in 1989, though, it aimed to become a larger player in the lucrative film entertainment business. It bought Cannon Pictures, a producer-distributor of low-budget action pictures (KICKBOXER [1989], DEATH WARRANT [1990], DELTA FORCE II [1990]), and it formed Pathé Entertainment to produce quality pictures in the $14 million budget range. Its initial releases included the Tom Selleck vehicle QUIGLEY DOWN UNDER (1990) and THE RUSSIA HOUSE (1990) with Sean Connery and Michelle Pfeiffer. In addition to its production and distribution activities, Pathé Communications was the largest exhibitor (462 screens) in the United Kingdom and the Netherlands and a co-operator of 48 screens in Scandinavia.[70] This was the third purchase of a Hollywood studio by an overseas firm, following Fox-News Corp. and Sony-Columbia (Matsushita-MCA was yet to come).

Like Turner before him, Giancarlo Parretti had considerable difficulties raising the funds to acquire MGM/UA. In the end, MGM's film library was the key to Pathé's ability to obtain financing, and the terms of the deal demonstrated the interlocking nature of the film industry oligopoly that had emerged at decade's end. Pathé raised funding by selling rights to titles in the film library. Time Warner paid $125 million for worldwide home video rights to the UA film library (over 950 titles) and the Cannon library (Pathé bought the Cannon Group film company several years previously). Turner Broadcasting Service paid $200 million for exclusive television rights in the United States for films from the UA library as well as MGM/UA films from 1986–89, including Rain Man, A Fish Called Wanda, Rocky I–IV and the first sixteen James Bond movies.

Once again, MGM/UA was being serviced by its prior decades of film production. This was a striking demonstration of the power of ancillary markets to rejuvenate the assets of production and distribution companies by extending the revenue life of motion pictures. MGM/UA was now, belatedly, a part of the international communications industry, though ownership by parent Pathé guaranteed it minor status among such titans as Sony-Columbia and Matsushita-MCA. With MGM/UA's purchase by Pathé and the MCA-Matsushita buy, Hollywood had become a media production center (along with music and publishing) driving the international home entertainment industry.

DISNEY

The Walt Disney Co. was an anomaly among the Hollywood majors in the 1980s. Because it was already a hugely successful and powerful international company, it rode out the merger wave. Disney was neither purchased by a parent communications firm during the 1980s nor turned into one (as was Paramount Communications, Inc.). In this respect, Disney did not participate in the merger-and-acquisitions mania. (At least not during the 1980s—as I noted in the introduction, Disney bought Capital Cities/ABC for $19 billion in 1995, thereby gaining a major broadcast television network.) Instead of merging with a larger company, Disney fought off hostile takeover attempts early in the decade, and it emerged from years of relative obscurity to become a film producer and distributor on a par with the other majors.[71]

In this regard, Disney's is a story of spectacular corporate success. In four years, it transformed its film entertainment operations so effectively that it rose from the bottom of the domestic market to the very top. From 1984 to decade's end, Disney saw a tremendous explosion in its film entertainment revenues (chart 2.6) and an accompanying rise in its share of the domestic film market (chart 2.7). In 1986, its share of this market jumped to 10 percent from the paltry 3–4 percent it had held since 1979, and it increased to 14 percent in 1987. In 1988, Disney led the majors with a market share of 20 percent, largely because of the spectacular success of WHO FRAMED ROGER RABBIT, the year's number one film. Disney had returned as a force in film entertainment.

CHART 2.6
Disney, Filmed-Entertainment Revenues, 1980–89 ($ millions)

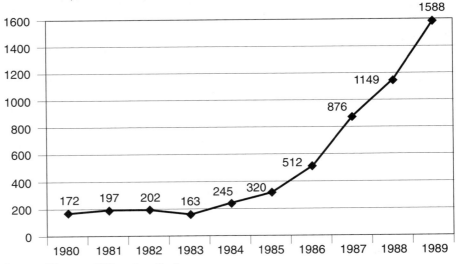

SOURCE: Disney, 10-K Reports, 1980–89.

CHART 2.7
Disney, Share (%) of Domestic Theatrical Market

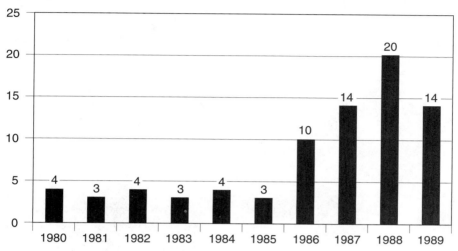

SOURCE: *Variety*, 17 January 1990, p. 15.

The market success achieved in 1986 (a year in which the company changed its name from Walt Disney Productions to the Walt Disney Co.) resulted from key management changes and a new strategic plan instituted in 1984. (Important facets of the new Disney strategy had been conceived earlier, under Ron Miller's tenure as CEO from March 1983 to September 1984. These included the launching of the Touchstone label for theatrical film; the production of SPLASH [1984], Disney's first big hit of the eighties; and a commitment to putting the Disney classics on video in order to exploit this market. The new management team of 1984 benefited from these initiatives that were already underway.) The year 1983 had been a terrible one for Disney's films. Revenues were down 18 percent, and the division posted a $33 million operating loss.[72] Disney's 1983 releases, TEX, TRENCHCOAT, and SOMETHING WICKED THIS WAY COMES, performed poorly, and the company had to write down a sizable loss on these pictures. Worse, at a time when the other majors were seeing big revenues from licensing their films to cable television, Disney was withholding its product in order to launch the Disney Channel on pay cable. By 1983, then, motion picture revenue was far below where it should have been, given the company's prestigious name and its library of film material.

In 1984, the new management team, headed by Frank G. Wells (president and chief operating officer), Michael Eisner (chairman and CEO) and Jeffrey Katzenberg (president of motion pictures and television) determined to return the company to prominence as a leader in film entertainment by increasing production and by exploiting the hitherto-underutilized ancillary markets. As Eisner and Wells explained to shareholders, "Increased motion picture production is an urgent priority with the aim of achieving parity with other major Hollywood studios and improving fundamental earnings in filmed entertainment."[73] Their goals included production of ten to twelve Touchstone features and three or four family films each year. Disney created Touchstone in 1983 to produce and distribute a more adult caliber of film than was possible under its existing corporate name. Its family pictures were failing to attract a broad or diverse audience,

Buoyed by the success of WHO FRAMED ROGER RABBIT, *Disney dominated the theatrical market in 1988 and achieved an impressive turnaround from its dismal fortunes earlier in the decade.*

and the Disney name was synonymous for many moviegoers with bland and dull filmmaking. Because of these problems, the company's revenues could not be increased without expanding the demographics for its pictures. Touchstone enabled Disney to surreptitiously market nontraditional (for Disney) product to nontraditional audiences.

The management team's new goals also included accelerating the production timetable for animated features by using computer assists to release a new animated feature every eighteen months. The studio also aimed to be a major supplier of programming for network television and the syndicated and pay-cable markets. Film revenues were up in 1984 because of the success of SPLASH, with Tom Hanks and Daryl Hannah, but Wells-Eisner-Katzenburg knew it would be at least two or three years before the effects of their plan could be assessed. To increase production and meet the plan's goals, Disney followed the industry norm by using limited partnerships to finance filmmaking and reduce and diversify its financial risk. In 1984, Disney raised $193 million through Silver Screen Partners II, which held a public stock offering and attracted twenty-eight thousand investors, making it the largest limited film partnership to that time. In 1986, Silver Screen III raised $300 million to fund films into 1988.[74]

Under Wells-Eisner-Katzenberg, the company continued to innovate and expand its operations. In 1985, Disney created and staffed pay-television and domestic syndication departments and licensed seven pictures for pay-cable presentation. After an absence of more than two years, Disney returned to network television with the NBC hit "Golden Girls" and, on Saturday mornings, "The Adventures of the Gummy Bears" (NBC) and "The Wuzzles" (CBS). Disney's home video releases were beginning to pay off, with rev-

Michael Eisner (left) and Jeffrey Katzenberg (right) were part of the management team that aggressively transformed Disney's film operations.

enues in the home video market increasing 46 percent over 1984. In 1986 Disney signed with Showtime/The Movie Channel, giving it exclusive pay-TV rights to all of Touchstone's feature releases over the next five years.

This proved to be a good deal for Showtime/The Movie Channel because in 1986 the features commenced under Wells-Eisner-Katzenburg came on line and began winning Disney whopping increases in market share. In 1986, these included DOWN AND OUT IN BEVERLY HILLS, released in January, RUTHLESS PEOPLE (summer release), and THE COLOR OF MONEY (fall release). In 1987, they included OUTRAGEOUS FORTUNE, TIN MEN, STAKEOUT, and the year's fourth highest renting picture, THREE MEN AND A BABY. In a canny strategy, Disney released these films during off-season points to minimize competition with the other majors' pictures. Disney's distribution unit, Buena Vista, released OUTRAGEOUS FORTUNE and DOWN AND OUT IN BEVERLY HILLS in consecutive Januaries, bypassing the Thanksgiving/Christmas season, when there is typically a glut of product in the nation's theaters. Again bypassing this season, Disney released THE COLOR OF MONEY in October and THREE MEN AND A BABY in early November.

In 1988, Disney's filmed-entertainment products had the greatest year in the company's history, and Disney added a third production arm, Hollywood Pictures, to its Disney (Buena Vista) and Touchstone lineup. WHO FRAMED ROGER RABBIT was the biggest film of the year, and Disney had three more films in the top ten: GOOD MORNING, VIETNAM; THREE MEN AND A BABY (continuing its run); and COCKTAIL. In 1989, Disney retained its strong market position with HONEY, I SHRUNK THE KIDS; DEAD POETS SOCIETY; TURNER AND HOOCH; and THE LITTLE MERMAID. In production during 1989 were more winners scheduled for release in 1990. These included PRETTY WOMAN and ARACHNIPHOBIA.

The eighties, then, became a dramatically successful decade for Disney films. Although Paramount and Warners performed more consistently as market leaders

Disney began its corporate makeover in 1984 with the Touchstone label and the promising success of Touchstone's initial release, SPLASH, which starred Daryl Hannah as a mermaid who falls in love with landlubber Tom Hanks.

during the period, no studio achieved such a remarkable turnaround in its fortunes as did Disney. Furthermore, Disney achieved this without merging into the communications industry. By decade's end, however, it was supplementing its international theme park and filmed-entertainment operations with tentative moves into the communications sector. In 1988, Disney ventured into television broadcasting by acquiring station KHJ in Los Angeles, and it formed a joint venture with Rupert Murdoch's News International to carry Touchstone movies on Murdoch's European-based Sky Television. Disney soon abandoned the venture, but, as its Capital Cities/ABC purchase demonstrates, it did not abandoned its plans to acquire a television distribution system.

Disney's success, though, brought to it the economic contradictions that tormented the industry as a whole. Disney's market presence in theatrical film, and its ancillary exploitation, placed it on a par with the other majors, and it found itself mired in the same problems they faced. Rising production costs were a condition of doing business, and they imposed a severe drag on profits. Disney sank nearly $50 million into its production of DICK TRACY in 1990 and spent nearly that much again promoting the picture. The film generated poor box office in relation to its costs. In reaction to this overspending, Jeffrey Katzenberg issued a notorious twenty-eight-page memo castigating the waste of blockbuster filmmaking and urging a more sensible and scaled-back approach to budgeting productions. "It seems that, like lemmings, we are all racing faster and faster into the sea, each of us trying to outrun and outspend and outearn the other in a mad sprint toward the mirage of making the next blockbuster."[75] Disney's success as a major replicated for it the industry's inescapable funding and production problems. The industry was locked into a pattern of capital-intensive filmmaking and distribution. The stars and effects that sold in the ancillaries and generated media coverage during theatrical release had become terribly, irrevocably costly. The escalation of production costs threatened the entire industry, and new revenue streams from the ancillaries merely delayed the day of reckoning without solving the fundamental problem.

The Boom in Exhibition

The industry's remarkable economic transformation extended to the exhibition sector and precipitated historic changes there. These changes were manifest in two areas: a large national increase in the number of theater screens and the size of the dominant theater circuits, and the dramatic reentry of the major studios into exhibition operations. Although admissions remained flat, by 1983 a wave of theater construction was under-way across the country, fed by the expanding production and distribution activities of the majors. Contrary to the prophets of doom who predicted that video and cable would kill the movie theater, exhibition circuits were flush with the excitement and energy of a rejuvenated industry. Theater construction was up 14 percent in 1983, and by mid-decade exhibition was seeing the biggest yearly increases in total screens since the late 1940s.[76] From 1980 to 1989, the nation's screen total jumped from 17,590 to 23,132 (table 2.7). The nation's largest theater circuits were adding sizeable numbers of screens to their holdings (charts 2.8–11). Racing Cineplex-Odeon, a rapidly expanding Canadian-based circuit that had entered the U.S. market in 1985, United Artists Communications, Inc., the nation's number two circuit by size, jumped from 1,063 screens in 1984 to 1,595 screens in 1986. By 1988 it had 2,677 screens. American Multi-Cinema jumped from 736 screens in 1983 to 1,614 in 1988.

Much of this activity was confined to multiplexes (i.e., multiscreen theaters) located in shopping centers. In this regard, the expansion of screens was tied to the real estate boom of the eighties, specifically the construction and leasing of retail and office space.

TABLE 2.7
Exhibition

	INDOOR SCREENS	DRIVE-IN SCREENS	TOTAL SCREENS
1980	14,029	3,561	17,590
1981	14,732	3,308	18,040
1982	14,977	3,043	18,020
1983	16,032	2,852	18,884
1984	17,368	2,832	20,200
1985	18,327	2,820	21,147
1986	19,947	2,818	22,765
1987	21,048	2,507	23,555
1988	21,689	1,545	23,234
1989	22,029	1,103	23,132

SOURCE: MPAA, 1996 *U.S. Economic Review.*

CHART 2.8
American Multi-Cinema, Total Screens

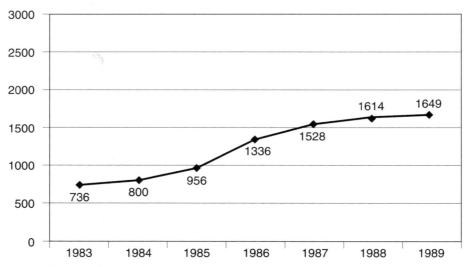

SOURCE: *Variety*, 1983–89.

CHART 2.9
Cineplex-Odeon, Total Screens

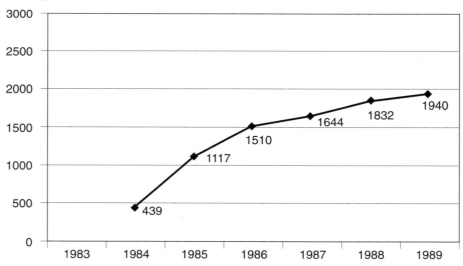

SOURCE: *Variety*, 1983–89.

CHART 2.10
General Cinema Corp., Total Screens

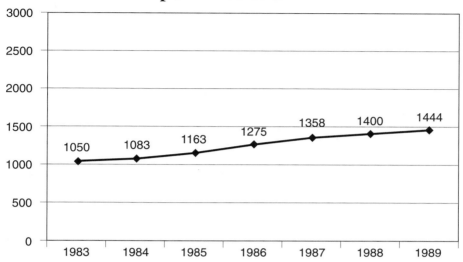

SOURCE: *Variety*, 1983–89.

CHART 2.11
UATC, Total Screens

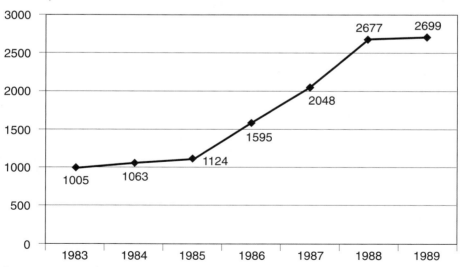

SOURCE: *Variety*, 1983–89.

This tie was especially important in light of the common practice by exhibition companies of renting existing properties rather than financing their construction from scratch. For many real estate developers, exhibition companies were another form of commercial tenant renting business space. Leasing and furbishing a five-screen multiplex might involve a cost to the exhibitor of only $750,000, much less expensive than it would be to build one.[77] Furthermore, real estate developers liked to have exhibitors in the mix of shopping center tenants because the theaters would bring in customers that other businesses could then attract. Movie theaters made good anchors for retail shopping malls. In 1983, 10,000 screens were located in only 400 locations.[78] The 2,677 screens UATC operated in 1988 were found in just 686 locations. General Cinema Corporation's 1,400 screens in 1988 were found in just 321 locations.

Multiplex pioneer Nat Taylor, a Toronto exhibitor, recalled that during the 1940s and 1950s, an era of stand-alone theaters, the idea of a multiplex would have seemed bizarre. "Nobody in those days could conceive of the idea that you could put two theaters in one location."[79] But Taylor and other exhibitors realized that with multiple screens, overflow business from the popular films would feed the slower attractions. By the 1980s, multiplexes were the dominant exhibition showcase. Making multiplexes adjuncts of shopping centers and malls, or placing them in shopping districts, ensured a steady flow of patrons into the theaters. The downside of multiplexing, though, was a reduction in the size of the auditorium, so that while there were more screens, there were also fewer seats relative to the big houses of decades past. The nation's 17,689 indoor theaters in 1948 had a seating capacity of 12 million, while the 14,977 indoor theaters in 1982 could seat only 5 million.[80] At its worst, the multiplexing trend produced screens the size of postage stamps in tiny auditoriums where the soundtrack of the film playing in an adjoining theater mixed with the one patrons were viewing in another.

But the expansion of exhibition in the 1980s had another effect that ran counter to the predominant multiplexing trend of smaller and inferior auditoriums. It helped produce an upgrade in the caliber and quality of presentation at many locations. For the canny exhibitor, improving presentation could be an effective marketing strategy, given the unsatisfactory conditions that prevailed at many multiplexes. High-class screening facilities would attract patrons. Typifying the fruits of this approach was Canada-based Cineplex-Odeon and its aggressive entry into the U.S. market in 1985.[81] In just a few years, through a careful but rapid series of theater buys, Cineplex expanded its holdings to become the second-largest circuit in the United States. It was yet another foreign company to gain sizable entry into the U.S. film industry.

In 1981, Cineplex operated 124 screens in Canada, and by 1984 its holdings had expanded to 439 screens. In 1985, launching its plan to base itself in the principal U.S. markets, it bought the Plitt circuit, the fourth-largest U.S. chain with 605 screens, for $130 million ($65 million for the circuit plus assumption of its $65 million debt). Its screen total now topped 1,000, and in 1986, after MCA bought a half interest in Cineplex, the circuit voraciously purchased a series of U.S. chains. In April, it bought the Septum circuit (49 screens, Georgia-based) for $11 million; in May, the Essaness circuit (41 screens in Chicago) for $15 million; in July the Neighborhood circuit (75 screens in Maryland and Virginia); in September, the RKO Century Warner Theaters (93 screens in Manhattan, New York, and New Jersey) for $180 million; and in December, Sterling Recreation (114 screens in Washington State) for $45 million. By the end of this spree in 1986, Cineplex had 1,510 screens in the United States and Canada, making it the number two circuit, behind UA Communications. In June 1987, Cineplex bought

In a dramatic sign of the vigorous activity in the exhibition sector, Garth Drabinsky, Chair and CEO of Cineplex-Odeon, aggressively expanded Cineplex operations in the U.S.

the Walter Reade Organization from Columbia Pictures (11 screens in Manhattan) for $32 million, and in December it bought the Washington D.C.–based Circle chain (75 screens) for $51 million.

From the start of Cineplex's dramatic and rapid expansion into the U.S. market, CEO Garth Drabinsky believed that the window of opportunity for multiplex growth was small because it was tied to the expansion of retail malls and would probably extend only through the end of the decade. "We see in the markets we're in that we are very much coming to an end of that expansion..." He added, "A very peculiar opportunity from 1978 to today may be drawing to a close—not as many shopping centers—we're reaching the end of an age. We got in at the middle and have taken advantage of it."[82] (Contrary to his prediction, though, the expansion of theater screens continued through the 1990s, rising by more than 20 percent to a 1996 screen total of 29,690.)[83]

Although Cineplex's startling growth was tied to the wave of multiplex expansion, Drabinsky was determined to offer a striking alternative to multiplex film presentation. Where many multiplexes offered a barren, boxlike environment for film viewing, Cineplex specialized in luxurious facilities. Cineplex flagship theaters harkened back to the age of the movie palace, and they were designed at great expense to give moviegoers a memorable and exciting experience. Drabinsky spoke of his sadness at seeing the ruination of once great moviehouses:

> When we went through New York City and purchased RKO and went into Brooklyn on Flatbush Avenue, we drove by theater after theater after theater, all boarded up and converted to bingo halls and gospel halls. Those fabulous theaters had been closed with total reckless abandon. It was heart-rending; it was a very unfortunate thing and never again will a wave of this type of theater be built in North America. They can't be built because of the cost.[84]

Drabinsky noted that Cineplex would try, in its way, to reignite the excitement of seeing a movie in a luxurious theater. Drabinsky was prepared to spend lavishly in order to upgrade the theater experience at Cineplex locations. Cineplex's architects and engineers and their support staff installed new seats, screens, projection, sound systems, and carpets. They also retained and refurbished existing special features in given theaters, such as ceiling frescoes at the Fairfax Cinema in Los Angeles and a wall mural and wall-mounted lights and fixtures at the Gordon theater, also in Los Angeles. They

commissioned sculptures and paintings and added cappucino and pastry bars to upgrade
the standard concession fare. As historian Douglas Gomery noted, "They added creature
comforts not seen since the Golden Age of the movie palace."[85] But all of this, including
Cineplex's appetite for expansion, did not come cheap. Drabinsky's aggressive move into
U.S. markets produced a gigantic national theater circuit and a mountain of debt. With
the company facing a $757 million debt load, its largest investors, MCA and Charles R.
Bronfman, forced Drabinsky to resign as president and CEO in 1989. Prior to his resig-
nation, Drabinsky battled with MCA and Bronfman for control of the company but lost.
His replacement, Allen Karp, instituted aggressive cost-cutting measures aimed at
reducing corporate debt. But the turnaround would be slow. In 1990, Cineplex's revenues were in the red for $178 million.[86]

THE MAJORS RETURN TO EXHIBITION

Cineplex's spectacular growth, and its ambitious renovation of existing theaters coupled
with the construction of new facilities, emblemized the robust expansion of exhibition
during the decade. Cineplex began as an independent exhibition chain, but by decade's
end MCA had purchased a 30 percent interest in the company, with Cineplex thereby
acquiring important backing from a major Hollywood studio and distributor. MCA's buy
into Cineplex was part of a historic realignment, commenced in mid-decade, between
the production/distribution and exhibition sectors of the business.

　　Nothing so vividly demonstrated the importance of exhibition in the ancillary eighties as the wholesale return of the Hollywood majors to theater operations. In 1986 and
1987, Tri-Star (and parent Columbia Pictures Entertainment), Gulf and Western, MCA,
and Warners all purchased major theater chains, marking their explicit return to classic
vertical integration of production, distribution, and exhibition. Under the 1948 consent
decrees, the studios had been forced to divest their theater operations. Since that time,
the majors had been unable to reenter theatrical exhibition on a major scale. Despite
this restriction, though, Hollywood's mergers and acquisitions had created substantial
vertical integration (e.g., the production/distribution/exhibition interests represented in
Tri-Star or in the News Corp.'s union of Fox and Metromedia television). Thus the wave
of theater purchases by the major studios occurred in a context already marked by a
return of vertical integration to the industry. Given the green light by a permissive
Justice Department, the majors now added theaters to their existing collection of delivery systems for motion pictures.

　　If the majors' theater buys seemed to violate the spirit of the 1948 consent decrees,
they did not violate their legal foundation. This is a significant point, given the choruses
of amazement that greeted these acquisitions. The consent decrees, accepted by the
majors Paramount, Fox, Warner, MGM, and RKO (but not the minors United Artists,
Universal, and Columbia, which at the time owned no theaters), were the outcome of
an antitrust suit that began in 1938 under which the government charged the five majors
and three minors with restrictive trade practices.[87] These included price fixing, stipulat-
ing the length of runs (known as "clearances"), and block-booking films to exhibitors.
These restrictive practices were the heart of the government's case and its main points
of contention, while the theaters owned by the majors merely provided a means for
implementing these practices.

　　When the case reached the Supreme Court, the court refused to find that theater
ownership by the majors was illegal in itself. Assessments about legality would depend on

the trade practices that accompanied, or were intended to be accomplished by, such ownership. Furthermore, while the case was still in district court, Paramount and RKO (which no longer exists) negotiated a consent judgment under which they received more favorable terms than Warners, Fox, and MGM, all of whom settled later. As a result, Paramount (along with the three minors because they then had no studios) remained free to acquire theaters, whereas the decrees negotiated by the other three majors (Warners, Fox, and MGM) stipulated that they seek court approval before engaging in exhibition. Thus, in the 1980s, Gulf and Western (Paramount), MCA (Universal), and Columbia were able to purchase theater chains outright, while Warners had to await court approval before it could do so. In all cases, however, the purchases were scrutinized by the Justice Department to determine whether they would facilitate restrictive trade practices. These buys were readily greenlighted by the government, except in the case of Warners which had to accept certain restrictions on its proposed exhibition partnership with Gulf and Western. (Fox stayed away from theater acquisitions.) The majors thus were able to reenter exhibition because, except in the case of Warners and Fox, there were no explicit restrictions against it, merely provisions against certain trade practices.

Why they chose to reenter exhibition is a matter for some debate. The majors apparently perceived that tangible benefits would come their way from doing so. These were mainly to derive from revising the negotiated business arrangements that typically prevailed between distributor and exhibitor. Under these arrangements, distributors had to negotiate the terms of payment from exhibitors leasing their films. These terms involved a split of box-office proceeds (typically a 90/10 distributor/exhibitor split) against a guaranteed minimum for the distributor. The minimum, termed a "floor," might be negotiated at an eight-week run with 70 percent of box-office for three weeks, 60 percent for two weeks, 50 percent for two weeks, 40 percent for one week, and 35 percent thereafter.[88] The distributor would collect revenues according to whichever formula (split or floor) produced the higher return, but these revenues were subject to change on a weekly basis, with the lion's share gradually shifting to the exhibitor the longer a film stayed in release. The majors apparently felt that owning theaters would simplify these arrangements and enable them to keep more of the revenues deriving from box office.

The majors saw another revenue benefit to such ownership. Distributors have always taken the bulk of box-office monies, so much so that exhibitors rely heavily on concession revenues for maintaining house profits. But exhibitors remit to distributors monthly or bimonthly, and this enabled them to maintain a "float" with distributor revenues that could accrue significant short-term interest. General Cinema Corp. acknowledged using the benefits of the float to finance its operations.[89] By owning theaters, the majors would eliminate revenues lost to the distributor by exhibitor floats. All revenues and interest would stay in-house.

In addition to these perceived financial advantages, the studio distributors apparently felt that major film releases could be strategically showcased in theaters to improve their ancillary business. Studio distributors believed they would have greater control over play dates, maintenance of theater quality, and more favorable rentals from exhibition. Finally, a herd mentality was apparent. Major studio distributors bought theaters because other majors were buying theaters. The majors rode a merger-and-acquisitions bandwagon during the eighties, and they jumped on because everyone else was jumping on.

The rush into exhibition occurred rapidly. In the span of two years, 1986 and 1987, the majors had, as *Variety* noted, returned to their pretelevision origins as vertically inte-

Cineplex's 18-theater multiplex at Universal City, California epitomized the upgrading of theatrical venues in the age of video. The marble-floored lobby featured a planetarium design on its ceiling (photo below), and the auditoriums were spacious and luxuriant.

grated producer-distributor-exhibitors.[90] (We have seen, though, that they had already integrated these areas before the wave of theater buys.) In January 1986, MCA purchased a 50 percent interest in Cineplex-Oden for $159 million (Cineplex had 1,056 screens at the time), funds and corporate resources that Cineplex then used for its buying spree. In June, Gulf and Western bought the Trans-Lux circuit (24 screens in New York and Connecticut) for $15 million and in October purchased Mann Theaters (360 screens) for $220 million. Paramount already owned Canada's Famous Players circuit (469 screens) and co-owned (with Universal) 76 screens in Europe. In December, Gulf and Western bought Festival Enterprises (101 screens) for $50 million. In October 1986, Tri-Star bought the Loew's chain of 230 screens for $300 million, and in 1988 Columbia Pictures Entertainment (which then contained Tri-Star) added the 317-screen USA Cinemas circuit to Loews holdings for $165 million.

Warner Bros. was slower than the other majors to enter exhibition, but in July 1987 it raised $500 million from a stock float and earmarked the funds for exhibition. In September a federal court ruling cleared Warners for entry into exhibition. Five months later, Warners agreed with Gulf and Western to buy a 50 percent interest in G&W's 472 U.S. screens for $150 million and become G&W's partner in their operation. This fit with G&W's desire to explore alternatives to full ownership in order to limit liabilities in the exhibition sector. The marriage, though, had to await an analysis by the Justice Department and a federal court ruling on the partnership's potential for trade infractions as specified by the consent decrees. The marriage was approved in December 1988, but Warners was ordered to operate at arm's length from the theater circuit by keeping the circuit's assets and executive staff separate from WCI holdings. The dash for theater circuits in the previous three years had made the original consent decree issues (of restrictive trade practices) newly relevant, especially because Cineamerica, the circuit jointly operated by G&W and Warners, had a strong regional concentration in the Los Angeles market. The federal judge who okayed the partnership noted its potential for trouble: "There appears to be continued anti-competitive behavior by exhibitors and distributors in this industry. We find this apparent climate of noncompliance with the Paramount decrees and with the antitrust laws to be fraught with serious problems. We cannot allow that climate to go unchecked and unsupervised."[91] (As evidence of continued anticompetitive behavior, the Supreme Court in 1990 upheld a lower court's conviction of 20th Century–Fox on block-booking charges.)[92]

By decade's end, however, the laudable ideal of competition existed in tension with an economic context in which there was an increasing concentration of media markets and of giant operators in those markets. The industry had moved throughout the decade toward ever bigger combinations of owner-operators and toward the vertical integration of film entertainment and its delivery systems. Time Warner exemplified this principle, and two of the era's spectacular acquisitions—Sony's buy of Columbia and Matsushita's buy of MCA—were founded on the conviction that the ultimate synergy was in the union of hardware and software. Sony and Matsushita would manufacture televisions, videocassette, and videodisc players, and their Hollywood subsidiaries would manufacture the programming the machines needed. In this way, their media empires would be self-supporting and self-sustaining. Many analysts, though, questioned whether the expense involved in attaining these unions of hardware and software was really justified. Herb Schlosser, former president of NBC, said, "The synergies are overrated. For $500 million you could license all the software in the world for a new system."[93] One did not need to buy a whole company to accomplish this.

Like the synergy that was to have prevailed between Coke and Columbia Pictures, the hardware-software synergy (aside from the enormous acquisition expense) is a less strategic one than those accomplished by the Time Warner merger or the Fox–News Corp. pairing. In these cases, the combination of programming and distribution outlets is key. The best synergies are those obtained by controlling film production, its distribution and consumption venues, and those markets and products that may be tied in to film products (e.g., music, books, and magazines). Thus the redesign of Gulf and Western into Paramount Communications, Inc., and the union of Time Warner are exemplary models of synergy, whereas the bubble-headed attempts to unite the movies with soft drinks or video hardware conjoin product lines that are nonsynergistic. These latter attempts resulted from the synergy fever that raged from the mid- to late 1980s and made the studios hot properties for acquisition. Everybody was looking to jump into the business. As Coke and others discovered, though, synergies were not omnidirectional. Movies did not combine well with diverse leisure-time products. They might work well inside entertainment and communications empires, but the film business had always been highly uncertain, marked by recurrent revenue spikes and troughs. Thus, synergies had a constrained potential, and they required careful design. But they did exist, and the maturation of alternative distribution venues gave them an unprecedented importance. No major could prosper without control of these venues, and the majors did prosper, surviving the "shake-out years," by gaining a significant measure of this control.

By decade's end, Hollywood had become a vital means for multinational communications conglomerates to service their global markets. These media giants, and the Hollywood industry that now belonged to them, attained a vertical integration far greater than what the old Hollywood majors represented with their theaters in the 1940s when antitrust action was taken against them. The new oligopoly was far more powerful, and it pervaded much bigger markets. Like the coming of sound in the late 1920s, the transformation of the American film industry in the 1980s is a point of transition that redefines all that follows and separates it from what has come before. Before there was cinema. Now, and in the future, there is software.

3

The Brave New Ancillary World

The mergers and acquisitions traced in the previous chapter had as their rationale the integration of multiple markets for generating film revenue. Before the 1980s, these were mainly theaters and broadcast television. By decade's end, these included the former as well as pay cable, home video, the marketing venues of product placement and product tie-ins, and the synergies that might be obtained through strategic cross-promoting in these areas. (During the eighties, the majors also saw significant revenues from the production and syndication of broadcast television programming. In 1980, for example, Gulf and Western's Leisure Time Group derived 20 percent of its revenues from series and films for television.)[1] As a result, film marketing grew more complex and required new strategies but could deliver greater revenues when the ancillaries worked in synergy, reinforcing one another.

Marketing films has always been a difficult business because it requires predicting what an audience will want to see one or two years in advance of a production. For decades, the industry has relied on market research methodologies, using questionnaire or focus group interviews to elicit from viewers information about their movie interest areas and responses to story concepts and character types that might form the basis for upcoming films.[2] In spite of the industry's recourse to social science methodologies as a means of lessening the uncertainty surrounding the marketing of its products, intuition, hunches, and guesses have played bigger roles than the industry has cared to admit. But amid all the formal and informal prognosticating about audience interests, the basic pattern of film distribution remained relatively stable for decades. Films with great potential popularity would receive a wide (or saturation) release, opening in 1,000–2,000 theaters nationwide, supported by a high-visibility media ad campaign. BATMAN, for example, opened on 23 June 1989 on 2,194 screens and grossed $40 million in its first weekend. By contrast, a platform release was reserved for pictures with solid commercial potential but that required a careful build to reach that potential. Opening such a picture in a few major urban areas and then moving to a wider break allowed good word-of-mouth and favorable critical reviews to build an audience. DRIVING MISS DAISY (1989) opened in four theaters in New York and Los Angeles in mid-December. One month later it was on 277 screens. Six weeks after opening, it was on 895 screens, and at the end of March, its release had expanded to 1,668 screens. During its thirty-six-

A careful, graduated release enabled DRIVING MISS DAISY *to find its audience and achieve significant box-office success. Jessica Tandy and Morgan Freeman starred in the period drama directed by Bruce Beresford.*

week domestic release, it grossed $107 million.[3] The subsequent non-theatrical revenue lives of BATMAN and DRIVING MISS DAISY were lengthy and multifaceted, and this distinguishing feature differentiated the eighties from previous decades of film distribution. Until the 1980s, after a film had opened on either a platform or saturation release, and once peak viewer interest had passed, it would go to second-run theaters. Prime-time network television presentation followed the completion of theatrical release.

With the growth and maturation of ancillaries in the eighties, however, release patterns shifted to reflect the relative importance of the new revenue sources. Table 3.1 shows the changes in revenue sources between 1980 and 1989. The most striking changes are the displacement of theatrical, as the largest source, by home video and the diminution of network television revenues from nearly 11 percent of the total to less than 1 percent. The initial release venue, however, remained theatrical. A theatrical release, with its attendant hoopla, helped create and sustain viewer interest as the film passed through subsequent release windows into the ancillary markets. Big-ticket items

TABLE 3.1
Film Industry Revenue Sources

	1980		1990	
	($MILLIONS)	PERCENT	($MILLIONS)	PERCENT
Theatrical: Domestic	1,183	29.6	2,100	15.9
Foreign	911	22.8	1,200	9.1
Home Video	280	7.0	5,100	38.6
Pay Cable	240	6.0	1,100	8.3
Network TV	430	10.8	100	0.8
Syndication	150	3.8	600	4.6
Foreign TV	100	2.5	1,000	7.6
Made for TV Films	700	17.5	2,000	15.2
Total	3,994		13,200	

SOURCE: Harold Vogel, *Entertainment Industry Economics* (New York: Cambridge UP, 1990).

like BATMAN or GHOSTBUSTERS would be eagerly anticipated by viewers awaiting their availability on video or cable television. Furthermore, performance in the theatrical market was predictive of revenues to be derived from video and cable releases. Though theatrical's share of the film revenue pie diminished during the 1980s relative to ancillary revenues, theatrical release remained the foundation for all that would follow from it. (The exhibition boom of the eighties demonstrated the continuing importance of this venue.) Before the eighties, broadcast television was the main nontheatrical ancillary. In the eighties, however, a film passed through other release windows before getting to network television.

The second release window was home video. (During its theatrical release, a film would also go to nonresidential pay-per-view, e.g., hotels.) Films were released to home video approximately six months after completion of the theatrical run. One to two months after home video release, a film went to home pay-per-view. The pay-cable window opened six to nine months after video release. After presentation on pay cable, a film might pass to broadcast television, but by now viewer interest had been almost fully exploited. By the mid- and late-1980s, network premieres of Hollywood films were no longer the events they once were. By the time a major film premiered on network television, viewers had already seen it, either in theaters, on pay cable, or on home video. Thus, networks, the last stop on the evolving release schedule, found that they could pay studios less for their top films, and studios, in turn, began exploring alternatives to network television, primarily sales to the syndication market.

In 1984, the president of MGM/UA TV noted the diminished importance of network revenues for nontheatrical presentation of feature films. "The three networks are just not buying pictures in groups any more, so we've got to get that revenue from somewhere else."[4] Accordingly, MGM/UA that year bypassed the networks entirely and offered a package of twenty-four prominent titles for TV syndication. None of these pictures, including FAME (1980), CLASH OF THE TITANS (1981), THE FRENCH LIEUTENANT'S WOMAN (1981), and MY FAVORITE YEAR (1982), had had any network exposure. Two of these titles—FAME and MY FAVORITE YEAR—had turned a nice dollar in theatrical distribution, and a third—THE FRENCH LIEUTENANT'S WOMAN—had been a favorite with critics. In 1987, Paramount got more than $2 million per title in license fees from more than 120 stations that bought a package containing such big box-office films as BEVERLY HILLS COP (1984), WITNESS (1985), STAR TREK II: THE WRATH OF KHAN (1982), and TRADING PLACES (1983). Each of these titles was a major box-office hit. Orion Pictures bypassed network television by offering a package for syndication that included HANNAH AND HER SISTERS (1986), F/X (1986), BACK TO SCHOOL (1986), and THE WOMAN IN RED (1984). Orion sold this package of twenty titles to sixty-five markets, clearing over $1 million per title in each market.[5] (Orion even offered these to the syndication market before pay cable. Syndie stations got to air each film three times over eighteen months before Orion would pull them for a three- to six-month pay-cable window.) As the studios redesigned their release windows to accommodate the ancillary markets, network television was the big loser, and syndication, pay cable, and home video were the important new kids on the block. Of these, by far the most significant in commercial and cultural terms was home video.

This surprised the studios because, as the decade began, home video was regarded by many in the industry as a frightening and dangerous drain on film revenue (I will discuss the reasons why in a moment) and because pay-per-view, via cable television, seemed to offer the greatest revenue bonanza coupled with maximum control of the

As television networks became less important ancillary outlets, the syndication market reaped the benefits. The Dan Aykroyd–Eddie Murphy comedy TRADING PLACES *was one of many prominent films that Paramount offered to syndicated stations.*

product. (Videotaping of movies by viewers threatened studios with a loss of control over the product because viewers could generate their own copies of movies.) Extolling the virtues of pay-per-view, MGM/UA's chair Frank Rothman enthused, "When 20 million homes are equipped to receive pay-per-view, we could charge $5 a home for ROCKY III, split the profits, and make $50 million in a single night."[6] But pay-per-view never took off the way home video did.

Pay-per-view is to be distinguished from pay cable. On pay cable, a viewer has access to a month's worth of Hollywood features in return for a basic subscription fee, whereas pay-per-view requires a viewer to pay for a single viewing of one movie. The studios liked the pay-per-view concept because they could control the exhibition of a film and realize a fee from each television set per exhibition. By contrast, with pay cable the studios leased their films in packages to services like HBO or Showtime and often felt that they were forced to relinquish the packages at below-market prices. Relative to pay cable, syndication, and videodiscs, home video offered viewers an enormous flexibility in its use, and this was a large part of its great appeal. With movies on cable, syndication, and disc, one could only watch them, but with a VCR one could "timeshift," that is, record a program from any of these sources for later viewing, and one could erase old material by rerecording over it. With two VCRs hooked together, one could make personal copies of pictures in videotape release. Furthermore, with a camcorder, home video became more than a medium for watching movies. One might also make them, as many families did who set aside their old 8-mm cameras and used video to capture their home movies (ironically substituting one medium with proven archival value for another, much less durable one). The studios liked videodiscs because they were a read-only medium on which one could not record. (One could record from them, however, by using a VCR, and the studios' animosity toward VCRs was well established). Videodiscs, though, never took off like videocassettes because VCRs were cheaper than disk players and let their users record program material as well as play it. Furthermore, in comparison with videotapes, discs were bulky and large.

Thus, home video emerged as the most user-popular ancillary distribution medium, despite the studios' initial resistance and their fears about an uncontrollable technology that would destroy copyright protection. We need to explore this resistance and these fears because they offer a fascinating account of the problems and challenges that the studios had to overcome before they could exploit the home video market. After exploring these problems and challenges, I will discuss the enormous impact of home video on the industry, and I will close by discussing the ideal of synergy as it operated through the relationships among the ancillary markets.

The Home Video Explosion

The rapid growth and diffusion of home video, its enthusiastic adoption by users, greatly alarmed the film industry. As table 3.2 shows, yearly sales of VCRs jumped from 802,000 in 1980 to 11–12 million per year during the second half of the decade. Sales of videodisc players, by contrast, remained sluggish, never substantially clearing 300,000 in any year. Sales of prerecorded videocassettes (chart 3.1) neared 50 million in 1985 and exceeded 200 million in 1989. A comparison (charts 3.2 and 3.3) of the adoption curves for VCRs and pay-cable subscriptions shows pay cable peaking faster than VCRs early in the decade (pay-cable subscriptions jumped from 9 million to 28 million between

Table 3.2
VCR** and Videodisc Player Sales
(Unit Sales in thousands)

Year	VCR	Videodisc
1980	802	40°
1981	1,500	157
1982	2,035	223
1983	4,091	307
1984	7,616	200
1985	11,336	75
1986	12,005	85°
1987	11,702	100°
1988	12,148	120°
1989	11,225	160°
Total	74,460	1,467

°Estimated
**Excludes Camcorders
Source: Electronic Industries Association in 1987–1991 *International Television and Video Almanac*; *Variety*, 17 June 1981.

Chart 3.1
Unit Sales of Prerecorded Videocassettes (millions)

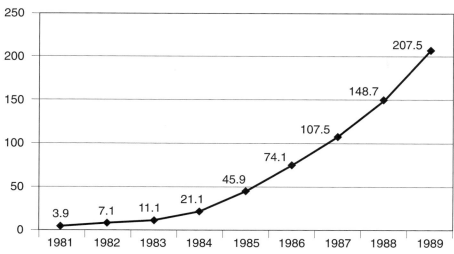

Source: MPAA, *1996 U.S. Economic Review.*

1980 and 1983), while VCR adoption saw a tremendous boom in the latter eighties, eventually surpassing the number of pay-cable subscriptions. In 1989, pay-cable subscriptions stood at 41 million as compared to more than 62 million VCR households. The number of television households with a VCR climbed steeply, from 2.4 percent in 1980 to nearly 70 percent in 1989.[7]

CHART 3.2
Pay-Cable Subscriptions (millions)

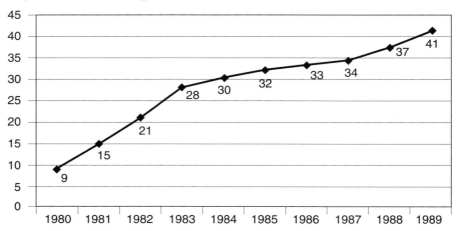

SOURCE: MPAA, *1996 U.S. Economic Review.*

CHART 3.3
VCR Households (millions)

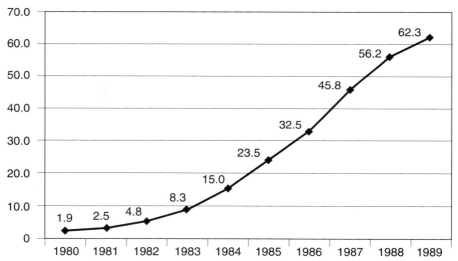

SOURCE: MPAA, *1996 U.S. Economic Review.*

These data show that long-established patterns of film viewing were changing. In previous decades, watching a movie meant going to a theater or turning on broadcast television, but this was no longer true in the 1980s. Marketing studies conducted at mid-decade showed that most people were now watching their movies on video rather than in theaters. A 1986 survey commissioned by Columbia Pictures found that while most of the public did not go to a movie theater in a given month, rates of videocassette viewing were skyrocketing in every age group studied. Teenagers, for example, tripled their video viewing to 58 million films in August–September 1985 while reducing their theatrical filmgoing by 20 percent. Columbia's president of marketing and distribution, Peter Sealey, pointed to the study's finding that three-quarters of the public did not attend a monthly film at the theater and contrasted this with the runaway sales figures for VCRs. The latter, he said, "is the most staggeringly fast penetration of households by any electronic appliance, I believe, in history—including television in its halcyon days." More than half of all VCR households in 1985 were renting an average of four video films per month. Drawing the contrast with theatrical attendance, Sealey concluded, "As VCR penetration goes up, this becomes the dominant factor in seeing a movie. It's the dominant market. It's profoundly larger than the theatrical market."[8] A 1987 American Video Association survey found a very robust video rental business nationwide, with average weekly rentals per store of 1,258 tapes, and in 1988 the Video Software Dealers Association disclosed that over 80 percent of the business lay in video rentals rather than sales.[9]

With the burgeoning popularity of video, the inevitable happened. Shortly after mid-decade, revenues from video outpaced those from theatrical box office. In 1987, home video revenues were $7.5 billion compared with a $4 billion box office. In 1989, the differential increased to over $11 billion for video against a $5 billion box office.[10] Wall Street took notice and by mid-decade began using home video revenues as a basis for appraising studio stock values. An analyst for Shearson Lehman pointed out that the video business, following theatrical, was hit-driven. "If a major has successful theatrical product, a high built-in demand for ancillary will have been created."[11] In the video sell-through market, the popular titles typically were big box-office films, a relationship that demonstrated strong synergies between the two markets and that provided a rationale for the exhibition sector's expansion beginning in mid-decade. As table 3.3 shows, the ten top-selling video titles in 1987 were also, largely, the top ten box-office films from 1986.

Furthermore, the business transactions covered in the previous chapter operated to enhance the financial rewards deriving from film-video synergies. The industry's main film producers and distributors, who received most of the box-office dollars, were also the video suppliers with the biggest market shares. Table 3.4 shows the 1989 estimated video market shares and revenues of the seven majors who were also the top seven home

TABLE 3.3
1987 Top Selling Video Titles
(Box Office Ranking 1986)

1. TOP GUN (1)
2. LADY AND THE TRAMP (40)
3. CROCODILE DUNDEE (3)
4. STAR TREK IV (4)
5. AN AMERICAN TAIL (15)
6. KARATE KID PART II (2)
7. LETHAL WEAPON (10)
8. THE GOLDEN CHILD (8)
9. THE COLOR PURPLE (6)
10. ALIENS (5)

SOURCE: *1989 International Television and Video Almanac*; *Variety*, 14 January 1987, p. 25.

Table 3.4

1989 Estimated Video Market Share and Revenues of the Majors

	Market Share	Video Revenue
Warner	14	481
Buena Vista	13	439
Paramount	9	310
CBS/Fox	8	272
MCA	7	246
MGM/UA	7	223
RCA/Columbia	6	215

Source: Video Magazine Store Research in *1991 International Television and Video Almanac*, p. 610.

video suppliers. Enhancing the importance of this ancillary was the fact that the video market is a global one. The majors derived video revenues from overseas sales, and these revenues had swollen to gargantuan proportions by decade's end. Videocassette sales, for example, generated $6.8 billion in top foreign markets in 1988.[12] The most profitable territories that year were the United Kingdom ($920 million in sales), Germany ($829 million), Japan ($751 million), and Canada ($480 million).

Challenges in the Video Market

With its exploding popularity and its gushing revenue stream, home video was, as *Variety* termed it, a goose that laid golden eggs. As a financial analyst for Merrill Lynch observed, "Without homevideo, the whole [film] industry would look a lot less healthy than it does."[13] Home video was a boon to Hollywood, but before the majors could exploit this ancillary market and dominate it, as they have come to do, a host of problems and challenges had to be surmounted. I turn now to these.

Piracy   The scariest aspect of home video for the majors lay in their perception of its threat to the revenues they derived from film production and distribution. To the majors, this threat assumed several forms, and the most urgent of these lay in the area of video piracy, that is, the unauthorized production and distribution of video copies of films that were then in domestic and overseas theatrical release. Before the advent of video, investigations of film piracy, conducted by the FBI with MPAA cooperation, focused on the nontheatrical 16-mm market. Videotape, though, created greater opportunities for making and distributing bootleg copies of motion pictures because the medium was so lightweight and portable and because duplication of tapes did not require the expensive lab work that film did. Thus, as videotape began its surge in popularity, the FBI and the MPAA shifted their antipiracy efforts to this medium, which the industry would calculate was producing a $1 billion loss worldwide.

In February, 1980, the FBI arrested thirteen people in eight U.S. cities on video piracy charges. Funding from the MPAA helped set up the sting operations that led to the arrests.[14] The FBI confiscated a large batch of illegal tapes including some (The Baltimore Bullet [1980] and The Jerk [1979]) that had been in circulation as videos prior to the picture's theatrical release. Piracy convictions throughout 1980 climbed sharply. By year's end, sixty people had been convicted, and ninety more had been arrested and were awaiting trial. By contrast, between 1975 and 1979, only eighty-four people were convicted on piracy charges (thirty-seven of them in 1979). In 1975, the FBI confiscated 5,867 pirated films and 1,195 pirated tapes. In 1980, the numbers were vastly different (312 films and 16,635 tapes), demonstrating the changing nature of piracy operations.[15] Video piracy would remain one of the industry's top concerns throughout the decade, and the problem would never, could never, be resolved. It only seemed to grow. In 1989, the FBI confiscated 659,615 illegal tapes.[16] The piracy problem required continuing vigilance from the MPAA and prominent announcements of temporary victories, as in 1989, when the MPAA counted one of its top achievements of that year a $250 million reduction in piracy losses in Japan.[17] But the electronic media had created an irresolvable problem for the majors that their antipiracy efforts could never hope to adequately control.

THE THREAT OF HOME TAPING   Electronic media (videotape in the 1980s, digital video and the Internet in the 1990s) make the duplication and transmission of information infinitely easier than the chemical- and heavy-industry-intensive media that preceded them. Film belonged to the latter category for much of its history as a chemically-based medium that required laboratory processing and elaborate machinery for its manufacture, distribution (trucks and planes), and exhibition (theaters with fixed projection equipment). All of these requirements erected barriers against the illegal production and distribution of motion pictures. They made it harder, though not impossible, for film pirates to operate. By contrast, video (and today's Internet distribution of digital images) eradicated many of these existing barriers, and as the medium of film changed from an industrial to an electronic format, the problem of uncontrollable manufacture and distribution of copyrighted images became far more acute.

Herein lay a second, but far more significant, threat to the revenues of the major film producers and distributors. This was the threat to copyright posed by the new electronic media and which the videotape boom of the 1980s was the first to make clear. Copyright protection of their work is the foundation safeguarding and securing the revenues derived by the majors from film production and distribution. As such, and for copyright purposes, films belong to the corporate entities that fund or distribute them. Directors may get possessive credit on screen (as in a credit that reads "A John Landis Film"), and stars may be the highest-paid members of a production crew, but the film itself remains the property of the studio, or the distributor or the agency, that puts up the operating capital and retains copyright control of the work.

For the majors, home video delivered a severe blow to copyright law and to its safeguarding of their profits. The home video boom was a nightmare come true for the Hollywood majors. Studio executives lay awake at night, sweating and trembling. They pictured families across America watching video movies taped from cable television and loaning these videos to friends, or worse yet, pictured families with two VCRs hooked together, making video copies of other tapes. To the majors, everyone with a VCR was now potentially a pirate. With the ease of home taping, studios could no longer control the distribution and consumption of their own films. MCA president Sidney Sheinberg complained about hometaping, "The trouble is, one can't technologically stop it, and people don't think it is illegal or immoral."[18] The majors resolved to fight the technology. Shortly after Sony Corp. introduced its Betamax videotape recorders (utilizing

MCA president Sidney Sheinberg voiced the anxieties of many in the industry about the threat to copyright posed by home taping.

one-half- inch tape, narrower than the three-quarter-inch VHS format marketed by Matsushita and which would become the standard) in late 1975, Universal (MCA) and Disney filed suit against Sony, claiming that its machines facilitated copyright infringement. Prosecuting their claims would take Universal and Disney eight years, and the issues would go all the way to the Supreme Court.

The case illuminated the terrific anxieties of the industry regarding home taping. For the first time, the majors confronted a distribution medium for film that they did not control. Even with television, initially construed by Hollywood as a rival medium, the studios controlled their product. They licensed films to networks for a limited period of restricted showings. Viewers did not determine when they would watch those films, and they could not make physical copies for subsequent viewing. By contrast, the VCR gave viewers unprecedented access to films and influence over the conditions of their viewing. The majors were accustomed to deriving revenues from each public exhibition of their films, whether in theaters, via cable, or over the airwaves, and studio officials proclaimed that uncontrolled VCR use would economically undercut the industry. Jack Valenti called VCRs "millions of little tapeworms" devouring the industry.[19]

To the majors, then, the VCR was an insidious technology, and in the hostility of their first responses to it, the industry replicated its initial paranoid reactions to the advent of television. As with television, the hostility would be replaced with an understanding that the new medium need be no enemy and could add big bags of cash to studio coffers. But first, the industry had to acclimate itself to the VCR and the video revolution it heralded. This entailed accepting the many ways in which video would change the industry's production and exhibition practices, and it also depended on successfully surmounting the challenges of exploiting the new market. Before all of this could happen, though, the industry's frontal assault, the litigation against Sony, had to run its course.

Focusing their anxieties on the litigation against Sony, the studios argued that home taping fell outside the fair use provision of copyright law (which permitted limited copying of protected works for nonprofit or educational usage) and that Sony was liable for damages, along with retailers who promoted sales of the machines by stressing the conveniences of home taping and time-shifting. The trial began in January 1979 in U.S. District Court, California, and concluded with an October decision against the claims of Universal and Disney. The judge found that home taping fell within the fair use provision of copyright law and that Sony was not liable for damages.

Disney and Universal appealed the decision, and they got a ruling this time against Sony. On 20 October 1981, the Ninth Circuit Court of Appeals ruled that home taping did constitute copyright violation. The decision overturned the lower federal court ruling. The appeals court decided, "We find no Congressional intent to create a blanket home-use exception to copyright protection and that home video-recording does not constitute fair use. In addition, the defendants are legally responsible for infringing activity for such use."[20] While the court's ruling on the fair use provision was unequivocal, the de facto situation posed problems for the relief Universal and Disney might expect. Millions of videotape recorders were already on the market and in homes, and recalling these machines would be a logistical nightmare. Possible solutions ran the gamut from royalty fees on VCR sales payable to the majors to a redesign of the machines to prevent them from recording. These were discussed but not implemented, and any effort to redesign the machines to disable copying would run counter to the singular feature that had been responsible for the public's quick acceptance of the technology and its rapid diffusion. The appeals court decision was highly unpopular, and it was widely ridiculed and condemned in the press, which pointed out that it criminalized a huge segment of the public.

It did not stand for long. Sony appealed, and the Supreme Court agreed to hear the case. In a landmark ruling on 17 January 1984, the court ended the majors' eight-year effort to curtail home taping by ruling that it was a fair use activity and that, because no copyright violation was involved, VCR manufacturers and retailers were not liable as contributory infringers. The court took a conservative view of the law. Writing for the majority, Justice John Paul Stevens noted that "in cases like this, in which Congress has not plainly marked our course, we must be circumspect in construing the scope of rights created by a legislative enactment which never contemplated such a calculus of interests." The court viewed home taping as a noncommercial, nonprofit activity that, contrary to studio claims, did not materially affect the market for Hollywood films. "One may search the Copyright Act in vain for any sign that the elected representatives of the millions of people who watch television every day have made it unlawful to copy a program for later viewing at home, or have enacted a flat prohibition against the sale of machines that make such copying possible."[21]

In a sense, the court was simply ratifying a decision that had already been made by popular fiat. The millions of video customers clearly believed that their noncommercial, in-home taping habits (as distinct from the for-profit copying and distribution of tapes by video pirates) were harmless and of little economic consequence to an industry that was posting record revenues. The mass marketing of VCRs, and the public's desire for them, were initiating an irreversible series of changes in society and in the film industry. Home video was an early hub for evolving concepts of "home entertainment centers," integrated audiovisual systems that moved entertainment programming into the home and away from public spaces more profoundly even than television had effected in earlier decades. The VCR revolution changed not only the distribution pattern of films but even how studios and parent corporations thought about what they produced.

On the negative side lay the clear result (for the studios) of their lost eight-year court battle: loss of control over distribution of their product, at least in the home sector, and the erosion of copyright protection for their work. Regarding the latter issue, MCA president Sidney Sheinberg (MCA's Universal had pressed the litigation against Sony) reflected:

> With the benefit of hindsight, I think it has been even more harmful than we
> thought. The harm is not only in the copying of material, which deprives us

of subsequent potential revenues—all the arguments that we made in the lit-igation—but in the continuing degeneration of the concept of copyright. Whether it's people plucking the HBO signal off the air or not paying for taps on cable systems or whatever, it's caused and fed a deteriorating respect for a basic and constitutionally motivated right.[22]

The industry's charges of copyright violation, and the litigation itself, masked a huge irony. During the years that Disney and Universal were pursuing the case against Sony and the industry was talking self-righteously about illegal incursions into its business operations by the manufacturers and distributors of video recorders, Hollywood itself went video. During those years it was moving aggressively into the video market that it professed to fear and loathe. The year 1981 was the first full year of operation for MCA Videocassette and for Disney's home video operations. By 1982 Disney had fifty-three titles in its home video catalog. That year it began overseas distribution of home video, marketing twenty-five titles in Western Europe, Australia, and South Africa, with plans to expand foreign markets to Spain, Italy, Latin America, and Asia.[23] In 1982, A WALT DISNEY CHRISTMAS and DISNEY'S AMERICAN SUMMER generated home video sales of more than $2 million, and at year's end the release of TRON generated over $1 million in initial orders. MCA Videocasette had placed eighty Universal films into home video release, and MCA jointly owned with Paramount a video distribution arm for foreign markets (the Cinema International Corp.). Paramount had commenced home video operations in 1980 with its division Paramount Home Video. Warner Bros. debuted Warner Home Video in 1979. Completing its first year of operation in 1980, Warner Home Video had forty-one titles in home video release in both Beta and VHS formats. In 1980, Columbia Pictures Home Entertainment completed its first year of operation and released videocassettes of twenty-four titles. In 1981, Columbia embarked on worldwide home video marketing, signing with RCA to form a joint venture, RCA Columbia International Video. The previous year, 1980, also saw completion of a very successful year for 20th Century–Fox's Magnetic Video Corp., which was distributing product for United Artists, ABC Video Enterprises, and Avco Embassy in addition to Fox films. Fox's ALIEN (1979) reached the million-dollar sales mark forty-five days after its home video release, and ALL THAT JAZZ (1979) attained this mark in one day.[24] MVC released 9 TO 5 (1980) and THE STUNT MAN (1980) less than two months after their first-run theatrical release was concluded.

Disney, Universal, and the rest of the Hollywood majors commenced an aggressive expansion into home video simultaneous with their lawsuit against Sony. Thus, the industry's rhetoric about VCR tapeworms belied the economic reality that the majors were exploiting the market they professed to decry. Between January 1979 and March 1980, the majors placed 477 titles into video release, an 854 percent increase over the 50 titles that had been available until then. Jack Valenti noted that this shift toward video release reflected a new commitment by the majors to the video market.[31] Furthermore, Sony's Betamax machines posed competition with the VHS market that Universal and the other majors had entered, and this provided a clear, albeit unacknowledged eco-nomic foundation for the lawsuit. Obliquely, the suit was about the competing claims of these two formats. Thus, the industry's rhetoric was not aligned with its business prac-tices. The economic rewards to be derived from successful video sales and distribution drove the majors almost immediately into this market even as they backed legislation designed to curb the freedom of viewers to tape movies. This was a contradiction between the majors' desire for traditional copyright protection and their willingness to embrace the market created by a new technology. While they wanted the market and would get it, the majors would never find a way in the eighties of securing their copyright interests against the onslaught of the new army of electronic tapeworms. Furthermore, the majors confronted another set of problems, legally related to copyright. These lay in the consequences of the first sale doctrine and the challenge of whether video revenue would be better construed as sale or rental income.

SALES VERSUS RENTALS Copyright law distinguishes between copyright ownership and lawful ownership of a copy of a protected work. The Copyright Act of 1976 gives copyright owners six exclusive rights, which govern the copying, distribution, and performance of protected works. These rights notwithstanding, however, the owner of a legally obtained copy "is entitled, without the authority of the copyright owner, to sell or otherwise dispose of the possession of that copy. . . ."* This provision has come to be known as the first sale doctrine. Of specific consequence to the industry, once a major sold a videotape to a retailer, the retailer was then free to rent the tape for home use and to keep the rental income. The studios had copyright control of their work, but if they sold video copies to retailers (whether chain stores or small mom-and-pop outlets), they failed to receive subsequent royalties from rental of those tapes. Congress extended specific exemptions to this provision for the record industry (the Record Rental Amendment of 1984) and the computer software industry (the Computer Software Rental Amendment Act of 1990) but not for videotapes.

Because of the peculiarities of this doctrine, the burgeoning rental market for videotapes threatened studios with a massive loss of royalty revenue. Across the country in the early 1980s, viewers were happily renting video copies of movies, rental outlets were happily counting their profits, and the majors were glumly watching the growth of a market from whose revenues they were excluded. Had life ever been so unfair for the industry's giants? As the rental market developed, the majors and the nation's retail outlets were in separate businesses. The studios packaged their tapes and sold them to national wholesaler-distributors, typically at discounts of 37 percent. For a title carrying a retail price of $99.95, for example, the studio would receive about $63 per unit. Because the studios sold to wholesaler-distributors, they were not involved in retail store transactions. The wholesaler-distributor then passed approximately 30 percent of its discounted price on to retailers (the $99.95 unit might be priced for retail at $70).[26] The distributor would thereby keep about $7 per unit. At the retail end, the hot rental period for major new studio releases lasts about ninety days. If the store can rent each unit of a new title for half of that period (forty-five times) at $3 per night, it will gross $135 per unit, turning a profit of $72. Of course, not all titles rent so successfully, and under the best of conditions, a video store has a rather narrow window of time in which to cover its costs and make a profit from its purchase of new studio pictures.

The studios, therefore, did not do business directly with video retailers, and this tended to intensify the estrangement and antagonism between the two groups that the First Sale problem had triggered. In response to this, the majors supported a legislative effort in Congress to repeal the first sale doctrine, and in 1981 and 1982 they experi-

---

* Provisions of the first sale doctrine, and litigation involving it, are reviewed by Steve Lauff, "Decompilation of Collective Works: When the First Sale Doctrine is a Mirage," *Texas Law Review* 76, no. 4 (March 1998): 869–904.

mented with several policies designed to give them better compensation from the rental market, although they risked considerable hostility from retailers in doing so. As a Warner executive explained, "We can't stand by and watch an ever-expanding universe in which rental revenues we do not participate in get larger and larger and continue to invest millions of dollars in films to fuel this market and not get any of it back."[27] Warner announced that it would no longer sell any video titles to retailers but would license them instead for a limited period of time. Retailers would pay a license fee, but because the tapes were not sold, Warner would retain ownership and would receive royalties. Twentieth Century–Fox and MGM announced similar policies.

Alternatively, Paramount, MCA, and Universal announced surcharge policies under which they would add a fixed amount to the base price of a cassette sold to retailers. The surcharge was intended to provide some royalty compensation for the rental revenues the studios would never see past the point of sale. Paramount's surcharge ranged from one to twenty-five dollars depending on the film's box-office performance. The disadvantage of this approach, and the reason that prompted Warners to go with a licensing policy, lay in its tendency to drive tape prices up to a level that affected retailers' abilities to achieve sufficient depth of copy, that is, stock enough copies of a popular title to meet customer demand. The higher the pricing per tape, the greater a retailer's capital outlay. Retailers facing this problem would respond by stocking fewer copies. Understandably, retailers were not happy with this policy, nor did they like the licensing approach. The objections of retailers, in fact, forced Warner to back off from its no-sell policy.

The efforts by the majors in 1981 and 1982 to increase income from the rental market by means of licensing and surcharge policies created a crisis for the infant home video industry because suppliers and retailers had assumed antagonistic positions. As far as the majors were concerned, the nation's video rental shops were in a different business altogether from their own, and the First Sale Doctrine helped to perpetuate this perception by severing video rental revenues from the other revenue streams the majors were accustomed to enjoying. Accordingly, the majors turned their attentions to another and potentially more profitable means of exploiting video. Viewing video rentals as an unwelcome intrusion upon their rightful business ventures, the majors went after the other video market: the "sell-through" market, that is, direct sales of video titles to customers.

The majors, though, were slow to perceive the viability of this market. Intent on recovering as much revenue from video as they could, they priced video titles far higher than most customers would support. Prices hovered around $80–90 per tape until Paramount, early in 1982, cut the nominal price of STAR TREK II (1982) from $79.95 to $39.95 in an effort to encourage higher sales. The price reduction was enormously successful, generating sales of over 100,000 tapes. This was a home video sales record, and it demonstrated that the sell-through market to consumers existed, provided tapes were reasonably priced. The following year, Paramount cut its price for AN OFFICER AND A GENTLEMAN (1982) to $39.95, and Embassy, following Paramount's lead, reduced BLADE RUNNER (1982) to $39.95. RCA/Columbia lowered tape prices even further with a $25 tag on its summer video release of HE-MAN AND THE MASTERS OF THE UNIVERSE. In July, Paramount moved more aggressively still, and antagonized exhibitors, by releasing the popular FLASHDANCE (1983) on video a mere six months after its theatrical release. In eight months, Paramount sold 250,000 copies. In November 1983, Paramount's RAIDERS OF THE LOST ARK (1981) set new records by posting initial unit sales of 500,000, carrying a retail gross of $30 million.[28] Unit sales reached 1.4 million by 1987.

At this point it was clear, largely through Paramount's series of bold price reductions, that consumers would pay to own inexpensive copies of favorite movies and that video could work for the studios, despite the unresolved problems associated with the rental end of the business. But it was not yet apparent just how big the video gold mine could be. Paramount, again, showed the industry the revenue potential of home video sales. TOP GUN, the number one box-office film of 1986, generated stunning video revenues. Within one week of its 1987 video release as a $26.95 cassette, Paramount sold 2.5 million cassettes, garnering wholesale revenues of more than $40 million, nearly half of the film's $82 million domestic theatrical rentals.[29]

Several factors were notable about these sales figures. For the first time, participation by video stores (rather than mass merchants) accounted for the majority of sales. Paramount found that most of its sales occurred in video rental stores, which the industry had been regarding as hopelessly lost sources of revenue. Rental outlets were participating in a sell-through program for the studios, signaling a rapprochement between these retailers and the majors after the contentious relations that prevailed earlier in the decade when the majors attempted their surcharge and licensing policies.

Second, TOP GUN was the first blockbuster film in video release to carry commercial sponsorship. The tape began with an ad for Diet Pepsi that was a stylistic and thematic

TOP GUN's *extraordinary video revenues demonstrated the size of the sell-through market and its fiscal importance for the majors. It was the first blockbuster video to carry advertising by a corporate sponsor.*

twin of the film. The ad shows a group of jet pilots returning to base after maneuvers. It is edited with quick, aggressive cutting and employs a rock music sound track like the film's. In the ad, "Mustang," (a thematic call-sign name, like the film's Navy pilot characters who are known as "Viper," "Iceman," and "Jester") has difficulty pouring his bottle of Diet Pepsi while flying, prompting one of the other pilots to ask, "Trouble with your refreshment system?" Mustang loops around, executing the kind of flashy stunts Maverick (Tom Cruise) does in the film, flying upside down, enabling the bottle's contents to flow into his mug. Satisfied at last, Mustang and the other pilots streak home.

The ad achieves perfect synergy with the film, its style and thematic content blending seamlessly with the film's imagery and the cold war issues that fuel its narrative. In the ad, the paraphernalia of aerial combat as dramatized throughout the film—the high-tech aerial guidance and surveillance systems, the evasive maneuvering and macho bantering of the pilots—is deployed to open a bottle of Pepsi, and Pepsi, in turn, becomes a "refreshment system" in the automated cockpit of the plane. In its content and style, the ad is virtually indistinguishable from the film, creating a symbiosis of the two products (Pepsi and TOP GUN). It was a remarkably shrewd maneuver. No one yet knew how well audiences would tolerate advertisements on their home videos (they didn't like them in theaters), and by blending ad and film so skillfully, Paramount and Pepsi were able to ease viewers into an acceptance of this new marriage between home video and product advertising. The TOP GUN–Diet Pepsi campaign was but one of many striking new synergies prevailing between merchants in the ancillary markets, and I discuss these relationships more fully later in the chapter.

The spectacular success of TOP GUN on video was overshadowed the following year by the long-awaited video release of E.T., which had been the top box-office film of

Reduced, consumer-friendly pricing helped make E.T. a home video phenomenon.

1982. MCA/Universal released the film as a $24.95 video that carried a $5 rebate offer from Pepsi. This price was a new low for a blockbuster release. MCA could barely keep the film stocked in video stores and other outlets. By year's end, MCA had sold over 15 million tapes and garnered over $175 million in revenue. As TOP GUN and E.T. demonstrated, the video gold mine for the majors lay in sell-through, not rental. Because of the First Sale problem, the majors were locked out of the billion-dollar rental market.

However, while sell-through would be a gold mine for the majors, they kept trying to find ways to divert rental revenues to their own coffers. In 1988 and 1989, for example, the majors considered implementing pay-per-transaction policies under which retailers could lease tapes at rates greatly below what they would have to pay to purchase them. In return, retailers would split the rental revenue with the supplier. The low cost of leasing would enable retailers to stock more copies of a hit title during periods of peak demand. By decade's end, pay-per-transaction had not been implemented by the majors, but its consideration shows their continuing restlessness and their dissatisfaction with the rental market. (The ambitious Divx digital video plan, marketed by Circuit City, Disney, Universal, and Paramount in 1998, showed that the industry had never relinquished its dream of a successful pay-per-transaction scheme.)

Other signs of this dissatisfaction in the later 1980s could be found in sometimes hilarious attempts to market technological solutions to the dilemma. Simpleton Resources Ltd. licensed a counter system to monitor how often a videotape had been played. It would have worked as a means of auditing the pay-per-view transactions the majors would split with retailers. (The Divx plan required viewers to dial in via modem to a central data bank with their viewing request and payment.) Rank Video Services developed a self-destructing videocassette (poof! after x number of plays) that could set an upper limit on the rental income per title lost to studios. (Divx discs would be unplayable for repeat viewings, and viewers could discard them after one viewing.) But such approaches threatened a return to the supplier-retailer opposition of the early 1980s, and with the sell-through revenue bonanzas the studios were reaping by mid-decade, some of their earlier urgency and anxiety had dissipated.

By decade's end, in its sell-through capacity, home video had emerged as the most important of the ancillary markets. Pay-cable revenues were a major source of income, but home video was bigger. Wall Street's Shearson Lehman calculated Paramount's 1986 theatrical and ancillary revenues, and its analysis breaks out the proportion from each category, something rarely disclosed in the majors' financial reports. As calculated (chart 3.4) by Shearson Lehman, Paramount received $320 million from domestic theatrical rentals, $207 million from home video, $120 million from pay cable, $120 million from overseas theatrical rentals, and $96 million from network TV.[30] In 1988, MCA's combined revenues (chart 3.5) from home video and pay television ($531 million) easily outpaced film revenues from theatrical exhibition ($249 million).[31] As we have seen, the majors initially believed that pay-per-view on cable television would bring them their biggest pot of ancillary gold, but by decade's end, this cable format failed to reach its anticipated maturity. In the meantime, licensing films for pay-cable presentation proved to be very lucrative, thank you.

VIDEODISCS

Videodiscs were another story altogether. In 1980–81, Warner, Paramount, Fox, Columbia, and MCA initiated videotape and disc operations. Disc and tape were seen

CHART 3.4
Paramount Pictures, 1986 Revenues

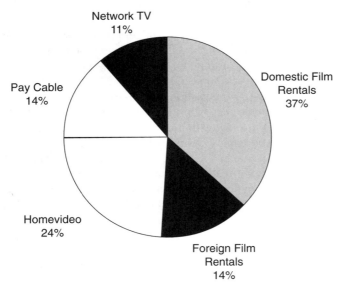

SOURCE: *Variety*, 23 September 1987, p. 1.

CHART 3.5
MCA, Inc., Filmed-Entertainment Revenues, 1988

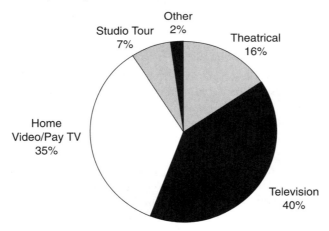

SOURCE: MCA, "Five Year Financial Highlights," Form 10-K, 1989, p. 5.

as joint components of the expanding home entertainment markets, and the majors commenced operations in both areas. Capable of producing better image quality than videotape, discs were introduced as a higher-end alternative to tape for the home market. Best of all from the standpoint of a copyright owner, videodiscs were a read-only medium (ROM, i.e., one could not record on a disc). Discs would therefore permit the studios to maintain better control over their product in the home markets, provided Universal won its lawsuit against Sony. In tracing the history of optical disc technology, David Robert Cellitti stresses the role played by MCA, in somewhat tense partnership with Phillips NV, in researching and pushing the format to market. MCA's involvement began in the 1960s, and MCA head Lew Wasserman believed that optical discs would the "jewel in the crown" of the company, permitting it to reap huge revenues from its library of films by licensing them for this format. Furthermore, Cellitti stresses that Wasserman felt it imperative to get the disc format to market before videotape could get a foothold. MCA's suit against Sony was, in this respect, about the competing formats. "MCA saw videotape as foe, not friend, to DiscoVision. It viewed the Betamax as a multifaceted monster that would gobble up copyrighted programming and cheat producers out of the millions coming to them in royalty fees."[32]

MCA head Lew Wasserman envisioned the optical disc format as an ideal ancillary medium, and his support was critical to its research and development.

By contrast with MCA's view, however, consumers judged discs' ROM status to be a distinct drawback. The great advantage of tape for consumers was its recordability. A consumer who bought a VCR could play movies and record them, while a consumer who bought a laserdisc player could only watch the discs. Compounding this disadvantage and hindering market acceptance was the competition between competing disc formats. In 1978, MCA debuted DiscoVision, its laser reflective optical system, which employed a laser beam to read information stored on the disc as a series of micropits and to translate this information into an NTSC television signal. Manufacturers and sellers of laser optical systems included MCA's DiscoVision, Magnavox, Phillips NV, Pioneer, and Sony. The laser optical system came in two formats. CLV (constant linear velocity) discs could hold up to one hour of programming per side but offered no interactive features. CAV (constant angular velocity) discs could hold only thirty minutes of material per side, but they offered freeze-frame, slow motion, and direct random frame access functions. These permitted viewers to break the linearity that celluloid film and videotape enforced upon a spectator's viewing habits. With a CAV disk, a viewer could instantly access any desired segment of a film and could resequence the viewing of multiple segments. CAV disks offered viewers new capabilities for reorganizing their viewing experience and the narrative structure of a film.

In 1982, RCA introduced a competing system, the capacitance electronic disc (which it called SelectaVision). This was a needle-groove system in which an electrode on a diamond stylus read signals from grooves on the disc surface. With its stylus and grooved discs, SelectaVision was reminiscent of phonograph records and thus seemed to consumers more like a carryover of an older technology than an exciting new one (and this at a time when audio CDs were challenging the primacy of grooved, vinyl audio discs).

RCA had invested close to $600 million in its SelectaVision system, a huge financial gamble. Unfortunately for RCA, even though it had licensed films from most of the Hollywood majors for release on this format, the system failed to gain an adequate customer base, and in 1984 RCA phased out SelectaVision. RCA's president, Thornton Bradshaw, cited "the enormous growth in VCRs, and the rapid development of a rental market for tapes" as the core factors behind the failure of SelectaVision. He added, "Selectivision was a technological success but a commercial failure."[33]

Optical reflectance disk systems remained on the market, but sales stayed low in comparison to videotape (chart 3.6). Faced with a market that failed to mature and with consumers' undeniable preference for the VCR, MCA abandoned its crown jewel. In the 1980s, it sold the patents and production plant to Japan's Pioneer Corp. It would be an error, however, to assume that the laserdisc market was simply a failure. It succeeded as a niche market by offering a specialty item to a limited but devoted segment of consumers. In comparison to tape, laserdiscs typically carried special features such as a film's theatrical trailer, outtakes, and commentary by filmmakers and film scholars. The image was sharper than tape and generally less noisy. Moreover, the video image on discs was frequently matted to preserve the film's proper aspect ratio, whereas viewers who saw films on videotape almost always saw them out of ratio (a matter discussed later in this chapter). Laserdiscs, therefore, became the medium of choice for videophiles and for serious film fans who cared about things like proper aspect ratio and good image quality. They retained this appeal and customer base through the remainder of the 1980s and well into the 1990s, at least until the advent in 1997 of DVD (digital

CHART 3.6
VCR and Videodiscs Sales

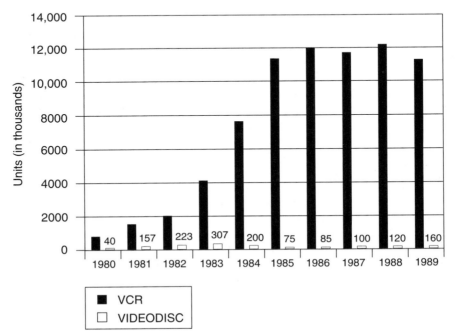

SOURCE: MPAA, *1996 U.S. Economic Review.*

videodiscs), which offered the highest-quality home video yet marketed. Although laserdiscs never generated a viable threat to home videotape and never gained widespread customer acceptance, they nevertheless remained alive as a market niche whose customers were tenaciously devoted to the format.

As a sign of its importance to the industry, home video claimed the second tier on the release hierarchy, right after theatrical exhibition. Home video had transformed the industry's expectations about the sources of its film revenues and had greatly amplified expectations about the overall size of those revenues. In these ways, it had a tremendous impact on the business. But the effects of home video were multifaceted, and an understanding of the economic and business ramifications is only the beginning.

Effects of Video on Film Production, Exhibition, and Consumption

Video's effects on distribution, as discussed earlier in this chapter, are easily recognized because of the widespread availability of videotape copies of movies and the popularity of home viewing; by the mid-1980s, many viewers would elect to "wait for it on video" rather than paying the higher prices charged for a theatrical screening. But the alterations in production practices due to video were just as momentous, and it will be useful to consider these first before turning to a discussion of the aesthetic impact of home video. Although film and video people historically have been separate and suspicious of one another—"it's like two competing tribes," said the head of a video production house in 1981—a series of factors was converging to give video an increasing presence and role during the production and post-production phases of filmmaking.[34] In production, video assists diverted some of the light from the camera's viewfinder to a video monitor that enabled the director and other relevant crew members to view the real-time picture as the camera "saw" it. They could also instantly replay the scene on videotape. This gave filmmakers quicker access to a visual record of their scenes than provided by the usual procedure of waiting to screen lab dailies (footage printed from each day's shoot). Stanley Kubrick used a video assist on THE SHINING (1980), and Francis Coppola employed it extensively on his late-seventies and early-eighties productions. Because the video assist used a prism to divert some of the light from the camera's viewfinder, however, it produced a somewhat degraded video image. The loss of clarity, color, and contrast on the video assist required that the cinematographer understand the precise disparity between the light values of the scene, how the camera was reading those values, and what the video assist was reporting about how the camera was reading the scene.[35]

The video assist also presented another problem: its use could slow a day's shooting as cast and crew members gathered about the monitor to watch the replay of their scenes. Clint Eastwood found that the presence of the assist seemed to invite actors to pass judgment on how a scene went or looked. "Everyone would have an opinion, but an opinion based on what they were supposed to do in the shot. They were only looking at themselves or their responsibility and it starts to become a decision by collective. There only needs to be one perspective and that's the director's. . . . So for me it's much more efficient to do without the assist."[36] Charles Harpole witnessed Robert Altman's use of a video assist on STREAMERS (1983) and has reported that Altman found it a

Stanley Kubrick was an early proponent of the video assist, which he employed to help monitor filming of The Shining.

mixed blessing. It slowed production as everyone gathered to watch video playback. "Further, he [Altman] was not sure he wanted actors to see themselves so soon after doing a scene and before they had shot all takes of the scene (perhaps diffusing their spontaneity). But Altman said he personally liked a small, live-feed monitor for himself because it was 'just like looking through the camera lens.'"[37]

Video also exerted a large influence on post-production (i.e., those stages of moviemaking that follow shooting). Typically, these stages include the editing of picture and sound as well as the recording of a music track and effects, the re-recording of dialogue, and the mixing of all of a film's sound elements. Video was an increasingly viable option for companies seeking to hold down post-production costs. Companies found that they could save money with the efficiencies of time offered by off-line video editing and electronic video effects. On Star Trek—The Motion Picture (1979), The Nude Bomb (1980), and In God We Tru$t (1980), 35-mm footage was transferred to videotape for the creation of electronic effects. In mid-1981, *American Cinematographer* headlined what it called "the emerging new film/video interface" in the industry.[38] While this interface was occurring in a multitude of ways, the most visible and provocative initial applications of video practices to feature film production were conducted by director Francis Ford Coppola on his ill-fated One from the Heart (1982).

Although Coppola had experimented with video editing on Apocalypse Now (1979), during production of One from the Heart he expanded the uses of video as a production tool. He hoped it would be a visionary application of new technology that would show the industry the road down which it might travel toward an all-electronic cinema.[39] Coppola used video and still photography to pre-visualize the picture using an electronic storyboard, that is, a videotape of sketches and photos of the planned pro-

Director James Cameron looks through the video assist.

duction design. He supplemented this with videotape records of the cast's rehearsals, and during filming he used a video assist that fed an electronic signal to Coppola's "command center." This was a mobile trailer from which Coppola directed his movie, watching the video signal on the monitor and issuing instructions to his cast and crew by means of a PA system. In post-production, the film was edited in a traditional manner (on celluloid) and by Coppola on Betamax cassettes. Coppola explored editing changes and alternatives on video as a cost-saving measure, and the film was then conformed with his alterations.

Coppola continued many of these procedures on his next production, THE OUTSIDERS (1983), but the box-office failure of ONE FROM THE HEART broke his power in the industry and made him into a journeyman director for the remainder of the decade. Furthermore, the evident failings of ONE FROM THE HEART—its aloof tone, underdeveloped characters, and narrative insufficiencies—invited widespread criticism of Coppola's attempt to use electronic technologies to direct a picture by "remote control." He nevertheless continued to use video editing systems on his subsequent films. While he had been employing linear editing systems on ONE FROM THE HEART and his next pictures, with THE GODFATHER, PART III (1990), Coppola used a random-access, computer-based video system. Throughout the decade, Coppola retained his commitment to interfacing film and video, and he was not alone in shifting to video for post-production editing. In the eighties, Oliver Stone, James Cameron, Carroll Ballard, Bernardo Bertolucci, and George Lucas joined him in this shift.[40]

While Coppola's flamboyant experiments garnered the media's attention, the industry was quietly and steadily changing on its own. Transferring footage to videotape, editing on tape, and then conforming the film negative to the edited tape saved time and money, and a variety of video-based editing systems were on the market for film-

makers in the early 1980s.[41] Linear systems like the CMX 600 had been around since
the 1970s but had not found much acceptance among filmmakers. With a linear system, the editor makes edits in a chronological fashion, one at a time, one shot after
another in sequence. The editor accesses material by searching through preceding
footage and frames until the desired segment is reached. Random access systems, like
the CMX 6000 or the Spectra Image/Laser Edit System, enabled filmmakers to locate
edit points without having to search in a linear way forward or backward through their
material. Lucasfilm's EditDroid, for example, on line at mid-decade, used a computer
interface to access video footage stored on laserdiscs. Computer-assisted editing systems facilitated recordkeeping, storing a database that contained information about
footage locations, edge code numbers, and shot descriptions. The computer's automated search function enabled the editor to use this information to find desired
footage rapidly. Random access systems also offered efficiencies of time and post-production dollars because they facilitated the quick execution of multiple editing commands. In the 1990s digital video-based editing systems would become the industry
standard.

But recourse to video-based editing systems, whether linear or random access, posed
problems. These were inherent in the different frame rates of the two media. While film
ran at twenty-four frames per second, video operated at thirty frames per second, with
each frame composed of two fields. Thus film and video frames did not correspond to one
another, and the general method of making film-to-tape transfers lay in converting each
successive film frame to, alternately, two, and then three, video fields (the "2-3 pulldown").
Some of the resulting video frames would therefore consist of two fields, each representing an adjacent film frame. The problem in moving to video for an edit of film material
and then converting back to film lay in being able to make the complex calculations of the
frame and field locations of each edit point necessary to keep the two formats in synch with
one another. By 1982, however, several companies were marketing devices to address this
problem. These included video that operated at twenty-four frames per second and computer programs that could correlate SMPTE (Standardized by the Society of Motion
Picture and Television Engineers, time code facilitates video editing by recording information about hours, minutes, seconds, and frames) with film key and edge numbers. By
mid-decade, Eastman Kodak offered film coated with a thin layer of magnetic oxide that
enabled the recording of machine-readable SMPTE time code and facilitated the automa-
tion of many film-handling operations that had been connected with the film-to-tape
transfers.[42] The frame rate problem remained a persistent one, though, bedeviling even
the digital editing systems (Avid, Lightworks) that succeeded the computer-assisted video
systems. Digital systems operated at a film speed of twenty-four frames per second, but
films were often converted first to videotape (using a 2-3 pulldown) and then digitized
from tape, thereby introducing a small loss of synch between the source film and its digital counterpart, greatly complicating the editing of sound.

Whether editing was done on film or tape, by mid-decade computer assistance was
becoming invaluable. The assistant editor on THE RIGHT STUFF (1983), for example,
used a computer program to keep track of the picture's 2,750 edits and its quarter million feet of footage.[43] By the latter half of the decade, the industry was increasingly looking toward nonlinear editing methods.[44] Computer-based systems offered a powerful
solution to the enduring problem of minimizing expensive post-production time, and
these systems may also have played a role in helping establish the ferociously fast-paced

tempos of American film in the nineties. The computer-based systems ranged from those that used the computer as an interface to facilitate editing on a nondigital video source (e.g., the Montage Processor) to those which stored footage digitally on disk (e.g., Avid, Lightworks).

A major problem involved the low resolution of the monitors on electronic editing systems. Because details did not show up well in long shots, the systems threatened to bias editors toward the use of shots with closer framings, an aesthetic shift that may or may not have been suited to the demands of a particular film. In the same way, the use of a video assist during cinematography threatened to substitute low-resolution video aesthetics for film's complex and sophisticated resolving powers.

Furthermore, as editor Walter Murch pointed out, an editor using a traditional Moviola or Kem (that is, editing on film) may actually come to know the footage better than one who has quicker access to it electronically. The random access features force an editor to rely on his or her notes: "The clearer you are about what you want, the faster they are." But the real issue, Murch suggests, is not how fast one can go but where one wants to go. As the edited structure of a sequence changes, the creative needs of the editor change as well, and the downside of random access systems is that much footage, labeled unusable, will remain unexamined because the notes have excluded it. By contrast, a traditional linear system forces the editor to scan a wealth of material in search of what is wanted. "Frequently—invariably in my experience—you find what you need instead: some shot that captures a moment better than the one you were after, but which you could not have described in advance of seeing it. You also get to know the material better, because you are constantly browsing through it, looking for different things, in different states of mind."[45] Accordingly, Murch recommended that a degree of linearity be built into digital editing systems.

In addition to the speed at which a feature could be edited, electronic editing facilitated the integration of electronic special effects, and these acquired a huge presence in nineties filmmaking. Effects once created on an optical printer would be created in the 1990s more convincingly through digital compositing. Though it took off in the nineties, the digital effects revolution began to appear (slowly) in the 1980s as increasingly complex programs became available for rendering light, texture, and motion on computer. Sixty seconds of sensational computer graphics in STAR TREK II—THE WRATH OF KHAN (1982), simulating a planet's transformation from a lifeless rock to a lush, verdant world, generated tremendous interest throughout the industry. But the initial applications of digital effects produced disappointing box-office results. TRON (1982) and THE LAST STARFIGHTER (1984) were greeted with a lukewarm public response. It was not until the next decade that digital effects work became an essential part of electronic post-production and a gold-mine for the industry in films like TERMINATOR 2 (1991), JURASSIC PARK (1993), and FORREST GUMP (1994).

By decade's end, then, post-production practices were undergoing major redesign. The traditional approaches to film editing vested in the physical acts of cutting, splicing, and searching through trim bins had given way to the "cleaner" and more powerful use of electronic and then digital technology to offer quicker and more flexible approaches. Editing and special effects work bonded intimately as related parts of a unified phase of electronic post-production. Thus, though it was not the ultimate beneficiary of these changes (digital would be the heir), videotape and videodisc helped spearhead the industry's electronic transformation of post-production.

ADDITIONAL EFFECTS ON PRODUCTION

REINFORCING BLOCKBUSTER FILMMAKING   The rise of the home video market reinforced existing economic imperatives in the industry, namely, the emphasis on blockbuster production. Each year, one or more films generated extraordinary box-office rentals and helped give their major distributor a commanding share of the theatrical market. This market was hit-driven, and each major aimed to distribute a top-renting blockbuster every few years. Paramount was the most successful such major during the 1980s. It had three number one films during the decade, more than any other studio. Columbia's slide during David Puttnam's tenure as CEO was tied to his failure to initiate any productions that had blockbuster potential and to his neglect of existing blockbuster franchises (e.g., his unwillingness to produce sequels to GHOSTBUSTERS, JAGGED EDGE, and THE KARATE KID). Home video reinforced the emphasis on hits and blockbusters because of the substantial revenue this ancillary market could produce and because home video customers tended to rent and buy the same films that were hits in theatrical release. The top-renting videos of 1989, for example, included such prominent theatrical hits as DIE HARD, RAIN MAN, COMING TO AMERICA, BIG, BATMAN, and GHOSTBUSTERS II.[46] The video-retailing industry offered special awards to recognize and honor the most popular rental and sales titles, and, no surprise, these were also the big theatrical hits. The American Video Association named TOP GUN video of the decade, and its choice of top videos by category for 1989 included BIG (best comedy), RAIN MAN (best drama), DIE HARD (best action-adventure) and WHO FRAMED ROGER RABBIT (best family-children's). In 1990, the Video Software Dealers Association named Arnold Schwarzenegger video star of the year and cited HONEY, I SHRUNK THE KIDS as best family film, LETHAL WEAPON II as best action-adventure, and LOOK WHO'S TALKING as best comedy. All were major box-office hits.[47]

Strong market synergies between theatrical and home video were dramatized by the success of pictures like DIE HARD, *a monster hit in both markets.*

While the thousands of titles available on video might promise to create more friends of old films among viewers, in practice this rarely occurred outside of specialty stores in major urban areas. The typical video shop emphasized new releases. The most depth of copy is found there, with a smattering of older titles elsewhere in the store. "Old", though, is a relative term. An old film on the video market might include (as I write this) the first DIE HARD film (1988), while any title twenty years or older qualifies for the "classics" section, the most moribund category in a video store. While home video, then, has kept more titles in active distribution from different periods in film history than ever before, the predominant trend has been a replication of the existing hit categories of the theatrical market and, because of this spillover, a consequent intensification of the need to be successful in that market.

STIMULUS FOR INDEPENDENT FILMMAKING   At the same time, however, home video exerted another, and somewhat countervailing, influence on production. Because of the sheer voraciousness of the public's appetite for movies, the need for product in this ancillary market helped produce a boom in the production and distribution of independent film. Downstream distribution outlets (the ancillaries) affected production and distribution upstream. The president of Fine Line Features and cofounder of Cinecom, important independents, pointed to the role of home video in creating opportunities for independent filmmakers:

> Perhaps the biggest boon that has ever occurred in the independent sector was the explosion of home video in the early eighties. It was a voracious market for anything with sprocket holes, and even the major studios couldn't provide enough product to satisfy the demand. All of a sudden there was enormous capital available to independent theatrical distributors as advances against the home video rights. Not only was all this money being used to acquire films, it also fueled the entrance of many independents into production.[48]

Releases by the majors were insufficient to meet demand, despite their willingness to pick up independent productions for distribution. From 1983 to 1987 independent productions distributed by the majors remained relatively constant, fluctuating between 49 and 64 pictures per year (see chart 3.7). By contrast, pictures distributed independently of the majors rose from 125 in 1983 to 242 in 1986 and 203 in 1987.[49] This constituted a major expansion of opportunities for independent filmmakers, and the eighties proved to be an important decade for such filmmaking. A host of independent distributors provided these filmmakers with access to markets and promoted their work. Among the most important of these distributors were Cinecom, Island, Miramax, New Line, Vestron, New World, Hemdale, and FilmDallas. Even the majors had distributor subsidiaries handling alternative films (e.g., Fox Classics, Orion Classics).

As a result of this bubble of opportunity, a wide array of significant directors and films became an enduring part of eighties film culture, offering alternative styles and visions to the more traditional product handled by the majors. Jim Jarmusch's minimalist STRANGER THAN PARADISE (1984, dist. Goldwyn) exerted tremendous influence and inspiration for aspiring independent filmmakers. The Coen brothers' BLOOD SIMPLE (1984, Circle Releasing) announced their audacious new talents and penchant for stylistic unpredictability. John Sayles's THE BROTHER FROM ANOTHER PLANET (1984,

CHART 3.7
Domestic Distribution of Independent Productions

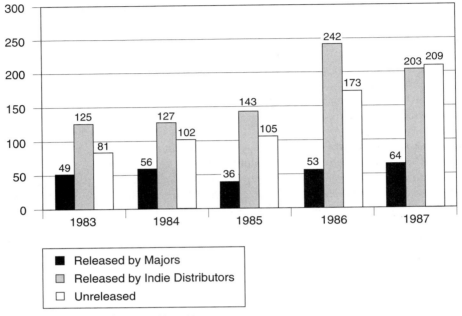

SOURCE: *Variety*, 24 February, 1988, p. 66.

Cinecom), and Alan Rudolph's CHOOSE ME (1984, Island) were among the most engaging of the decade's independent pictures. Important new talents with original pictures included Wayne Wang (DIM SUM, 1984, Orion Classics), Joyce Chopra (SMOOTH TALK, 1986, Spectrafilm), Gus Van Sant (MALA NOCHE, 1986, self/Frameline), Spike Lee (SHE'S GOTTA HAVE IT, 1986, Island), David Byrne (TRUE STORIES, 1986, Warners), Robert Townsend (HOLLYWOOD SHUFFLE, 1987, Goldwyn), Tim Hunter (RIVER'S EDGE, 1987, Island), Abel Ferrara (CHINA GIRL, 1987, Vestron), David Burton Morris (PATTI ROCKS, 1988, FilmDallas), Fran Kuzui (TOKYO POP, 1988, Spectrafilm), Kenneth Bowser (IN A SHALLOW GRAVE, 1988, Skouras), Gary Sinise (MILES FROM HOME, 1988, Cinecom), Bob Balaban (PARENTS, 1989, Vestron), Michael Lehman (HEATHERS, 1989, New World), Patrick Duncan (84 CHARLIE MOPIC, New Century Vista), Steven Soderbergh (SEX, LIES, AND VIDEOTAPE, 1989, Miramax), and Nanacy Savoca (TRUE LOVE, 1989, MGM). In addition, established directors found that the independent circuit enabled them to continue working steadily or found that independent distribution enabled them to realize a special kind of picture the majors would not touch. These filmmakers included Henry Jaglom (ALWAYS, 1986, Goldwyn; SOMEONE TO LOVE, 1988, Castle Hill), John Sayles, Alan Rudolph, Paul Newman (THE GLASS MENAGERIE, 1987, Cineplex), and John Huston (THE DEAD, 1987, Vestron).

   The ancillary markets provided a historic economic boost for this filmmaking wave. Distributors were able to acquire lines of credit against ancillary revenues, and this influx of capital helped bring a variety of new distribution firms, and new investors, into the business. Sam Grogg, a managing partner of FilmDallas, one of the most innovative

The ancillaries helped expand the aesthetic range of commercial cinema by rejuvenating independent film. Pictures like SEX, LIES, AND VIDEOTAPE, *with Andie MacDowell and James Spader, benefited from the enhanced financing and distribution opportunities of the late eighties.*

of the new distributors, stressed that the ancillaries created new investment opportunities for venture capital and thereby permitted the growth of alternate centers of production and distribution, like the one his firm serviced around Dallas, Texas:

> The newly developing production centers acted as beacons during the 1980s to draw entrepreneurs from across the country to consider involvement in the upswing of the booming film industry—cable had matured, new superchannels were leading new markets for movie sales, videocassette rentals were growing at phenomenal rates and the international market was on the rebound. This was new information to attract new investors, and soon the motion picture industry became a viable, albeit minor, facet of the standard investment portfolio.[50]

During its three and one-half years of operation, FilmDallas raised over $20 million for its film production, acquisition and distribution operations.[51] The firm innovated by offering a mutual fund–type structure for investors, who could purchase limited-partnership units ($50,000 per unit). Under this arrangement, investors did not have to make the choice to back a specific film (a dicey decision that many did not wish to make or feel qualified to make). Instead, their funds were administered by a money manager who evaluated production and distribution opportunities and allocated capital among these opportunities according to three criteria. The fund restricted its investments in any one film project to $500,000, and the projects carried a budget ceiling of $2 million.

FilmDallas thereby limited its investments to 25–50 percent of a film's budget, enough to ensure a corporate voice in shaping production while being protected by sharing the risk with other investment firms. Furthermore, FilmDallas limited half of its investments to films produced near Dallas, a policy pleasing to local investors.

Most canny of all, FilmDallas weighted revenue returns to favor investors, who received 99 percent of the returns until they had recovered their investment, with a 50-50 split thereafter. The intent here was to instill investor confidence in the decisions of the production fund managers. Following these principles, FilmDallas backed three of the decade's most prestigious and endearing independent films. Alan Rudolph's CHOOSE ME (1984) carried a $500,000 FilmDallas investment in equity and distribution. For $500,000 FilmDallas acquired North American distribution rights to Hector Babenco's KISS OF THE SPIDER WOMAN (1985), starring William Hurt and Raul Julia. FilmDallas invested a similar amount in the production and distribution of THE TRIP TO BOUNTIFUL (1985), which earned Geraldine Page a best actress Oscar for her poignant portrait of an aging woman who wants a last look at her childhood home. While FilmDallas saw only a 60 percent return on investment from CHOOSE ME, the other two productions generated a 175–200 percent return on investment.

Typical of the life span of many independent distributors, FilmDallas operated for only a few years, but its innovative strategies for creating investment opportunities point to the energies unleashed in the industry by the explosion of ancillary markets and the

The canny investment strategies of FilmDallas made possible some of the decade's most distinguished independent films, including THE TRIP TO BOUNTIFUL, *with Geraldine Page and (in a brief appearance) Rebecca De Mornay.*

demand for product that they established. By decade's end, FilmDallas was gone, and Cinecom, New World, Alive, and Vestron had folded or were in decline. The market forces that they confronted were harsh. Independent films at best were small money-makers. They lacked the production budgets and stars that were strong predictors of success in theatrical and ancillary markets, and the industry was consolidating to give the majors more control over exhibition and ancillary distribution. Furthermore, independent distribution was subject to the same vagaries that plagued the majors' product. Many pictures died in the pipeline and never received a theatrical release. In 1986 and 1987, 382 independent films failed to receive distribution. Approximately 25 percent of these unreleased titles went directly to video.[52] For such films, lacking stars and glitzy production values, video could be an instant graveyard.

Furthermore, while the home video market helped create opportunities for independent film, the independent market was just as hit-driven as the market for the majors' products. In 1987, HOLLYWOOD SHUFFLE and RIVER'S EDGE accounted for more than 40 percent of rentals among the eighty-two pictures with budgets under $2 million. HELLRAISER and WITCHBOARD generated more than 40 percent of rentals among the sixty pictures with budgets of $2–4 million. DIRTY DANCING and NIGHTMARE ON ELM STREET 3 produced 50 percent of the rentals among the forty-three pictures with budgets of $4–6 million. None of the remaining twenty titles with budgets over $6 million fared well at the box office.[53]

Independent distribution was a precarious undertaking, with no promise of big revenues, and the executives who ran these firms were often driven by their sheer love of moviemaking and the excitement they felt in helping a RETURN OF THE SECAUCUS SEVEN (1980) or a SHE'S GOTTA HAVE IT (1986) find a niche audience. Thus, while home video offered an important outlet and stimulus for independent production, the independents were constrained by the same market dynamics that had traditionally operated to marginalize their product relative to that handled by the majors. By the middle of the decade, the odds that an independent filmmaker could get funding and some distribution for a picture were much better than they had ever been, but overall market share remained extremely small, and many of these productions were forced to assume the second-string status of a direct-to-video release.

STIMULUS FOR ADULT (PORNOGRAPHIC) FILMMAKING   The home video revolution boosted film production in yet another area. The adult film industry enjoyed a decade-long, striking expansion in the production and distribution of sex films. Because of home video, porn films moved out of dingy theaters in seedy urban areas and into the living rooms and bedrooms of private homes nationwide. This shift and spread of adult filmmaking alarmed social watchdog groups and helped trigger a series of hotly contested battles between the industry and various citizen groups allied with federal and state prosecutors. I examine these battles and controversies in chapter 8. At this point, it is sufficient to note the extraordinary impact that the video revolution had on adult filmmaking and thereby on the culture at large. Home video gave adult films the cultural prominence and visibility they had never possessed in previous decades (especially prior to the 1970s, when they came aboveground on the theatrical exhibition circuit in the form of DEEP THROAT, THE DEVIL IN MISS JONES, and BEHIND THE GREEN DOOR). In the early 1980s, the production of pornographic feature films shifted from film and theatrical exhibition to videotape, with a resulting decrease in production costs.

As a result of this shift, adult video releases skyrocketed in the first half of the decade, climbing from four hundred titles in 1983 to sixteen hundred in 1985 before falling back to around thirteen hundred per year for the rest of the decade (chart 3.8). Revenues from tape sales (chart 3.9) expanded from $225 million in 1983 to $425 million in 1986.[54] Adult filmmaking had become a major economic force in the American film trade, and the adult industry modeled itself on Hollywood, promoting its films with name directors and celebrity stars and holding an annual awards ceremony, like the Oscars, to recognize the industry's best pictures and talents. Admittedly, it was a microcosmic community, but within its boundaries, like that of Hollywood, filmmaking and distribution were name-driven. Prominent directors included Henri Pachard, Paul Vatelli, Fred J. Lincoln, Chuck Vincent, and Anthony Spinelli. Male stars included Eric Edwards, John Leslie, Richard Pacheco, Tom Byron, Ron Jeremy, Paul Thomas, Jaime Gillis, and Mike Horner. Female stars included Keisha, Annette Haven, Vanessa Del Rio, Ginger Lynn, Seka, Marilyn Chambers, Barbara Dare, Lisa DeLeeuw, and Bridget Monet. (One of the biggest female stars of the eighties was Traci Lords, and her fame quickly turned to scandal when it transpired that she was under legal age when she began making porn films.) These stars attained their (often brief) fame in the video market. Packaging of videotapes called prominent attention to stars and directors, and cheapie compilation tapes were common. These were composed of sex scenes excerpted from the many films in which a popular performer such as Annette Haven, Seka, or Vanessa Del Rio had appeared.

Home video helped kill porn moviehouses throughout the nation, but it offered a much more lucrative venue for production and distribution, and in so doing, it placed porn on the cultural landscape in hitherto unprecedented ways. While some of the nation's biggest video retailers, such as Blockbuster Video, refused to stock adult films, many smaller outlets reserved a back room for the videos or placed them under the counter and made them accessible to patrons consulting a printed list of titles. In this way, adult films achieved a pervasiveness they had not previously enjoyed. Their acces-

CHART 3.8
Annual Number of Adult Video Releases

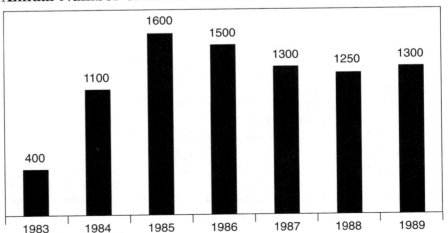

SOURCE: *Variety*, 17 January 1990, p. 36.

CHART 3.9
Adult Video Sales Revenues ($ millions)

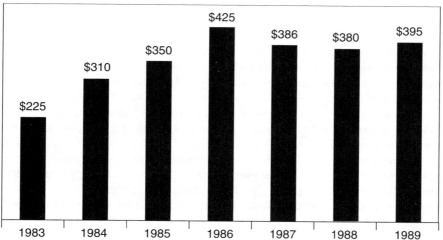

SOURCE: *Variety*, 17 January 1990, p. 36.

sibility generated staunch opposition among some citizen groups, while it reinforced the conviction of others that their First Amendment rights permitted them to read and view legal material of their own choosing in the privacy of their homes.

While this conflict of outlook was explosive and not amenable to compromise, the adult video industry prospered during the decade and exerted two kinds of major influences on filmmaking outside its purview. It stimulated mainstream filmmakers to adopt more explicit portrayals of sexuality in such pictures as 91/2 WEEKS (1986), WILD AT HEART (1990), and HENRY AND JUNE (1990), and it gave birth to a spinoff subgenre, the so-called R-rated, or unrated, softcore film that is readily available above counter in most video stores (e.g., MIRROR IMAGES [1991], ANIMAL INSTINCTS [1992], SECRET GAMES [1992]).[55]

Effects on Viewing and Film Aesthetics

As discussed thus far, the effects of home video reconfigured existing film formats and modes of production. It destroyed 8-mm and Super 8 as amateur formats when families turned to camcorders to preserve memorable moments of family history. Home movies shifted to video, and retailers helped accelerate the changeover by advertising special deals on the conversion of existing 8-mm home movies to videotape. The irony in this was that video is a much poorer archival medium than film. It wears out faster from frequent use, and it has a shorter shelf life than film. While video boosted the production of independent films and adult films, it closed moviehouses across the nation that specialized in art and repertory films. It also crippled the 16-mm nontheatrical market, which had serviced schools and universities, airlines, and television stations. In comparison to 16-mm, video copies of movies were much easier to transport and much less cumbersome to present.

Home video made movies far more accessible to viewers and has greatly affected their viewing habits. These developments may be difficult to appreciate now when so many movies are available in a host of nontheatrical formats and so much viewing occurs in these contexts. Before the advent of video, one either saw movies in current release at local theaters or on broadcast television. Neither outlet, though, offered viewers systematic access to films of different periods, styles, or countries. In the 1980s, by contrast, one needed only to walk into a reasonably well stocked video store to be confronted with a dizzying array of home viewing choices, including a wide range of genres, stars, directors, and classic and foreign films. This abundance gave viewers immediate access to film history, an unprecedented universe of films, and it gave these films greater and more sustained cultural visibility than ever before (even if, in practice, most viewers chose to rent new releases).

This phenomenon had a down side: film became devalued as a consumer item. Before video, when access to individual films was more restricted, the opportunities to see or screen them were more privileged. A chance to see CITIZEN KANE (1941) or SEVEN SAMURAI (1954) or A STAR IS BORN (1954) was special because it was rare, and value was based in scarcity. By contrast, with access to nearly any film on video, one's encounter with an individual title, no matter how fine or special that title, grew more unremarkable. The home video experience meant movies on a small television in a room undesigned for good image or sound. (In the latter 1990s "home theater" systems revolutionized home viewing. Digital video, six-channel sound, and a large, widescreen projection monitor restored "cinema" back into video by producing a high-caliber viewing environment with sound quality superior to that offered in many theaters.) Videotape was a low-grade medium designed for transient viewing. The low-priced, mass-produced videocassette tended to trivialize the medium because cassettes were so plentiful, so *small*, and so disposable, and because they were viewed on television sets. In this way, until the advent of home theater systems, video subjected film to the television experience.

Videotape and film were, and are, quite dissimilar. Tape had virtually nothing in common with celluloid, which contains on its surface the actual still images that come to life in the cinema. These images hold traces of the light that was originally in the scene before the cameras. One can hold a strip of film and see these pictures, can reactivate these traces. By contrast, the videocassette itself, as object, is uninteresting. Lightweight, encased in cheap plastic, it contains no pictures, merely a magnetic signal that requires decoding. The excitement that comes from holding the actual film image in one's hands cannot be replicated with video. Film is now more abundant on videotape, but it is not the same medium and does not have the same emotional charge. This is due to the very different aesthetic experiences induced by film and video imagery.

AESTHETIC PROBLEMS OF FILM-TO-VIDEO TRANSFERS

Because the video and cable markets proved to be so important, the majors quickly moved to upgrade the quality of their video product. Their willingness by mid-decade to permit transfers from invaluable first-generation negative or interpositive materials facilitated a quantum improvement in the sharpness, clarity, and color rendition of video versions of movies, as compared to transfers made in the initial years from release print (positive film) materials. Rank-Cintel color telecines, used to make transfers, featured a capstan drive mechanism that was much gentler on film than a sprocket system could be, and this helped persuade the majors to make first-generation material available.[56] Ironically, as a result, video taught viewers that films, irrespective of their period, should look good. Murky, scratched 16-mm prints, which used to suffice for films out of the-atrical distribution, quickly became unacceptable. This was an undeniable blessing, and it accelerated the cause of film preservation and restoration. Old films became com-mercially valuable again as programming for the home video market. On the other hand, the "videoization" of film has imposed an alternate set of conditions on the medium.

The process of converting film to video is called a transfer, and it was carried out using a flying spot scanner. Each film frame was scanned by a beam of light, moving one scan line at a time. The quality of the light was affected by the densities of the film frame through which it passed, and the scanner converted these changes into an ana-log electronic signal that was recorded on videotape. The telecine operator became, in effect, a co-director, co-cinematographer, and co-editor of the film because he or she made a variety of decisions regarding how the celluloid image was to be reformatted for video. The telecine permitted the operator to zoom or cut in to a portion of the film frame and to make adjustments for brightness, contrast, and color levels.[57] Color film, for example, could handle brightness ratios of 130:1, whereas videotape could manage a ratio of 40:1. This is a sizable disparity, and it was up to the telecine operator to nego-tiate this difference.

Because film and video handle brightness, contrast, and color so differently, it would be more accurate to call the conversion process a translation. Charles Shiro Tashiro writes, "While film and video share common technical concerns (contrast, color, density, audio frequency response, etc.), their means of addressing those concerns differ. The conscientious film-to-video transfer is designed to accentuate the similarities and mini-mize the differences, but the differences end up shaping the video text."[58] Video lacks the resolving power of film and is subject to more distortion (evident in the shimmering that densely textured patterns produce). Its abilities to handle contrast and color are also inferior. Chroma noise is common; highly saturated reds, for example, create noise or bleeding in the video signal, even in a digital video signal. The brightness range of video is also more reduced, in part because the television screen is usually viewed in an illu-minated environment, unlike the darkened movie theater. These differences mandated alterations in the film original when it was transferred, or translated, to video.

High-contrast cinematography, with a lot of shadow definition, translated poorly to video because of its reduced contrast range. The transfer engineer would have to flatten the tonal range by boosting midtones and brightening shadows and dark areas. This pro-duced a grayer image but one that looked cleaner and brighter on video. What was acceptable and judged a good look by the video engineer, according to the standards of the video signal, however, often did an injustice to the cinematographer's lighting design and compositional principles. Viewers confronted with transfers in which the dynamic contrast range of a film original was flattened for video might erroneously attribute the blandness of the imagery to the film rather than to its video surrogate.

The videotape transfer of Michael Mann's THE LAST OF THE MOHICANS (1992), for example, rendered the forest locations a murky blur. The tape could not capture the impressive contrast range or resolution of Dante Spinotti's cinematography. In effect, the film (on video) looked washed out. Writing about the issues involved in making video transfers, Dominic Case points out, "It is common, when faced with difficulties in telecine, to blame the original photography. A typical comment might be that the nega-tive is underexposed; to see into the shadows there must be more density in the negative.

But exposing for the shadows is not the answer. . . . A properly graded print will show more detail in the shadows in the cinema . . . but on telecine, the shadows become a murky black instead of a murky gray."[59] Because of video's more restricted contrast range, murky blacks will obliterate detail. They are deemed unacceptable, and the telecine operator must adjust brightness and contrast levels to eliminate them. (Digital video has a better contrast range, and the blacks really look black on high-end digital home theater systems.)

Other problems in going from film to video involve issues of aspect ratio or the different configurations of cinema screen and television screen. These are particularly problematic when some form of widescreen cinematography has been employed in the film original. The transfer engineer may pan-and-scan the film, reproducing only a portion of the original frame and introducing electronic cuts and camera movements that were never in the film. The telecine facilitates this by enabling the operator to select or enlarge portions of the film frame. Pan-and-scan fills the viewer's TV screen with a picture, but it destroys the cinematographer's compositions by reproducing only part of the widescreen frame. The unitary space of an extended framing is replaced by alternating close-ups joined by electronic edits. The movie thereby is made to serve the video medium. It is converted into television. As Tashiro points out, "It is more important to fill the TV frame than it is to maintain cinematic composition."[60]

Photos 3.12 and 3.13 illustrate the problems inherent in converting widescreen aspect ratios for television. The two images from Martin Scorsese's RAGING BULL demonstrate the differences between framing for a theatrical ratio of 1.85:1 and the 4:3 framing used for video and television. A 1.85:1 ratio is produced by masking the top and bottom portions of the image. During production, the cinematographer's viewfinder is marked so that the compositions and dramatic action can be reliably contained within the 1.85:1 area. During exhibition, the film is projected as a matted image to produce the widescreen ratio. Note how the 4:3 image of RAGING BULL includes additional information at the top and bottom of the image, information blocked by the matte in the 1.85 framing. The resulting 4:3 composition might be judged an acceptable one, and it would necessitate no panning and scanning during telecine conversion. Thus, one justification for shooting 1.85 is that it can protect a film from having to be panned and scanned when being prepped for the home video market. On the other hand, the 4:3 ratio introduces subtle differences into the composition. Note how the space between the brothers (Jake and Joey La Motta) is more pronounced in the 1.85 framing. As the theme of the film is Jake's isolation from family and friends, the 1.85 framing produces a better visual statement of this theme.

The problems of converting between different aspect ratios grow more pronounced when the theatrical ratio is a wider frame, such as 2.35:1. The photos from 10, placed in video release by Warners in 1980, demonstrate these problems. Photos 3.14 and 3.15 show how a 4:3 framing may include both characters on screen, but doing so necessitates a more severe alteration of the composition than in the case of a 1.85:1 framing. The widescreen framing of Dudley Moore and Julie Andrews is quite relaxed, with ample space on either side. The 4:3 framing produces a tight, cramped composition that looks like television. When character positioning is more dispersed across the 2.35:1 frame, as in photo 3.16, the 4:3 conversion can reproduce only a portion of the dramatic action. The two-shot of Dudley Moore and Robert Webber becomes, for video, a close-up of Moore (photo 3.17). If a filmmaker shoots 2.35:1, as the director of 10, Blake Edwards, usually did, it almost always involves a deliberate choice to work in a purely

Widescreen (1.85:1) and 4:3 framing of RAGING BULL.

theatrical aspect ratio. Put differently, it means the director is making movies for the "big screen," not the home screen. To get such a film to the home screen requires that it be mutilated by pan-and-scan or that it be letterboxed.

Letterboxing, which masks the top and bottom of the video frame to produce a widescreen ratio in the center, is the alternative to pan-and-scan. Letterboxing was a distinctly unpopular format throughout most of the 1980s, when the huge majority of videotape transfers were done as pan-and-scan. Letterboxing was more commonly used on videodiscs because manufacturers and suppliers conceived of the video market as having two tiers. Videotape appealed to casual viewers who preferred to have their TV

Widescreen (2.35:1) and 4:3 framing of 10.

screens filled with a picture and were less concerned about composition or arcana like aspect ratio. Videodisc users, supporting a higher-end format, tended to value their ability to see the original film compositions. This was probably always a false dichotomy, and toward the end of the decade letterboxing began appearing in the tape market as a viable format (though still used less widely than pan-and-scan). The advent of big-screen televisions in the 1990s facilitated more widespread use of letterboxing because the matted image did not look so shrunken on a larger screen. Widescreen, 16 x 9 (screen ratio) televisions offer the best pre-HDTV replication of the cinema image.

The trade-off with letterboxing (on normal-sized direct-view televisions, which are what most viewers in the 1980s possessed) is a shrunken picture that sits as a thin band across the center of the TV screen. Thus, this format also subjects cinema to television.

"If film is usually considered larger and grander than TV, widescreen film letterboxed in a 1.33 TV frame subjects film to television aesthetics by forcing the film image to become *smaller* than the TV image. Thus, in the act of privileging film over video, video ends up dominant."[61]

This is particularly damaging to films that have an epic scope and sweep. In 1989, the restored LAWRENCE OF ARABIA (1962) was released in 70-mm widescreen and subsequently transferred to letterbox video. The 70-mm image engaged the viewer's peripheral vision, intensifying the perception of depth and the experience of three dimensions on screen. Because of its shrunken size, the image appears much flatter on letterboxed video, and all scale is lost.[62] In the magnificent long-shots of Lawrence crossing the desert by camel, he appears on video as a black speck moving across the TV screen. But at least LAWRENCE OF ARABIA was letterboxed, a video format that, for all its flaws, remained preferable to pan-and-scan. Another prominent restoration, 1983's A STAR IS

BORN, a 1954 picture filmed in Cinemascope, featured newly struck prints with additional footage long believed lost. However, the restoration was promptly unrestored when it was transferred to video as a pan-and-scan. Major characters in Cinemascope two-shots disappeared from the video version. The George Cukor–Judy Garland musical, badly cut for studio release in 1954, had been cut yet again—this time compositionally—even though the video was advertised as the restored, uncut version.

The differences between film and video discussed thus far involve image attributes that were sufficiently subtle that many viewers in the 1980s did not perceive or care about them. One area of video alteration, by contrast, was so explicit that it aroused a ringing chorus of condemnation from members of the film community, politicians, and the public. This was the colorization of black-and-white movies. Following his 1986 purchase of the MGM library, Ted Turner arranged for one hundred of these films to be colorized by Color Systems Technology. Included in the package were such popular favorites as CASABLANCA (1942) and THE MALTESE FALCON (1941). At the same time, the Hal Roach Studios began its own program of colorization, adding hues most notoriously to the public-domain and beloved IT'S A WONDERFUL LIFE (1946). While colorized tapes of IT'S A WONDERFUL LIFE sold briskly, the Hollywood community was outraged. Prominent directors, including John Huston, Woody Allen, and Martin Scorsese, testified before Congress that colorizing desecrated the artistry of older films and violated the rights of the artists who worked on those pictures.

As a result of this outcry, in September 1988 Congress passed the National Film Preservation Act, and President Reagan signed legislation creating a National Film Preservation Board with authority to designate twenty-five films per year as national treasures. (The first batch of twenty-five films, selected in 1989, are listed in appendix 4.) Recommendations from industry groups like the Directors Guild, the American Film Institute, and the National Society of Film Critics helped determine the selections. Archival copies of these films were preserved and deposited in the Library of Congress. Colorized versions of existing films (or other alterations of the original for video release) now must carry a disclaimer informing viewers of the changes. For colorization, the proposed disclaimer read, "This is a colorized version of a film originally marketed and distributed to the public in black and white. It has been altered without the participation of the principal director, screenwriter and other creators of the original film." Films altered by editing for television or through the reformatting of their aspect ratios carry similar announcements. The board could not prohibit films from being substantially altered for distribution across the ancillary markets, but at least viewers would be informed about the changes that were made.

The issue of colorization resonated especially strongly, and with some irony, at a time when color films were losing their hues. It seemed perverse for the industry to turn black-and-white films to color while color films turned to mud. During the early and mid-1980s, a crisis of color fading beset the industry and was exacerbated by the value the ancillary markets now placed on older films. The term "fading" actually represents only a part of what happens in the process of color film decay. As dyes fade, their loss affects the apparent intensities of remaining colors, which then appear to deepen. Thus, faded prints typically take on an intensely monochromatic quality, looking very brown, pink, or red.

Galvanized by director Martin Scorsese's 1980 campaign to persuade Kodak to develop film stocks with greater dye stability, filmmakers throughout the industry voiced outrage over the muddy browns and garish pinks that had become the fate of aging color film. Cinematographer Nestor Almendros said, "In ten years, the films I've made I'm sure will have vanished." Jack Tillmany of San Francisco's Gateway Cinema remarked of the existing print of Tony Richardson's TOM JONES (1963) screened by his cinema, "The vivid greens that were so vital to the marvelous photography of the film are now just a memory. The whole damn thing has turned fire engine red. Tom Jones is now romping across a red countryside under pink skies. Thank you, Eastman Kodak." Steven Spielberg remarked, "After only five years the blue is leaving the waters of JAWS, while the blood spurting from Robert Shaw's mouth gets redder and redder."[63] In his own film-making, Scorsese took steps to insulate his work from the ravages of color loss. He made black-and-white separations from NEW YORK, NEW YORK (1977) that could be used, if necessary, to reconstitute the film's colors, and he shot RAGING BULL (1980) in black and white. (Ironically, 16-mm copies of this film were printed on color stock. These were badly timed, introducing color distortions into the film!)

The film stocks manufactured by Eastman Kodak, which began in the 1950s to supplant the Technicolor imbibition (IB) process, proved to have unreliable dyes. Under the Tech IB system, color was applied in a dye transfer process using relief matrices, whereas the Eastman stocks placed dye-forming compounds in a multilayer film stock that required only basic lab processing to achieve full color reproduction.[64] Technicolor closed its Hollywood dye transfer plant in 1974, and during the 1980s an operating dye transfer plant remained in China at the Beijing Film Lab. At the time of the Hollywood lab shutdown, Technicolor scrapped and destroyed its priceless black-and-white matrices (which could have been used to print restored Tech IB copies of old movies) and existing 16-mm answer prints.

Eastmancolor, introduced by Kodak in 1949, gained widespread industry acceptance in the early 1950s because it could be processed with greatly simplified lab work relative to Technicolor. Cost and time advantages followed from this. Color prints could be made directly from camera negative by means of contact printing (passing light through the negative onto the positive stock), whereas the imbibition process required the expensive production of the relief matrices used for dye transfer. The Eastman prints looked sharper than Tech IB prints. The Tech process required that the dyes be transferred separately from three matrices onto the release print, introducing registration problems; that is, the alignment of the matrices was not always exact. The resulting clarity and sharpness of Eastman prints, coupled with their economy of production, quickly won the industry's enthusiasm.

But there was a terrible flaw. The dyes used in Eastman's multilayer film did not last, particularly the cyan and yellow layers, which were the first to fade, depending on the particular stock. Many factors contributed to fading, including oxidation from the air, moisture contained in the gelatin in film emulsion, and reactions from the chemicals in the film. As dyes fade, contrast also diminishes because the density of the film image is changing. Thus, faded prints have a washed-out look that reflects the alterations in both color and contrast. Worse yet, in the late 1960s Eastman Kodak introduced a method of making release prints from reversal color negative (Color Reversal Internegative, or CRI) and marketed it at a lower price than the Technicolor alternative. This was a classic instance of economizing on mass production at the expense of long-term quality. CRI films had especially unstable color, worsening an already bad situation, and Kodak phased out the process by 1988.

For many years, neither Kodak nor the film studios much cared about faded color in motion pictures because little to no fading occurred during the limited life of a release print, which was generally as short as six months. The industry-wide disregard for issues of color longevity could be defended as a business policy only when the theatrical market was the primary venue for film consumption and little ancillary revenues were to be derived from other avenues of film distribution. But by the early 1980s, this was a patently outmoded policy and a very costly one. The American color film heritage of the 1950s–1970s had by then faded into monochromatic pinks, browns, and reds, making these prints and negatives unfit for exploitation in the nontheatrical markets. Under any circumstances, this was a horrifying development, but for the majors who could now reap millions from their libraries in ancillary distribution, color fading was a monumental disaster.

At the prompting of director Martin Scorsese and other industry figures, Kodak in 1982 issued new low-fade film stock (color print film 5384/7384) with much better dye stability.[65] Dyes in this film were projected to last ten times as long as Kodak's previous low-fade stocks (SP 5383/7383, LFSP 7379, and LF 7378), the worst of which experienced a 20 percent loss of color density in as short a period as ten years under storage at 75°F. Because cold storage can prolong the color life of motion picture film, the studios actively investigated controlled, long-term storage of valuable negatives, and some, like Disney, also made black-and-white separations of films deemed especially valuable.[66] But these were stopgap measures. As a photomechanical process, color film is subject to inherent decay, and it may be that the digital encoding and storage of color information will offer the best solution to the problem. (Digital methods, though, create a new set of problems, involving the retrieval and playback of information on platforms whose designs quickly become obsolete.) Thus, during the 1980s, the crisis of color fading in motion pictures stabilized with the introduction of the new Kodak stocks but not before alarms sounded throughout the industry over the essential fragility of the celluloid upon which so much revenue depended and on which so much of the industry's history was encased.

Marketing Synergies

The ancillary markets changed film production, exhibition, and aesthetics. They also had an enormous impact upon the marketing of motion pictures. Pursuing policies of synergy, the majors found ways of using theatrical exhibition and ancillary distribution to reinforce the performance of film across these areas. The revenue potential of the ancillaries was thus multiplicative rather than additive.

Two marketing practices achieving maturity in the 1980s illustrate these synergies especially well. These were (1) the cross-promotion of film in either multiple ancillaries or in exhibition coupled with ancillary on a simultaneous basis, and (2) the licensing of film-related product placement and merchandising. Just as it led the industry in pricing videos of popular films to stimulate the sell-through market, Paramount innovated cross-links between theatrical and ancillary distribution. Paramount's Flash-dance (1983) was released on video while the film was still in theatrical release, albeit near the end of that release. The film's box office, which had begun to dip after the film had been in release for several months, climbed 14 percent following the announcement of its videocassette debut.[67] This uptick was apparently due to a decision by consumers who were contemplating a video purchase to watch the film on the big screen before buying.

Struck by the phenomenon, Paramount scheduled a theatrical re-release of FOOTLOOSE (1984) to coincide with the film's debut on home video. For its release of INDIANA JONES AND THE TEMPLE OF DOOM (1984), Paramount again looked to home video to boost theatrical receipts, though this time across two different Indiana Jones films. Every videocassette of RAIDERS OF THE LOST ARK (1981), released for sell-through at $39.95, carried a trailer for TEMPLE OF DOOM, and all promotional material for RAIDERS carried ads for TEMPLE OF DOOM. Anticipating huge sales for the RAIDERS videocassettes, Paramount used the video release to give its sequel a major push.

In addition to this upstream influence on theatrical, the ancillaries offered tremendous potential for downstream cross-promotions. As we saw in previous chapters, the majors and their parent corporations had recorded-music operations in addition to their film activities, and they built enormously lucrative linkages between these areas. During the eighties, the majors targeted a core audience that could be reached simultaneously through film and pop music. This was an audience that could be counted on to see pictures like FLASHDANCE, RISKY BUSINESS (1983), TOP GUN (1986), and BATMAN (1989), an audience that purchased huge amounts of recorded music and regularly watched MTV. It didn't take a fortuneteller to see the obvious connections, considering that the youth audience had been a vital demographic for Hollywood film for decades. The music director for Columbia Pictures noted, "The target audience for MTV is the same target for pictures. You need the 12 to 25 demographic."[68]

In 1983, FLASHDANCE, a glib but stylish movie about a woman who welds steel by day and disco dances by night, demonstrated the wad of cash that such cross-promotion could generate, and it established the trend of using music and music videos to promote movies, and vice versa. FLASHDANCE featured several aggressively staged and edited musical numbers. These were issued on a highly popular sound-track album, which was also marketed as a disco/pop album. In its first twenty-four days of national release, FLASHDANCE (the film) grossed over $20 million, and the album attained platinum status with sales of 1 million copies. Singer Irene Cara performed the film's title track. Released early, it was already a hit single when the film opened, and Cara's song was featured on all the radio and television advertising for the picture. Paramount's senior vice president of worldwide marketing noted, "If you have a single playing on the radio, the spots are like cross-pollination."[69]

To extend the promotional cross-marketing, FLASHDANCE director Adrian Lyne edited four music videos ("What a Feeling," Imagination," "Maniac," and "Romeo") using footage from the film, and these ran extensively on MTV before and during the film's release. "Maniac," for example, featuring Michael Sembello's music, was released to MTV four weeks before the film's opening. The tune was also issued as a single. The FLASHDANCE singles, music videos, sound-track album, and movie all functioned as commercials for one another, reinforcing a consumer's perceived need to have or to see them all.

Following the success of FLASHDANCE (the sixth-biggest film of its year), the majors rushed into the production of music videos for MTV because this was such an effective way of enhancing film and recorded-music revenues. For production of the Phil Collins music video of "Against All Odds," from the 1984 film of the same title, Columbia Pictures built a completely new set to match the film's imagery. Production cost for the video was forty-five thousand dollars, and MTV was comfortable running the video because it did not look overtly like a film trailer. MTV was reluctant to carry videos that were clear film promos, even though all film-culled music videos were obviously publicity material. The studios could produce inexpensive music videos by simply re-editing

Its aggressive editing and music score gave FLASHDANCE the attributes of a rock music video, and Paramount shrewdly cross-promoted it in theatrical, home video, and music video markets.

scenes from a film and laying a pop singer's music over the footage, but MTV balked at carrying such blatantly promotional pieces. The tie-ins needed to be more subtle to satisfy the giant cable programmer. Warners produced a Bob Seger video, "Old Time Rock and Roll" (from RISKY BUSINESS), which MTV rejected because the film footage was too prominent. The video was dismissed by an MTV executive as "a trailer set to a Bob Seger song."[70] Warners recut the video to include and emphasize Seger concert footage (obtained from Capital Records, Seger's label), at which point MTV accepted the video.

In 1984, Paramount scored another big success with its sound track for FOOTLOOSE, a quasi-musical starring Kevin Bacon as a dancer in a repressive, small Midwest town. Production of the sound track illustrated the close corporate partnerships that successful ancillary promotion entailed.[71] FOOTLOOSE started as a Fox production directed by Michael Cimino (who was still finding employment post–HEAVEN'S GATE), but Cimino was fired from the production, which then passed to Paramount and director Herbert Ross. To ease its production costs, Paramount wished to cofinance the sound track (scores featuring performances by popular musicians could be very expensive because their fees were on top of those paid to a composer to produce an original score for the picture). CBS Records (a subsidiary of Columbia Pictures) offered a $250,000 advance and agreed to permit singer Kenny Loggins, whom it had under contract, to record one song for the picture. Paramount felt Loggins's participation was essential to establish the film's tone of Americana. CBS, however, required that Paramount also sign two non-CBS artists whose albums had gone gold (sales of 500,000 copies). From Geffen Records (financed by Warner Bros.), Paramount signed rock singer Sammy Hagar and

FOOTLOOSE capitalized on the lucrative tie-ins between movies, music, and video that cross-market synergies made possible.

got the rhythm-and-blues group Shalamar from Solar/Elektra (also a Warner label). Thus, several majors effectively split the revenues from this ancillary promotion. Warner's artists received royalties for their participation. Paramount retained financial control of the Loggins video, and Columbia-CBS got the sound track and planned to make its own video from another track on the album.[72]

These somewhat byzantine relations proved to be very profitable as FOOTLOOSE earned $34 million in rentals (putting the film in eleventh place on the 1984 box office), and the sound track sold very well. Like Paramount, Warner Bros. scored a major cross-promotional hit that year with PURPLE RAIN. The film, starring rock musician Prince, had an opening three-day, $7 million box office. Warner's strategic prerelease of music from the picture in advance of the film's opening helped drive the picture's box-office performance. The film opened 27 June 1984, but Warner released the Prince single "When Doves Cry" on 16 May. This was also far in advance of the sound-track recording's release, which occurred 25 June, just before the film's national break. The PURPLE RAIN sound track sold over 2 million copies by the end of July; 205,000 of them were sold on the film's opening day.[73]

The tie-ins between films and music videos often aimed to fuse production design, theme and characters in the two media. This fusion would operate like a brand label, unifying as products with a common corporate identity the film and its music and music video spin-offs. Each product would thereby reinforce in the consumer's mind the arch-image and identity of the franchise. FOOTLOOSE, PURPLE RAIN, and other cross-promoted entities were therefore greater than their incarnation in any single product, whether it was film, video, or recorded music. If the synergies worked, consumers would be stimulated to desire all incarnations of the multiplicative product. The lighting and color design of Kenny Loggins "Danger Zone" videos, from TOP GUN, resembled those used in the film. The main characters from THE JEWEL OF THE NILE (1985) and JUMPIN' JACK FLASH (1986), and the stars who play them, appear inside (i.e., not as clips) the music videos from those films.

On occasion, a major studio might issue an alternate sound-track album for a film to showcase a popular performer whose music was used in the picture. Warners issued an instrumental sound track for BATMAN, featuring the Danny Elfman score, as well as an album of songs by Prince, who had two songs in the picture, with liner notes tying the vocals to scenes in the film and to particular characters. This, in effect, was a musical reorganization of the picture, a vocal reinterpretation of the film by Prince. As Justin Wyatt has written, "The effect of these songs is to resituate the original narrative of the film from the perspective of Prince's pop persona, emphasizing the style and sexuality of the characters, rather than focusing on the adventure and action in the filmic narrative. Similar to the promotional music video, this restitution possesses a strong economic motive based on multiplying possible points of connection with the film."[74] Because of the way Prince reworked and reinterpreted the movie, BATMAN director Tim Burton was unhappy with Warner's decision to release the album, but he felt helpless in the stratosphere of blockbuster economics to influence the studio's marketing decisions. Describing his unhappiness, Burton said, "They're saying to me, these record guys, it [the film] needs this and that, and they give you this whole thing about it's an expensive movie so you need it [an album by a superstar]. And what happens is, you get engaged in this world, and then there's no way out. There's too much money."[75]

The effect of these ancillary promotions is to multiply different versions of a given film such that one can no longer reliably identify its singular or truest incarnation. TOP GUN exists simultaneously as a hit feature film, a stylish Pepsi commercial, a group of popular songs, and a Kenny Loggins video, with common thematics and stylistics dispersed across these media. BATMAN exists as two very different record albums, a movie, and several varieties of comic strip. As software, these can be marketed to a variety of "platforms": movies, television, recorded music, and publishing. In such a situation, notions about an original text or format become problematic. BATMAN (or PURPLE RAIN or FOOTLOOSE) is more than a film. It is a huge interconnected series of media formats, marketing strategies, and ancillary outlets designed to return revenue to multiple Warner operating divisions.

The ancillary markets have made more relevant than ever Walter Benjamin's old remarks about how works of art in an era of mechanical reproduction lose the aura associated with an original version. "To an ever greater degree the work of art reproduced becomes the work of art designed for reproducibility," Benjamin noted.[76] This is an exact description of the conditions underlying blockbuster production and its promotion in the ancillary markets, where the replication of product identity provides the means of revenue return. Thus, the majors were most enthusiastic about backing those pictures projected to perform well across theatrical and ancillary markets and from which they could reap the revenues accruing from cross-promotional and spin-off activities. To accomplish this, the product had to be capable of mass production in a variety of formats unified by a common label, style, and corporate identity. As Paramount head Michael Eisner stressed in 1981, a film might give rise to many different marketing and licensing activities, but the revenues needed to be huge and all revenue streams had to stay in-house. An entertainment industry executive at Wells Fargo Bank pointed out that the reproducibility of a film was the key to obtaining bank financing: "Whenever a producer can show his financial backers that he has spin-off products to promote—such as a record album or a television series, or an eye-catching product—he is apt to get a more interested hearing. In fact, motion picture projects have been financed largely on the basis of their downstream sales potential."[77]

Helping to disperse and disintegrate a unitary identity for a given film, adding to its replicative value, and functioning as a vital source of ancillary income are the product tie-ins. These are streams of merchandise featuring characters or logos from popular films, which the studios control through their licensing divisions. BATMAN or GREMLINS (1984), big merchandising bonanzas, assumed a myriad of forms as their imagery and characters showed up in the wares of national retailers. Product tie-ins are not a phenomenon of the 1980s. In the mid-1970s, JAWS (1975) and STAR WARS (1977) showed how lucrative spun-off merchandise could be. In the eighties, product tie-in revenue became part of the booming ancillary mix and helped supplement the general nontheatrical gold mine. Warner's Licensing Corp. of America made deals with fifty manufacturers to put the likenesses of Gizmo and other gremlins on their merchandise.[78] These included Hallmark Cards, Hasbro Toys, Avon Books, Disney's Buena Vista Records (for children's recordings), as well as makers of clothing, watches, beach towels, and video games. Warner couldn't lose money from sluggish retail sales because the Licensing Corp. took cash in advance from suppliers plus a portion of their revenue from wholesale.

Other prominent product tie-ins of the period included the campaigns to cross-promote Paramount's DAYS OF THUNDER (1990), a Tom Cruise vehicle about a race car driver, and Chevrolet (the tie-in being the Chevy Lumina that Cruise drives in the movie), Exxon Corp. (Superflo motor oil), Coca-Cola (Mello-Yello soft drink), and

Nonhuman characters facilitated product licensing, and they proliferated in eighties films as this revenue stream grew in importance. GREMLINS.

Hardee's (hamburger purchases in exchange for the toy race cars). Because advertising and print costs could consume as much as an additional 40 percent of a picture's budget, studios found product tie-ins to be a sigificant means of defraying marketing costs. Disney's promotional campaign for WHO FRAMED ROGER RABBIT (1988) got a big boost from an additional $12 million in advertising by McDonald's and $10 million in ads placed by Coca-Cola. These ads featured the animated characters from the movie, thereby serving as promos for the film as well as for fast food and soft drinks.

If the product tie-in was not a unique eighties phenomenon, despite its vital economic importance for the industry during the decade, the placement of product advertising inside films was a singular and remarkable development during the period. In the old days, Hollywood's Production Code and Advertising Code forbid on-screen advertising, enjoining filmmakers to avoid shots of brand name labels or logos on products. Writing in 1947, Ruth Inglis observed, "Although occasionally high-pressure publicists for national products try to inject their sponsors' wares into films and at times bribe studio employees to achieve their ends, every effort is made to avoid unnecessary close-ups of radios and other items showing the name of the product, outdoor scenes showing advertising signs or billboards, and dialogue mentioning trade names."[79]

In the 1980s, by contrast, films explicitly showcased the wares of advertisers. If a character drank a beer or ate a bowl of cereal on screen, the item would carry a recognizable brand name. This practice became known as product placement. Prior to production, the studio would make a deal with a product placement agency (e.g., Associated Film Promotions) to present a clients' goods on screen in exchange for a fee or, in some cases, hard-to-find props required by the story. Pepsi, for example, supplied rare items needed for a 1950s soda fountain in BACK TO THE FUTURE (1985) and received prominent on-screen visibility in return. A senior vice president of publicity for Columbia Pictures noted that "product placement can help cut a budget— maybe not in terms of using a tube of toothpaste, but if you have an action picture that needs cars or a sports film that requires sporting goods, it can certainly help."[80] Most commonly, studios charged fees for placements. The California Raisin Board paid twenty-five thousand dollars for a billboard in BACK TO THE FUTURE advertising its product. Associated Film Promotions, the largest placement agency in the industry, had over one hundred major corporate clients seeking screen time for their products. These firms included General Motors, Cadillac, Proctor and Gamble, Anheuser-Busch, Burger King, and Kodak.

Executives with the studios and product placement agencies extolled the practice for two reasons. First, it netted the studios funds needed for production, and for merchants it was a cost-efficient form of advertising. One product placement executive noted, "The average film can realize $200,000 in product placements. . . . If [the film earns] $20 million, which is average, you've reached 5.5 million people, and more importantly, when it is seen around the world—on video, HBO, maybe primetime TV—it's incredibly cost efficient. When you're talking $10,000 to $50,000 [for a product placement], the cpms are pennies. . . . People feel good when they see impressions in movies. It pays to have Tom Hanks driving a Subaru."[81]

Proponents also claim that product placement helps create a greater sense of realism in a film. Al Ruddy, who produced THE GODFATHER (1974), explained why it was so important for the Teenage Mutant Ninja Turtles to eat Domino's Pizza on screen: "That scene is funny because kids know Domino's Pizza, and they know you get money off when it's late. Also, when you have fantasy characters and can ground them in reality like that, it's great for the movie. . . . You can't have Mel Gibson picking up a pack of Ajax cigarettes and drinking Aqua beer, because people won't believe it."[82]

In the 1980s, the boundaries between film and advertising were blurring. This was an inevitable result of the growth of interlocking media markets and the corporate super-powers who owned them. The CEO of Associated Film Promotions remarked, "Life in the 20th century is a life of commercialism. Films are becoming more real. Face it, doesn't life look like a commercial?"[83] In some cases, product merchandising might drastically influence the box-office success of a film. Hugely popular in the United States, TEENAGE MUTANT NINJA TURTLES (1990) bombed on its release in Japan, apparently because there were no product tie-ins on toy store shelves to support the film. Despite lots of publicity, theater attendance was sparse. The Japanese distributor claimed that American copyright holders would not sell the Japanese rights to merchandise based on the film's characters at a reasonable sum, attributing the movie's failure to a lack of merchandise support.[84]

Because film-related merchandising furnished a vital source of ancillary revenue for Hollywood, the biggest films were increasingly shaped by the imperatives of this marketing venue. Again, as Walter Benjamin noted, those works reproduced are those designed for replication. Thus, major films of the era featured cartoon or mechanical characters: Dick Tracy, Batman, Superman, E.T., the STAR WARS heroes, the Ninja Turtles. With their stylized appearances, these characters lent themselves easily to reproduction as a myriad of product lines, more easily than do ordinary human beings. The economic imperative behind the proliferation of eighties film fantasies about non-human characters is the need to feed ancillary merchandising. The ancillaries drove blockbuster production, which in turn, seeded the ancillaries. Anticipating a huge merchandising boom in GREMLINS-related products, the licensing director for Amblin Entertainment noted, "Whenever you have a non-human type of character, it lends itself to merchandising."[85] The extraordinary success of BATMAN, ROGER RABBIT, and the Ninja Turtles stimulated a rush of development deals to bring to the screen such eminently merchandisable characters as Barbie, the Flintstones, Captain America, Dr. Strange, Iron Man, the Fantastic Four, and others.[86]

The use of popular film characters as advertisements for product lines functioned globally as a vital part of multinational economics. The majors derived significant film rentals from overseas markets. In 1984, for example, overseas rentals totaled $935 million as compared with $1.2 billion domestic. Table 3.5 shows earnings derived from the top ten overseas markets. Film-related product merchandising stimulated overseas markets because of the international popularity of Hollywood movies. In 1993, MCA/Universal anticipated greater revenues from international sales of JURASSIC PARK–licensed products than from domestic sales. Describing how its film, video, and recorded-music products were used in countries ranging from England and Germany to Taiwan, Kenya, New Guinea, and Thailand, Warner Communications, Inc., proudly announced its role in helping to create a global web of interlinked cultural and commodity consumption: "There is a natural demand for entertainment the world over, and WCI's products have become an integral part of many different cultures in a variety of ways. . . . One reason for the success of Warner Communications internationally is the fact that its product knows no geographical boundaries."[87]

Herein lay the connection between film production by the majors, the ancillary markets, and the consolidation of multinational corporate influence. Despite a film's initial theatrical release, production occurred to service the ancillaries, and blockbuster films

TABLE 3.5
Top Ten Export Markets for U.S. Majors, 1987

	1987 RENTALS ($MILLIONS)
Japan	$138
France	101
West Germany	98
Canada	97
UK/Ireland	73
Italy	70
Spain	49
Australia	32
Brazil	24
Sweden	24
Total	$706

SOURCE: *Variety*, 19 May 1988, p. 30.

stimulated a huge array of marketing and merchandising throughout the world's restaurants, toy stores, and other retail outlets. Since the appeal of film characters (especially cartoon or mechanical characters) crossed media classes and product lines, it was essential for the majors and their parent corporations to maintain control over these markets and distribution channels. Lauding the advantages of its vertically integrated, multinational structure, Time Warner asserted, "No competitor can match our lineup of quality products. But just as impressive is how we distribute them. We are the only company of its kind that owns and controls 100 percent of its worldwide distribution networks. We can control the flow of our products to market and aren't required to share our distribution profits in the process."[88] Understood in strict economic terms, production by the majors was about the manufacture and distribution of commodities (not films) on a national and global scale. The rise of new distribution technologies in the 1980s reestablished the primacy of the American industry as the global leader in filmed entertainment and enabled the majors to solidify their hold on domestic and overseas entertainment markets.

Without the ancillary markets and the new distribution technologies, film production could not have attained the economic centrality it now possesses. But did the ancillaries enhance the *profits* to be derived from film production? Did they give the industry greater security by enhancing its rate of return from production? They augmented theatrical exhibition with a host of additional revenue sources, and the amount of revenue derived from these sources shifted during the eighties to the detriment of theatrical. But a compelling case can be made that these sources operated in a substitutional manner; that is, home video revenues replaced those lost to theatrical as the preferred venue of film viewing shifted from theaters to the home, as pay-cable revenues replaced those lost from broadcast. In the meantime, the costs of film production escalated, and only a handful of films released in a given year generated sufficient distributor rentals to break even on print and publicity costs.

Furthermore, major film flops could not be saved in the ancillaries. The belief that home video or cable could rescue a production from landing in the red, if its theatrical release failed to close in on the negative cost break-even point, remained a myth. Most films failed to recoup enough from theatrical, and home video, like theatrical, was hit-driven. Only a few films generated the big revenues. Big-budget films that failed theatrically could, at best and in a few cases (e.g., DUNE [1984], THE COTTON CLUB [1984], RHINESTONE [1984]), generate enough revenues from home video to cover some of the theatrical marketing costs.[89] Unless a film was very low budget, though, home video could not recoup a big theatrical loss. As *Variety* pointed out,

> There is little homevideo revenue left over to pay back the substantial negative cost still on the books from a theatrical flop. Homevideo success in such a case is significant for the company's cash flow and especially for its homevideo profit center, but profit participants due a percentage on the theatrical flop are unlikely to be close to paydirt.[90]

Harold L. Vogel, vice president of Merrill Lynch Capital Markets, has pointed out that aggregate industry profits from 1984 to 1988 increased by only 14 percent, and operating margins remained well below those prevailing in 1974–79. Vogel suggests, "What is gained in one market may be at least partially lost in another; that is, in the aggregate, ancillary-market cash flow is often largely substitutional and thus does not necessarily lead to net increments in total revenues."[91] Film production has always been a difficult enterprise from which to secure net profits, and this axiom retained its relevance in the age of the ancillaries. By extending the release cycle of a film and increasing the number of gross and net profit participants in revenues deriving from the multitude of distribution venues in which a film is marketed during its life cycle, the ancillaries have greatly complicated assessments of profitability. The target is always in motion, break-even points are floating, and net profits remain as elusive as ever.

Aside from this paradox, perhaps the most striking fact about the ancillaries is that film vanished from them. Film as film, that is, on celluloid, no longer existed beyond its theatrical venue. After that point, the electronic formats took over. Film became video for its distribution in pay-per-view, pay-cable, tape, disc, and broadcast television markets. Hollywood film in the 1980s became the engine driving the interlinked global entertainment markets. The majors needed films, but they needed celluloid only to supply theaters with product as the launching pad for the new array of electronic formats. As soon as high-resolution digital video delivery systems became viable for large auditoriums, film would vanish from those, too. Though it still held a place at the table, film now was history. The ancillaries had seen to that.

4

Independents, Packaging, and Inflationary Pressure in 1980s Hollywood

Justin Wyatt

The seventy-fifth anniversary edition of *Variety*, dated 14 January 1981, split its financial page between two different stories: "For Screen or Tube Financing, the Buzz-Word Is Package" set beside "Loss of Control over Film Costs Stressed by Heaven's Gate Fiasco." This match proved to be most prophetic: packaging and spiraling costs were indeed two of the most durable issues in the industry of the decade. While the Heaven's Gate story placed the Michael Cimino film against other high-budget films from the majors (Universal's Flash Gordon and Paramount's Popeye), the statistical summary noted the much more obscure Raise the Titanic, also released in 1980 and budgeted at an identical level to Heaven's Gate ($36 million). Produced by Lord Lew Grade's British company, ITC, Raise the Titanic lacked media hooks such as an Oscar-winning auteur, year-long production schedule, and a beleaguered studio under siege. The film was significant nonetheless as an early example of the ballooning budgets and expectations that were attached to certain high-level independent productions in the 1980s (and that continued to play a significant role in the following decade as well). In this chapter, I consider the influence of independent companies (i.e., those unaffiliated with the major studios) as a force within the industry of the decade and as a factor in shifting mainstream Hollywood filmmaking toward even more fiscally conservative, pre-sold forms of production. The most significant of these companies was Carolco Pictures, although several other independents—including the Cannon Group, De Laurentiis Entertainment Group, and Vestron Pictures—also made valiant attempts to achieve "instant major" status during the brief period of expansion for the independents in the 1980s.

Unraveling Independents in the 1980s: The Case of Carolco: Action Stars and Spiraling Salaries

To describe a company such as Carolco as an "independent" illustrates the complexity of the term within the filmmaking world of the 1980s. In another context, an independent of the period might be constituted by a studio classics division (Columbia, 20th Century–Fox, Universal, United Artists) operating in relative autonomy from the commercial dictates of the larger studio, by a production company attached to a major (Imagine Entertainment and Universal), or by an individual production, without distribution, financed independently of the majors altogether. Admittedly, Carolco Pictures is a separate entity from the major studios and therefore qualifies as an independent— Carolco is independent in operation from the majors. Simultaneously, though, Carolco, as with many other independents, is dependent on the majors, for domestic distribution and occasionally for financing. This relationship, pitched between independence and dependence, characterizes several of the most prominent independent companies of the era. Nevertheless, despite the dependence on the studios, the power and potential freedom of the independents increased markedly for a brief period in the mid-1980s, fueled by the increased opportunities offered by video, cable, and other new markets.

In terms of business formation, these independent companies were distinguished not only by an initial desire to remain limited in scope compared to the major studios but also by an equal need to compete with the majors on their own terms, that is, by producing costly, star-driven vehicles. Carolco Pictures, run by Mario Kassar and Andrew Vajna, might be the paradigm for these ventures. Referred to by *Newsweek* as "the most successful independent filmmakers," Carolco was formed in 1976 by the two entrepreneurs. Despite a slow start at the beginning of the 1980s, the pair gained momentum with the 1982 release of FIRST BLOOD and enormous commercial success with the sequel, RAMBO: FIRST BLOOD PART II in 1985. After that time, Carolco focused on large-scale, star-driven action spectaculars (RED HEAT [1988], RAMBO III [1988], AIR AMERICA [1990], TOTAL RECALL [1990], TERMINATOR 2: JUDGMENT DAY [1991]) and an eclectic mix of more modestly budgeted action dramas (EXTREME PREJUDICE [1987], NARROW MARGIN [1990]), historical dramas (MOUNTAINS OF THE MOON [1990]), and thrillers (ANGEL HEART [1987], JOHNNY HANDSOME [1989], DEEP STAR SIX [1989], JACOB'S LADDER [1990], BASIC INSTINCT [1992]). Commercially, Carolco achieved blockbuster grosses only with the action spectacles, including worldwide grosses of $490 million for TERMINATOR 2, $300 million for RAMBO II, $262 million for TOTAL RECALL, $189 million for RAMBO III, and $120 million for FIRST BLOOD. While Carolco remained in existence until filing for bankruptcy protection in 1994, the company deteriorated considerably with each passing year of the 1990s.[1] As one industry veteran commented in 1991, the extravagance and daring of the independent Carolco was "the style of the Eighties," dependent on complex financing and the elaborate exploitation of different interlocking domestic and foreign release markets.[2]

Before Carolco's inception, both partners had some experience with international film distribution. Vajna segued at age twenty-five from owning the largest wig-making factory in the world to purchasing two Hong Kong movie theaters and making initial plans to enter the world of film production and distribution. In 1973, he produced an uninspired kung fu thriller, THE DEADLY CHINA DOLL, for a bargain basement budget of $100,000. Nevertheless, the film garnered $1.2 million domestically and $2.5 million internationally.[3] With a slightly more linear job history, Kassar became a film sales agent for the Middle Eastern market at age eighteen. Realizing that better deals could be negotiated by including both the Far East and the Middle East, Vajna and Kassar joined forces at the Cannes Film Festival in 1975 to form Carolco, a film distribution company. The goal for the company was relatively simple: to buy and resell foreign rights to domestic films and eventually to form partnerships for financing low-budget films.[4] Vajna and Kassar served as executive producers for two films that received good reviews but poor commercial reception: the George C. Scott ghost thriller THE CHANGELING (1979) and the CIA espionage drama THE AMATEUR (1982). Working as associate producers on VICTORY (1981), a John Huston film about a soccer rivalry between World War II POWs and their German captors, Vajna and Kassar encountered VICTORY's star, Sylvester Stallone, destined to be the star of their first breakthrough film, FIRST BLOOD.[5] The partners risked much of their capital, $385,000, by acquiring the rights to the novel *First Blood*, about an unhinged Vietnam War veteran named John Rambo. The marketing assets for the film were bolstered significantly by hiring Stallone to play Rambo, a deal that could be achieved only through Carolco's securing European bank loans for the star's salary. With a worldwide gross of $120 million, the financial success of FIRST BLOOD established Carolco as a true player in the Hollywood community.

Timing the sequel for FIRST BLOOD to coincide with the tenth anniversary of the United States' withdrawal from Vietnam, Kassar and Vajna maximized publicity opportunities for the film (including sponsoring a thirty-minute documentary about American soldiers missing in action). By centering the plot on a Green Beret veteran's return to Vietnam to rescue soldiers missing in action, the filmmakers were able to offer a counternarrative on the Vietnam War that erased the largely negative images present in such films as APOCALYPSE NOW, COMING HOME, and THE DEERHUNTER. As Vajna commented about the marketing approach behind the film, "We were hoping the press would pick up on it as a Vietnam controversy, and I think that we were able to accomplish that."[6]

Further enhancing the film's marketing abilities, President Ronald Reagan remarked, on the eve of the release of American hostages hijacked to Lebanon, "I saw RAMBO last night, and next time I'll know what to do."[7] David Rosenfelt, senior vice president of marketing for RAMBO's distributor, Tri-Star Pictures, assessed the effect of this coverage by noting that the film "became a kind of rallying point for a new American self-assertiveness invoked by none other than the President of the United States."[8] Stallone bolstered this interpretation: "People have been waiting for a chance to express their patriotism. RAMBO triggered long-suppressed emotions that had been out of vogue. Suddenly, apple pie is an important thing on the menu."[9] RAMBO: FIRST BLOOD PART II substantially benefited from this media barrage and relatively weak competition in the summer 1985 release schedule.[10] Suddenly, Vajna and Kassar were being lauded in the industry trades, with *Variety* even referring to the pair as "the Cinderella twins of the motion picture industry."[11]

With $300 million in worldwide gross for this film, Carolco's strategy became set: rights in some foreign and ancillary markets were pre-sold to offset the initial budget; overhead was limited because the company did not require physical studio space or a distribution outlet for a steady stream of product (Carolco became increasingly focused on a small number of features); and production centered on action, "event" movies driven by star power. Action stars such as Stallone and Arnold Schwarzenegger were attracted to work for Carolco primarily because of the unprecedented salaries offered by the company. As producer David Puttnam describes the phenomenon, "Carolco in particular became an instant 'major' by offering the stars more money than the established studios offered."[12] Losses on other Carolco product, such as ANGEL HEART, JOHNNY HANDSOME, and EXTREME PREJUDICE, were easily offset through the decade by a single breakthrough hit. Crucially, Carolco distributed all their films domestically through agreements with major distributors, such as Tri-Star Pictures.

The big-budget, minimum overhead strategy was engineered partly by the third member of the Carolco management team, tax attorney Peter Hoffman, who was named president of the company in 1986. To secure the lavish budgets, Hoffman ingeniously developed an intricate plan to limit Carolco's tax liability in the United States. Despite the Carolco headquarters in Los Angeles, Carolco retained all its income from foreign sales, at least half of the company's revenue, by funneling it into a subsidiary in the Netherland Antilles. Such funds, valued at $90 million in 1987, were untaxed domestically so long as Carolco did not bring the money back for distribution as dividends.[13] Of course, the company chose not to pursue such action, leaving the money offshore to fund further movies.

As Carolco narrowed its focus to action epics, the costs began to climb: the third RAMBO cost $60 million, far more than the budgets of the first two combined, with Stallone claiming $16 million of that amount for his services. To defray some of these costs, Carolco offered 2.8 million shares of stock, timed to coincide with the opening of RAMBO III in May 1988. The third film fell markedly from the box-office measures set by its predecessor, plunging 44 percent to gross $39 million in the first nineteen days, in comparison with RAMBO II's $70 million gross. Citing strong returns from foreign territories such as Puerto Rico, the Virgin Islands, Japan, Thailand, and the Philippines, Peter Hoffman claimed that the disappointing domestic returns would be more than compensated through foreign income. "The U.S. is only half the market for *Rambo*," Hoffman insisted after RAMBO III's domestic release.[14] As an indication of the limited potential for North America, Carolco chose to sell distribution rights domestically to Tri-Star Pictures in return for 35 percent of net revenues from release. To a certain extent, the financial investment in the film was offset by almost $80 million in guarantees from theatrical, foreign, and video rights that had been sold before the film's release.[15]

Much of the film's press coverage concerned the extravagant budget for the film, including the $16 million salary for Stallone.[16] The film could indeed serve as a model for future Carolco productions: pre-sold, action-oriented, star-driven, and dependent on a worldwide audience base. Apart from the RAMBO series, Carolco also garnered strong returns from the Arnold Schwarzenegger vehicles RED HEAT (1988), TOTAL RECALL (worldwide gross of $262 million in 1990), and most impressively, TERMINATOR 2 (worldwide gross of $490 million in 1991).

The financial success was accompanied by an inevitable expansion. Hoffman was determined to develop a more stable flow of income for the company, and to this end, Carolco diversified into allied entertainment fields. In 1986, Carolco purchased a 25 percent stake in IVE, a small home video company, which was merged in 1988 with a much larger distributor, Lieberman, in which Carolco had purchased a 52 percent interest a year earlier. Under the direction of Jose Menendez, the new company, dubbed Live Entertainment, also added a 144-store retail music division, including the music chains Strawberries and Waxie Maxie. Live's video division relied on the Carolco releases, and in turn, Live supplied guarantees that helped to fund their future film productions, such

as a $10 million investment in TERMINATOR 2. By 1991, Carolco had increased its stake
in Live to 6.5 million shares, approximately a 54 percent stake. With strong promotion
and marketing, the association proved beneficial for both parties—particularly because
Live was able to achieve strong home video shipments for such Carolco commercial disappointments as NARROW MARGIN, JACOB'S LADDER, and AIR AMERICA.[17] With less
auspicious results, Carolco also diversified by purchasing a television syndication company and the film library of the Hemdale Film Corporation.[18]

Critically, Hoffman attempted to shift the production focus to some A-pictures
(action blockbusters) and "a nice flow of under-$15 million movies." With this produc-
tion strategy in place, by the late 1980s, Carolco balanced large-scale action movies with
eclectic, largely commercially unsuccessful fare such as the courtroom drama MUSIC
BOX (1989), the period exploration drama MOUNTAINS OF THE MOON (1990), Steve
Martin's comedy L.A. STORY (1991), and the narratively complex thriller JACOB'S
LADDER (1990). While Carolco could benefit from the big-selling star-centered action
spectacles and sequels, the marketing challenges represented by the mid-tier productions were considerable. JACOB'S LADDER, for instance, spins a difficult-to-condense
story about a Vietnam veteran, not John Rambo this time, experiencing disturbing nightmares and daytime hallucinations. Falling between the psychological thriller and horror
genres in terms of audience appeal, the film also lacks an exploitable premise, stars, and
linear storyline. In defense of the mixed schedule of films, Hoffman described the ambitious production plan in terms of vertical integration: "With a balanced program of pictures augmented by our foreign distribution business and our worldwide video arm,
Carolco will have the nucleus of a strong, diversified growth company for the '90s."[19]

*Carolco's JACOB'S LADDER performed well on video in comparison to its lackluster
theatrical run.*

The Carolco management team was fractured eventually by the overspending. In 1987, Vajna attempted to fire Stallone during the filming of RAMBO III because of excessive budget increases. This move paved the way for Vajna's exodus from the company: in 1989, Hoffman arranged for loans to allow Kassar to purchase Vajna's stock for $108 million.[20] With Vajna gone, Kassar's spending on production and on his own compensation jumped considerably. In spite of an annual salary of $1.2 million, Kassar engineered a dubious share buyout: in September 1990, Carolco bought shares from Kassar at $13 per share, an 80 percent premium over the market price and at a nearly 40 percent higher price than Kassar paid for them merely nine months earlier. Some shareholders decided to sue Kassar, leading to an injunction freezing his stock in the company. In addition, cost overruns on production, overhead, percentages to stars, and an extravagant and highly publicized lifestyle (giving Arnold Schwarzenegger an airplane, paying Stallone $1 million per year for bodyguards) contributed to rather erratic stock returns: earnings of $.47 per share in 1987, $1.15 in 1988, and $.46 in 1989.[21]

The stock buyout scandal created another rift, this time between Kassar and Hoffman. Kassar claimed that the deal was designed by Hoffman to weaken Kassar's control of the company and to (further) taint his public image. Hoffman, in defending the deal, assigned the negative publicity to the movement within the media against the excesses of business in the late 1980s: "People tied it to Mike Milken, greed, Hollywood craziness. Nobody cared what the facts were."[22] Hollywood financial excess had indeed become synonymous with Carolco, a situation partly due to Kassar running rampant and partly due to the media seizing Carolco as the most visible target for Hollywood overspending.

A marker of Hollywood's response to this adverse publicity was Jeffrey Katzenberg's 1991 twenty-eight-page internal memo to his Disney staff, leaked to the Hollywood trades and reprinted, in part, within *Variety* as "The Teachings of Chairman Jeff." Katzenberg ranted against the movement toward blockbuster, star-driven projects, believing that Hollywood had lost its focus on simple, well-told stories in the process. Despite Disney's number one position in the previous year, Katzenberg cautioned against optimism within his company, citing to their own reliance on pre-sold blockbuster projects such as DICK TRACY. Instead, he urged his executives to examine the extraordinary popularity of such recent films as PRETTY WOMAN, GHOST, and HOME ALONE (all 1990), all of which share two attributes, according to Katzenberg: a good story, well executed.[23]

Katzenberg mentioned specifically the ballooning of star salaries, especially the setting of new plateaus each time a studio or production company chose to pay a star an exorbitant salary. This statement was perceived as a thinly veiled stab at Carolco. Three months earlier, Carolco's Hoffman had responded to accusations that Carolco had single-handedly driven production and talent costs to new levels by countering that Disney was really to blame. "Disney is driving up costs in the most aggressive and dangerous way. . . . tell Disney to stop spending at the present levels and we will," exclaimed Hoffman, citing Disney's DICK TRACY for spending $48 million on advertising alone (it should be noted that at that time Disney was partnered with Cinergi Productions, run by Carolco co-founder Vajna).[24]

In the immediate aftermath of the Katzenberg memo, Carolco seemed to reinforce all of the negative characteristics identified by Katzenberg. Certainly the costs of the Carolco films escalated even further, with Arnold Schwarzenegger receiving $10 million and a percentage for the science fiction/action film TOTAL RECALL and $14 million for TERMINATOR 2: JUDGMENT DAY.[25] By 1991, Carolco's financial successes were outweighed by lavish spending on production and the institutional development of the company. Even though TERMINATOR 2 was pre-sold (mainly in foreign territories) to a sum of over $90 million and the film grossed nearly $500 million worldwide, Carolco realized little growth. Dampened also by an ongoing recession within the American economy, Carolco's success with the Schwarzenegger sequel was offset by its inability to complete a deal for the full ownership of the video distributor, Live Entertainment. While the Carolco stock did jump before the film's release, the unconsummated video merger led arbitragers to short-sell the stock, leading to downward pressure on the Carolco stock price. By the time the deal finally dissolved, in December 1991, the stock had fallen to $3 a share, a drop of over 70 percent from only six months earlier.[26] Added to the extravagant overhead spending, dubious deals, broken partnerships, and negative publicity, Carolco was heading downward almost as quickly as their miraculous rise in the mid-1980s.

When third-quarter earnings in 1991 revealed that Carolco had lost $91 million in the first nine months of the year, funding sources started to become more scarce. Credit Lyonnais and Bankers Trust reportedly called in loans, and the company was forced to terminate forty-nine employees.[27] Three partners—RCS Video International Services B.V., Le Studio Canal+, and Pioneer LDCA, Inc.—did agree to provide Carolco another $45 million, in addition to the $150 million that they had already invested. By 1992, Carolco's precarious financial situation affected their ability to secure a fair distribution deal for their $60 million Stallone epic CLIFFHANGER: in return for half of the film's budget, Tri-Star Pictures strong-armed Carolco for all North American rights (theatrical, home video, and ancillary rights) and rights in such foreign territories as France, Germany, Australia, New Zealand, and Mexico. As Tri-Star chairman Mike Medavoy commented on the arrangement, "We've got a terrific deal on this picture."[28]

Even with the outside cash infusion, further overseas business transactions, and structural reorganization, Carolco continued to flounder. With the financial difficulties, Carolco's abilities to green-light star-driven event pictures, their specialty, became more strained; for instance, CRUSADE, starring Arnold Schwarzenegger, was postponed as a project in 1994 after its budget passed $100 million. To raise additional capital, the company also sold off rights to a number of projects, including SHOWGIRLS (1995).[29] *Variety* reported the flurry of sales under the appropriate title of "At the Carolco Garage Sale."

The garage sale was needed to fuel a large-scale project that veered from many of Carolco's "rules" for commercial success. On the brink of bankruptcy, Carolco attempted to revive the company with Renny Harlin's pirate movie CUTTHROAT ISLAND (1995). By this point, Carolco could not secure star power for their film: Michael Douglas departed the project early on, replaced by minor star Matthew Modine, and the film's co-star, Harlin's wife, Geena Davis, had not appeared in a hit film since 1992's A LEAGUE OF THEIR OWN. With a production cost pegged between $90 million and $100 million, Carolco needed a strong showing to reestablish prominence in the international marketplace. Without a star, Carolco and domestic distributor MGM attempted to position the film in terms of spectacle: as one MGM executive commented, "We plan to position this as a big-event movie....The scope of this film will be the big star."[30] Box-office performance was weak, with Carolco estimated to have lost at least $50 million after the completion of the theatrical run.

Before the release of the film, Carolco filed for protection from creditors under Chapter 11 of the U.S. Bankruptcy Code. Such a filing allowed Carolco to sell off most of its assets to 20th Century–Fox for $50 million in November 1995.[31] Kassar resigned as chairman while the company filed for bankruptcy. By January 1996, Kassar had already secured a three-year deal to produce films for Paramount Pictures. In announcing the deal, Paramount chairman Sherry Lansing cited Kassar's abilities to sell overseas rights to raise production financing, or, in Lansing's terms, his capacity to bring "creative financial arrangements to the films he makes."[32]

Within the Wider World of 1980s Independents: Fleeting and Overextended

Despite its presence as an independent, Carolco engaged in an escalating competition with the mainstream studios. In part because of its outsider status, Carolco continued to receive much of the blame for spiraling costs during the late 1980s through the mid-1990s. The effect of Carolco on production costs, above and beyond star salaries, was widely covered in the industry around the time of the Katzenberg memo. With Stallone, Schwarzenegger, and others receiving record salaries from Carolco, the benchmark for salaries was raised higher and higher.[33] As entertainment lawyer Tom Hansen commented in 1990, "It is an industry where everyone looks at what everyone else makes. That creates a type of momentum."[34] As their allegiance to the packaged film became stronger, Carolco also influenced salaries for screenwriters: most notoriously with the $3 million paycheck for Joe Eszterhas's BASIC INSTINCT. Following a trickle-down effect, salaries for other creative talent were bid up to match these new levels, as producer Lee Rich explains: "when stars get more, an Oscar-nominated cinematographer who earned $6,000 a week two years ago may make close to $12,000 today."[35] Consequently, the negative cost of production rose dramatically in the late 1980s: with average feature production cost jumping 48 percent from $18.1 million in 1988 to $26.78 million in 1990 (marketing—prints and advertising—costs also increased a substantial 38 percent during this period).[36]

The extent to which Carolco was responsible, both directly and indirectly, for the inflationary trend in Hollywood is debatable. Yet the period of this inflation certainly correlates with the burst of independent companies in the wake of video and cable.[37] Carolco's success during the decade should be placed in the wider context of the increased opportunities for independent film initially presented by the video and cable markets. Gauged in terms of the number of independent films receiving MPAA ratings, the market increased substantially during the mid-1980s: 206 independent films were released in 1983, compared to 316 only five years later, in 1988. Despite early hopes, video proved to be an unreliable market for the independents.[38] Indeed, both rental and "sell-through" (to the home market) videos have been characterized as an A-title business. Many of the independent companies initially helped by video and cable eventually cut production severely or exited from the market altogether (e.g., Island, Alive, Cannon, FilmDallas, Vestron, Atlantic Releasing, Avenue, MCEG, Weintraub Entertainment Group, DeLaurentiis Entertainment Group).

While Carolco was perhaps the most visible of these independents, several other companies also illustrate the boom period of the 1980s. Joined through strategies seeking to compete with the majors, these independents eventually succumbed by the end of the decade to various institutional and structural factors. The Cannon Group, the De Laurentiis Entertainment Group (DEG), and Vestron Pictures represent a cross-section of these independents, following Carolco in terms of significance (and threat) to the major studios.

Along with Carolco, Cannon was also instrumental in using the pre-sale market. Purchased by Menahem Golan and Yoram Globus in 1979, Cannon specialized in low-budget, English-language exploitation films whose budgets were recouped before production commenced.[39] Golan and Globus were known previously as independent Israeli filmmakers: Globus's expertise was primarily in financing and marketing, and four of Golan's films—THE HOUSE ON CHELOUCHE STREET (1974), OPERATION THUNDER-BOLT (1977), I LOVE YOU ROSA (1972), and SALLAH (1964)—received Academy Award nominations for best foreign film. Globus also had credentials in the world of independent film, having worked as an assistant to Roger Corman and having his films distributed by Samuel Arkoff. The pair became majority stockholders of the financially troubled Cannon responsible for films such as GAS PUMP GIRLS and SLUMBER PARTY '57.

Quality and artistic merit were rarely guiding issues for Cannon. International marketability was much more important to the company, which experienced early success with ENTER THE NINJA (1981) and DEATH WISH II (1982). A typical sales campaign for Cannon would mix exploitation of all types: teen sex comedies, soft-core pornography, action thrillers, and horror films. Consider the sales pitch in 1981 for a roster of movies such as LEMON POPSICLE III: HOT BUBBLEGUM, LADY CHATTERLY'S LOVER, and DR. HECKYL AND MR. HYPE. Cannon would generally sell rights to cable television, video, and some foreign markets to cover some or all of the negative costs. Within the industry, comparisons were made to Roger Corman; Corman even chose to describe Menahem Golan as "a master of the pre-sell on the international market."[40] The product for the pre-sold films fell firmly within the realm of exploitation: from explorations of current trends in dance (BREAKIN' [1984]) to action star Chuck Norris's Ramboesque MISSING IN ACTION (1984). Cannon remained allied with the majors through distribution, most notably through a multiyear deal with MGM/UA, which became the domestic distributor for Cannon.[41]

The practice of pre-selling rights to motion pictures before production allowed Cannon to set an aggressive slate of films, shooting twelve films in 1982, compared to eight at Columbia and seven at Paramount. While the strategy may have been able to produce capital for production, the upside potential was also limited: selling off various rights and territories inevitably meant that Cannon would not benefit from a large-scale hit because the rights had already been sold. Consequently, Cannon was not able to realize the full box-office success in the same way as other distributors. Of course, as film after film failed to produce anticipated revenue, the method of pre-selling became increasingly difficult to implement with Cannon's disgruntled client list.

Cannon's bid for major status grew from attempts to break the exploitation mold with art house product, such as an adaptation of the Jason Miller stage play THAT CHAMPIONSHIP SEASON (1982), John Cassavetes's LOVE STREAMS (1984), and most improbably, Jean-Luc Godard's KING LEAR (1987).[42] All of the highbrow films distributed by Cannon were commercial and mostly critical failures, including the sensitive drama about a disturbed World War II veteran MARIA'S LOVERS (1984), Robert Altman's adaptation of Sam Shepard's FOOL FOR LOVE (1985), and Julie Andrews as a concert violinist with multiple sclerosis in DUET FOR ONE (1986). Only RUNAWAY TRAIN (1985), an action thriller starring Jon Voight, Eric Roberts, and Rebecca DeMornay, achieved both respectable commercial and critical success, including Academy Award nominations for Voight and Roberts.

Parallel to Carolco, Cannon began to reward the action stars with large salaries, paying Stallone a reported $12 million for the Golan-directed arm-wrestling drama OVER THE TOP (1987) to a seven-year deal with Chuck Norris valued at $21 million.[43] Combined with no breakthrough box-office hits on the art house front and a production schedule larger than any of the majors, Cannon's aggressive expansion in the mid-1980s was met with an almost equally quick fall. MGM/UA canceled the distribution deal with Cannon after fourteen months, supposedly over the critical and financial embarrassment of the Brooke Shields romantic desert melodrama SAHARA (1984). Cannon was sued by the Securities and Exchange Commission in 1987 for fraudulently misrepresenting earnings, and the share price dropped from a high of 451/2 in 1986 to 4 in 1988.[44] The company was able to remain in business for a short time after this debacle with an investment of $250 million by Italian financiers Giancarlo Parretti and Florio Fiorini. In return, the pair immediately starting liquidating Cannon's assets, including selling a half-interest in a large British exhibition chain and London's Elstree Studios.[45]

Cannon's mixture of too many middle-of-the-road art house and exploitation films generally revealed the company's origins in low-budget exploitation fare. Both DEG and Vestron, the other most visible independents, embarked on more ambitious expansion programs that attempted to position the independents as new majors. Although for different reasons, both companies ultimately fell far short of their goal, losing status and influence by the late 1980s.

DEG was established in 1985 by Dino De Laurentiis, known as the Cecil B. De Mille of Italy for such extravagant dramas as THE BIBLE (1966) and ULYSSES (1967), as well as the sci-fi comedy BARBARELLA (1968).[46] After moving to America in 1972, De Laurentiis was responsible for some substantial hits in the mid-1970s as an independent

Production costs soared on OVER THE TOP, ensuring that the film would have great difficulty recouping its costs in the theatrical market.

Dino De Laurentiis brought his company on line at mid-decade.

producer affiliated with Paramount: SERPICO (1973), DEATH WISH (1974), THREE DAYS OF THE CONDOR (1975), and his strongest film commercially, KING KONG. After KONG's blockbuster success in 1976, De Laurentiis spent the next decade unsuccessfully attempting to replicate the formulas of JAWS (with a killer whale film, ORCA [1977]), and STAR WARS (with the remake of FLASH GORDON [1980]) before realizing one hit with the Schwarzenegger vehicle CONAN THE BARBARIAN in 1982.

Despite this uneven track record in the United States (with the well-publicized, big-budget flops HURRICANE [1979], RAGTIME [1981], and DUNE [1984]), De Laurentiis jumpstarted DEG with considerable aplomb: purchasing Embassy Pictures for its distribution arm, building a thirty-two-acre movie studio in Wilmington, North Carolina, and raising $240 million from stock offerings and bank loans.[47] De Laurentiis chose to augment big-budget projects ($25 million for *Tai-Pan* [1986], $21 million for KING KONG LIVES [1986]) with smaller-budget films, many of which had been discarded as projects by the majors. With a slate even more diverse than those from Cannon and Vestron, DEG failed to break even on their entire roster of 1986 films, which included a thriller about possessed trucks written and directed by Stephen King (MAXIMUM OVERDRIVE), two highly exploitable children's films (MY LITTLE PONY, TRANSFORMERS), a Michael Mann thriller featuring the character of Hannibal Lecter (MANHUNTER), David Lynch's critically praised dark vision of small-town American life (BLUE VELVET), and a sequel to De Laurentiis' greatest hit (KING KONG LIVES).[48]

De Laurentiis had been known for his lavish spectacles matched with hyperbolic advertising claims; the attempt to offer modestly budgeted fare proved to be more challenging.[49] Nevertheless, De Laurentiis still attempted to apply his famous showmanship to this product. Perhaps the most striking example of De Laurentiis's marketing audacity can be located in the DEG design for the film MILLION DOLLAR MYSTERY (1987). The film offered one audience member a prize of $1 million for discovering the location of a hidden stash of that amount through clues in the comic plot revolving around the search for $4 million buried somewhere in the United States. Audience members were encouraged to solve the puzzle and write in the location on an entry form. The winner was to be selected by lottery from all the correct entries. As DEG marketing chief Lawrence Gleason commented at the time of the release, "We have a bigger star than Stallone. Greed."[50] While the gimmick attracted some attention in the press, the lame comic adventure repelled audiences—ironically, the box office take was less than $1 million, so DEG could not even recoup their prize money, let alone the $10 million negative cost of the film.

Lisbeth Barron, an analyst at the investment company Balis, Zorn and Gerrard, linked the problems at DEG to those of other independents: "[DEG], in addition to

DEG used an unusually aggressive marketing ploy to promote MILLION DOLLAR MYSTERY.

Cannon Group and several others, fell into kind of a snowballing situation. When they decided to handle their own distribution, they took on a lot of overhead expenses and they had to make a lot of pictures to bring in as much money as possible. They believed that they were safe because they were doing a lot of pre-selling, which covered their production expenses. Except that it's prints and advertising where most money is lost."[51] Despite some critically well received art house films, such as BLUE VELVET, CRIMES OF THE HEART (1986), and WEEDS (1987), DEG did not realize a single substantial hit; the company's attempts at becoming an instant major failed miserably. De Laurentiis was removed as chairman of his own company in February 1988, and by August, DEG had filed for Chapter 11 bankruptcy proceedings.[52] At Mario Kassar's request, the DEG studio in Wilmington was purchased in 1989 by the still solvent Carolco Pictures.[53]

In contrast to DEG, which grew from De Laurentiis's lengthy career and experience in producing, Vestron Pictures was a specific outcome of the surge in video in the early 1980s. Founder Austin O. Furst began purchasing home video rights to films in 1981, starting the Vestron library with the Time-Life feature film collection. This preemptive move helped Vestron establish a secure early foothold in the video market. In addition to the Time-Life films, Vestron was able to purchase the home video rights to recent major films before the studios realized the potential of starting their own video companies. Video sales for Vestron grew to the $200 million mark within a short four-year period. A 1982 deal with Orion Pictures that assigned Vestron video rights to several Orion films for $10 million was crucial to the early success of Vestron.[54] As the majors began to form their own video arms, Vestron's activities broadened to production and distribution, aided by a stock offering in October 1985. At that time, financial analysts warned that Vestron Pictures was working within an incredibly fragile market niche, vulnerable due to the studios' formation of their own video companies and an overvaluation of the Vestron team's talent in the Merrill Lynch and Smith Barney stock offering.[55]

Despite such premonitions, Vestron was able to sell stock at $13 a share, below the antic-
ipated $16–19 a share but respectable nonetheless.

Soon after the stock offering, Vestron's reputation as a scrappy independent influenced one of its potentially most profitable deals, the video release of the Academy
Award winner for best picture, PLATOON (1986). With the rights pre-sold to Vestron in
1985 for the modest sum of $2.6 million, producer Hemdale Films, feeling that the deal
undervalued the hit film, failed to deliver the negative to Vestron, prompting Vestron to
withhold all payment. In the interim, Hemdale negotiated a $11 million deal for the
video release with HBO Video.[56] Analysts estimated that the confusion further dampened Vestron's stock, which dropped from the initial price of 13 to 41/2 by August 1987.[57]
Within the press, journalists cited as reasons for the disagreement both the disadvantageous terms for Hemdale and Vestron's reputation for peddling exploitation fare.

Furst's response to the falling stock price was audacious: he vowed to expand into
film production to ensure a steady flow of product for the video arm of the company.
With another public stock offering to fund the diversification, Furst hired William
Quigley, vice president of Walter Reade Theatres, to run Vestron Pictures. Quigley's
distribution choices were a curious mix of art house product (John Huston's adaptation
of James Joyce's THE DEAD [1987]; a fascinating but uncommercial study of a British
child's hallucinatory world, PAPERHOUSE [1988], Ettore Scola's multigenerational saga
THE FAMILY [1987]), horror (THE UNHOLY [1988], WAXWORK [1988]), teen comedies
and dramas (the post–high school angst drama PROMISED LAND [1988], teen heart-
throbs Corey Feldman and Corey Haim in the trendy "body switching" genre film
DREAM A LITTLE DREAM [1989], Howie Mandel in the darkly comic LITTLE MON-
STERS [1989]), and "auteur" movies such as Roger Vadim's American remake of his own
AND GOD CREATED WOMAN (1987) and four Ken Russell films (GOTHIC [1986], THE
LAIR OF THE WHITE WORM [1988], SALOME'S LAST DANCE [1988], THE RAINBOW
[1989]). With the budgets kept low and the number of releases high, Vestron followed
a route similar to that of both Cannon and DEG by mixing exploitation fare with art
house product.

While the quality of Vestron's product was uneven at best, occasionally the extensive
release schedule allowed a unique and distinctive film to be produced that would never
have been considered by the major studios. Julien Temple's EARTH GIRLS ARE EASY
(1989) qualifies as one of these curious and worthwhile films. A musical-comedy satire
on the aggressively laid-back California lifestyle, EARTH GIRLS details the experience of
three furry aliens who crash land in a Valley girl's pool. The owner, played by Geena
Davis, and her best friend, comedienne Julie Brown, rather than being frightened by the
invaders, attempt to socialize the aliens—Jeff Goldblum, Damon Wayans, and a then-
unknown Jim Carrey—to life in Southern California. One of the film's most amusing set
pieces offers Julie Brown's musical explanation of the power of "blondeness," "'cause I'm
a Blonde," with lyrics beginning, "Because I'm a blonde, I don't have to think/I talk like
a baby, and I never pay for drinks." The film was tagged as "an out-of-this-world, down
to earth comedy adventure," which fails to convey the film's social satire, music, and
romance. From a commercial perspective the film is largely unmarketable, with its mix
of genres and quirky charms. Consequently, a studio would certainly not be interested
in such a commercially risky project.[58] Vestron, on the other hand, with its large scale
production and distribution schedule fostered the film's development. Similarly, commercially untenable yet artistically interesting and distinctive projects cropped up at
DEG (BLUE VELVET) and Cannon (LOVE STREAMS).

Despite a large number of commercial failures, Vestron managed to achieve one breakthrough hit with DIRTY DANCING in 1987.[59] Grossing over $60 million in a six-month span, DIRTY DANCING, a period romance with music, was sold aggressively by the company through the sound-track album (termed "the upset of the year' in pop music, selling 1 million albums in five weeks), a concert tour, and sell-through video release.[60] As William Quigley, president of Vestron Pictures, commented at the time, "We took out a film as if we were Paramount. And guess what? We beat almost everybody there. All the majors included."[61] Within a two-year period, though, Vestron shut down its production arm after an overly ambitious slate of movies failed to yield an even middling success. Cash flow problems at the end of 1988 led Security Pacific National Bank to cancel a $100 million loan for the company.[62] After the bank withdrew the loan, Vestron Pictures was dismantled. In a move that illustrates the convoluted world of the independents, in 1990, Live Entertainment, controlled by Carolco Pictures, purchased Vestron, primarily for the Vestron library of twelve hundred films and the remains of Vestron's video infrastructure.[63] Several Vestron films waiting for theatrical release, such as the thriller PAINT IT BLACK (1989), debuted on home video instead owing to the company's demise.[64]

Cannon, DEG, and Vestron are companies that aspired to majordom during the period of expansion in the mid through late 1980s, seeking to compete directly with the majors through aggressive distribution and diversification. While these companies represented the most serious threat to the majors and helped to encourage the bidding war for talent led by Carolco, several other independent distributors also appeared briefly to be contenders for major status. New World Entertainment is perhaps the most significant, although a single hit for a smaller independent, or "boutique studio," of the period gave each of these companies some credibility and promise in the wider marketplace.

DIRTY DANCING was a major hit for Vestron in 1987, but it could not save the company from its financial troubles.

Unlike Cannon, DEG, and Vestron, New World's growth (and quick decay) derives as much from an attempt to position the company in broadcast programming and in children's toys and comic books as from motion pictures. As Robert Rehme, chairman of New World, commented in an article calling for more stability in the independent film marketplace: "Diversification, as at New World, is essential so that a company is not dependent on any one stream of revenue. Areas of investment can include theatrical, film, television, video, publishing, children's programming/animation, licensing, and merchandising. . . . a solid formula is to be a fully integrated distribution company which distributes its product in every medium."[65] New World Entertainment entered the 1980s as an exploitation company formed by Roger Corman, known for youth-oriented, low-budget horror, action, and sex comedies.[66] Hollywood lawyers Harry Evans Sloan and Lawrence L. Kuppin purchased the dying company with $2 million and $10 million in bank loans in 1983.[67] Keeping budgets under $5 million, New World distributed over twenty-five films per year during their boom period in the mid-1980s, enjoying substantial hits with HOUSE (1986) and SOUL MAN (1986). Unlike the other striving independents, New World expanded immediately into broadcast production and station acquisition.[68] Since first-run television incurs deficits for the producers (with the hope that retaining rights to off-network syndication will compensate in the long run), New World immediately started to feel financial pressure with their shows "Crime Story," "Sledge Hammer," and "Rags to Riches."[69] In a move that could have easily been cushioned by a studio operating within a conglomerate, New World acquired Marvel Comics for $50 million in hopes of entering the animation market and made ambitious bids for both Kenner Parker Toys and Mattel, Inc.[70] Such determined diversification, however, left New World unprotected for the October 1987 stock market crash. With heavy debt after the crash, New World sold Marvel Publishing in January 1989, followed by their agreement in March 1989 to fold the company into Giancarlo Parretti's Pathé Entertainment.[71]

The other independents in the 1980s failed to reach the prominence of Cannon, DEG, Vestron, and New World, although several were able to develop a single breakthrough hit: Atlantic Releasing with TEEN WOLF (1985), Cinecom Entertainment Group with A ROOM WITH A VIEW (1985), and Hemdale with PLATOON. By the end of the decade, Miramax Films and New Line Cinema were developing strategies to compete with the majors during the 1990s.[72] After its owners' brief career in the concert business and as theater owners in Buffalo, Harvey and Bob Weinstein's company Miramax Films ventured into distribution in 1979 through road-showing a Genesis concert movie. This move was followed in 1983 by the very aggressive release of ERENDIRA, a Brazilian film scripted by Gabriel García Márquez. Discarding the original ad campaign featuring veteran actress Irene Pappas, the Weinsteins focused advertising and publicity on one of the supporting cast members, the seductive Brazilian actress Claudia Ohana—even to the extent of securing an appearance for Ohana in *Playboy* magazine. Given the effective marketing, the film grossed almost $3 million domestically on an initial investment of $50,000 by the brothers. Subsequently, Miramax was able to employ the same strategy—low pickup costs and calculated niche marketing—to garner small profits on such films as WORKING GIRLS (1986), I'VE HEARD THE MERMAIDS SINGING (1987), and PELLE THE CONQUEROR (1988). Achieving greater visibility at the end of the decade, the Weinsteins doubled their business from 1988 to 1989, grossing $28 million in 1989.[73] Buoyed by this success, the Weinsteins nonetheless refused a quick expansion in the Vestron model. As Bob Weinstein explained, using vocabulary reminiscent of the then-popular Al Ries and Jack Trout volume MARKETING WARFARE, "The major studios are the big American army. If we went straight up against them, they would nuke us. We're the guerillas. We snipe and we hit and we win a few battles, then we retreat. We're good at being niche players. We don't want to grow up and be another Walt Disney."[74] By this point, Miramax had perfected their tactic of fostering media controversies around exploitable, often sexual, subject matters and sometimes disputed MPAA rating. SEX, LIES, AND VIDEOTAPE; SCANDAL; and THE COOK, THE THIEF, HIS WIFE, AND HER LOVER, all released in 1989, suggest Miramax's brilliance at marketing and publicizing controversial content.[75]

New Line Cinema became a market presence in the 1980s through offering franchises, such as the NIGHTMARE ON ELM STREET series, to ensure a steady flow of income to support more commercially dubious projects. Before the move to franchising, New Line Cinema, formed in 1967, existed on marginal and cult films such as PINK FLAMINGOS (1972), THE TEXAS CHAINSAW MASSACRE (1974), and SMITHEREENS (1982). At the same time as Miramax's ascendancy, New Line also became a force in the independent marketplace through their franchising of the NIGHTMARE series, along with the TEENAGE MUTANT NINJA TURTLES and HOUSE PARTY movies.[76] Both New Line and Miramax are central to the reformed independents of the 1990s, made powerful through their eventual affiliation with studios and larger media conglomerates (Miramax with Disney/Capital Cities/ABC, New Line with Time Warner/Turner).

As the examples of Cannon, DEG, and Vestron illustrate, the market for independent film, which seemed so promising in the middle of the 1980s, proved to be more limited by the end of the decade. In 1989, a Variety article titled "Domestic Market for Indie Pix Soft" illustrates this trajectory: while negative costs doubled in the four-year period of the production boom, domestic film rentals for independent pictures fell by 33 percent.[77]

New Line's successful releases included the TEENAGE MUTANT NINJA TURTLES.

Independent films tended to perform especially poorly at either end of the cost spectrum: in 1988, 48 of 132 independent films budgeted at under $2 million failed to receive a full theatrical release, with producers choosing to send the films directly to video; in the same year, many higher budgeted ($15 million and over) independent films also stumbled at the box office. The latter phenomenon continued from the previous year, in which all independent releases budgeted at $6 million or more were unqualified commercial failures. Within the box-office gross for independent film, rentals tended to be skewed by a couple of large hits: in 1987, for instance, almost 50 percent of rentals for all independent film were accounted for by two films, DIRTY DANCING and A NIGHTMARE ON ELM STREET 3: DREAM WARRIORS.[78]

Independents in the Second Wave of Global Conglomeration

The fate of Carolco and other independents, such as Cannon, DEG, and Vestron, must be placed within the increasing globalization of media production at the end of the 1980s. As Tino Balio notes, this period was marked by a shift toward horizontal integration: studios partnering with other producers and distributors.[79] This move reflected both an attempt to operate on a global level by the studios and to become more narrowly focused on media rather than on a vast array of unaffiliated companies. The formation of Time Warner in 1989, the acquisition of CBS Records in 1987 and Columbia Pictures Entertainment in 1989 by the Sony Corporation, and the purchase of MCA (parent of Universal Pictures) by Matsushita in 1990 all evidence this trend to media-oriented global conglomerates.

The implications of this shift for the independents were far-reaching. First, these global conglomerates possessed the resources to create high-budget, packaged (star, concept, genre) movies in the Carolco fashion. The desire by these conglomerates to enter the film business at almost any cost can be seen with Sony's installation of Peter Guber and Jon Peters as chairmen—a deal that created a breach-of-contract suit by Warner Bros. that cost Sony as much as $800 million to settle.[80] With the global media conglomerates playing a more significant role in Hollywood, the function of independent packagers such as Carolco was largely usurped. Added to the ultimately false hope of a larger market due to video and cable, the independents—Carolco and those companies attempting to be studios, such as DEG and Vestron—withered by the turn of the decade.

Part of this diminution occurred through the foreign takeover of some independent companies as globalization became central to the media industries. Italian financiers Parretti and partner Fiorini began consuming independent film companies in 1987 to build a base for production and distribution in the international market: buying Cannon and France's Pathé Cinema, bidding on DEG, and in 1989, purchasing New World Entertainment.[81] While Parretti would eventually control major MGM/UA, his actions served to consolidate several of the independents who had held such promise only half a decade earlier.

In the early 1990s, these factors—the second wave of media conglomeration and the consolidation of independents—served to constrain the world of independent film. Ultimately the position held by the independents in the 1980s was undone by the hegemony of the studio system: primarily through the majors controlling domestic distribution (even in the heyday of the independents, several companies, including Cannon and

Carolco, chose to cut distribution deals with the majors) and through the horizontal integration of the studios with smaller distributors. Ownership ties between Time Warner and independent New Line Cinema, Disney and Miramax Pictures, and Sony and Castle Rock demonstrate the blurred boundaries between the independent and the studio by the 1990s.

These ties between the majors and the independents were rooted in the experience of the 1980s independent distributors. While Carolco achieved a high level of commercial success with "packages," the movement toward focused, star- and genre-driven spectacles made the company compete more and more directly with the studio product. Similarly, smaller companies—DEG, Vestron, Cannon—through expansion attempted to offer product very similar to the majors. By minimizing the differences between the films of the majors and the independents, the independents of the 1980s were, in fact, creating a situation in which they could be easily assimilated within the contemporary studio system. By the mid-1990s, the blurring between independent and mainstream had become complete, and the possibility of independent companies offering a clear commercial and aesthetic challenge to the majors was slight at best.

5

The Talent Oligopoly

The industry's evolution during the 1980s concealed a paradox. Complicating their drive to keep all revenue streams in-house, the majors failed to control a vitally important resource—the talent required for making films. During the 1930s and 1940s, the major studio-distributors maintained repositories of in-house talent that they kept under long-term contract. Such an arrangement assured relatively stable relations with the personnel needed for production, and the old-line studio moguls treated most of their directors, screenwriters, and actors like what they were—studio employees. As producer Bernie Brillstein noted, "When Spencer Tracy [under contract to MGM's Louis B. Mayer] wanted to make a movie for Columbia, he had to beg Mayer to let him."[1]

By contrast, in the 1980s the majors labored under the constraints that had prevailed since the 1947 divestiture ruling and the industry changes that it helped to instigate. Chief among these were the dissolution of in-house talent repositories and the major studios' abilities to function as centers of film production, rather than, as in the eighties, centers of financing and distribution with downscaled production operations. As a result, the majors had to bid for the services of actors, directors, and screenwriters. Talent agents represented performers, writers, directors, and other personnel for hire, while entertainment lawyers would take the point when negotiating for a producer aiming to get a project going or when negotiations turned on fine legal distinctions. As deal making became essential to film production and the number of people with whom deals had to be struck increased, the industry grew more decentralized. This development was antithetical to the major's efforts to consolidate power in the 1980s, and the tension it created no doubt fueled the industry's drive to control those segments of the maket that it could. Writer-director Frank Pierson noted the dispersion of deal-making authority in the eighties' industry: "The major difficulty today is that the studio system has become so fragmented that virtually every single idea is developed as a separate enterprise of its own."[2] Industry agent Rick Ray stressed that the dispersion of authority created an impediment to film production:

> One of the major changes in the business is that while there used to be a small coterie of studios to which you would go [to make a picture], today we have an operative list . . . [of] hundreds of people, any one of whom can be instrumental in getting something sold or getting something off the ground. [Consequently] it's fifteen times as difficult today as it used to be. You have a widely separated industry sprawled all over the place.[3]

Analyzing the industry's financing practices, Institutional Investor emphasized the importance of deal making in the culture of Hollywood: "Hollywood is about making deals—and movies on the side. And to watch the money move, you need go no farther than the right restaurants. At Le Dome, Mortons, the Palm Court, within marbled and mirrored walls, behind palms, amid the ringing of cellular phones, billions of dollars are spent brokering talent, distribution rights, film libraries, whole companies."[4]

The emergence of agents and lawyers as industry power brokers, packaging and facilitating deals, was not a phenomenon originating in the eighties, but in that decade the results of their clout assumed stark clarity. The results were threefold: they fueled the inflation that gripped the industry, cartelized talent, and delimited the powers of studio executives. The first of these, inflation, has been covered in detail in other chapters. The agents' contribution to this lay in the 10 percent commission that they routinely levied on the salaries they negotiated for their clients. This created an incentive to negotiate for ever higher salaries. The higher the salary, the bigger the commission, and as the pay of star actors, directors, and screenwriters escalated throughout the period, agents got richer. Jack Nicholson commanded a $50 million fee for playing the Joker in BATMAN (1989). Joe Eszterhas became the hightest-paid screenwriter in the business, earning $1.25 million per script for FLASHDANCE (1983) and JAGGED EDGE (1985). The escalating of fees commanded by the industry's top talent fueled the industry's inflationary spiral, adding greatly to negative costs. The situation was exacerbated by the majors' need to compete with each other for the services of leading actors, writers, and directors. With these talents in short supply and great demand, the majors bid exorbitantly to secure them.

The majors had no choice in the matter. The industry's three leading talent agencies—William Morris, Creative Artists Agency (CAA), and International Creative Management (ICM)—were, effectively, a cartel. To get talent, the majors had to do business with them, and in doing so studio executives found that their powers were considerably more limited than in earlier decades, when majors would simply acquire literary or other creative properties for their in-house filmmakers to go to work on. With talent now outside the majors, executives found themselves relying on agents for information about properties in development, the availability of stars or directors and their interest in specific projects, and the availability of packaged talent, that is, a script, star, and director all signed to a project and usually represented by the agent who had assembled the package. In this way, agents insinuated themselves into the industry's networks of power and became indispensible for the operation of the business. Moreover, the balance of power began to shift from the majors to the agents because the latter controlled the talent. ICM's best-known agent was Sue Mengers, in the 1970s one of the industry's most powerful figures and in the 1980s coming out of retirement to head (briefly) the William Morris agency. Mengers pointed to the power shift that had occurred: "Right now agents have more power than the studios. Studios need the agents because the agents are the major suppliers of talent and material." Mengers contrasted this with the marginal and despised role played by agents in earlier periods when the industry might still shut them out of the production process. "What used to drive us crazy is that we would work very hard to help put a picture together and then the picture would be finished, there would be a preview, and we would be told that no agents were allowed." She noted with satisfaction that the majors had been forced to deal with agents as powerful and respected intermediaries. "Only recently has that [marginalization of agents by the majors] stopped because some of us said, 'The hell with you. How dare you? We made as much of a contribution to this film as this studio did.' Slowly now the image of the agent is returning to one of much more importance, much more respect."[5]

The career corridor that connected agents with top executive posts in the majors was the clearest sign of this importance and respect. ICM agent Mike Medavoy left ICM to become production chief at Orion. Guy McElwaine left ICM to become chairman of Columbia Pictures. After managing his own agency, Creative Management Associates (CMA), Freddie Fields went on to become president of MGM/UA. Easily the most spectacular agency head in the eighties, Michael Ovitz segued from building CAA into the most powerful of the industry's power brokers to stage-managing the Matsushita buy of MCA/Universal, and still he aimed for a bigger power base. An Ovitz colleague pointed out, "CAA is just a bridge he is building so that he can take over Columbia Pictures, MGM/UA or MCA. Michael would like to end up as the Lew Wasserman of his day."[6] (Wasserman was the long time head of MCA.) In the 1990s, Ovitz got his wish when he became the head of Disney.

The career trajectory tying agents to top industry posts was a function of the close ties between agents and their clients. The majors, and their corporate owners, valued those individuals who knew talent and had the savvy to assemble and market it. These skills were integral to the business of filmmaking, and the move by agents into the executive suites of the majors was a tacit recognition that agents controlled an information base essential for the industry. As agent Robert Littman pointed out, "One of the reasons agents are constantly hired as heads of studios is because the establishment, the banks and lawyers, think that agents are the people with the closest relationship with their clients."[7] Thus, the paradox of eighties Hollywood was that, to a significant degree, the agents got films made, and the majors attempted to recoup this ability by hiring agents to helm top executive posts. But from the standpoint of talent, the majors were on the outside and were forced to compete for the services they needed in order to get product to fund their distribution arms. And the secret of any cartel's success is to wield power by virtue of its horizontal control of the market. By controlling talent, agents came close to controlling the business. And the top stars, directors, and writers found that their greatest profit potential came from NOT aligning themselves with the majors. As the *Economist* noted, "Well-organised talent . . . will always make more money from feeding the new conglomerates' distribution machines than from joining them," and concluded, "The entertainment industry has found itself on the wrong side of the most painful form of cartel—one that controls its raw material."[8]

The cartelizing of top industry talent was a function of the competition between William Morris, CAA, and ICM as they vied for industry dominance. This competition produced dramatic changes in the fortunes of these firms, and the most spectacular of these was the decline of Morris and the ascendancy of CAA. In the mid-1980s, Morris was a behemoth, the largest talent agency in the world, with 550 agents and two thousand clients. Unlike CAA, which was a Hollywood-specific agency when it began in 1975, Morris represented clients in advertising, music, television, and many nonmedia fields as well as film. Its television revenues were especially important. In 1988, when the company was on a slide in Hollywood, losing many big-name movie clients, the firm earned record revenues of $60 million.[9] Much of this was due to the success of "The Cosby Show," which it helped package, as well as other popular prime-time shows ("Matlock," "A Different World," "Murphy Brown"). (Unlike the practice with film clients of extracting a 10 percent commission from their individual salaries, an agency that packages a network show, as Morris did with "Cosby," may claim 6–10 percent of the show's production budget.)[10]

Unlike CAA and ICM, Morris was also the oldest of the top Hollywood agencies, founded in 1887 by William Morris, a German immigrant. The agency helped guide the careers of such figures as Charles Chaplin, Elvis Presley, and Marilyn Monroe. When Morris died in 1932, control of the agency passed to Abe Lastfogel, who ran the firm until his death in 1984. With Lastfogel's long tenure at the helm, the Morris agency was distinguished by an extraordinarily stable bureaucracy. Top executives stayed in their posts for many years, and as they aged, the Morris image assumed graying tones. On the one hand, this was a positive feature in the Hollywood milieu, where turnover in executive positions was extremely fast. In this climate, the Morris agency seemed mature and orderly, a bedrock in a volatile community. On the other hand, though, this feature made the agency appear stodgy, slow to respond and out of touch with rapidly changing developments in a fast-moving town. This perception helped feed the crisis that bled Morris of its film agents and clients in the latter half of the eighties. In 1989 Forbes posed this Hollywood joke: "How do you commit the perfect murder? Kill your wife and go to work for the Morris Agency. They'll never find you."[11] In 1991, FORBES asked, "Is the William Morris Agency finally ready to admit that Marilyn Monroe is dead?"[12]

As the eighties began, Morris boasted a healthy share of the Hollywood market and reaped benefits from the historical prestige accruing to its name. Its film agents included Lenny Hirshan (representing Clint Eastwood, Jack Lemmon, and Walter Matthau), Ed Bondy (representing Ann-Margret, Michael Douglas, Diane Keaton, Henry Winkler, and John Travolta), Ed Limato (representing Richard Gere and Mel Gibson), and Rick Nicita (representing Sissy Spacek, Christopher Walken, and Eric Roberts).[13] These agents, though, were lesser figures compared with Stan Kamen, the most powerful Hollywood agent in the first half of the decade. Kamen's name was legendary around town, and his roster of clients and studio contacts was unrivaled. Kamen's power derived in large part from his close relationships with studio executives and others in the Hollywod power elite, and it no doubt helped to reify the tradition of these partnerships. Kamen was particularly close to producer Ray Stark (SEEMS LIKE OLD TIMES [1980], ANNIE [1982], THE SLUGGER'S WIFE [1985], BRIGHTON BEACH MEMOIRS [1986], BILOXI BLUES [1988], STEEL MAGNOLIAS [1989]), a powerful figure who had the clout to get his projects made with backing and distribution by the majors. Stark's CALIFORNIA SUITE (1978) (directed by Herbert Ross for Columbia Pictures) featured a plethora of Morris clients: Alan Alda, Jill Clayburgh, Bill Cosby, Jane Fonda, Walter Matthau.[14] Kamen's friendship with Barry Diller at Paramount and with Alan Ladd, Jr., at Fox helped him place his client Alan Pakula with Paramount as the director of STARTING OVER (1979) and client Robert Redford with Fox as the star of BRUBAKER (1980).

One of the ultimate Hollywood insiders, Kamen used his connections with the majors to make things happen for his clients. Barbra Streisand, for example, was keenly interested in YENTL, a property about a Jewish woman passing as a young man, but she had been unable to attract studio interest in it until she brought it to Kamen. Streisand and her agent, Sue Mengers, had had a falling out after Mengers pressed Streisand to make ALL NIGHT LONG (1981), an unusual comedy about a drugstore manager (Gene Hackman) who romances a housewife (Streisand). As directed by Jean-Claude Tramont (Mengers's husband), the film was sweet and charming in a low-key way, but Streisand disliked her role and felt that Hackman was the real star of the picture. By the time of the picture's release, considerable tension had developed between Streisand and Mengers, and this was augmented by Mengers's opposition to the YENTL project. (Despite this opposition, Mengers managed to make a deal for it with Orion, but in 1980 Orion withdrew its backing.) Committed to YENTL, Streisand contacted an entertainment lawyer who put her in touch with Kamen, and he began shopping the project around town with the objective of attracting a studio backer. With Streisand's help, he secured the backing of United Artists, and in this regard, his relationship with UA demonstrates how powerful an agent of Kamen's stature was in the deal-making process. At the time Kamen was pitching a deal for YENTL, UA was staggering through the failure of HEAVEN'S GATE (1980), a project that Kamen had helped negotiate for his client, Michael Cimino. Cimino's spendthrift ways had bankrupted UA, yet even as the company went down, it continued doing business with Kamen. The agent emerged unscathed from the fiasco, and this remarkable development provides an important insight into the place agents occupied in the industry. They were valued for their ability to make things happen, to bring people together and get productions going. What occurred after that point was moot. A film's success or failure was the responsibility of the talent and the studio. If the agent could make the deal, he or she had power, and from that power came the longevity to survive in a business littered with productions that had flamed and crashed at the box office. The agent made the deal, prospered, and moved on to the next one.

On the other hand, however, an agent's power rested on such intangibles as the belief of clients that he or she was giving them better representation than a rival agency might provide. An agent created business opportunities by courting and signing clients, and with over two hundred talent agencies in Hollywood, the danger always existed that rivals would poach clients. The defection of one or two big-name clients would damage an agent's symbolic cachet, and Kamen saw ominous signs of this occurring by the mid-1980s. In rapid succession, he lost Burt Reynolds, Robert Redford, Sylvester Stallone, and Jane Fonda, all but Reynolds to CAA. The desertions left an indelible impression that Kamen's industry power was slipping, and this decline unfortunately occurred as the end of Kamen's life rapidly approached. On 25 October 1984, the industry hosted a benefit recognizing Kamen's contributions to motion pictures. The industry's power base turned out to honor him. Attending were MCA head Lew Wasserman, MGM/UA's Frank Yablans, Fox chair Barry Diller, Warner Bros. chair Robert Daly, agent Sue Mengers, NBC chair Grant Tinker, actor Warren Beatty (a power broker in his own right, much more so than an actor), and assorted producers, directors, and stars. It was a brief but public moment of glory, after which Kamen fell ill with AIDS, and as his health declined, he witnessed the defection of his clients and other Morris agents. On 20 February 1986, Kamen died, and his passing emblemized an official transition of power, the death of one king and the enshrinement of another.

Michael Ovitz had been making serious inroads on the Morris clientele for years prior to Kamen's death, and he had built CAA by mid-decade into the industry's emerging star. The effloresence of CAA came at the expense of Morris and was so striking because of CAA's stunning success at raiding Morris of its top clients and agents. For the Morris agency, CAA's success was especially irksome because Ovitz and his four founding copartners had been Morris agents. The five abruptly left Morris following the 1974 year-end firing of Phil Weltman, who had been a mentor for the younger group. Five years after its founding, CAA remained a small player in Hollywood, with just nineteen agents and two hundred clients.[15] While it represented some fairly prominent Hollywood figures—directors Richard Donner and Ivan Reitman, for example—CAA lacked a roster of major clients that could propel it to the forefront of the industry. Noted for his shrewdness, persistence, and determination (sharklike, said his detractors), Ovitz set out to win major names. So impressive was his success in signing them that he became a bigger player in the eyes of the industry than any of those he brought to CAA. He carefully cultivated relationships with prominent entertainment lawyers, and these steered him to many of their big-name clients. Sean Connery had established his reputation as the first (and for many still the only) James Bond, but after leaving the Bond franchise with DIAMONDS ARE FOREVER (1971), Connery's career had been in a stall, and he was eager for new representation. Orion Pictures' Mike Medavoy put him in touch with tax lawyer Gary Hendler (whose clients included Sydney Pollack, Robert Redford, and Paul Newman, all of whom Ovitz would sign for CAA), and Hendler steered him to Ovitz. Connery was impressed with Ovitz's directness and vision for CAA, in particular his emphasis on packaging the right people and properties and his reluctance to make easy and empty promises:

> He wasn't making any great, monumental claims. He said that he wanted an office that would have the best writers and directors, with the best actors and actresses. He foresaw the idea of packaging. Putting together creative and talented people was very much in his game plan. Nobody talked quite that way to me. They all talked about how good they had done in the past.[16]

Connery signed with Ovitz in February 1979 and was the agency's first big-name client. The following year, Paul Newman signed with CAA. Like Connery, he was looking to

After signing with CAA, Paul Newman's career flourished, and he found one of his best roles of the decade as a faded Boston lawyer in Sidney Lumet's THE VERDICT.

rejuvenate his career after a series of films with poor box office, and he too was impressed with Ovitz's market savvy and complex character:

> He's a cross between a barracuda and Mother Teresa. He's a tough and crafty businessman, and I mean that in the best sense of the word. He's sly like a fox, but that's the only way you can survive in that agency business. But he also has a generosity of spirit that people are not accustomed to seeing. . . . I expect that he'll own most of southern California in the next seven or eight years. . . . Ovitz is like a driver who knows how to lead a race and how to win. He's a great mediator.[17]

If Newman was fascinated with Ovitz and his multifarious personality, he was not alone. Michael Ovitz would become the most discussed and debated agent in Hollywood history, the center of tremendous industry and media attention. Yet in the early and mid-1980s, he was a largely private and secretive figure who avoided personal publicity and preferred that little information about CAA be made public. During these years he became widely known inside the industry, if not in the media, for his stunning coups in winning clients for CAA.

After Newman, Ovitz next bagged Dustin Hoffman, another signing that transpired through the interstices of an entertainment lawyer, Bert Fields, who had Hoffman as one of his clients. Hoffman signed with Ovitz in 1980, and in 1981 Ovitz won another Hendler client, director Sydney Pollack. Pollack introduced Ovitz to his friend and frequent collaborator Robert Redford, and sixteen days after he had signed Pollack, Ovitz won Redford to CAA. Redford signed in March, and in July Ovitz made a direct pitch to Sylvester Stallone and signed him to CAA.

By signing these major players, Ovitz made CAA into an industry presence, and he demonstrated vision (or luck) in his dealings with clients who had not yet established viable careers. Producer Stanley Jaffe asked Ovitz to look at his just completed film, Taps (1981), and a young actor named Tom Cruise, who had a small, supporting role alongside topliners George C. Scott and Timothy Hutton. Ovitz told author Robert Slater about the tremendous impression Cruise made upon him during their initial meeting: "He sat down on the couch across from us, and we were knocked out. He had this quiet energy. His eyes sort of danced. He had this infectious smile. He was the single politest man I'd ever met. No arrogance or cockiness. I just fell in love with the guy. He was terribly centered." Convinced that Cruise could have a tremendous career, Ovitz signed him with CAA, and Cruise, in turn, was impressed with the respect accorded him by CAA, in particular the way Ovitz and the agency treated him as a major star (which, as yet, he was not). Regarding Ovitz, Cruise said, "He didn't treat me any differently. I wasn't making him that much money compared to Paul Newman, Dustin Hoffman, or Sydney Pollack. . . . He made me feel like I had a home at CAA, and with him."[18]

In the next few years, Ovitz signed Al Pacino, Robert De Niro, and Jane Fonda. The process accelerated after Stan Kamen's death. Illustrating the symbiotic relationship prevailing between talent agencies and the majors, Warner Bros. chair and co-CEO Terry Semel spoke with a number of regular Warners performers to persuade them to go with CAA now that Kamen was gone. These included Barbra Streisand, Goldie Hawn, Chevy Chase, and Meryl Streep, all of whom signed with CAA. Ovitz's firm had impressed Semel with the aggressive way it promoted its clients' careers. Semel said, "We saw Stan's death as a good opportunity for some of our clients to go to CAA. CAA

His supporting role in TAPS *brought Tom Cruise to the attention of CAA and the threshold of a major career.*

was a good place, with aggressive people who were probably going to lead the 1980s and 1990s in their field. We are the largest producer of movies in the last twenty years, and CAA was building the largest list of stars."[19] A few months after Kamen's death, most of his clients had gone over to CAA.

His extraordinary roster of talent gave Ovitz production capabilities and industry connections that surpassed those of his competitors. Legendary Hollywood agent Irving ("Swifty") Lazar commented, "There hasn't been a phenomenon such as CAA since 1947, when Lew Wasserman and MCA dominated Hollywood. Comparing CAA to its strongest competition is like comparing Tiffany's to the A&P."[20] At its most striking level, Ovitz's success gave him tremendous leverage over film production. In supplying material for production, CAA maintained a close working relationship with the majors as well as with smaller production companies, such as Castle Rock Entertainment. Castle Rock had been formed by CAA client Rob Reiner, whose career shift from acting (most notably on television's "All in the Family") to directing (STAND BY ME [1982], THE PRINCESS BRIDE [1988], WHEN HARRY MET SALLY [1989]) Ovitz had coached. CAA's relationship with Castle Rock was special. In exchange for finding material and properties for the production company, CAA received $50,000 on every Castle Rock production and $200,000 for those directed by Reiner.[21]

In developing material for production, CAA used an aggressive and shrewd appoach. Despite CAA's nominal status as an agency outside the majors, this approach enabled Ovitz to effectively green-light productions. Though CAA was not a production company or a distributor, it nevertheless got films made, through the packaging of talent, almost as if it were a firm that functioned in these capacities. "Packaging" was not new to the business, but Ovitz made it the hallmark of the CAA approach, and it is the business practice that is perhaps most closely associated with his tenure. By floating to the majors a package of readily assembled talent (screenwriter, director, stars), Ovitz could leverage production deals in a highly persuasive way. Accepting the package made the studio executive's job much easier. It eliminated the need to expend resources securing a property and the requisite talent and negotiating with all of the agents that would be involved in striking separate, individual deals for the project. Instead of diffusing energy and resources in this fashion, it was more tempting to sign off on the package. Indeed, it was often imperative because a competing major would get it if declined. Thus, with packages, Ovitz encroached upon actual filmmaking territory, and some industry figures resented this as an intrusion on their prerogatives. Producer Don Simpson, for example, bristled at the production authority that was inherent in the package deal on the part of its assembler. He recalled fighting with CAA over the right to make decisions about who would participate in a given production. "We would get into big fights. I would say I'm not interested in so-and-so. I'm interested in the idea and the writer. We will make the choices as to who will produce it, and who will direct it."[22]

Ovitz's first major package resulted in TOOTSIE (1982), which featured the participation of CAA clients Dustin Hoffman, Bill Murray, and Sydney Pollack (working in a dual capacity as a performer in the film and the film's director).[23] Ovitz determined to bring Pollack into the project when its original director, Hal Ashby, left. Pollack was reluctant to participate because, at the time, he enjoyed making dramas and doubted the material and his facility with comedy. But Ovitz pursued him relentlessly, with a barrage of phone calls, and eventually offered to secure him his full director's salary for a week of work on the screenplay with its writers and Dustin Hoffman. Ovitz apparently hoped that this week of close work would hook Pollack on the material, and it evidently did. Pollack signed on, and Ovitz notified Columbia that the package was complete. TOOTSIE was the second highest grossing picture of its year, and it was an early public acknowledgment of Ovitz's emerging status in the industry. In the film, Pollack plays a power-brokering talent agent, and on the wall of his office hangs the CAA logo.

Other films packaged by CAA included RHINESTONE (1984), GORILLAS IN THE MIST (1988), and RAIN MAN (1988). While the latter two films are fine and distinguished pictures, the former exemplifies the waste and irrationality that often typify Hollywood production. The momentum created by an enticing package could overrule sound creative decision making, particularly assessments about whether the right talent was participating in a given project. In short, packaging could drive production decisions and result in films that were deformed in various ways, worse than they might have been, or in pictures that shouldn't have existed. According to one studio executive, "CAA packages are a prefab, take-it-or-leave-it way of making movies. Some pictures get made that maybe shouldn't be made."[24]

RHINESTONE began with a strong script by Phil Alden Robinson and a decision by Fox executive Joe Wizan that the picture should be made with major stars. Dolly Parton, a CAA client, signed on for the female lead, and as Fox considered prospects for the male lead, CAA suggested they take Sylvester Stallone. Stallone had just finished ROCKY III (1982) and had directed John Travolta in STAYING ALIVE (1983), which had been trashed by the critics but had done reasonable business. After STAYING ALIVE, RHINESTONE would be Stallone's second musical. He signed on and began to rewrite Robinson's script, altering the characters, removing the texture, enlarging his role, and making his character tougher. Stallone also selected the picture's director, choosing Don Zimmerman, his editor on ROCKY III. Zimmerman had never directed

An unsuccessful example of industry packaging: RHINESTONE.

before, and he soon found that Stallone was the film's de facto director. With his authority on the set undermined, Zimmerman lasted three weeks before he was fired. The director chosen to replace him, Bob Clark (PORKY's [1981]), was another CAA client. Although Clark inherited a script, now substantially different from Robinson's original, over which he had had no influence and a willful star who seemed to prefer to direct himself, he completed the film without further incident. When Fox released the picture, however, viewers stayed away, and the picture recouped only a portion of its $28 million budget. It became one of many poorly performing Fox films, a record that influenced owner Marvin Davis's decision to unload the studio. Robinson publicly criticized the poor handling of his script and said, "I think the lesson for the town is that you can't let a good script be thrown away." Zimmerman felt that the power dynamics in the business were out of balance and that many individuals were invested with creative authority not properly their own. "The lesson to learn is the danger of the Hollywood syndrome. Basically the power has left the producing element and has just run out of control."[25]

Screenwriter Joe Eszterhas believed he had come up against that power and wrath in what became a highly visible and public clash with Ovitz. Before signing with CAA, Eszterhas had been represented by ICM's Guy McElwaine, but McElwaine had left the agency business to run Columbia Pictures. When McElwaine decided to return to ICM in 1989, Eszterhas felt that he should go with him. He claims that when he informed Ovitz of his wish, the CAA head threatened to sue him, to tie him up in court and ruin his career should he leave CAA. In what became the incident's most notorious tag line, Ovitz said, according to Eszterhas, "My foot soldiers who go up and down Wilshire Boulevard each day will blow your brains out."[26] The flap was widely reported in the media, and it tarnished Ovitz's image with its suggestions of a none-too-benign exercise of power.

While the packaging of RHINESTONE had worked to the detriment of the picture, in the case of RAIN MAN CAA's influence produced a decidedly happier result. The critically acclaimed film examined the relationship between two brothers, one of whom is autistic. For a long time at the outset the picture was mired in seemingly insoluable problems as one director after another withdrew. The package had been set up for United Artists with Martin Brest directing and Dustin Hoffman starring. Hoffman, playing the autistic Raymond, wanted Mickey Rourke to play the role of Raymond's younger brother, but Tom Cruise's agent at CAA felt the role was right for him. With Ovitz backing Cruise for the part, he won the role. "Mike fought for me, and they cast me in it," Cruise recalled.[27] Brest, though, failed to find the script sufficiently interesting and abandoned the project. Operating a bit like a studio mogul of old, Ovitz went to CAA's in-house talent reservoir and recruited the people he needed. He contacted two directors, both CAA clients. Sydney Pollack declined, believing that the film's last act, when the brothers travel by car to Las Vegas, presented an insoluble structural weakness. Barry Levinson (DINER [1982]; GOOD MORNING, VIETNAM [1987]), though, felt he could make it work by stressing the deepening relationship between the brothers, and he agreed to direct. When the picture was released, it generated huge box office as the year's top-earning film and garnered superb reviews from the nation's critics. But for more than two years it had been a project in limbo, a script with stars attached but no director and with management at UA who doubted that a director could be found. During this period, Ovitz held the project together by convincing Hoffman and Cruise that the picture would get made and that it would be an important film. Hoffman, Levinson and the chairman of United Artists all agreed that Ovitz's commitment to the project and his determination to make it happen were the critical factors in keeping it alive, and each acknowledged his pivotal role in the genesis of the film.

Ovitz was clearly functioning as more than a talent agent. To promote the careers of CAA clients, he used his considerable industry power and close connections to the majors to package productions, and then, when the project was under way, he worked like a film producer, ensuring that the projects stayed on track. His ambitions carried him beyond the parameters of talent promotion as it had been traditionally defined (i.e., finding work for clients) and toward a more expansive kind of power brokering where he might facilitate not just an individual's career or a film's production but corporate transactions at their highest level and even the daily operations of a film major. Toward the end of the decade, Ovitz put these ambitions into play by participating in the efforts of Sony and Matsushita to buy a Hollywood major.[28] In 1988, Sony hired Ovitz as a consultant, and he fed the Japanese corporation information on several prospective buys. But these—MCA and MGM/UA—the electronics giant turned down. Sony was interested in Columbia Pictures Entertainment, and Ovitz analyzed the value of CPE for Sony. After the purchase, Sony asked Ovitz to head the studio and offered to buy and then resell CAA in a deal that would have made Ovitz $100 million. But he asked, in addition, to run Sony's record division, an arrangement that would have doubled the value of Sony's offer, and Sony declined. Ovitz was out, and Jon Peters and Peter Guber were in (see ch. 2).

Concurrent with the Sony transactions, Ovitz sought a buyer for MCA and looked at other Japanese multinational corporations. Matsushita expressed interest, and Ovitz lined up a CAA team to facilitate the international dealings. Ovitz made several trips to

CAA's solid support and its packaging of talent helped ensure the success of Rain Man, *despite the project's troubled production history.*

Hawaii and Japan, and although negotiations stalled during the next year over the price of MCA stock, the deal eventually went through. In both the Sony and Matsushita deals, the Japanese placed a high value on Ovitz's services and relied on him as an intermediary rather than going directly to Columbia or MCA. The commodity that Ovitz offered the Japanese was information, gleaned from the core business elements of the industry. In this regard, Ovitz performed a function in the negotiations that usurped the more traditional role played by the community of investment bankers. As one banker said, "All of us knew Sony and Matsushita had interests in the movie companies. But they didn't need us. The only thing that was important to them was to have high-level contacts, insiders who could advise them on who was the best management." Joe Cohen, a Hollywood financial consultant, pointed out that the Japanese wanted information from people who really knew the business. "The Japanese understand one thing—Wall Street doesn't understand Hollywood at all. And the guys who know this town can be counted on one hand."[29] The Japanese valued Ovitz's prominence in the industry and the unique stock of confidential information that he had accrued. His role as consultant in these two megadeals boosted his already impressive industry cachet. Fittingly, his power, long known inside Hollywood, was now publicly acknowledged. In May 1990, *Premiere* magazine published its first list of the Hollywood power elite. Topping the list of one hundred names was Michael Ovitz.

The third major Hollywood agency, International Creative Management, was neither as old as Morris nor as focused in its corporate structure as CAA. ICM founder Marvin Josephson cobbled together a series of smaller talent agencies—the Ashley Famous Agency, purchased in the 1960s, and Creative Management Associates, purchased in 1975—and housed them under a conglomerate umbrella company, Josephson

International. In the early 1980s, Josephson International diversified with purchases of office supply companies, radio stations, and a stock brokerage firm and saw dismal results. With its new acquisitions losing money, Josephson unloaded them and took ICM private. While this resulted in a $62 million bank debt, Josephson installed new officers at the head of ICM and launched an aggressive bid to expand the company's share of the talent agency market. In the early 1990s, ICM returned to profitability and had 150 agents representing more than two thousand clients.[30] ICM's bid for expanded power in Hollywood coincided with the weakening of the Morris agency, which enabled ICM to mount some spectacular raids of the Morris constituency. In 1988, ICM snagged top Morris agent Ed Limato, who brought his clients Michelle Pfeiffer, Mel Gibson, and Richard Gere with him. Then in 1991 ICM bled Morris badly by taking five of its agents and their clients, including Julia Roberts, Tim Robbins, Andie MacDowell, Anne Bancroft, Jason Robards, Anjelica Huston, James Spader, and directors Alan Pakula and Norman Jewison. With this shift in the balance of power, ICM emerged into the number two agency spot, behind CAA.

While the majors established intimate relationships with the talent agencies, they took steps to circumvent their power. The multipicture contract was one such step. The majors sought to sign prominent directors, actors, producers, and screenwriters to multiple picture deals. While the terms of these deals were very favorable for talent, the studios also gained by minimizing the need to strike deals on each project with a talent agency intermediary. Paramount, for example, signed producers Don Simpson and Jerry Bruckheimer to a multipicture deal. More famously, Paramount signed Eddie Murphy, then at the crest of his eighties career, to an exclusive five-picture contract that was promptly revised and renewed after completion of the first picture, BEVERLY HILLS COP II (1987). Under the terms of the revised contract, Murphy's per picture salary was just under $16 million, in a comparable range with Sylvester Stallone's salary as one of the top-paid actors in the business. Furthermore, Murphy would be entitled to develop and produce additional features and television shows for his companies, Eddie Murphy Productions and Eddie Murphy TV Enterprises. During a press conference held to announce the new contract, Murphy said that he felt justified in pressing Paramount for new terms because of the success of BEVERLY HILLS COP II, which was the highest-grossing film of the year. The renegotiation of existing contracts is a normative affair in Hollywood, Murphy said, and it was natural to aim for as much money as he could get. "When you make a deal to . . . do like five pictures, and the first did so well, we went back and said, 'Hey, let's renegotiate.' This is a business where you renegotiate deals. Do I believe in living up to contracts? Yes. Do I believe in being underpaid for something I do? No."[31]

While Paramount believed it made good business sense to strike a multipicture deal with Murphy, its strategem was defeated, to some extent, by Murphy's popular success, which compelled Paramount negotiate anew with his lawyers and agency. Furthermore, Murphy's association with Paramount brought the studio one of the messiest Hollywood lawsuits of the decade, a suit that clarified some fundamentals about the relationship between the majors and the agencies. After the release of Murphy's COMING TO AMERICA (1988), syndicated columnist Art Buchwald and film producer Alan Bernheim sued Paramount, claiming the picture was based on a treatment (a several-page prose summary of a proposed film) that Buchwald sold Bernheim in 1983. As Bernheim was a Morris client, the trial pitted Paramount against the Morris agency, whose business depended on safeguarding the privacy of its clients' business affairs. On 8 January 1990,

Eddie Murphy's string of hits for Paramount included his
BEVERLY HILLS COP *films, and the studio sought an ongoing*
relationship with him by offering a multipicture contract.

the trial judge upheld Buchwald's claim that the film was based substantially on his treatment and found Paramount to be in breach of contract for failing to honor Buchwald's claim to a share of the film's profits. In a development that generated a great deal of media coverage and speculation about the vagaries of Hollywood profit taking, Paramount claimed that the film's net profits had been zero, despite a gross of more than $300 million. Buchwald's attorneys were especially outraged by some of the expenses Paramount cited to explain where the money had gone. These included such star perks as $115,000 for Murphy's twenty-four-hour limousine and driver.[32]

During the damage phase of the trial, with Morris's West Coast business affairs chief slotted to testify for Buchwald, Paramount went after the Morris agency. It subpoenaed every Morris film contract and deal memo involving writers and producers from 1975 to 1987.[33] This was confidential information, and the prospect of its revelation terrified Morris. It would have gutted the agency's reputation for discretely managing its clients' affairs and would have precipitated another hemorrhage of talent from the firm. Had the subpoenas not been quashed, Paramount would have gleaned information on how its competitors' motion picture deals had been structured and what its competitors had

The case of the vanishing profits: COMING TO AMERICA, *with Eddie Murphy and Arsenio Hall.*

paid for talent. In this regard, the Buchwald case demonstrated the inherently adversarial relationship that prevailed between the majors and the talent agencies. The agencies facilitated the majors' abilities to conduct business, but the agencies served their clients, not the majors, and derived income by making the majors pay a high price for the talent they wanted. Ordinarily, the normative and accepted rituals of deal making in Hollywood concealed the adversarial nature of this relationship, but the Buchwald case exposed the alignments of power for all to see.

With CAA, Morris, and ICM holding the reins of talent and promoting their clients' careers, how did the careers of the performers themselves fare during the decade? Eddie Murphy, Dustin Hoffman, Paul Newman, and Sylvester Stallone were among the decade's highest-paid actors. All, of course, are men, and star salaries skewed sharply according to gender, with male stars receiving disproportionately higher pay than women. Exemplifying peak earnings was the $16 million Stallone reportedly earned per picture in 1987. No female star worked in this remunerative stratosphere, and the performers who commanded the largest box office in the domestic and international markets were, without exception, male. This gender skew, however, went beyond issues of pay. A 1990 study by the Screen Actor's Guild found a diminishing proportion of feature film roles going to women in the 1980s. According to SAG, 71 percent of film roles went to male performers. Furthermore, women over forty, who had aged beyond what the industry typically found desirable or glamorous, worked in only 9 percent of all film roles.[34]

The Screen Actors Guild Women's Committee sponsored a 1990 conference to address the shortage of women's roles. At the conference, Meryl Streep complained that contemporary film failed to measure up to the standards Hollywood established in earlier decades, when a gallery of strong female roles and performers existed on screen. She questioned whether contemporary film was addressing itself to the dreams and imaginations of its young female viewers:

> I'm in the prime of my life and I want to play the lead. . . . I grew up with the legacy of those great female stars, Bette Davis, Katharine Hepburn, Barbara Stanwyck. They inspired me. They made me happy to be a girl. I thought, if she's so important, if she matters, then I matter. If we no longer have these images of women to admire, then we stifle the dreams of our daughters. When we see women on screen getting slapped, kicked and asking for help, this is not an indication that actresses are confused about the roles they accept. It's an indication of what gets a green light, of what sells.

Streep criticized the economic factors that had skewed film production toward the action blockbuster. The overseas market had made action films extremely popular, and such stars as Sylvester Stallone and Arnold Schwarzenegger commanded huge international followings, which, in turn, permitted them to negotiate for stratospheric salaries. Streep suggested that these action films sold well overseas because "People don't need to understand English to know something is exploding and to enjoy that spectacle. They don't call it the bottom line for nothing. Where have the classic films gone? Look under the wheels of the blockbusters."[35]

Despite the strong gender skewing of film roles and salaries in the 1980s, a gallery of front-rank female stars existed, and many commanded great popularity throughout the decade. Furthermore, these stars represented an impressive range of personas and genres, from light comedy, slapstick, and sultry glamour to old-fashioned Bette Davis toughness. But as SAG's figures indicated, they didn't receive the compensation of their male peers, nor were they as frequently the lead performer around whom a film was constructed. Though she worked in films infrequently, Barbra Streisand was probably the most powerful female filmmaker-star of the period. Other than ALL NIGHT LONG, which was a product not of her design, she only made two films during the eighties, but these—YENTL (1983) and NUTS (1987)—were projects on which she exerted chief creative authority as star and producer and (on YENTL) director. Streisand designed these vehicles for herself, and she controlled the screen and gave herself the camera to a degree that her fans loved but others found discomforting. When she was criticized, the films were labeled as vanity productions, but it is difficult to believe that male stars would receive an equivalent criticism. In any event, no other female star replicated Streisand's commanding authority over production matters.

Meryl Streep (THE FRENCH LIEUTENANT'S WOMAN [1981], STILL OF THE NIGHT [1982], SOPHIE'S CHOICE [1982], SILKWOOD [1983], FALLING IN LOVE [1984], PLENTY [1984], OUT OF AFRICA [1985], HEARTBURN [1986], IRONWEED [1987], A CRY IN THE DARK [1988], SHE-DEVIL [1989]) established a career in the eighties primarily in dramas that allowed her to display a dazzling gift for voice and the physical extension of character. At decade's end, she switched to comedy (SHE-DEVIL), performed it with flair and distinction, and continued to work in a lighter vein (while continuing her dramatic roles) into the next decade. One of the finest screen performers of

Director and star of YENTL, *Barbra Streisand carefully chose her film projects and attained a significant measure of power in the industry.*

all time, Streep's extraordinary gifts were often minimized by critics charging that she mainly did accents, but her range was unmatched by any other performer. SOPHIE'S CHOICE and OUT OF AFRICA contained her finest performances of the eighties, as, respectively, a mother forced to decide which of her children would die in the Nazi death camps and writer Isak Dinesen during the years she spent on an African coffee farm. Both were melancholy films, and while critics complained that Streep seemed to specialize in lugubrious roles, her presence in both films was luminous. As an actor, Streep simply had no limits, and her gallery of characters was unmatched in its depth or range by the work of any of her peers.

Jessica Lange (THE POSTMAN ALWAYS RINGS TWICE [1981], TOOTSIE [1982], FRANCES [1982], COUNTRY [1984], SWEET DREAMS [1985], CRIMES OF THE HEART [1986], EVERYBODY'S ALL AMERICAN [1988], FAR NORTH [1988], THE MUSIC BOX [1989]) and Sissy Spacek (COAL MINER'S DAUGHTER [1980], RAGGEDY MAN [1981], MISSING [1982], THE RIVER [1984], MARIE [1985], VIOLETS ARE BLUE [1986],

Meryl Streep in IRONWEED. *Gifted with an astonishing versatility, Streep was perhaps the finest actor in eighties cinema.*

CRIMES OF THE HEART [1986], THE LONG WALK HOME [1990]) specialized in straight drama and created a gallery of commanding characters. Lange succeeded Lana Turner as the seductive Cora in Bob Rafelson's remake of POSTMAN, and the following year she balanced a fine comic performance in TOOTSIE with a stark portrait of the tormented Hollywood actress Frances Farmer. Lange's screen presence was more intense and aggressive than Spacek's, but Spacek showed how commanding quietude and gentility could be, especially in MISSING, where she furnished the voice of conscience amid the chaos of post-Allende Chile.

With a flinty personality, Debra Winger brought a Bette Davis toughness to her roles (URBAN COWBOY [1980], AN OFFICER AND A GENTLEMAN [1982], TERMS OF

ENDEARMENT [1983], LEGAL EAGLES [1986], BETRAYED [1988]), a grit that no Hollywood actress had shown in a generation. Winger worked relatively infrequently (five films in ten years), and her industry reputation for being "difficult" seemed to have impeded the development of her career. But she could play tough (AN OFFICER AND A GENTLEMAN) as well as sweet (TERMS OF ENDEARMENT). In the latter film, she was heartbreaking as a woman trying to repair her relationship with her mother and dying young of that strange Hollywood malady that puts beautiful actresses gently to sleep. It was a hokey narrative device, no more credible here than in LOVE STORY (1971), but it touched audiences with its essential truth about the unfairness of life. Succumbing to fatal illness, in TERMS OF ENDEARMENT Winger enjoyed her greatest rapport with a popular audience.

With her extraordinary, husky voice, Kathleen Turner achieved an overnight stardom in BODY HEAT (1981), in which she and writer-director Lawrence Kasdan revived the classical femme fatale. As the seductive and duplicitous Matty, Turner led venal Florida

Classical movie glamour: Kathleen Turner in BODY HEAT.

lawyer (William Hurt) to a much deserved ruination. As the alluring siren, Matty was wonderfully written but a hard role to play because of her mythic qualities. Turner, though, making her initial appearance in the film as an impossibly beautiful vision in white, fashioned Matty into one of the decade's most memorable screen characters. Here and in her subsequent films, Turner represented a mature Hollywood glamour that was quite beyond the adolescent appeals of the younger generation of "brat pack" stars. As the epitome of this classical glamour, Turner supplied the voice of cartoon siren Jessica Rabbit in WHO FRAMED ROGER RABBIT (1988). Mainly drawn to literate projects with strong scripts, Turner proved adept at both drama and light comedy (THE MAN WITH TWO BRAINS [1983], ROMANCING THE STONE [1984], PRIZZI'S HONOR [1985], THE JEWEL OF THE NILE [1985], PEGGY SUE GOT MARRIED [1986], SWITCHING CHANNELS [1988], THE ACCIDENTAL TOURIST [1988], THE WAR OF THE ROSES [1989]).

While Lange, Turner, Streep, and Winger played strong women, the decade's warrior-woman prize went to Sigourney Weaver for her popular Ripley character in the ALIEN series (1979, 1986, 1992, 1998). Weaver's Ripley was a battle-hardened soldier capable of doing combat with the slimy, reptilian creatures that populated this series. The climax of the cycle, for Weaver as Ripley, came in the second feature, ALIENS (1986), wherein she wages a fierce, maternal war (both antagonists are protecting their young) on the huge alien queen of the nest. In these films, Weaver feminized the action roles typically slotted for men and helped open a space for women as strong, active, and physical characters in the action genre. Though her amazon-warrior roles have been the most memorable of her career, Weaver alternated these with comedies and nonaction dramas (THE YEAR OF LIVING DANGEROUSLY [1983], DEAL OF THE CENTURY [1983], GHOSTBUSTERS [1984], ONE WOMAN OR TWO [1985], HALF MOON STREET [1986], GORILLAS IN THE MIST [1988], WORKING GIRL [1988], GHOSTBUSTERS II [1989]).

While these other actresses portrayed sympathetic and often heroic characters, Glenn Close portrayed the decade's vivid female villains in FATAL ATTRACTION (1987) and DANGEROUS LIAISONS (1988), after starting the eighties in earth-mother roles (THE WORLD ACCORDING TO GARP [1982], THE BIG CHILL [1983], THE STONE BOY [1984], THE NATURAL [1984]). Close brought an extraordinary zest and relish to her villains that suggested she enjoyed playing these characters far more than the blander roles in her other pictures. Her vengeful harpy in FATAL ATTRACTION, menacing stockbroker Michael Douglas and his family, was the kind of villain audiences love to hate, and it was a bravura performance that electrified the film.

Light comedy and comedy-drama afforded three stars the opportunity to build or maintain major careers. In the seventies, Sally Field had been burdened by her association with TV's "The Flying Nun" and Burt Reynolds's moonshine comedies, but in the eighties she broke free of these and established her own career in ABSENCE OF MALICE (1981), KISS ME GOODBYE (1982), PLACES IN THE HEART (1984), MURPHY'S ROMANCE (1985), SURRENDER (1987), PUNCHLINE (1988), and STEEL MAGNOLIAS (1989). She was especially appealing with subdued charm alongside James Garner in MURPHY'S ROMANCE, a May-September love story directed by Martin Ritt. Cher successfully segued from her retro status as musician to a front-rank film career: COME BACK TO THE FIVE AND DIME, JIMMIE DEAN, JIMMIE DEAN (1982); SILKWOOD (1983); MASK (1985); MOONSTRUCK (1987); SUSPECT (1987); THE WITCHES OF EASTWICK (1987). Cher proved to be an especially fine performer in drama and comedy-dramas, and her performance in MOONSTRUCK, as a lonely woman verging on middle age, is a masterpiece of comic poignancy. Goldie Hawn had transitioned from TV's "Laugh-In"

*Sigourney Weaver prepared to do battle with the alien queen
in* ALIENS. *The great female warrior of eighties cinema, Ripley
was Weaver's most significant and enduring character.*

to a prolific seventies film career whose momentum carried her through the eighties,
even as the popularity of her pictures slipped somewhat in the latter half of the decade:
PRIVATE BENJAMIN (1980), SEEMS LIKE OLD TIMES (1980), BEST FRIENDS (1982),
PROTOCOL (1984), WILDCATS (1986), and OVERBOARD (1987). Hawn also starred in
and produced SWING SHIFT (1984), a comedy-drama about housewives working in factories during World War II. This picture devolved into one of the decade's notoriously
ruined films, the casualty of an apparent battle between Hawn and director Jonathan
Demme over the concept and shape of the picture. The battle resulted in a re-edit of
the film against Demme's wishes and the release of a picture that lacked coherency and
structure. The original version of SWING SHIFT was never publicly exhibited.

In addition to the work of these actresses, the decade also saw the appearance of five
performers who began to establish careers that would ripen into stardom in the nineties:
Julia Roberts (FIREHOUSE [1987], MYSTIC PIZZA [1988], BLOOD RED [1988], and
STEEL MAGNOLIAS [1988]); Holly Hunter (THE BURNING [1981], SWING SHIFT
[1984], RAISING ARIZONA [1987], BROADCAST NEWS [1987], MISS FIRECRACKER
[1989], ALWAYS [1989]); Laura Dern (FOXES [1980], TEACHERS [1984], MASK [1985],

SMOOTH TALK [1985], BLUE VELVET [1986], FAT MAN AND LITTLE BOY [1989]); Sandra Bullock (A FOOL AND HIS MONEY [1988], WHO SHOT PATAKANGO [1989]); and Meg Ryan (RICH AND FAMOUS [1981], AMITYVILLE 3-D [1983], TOP GUN [1986], INNERSPACE [1987], D.O.A. [1988], THE PRESIDIO [1988]), whose breakthrough picture came at decade's end, WHEN HARRY MET SALLY (1989).

The finest male actors of the decade included Paul Newman, Al Pacino, Robert De Niro, Gene Hackman, Jack Nicholson, and Dustin Hoffman. After signing with CAA, Newman's career revived, and he turned in a series of prestigious performances in well-received films (ABSENCE OF MALICE [1981], THE VERDICT [1982], THE COLOR OF MONEY [1986]) and colorful supporting roles as General Leslie Groves and Huey Long in, respectively, FAT MAN AND LITTLE BOY (1989) and BLAZE (1989). Robert De Niro created an impressively varied gallery of characters (including a boxer, a priest, an eccentric media star wannabe, several gangsters including Al Capone, a Spanish con-

As the decade ended, Julia Roberts found her breakthrough role to stardom in PRETTY WOMAN. *Garry Marshall's film vividly showcased her charisma and charm.*

quistador, and the Devil) in Raging Bull (1980), True Confessions (1981), The King of Comedy (1983), Falling in Love (1984), Once upon a Time in America (1984), Brazil (1985), The Mission (1986), Angel Heart (1987), The Untouchables (1987), Midnight Run (1988), and We're No Angels (1989). In Raging Bull and The King of Comedy, De Niro continued his ongoing collaboration with director Martin Scorsese, and his overweight characters in Raging Bull and The Untouchables were extreme manifestations of his famous ability to physically transform himself in order to inhabit a role.

Dustin Hoffman and Al Pacino worked relatively infrequently during the decade. Hoffman appeared in only four features (Tootsie [1982], Ishtar [1987], Rain Man [1988], and Family Business [1989]), but two of these (Tootsie and Rain Man) solidified his status as one of the industry's most gifted actors, as did a memorable performance as Willy Loman in the Volker Schlondorff–directed television production Death of a Salesman (1985). Pacino's career slumped in the eighties, with the loathsome Cruising (1980), an unsuccessful comedy (Author, Author [1982]) and a giant box-office dud (Revolution [1985]). Scarface (1983) provided Pacino with memorably flamboyant material that he used to etch a classic gangster character, and Sea of Love (1989), a classy film noir directed by Harold Becker, signaled a revival in Pacino's career that lasted throughout the next decade. Another major star who rarely appeared in eighties cinema was Robert Redford (Brubaker [1980], The Natural [1984], Out of Africa [1985], Legal Eagles [1986]). Instead of performing with some regularity, Redford turned his attention to the causes of Western environmental conservation and the creation and promotion of his Sundance Film Institute.

In contrast with the infrequently appearing Hoffman and Pacino, Jack Nicholson and Gene Hackman were among the decade's most prolific performers. Nicholson alternated between quiet, thoughtful performances that showed the exquisite subtleties of which he is capable (The Postman Always Rings Twice [1981], Reds [1981], The Border [1982], Prizzi's Honor [1985], Heartburn [1986], Ironweed [1987]) and over-the-top, scene-chewing displays that unbalanced the films in which they appeared (The Shining [1980], Terms of Endearment [1983], The Witches of Eastwick [1987], Batman [1989]). Gene Hackman appeared in a remarkable range of material, from light comedy to physical action, but always managed to deliver performances of restraint and nuance that showed what a careful and disciplined performer he is (Superman II [1980], All Night Long [1981], Reds [1981], Eureka [1981], Under Fire [1983], Uncommon Valor [1983], Misunderstood [1984], Twice in a Lifetime [1985], Target [1985], Power [1986], Hoosiers [1986], No Way Out [1987], Superman IV [1987], Another Woman [1988], Bat 21 [1988], Full Moon in Blue Water [1988], Split Decisions [1988], Mississippi Burning [1988], The Package [1988]). Hackman had an old-Hollywood naturalness to his style that made everything he did look easy, as if no work or effort were involved. In this regard, he epitomized the virtues of the classical Hollywood screen acting tradition.

Harrison Ford was another star who showed something of this tradition in his performances, which were straightforward and unpretentious in their skill of execution. Throughout the eighties, he was closely identified with the films of George Lucas and Steven Spielberg (The Empire Strikes Back [1980], Raiders of the Lost Ark [1981], Return of the Jedi [1983], Indiana Jones and the Temple of Doom [1984], Indiana Jones and the Last Crusade [1989]), but he also gave quiet and sincere performances in Blade Runner (1982), Witness (1985), The Mosquito Coast (1986), Frantic (1988), and Working Girl (1988).

Measured in terms of pay and box-office popularity, Tom Cruise, Eddie Murphy, Sylvester Stallone, and Arnold Schwarzenegger established tremendously powerful careers. After his debut in Taps (1981), Cruise appeared in several small pictures (All the Right Moves [1983], Losin' It [1983], The Outsiders [1983]) before his breakthrough role as a brash young entrepreneur in Risky Business (1983). In most of his subsequent films, his patented image was of a cocky, self-assured, and charismatic young achiever. Except for a few misfires (Legend [1985], Cocktail [1988]), Cruise proved to be a shrewd judge of projects, and he worked with the decade's major talents on a series of high-profile films: director Martin Scorsese and Paul Newman (The Color of Money [1986]), producers Don Simpson and Jerry Bruckheimer (Top Gun [1986]), Dustin Hoffman (Rain Man [1988]), and director Oliver Stone (Born on the Fourth of July [1989]). In the latter film, Cruise gave an astonishing performance as a crippled Vietnam veteran and proved that he had a wider range than commonly supposed and which he rarely tested.

Eddie Murphy successfully parlayed his "Saturday Night Live" popularity into a high-powered film career that peaked at mid-decade with a string of hits for Paramount: 48 Hrs. (1982), Trading Places (1983), Beverly Hills Cop (1984), The Golden Child (1986) Beverly Hills Cop II (1987). A nasty strain in his humor surfaced in Eddie Murphy Raw (1987), a reaction to problems brought on by his sudden, meteoric success and his behavior in relation to that success. Murphy battled a paternity suit, and his humor was laced with animosity toward women. "I did Raw at a really bitter stage of my life. I look at it now and cringe. It's not so much that I think Raw wasn't funny, but I can't believe what I was feeling then."[36] His subsequent films (Coming to America [1988], Harlem Nights [1989]) failed to achieve the success of the earlier ones, and his decision to do a third Beverly Hills Cop film (1990) was taken as the signal of a floundering career. This was especially unfortunate in light of the racial restrictiveness of eighties cinema. After Richard Pryor, whose career went into eclipse at mid-decade, Murphy was the only major black star in Hollywood cinema and the only one around whom the industry would construct an expensive film. Pryor's pictures had included Stir Crazy (1980) and Bustin' Loose (1981), which teamed him with Gene Wilder as a memorable comic duo; Some Kind of Hero (1982); the concert film Richard Pryor Live on the Sunset Strip (1982); Superman III (1983), and Jo Jo Dancer, Your Life Is Calling (1986), an autobiographic film that Pryor also directed.

Sylvester Stallone and Arnold Schwarzenegger represented the advent in Hollywood of the international action blockbuster. They were arguably among the most popular film performers in the world, and their films were often the most cartoonish of the decade. Stallone achieved success when he played two characters, Rocky (1976, 1979, 1982, 1985, 1990) and Rambo (1982, 1985, 1988), and could not otherwise find much of a domestic audience (Nighthawks [1981], Victory [1981], Rhinestone [1984], Cobra [1986], Over the Top [1987], Tango and Cash [1989], Lock Up [1989]). His films were loud, simplistically-plotted, and redolent with violence and mayhem. The same was true for Arnold Schwarzenegger's work, although he successfully embarked upon a more substantial revision of his image and career. Beginning with very low prestige actioners (Conan the Barbarian [1982], Conan the Destroyer [1984]), in which the critics lambasted his acting, he then displayed an ironic, good-naturedly self-mocking quality in The Terminator (1984) that carried over into subsequent films (Commando [1985], Raw Deal [1986], Predator [1987], The Running Man [1987], Red Heat [1988]), where his performances winked at the audience to say that he knew what everyone else knew, namely, that the films were live-action cartoons. In contrast to Stallone's stolid seriousness, Schwarzenegger clearly had fun with his characters. This may explain why he was much more successful than Stallone at getting an audience to accept him in a range of roles (e.g., Twins [1988], Kindergarten Cop [1990]). Despite the relative joviality of Schwarzenegger's persona, however, he and Stallone established a popular cinema based on spectacles of mass slaughter, with the mayhem punctuated by cynical one-liners (e.g., Schwarzenegger in Total Recall [1990] shoots his wife in the head and quips, "Consider that a divorce"). In their work, and the work they inspired, action films became synonymous with explosions and high body counts, narrative went out the window, and popular culture became inured to ever higher doses of screen violence. This was hardly a progressive or life-affirming feature of eighties cinema.

A handful of actors established careers that would flourish into major stardom in the next decade or had already begun to do so in the later eighties: Nicolas Cage (Fast Times at Ridgemont High [1982], Rumble Fish [1983], Racing with the Moon [1984], The Cotton Club [1984], Birdy [1984], Peggy Sue Got Married [1986], Raising Arizona [1987], Moonstruck [1987], and Vampire's Kiss [1989], in which Cage earned a note in acting history for eating a live cockroach on screen); Tom Hanks (He Knows You're Alone [1981], Bachelor Party [1984], Splash [1984], The Man with One Red Shoe [1985], Every Time We Say Goodbye [1986], The Money Pit

Arnold Schwarzenegger's star-making role as The Terminator *made him an action film hero with an international following.*

The latter eighties found Nicolas Cage on the verge of a major career. Pictured here with Cher in MOONSTRUCK.

[1986], NOTHING IN COMMON [1986], DRAGNET [1987], BIG [1988], PUNCHLINE [1988], THE 'BURBS [1989], TURNER AND HOOCH [1989]); Kevin Costner (NIGHT SHIFT [1982], SILVERADO [1985], THE UNTOUCHABLES [1987], NO WAY OUT [1987], BULL DURHAM [1988], FIELD OF DREAMS [1989]); Morgan Freeman (LEAN ON ME [1989], DRIVING MISS DAISY [1989], GLORY [1989]); and Denzel Washington (CARBON COPY [1981], A SOLDIER'S STORY [1984], POWER [1986], GLORY [1989]).

As it had been throughout its history, Hollywood in the eighties remained a business critically dependent on its stars. They ensured a public following for the pictures in which they appeared and a hedge against the inherent uncertainties of making and marketing movies. The agencies had assembled under their auspices the pool of industry talent, and they became, for the majors, a force to reckon with. This oligopoly did not compete with the majors but furnished the industry's raw materials. Doing so, it exerted a continuing upward pressure on the costs of doing business. Despite the wasteful aspects of this arrangement, the uneasy partnership between the agencies and the majors defined the nature of contemporary production and gave the top industry talent a considerable authority over the production process.

6

The Filmmakers

Despite consolidation by the majors, film production in the 1980s showed a healthy diversity. In part, this was due to the ancillary markets that voraciously demanded new product. But it was due as well to the robust energy of American film culture and the inherent requirements of film production.

Studio executives aimed to rationalize their capital expenditures, and this impulse had considerable institutional support in the industry. Talent agencies took "packages" to the studios. These commanded a hefty fee, but they enabled studio executives to justify the decision to green-light a production. Market research also helped guide executive decision making, though the industry remained quite secretive about the extent to which it used such research. Film projects were concept tested before scripts were written, and scripts were subjected to focus group evaluation to predict audience responses to the hypothetical film. Based on this testing, scripts could undergo further revisions.[1] If a script found its way into production, the resulting film might be subject, before release, to another round of market research, the results of which could dictate additional editing to revise characters, rework the ending, or drop scenes that elicited big negatives. The ending of FATAL ATTRACTION (1982), for example, tested poorly with audiences, so an alternative, less subtle conclusion was shot in which the villainess died on screen in a grisly manner that test audiences found emotionally satisfying.

Millions of dollars were at stake on a major production, yet predicting what an audience wanted to see was maddeningly difficult, especially with a time lag of one or more years between the onset of a production and the release of a finished picture. For these reasons, packaging, market research, and other decision-making props assumed a major institutional presence in the industry. Yet filmmaking remained an elusive enterprise, resisting the efforts of production and marketing executives to predetermine its variables. Films still had to be *created*. They were not paint-by-number exercises, and therefore, filmmakers commanded significant freedoms to devise shots, tell stories, and present characters. The imperative for the front office to allocate resources on the basis of predictable outcomes was, and always would be, in tension with the vagaries of the creative process. The front office needed talent, literally banked on it, but also had to let it alone to do its work. This made for many unhappy marriages but also for solid successes, and it helps explain why so much diversity existed in the productions of the 1980s or in any decade. The industry was large enough that filmmakers could work at varying degrees of proximity to the major studio-distributors, with correspondingly greater or lesser pressures to be accountable to the box office.

This latter characteristic helps explain why the so-called epoch of the blockbuster was actually less influential on filmmaking across the board than is popularly supposed. The high-tech, high-gloss, high-concept style of filmmaking (e.g., RETURN OF THE JEDI [1983], TOP GUN [1986]) attracted a great deal of media coverage, with hypotheses that this style was taking over Hollywood in the eighties. Certainly there were filmmakers whose careers flourished because of their savvy commercial sense and whose films often seemed definable in these terms. These included Adrian Lyne (FLASHDANCE [1983], 9 1/2 WEEKS [1986], FATAL ATTRACTION [1987]), Ron Howard (SPLASH [1984], COCOON [1985], PARENTHOOD [1989]), and Rob Reiner (THIS IS SPINAL TAP [1984], STAND BY ME [1986], THE PRINCESS BRIDE [1987], WHEN HARRY MET SALLY [1989]). But the influence was less far-reaching than the publicity generated by these films implied. Furthermore, the industry's productions were eclectic, and it will be helpful here to show some of this variety in reference to filmmakers who do not receive extended profiles later in the chapter. Blake Edwards, for example, maintained a steady output during the period, and his films were resolutely antithetical to blockbuster style. The editing rhthms of Edwards's pictures established a slow, contemplative pacing, in which character development unfolded in all of its subtleties and in which pauses, longeurs—what comes between the dialogue—counted for so much. S.O.B. (1981) was an acidic portrait of the film industry and featured the late, great William Holden's final performance. VICTOR/VICTORIA (1982) was a sophisticated comedy about the politics of gender and sexual preference. THAT'S LIFE (1986) was a mellow, introspective portrait of an aging man's assessment of his life and family. With many of Edwards's family members in the cast, it amounted to a personal and revealing self-portrait. Bereft of his collaborator, the late actor Peter Sellers, Edwards tried to keep the Pink Panther series going, but with poor results. Without Sellers's brilliant portrait of the bumbling Inspector Clouseau, TRAIL OF THE PINK PANTHER (1982) and CURSE OF THE PINK PANTHER (1983) came off poorly. But THE MAN WHO LOVED WOMEN (1983), MICKI AND MAUDE (1984), A FINE MESS (1986), BLIND DATE (1987), SUNSET (1988), and SKIN DEEP (1989) demonstrated Edwards's gift for creating a sophisticated blend of sight gags, slapstick, and dialogue-based comedy. Furthermore, Edwards consistently shot his films in a 2.35:1 aspect ratio, making him, along with John Carpenter, one of the widescreen format's most consistent and skillful practitioners.

Many other filmmakers elaborated stylized pictures removed from the standard industry templates. Jonathan Demme, for example, made an eclectic group of films that by decade's end had moved toward the mainstream. MELVIN AND HOWARD (1980) was an incisive, low-key character piece about millionaire Howard Hughes and Melvin Dummar, an ordinary guy to whom Hughes allegedly bequeathed a fortune. STOP MAKING SENSE (1984) and SWIMMING TO CAMBODIA (1987) recorded performances by, respectively, the band Talking Heads and monologuist Spalding Gray. SOMETHING WILD (1986) changed gears unexpectedly on its audience, shifting from an endearing comedy about a straitlaced businessman (Jeff Daniels) and a kooky woman (Melanie Griffith) to graphically violent melodrama. MARRIED TO THE MOB (1988) was an attempt at mainstream comedy in a story about a gangland moll (Michelle Pfeiffer) on the run from the Mafia. Demme ended the decade at work on the singularly grim and unpleasant SILENCE OF THE LAMBS (1990), a violent look at serial killers that, for all its bleakness, enjoyed the biggest audience success of his career.

John Huston alternated formulaic efforts (VICTORY [1981], ANNIE [1982]) with more personal, unusual projects. UNDER THE VOLCANO (1984) was a finely textured

Blake Edwards's directing career flourished in the 1980s with a series of elegant, witty comedies of manners. Victor/Victoria *spoofed Sexual bigotry in a Depression-era tale of a cabaret singer (Julie Andrews) who finds popular success when she masquerades as a man.*

and atmospheric portrait of a drunken diplomat's self-destruction in Mexico on the eve of World War II. Albert Finney's magnificent performance and Huston's eye for Mexico combined to etch a memorably tragic vision of the squalid way stations visited by the diplomat on his way to a hell freely chosen. Prizzi's Honor (1985) was a droll portrait of gangland assassins (Jack Nicholson and Kathleen Turner) who fall for each other, and The Dead (1987), Huston's last film, was a luminous adaptation of the James Joyce short story about loss and aging in the context of a dinner party at turn of the century.

Philip Kaufman defined his own filmmaking territory with a pair of unusual productions. The Right Stuff (1983) could have been a standard-issue glory fest about the early days of the NASA space program, but Kaufman turned it instead into a quirky, episodic, and unexpectedly comic film whose style and rhythms remained creatively offbeat. Adapted from the Milan Kundera novel about a Czech doctor and the two women he loves, The Unbearable Lightness of Being (1988) played more like a foreign art film than a Hollywood production. With cinematography by longtime Ingmar Bergman collaborator Sven Nykvist and with a cast including Juliet Binoche, Lena Olin, and Daniel Day-Lewis, the film's leisurely three-hour pace, character-centered drama,

Albert Finney's remarkable performance as the alcoholic diplomat in UNDER THE VOLCANO *helped make this one of director John Huston's most distinguished pictures in a long and versatile career.*

and political subtext were characteristics perhaps more typical of European productions than American ones. As with THE RIGHT STUFF and the Tom Wolfe novel on which it was based, Kaufman directed a sterling adaptation of a notoriously difficult book. Continuing this string of unusual and thoughtful films, Kaufman ended the decade filming a lush, intelligent, and sensual account of writer Henry Miller's Paris sojourn in the twenties. When released, HENRY AND JUNE (1990) was the first film to carry the industry's new NC-17 rating, designating it as having nonpornographic, sexually adult content.

Directors Norman Jewison (BEST FRIENDS [1982], A SOLDIER'S STORY [1984], AGNES OF GOD [1985], MOONSTRUCK [1987], IN COUNTRY [1989]), Alan Parker (FAME [1980], PINK FLOYD—THE WALL [1982], SHOOT THE MOON [1982], BIRDY [1984], ANGEL HEART [1987], MISSISSIPPI BURNING [1988]), and Bruce Beresford (TENDER MERCIES [1983], CRIMES OF THE HEART [1986], DRIVING MISS DAISY [1989]) specialized in a diverse range of film topics and characters, including projects with clear commercial potential (MOONSTRUCK, DRIVING MISS DAISY) and those targeted for

smaller audiences (BIRDY, TENDER MERCIES). After making two science fiction classics—ALIEN (1979) and BLADE RUNNER (1982)—Ridley Scott turned his talents for
visual design to a series of different productions: LEGEND (1986), an Arthurian adventure; SOMEONE TO WATCH OVER ME (1987), a contemporary romantic thriller; and
BLACK RAIN (1989), a crime drama set in Japan and which made explicit the
Japanophobia that was latent in BLADE RUNNER. These other pictures were unbalanced
by their bravura production design and cinematography. While they were handsome to
look at, their narratives were insufficiently developed. This was especially apparent in
SOMEONE TO WATCH OVER ME, a picture with a formulaic storyline overlaid by glossy
visuals. Scott's BLADE RUNNER created an enduring template for subsequent science
fiction (more on this later), but his other films fell short of the classic status that that picture has attained.

Postulating a profound influence by blockbuster filmmaking requires that one minimize the variety of production that actually prevailed. This chapter aims to emphasize
that variety, and if the result is a less linear or teleological aesthetic history of the period,
I believe that accords well with the industry's output. By contrast with this one, however,
chapters 7 and 8 furnish a more topological account. There I cover the aesthetic and
social patterns that emerged in eighties filmmaking and the ways in which segments of
the moviegoing public responded. The aesthetic history of eighties filmmaking was
formed from the tensions created between these centripetal and centrifugal forces. In
the present chapter, I begin by considering key filmmakers in "below the line" departments. I then examine those above the line (directors and producers). "Above" and
"below the line" are terms used by the industry in factoring production costs. "Above the
line" designates those expenses incurred during production by the principal talent:
director, producer, star, writer. "Below the line" designates those costs incurred during
production in all other capacities.

Below the Line: Cinematography, Production Design, Editing, and Scoring

Filmmaking is a collaborative act, and a film's aesthetic design results from the creative
input of a range of production personnel. The director typically has the ultimate creative
authority, and other members of the production team understand that their task is to
help the director realize his or her vision for the project. In practice, though, directors
rely on the vital contributions from crew members in areas that have direct bearing on
the way a film is going to look and sound. So important are these areas that many directors maintain enduring relationships with individual cinematographers, production
designers, editors, or composers, and the artists who excell in these areas can exert
tremendous influence over the look and feel of the finished film. Furthermore, front-
rank artists in these departments are highly prized by the industry and may establish
thriving careers on an international level. In this section of the chapter, I examine
American film from the standpoint of these "below the line" production personnel, noting their important and enduring collaborative relationships with individual directors.

Demonstrating the globalization of film culture, a group of elite cinematographers
collaborated with directors in multiple national film industries, European as well as
Hollywood. Nestor Almendros shot French director Francois Truffaut's THE LAST

METRO (1980) and Eric Rohmer's PAULINE AT THE BEACH (1983) and collaborated with Hollywood directors Robert Benton, Mike Nichols, and Martin Scorsese on, respectively, PLACES IN THE HEART (1984), HEARTBURN (1986) and NEW YORK STORIES (1989). After shooting a number of Wim Wenders's films in the seventies, Robby Muller worked for Peter Bogdanovich on THEY ALL LAUGHED (1981), Jim Jarmusch (DOWN BY LAW [1986], MYSTERY TRAIN [1989]), Wenders again (PARIS, TEXAS [1984]), William Friedkin (TO LIVE AND DIE IN L.A. [1985]) and John Schlesinger (THE BELIEVERS [1987]). Sven Nykvist shot Bergman's last films in the eighties (AFTER THE REHEARSAL [1983], FANNY AND ALEXANDER [1983]) and, in Hollywood, Paul Mazursky's WILLIE AND PHIL (1980), Bob Rafelson's THE POSTMAN ALWAYS RINGS TWICE (1981), Bob Fosse's STAR 80, and Philip Kaufman's THE UNBEARABLE LIGHTNESS OF BEING (1988). Dante Spinotti maintained a prolific career shooting Italian films and such Hollywood features as CRIMES OF THE HEART (1986), MANHUNTER (1986), and BEACHES (1988). Vittorio Storaro continued his long collaboration with Bernardo Bertolucci (THE LAST EMPEROR [1987]) and his more recent partnership with Francis Coppola (ONE FROM THE HEART [1982], TUCKER: THE MAN AND HIS DREAM [1988], NEW YORK STORIES [1989]). The relationships maintained by these cinematographers demonstrated the international scope of the contemporary Hollywood industry and its ability to attract top talents from overseas.

Hollywood's own cinematographers created outstanding and memorable visual designs for the period's films. John Alonzo captured superlative and beautiful landscapes for TOM HORN (1980) and employed strikingly garish colors to suggest the vulgarity and frenzy of the Miami drug trade in SCARFACE (1983). Michael Chapman's versatility carried him from the stark black-and-white of Scorsese's RAGING BULL (1980) to Gothic horror (THE LOST BOYS [1987]), physical action (SHOOT TO KILL [1988]) and high-budget, effects-based work (GHOSTBUSTERS II [1989]). Freddie Francis excelled at period work in THE FRENCH LIEUTENANT'S WOMAN (1981) and GLORY (1989). David Watkin's camerawork was extraordinarily subtle in literate, character-centered dramas and comedy (OUT OF AFRICA [1985], MOONSTRUCK [1987]). Laszlo Kovacs had been closely identified with key counterculture and new wave films of the sixties and seventies (EASY RIDER [1969], FIVE EASY PIECES [1970]), and he worked prolifically in the eighties on an eclectic group of mainly middle-of-the-road pictures: HEART BEAT (1980), THE TOY (1982), GHOSTBUSTERS (1984), MASK (1985), LEGAL EAGLES (1986). Only FRANCES (1982), a portrait of the tortured life of Hollywood actress Frances Farmer, harked back to Kovacs's celebrated rebel pictures. Haskell Wexler sustained his unusual career mix of mainstream commercial projects (THE MAN WHO LOVED WOMEN [1983], BLAZE [1989], THREE FUGITIVES [1989]) and left-wing political films (NO NUKES [1980], LATINO [1985], MATEWAN [1987]). Zilmos Zsigmond, one of the industry's most brilliant cinematographers, had the misfortune to do some of his best work in two films that bookended the decade as examples of industry waste: HEAVEN'S GATE (1980) and THE BONFIRE OF THE VANITIES (1990).

Strong directors developed a recognizable style across their films in large part through their ongoing collaborations with individual cinematographers. John Bailey's work served the literate, dialogue-driven filmmaking of Lawrence Kasdan (THE BIG CHILL [1983], SILVERADO [1985], THE ACCIDENTAL TOURIST [1988]) as well as the more aggressively visual filmmaking of Paul Schrader (CAT PEOPLE [1982], MISHIMA [1985], LIGHT OF DAY [1987]). After shooting several films in Germany for Rainer

Werner Fassbinder, a director not noted for elaborate visual choreography, Michael Ballhaus began a close collaboration with Martin Scorsese (AFTER HOURS [1985], THE COLOR OF MONEY [1986], THE LAST TEMPTATION OF CHRIST [1988]), permitting him to execute florid camera moves and the complex lighting designs they required. Director Sidney Lumet appreciated Andrzej Bartkowiak's ability to shoot fast and employ lenses, lighting, and color for symbolically expressive effects in PRINCE OF THE CITY (1981), DEATHTRAP (1982), THE VERDICT (1982), DANIEL (1983), GARBO TALKS (1984), THE MORNING AFTER (1986), POWER (1986), and FAMILY BUSINESS (1989). Brian De Palma relied on Stephen Burum to create a flamboyant visual style for BODY DOUBLE (1984), THE UNTOUCHABLES (1987), and CASUALTIES OF WAR (1989), and Burum created memorably expressionistic images for Francis Coppola on RUMBLE FISH (1983). Ernest Dickerson's fluid camera and insistent color designs helped give Spike Lee's work (SHE'S GOTTA HAVE IT [1986], SCHOOL DAZE [1988], DO THE RIGHT THING [1989]) its memorably visual qualities in the latter part of the decade, when Lee appeared as the precursor of a new wave of black filmmakers. In the eighties, when Jonathan Demme moved up from the exploitation films he made for Roger Corman's New World International, he took cinematographer Tak Fujimoto with him to create MELVIN AND HOWARD (1980), SWING SHIFT (1983), SOMETHING WILD (1986), and MARRIED TO THE MOB (1988). Chris Menges's work for Roland Joffe gave historical tragedy physical presence and emotional resonance in THE KILLING FIELDS (1984) and THE MISSION (1986). In more historically oriented productions, Robert Richardson's partnership with Oliver Stone yielded some of the decade's political classics: SALVADOR (1986), PLATOON (1986), WALL STREET (1987), TALK RADIO (1988), and BORN ON THE FOURTH OF JULY (1989).

Bruce Surtees was essential to Clint Eastwood's filmmaking throughout the decade, with FIREFOX (1982), HONKY TONK MAN (1982), SUDDEN IMPACT (1983), TIGHTROPE (1984), and PALE RIDER (1985). Outside his Eastwood films, Surtees shot two of the decade's most popular pictures, RISKY BUSINESS (1983) and BEVERLY HILLS COP (1984). Blake Edwards relied on Harry Stradling for much of his eighties widescreen work: S.O.B. (1981), MICKI AND MAUDE (1984), A FINE MESS (1986),and BLIND DATE (1987). In his collaborations with John Carpenter, Dean Cundey did some of the decade's best widescreen filming, on ESCAPE FROM NEW YORK (1981), THE FOG (1981), THE THING (1982), and BIG TROUBLE IN LITTLE CHINA (1986), and his subsequent association with Steven Spielberg and Robert Zemeckis (BACK TO THE FUTURE [1985], WHO FRAMED ROGER RABBIT [1988], BACK TO THE FUTURE PARTS II AND III [1989, 1990]) lifted him out of low-budget horror and into the industry's expensive, state-of-the-art productions. On those films that he directed, Spielberg maintained a long relationship with Allen Daviau (E.T. [1982], TWILIGHT ZONE: THE MOVIE (1983), THE COLOR PURPLE [1985], EMPIRE OF THE SUN [1987]) and Douglas Slocombe (RAIDERS OF THE LOST ARK [1981], INDIANA JONES AND THE TEMPLE OF DOOM [1984], INDIANA JONES AND THE LAST CRUSADE [1989]).

Woody Allen's filmmaking had always been extremely literate, with its foundation in solid screenplays penned by Allen. When he began to collaborate with cinematographers renowned for their magisterial control of light, however, his work became truly cinematic, with visual designs as fully articulated as the work's verbal dimensions had been. Allen learned about light from three extraordinary collaborators: Gordon Willis (STARDUST MEMORIES [1980], A MIDSUMMER NIGHT'S SEX COMEDY [1982], BROADWAY DANNY ROSE [1983], ZELIG [1983], THE PURPLE ROSE OF CAIRO

[1985]); Carlo Di Palma (HANNAH AND HER SISTERS [1986], RADIO DAYS [1987], SEPTEMBER [1987]); and Sven Nykvist (ANOTHER WOMAN [1988], CRIMES AND MISDEMEANORS [1989]).

Several prominent directors of the nineties first established careers as cinematographers in the eighties. Barry Sonnenfeld, director of THE ADDAMS FAMILY (1991) and MEN IN BLACK (1997), worked closely as cinematographer for Joel and Ethan Coen (BLOOD SIMPLE [1984], RAISING ARIZONA [1987], MILLER'S CROSSING [1990]) and Rob Reiner (WHEN HARRY MET SALLY [1989], MISERY [1990]). The action-oriented director of SPEED (1994) and TWISTER (1996) Jan De Bont first worked as a cinematographer with surprising versatility: THE JEWEL OF THE NILE (1985), JUMPIN' JACK FLASH (1986), RUTHLESS PEOPLE (1986), DIE HARD (1988), BERT RIGBY, YOU'RE A FOOL (1989), and BLACK RAIN (1989).

The production designer is a key collaborator with the director and cinematographer because the work in these areas intersects and overlaps. The colors employed on a film's sets, for example, will have consequences for how those sets are lit and shot, and decisions about camera placement will affect how a set should be dressed. Production design refers to the visual organization of a film's physical environments, whether they be real locations or artificial creations on a sound stage. Much filmmaking in the eighties afforded production designers elaborate opportunities to create intricate and expansive visions of past and future in the disparate modes of fantasy and historical realism. Production design in these films was often the dominant element of *mise-en-scène*, and the designers who excelled at conjuring these visions were responsible for some of the decade's memorable and enduring imagery. Legendary production designer Ken Adam (DR. STRANGELOVE [1964], GOLDFINGER [1964], BARRY LYNDON [1975]) provided imaginatively stylized sets for one of the decade's most unusual films, PENNIES FROM HEAVEN (1981), contrasting the bleakness of Depression-era America with the cheery opulence of that period's Hollywood musicals. Dante Ferretti, who constructed elaborate fantasies for Pier Paolo Pasolini (THE DECAMERON [1971]) and Federico Fellini (ORCHESTRA REHEARSAL [1979]), designed for Terry Gilliam's THE ADVENTURES OF BARON MUNCHAUSEN (1989) a pseudo-historical magic kingdom that contained some of the period's most elaborate and outlandish sets in a fantastical portrait of nineteenth-century Germany. Ferdinando Scarfiotti's memorable work for Bernardo Bertolucci in the seventies (THE CONFORMIST [1971], LAST TANGO IN PARIS [1973]) gave him the international prominence that led to Hollywood productions and some of the decade's most stylized design in FLASH GORDON (1980), CAT PEOPLE (1982), and, again for Bertolucci, THE LAST EMPEROR (1987). Richard Sylbert's brilliant work on CHINATOWN (1974) was among the best of that decade, and while no comparable classic beckoned him in the eighties, he nevertheless did very strong work establishing historical periods on REDS (1981), FRANCES (1982), and THE COTTON CLUB (1984). Patrizia von Brandenstein also excelled at period design, with an emphasis on opulence, in RAGTIME (1981), AMADEUS (1984), and THE UNTOUCHABLES (1987), though her work also included more austere and gritty projects (SILKWOOD [1983], NO MERCY [1987]). Bo Welch's elaborate fantasy showpieces were integral to the *mise-en-scène* of THE LOST BOYS (1987), BEETLEJUICE (1988), and GHOSTBUSTERS II (1989), and, though he did not practice this as often, he also excelled at subdued naturalism (THE ACCIDENTAL TOURIST [1988]). Anton Furst's Gotham City—dark, dank, oppressive—established an unforgettable *mise-en-scène* for BATMAN (1989) and dominated that picture's visual design. The most influential production design of the eighties, however, was

The period settings of AMADEUS *were sumptuously visualized by Patrizia Von Brandenstein's Academy Award–winning designs.*

Lawrence G. Paull's work on the science fiction classic BLADE RUNNER (1982), offering a ghetto environment of crumbling buildings and urban squalor coexisting with architectural opulence and high-tech modes of transport. It established a template of the futurist megalopolis that endured on screen for the next fifteen years, until director Luc Besson, cinematographer Thierry Arbogas, and production designer Dan Weil on THE FIFTH ELEMENT (1997) felt compelled to break with it and offer an antithetical vision.

    As they did with cinematographers, many prominent directors maintained continuing collaborations with production designers. Dean Tavoularis's brilliant work was essential for Francis Coppola's efforts to break with realism and substitute stage-bound expressionism on HAMMETT (1982, Coppola producing), ONE FROM THE HEART (1982), and RUMBLE FISH (1983). Tavoularis's other Coppola collaborations were more subdued and included THE OUTSIDERS (1983), PEGGY SUE GOT MARRIED (1986), GARDENS OF STONE (1987), TUCKER (1988) and NEW YORK STORIES. Steven Spielberg and George Lucas found Norman Reynolds's affectionately retro designs indispensible for THE EMPIRE STRIKES BACK (1980), RAIDERS OF THE LOST ARK (1981), RETURN OF THE JEDI (1983), and EMPIRE OF THE SUN (1987). Mel Bourne, who provided

Woody Allen with a versatile array of locales for the disparate STARDUST MEMORIES, A MIDSUMMER NIGHT'S SEX COMEDY, BROADWAY DANNY ROSE, and ZELIG, was succeeded by Stuart Wurtzel (THE PURPLE ROSE OF CAIRO, HANNAH AND HER SISTERS) and Santo Loquasto (RADIO DAYS, ANOTHER WOMAN, SEPTEMBER, CRIMES AND MISDEMEANORS, NEW YORK STORIES). Pato Guzman regularly collaborated with Paul Mazursky, producing designs for WILLIE AND PHIL (1980), TEMPEST (1982), MOSCOW ON THE HUDSON (1984), DOWN AND OUT IN BEVERLY HILLS (1986), and MOON OVER PARADOR (1988). Rodger Maus was Blake Edwards's preferred designer (S.O.B., VICTOR/VICTORIA, THE MAN WHO LOVED WOMEN, MICKI AND MAUDE, A FINE MESS, BLIND DATE, SUNSET). Sidney Lumet relied on Philip Rosenberg for DANIEL, GARBO TALKS, RUNNING ON EMPTY, and FAMILY BUSINESS. Bruno Rubeo made politics concrete in the memorable locales and sets he designed for Oliver Stone on SALVADOR, PLATOON, TALK RADIO, and BORN ON THE FOURTH OF JULY. In the seventies, Polly Platt regularly collaborated with Peter Bogdanovich, and his relative inactivity in the eighties led her to a more diverse range of productions: THE MAN WITH TWO BRAINS (1983), TERMS OF ENDEARMENT (1983), and THE WITCHES OF EASTWICK (1987).

Bill Kenney's work for Sylvester Stallone (RAMBO [1985], ROCKY IV [1985], RAMBO III [1988]) established him as a premier visual stylist for action blockbusters, while his designs for Lawrence Kasdan on BODY HEAT conveyed that film's intricate thematic motifs with much subtlety. Especially memorable was the design Kenny created for Matty's "lair," a balcony festooned with wind chimes that audibly conveyed the story's undercurrents of desire and menace. Wynn Thomas's transformation of a Brooklyn city block (strategically without trees that would offer shade) and selective application of

Anton Furst created a heavy, dark and oppressive Gotham City in BATMAN, *a design that predominated in the picture's* mise-en-scène.

color (red) enabled Spike Lee to convey the heat of oppressive weather and smoldering racial tension so palpably in Do the Right Thing (1989).

The decade also saw outstanding and significant work by the industry's film editors. Like production design, editing is a supremely important production component about which the general moviegoing public knows little. Editors are hardly household names in the way that some directors are, yet it is the editor's work that gives rhythm and pace to the film, provides narrative structure, and shapes and crafts many aspects of an actor's performance. The singular achievements of the decade's filmmaking were often a function of the editor's work. Nino Baragli surpassed even his customary brilliance with his editing of Sergio Leone's Once upon a Time in America (1984), creating a kaleidoscopic narrative that juggled multiple time frames with astonishingly fluid transitions. John Bloom surmounted the daunting challenge of telling a story backward in Betrayal (1983), starting with the ending and working toward the beginning, and he made the shots work using this peculiar time scheme. Bloom also provided one of the decade's best examples of editing for tight narrative effect in Under Fire (1983), an extremely well cut film. Thelma Schoonmaker, Scorsese's regular editor, provided edgy rhythms and lightning fast transitions in Raging Bull, The King of Comedy, After Hours, The Color of Money, and The Last Temptation of Christ.

Dede Allen had given Arthur Penn's work (Bonnie and Clyde [1967], Night Moves [1975]) its peculiarly off-kilter rhythms. While she found no comparable projects for her unusually angled shot transitions in the eighties, her work on Reds (1981) and The Milagro Beanfield War (1988) crisply organized each project's abundant wealth of source material. Another brilliant editor of late-sixties American cinema, Lou Lombardo (who edited The Wild Bunch [1969] to seminal effect) worked sporadically in the eighties and mainly on low-key films (Moonstruck, In Country [1989]) where his editing choices showed the intelligence and subtlety that rarely wins Oscars. The wonderful comic effectiveness and timing of Moonstruck, for example, depends as much on Lombardo's editing as on John Patrick Shanley's script or the performances by Cher, Nicolas Cage, and the rest of the cast. Legendary editor Anne V. Coates (Lawrence of Arabia [1962]) worked in the eighties with no directors the stature of David Lean, but her editing (with Antony Gibbs and Stanley Warnow) held Ragtime (1981) together amid its plethora of characters and subplots and produced a workable film from a difficult-to-adapt novel. Ray Lovejoy cut Stanley Kubrick's 2001: A Space Odyssey (1968), and he worked again with Kubrick on The Shining and supplied that picture with an entirely different—tenser, more foreboding—texture than the stately science fiction classic had possessed. Lovejoy also proved adept at editing for blockbuster effect. His cutting in Aliens sustained that sequel's narrative momentum with a speed and tension that its predecessor did not have, and his editing on Batman finessed that film's gaping narrative problems by simply rushing past them. For Walter Murch (whose classic work in the seventies included The Conversation and Apocalypse Now and in the nineties The English Patient), the eighties were a relatively quiescent decade as film editor: Disneyland's "Captain Eo" (1986), and The Unbearable Lightness of Being (1988). After cutting in the seventies The Godfather, Parts I and II and The Deer Hunter, Peter Zinner, too, worked on less prominent projects in the eighties, the most notable being An Officer and a Gentleman (1982).

Character-centered and dialogue-based filmmakers needed sensitive editors to find the dramatic nuances in the material, the appropriate take of an actor's performance, and the right edit points to shape the subtleties of a scene. Barry Levinson relied on Stu Linder to give DINER (1982), THE NATURAL (1984), TIN MEN (1987), and RAIN MAN (1988) the careful shaping that the material demanded, and Lawrence Kasdan relied on Carol Littleton for BODY HEAT (1981), THE BIG CHILL (1983), SILVERADO (1985), and THE ACCIDENTAL TOURIST (1988). Clint Eastwood's improvisatory approach to film-making, wherein he allowed the actors to find their characters and behavior on the set while shooting, found its complement in the stately, unhurried pacing supplied by Joel Cox's editing (Cox succeeding Ferris Webster for Eastwood) on BRONCO BILLY (1980), SUDDEN IMPACT (1983), TIGHTROPE (1984), PALE RIDER (1985), HEARTBREAK RIDGE (1986), BIRD (1988), and PINK CADILLAC (1989). The pacing of the Cox-Eastwood films was at striking variance from the accelerating speed of much filmic storytelling in the eighties, especially in action films. Their eighties work anticipates and collectively points toward their supreme achievement in "real time" editing, THE BRIDGES OF MADISON COUNTY (1995).

The editor's contribution to a director's work is evident in other enduring partnerships that spanned the decade. Woody Allen and Francis Coppola's projects were remarkably eclectic in style and subject matter, yet they retained regular editors despite the changing aesthetic nature of their productions. Susan E. Morse edited every Allen film of the eighties, regardless of its subject matter or visual design, and as we have seen, Allen worked with a variety of cinematographers and production designers in those years. His insistent use of Morse demonstrates the essential nature of her collaboration. Barry Malkin cut Coppola's RUMBLE FISH, THE COTTON CLUB, PEGGY SUE GOT MARRIED, and GARDENS OF STONE as well as the Coppola-produced HAMMET. He also cut Arthur Penn's FOUR FRIENDS (1981), and the difference an editor makes on a director's films is evident by comparing his more linear approach to Dede Allen's fractured and off-center cutting. Brian De Palma's work was more consistent stylistically than Allen's or Coppola's, and he relied on Bill Pankow for BODY DOUBLE (1984), THE UNTOUCHABLES (1987), and CASUALTIES OF WAR (1989). Sydney Pollack used Fredric and William Steinkamp on all of his eighties work (TOOTSIE [1982], OUT OF AFRICA [1985], HAVANA [1990]). In its comic sophistication and narrative elegance, Blake Edwards's work exemplified the merits of classical Hollywood filmmaking, and illustrative of this, he relied on Ralph E. Winters, whose editing credits go back to MR. AND MRS. NORTH (1941) and GASLIGHT (1944) and who cut, for Edwards, S.O.B., VICTOR/VICTORIA, CURSE OF THE PINK PANTHER, THE MAN WHO LOVED WOMEN, and MICKI AND MAUDE.

Action film storytelling accelerated at a lightning pace during the decade, with edit points barely separated by a handful of frames. Mark Goldblatt's ferocious work on THE TERMINATOR (1984) was the most impressive example of editing for sheer narrative momentum since Carl Pingitore and Don Siegel's work on DIRTY HARRY (1971). Goldblatt also worked on the fast-moving COMMANDO (1985), RAMBO (1985) and JUMPIN' JACK FLASH (1986). Chris Lebenzon and Billy Webber's editing of TOP GUN, Paul Hirsch's editing of THE EMPIRE STRIKES BACK (1980), and Michael Kahn's work on RAIDERS OF THE LOST ARK (1981) and INDIANA JONES AND THE TEMPLE OF DOOM (1984) raised the threshold for narrative pacing and, through their influence, helped many of the period's most popular films increasingly resemble roller-coaster rides.

Unlike other below-the-line production components, film scoring faced a threat to its very existence in the eighties. The majors' desire to exploit ancillary markets placed increasing pressure on filmmakers to use pop music (either by currently popular artists or the recycled hits of yesterday) in place of an original score. Most film composers regarded the pop solution as a quick and dirty way of getting a soundtrack and artistically inferior to an original score, whose purpose, unlike the pop song, is to serve the film. To the extent that the pop song strategy prevailed, the art of original scoring languished, and many films were released whose soundtracks were clearly just a means of selling records. On the other hand, however, the eighties produced fine original film scores, and enough productions avoided pop music to enable major composers to continue their careers by producing work of distinction.

John Barry, for example, had famously written the brassy and jazz-inflected scores for the James Bond films in the sixties. In the eighties he produced lushly romantic compositions for BODY HEAT, OUT OF AFRICA, and DANCES WITH WOLVES (1990). Barry's ability on these films to write soaring music for full symphony orchestra resulted from John Williams's demonstration in the Spielberg-Lucas films (RAIDERS OF THE LOST ARK, STAR WARS, etc.) of the symphony as a vital scoring resource. In the sixties and early seventies, the symphonic score had fallen out of favor, replaced by smaller groups of musicians playing rock-based music. Williams brought the symphonic score back into prominence with his stirring music for the blockbusters and enabled others to work in this mode (e.g., Randy Newman's THE NATURAL [1984]). James Horner's soaring GLORY, replete with the Harlem Boys' Choir, was one of the decade's outstanding symphonic compositions. In this expansive mode, Maurice Jarre's score for A PASSAGE TO INDIA concluded his collaborations (LAWRENCE OF ARABIA, RYAN'S DAUGHTER [1970]) with director David Lean.

With his remarkable versatility, Jerry Goldsmith worked inside and outside of this tradition as the needs of a production warranted. His scores for the RAMBO series (1982, 1985, 1988) were full-blooded orchestral works, while his work on GREMLINS (1984) showed his ability to write memorable themes that provided a perfect musical embodiment for a film's emotional coloration. His score for UNDER FIRE aimed to musically characterize regional revolution in Central America by using indigenous instrumentation (pan flutes), and he managed to do this while accommodating room for impressive guitar solos by Pat Metheny. Like Goldsmith, Henry Mancini was prolific and adept at working in a variety of musical modes. Mancini's witty scoring was a superb accompaniment to Blake Edwards's comedies, and together they represented one of American cinema's most important director-composer teams. Mancini scored Edwards's S.O.B., VICTOR/VICTORIA, TRAIL OF THE PINK PANTHER, THE MAN WHO LOVED WOMEN, THAT'S LIFE, A FINE MESS, BLIND DATE, and SUNSET. Mancini was equally adept at scoring drama, and his music for Edwards' earlier "Peter Gunn" television series and feature DAYS OF WINE AND ROSES (1962) added classic and enduring musical themes to the repertoire. In 1989, Edwards returned to television with a new Peter Gunn movie and another Mancini collaboration in a superb dramatic score.

Italian composers Giorgio Moroder and Ennio Morricone wrote striking scores using novel instrumentation, relatively simple themes subject to intensive repetition, and the integration of electronics with the conventional symphony. Moroder's insistent disco rhythms gave an unmistakably pop sound to the scores for AMERICAN GIGOLO (1980), CAT PEOPLE (1982), FLASHDANCE (1983), SCARFACE (1983), and TOP GUN (1986), and his synth-pop sound was unmistakable on THIEF OF HEARTS (1984), for which he was the soundtrack producer, and the 1984 restoration of METROPOLIS (1926), which he produced and coscored. Ennio Morricone, most famous for his scores for Sergio Leone's spaghetti Westerns, was one of the most prolific film composers in the business. In the eighties, he wrote music for over sixty films. This quantity of output, however, accompanied great variations in quality, with Morricone often seeming to plagiarize himself by recycling his own material (e.g., IN THE LINE OF FIRE [1993] and THE UNTOUCHABLES [1987]). Morricone worked as an international composer in the eighties, and his scores for Hollywood pictures accompanied a great deal of work in the Italian cinema. His best Hollywood scores left an indelible imprint on the films and in the viewer's mind. By turns lyrical and violent, accentuating rarely employed instruments like pan flutes or harmonica, Morricone's music fused with the images and became an organic part of the experience of ONCE UPON A TIME IN AMERICA (1984), THE MISSION (1986), THE UNTOUCHABLES (1987), and CASUALTIES OF WAR (1989). One casualty for Morricone in the eighties was his score for THE THING (1982). Director John Carpenter discarded much of Morricone's composition and retained those passages that were stylistically consistent with the scores Carpenter had himself written for his other films.

Bill Conti had secured his career by scoring the ROCKY series, beginning in the latter seventies, and writing the popular Rocky theme ("Gonna Fly Now"). With John Williams's themes from the RAIDERS and STAR WARS series, this was one of the decade's best-known musical leitmotifs. Conti specialized in stirring, rousing scores (others included VICTORY [1981] and THE RIGHT STUFF [1983]), and he broadened his association with ROCKY director John Avildson by scoring Avildson's KARATE KID series (1984, 1986, 1989).

Prominent scoring newcomers in the eighties included Angelo Badalamenti, whose haunting and eerie music David Lynch used to great effect in BLUE VELVET (1986), WILD AT HEART (1990) and, on television, "Twin Peaks" (1990). Scoring his first films for release in 1979, James Horner emerged as a major talent in the eighties, with full bodied, epic scores for STAR TREK II: THE WRATH OF KHAN (1982) and STAR TREK III: THE SEARCH FOR SPOCK (1984). But along with GLORY, it was FIELD OF DREAMS (1989) that represented his finest work of the decade. Horner's FIELD OF DREAMS score was an intriguing combination of symphony orchestra and electronic instrumentation, using the former to capture the nostalgic romance of baseball and the latter to emblemize the supernatural aspects of the story. Mark Isham's scores for Alan Rudolph's films (TROUBLE IN MIND [1985], MADE IN HEAVEN [1987], THE MODERNS [1988]) relied on unusual instrumentation and sonic effects, with the TROUBLE IN MIND score a particular standout with its noirish mix of solo trumpet, blues, and vocal cries. Lennie Neihaus worked without bombast, in a self-effacing way, with his music for Clint Eastwood on CITY HEAT [1984, Richard Benjamin, director], TIGHTROPE [1984, Richard Tuggle, director], PALE RIDER [1985], HEARTBREAK RIDGE (1986) and BIRD (1988). Although he did some scoring in the seventies, Basil Poledouris emerged in the eighties as a major composer, producing the best Western movie score of the last thirty years for the television miniseries "Lonesome Dove" (1989). It was an epic score, with big-screen sweep and grandeur, and it stands with Victor Young's SHANE (1953) and Elmer Bernstein's THE MAGNIFICENT SEVEN (1960) as a classic in the genre. Other significant composers who established their careers in the eighties were Howard Shore (PLACES IN THE HEART [1984], AFTER HOURS [1985], THE FLY [1986], BIG [1988]) and Alan Silvestri (BACK TO THE FUTURE [1985], WHO FRAMED ROGER RABBIT [1988], BACK TO THE

FUTURE, PART II [1989], THE ABYSS [1989]). The most important new film composer in the eighties, however, was Danny Elfman, whose unique orchestrations and intricate rhythms made incalculable contributions to Tim Burton's PEE-WEE'S BIG ADVENTURE (1985), BEETLEJUICE (1988), and BATMAN (1989). Elfman quickly established a unique musical voice and a superb ability to catch the action on screen, essential attributes that the great film composers have possessed.

Above the Line

To create an organizational schema, I have grouped the decade's major directors in terms of those who had an exemplary box-office track record (the hit makers: Steven Spielberg, George Lucas, Don Simpson and Jerry Bruckheimer, John Hughes, John Landis, Jon Peters and Peter Guber, Robert Zemeckis); those whose careers foundered (the embattled auteurs: Robert Altman, Peter Bogdanovich, John Carpenter, Francis Ford Coppola, Brian De Palma, Arthur Penn, Martin Scorsese); those who worked steadily and solidly throughout the decade (the working directors: Woody Allen, Clint Eastwod, Sidney Lumet, Sydney Pollack); those who represented a new constituency and who added their voices to American film (the newcomers: women directors and producers, Tim Burton, James Cameron, Joe Dante, Lawrence Kasdan, Barry Levinson, Spike Lee, Oliver Stone); and those who worked outside the major channels of production and distribution (the independents and outsiders: Joel and Ethan Coen, Jim Jarmusch, David Lynch, Alan Rudolph, John Sayles, Paul Schrader). I have sequenced the filmmakers alphabetically in each section, except for the first one which deals with the hit makers. Because of the seminal status of Steven Spielberg, George Lucas, and producers Don Simpson and Jerry Bruckheimer, it is appropriate to begin that section with their careers.

THE HIT-MAKERS

Year after year, the industry's big blockbuster films were its most visible products, garnering the greatest media attention and public interest. The success of the blockbusters points to a related phenomenon of the period, namely, the ascendency of the producer as both creative auteur and as custodian of studio capital. Following the HEAVEN'S GATE disaster, with its lesson about the perils of letting an ambitious director work unsupervised, studio supervision of film production tightened, and a new era of powerful producers commenced. This was a concomitant of blockbuster filmmaking and helped provide an extra index of security for the majors. Potential blockbusters would not be entrusted to directors working without tight supervision. Most of the period's reliable hit makers functioned as powerful producers, if not also as directors.

STEVEN SPIELBERG   Measured strictly by box office, Steven Spielberg was easily, and clearly, the decade's most important filmmaker. His career skyrocketed during this period and arguably was informed by the period's zeitgeist. But to measure Spielberg's filmmaking accomplishments only by the spectacular box-office returns they generated is to misjudge his career and his talent. The discontinuity between academic and high-brow cultural criticism and the public is nowhere more apparent than in the critical reception accorded Spielberg and George Lucas. These filmmakers achieved an extra-ordinary rapport with the popular audience, yet the critical merit of their filmmaking has remained controversial. It is true that Spielberg's popular films evoke an uncomplicated range of emotions. Furthermore, in the eighties Spielberg had not yet become intimate in his art with the evil and moral darkness that he depicted so powerfully in SCHINDLER'S LIST (1993) in the character of the Nazi commandant Amon Goeth (Ralph Fiennes). But serious critics failed to give him his due. One finds in the work of Spielberg and Lucas some decidedly old-Hollywood virtues—a delight in economical, no-nonsense storytelling, an embrace of sentiment, an emotional immediacy unaccom-panied by irony, and a love for the medium that is enthusiastic and that lacks tortured, postmodern self-consciousness. Given such qualities, it is no wonder the public embraced these filmmakers.

Spielberg's first picture of the decade, RAIDERS OF THE LOST ARK (1981), followed his seventies hits JAWS (1975) and CLOSE ENCOUNTERS OF THE THIRD KIND (1977) and seemed to certify him as a blockbuster filmmaker par excellance. But RAIDERS is more ambitious and accomplished than the appellation of "blockbuster" conveys. Based on a story by George Lucas (who also co-produced), it shows its makers' deep love for the medium, in particular the adventure stories and cliffhanger serials they recalled from their youth (and it has a basis in pulp novels as well—Indiana Jones is a Doc Savage-like character).[2] The opening act is an amazing demonstration of storytelling skill, bringing the viewer in at the climactic end of one movie, which concludes before the main narrative of RAIDERS will begin. Jones's efforts to capture a valuable idol from a booby-trapped cave generate an escalating series of climaxes and hair breadth escapes

Indiana Jones (Harrison Ford) on the run in the exciting prelude of RAIDERS OF THE LOST ARK.

that provide a splendid filmic conclusion—except that RAIDERS is only just beginning. The challenge Spielberg (and Lucas) set themselves here demonstrates their skill. By opening the film in this adrenaline-charged manner, they set a pace and level of thrill that they had to continually top, and they do. This is as self-conscious an act of narration and filmmaking as one will find (and which culminates in an overt homage to CITIZEN KANE [1941] at the end), yet the film's popularity has tended to obscure the filmmaking work and the narrative ambitions that are involved.

Spielberg followed RAIDERS with two more popular hits: E.T.: THE EXTRA-TERRESTRIAL (1983) and INDIANA JONES AND THE TEMPLE OF DOOM (1984). Once again, to the dismay of serious film critics, the popular audience made a clear statement about the importance of feeling and emotion in cinema and the enthusiastic narrative skill that Spielberg brought to his work. E.T. , in particular, touched viewers in a powerful manner that few filmmakers ever achieve in their work. Many critics distrusted the emotional response that Spielberg's films evoked from viewers, and this disconnect from the popular audience soon became apparent, as well, among Spielberg's filmmaking peers. Though his films (RAIDERS, E.T., THE COLOR PURPLE) were nominated for best picture Oscars, none of them won this award, nor did Spielberg receive a best director Oscar during the decade. Moreover, he failed even to be nominated for THE COLOR PURPLE. The Motion Picture Academy of Arts and Sciences seemed to be sending a clear message that a schism prevailed between box-office success (at the extraordinary level that Spielberg's pictures enjoyed) and artistic success.

In 1986, the Academy did bestow an honor upon Spielberg, awarding him the Irving G. Thalberg Memorial Award. In his acceptance speech, Spielberg lamented that much contemporary film was poorly written and urged filmmakers to create a more literate cinema, in which ideas and ennobling themes could be explored. These remarks surprised many listeners, who did not associate Spielberg with an especially literate style of filmmaking. But he now endeavored (and, indeed, had already started with 1985's THE COLOR PURPLE) to honor this principle. In respect of this, his work in the eighties is bifurcated. The first half of the decade finds Spielberg working in a populist mode, fashioning films that connect with the greatest possible number of viewers (RAIDERS, E.T., INDIANA JONES AND THE TEMPLE OF DOOM, and a segment of TWILIGHT ZONE: THE MOVIE [1983]). By contrast, most of his features in the second half of the decade are films without clear blockbuster potential: THE COLOR PURPLE, EMPIRE OF THE SUN (1987), ALWAYS (1989). Only INDIANA JONES AND THE LAST CRUSADE (1989) finds Spielberg back in a popcorn-movie mode. Based on the novel by Alice Walker, THE COLOR PURPLE relates a story about the life of a poor black woman (played by Whoopi Goldberg in her film debut) who endures years of abuse from her husband before she can assert her independence. EMPIRE OF THE SUN was another ambitious literary adaptation, based on J. G. Ballard's novel about a young British boy separated from his parents in Shanghai when the Japanese invade China in the prelude to World War II. ALWAYS was a remake of a popular World War II movie about a pilot, killed in a crash, who returns to offer spiritual shelter and protection to the woman he loves. Though each of these films has evident failings, it was clear that Spielberg was an ambitious filmmaker who aspired to new challenges and that he was seeking to expand his range.

Of greatest significance is a point that was hard to see at the time—that World War II had a special resonance for Spielberg and that he would become one of its most significant cinematic chroniclers. The Indiana Jones films are set in and around that period, with Nazis as Jones's most dangerous antagonists. The storyline of THE COLOR PURPLE runs into the late thirties, and servicemen in uniform appear as extras in the background of one scene. EMPIRE OF THE SUN deals directly with the war, and ALWAYS resituates what was originally a wartime narrative (the original picture, A GUY NAMED JOE, was released in 1943) into more contemporary terms. These pictures in the latter eighties enabled Spielberg, with some awkwardness, to segue to a more adult-themed filmmaking and to make his initial forays into the historical period, and the moral issues, that he would take up with much greater assurance and accomplishment in SCHINDLER'S LIST (1993) and SAVING PRIVATE RYAN (1998). Thus, to dismiss Spielberg as a popcorn-movie maker is doubly wrong. It minimizes the real accomplishments of his hit movies, and it overlooks the new directions in which he took his filmmaking in the latter half of the decade.

Spielberg's talent was evident as well in the impassioned pace with which he worked. He completed seven features during the decade—an extraordinary level of output—and he left his mark as director or producer on a huge outpouring of film and television programming. As a producer of work by other filmmakers, he gave important career boosts to directors Lawrence Kasdan, Joe Dante, and Robert Zemeckis. Like the powerful producers of classical Hollywood, such as Arthur Freed, Spielberg left his mark on the style of the pictures he produced. Like his own most popular work as director, these tended to involve special effects and to evoke lighthearted, adolescent adventure. His work as producer included USED CARS (1980), CONTINENTAL DIVIDE (1981), POLTERGEIST (1982), TWILIGHT ZONE: THE MOVIE (1983), GREMLINS (1984), YOUNG SHERLOCK HOLMES (1985), THE GOONIES (1985), BACK TO THE FUTURE (1985), "Amazing Stories" (1985, TV series), AN AMERICAN TAIL (1986), THE MONEY PIT (1986), °BATTERIES NOT INCLUDED (1987), INNERSPACE (1987), THE LAND BEFORE TIME (1988),

Whoopi Goldberg as Celie in THE COLOR PURPLE, *Spielberg's initial foray into adult-themed filmmaking.*

WHO FRAMED ROGER RABBIT (1988), DAD (1989), and BACK TO THE FUTURE, PART II (1989).

Spielberg's work was a major influence on the blockbuster turn in contemporary cinema, but his ambitions as a filmmaker clearly transcended this category of production. The 1980s were the transitional decade for him, taking his work from the seminal popularity of pictures like E.T. , and his seventies hits, and toward the ambitious and complex issues of human evil and moral redemption that he regularly examined in the nineties (SCHINDLER'S LIST, AMISTAD (1997), SAVING PRIVATE RYAN).

GEORGE LUCAS   The STAR WARS films of George Lucas are seminal works of modern cinema, exerting a profound influence on popular culture, and they are among the most ambitiously conceived epics of film narrative ever made. The second and third installments of the series (which are episodes five and six in the narrative cycle)— THE EMPIRE STRIKES BACK (1980) and RETURN OF THE JEDI (1983)—climaxed and brought to conclusion the narrative elements that had been broached in the mid-seventies with STAR WARS. (Accentuating the scope of these ambitions, Lucas launched in the late nineties an additional three films, which form the "back story" to the conflict between the Empire and the rebel forces.) The hugeness of this project and the expanse and wealth of story information that Lucas gave to his mythopoeic world were unprecedented in contemporary cinema. By beginning his saga in the middle of the story (STAR WARS is episode four), Lucas abruptly plunged his viewers into a well-defined mythic universe, and each subsequent film elaborated upon the intricate network of characters and locations that Lucas was fashioning, installment by installment. By the end of RETURN OF THE JEDI, this imaginative universe contained a galaxy of uniquely differentiated and vividly rendered planets where critical episodes of the storyline occur. THE EMPIRE STRIKES BACK opens on the ice world of Hoth and a deadly clash between the Empire and the rebel forces, which have gone into hiding after launching (from the planet of Yavin 4) their assault on the first Death Star in STAR WARS. The heroes, Luke, Han, and Princess Leia, escape the battle, with Luke journeying to the jungle world of Dagobah, where he encounters the Zen-like but diminutive Yoda. Han and Leia seek refuge on Bespin in the Cloud City run by Lando Calrissian. Darth Vader, though, sets a trap, freeze-dries Han, and sends him to Tatooine, the desert world where Luke grew up and where the toadlike gangster Jabba the Hut has his headquarters. The climax of the Empire-rebel struggle occurs in RETURN OF THE JEDI on Endor, a forest planet that is home to the Ewok, a race of furry, cute, but fierce Rebel allies. Filling out this remarkably detailed gallery of places and characters are bounty hunters (Boba Fett, Greedo), monsters (the sand-dwelling Sarlacc), and Wild West cantinas (Mos Eisley).

Much of the series' popular appeal certainly lies in the elaborateness of its conception and the vivid and engaging details with which Lucas filled it out. But this appeal ran deep and captured the fancy of a generation of young viewers. Here the archetypal elements of the story are relevant. Lucas was familiar with folklore and mythology, particularly the work of Joseph Campbell on the structural characteristics of myth. Adroitly handled by Lucas and his team of filmmakers, the mythic substrata of the stories carried the emotional urgency of primal issues. Luke's struggle with the Dark Side and the revelation (a narrative surprise at the conclusion of THE EMPIRE STRIKES BACK) of his relationship with Darth Vader gave the fantasy moral force and emotional resonance.

THE EMPIRE STRIKES BACK (1980).

As Lucas has acknowledged,

> The struggle between good and evil within us has been around since the beginning of time. All mythology and all religions address it, and it's the most intimate struggle that we cope with—trying to do the right thing and what's expected of us by society, by our peers, and in our hearts. The issues of falling from grace and being redeemed, and the strength of family and love—they're all very primary issues.[3]

The enthusiastic public reception for the films demonstrated the powerful rendition that Lucas had given these issues and the engaging manner in which he put them across. The archetypal force of these films is so immediate, the narratives and characters so lacking in irony, that intellectuals and critics were dismayed and somewhat uncomfortable with the communion that Lucas had achieved with his audience, as if the films' extraordinary popularity compromised their artistic worth. Interestingly, in this regard, Lucas did not, and had never, seen himself as a Hollywood filmmaker. "I am an independent filmmaker. People say my movies are just like Hollywood movies. And I say, 'I can't help it if Hollywood copies.'"[4] Lucas's independence was both financial and artistic. By controlling the sequel rights to STAR WARS and the related product licensing, Lucas reaped a fortune, which he used to establish his production facilities. These gave him an artistic freedom from studio interference. And he put his fortune into the films, using the success of each to finance the next. "I took the money I'd made from AMERICAN GRAFFITI and stuck it into starting ILM, and then I took the money from STAR WARS and popped it into THE EMPIRE STRIKES BACK, and the money from EMPIRE into RETURN OF THE JEDI. Each film has paid for the next."[5]

His desire for artistic independence fueled the development of film production facilities that were geographically removed from Hollywood, with the divergent locale embodying the philosophical split from the studios, and that were on the cutting edge of research and development into sound recording and special effects. Lucas founded in 1975 the special effects house Industrial Light and Magic, based in San Rafael, California. In 1980, he began construction in Marin County, California, of Skywalker Ranch, the headquarters of Lucasfilm Ltd., his production company. The facility would contain an extensive research library and state-of-the-art sound recording facilities that served the postproduction of Lucas's pictures as well as THE GODFATHER, PART III (1990), TERMINATOR 2 (1991), BUGSY (1991), JFK (1991), and other films by directors who were attracted to the sophisticated resources that Skywalker Ranch offered. In developing these facilities, Lucas held a long-range view of the industry's future. He wanted the resources that could train the next generations of special effects wizards and that could ease the industry's transition toward electronic methods of filmmaking, which he believed could help make cinema into a medium like painting, where the artist can control, with exacting precision, all aspects of the image. In this respect, Lucas took an industry lead in developing electronic and computerized approaches to image and sound editing—the EditDroid and SoundDroid systems—and a general upgrading of post-production tools. Pursuing these interests—and getting ILM into solvent shape—effectively stalled his directing career. After directing the original STAR WARS (1977), he served as producer on the two follow-up films and did not direct any features during the decade (though he did shoot second-unit footage on RAIDERS OF THE LOST ARK, WILLOW, TUCKER, and other pictures). Furthermore, the completion of RETURN OF THE JEDI put the series into a long hiatus, with sixteen years elapsing before release of THE PHANTOM MENACE (1999).

But though he did not direct, Lucas used his role as a producer, and his company, to exert considerable influence on picture making during the period. As producer, Lucas worked on KAGEMUSHA (1980), BODY HEAT (1981), RAIDERS OF THE LOST ARK (1981), TWICE UPON A TIME (1983), THE EWOK ADVENTURE (1984, TV movie), INDIANA JONES AND THE TEMPLE OF DOOM (1984), EWOKS: THE BATTLE FOR ENDOR (1985, TV movie), "Ewoks" (1985, TV series), HOWARD THE DUCK (1986), LABYRINTH (1986), THE LAND BEFORE TIME (1988), TUCKER: THE MAN AND HIS DREAM (1988), WILLOW (1988), and INDIANA JONES AND THE LAST CRUSADE (1989). Lucas used his industry influence to help filmmakers he admired get their projects into production and distribution—Akira Kurosawa and KAGEMUSHA, Lawrence Kasdan and BODY HEAT, Haskell Wexler and LATINO (1985).[6] In addition to this feature and television work, Lucas designed the Disney theme park attractions "Captain EO" (1986, directed by Francis Coppola and featuring Michael Jackson) and "Star Tours" (1987), an effects ride tied in to the Empire-rebel conflict of STAR WARS.

In tandem with this work, Lucas and ILM researched and developed the next generation of production tools. Indeed, Lucas's greatest influence on American film was here, in his championing of digital production methods and effects technology. As noted, Lucasfilm brought a random-access, computer-assisted electronic editor (Editdroid) on line at mid-decade and an all-digital sound editor (SoundDroid) a few years later.[7] To ensure optimum, state-of-the-art sound, the Technical Building (a sound post-production facility at Skywalker Ranch) was constructed with elaborate acoustical design features. These included mechanical and electrical systems to optimize room acoustics and to isolate sound from low-level background noise.[8] The facility enabled Lucasfilm to lead the industry in sophisticated sound design, and its recording stage attracted a variety of

Lucas was an active producer of other filmmakers' work, most notably on Spielberg's three Indiana Jones films. Here Lucas and Paramount executive Michael Eisner have some fun with a famous prop from RAIDERS OF THE LOST ARK.

George Lucas used his power and prestige in the industry to enable Japan's Akira Kurosawa to complete KAGEMUSHA, which was released by 20th Century–Fox, Lucas's distributor for the STAR WARS pictures.

other filmmakers and musicians (the Grateful Dead, the Kronos Quartet, Linda Ronstadt).

Lucas's effects house, Industrial Light and Magic, designed effects for the Lucas productions as well as a wide range of other prominent films. These included DRAGONSLAYER (1981), THE DARK CRYSTAL (1982), STAR TREK II: THE WRATH OF KHAN (1982), E.T. (1982), STARMAN (1984), STAR TREK III: THE SEARCH FOR SPOCK (1984), INDIANA JONES AND THE TEMPLE OF DOOM (1984), OUT OF AFRICA (1985), MISHIMA (1985), THE GOONIES (1985), BACK TO THE FUTURE (1985), COCOON (1985), THE GOLDEN CHILD (1986), STAR TREK IV: THE VOYAGE HOME (1986), THE MONEY PIT (1986), EMPIRE OF THE SUN (1987), STAR TREK: THE NEXT GENERATION (1987), *BATTERIES NOT INCLUDED (1987), INNERSPACE (1987), HARRY AND THE HENDERSONS (1987), THE WITCHES OF EASTWICK (1987); THE LAST TEMPTATION OF CHRIST (1988), COCOON II (1988), THE ACCIDENTAL TOURIST (1988), WHO FRAMED ROGER RABBIT (1988); ALWAYS (1989), BACK TO THE FUTURE, PART II (1989), THE ABYSS (1989), GHOSTBUSTERS II (1989), INDIANA JONES AND THE LAST CRUSADE (1989), STAR TREK V: THE FINAL FRONTIER (1989), and FIELD OF DREAMS (1989). Through these pictures, ILM put its imprimateur upon a decade's worth of film and became synonymous with cutting-edge special effects.

In 1989 and 1990, ILM's work with director James Cameron on THE ABYSS and TERMINATOR 2 broke new ground in the use of digital effects to create the films' slithery water creature and gleaming, shape-shifting terminator. Since then, ILM helped move the industry toward more extensive computer-based methods of filmmaking, which, Lucas believed, will give filmmakers significantly greater creative freedom because filming and post-production processes will be completely digital. "Before, once you photographed something, you were pretty much stuck with it. Now . . . you can have complete control over it just like an artist does, and that to me is the way it should be."[9] With digital tools, Lucas points out, "you can make shots conform to your idea after the fact, rather than trying to conform the world to what your idea is."[10]

Of course, many filmmakers and viewers might find this compulsion for total control over filmic elements to be stifling of creative freedom, the very ideal that Lucas said he was pursuing. His passion for preplanned design was an approach to filmmaking at odds with more aleatory, improvised methods. But cinema is open to both approaches, and Lucas's design-centered aesthetic was not dissimilar to Hitchcock's passion for control, with the proviso that Hitchcock's understanding of the audience was perhaps more nuanced than Lucas's. And it is very few filmmakers who create the essential epic mythos of modern cinema and one with a cultural force that transcends the medium and imbibes the period to become its inescapable artifact. ILM was the engine driving the effects and digital revolutions in modern film, and Lucas became the industry's technological visionary, fixed on the digital future of film and transforming it away from its photomechanical base.

DON SIMPSON AND JERRY BRUCKHEIMER   Along with Spielberg and Lucas, Don Simpson and Jerry Bruckheimer were the decade's most successful blockbuster filmmakers. It is not incorrect to refer to them as filmmakers even though they received no director's credit on their films, nor did they direct such films. They didn't have to. As producer-auteurs (FLASHDANCE, BEVERLY HILLS COP, TOP GUN), they imposed a powerful visual and narrative style on the films they guided through production, and in this

respect there was something of old Holly-
wood about their character and methods.
Powerful producers were plentiful during
Hollywood's classical period (David O.
Selznick, Arthur Freed, Walter Wanger,
Mark Hellinger), but the cult of the director
that developed in the late sixties and seventies tended to delegitimize the producer's
creative contributions. Director Martin
Brest (GOING IN STYLE [1979], BEVERLY
HILLS COP) noted that in the seventies
"producer" was a dirty word.[11] By contrast,
in the eighties the legacy of HEAVEN'S
GATE and the spectacular success of Lucas
and Spielberg and of Simpson-Bruckheimer
Productions marked a resurgence of the
producer as a key auteur.

Indeed, Simpson absolutely considered
himself to be the author of those pictures
that he produced, and he forcefully proclaimed this creative ownership as a means
of countering a studio's inevitable assertion
of creative property rights. Describing the
Simpson-Bruckheimer approach, Simpson

*Don Simpson and Jerry Bruckheimer
were Hollywood's top-gun producers
and helped popularize the "high concept" brand of filmmaking.*

said, "We're not only hands-on, we're feet-on. We don't take a passive role in any shape
or form."[12] Bruckheimer noted that it was strategically important to insist on the producer's creative authority when dealing with powerful studio-distributors because, otherwise, the studio would usurp the producer's autonomy. "Don . . . felt, and he was right,
that unless you say, 'I made this movie,' it will be Paramount's TOP GUN, it will be a studio movie."[13] Simpson was skeptical about the claims to sole authorship by many directors, and he regarded the director on Simpson-Bruckheimer productions as another
for-hire member of the crew, a member that had one function—to serve the production.
"I don't believe in the auteur theory. Some directors who shall remain nameless do
regard movies as an extension of their internal emotional landscape, but Jerry and I
decide on the movie we want to make. We then hire an all-star team who can implement
the vision. The movie is the auteur, the boss. . . . No one person, director or writer, is
above the call of the final result."[14]

Simpson was an executive at Paramount and the president of worldwide production
from 1981 to 1982 when he switched (or was forced out of the studio, depending on who
is telling the story) to independent production with Bruckheimer, whose background
was in advertising. Considering Paramount home, Simpson-Bruckheimer turned out a
stream of hits for the studio during the eighties. The production duo's chart-topping success began with their first collaboration in 1983, FLASHDANCE, followed by THIEF OF
HEARTS (1984, and not a huge hit like the others), BEVERLY HILLS COP (1984), TOP
GUN (1986) and BEVERLY HILLS COP II (1987). By decade's end, their films had generated revenues for Paramount of $2.27 billion. Paramount, in turn, was so committed
to keeping the production duo that the studio tore up their existing contract in 1985 and

signed them to a new, multimillion-dollar, four-year deal that gave them points on all the films they produced and a share of ancillary revenue.

More than any other eighties productions, the Simpson-Bruckheimer films embodied the "high concept" approach to moviemaking. The storylines were simple and easily described but were punched across by aggressive editing and a skillful blend of visual imagery and popular music. FLASHDANCE and TOP GUN embodied a rock video style of filmmaking in which the emphasis was on bite-sized narrative segments and a fusion of image and music. The narrative in TOP GUN is exceptionally direct and unembellished ("clean" in Simpson's lexicon). Tom Cruise plays a Navy fighter pilot in training at the elite Top Gun school, where he learns the latest methods of aerial combat. He romances a teacher at the school (Kelly McGillis), loses his best friend in a flying accident, suffers a crisis of confidence and nerve, and recovers his skills in time to save a comrade in a dogfight with Soviet fighters. This bare-bones narrative gets a high-gloss visual treatment amid extended sequences cut to music and that featured little or no dialogue.

Simpson and Bruckheimer combined their complementary backgrounds to perfect their high-concept formula, merging a lean, propulsive story (Simpson) and commanding visuals (Bruckheimer). Simpson said, "We entered into this relationship from two disparate positions. With my background as writer and actor, my responsibility was always in telling and conceiving the story. I brought the verbal to the relationship. Jerry was the film editor and photographer, so he brought the visual. Verbal and visual; we were the 'V & V' twins." For Simpson, the blockbuster aesthetic must be "clean"; that is, it must use a design that is clear and immediately accessible. This was the essence of high concept—a catchy premise uncluttered by excessive narrative development or dramatic ambiguities and layered with slick images like icing on a cake. "The aesthetic is: 'that's clean' . . . which can apply to art, a jacket, a shot in a movie, even a girl. It means 'it works.' The design works." Simpson's description of how he chose a project was also a statement of how their high-concept films worked on viewers: "I never start out intellectually. I commit my instincts. It's gut to heart to mind to mouth."[15]

Simpson-Bruckheimer's incorporation of music as a key element of high-concept design proved to be tremendously influential. Portions of FLASHDANCE and TOP GUN are essentially rock videos, extended montage sequences cut to music, which facilitated synergies with recorded music merchandising (see ch. 3). FLASHDANCE and subsequent Simpson-Bruckheimer films were carefully marketed in tandem with the release of singles and albums featuring music from the sound track. The popularity of each market (recorded music and film) reinforced the performance of the other. The BEVERLY HILLS COP sound track sold over a million copies (platinum status) the year of the film's release, and the FLASHDANCE sound track broke 5 million copies.

The high-concept approach became a durable and essential staple of Hollywood filmmaking and transcended the works produced by Simpson and Bruckheimer. TWINS (1988), for example, made at Universal under production chief Tom Pollock, hinged its narrative premise and marketing appeals on the singular prospect, and image, of muscular Arnold Schwarzenegger and diminuitive Danny DeVito as fraternal twins. The image and the idea vividly encapsulated the film. Even as they bequeathed high concept to American cinema, Simpson and Bruckheimer's box-office success faltered at decade's end. In 1988, Paramount renegotiated their contract, promising over $300 million for five pictures of their choosing plus a percentage of the gross. The first picture under this deal, DAYS OF THUNDER, starring Tom Cruise as a race car driver, went into production with a problematic script, unusual for a Simpson-Bruckheimer picture because Simpson

The image of Arnold Schwarzenegger and Danny DeVito encapsulates the high-concept premise of TWINS.

was renowned for giving scripts close attention. He would issue twenty- and thirty-page memos to writers specifying revisions and then oversee as many rewrites of the material. (Screenwriter John Gregory Dunne found Simpson's analyses to be intelligent and keenly attuned to issues of narrative structure.) Worse, DAYS OF THUNDER went over budget, costing Paramount $70 million and generating relatively disappointing box office, short of the TOP GUN–on-wheels potential the studio wanted.

In the wake of this "failure," Paramount demanded a restriction on their gross participation perk, whereupon Simpson and Bruckheimer left Paramount for Disney, ending their spectacular alliance with the decade's most successful major. At Disney, cost cutting was the norm, and Simpson-Bruckheimer's lavish ways were ill suited for their new employer's corporate climate. They had difficulty putting projects together. THE REF, their next release, did not appear until 1994, and it performed poorly. But in 1995–96, they came back with three huge hits, CRIMSON TIDE, DANGEROUS MINDS, and THE ROCK. By now, though, Simpson's drug use, which had been a chronic feature of his life, was out of control, and Jerry Bruckheimer dissolved the partnership. Simpson quickly self-destructed. Drug and psychological problems overwhelmed him. Five months later, in January, he died of a drug overdose.

It was a dispiriting fall from power and a cautionary tale of Hollywood excess. Yet throughout the eighties, Simpson and Bruckheimer's hits helped make Paramount the most successful major of the decade, dramatized the windfall profits that ancillary synergies could produce, and helped turn film narrative into a series of adrenaline-pumping audiovisual montages. And although Simpson could not control the chaos of his private life, before his partnership with Bruckheimer ended, they had given the industry the quintessential elements of blockbuster marketing.

JOHN HUGHES   The decade's king of teen comedy was John Hughes. Beginning with his first film as director, SIXTEEN CANDLES (1984), Hughes worked prolifically, directing a film a year through the remainder of the decade. By contrast, in the nineties, he was virtually quiescent as a director, though not as a writer. Thus, to date, he remains essentially a filmmaker of the eighties.

SIXTEEN CANDLES established the essential Hughes milieu of adolescent longing and angst played as lighthearted comedy. Shot for less than $6.5 million, the picture broke the rules of teen comedy and set new ones. Hughes felt that sixteen-year-olds were poorly served by the films aimed their way, so he pitched the SIXTEEN CANDLES story with a female character at its center and with sex deemphasized. Samantha (Molly Ringwald) is a high school student fast approaching her sixteenth birthday, and she struggles with her crush on the school's most popular guy while trying to fend off the awkward affections of the school geek. "It was my intent to write it from the female point of view, because this genre is generally about males, and sex is a predominant theme. . . . When you're 30, you forget that at 16 sex was *not* your primary motivation; you were much more interested in having a boyfriend or girlfriend."[16]

Hughes's sensitivity to the moviegoing interests of young viewers, and to the real-life issues that subtended their moviegoing, made his pictures phenomenally successful and influential within their demographic niche and established a galaxy of new performers. In Sixteen Candles, The Breakfast Club, (1985), and Ferris Bueller's Day Off (1986), Hughes's casting choices helped launch the careers of a gallery of young actors that became known, somewhat derisively, as the brat pack: Molly Ringwald, Judd Nelson, Ally Sheedy, Emilio Estevez, Anthony Michael Hall, and Matthew Broderick.

As a writer-director, Hughes had a gift for capturing authentic-sounding teen dialogue, which he achieved partly by inventing new slang terms, and he centered the films' action within the somewhat solipsistic worlds of their young characters. Thus, adult life in these films is properly distanced from the ideals, longings, and shenanigans of his teens. But unlike Spielberg, who sometimes imposed childlike responses on his viewers, Hughes's strategy was more sociological. He did not say, like Spielberg, that it's better to be a kid. Instead, he was interested in observing and recording the codes and rituals of teen life. He played to that audience without attempting to regress his viewers to that level, emphasizing story and characters and letting the jokes emerge later and from this grounding. "I never start with the jokes. I look at an issue and try to find the story in

Molly Ringwald's endearing performance helped make Sixteen Candles *one of John Hughes's most accomplished teen comedies.*

it. . . . You get a lot of bad comedy from people sitting around a bar saying 'wouldn't it be funny if . . .'"[17]

Hughes's most stylish and popular film in the teen series was FERRIS BUELLER ($29 million in domestic rentals), about "one man's tireless crusade to take it easy." While cutting classes, Ferris embarks on a wild series of misadventures about which his parents and other adults remain completely clueless, as Hughes stylishly captures the solipsism of adolescence.

Hughes profitably ventured outside the teen genre with two popular John Candy vehicles (PLANES, TRAINS, AND AUTOMOBILES [1987], also starring Steve Martin, and UNCLE BUCK [1989]), but he is best known for the Brat Pack cycle that he helped popularize. If in the nineties he turned his energies to writing and producing, Hughes's eighties films defined the quintessential look and sound for an affluent, suburban youth culture. In an era of special effects, Hughes showed that one could be successful on modest budgets, with smart, funny writing and with pictures rooted in a real sociocultural milieu.

JOHN LANDIS   Landis suffered the indignity of being the only American director prosecuted for the death of actors under his filmmaking supervision. The trial, its publicity, and its aftermath hung like a pall over his career during the decade and affected his already rocky relationship with the nation's film critics. The pictures he made during this period, before, during, and after the trial, contained some notable hits but also some overbudgeted, overproduced misfires.

He began the decade as an auspicious and commercially promising filmmaker. NATIONAL LAMPOON'S ANIMAL HOUSE, which Landis directed, was one of the biggest hits of 1978, and it made him into a golden boy at Universal. Steven Spielberg admired and liked the picture, and he and Landis became friends. Eager to support their new filmmaker, Universal executives funded THE BLUES BROTHERS, a comedy Landis fashioned around "Saturday Night Live" performers John Belushi and Dan Aykroyd and the characters and sketch material they had created on that popular television show. But instead of being a character-driven comedy, the movie escalated into a series of overproduced musical numbers, explosions, and car crashes. The budget went beyond what Universal had anticipated, with press reports of a production cost in excess of $30 million. When the picture was released in 1980, critics were appalled at the expenditure of so much money on so noisy a film. The *Washington Post* called it a "ponderous comic monstrosity," and critic Kenneth Turan remarked that "it has more car crashes than a demolition derby" and "fewer laughs than an afternoon at traffic school."[18]

Despite these reactions, the picture sustained a devoted cult following that ensured its relative success at the box office. Intent to prove that he could work within a modest budget, Landis next made AN AMERICAN WEREWOLF IN LONDON (1981) for Polygram Pictures and producers Jon Peters and Peter Guber. Landis again aimed for the outrageous. He had filmed ANIMAL HOUSE with grossly funny and wickedly lewd humor. This time, he deliberately blended slapstick comedy with graphic violence and gory special effects. The monster wreaks extremely bloody carnage and corpses decay in lingering detail while Landis stages wacky car crashes. He described his approach in these terms: "Let's say you were walking in Times Square and feeling *very* high—like you feel after a good movie or a great concert. . . . And let's say at that particular moment you were approached by . . . Dracula, and he *attacks* you and starts biting your neck with his long eyeteeth. . . . That sort of fast transition is going to happen all the time in this movie, and that's what nobody liked about the script."[19]

AN AMERICAN WEREWOLF was a modest success, and it helped sustain Landis's reputation as an iconoclastic director whose irreverent work was especially appealing to
young viewers, that vital industry demographic. When Universal floated the idea to
Spielberg of doing a movie based on Rod Serling's "Twilight Zone" television show,
Spielberg expressed his interest, and Landis was one of the directors recruited to helm
a segment of this anthology film. It gave him an opportunity to work with Spielberg, who
was directing another segment for the film and serving as the picture's producer.

Landis scripted a dark tale about a bigot, played by Vic Morrow, who inexplicably
finds himself trapped in other times and places—the American South, Vietnam,
Germany during the Nazi era—where he becomes the target and victim of racial hatred.
The character learns what it is like to be the object of irrational animosity. Morrow's
character gets a chance at redemption, though, when he lands in Southeast Asia during
the Vietnam War and rescues two Vietnamese children from a helicopter attack on their
village. The filming of this sequence produced a grotesque accident, one for which
Landis and four associates were held accountable. They were charged with involuntary
manslaughter in the events that led to the deaths on 23 July 1982 of Morrow and two
child actors, Myca Dinh Le and Renee Chen.

During action in which Morrow fled the burning village carrying the children, a helicopter piloted by Dorcey Wingo (one of Landis's codefendents) was hit by a special
effects explosion and careened out of control, crushing one of the children and decapi-
tating Morrow and the other child. The prosecution argued that Landis exhibited gross
negligence in asking his effects crew to produce explosions so large they were unsafe and
in asking the pilot to fly unnecessarily close to the fireball for the sake of a more impressive shot. Reporting on the accident, California's OSHA found thirty-six safety violations
on the set.[20] Making matters worse, the production had employed the children illegally.
They had no work permit, and they were working well after dark.

When a judgment was finally rendered nearly five years later, on 29 May 1987, Landis
and his four codefendents were acquitted of the charges brought against them. But in
the interval and through the massive publicity the case and the trial had generated,
Landis and TWILIGHT ZONE: THE MOVIE came to symbolize, fairly or not, a reckless
handling of actors in pursuit of the biggest explosion or the most stupefying effects
sequence. Worse yet, the picture as released retained its Vic Morrow segment. Morrow
and the children died "on camera," that is, during filming, but the footage showing their
deaths did not appear in the finished film. The Vietnam sequence was dropped. As it
now exists in TWILIGHT ZONE: THE MOVIE, Landis's segment ends with Morrow's character trapped in Nazi Germany and shipped off with Jews to an extermination camp. It
makes for creepy viewing. Its violence and general nihilism are compounded by a
viewer's knowledge of the accident and resulting deaths. Furthermore, the retention of
the Morrow segment in the finished film enhances the unpleasant aura of exploitation
that hangs over this picture.

Landis continued working through this five-year debacle from the accident to the
end of the trial. His next picture, TRADING PLACES, was the third biggest box-office film
of 1983 and helped skyrocket Eddie Murphy to superstardom. It was a well-written,
clever comedy about a pauper (Murphy) who becomes rich on the whim of a wealthy
benefactor and must contend with the awkwardness of his new class identity. As a comic
vehicle, it allowed Murphy full reign in expressing his streetwise sassiness to skewer
upper-class pomposity. Audiences loved Murphy and loved the film. But after this picture, and as the publicity fallout from the TWILIGHT ZONE case intensified, Landis's

The ill-fated Vic Morrow in Twilight Zone: The Movie.

career went into an eclipse. He kept working, but his subsequent films failed to achieve solid commercial success in relation to their production costs. In addition, the critics were unkind to Into the Night (1985), Spies Like Us (1985), and Three Amigos! (1986), pictures that were often clever but also seemed derivative of earlier films and genres and too full of in-jokes and cameos by Landis's friends. Of these subsequent films, only Coming to America (1988), teaming him again with Eddie Murphy, gave Landis a measure of his earlier success. He ended the decade on this slow fall from his former box-office fame and remained most renowned for the Twilight Zone disaster. His work epitomized the brashness of megabuck studio filmmaking in which explosions, car crashes, and a general vulgarity of tone became prized assets for which the studios would spend millions.

Jon Peters and Peter Guber Never as powerful as Don Simpson and Jerry Bruckheimer, Peters and Guber had a fitful, precarious cachet in eighties Hollywood because of their (sometimes remote) association with three of the decade's big hits: The Color Purple (1985), Rain Man (1988), and Batman (1989). Unlike Simpson and Bruckheimer, though, they were not hands-on producers but instead tended to be packagers of scripts, directors, and stars, and in this regard their work personified the importance of marketing in eighties Hollywood.

Early in their careers, Peters and Guber showed the flair for promotion that gained them prominence in the industry. Promoted from Barbara Striesand's hairdresser-lover to the producer of her film A Star Is Born (1976), Peters helped design its ad campaign featuring a nude embrace between Streisand and co-star Kris Kristofferson. The picture grossed over $90 million, and its success enabled Peters to form in 1977 his own

Jon Peters and Peter Guber.

production company, the Jon Peters Organization. Guber's breakthrough hit was THE DEEP (1977), based on a novel about sunken treasure by *Jaws* author Peter Benchley. Guber based the film's marketing around actress Jacqueline Bisset's wet T-shirt, and the picture, despite its mediocrity, became the second biggest box-office film of 1977. "That T-shirt made me a rich man," Guber remarked.[21]

In 1980, Peters and Guber joined forces as joint producers at PolyGram Pictures, where they produced a string of films in 1981 that generally failed to find much popular acceptance: KING OF THE MOUNTAIN, THE PURSUIT OF D. B. COOPER, ENDLESS LOVE, and AN AMERICAN WEREWOLF IN LONDON. As a result, PolyGram's European financiers sought to cut their loses (up to $80 million) and get out of the movie business. Peters and Guber left the company, set up shop as the Guber-Peters Co. in 1982, and found a home at Warner Bros., which agreed to finance and distribute their productions. Nearly all of the initial films were box-office losers: VISION QUEST (1985), THE LEGEND OF BILLIE JEAN (1985), CLUE (1985), HEAD OFFICE (1985), YOUNGBLOOD (1986), THE CLAN OF THE CAVE BEAR (1986). The exception was THE COLOR PURPLE (1985), directed by Steven Spielberg. Guber-Peters were associated with this picture because they owned the rights to the novel, but Spielberg had them barred from the set during filming and never collaborated with them on the project.[22] Nevertheless, Guber and Peters treated *Color Purple* as the jewel in their crown.

Another string of box-office disappointments (WHO'S THAT GIRL [1987], INNERSPACE [1987], CADDYSHACK II [1988]) was offset by THE WITCHES OF EASTWICK, the sixth biggest revenue-generating film of 1987. Director George Miller wanted a low-key and witty film about a clash between the devil and three small-town women, but Peters pushed aggressively for a heavy dose of special effects. Peters won, and the resulting picture was a box-office winner.

After a precipitous attempt to buy the remains of MGM/UA from Kirk Kerkorian in 1988, Peters and Guber had two huge successes that strengthened their reputation as hit makers. RAIN MAN was the top film of 1988's box office; as with THE COLOR PURPLE, however, Peters and Guber had a stake in the script but were absentee producers on the project itself, visiting the set only once.[23] By contrast, on BATMAN (1989), a huge moneymaker for Warners, Peters took a more active role, recruiting Jack Nicholson to the project, urging director Tim Burton to add more action and romance, and helping design the very successful ad campaign.

Despite their uneven track record, Sony felt that Guber and Peters were essential for the success of its newly acquired Columbia Pictures. Accordingly, the electronics giant bought out their Warners contract for $200 million and appointed them to run Columbia Pictures. Sony's action was widely criticized as excessive and unnecessary, but it seemed to be a formal acknowledgment of the producer-as-superstar status that had become such a distinguishing feature of eighties Hollywood. But their five-year tenure at Columbia proved to be a disaster. Prominent box-office bombs—BUGSY (1991), HUDSON HAWK (1991), CITY OF JOY (1992), THE LAST ACTION HERO (1993), I'LL DO ANYTHING (1994), GERONIMO (1993)—led to Guber's firing as Columbia head and Sony's posting of a $3.2 billion loss in its second quarter 1994. An era of overspending on inflated productions helped produce this massive loss and brought an end to Guber's power-broker posting.

Ironically, given the poor showing of their Columbia films, Guber and Peters's strengths had always been in marketing and promotion, and their regard for films as revenue-generating commodities was certainly in synch with the predominant thinking in the majors' executive suites. But their uneven track record contained only a few prominent hits (on some of which they had a distant association), and this mixed performance ensured that Guber and Peters remained occasional players in the highly uncertain and unstable world of the hit-making studio executive.

ROBERT ZEMECKIS   A Spielberg protégé, Robert Zemeckis directed several of the 1980s' top hits (BACK TO THE FUTURE, WHO FRAMED ROGER RABBIT, both Spielberg productions), and he moved to the forefront of special effects filmmaking by virtue of ROGER RABBIT and, in the 1990s, DEATH BECOMES HER (1992) and FORREST GUMP (1994). A university film school attendee, Zemeckis' award-winning student film, FIELD OF HONOR, earned Spielberg's attention, and Zemeckis subsequently co-wrote the story for Spielberg's 1941 (1979). The following year, he directed a fast, funny satire of car salesmen in the Spielberg-produced USED CARS (1980), which was released to poor box office ($5 million in rentals). The industry tagged USED CARS, Zemeckis's earlier I WANNA HOLD YOUR HAND (1978), and 1941 as failures, and he was temporarily unemployable. No studio would touch his screenplay for a film called "Back to the Future"! As a result, he was unable to land a directing job for several years.

But he returned with a picture that attracted a great deal of attention. ROMANCING THE STONE, produced by actor Michael Douglas, earned $36 million in rentals, placing it in the top ten for 1984. The film was an old-fashioned, lighthearted adventure-romance about unlikely lovers (Douglas and Kathleen Turner) in peril in South America, and it contained none of the gadgetry and special effects for which Zemeckis's work would become known. He passed on doing the sequel (THE JEWEL OF THE NILE [1985]) and concentrated on his BACK TO THE FUTURE project, about young Marty McFly's (Michael J. Fox) comic adventures time-traveling in a sporty DeLorean auto.

BACK TO THE FUTURE (1985) is one of the quintessential eighties films. Tremendously successful, it spawned two sequels (1989, 1990), and it epitomized the collective yearning for a pristine past that the Reagan years had defined as a core national aspiration. Dr. Brown (Christopher Lloyd), Marty's loony inventor friend, creates a time machine that enables Marty to travel back in time to his hometown in 1955, where he meets his parents when they were high school teens. To ensure that their future (and his present life in the eighties) will come true as he has known it, Marty has to act as matchmaker, encouraging their courtship. Oedipal complications ensue, however, when his mother develops a crush on Marty, whom she perceives as an attractive and mysterious visitor in town. Downplaying this narrative wrinkle, Zemeckis concentrates on Marty's efforts to make the past right (i.e., get his mom and dad to fall in love), much as President Reagan was exhorting the nation to return to its collective past in order to find its cultural bearings amid an uncertain present. As in Reagan's rhetoric, the past here is a more shining and idealistic time than is the present. Marty's hometown in the eighties

Traveling back in time, Marty McFly (Michael J. Fox) gives his teenage parents romantic counseling in BACK TO THE FUTURE, *one of the decade's quintessential films.*

is blighted with litter, homeless drunks sleeping in public, and porno movies at the corner theater. By contrast, in the fifties the town was spotless and bursting with the aspirations of youth. Moreover, as Reagan urged the nation, Marty uses the past to remake the present. At the end of the film, he learns that his intervention into his parents' lives in 1955 has made them happier, more self-fulfilled, and successful in the eighties. In these ways, BACK TO THE FUTURE venerates small-town America in terms consistent with the rhetoric of the Reagan presidency (while, nevertheless, aiming a few jokes at Reagan for being an actor-turned-president). The film owed much of its success to this artful manipulation of the eighties zeitgeist (shared by another of the period's hits, FIELD OF DREAMS [1989]), but its popularity was also a function of its warm and affectionate portrait of Marty's deepening involvement with his parents and his discovery of the conditions that made them who they are.

BACK TO THE FUTURE commenced the special effects turn in Zemeckis's filmmaking, an emphasis that would become one of his distinguishing directorial characteristics. Dr. Brown's time-traveling auto leaps through the decades in a burst of light and leaves a double trail of flame in its wake. To create these and other effects, Zemeckis began a collaboration with Industrial Light and Magic that continued on his subsequent films and produced a series of Academy Awards for best effects (WHO FRAMED ROGER RABBIT, DEATH BECOMES HER, and FORREST GUMP).

The evil Dr. Doom (Christopher Lloyd) threatens a toon with extinction in the sophisticated and delightful WHO FRAMED ROGER RABBIT.

Preceding the digital effects revolution, WHO FRAMED ROGER RABBIT (1988), Zemeckis's next film, was the climactic achievement of traditional compositing and matte effects work.[24] Its seamless blend of live-action and animated footage, in a tale of a private eye (Bob Hoskins) investigating a crime in Toontown amid its cartoon denizens, would today be accomplished through computer animation and compositing of all-digital elements. But such was the skill with which Zemeckis and ILM executed the blend of live action and animation, and so witty were the results, that Roger and his cohorts became the year's most popular film characters.

Zemeckis carefully integrated the effects work with a clever story that linked disparate styles: film noir and famous cartoon characters from classic animated entertainment. Eddie Valiant, the private eye, works 1947 Hollywood, and like noir heroes he's haunted by past trauma. A cartoon character killed his brother. "Just like a toon to drop a safe on a guy's head," a cop mutters about the deed. Like Jake Gittes in CHINATOWN, Valiant is drawn into a complex web of crime hinging on a corrupt land deal. To investigate he must return to Toontown, where the cartoon characters who work in Hollywood movies live and where he'll confront the scars of his past. Against this noir tableau, the film introduces a gallery of cartoon greats (mainly from Warners and Disney films) who make nostalgic and funny cameo appearances: Bugs Bunny, Tweety Bird, Dumbo, Porky Pig, Pinocchio, Donald Duck, Yosemite Sam, Mickey Mouse, and, in her black-and-white glory, Betty Boop. To these old favorites the film adds two new animated characters. Roger is a well-meaning but buffoonish and long-suffering rabbit who lacks Bugs's impish savoir faire, and his wife, Jessica Rabbit, is an impossibly voluptuous human, voiced by Kathleen Turner, and given the film's best line of dialogue: "I'm not bad. I'm just drawn that way."

The film's extraordinary accomplishment lies in the unprecedented sophistication of its integration of live action and 2D animation. The film featured 1,031 optical shots where live action and animated footage were composited together, and this material was photographed using the eight-perforation, horizontal VistaVision process. With its larger frame size, VistaVision provided optimal clarity and resolution to offset generational loss during optical printing (which necessitated the rephotographing of layered elements in order to create the final composited image).

Zemeckis, cinematographer Dean Cundey, and the ILM effects artists aimed to give the 2D animation a compelling three-dimensional look because the aesthetic conceit of the film is that Bob Hoskins and the other performers are interacting with the cartoon characters. To accomplish this, Zemeckis and Cundey resolved to shoot the film with complex camera moves and lighting textures (smoke, fog) that typically are not used in cartoons. For example, when Valiant goes to the Ink and Paint Club to watch Jessica sing, its cartoon patrons move behind the room's curtain of smoke. To make it easier for the actors and the cinematographer, the shots were rehearsed with full-figure models standing in for Roger, Jessica, and the other toon characters. Lighting, camera moves, and the actors' performances were established with reference to these figures, which were then removed during shooting. For the sequence where Valiant visits Toontown and Hoskins was the blue-screen element (acting against a blue screen for subsequent compositing with an animated landscape), the animators' layouts of the background were matted in on a TV monitor, enabling Zemeckis to visualize the full shot and plan camera and character moves. To enhance the 3D appearance of the toon characters, the animators added an uncommon degree of shadow and lighting information, and these effects were augmented further during the compositing stage. In addition to the light and color linkages, the camerawork connected the live action and animated environments, as when Zemeckis and Cundey shifted focus within a shot between live actors and the cartoon figures. These ingenious techniques worked splendidly. After an initial gasp, the viewer completely accepts that the cartoon characters exist in real time and space.

An uncommonly clever and well executed film, WHO FRAMED ROGER RABBIT is a uniquely innovative and ambitious achievement. Filmed with intelligence and filled with a love for cinema, especially the old cartoon classics, it speaks eloquently and with delight to young and old viewers, enchanting the old with familiar toon faces and amusing the young with stupendously well executed slapstick. It is one of the decade's key films, marking the passage of eras. Achieving that ever-difficult integration of art and technology, it epitomizes the glories of traditional methods of special effects compositing at the onset of a digital future. Like SUNRISE (1927) at the close of the silent era, it is a *summa* of the old style that offers an implicit challenge to the new.

With that of Lucas and Spielberg, Zemeckis's work personified the contemporary fusion of narrative and special effects, and as ROGER RABBIT shows, Zemeckis understood that effects were not the movie and should be carefully motivated and used with intelligence. In the nineties, the digital revolution enabled Zemeckis to be even more audacious, taking presidents Kennedy and Clinton and compositing them with the narrative and characters of FORREST GUMP and CONTACT (1997).

The well-rendered familial drama of BACK TO THE FUTURE and the emotional darkness in ROGER RABBIT, DEATH BECOMES HER, GUMP, and CONTACT indicated that Zemeckis was an ambitious filmmaker who placed effects in service to cinema and not vice versa. He was the only filmmaker to have emerged from Spielberg's shadow with a technical prowess equaling or surpassing his mentor. He was one of the few contemporary directors whose work conjoined cutting-edge effects with a sophisticated grasp of narrative and an aspiring artistic sensibility.

THE EMBATTLED AUTEURS

The 1980s were a difficult decade for some of the industry's most ambitious and talented filmmakers. In the 1960s and 1970s, these directors achieved significant critical, and sometimes great commercial, success, yet in the 1980s they struggled to obtain financing for productions and several careers foundered. One of the most striking facets of eighties cinema is the list of major filmmakers whose careers stalled during the decade.

It is tempting to ascribe this phenomenon to changed economic circumstances. With the problem viewed this way, the majors were pursuing blockbusters and funding those filmmakers most likely to create them, and these did not include the seventies auteurs. Their films had been driven more by art and poetic sensibility than by the box office, and in the eighties the line between thinking films and commercial ventures became more absolute. Furthermore, tighter production controls were implemented post–HEAVEN'S GATE with the result that maverick auteurs were kept on a shorter leash. While there is certainly some truth to these contentions, they fail to explain why other fine directors maintained strong career continuity in the eighties and why so many new and original filmmakers were able to begin their careers in this period. Plainly, many opportunities for work existed inside and outside of the industry. Ascribing the failed-auteur syndrome to the politics and economics of blockbuster production is too simplistic an explanation, and it provides an overly schematic portrait of the industry and the decade's filmmaking, which was too broad and eclectic to be characterized by an "us versus them" or "art versus commerce" dichotomy. But the phenomenon was real. Major filmmakers who were regarded ten years previously as the luminaries of American film culture were adrift in the eighties and encountered great difficulties sustaining their careers. The factors responsible for this turn of affairs were complex and varied, and they differed according to the filmmaker. They included the effects of intransigent personalities, hostility to the system and the prospect of working for the majors, and creative crises precipitated by personal estrangement from the sociocultural moment and the exhaustion of one's available talents. As this constellation of problems descended on the seventies auteurs, their collective crisis in the eighties began.

ROBERT ALTMAN   Altman's fall in the eighties epitomized the fate of seventies auteurs. During the eighties, his career absolutely collapsed as a feature filmmaker receiving funding and distribution from the majors. He was unemployable within the system, despite having made such seventies classics as MCCABE AND MRS. MILLER (1971), THE LONG GOODBYE (1973), and NASHVILLE (1975). To the studios, his aleatory filming methods, cavalier treatment of scripts, and disdain for conventional narrative amounted to irresponsible filmmaking, and the poor box-office performance of his late-seventies pictures set him up for a crisis.

It came with 1980's POPEYE, made for Paramount and Walt Disney. The production went over budget and was plagued with shooting difficulties not of Altman's making. In the context of a troubled production, however, studio executives found Altman's meandering narrative style and improvisatory filming methods to be unacceptable, and he took the fall for the picture's delays. Moreover, POPEYE was not a huge hit. Its worldwide rentals were respectable, yet because it fell short of blockbuster status, the industry perceived the film as a failure. After a string of box-office bombs in the latter 1970s, virtually no studio would now touch Altman. MGM was an exception, reluctantly signing him in 1983 to direct O.C. AND STIGS, an awkward comedy about two teenagers tormenting the adults around them. The finished picture tested badly with preview audiences, and MGM deemed the work unreleasable.

For Altman, the eighties now became a decade of drift and continual struggle to find work. In 1981, he sold his Lion's Gate production facility and relocated to New York, and then, in 1985, to Paris. He turned to filming plays on ultralow budgets. COME BACK TO THE FIVE AND DIME, JIMMY DEAN, JIMMY DEAN (1982) was shot on super-16mm for $850,000 and was distributed by Cinecom, a small independent. Relative to the others in the cast, Cher was the biggest name, but this was only her second film, and she had not yet established much of a film career. Furthermore, although the play about a group of women holding a twenty-year reunion of their James Dean fan club had some fine moments, on the whole it was a weak vehicle to serve as the basis for a feature film. STREAMERS (1983) was based on a harsh David Rabe play about Vietnam-era soldiers, and Altman had to supply the financing for the production. SECRET HONOR (1983), based on a one-man play about Nixon's dark days, was shot on 16mm at the University of Michigan. FOOL FOR LOVE (1986), from the Sam Shepherd play, was made for Cannon, a somewhat disreputable distributor that normally handled violent action pictures. Altman subsequently veered away from theatrical filmmaking and into directing plays for television (THE LAUNDROMAT, 1985; THE DUMB WAITER, 1987; THE ROOM,

Robin Williams as Popeye with Shelley Duvall as Olive Oyl. Holding blockbuster expectations, Walt Disney Productions and Paramount Pictures were disappointed with POPEYE's *box-office performance.*

1987; THE CAINE MUTINY COURT MARTIAL, 1988) and a series for HBO ("Tanner '88," 1988).

Critical reactions to Altman's journeyman period were highly variable. Some of it (STREAMERS, SECRET HONOR) drew high praise, but many commentators found Altman's work too glib, and without the controlled ironies of his early seventies masterworks. Moreover, many of the plays he was filming seemed relatively negligible, and little from this period has the cultural resonance and piercing intelligence of MCCABE AND MRS. MILLER, THE LONG GOODBYE, or THIEVES LIKE US (1973). Altman, though, proved to be a survivor. When the industry shut him out, he found ways to keep working as a filmmaker, and in the following decade he returned to prominence with THE PLAYER (1992). This trenchant, caustic satire about the deal-driven, sequel-obsessed film industry was a big hit with Hollywood insiders and featured a galaxy of cameos by industry players. Altman followed this picture with a second prominently marketed critical hit, SHORT CUTS (1993), based on a series of Raymond Carver short stories. With these films and his demonstration that he, too, could be a player in the industry, he regained status as a filmmaker with projects attracting distribution by the majors.

One must be careful when assessing Altman's troubles in the 1980s. The temptation to celebrate the director and denigrate the Hollywood system is seductive and romantic, and there are many proponents of this view. But the lesson to be drawn from Altman's eighties travails is not that the system was necessarily intolerant or that blockbuster economics had foreclosed on the seventies auteurs. To do so is to miss the significant counterexamples. Oliver Stone, Woody Allen, Tim Burton, and Spike Lee had successful screen careers as respected filmmakers with alternative film styles and with devoted audiences outside the blockbuster demographic. But they were, perhaps, more committed to working within the system. Altman had antagonized the majors, and like other iconoclasts before him (Sam Peckinpah, Erich von Stroheim), he found that the majors eventually fulfilled his expectations by denying him their resources.

PETER BOGDANOVICH   Critic-turned-director Peter Bogdanovich was extremely prolific in the 1970s, completing a film nearly every year from THE LAST PICTURE SHOW (1971) to SAINT JACK (1979). Hailed by the critics in that decade as a major and brilliant new director, Bogdanovich had gotten off to a spectacular start. In the 1980s, though, his career crashed, and he rarely worked as a film director. He completed only three films, and two of these were hardly seen by audiences. THEY ALL LAUGHED (1981), a romantic comedy with Audrey Hepburn and Ben Gazzara, was marred by tragedy when Bogdanovich's lover, Dorothy Stratten, was murdered by her estranged husband shortly after finishing her role. A distraught Bogdanovich retreated from filmmaking and remained inactive for several years. In the wake of Stratten's death, the picture was shelved by its distributor. Bogdanovich returned to directing with MASK (1985), a tender story of a disfigured youth and his devoted and protective mother (Cher in another winning performance that added more luster to her acting career). Bogdanovich here did not try to recycle a genre or star persona from classic Hollywood, as he had in previous work, and thus the picture's contemporaneous qualities helped it find its audience. The picture was a relative box-office success, Bogdanovich's first in a long while.

With his next film, though, he was back to mining old Hollywood material with the poor results that had recently become the norm for him. ILLEGALLY YOURS (1987) was another attempt at screwball comedy (WHAT'S UP DOC? had been very successful in 1972). Whereas WHAT'S UP DOC? was derivative of Howard Hawks, with Ryan O'Neal in glasses imitating Cary Grant from BRINGING UP BABY (1938), ILLEGALLY YOURS offered Rob Lowe in glasses imitating Ryan O'Neal in WHAT'S UP DOC? This recycling evidenced Bogdanovich's creative problem, an apparent inability to keep creating innovative work on the order of THE LAST PICTURE SHOW. While his seventies films were often variants of Hollywood's early classics, now he seemed to be rehashing his own material and trading on his earlier success. Bogdanovich had been a film critic before he became a director, and a critic is creative in a second-order way, being dependent on those works and artists who furnish the basis and material for the critic's livelihood. As director, Bogdanovich remained mired in the critic's predicament. He needed existing templates from which to fashion his work, as he had done with screwball comedy and the musical (AT LONG LAST LOVE [1975]), with stars (Boris Karloff and TARGETS [1968]) and directors (John Ford, Howard Hawks, and THE LAST PICTURE SHOW [1971]). When these ran out, his fount of original material did not sustain him, and his career foundered. ILLEGALLY YOURS, his last picture of the eighties, was barely released by its distributor, and Bogdanovich then largely faded from view as an active filmmaker.

JOHN CARPENTER   On the basis of three witty and shrewdly filmed B pictures—DARK STAR (1974), ASSAULT ON PRECINCT 13 (1977), and HALLOWEEN (1978)—John Carpenter seemed poised on the threshold of a major career in the 1980s. HALLOWEEN made him famous for horror, and he single-handedly defined the modern slasher film in

Kurt Russell battles an alien menace in THE THING, *a nearly career-ending picture for director John Carpenter.*

this creepy tale about a serial killer who returns to his hometown and sharpens his knives on Halloween eve. Establishing the killer's presence and perspective with extended subjective camerawork, Carpenter gave the film a brilliant visual style and elaborated the slasher film's key signature device, the floating, optical point-of-view shot. Moving from horror to science fiction, Carpenter made another nearly as influential picture. ESCAPE FROM NEW YORK (1981) was a seminal work in the era's dystopic sci-fi cycle, picturing the United States as a fascist police state overrun with crime and decay. Its images of crumbling cityscapes would, along with those of BLADE RUNNER (1982), provide the essential iconography for a decade's worth of grimly pessimistic science fiction films.

On each of these early pictures, Carpenter displayed a flair for working on low budgets while getting maximum effects and a cinematic self-consciousness that pleased critics and led them to expect more and better things from him. When he was finally allowed to graduate from B pictures and make a major studio film, he did THE THING (1982), a tense, well-made update of the Howard Hawks–Christian Nyby fifties classic.

The picture remains one of the decade's important films, but it virtually ended Carpenter's career. With then-state-of-the-art gore effects, achieved with latex and miniature models, Carpenter's THING featured a striking visual design, locating evil and terror in the formlessness of the frozen Antarctic snowscapes. Moreover, it updated the original film by offering a potently metaphoric treatment of the monster so that the film became a symbolic commentary on its social era. Whereas Hawks's film showed the monster defeated by the teamwork and camaraderie of its human opponents, Carpenter showed a dysfunctional society in the community of Antarctic researchers. The group is riddled with tension and mistrust, and the men fail to work together to defeat the intruder. Accentuating the tension are anxieties about who is human and who not, the alien having taken over an undisclosed number of the men at the research post. To destroy the alien, the men destroy themselves and the compound that sustains them amid the frozen wastes of the icy wilderness. At film's end, two survivors warily face one another—significantly, a white man and a black man—each convinced the other is a monster. About the film's pessimistic social vision, Carpenter noted, "I was seeing this movie as a parable of our times. . . . It's also a lot like the world we live in right now [in the 1990s]. Not only can we not trust that we don't have diseases or that we're not some sort of killer inside, but we also don't trust each other, in general, because of the skin color or ideology. I think it's a film that's as true to its time as Hawks' version in 1951 was true to its time."[25]

Unfortunately for Carpenter, the picture was greeted with great hostility upon its release. The prevailing mood in Reagan America was resolutely upbeat, and in this context the film's tone seemed perverse and hateful. E.T. was the alien everyone wanted to see. Carpenter believed that its poorly timed release hurt his picture by pitting it against E.T. and the era's zeitgeist, which that film embodied. "What happened was it was 1982, the summer of E.T. THE THING was the exact opposite of E.T. It wasn't a friendly, fun movie. It was a bleak and grim film. The perception in Hollywood, among my peers, was THE THING was a really big, gigantic bomb."[26]

Carpenter's career never quite recovered from the collective impression that he had used studio funding to make an odious picture. The film's special effects were attacked for being gruesome and unpleasant, possibly because of the backlash then forming against the huge wave of low-budget slasher films in distribution in 1981–82. "THE THING was probably the movie that changed my creative career more than any other. That movie was universally hated by critics and audiences. . . . It really affected me because my agent and people around me were calling and saying you have got to change your ways. I lost a job at Universal because of that film. I thought I made this great film."[27]

Carpenter's career now faltered. He made a mechanical Stephen King adaptation, CHRISTINE (1983), sweet, Spielbergish sci-fi, STARMAN (1984), and a wild homage to Hong Kong movies, BIG TROUBLE IN LITTLE CHINA (1986). He then was demoted by the majors back to B movies, where he finished the decade with PRINCE OF DARKNESS (1987) and THEY LIVE (1988), the latter a nifty sci-fi political satire about the harsh social policies of Reagan America. Unable to sustain a career as a front-rank industry insider, Carpenter began and ended the decade in B pictures, where he perhaps experienced a better fit between the materials and working methods and his sensibilities. With THE THING, he had created one of the decade's memorable films, but the legacy of that picture was a broken career.

FRANCIS FORD COPPOLA   Francis Ford Coppola's seventies triumphs THE GOD-FATHER (1972) and THE GODFATHER, PART II (1974) had given him an artistic prestige and power that was unparalleled among his director peers. In the 1980s his creative ambitions and poor business sense dissipated that power and turned him into an itinerant filmmaker no longer able to dictate his terms. In 1980, Coppola bought a ten-acre lot in Hollywood and launched Zoetrope Studios, his grand and ambitious effort to start a new studio that would be filmmaker-friendly, operate with in-house talent as did the classical studios of old Hollywood, and boldly innovate production with new technologies including the storyboarding and previsualization of shots on computer and high-resolution video and the use of satellite distribution.

Unable to secure complete funding for his first Zoetrope film, ONE FROM THE HEART (1982), Coppola nevertheless plunged on and started production. His ambition to create extravagant and stylized imagery, his willingness to undertake ongoing and expensive revisions of production design even after shooting began, and his uncertainty over what the film should be about resulted in a needlessly expensive $27 million production. Amid the picture's grandly stylized sets and imagery, the storyline—about two lovers who squabble, separate, and then reconcile—was thin to the point of translucence, too slight and unembellished to support the weight of Coppola's visual design. ONE FROM THE HEART was thus terribly out of balance, dazzling audiences with its images while leaving them feeling that the picture was empty at its core. Paramount dropped its plans to distribute the picture, and Coppola secured a last minute distribution deal with Columbia. But the damage was done. Reviews were poor, and the picture flopped commercially and was pulled from release.

Coppola's assets were bound to the fate of this film, and its failure led to the collapse of Zoetrope Studios and his effort to become a visionary force in the production and distribution of American film. (Jon Lewis provides a detailed account of these tribulations in *Whom God Wishes to Destroy: Francis Coppola and the New Hollywood*. Durham:

Dean Tavoularis's production design was a visual highlight of ONE FROM THE HEART.

Duke University Press, 1995.) He put Zoetrope up for sale before the studio had completed its second year of operation, and his career was now adrift. The majors were unwilling to fund other expensive Coppola projects, and he seemed unable to connect with the box office on those projects that he originated (e.g., RUMBLE FISH [1983], GARDENS OF STONE [1987]). His cachet with the majors was eroded further when he became enmeshed in an acrimonious battle during the production and release of THE COTTON CLUB (1984) with producer Robert Evans, the picture's financiers, and distributor Orion. Coppola and Evans had worked together to create THE GODFATHER (1972), a genuine classic, but their relations had been strained and angry, with highly publicized disputes over the editing of the picture. While their hostilities had been relatively contained on THE GODFATHER, they exploded into open warfare on THE COTTON CLUB. The film, originating from a series of troubled scripts, was an uneasy mixture of the musical and gangster genres in its portrait of the popular Harlem nightclub. Coppola and Evans feuded over the conception, shooting, and editing of the picture, and their battles helped erode each man's career. For Evans, it was to have been his comeback as producer; for Coppola, it was a return to the gangster terrain that had made his name. But the film was neither here nor there. The narrative line was cluttered, and the gangster material failed to integrate with the music and the film's depiction of black culture, displacing those elements despite their evident historic importance. The film satisfied neither viewers looking for a gangster movie nor those looking for a portrait of Harlem's cultural vibrancy. The picture was greeted with mixed reviews, given a weak release by Orion, and returned only $13 million in domestic rentals on its $47 million production cost.

Coppola's next film, PEGGY SUE GOT MARRIED (1986), was a box-office success, but Coppola was a director for hire on the project. After the damage inflicted on his reputation by ONE FROM THE HEART and THE COTTON CLUB, he had not been the producer's first choice as director. Coppola signed for the project knowing that he was inheriting a preassembled package of script and star (Kathleen Turner) and that his debt load now compelled him to work as a journeyman director. Turner's winsome and emotionally expansive performance as Peggy Sue, who revisits the world of her youth during a period of marital crisis, gives the film tremendous heart, and Coppola supports her with a visual design that is shrewd and intelligent but not intrusive or showy. It was Coppola's best work in many years, and it showed what he could do when kept on a tight leash so that his aesthetic ambitions did not unbalance a picture.

His next picture, GARDENS OF STONE, was a thematically murky portrait of the Honor Guard at Arlington National Cemetery during the years of the Vietnam War. This was Coppola's first return to the subject of the Vietnam War since APOCALYPSE NOW (1979). As with that film, however, GARDENS OF STONE failed to manifest a discernable point of view, and its conceptual disorganization was perhaps a result of the personal tragedy that befell Coppola during production when his son was killed in a boating accident. Because GARDENS OF STONE failed to find an audience upon release, Coppola was again shackled when he commenced production of TUCKER: THE MAN AND HIS DREAM (1988). The film portrayed Preston Tucker's entrepreneurial efforts to build an innovative car in the 1940s independently of the Big Three automakers. But Coppola's present status meant that he'd have to make a different sort of picture than the one he had planned. Paramount agreed to fund and distribute the film after George Lucas interceded for him. As the film's executive producer, Lucas maintained tight supervision and made sure that Coppola took the film in an upbeat direction to ensure its mar-

Jeff Bridges played the dreamer and visionary in Tucker, *whose dilemmas were akin to those of director Francis Ford Coppola.*

ketability. Under Lucas's shaping, the film became a celebratory and romantic story about American entreprenurial vision instead of a dark fable about genius thwarted in the corporate marketplace (a fable that Coppola may have felt paralleled his own career). Coppola's weakened position left him no choice but to accede to Lucas's suggestions. As Coppola ruefully observed, "He [Lucas] wanted me to candyapple it up a bit, make it like a Disney film. . . . it's not the movie I would have made at the height of my power."[28]

At decade's end, Coppola acceded to further compromise—a return to the Godfather saga for a third film, released in 1990 and rushed through post-production with unsolved narrative problems. It was a picture he had been refusing to make for years, and it seemed inevitably like a step backward. He began the decade as a bold visionary seeking to transform American film. But in so trying, he harnessed his ambitions to expensive productions that flamed with audiences, and instead of transforming the industry, his place in the industry was transformed. With the failure of Zoetrope, Coppola had to extricate himself from a mountain of debt and so undertook his years as a journeyman director for hire, compelled to craft less audacious works. His eighties travails resulted from tensions between his expansive and expensive artistic goals, the need for box-office success inherent in costly productions, and his reluctance to work for that success. It was a ruinous set of contradictions that sabotaged Coppola's career and made for a dispiriting finish to an exciting beginning.

Brian De Palma   Attracted to filmmaking because it permitted exploration of his strong visual ideas, Brian De Palma found significant success in the 1970s, but when the nation's moral climate shifted in the 1980s, he found himself under fire and his work the target of protest. Sisters (1973), Phantom of the Paradise (1974), and Carrie

(1976) garnered him a solid critical reputation as an intelligent stylist of horror material. In the eighties, though, his work was criticized for its violence, especially against women, and for being overly derivative of Hitchcock. The prominent violence against women in De Palma's films—in DRESSED TO KILL (1980) and BODY DOUBLE (1984) they are slashed, stabbed, and impaled—generated tremendous opposition because the feminist critique of violence against women in media was acquiring much cultural force in the early and mid-1980s. (I explore this development in relation to Hollywood film and De Palma's work in ch. 9.)

Amid a rising chorus of criticism, De Palma baited his critics in ways that further enraged them. SCARFACE (1983), a three-hour update of the 1932 Howard Hawks gangster classic, featured abundant violence, including a notorious chainsaw killing that prompted the MPAA to threaten the film with an X rating unless De Palma trimmed the gore. He lashed back at his critics, saying "I want to be *infamous*. I want to be *controversial*. It's much more colorful. . . . if they want an X, they'll get a *real* X."[29]

Despite or perhaps because of its excesses, SCARFACE emerged as a quintessential eighties film, as much in tune with and as reflective of its era as the Howard Hawks's original was of Depression America. Producer Martin Bregman wanted to make a type of gangster picture—a classical rise-and-fall story—and to show a character type, like James Cagney's psychopathic Cody Jarrett, that audiences had not seen for many years. De Palma's update of the picture relocated its action to Miami and made its gangster hero a Cuban who had been expelled from Castro's Cuba as part of the Mariel boat exodus of 1980. Tony Montana (Al Pacino) arrives in a Miami awash in narco dollars and quickly rises to a position of prominence and power in the cocaine trade. The film is especially vivid in evoking the eighties as a decade of avarice, greed, and moral corruption. Pacino's Montana is perfect for the times, all appetite, a shark, dead-eyed and ferocious, killing his way to the top of the narco food chain. Tony boasts to a friend, "Me, I want what's coming to me. The world and everything that's in it."

Tony briefly attains his wish with the help of compliant U.S. businesses. With a script by Oliver Stone, the film indicts American capitalism for being a bed partner with Montana and the South American drug kingpins. Legitimate American banks launder Montana's drug money, and a U.S. government representative is shown in attendance at a strategy session held by a drug lord and his associates in the Bolivian government and military. Eventually, Montana succumbs to the product he peddles, and as the pile of cocaine on his desktop becomes a mountain, he is assassinated by the Bolivians in an extended scene of slaughter during which a defiant Tony achieves his moment of apotheosis in death.

Awash with blood and cruelty, De Palma's SCARFACE is unremittingly savage and cold. The chainsaw killing is one of the decade's most infamous scenes of violence. When Tony and Angel, a Cuban friend, are ambushed by a gang of Columbian drug dealers, the gang's leader forces Tony to watch as he cuts Angel to pieces with the saw. The scene originated in Oliver Stone's script, based on accounts Stone had heard and read of drug killings done in this manner. De Palma resolved to include this detail in the film in order to dramatize the intensified violence spawned by the narco trade.

The sequence is truly horrific, but like the shower scene in PSYCHO (1960), much of it works by suggestion and implication, lodged in the viewer's imagination with terrible clarity by images that are not graphically detailed. The dismemberment occurs off camera, and it is the horrid roar of the saw, Pacino's frenzied expressions as he watches, and the blood spattered on walls and floor that give the scene its terrible power. De Palma

The flamboyant violence in Brian De Palma's SCARFACE *enraged many critics and helped make the picture as controversial in its era as the Howard Hughes–Howard Hawks original had been in its time.*

shows nothing of the actual cutting, but the scene (and the film) was vehemently attacked by virtually every national film critic. The scene's ingenious construction—its compositional design and editing—elicited this outrage, rather than anything explicit De Palma had shown. In part because of this scene's hideous intensity, the picture was villified, as Hawks's SCARFACE had been villified in the 1930s for its violence. Both films outraged their respective critical establishments, and in this way De Palma's remake was truest to its source. The film's energy and savagery, united with its political portrait of the drug trade, make for a powerful and memorable evocation of eighties narco-corruption.

De Palma followed SCARFACE with BODY DOUBLE (1984), a retread of Alfred Hitchcock's REAR WINDOW (1954) and VERTIGO (1958) set in the world of pornographic filmmaking with generous doses of sex and violence. It was the sex-violence picture De Palma had threatened to make when he condemned his critics on SCARFACE with the threat to make a real X. The impalement of a woman with a power drill was the film's most incendiary scene, though the picture as a whole was widely condemned for its tawdriness.

Uncharacteristically, De Palma next tried a comedy, WISE GUYS (1986), before directing his only solid hit of the decade, THE UNTOUCHABLES (1987), a well-mounted feature version of the popular television show. The picture has a narrative economy, momentum, and power that is unusual for a De Palma film, and this exceptional storytelling, along with a winning star performance by Sean Connery, made THE UNTOUCHABLES an uncommonly well rounded, well mounted production. It was precisely the kind of solid commercial filmmaking that De Palma almost never practiced.

It was the fifth biggest box-office film that year, and this clout permitted De Palma to make CASUALTIES OF WAR (1989), a project he was genuinely close to and which he hoped would make an important statement about the Vietnam War. But the picture was unceasingly grim and brutal. It depicted a group of American soldiers who kidnap a Vietnamese woman, repeatedly rape her, and then murder her. While De Palma no doubt wanted viewers to condemn the soldiers, the close visual attention devoted to the woman's brutalization seemed almost pornographic in its fixation. As a result, and because of the turn his reputation had now taken, CASUALTIES OF WAR was criticized for its lurid violence against women (though the film had its source in real events), and it did miserable business. De Palma then compounded his slide by directing a picture widely perceived (like ISHTAR) as a great modern stinker, THE BONFIRE OF THE VANITIES (1990), an adaptation of the popular Tom Wolfe novel.

Despite his florid visual stylishness, De Palma's career in the eighties foundered because the sexual politics of the period were incompatible with the violence in his films, particularly when aimed at women. Impaling them with power drills and slashing at them with razors damaged his reputation among critics and in the industry itself. To date, De Palma's work has not fully recovered from this tarnishing.

ARTHUR PENN   Penn directed a group of key pictures in the late 1960s and early 1970s (BONNIE AND CLYDE [1967], ALICE'S RESTAURANT [1969], LITTLE BIG MAN [1970], NIGHT MOVES [1975]) that captured the verve of the counterculture, its subsequent collapse, and the ensuing despair of the post-Watergate period. His sense of connection with the cultural politics and struggles of those decades gave his work tremendous vitality. By contrast, the politics of the later 1970s and 1980s puzzled and dispirited him, and his filmmaking could not flourish in response to its social moment. When America left the contentious sixties behind, Penn lost the crucible for his work, those conditions to which it, and he, had risen so memorably. In concert with this, the onset of the blockbuster era depleted his spirits even more. While maintaining the cautions expressed at the outset of this chapter, it seems clear that Penn was a major casualty of the industry's move toward blockbuster production and projects that had synergy across the ancillary markets. Penn felt considerable antipathy for this type of filmmaking, and this, conjoined with his political estrangement, left him effectively paralyzed as a filmmaker. Out of synch commercially and culturally, he nearly ceased work as a director in the eighties, except for three intermittent productions.

FOUR FRIENDS (1981), about the impact of the sixties on a quartet of young people, was based on a script over which Penn had little input, and the resulting film was intriguing if erratic in its execution. While it showed his continuing interest in the political culture of the 1960s, its themes and formal design lacked the energy and innovation of the work he had done in that period. His other two pictures during the decade were uninspired genre pieces. TARGET (1985) teamed him again with actor Gene Hackman, with whom he had done stupendous work in BONNIE AND CLYDE and NIGHT MOVES. But it was a routine espionage thriller that originated from Penn's desire to prove to the majors that he was not, as they perceived him, "some kind of arty, very distant, strange character who couldn't shoot an action sequence."[30] Indeed, TARGET has some well-staged action scenes, but the picture rarely rises above them, and its sheer ordinariness seemed hard to square with the talent that had made BONNIE AND CLYDE and NIGHT MOVES. DEAD OF WINTER (1987), a horror-chiller, Penn made as a favor to some young friends who had gotten backing from MGM but could not deliver a director who could handle the production.

Although Penn felt that these were acceptable pictures, they were far from his groundbreaking work of the late sixties. Penn's voice as a film director became quiescent during the eighties, although other strong stylists such as Scorsese and Altman found ways to keep working. Penn acknowledged about their continuing work, "I went to the movies of Altman and Cimino and Scorsese with admiration and maybe a little touch of envy. I couldn't find my subject, my story. I had trouble finding a focus."[31] Penn remained disillusioned by the high cost of studio productions and by his perception that this expense militated against the possibility of doing good work in the system. This was perhaps a self-defeating outlook since it ensured that he would not get the chance to do good work in the system, even as others were, or that he would do it if given the chance. He remained somewhat bitter about his prospects: "The Hollywood studios will continue, probably in the Disney model, which is to send out memos saying, 'We gotta cut costs,' but they don't know how to cut costs. Costs are in inverse proportion to *ideas*! And they'll never escape their sort of formulaic predestination, they don't have the mechanism to shed that skin."[32] As a result of this outlook, one of the American cinema's most gifted directors faced a virtual career shutdown in the eighties, despite the opportunities the boom in independent production afforded other directors. Penn did not, or was unable to, take advantage of this boom, and his eighties work remained sporadic and lackluster.

MARTIN SCORSESE   Martin Scorsese began the 1980s as a highly respected filmmaker but one who was on the fringes of the system, in part because his films were quirky and moved in different directions from the studio product. MEAN STREETS (1973), ALICE DOESN'T LIVE HERE ANYMORE (1974), TAXI DRIVER (1976), and NEW YORK, NEW YORK (1977) were all pictures that worked against the narrative and stylistic expectations of viewers and studio executives, and none were major hits, although TAXI DRIVER did well and generated a great deal of critical and media attention. NEW YORK, NEW YORK was a famous failure, in both its conceptual design (an effort to mix film noir and the movie musical) and its box-office performance. Scorsese was not a filmmaker to whom the majors entrusted large budgets and big productions, but he commanded a measure of respect throughout the industry. Producer David Field noted, "I thought sure the studios should make sure that Marty always had the money to make the movies he wanted to make. He is one of these rare people, and we should just do that. Of course, you say that in a studio meeting, and people re-examine what they think of you as an executive. But I do feel that way about him."[33]

Scorsese began the eighties with a picture that is now widely regarded as one of the decade's best. Based on the life of boxer Jake La Motta, a middleweight champ, RAGING BULL (1980) is a powerful portrait of a man who channels his rage inside the ring to great success while his inability to control it outside the ring destroys his life. The boxing sequences were shot with exceptional ferocity by cinematographer Michael Chapman (using hand-held work, slow motion, Steadicam, variable camera speeds, and a flashbulb simulator), but it is the scenes of domestic violence between La Motta and his wife that are the most disturbing, particularly those eerie moments of tense calm before La Motta explodes, when his paranoia about his wife's fidelity drives him to twist every casual remark into a lunatic proof of her adultery. Scorsese makes no attempt to explain La Motta's violence by, for example, attributing it to some personal trauma. Instead, the rage simply *is*. It exists, beyond explanation, and Scorsese finds it sufficiently compelling to study at close range and with judgment suspended, save for a

Martin Scorsese's vivid and powerful RAGING BULL *remains one of the decade's most ambitious and uncompromising pictures.*

compassion that is reserved for La Motta's (but not his victims) moments of greatest defeat and alienation. The most intense and sustained of these occurs when La Motta, bereft of wife and family, is imprisoned for selling liquor to a minor and beats his fists and head against the concrete cell in a prolonged act of self-laceration. It is a harrowing moment, but it provides only a limited illumination of the character. Instead of reassuring answers, the film operates like CITIZEN KANE (1941) and PSYCHO (1960), earlier classics that highlighted the complexity and opacity of human personality. The film's La Motta is a stark and harrowing creation and a hauntingly enigmatic character.

The film is a highlight in the career collaboration between Scorsese and Robert De Niro, who plays La Motta and physically inhabits the character in extraordinary terms, taking him from a lean, muscular youth to bloated middle age. De Niro was intrigued at the prospect of showing a character emotionally falling apart by gaining weight, and he put on sixty pounds to play La Motta in his corpulent years. It became one of the most famous physical transformations by an actor in American cinema. As he had done with TAXI DRIVER, Scorsese here placed a violent, paranoid individual, played by De Niro with manic intensity, at the center of the film and built its design around his character flaws and pathology, as if daring the audience to admire the work or draw close to the character. Unlike in TAXI DRIVER, however, Scorsese and De Niro humanized La Motta so that he emerges as a suffering individual, tormented by his enduring alienation from others and his own rage and anguish. In this regard, Scorsese and De Niro responded to a pre-production challenge from United Artists. The UA executives were uneasy about the darkness and brutality in the script, and one said that LaMotta, as written, seemed to be a cockroach. Stung by that complaint, Scorsese and De Niro invested the material with great feeling, and it became for them a film about a man who lost everything but regained it spiritually. (The losing is clear enough, but the spiritual regeneration is barely implied.) Not concerned about audience reactions to this unconventional character, Scorsese was uncompromising in his treatment of the material because he felt this picture might be his last. "The idea had been to make this film as openly honest as possible, with no concessions at all for box office or audience. I said, 'That's it. Basically, this is the end of my career, this is it, this is the final one.' I was very surprised when it was received well."[34] The film is a bravura display of technique, with its extraordinary black-and-white cinematography and crisp, fluent editing by Thelma Schoonmaker. Scorsese shot the picture in black and white because of the unstable color dyes in Kodak's film stocks, and, as with all of his eighties pictures, he used the 1.85 aspect ratio to prevent the film from being panned and scanned in its television and video releases.

In the purity of its aesthetic design and the passionate intensity with which it was made, RAGING BULL is unique among Scorsese's eighties films. His other pictures bear the marks of their production circumstances, in terms of quick shoots, low budgets, or calculated design for box office effect. His next picture, THE KING OF COMEDY (1983), with De Niro as an obsessed celebrity hound, was distributed by Fox as a pickup (i.e., a production that Fox did not fund), and preview audiences disliked it. It remains, though, an interesting study of the symbiotic bond between celebrities and their fans, and its low-key emotional restraint contrasts nicely with the inflamed passions of RAGING BULL. By year's end, it had earned a paltry $1.2 million in rentals and had further eroded Scorsese's commercial prospects in the industry. As if to demonstrate this, after agreeing to finance the project, Paramount pulled the plug at the last moment on Scorsese's long-cherished plan to film Níkos Kazantzákis's novel *The Last Temptation of Christ*. Stung by this decision and to demonstrate his continued viability as a filmmaker, Scorsese immediately launched into production of the low-budget ($4 million) AFTER HOURS (1985), a black comedy about a young man's bizarre misadventures in Manhattan. "The trick was to survive," Scorsese said. "That was the idea. The trick was to survive after THE LAST TEMPTATION OF CHRIST was canceled by Paramount in 1983. That was four weeks before shooting was to have started. We had everything ready. It was devastating."[35] AFTER HOURS is a shaggy dog story about Paul Hackett's (Griffin Dunne) efforts to survive, mentally and physically, a series of misadventures with an erratic array of Manhattan kooks, eccentrics, and psychopaths on an evening when he is trapped in Soho without any money. A comedy filmed with aggressive camera moves, the picture was very dark in tone, perhaps in response to Scorsese's career straits.

Given these career problems, his next picture, THE COLOR OF MONEY (1986), was a canny move, and with it he began to establish his credentials as a filmmaker on whom the majors could bank. It required from him, though, a much less personal kind of filmmaking than he had demonstrated in RAGING BULL. His iconoclastic pictures had won critical raves and the respect of executives such as David Field, but they had not advanced his status as a bankable director, someone whose name could be reliably packaged. This was something Scorsese deeply desired. He cherished the industry stature and prestige accorded such accepted masters as William Wyler, John Ford, and Alfred Hitchcock. Like them, he wanted to have a prized place inside the industry from which he could make personal films like THE HEIRESS (1949), VERTIGO (1958), or THE SEARCHERS (1956). Although he would not attain this standing until the early nineties, THE COLOR OF MONEY was a necessary project to begin the transformation. With it, he showed the industry that he could work with a major star and could build a picture around the requisites of that star's persona. In this case, the star was Paul Newman in a repeat of his role as Fast Eddie Felson from Robert Rossen's near-great THE HUSTLER (1961). Scorsese observed, "We wound up working about nine months on the script and, in that process, we really started to shape the film for Paul. We realized we were making a star vehicle movie."[36] Michael Eisner, a Scorsese supporter and the president of Disney (the film's distributor), resolved to promote the picture with full studio resources out of respect for Newman and Scorsese and because the picture was part of Disney's efforts to remake its film division with more adult-oriented films. As a result of Disney's solid backing, the picture was among the top twenty box-office films of 1986. As an artistic successor to THE HUSTLER, however, it was a disappointment. It lacks the earlier film's psychological depth, and, although Newman clearly relished the chance to play Felson again, the material as written does not have the eloquence of Rossen's script, nor

Paul Newman reprised his role as Fast Eddie Felson in THE COLOR OF MONEY, *an important transitional film in Scorsese's career.*

does it give Newman the great soliloques he had in the earlier picture. Furthermore, the screen time given Tom Cruise as a young hustler displaces Felson to an often-subordinate role. A rare opportunity to extend a near-classic film had slipped away.

The financial success of THE COLOR OF MONEY began to turn things around for Scorsese. Michael Ovitz, of Creative Artists Agency, took Scorsese as a client, and Ovitz approached Universal about making THE LAST TEMPTATION OF CHRIST. Universal president Tom Pollock liked the book and admired Scorsese. The studio agreed, and the $7 million project was cofinanced by Garth Drabinsky's Cineplex Odeon, which assured exhibition outlets for the controversial production. Scorsese resolved to make a serious religious film in which Christ would be made real through an exploration of his human aspects. In this regard, he wished to overcome the tendency in Biblical films of treating Christ as a wooden figure, and the extent to which he succeeded was apparent in the controversy that embroiled the production when fundamentalist groups attacked it as sacriligious. Elated to be at last undertaking this film, Scorsese applied himself to the task with his customary intensity. The sixty-day shoot was completed under arduous conditions in Morocco, and Scorsese often had to work without the benefit of viewing rushes. The finished work is an uncommonly gritty biblical film, in which the flies, heat, and desert sand have a palpable presence lacking in earlier Hollywood Bible pictures and in which the physicality of fleshly existence is vividly contrasted with the spiritual domain. I consider this film and the controversy that surrounded it in more detail in chapter 8.

With the completion of his dream project, Scorsese returned to Disney for "Life Lessons," an exhuberantly filmed portrait of a narcissistic painter, played by Nick Nolte. It comprised his segment of NEW YORK STORIES (1989), an anthology picture with other segments directed by Woody Allen and Francis Coppola. This short film was his final picture released in the eighties. Through his career crisis, he had reinvented himself as a filmmaker whom the majors might reliably support and whose critical cachet would benefit them even if Scorsese's box office was never huge. Scorsese's crisis was thus neither as long nor as severe as Robert Altman's or Arthur Penn's, in large part because Scorsese genuinely wanted the acceptance and respect of the industry and was willing to make a COLOR OF MONEY to show he could do successful industry vehicles. His nineties work—GOODFELLAS (1990), CAPE FEAR (1991), THE AGE OF INNOCENCE (1993), CASINO (1995), KUNDUN (1997)—had solid financial backing and, for the most part, met with critical and relative commercial success, as he alternated genre pictures with more difficult and ambitious projects (INNOCENCE, KUNDUN). During the eighties, then, Scorsese successfully negotiated a major career transition. He moved from the fringes of the industry to a position of power while continuing to make, for the most part, challenging and ambitious films.

THE NEWCOMERS

While the 1980s were a rough decade for the major auteurs of the 1970s, a diverse group of younger directors successfully established their careers, adding important new voices to the American cinema. To varying degrees, the industry proved itself to be receptive to their talents, and they were able to build and sustain careers as next-generation filmmakers. American film culture benefited from the work of these new filmmakers, and the range of their creative voices demonstrated the industry's relative flexibility and readiness to fund work exhibiting diverse styles and sensibilities.

WOMEN DIRECTORS While Hollywood was still primarily a boy's town in the eighties, with men ensconced in the industry's primary power roles, an increasing number of women began to fill roles as directors and producers. While a compelling case can be made that grouping directors in terms of gender imposes distinctions that ghettoize women—for example, by implying that women would make "women's" pictures—it is nevertheless important to note the emergence of a group of women filmmakers as an important development in eighties cinema. The industry, though, was far from being an equal opportunity employer. In almost every case, women working as directors had to overcome unique challenges (e.g., men who did not like taking orders from a woman, male executives resistant to certain story situations) and confronted serious impediments to the continuity of their careers. Many, such as Susan Seidelman, Amy Heckerling, and Joan Micklin Silver, found that a successful low-budget, often independent feature enabled them to make the transition toward bigger-budget productions, whereupon they experienced difficulties sustaining a career at this level of industry financing. Furthermore, because few women were functioning as directors with funding or distribution from the majors, those who were often found their visibility to be a source of additional pressure. As director Randa Haines (CHILDREN OF A LESSER GOD [1986]) expressed, "Every woman working maybe even still today feels that she's carrying an added responsibility, that every time a woman succeeds at doing something, it opens the door a little bit further for everybody else, and if you fail, it closes the door just that little bit."[37]

Measured in terms of the industry clout that box-office success provides (e.g., access to major stars, top cinematographers, aggressive promotion and distribution), the most successful of this new group of filmmakers was Penny Marshall. She parlayed a successful television acting career ("Laverne and Shirley") into an opportunity to direct features. Marshall agreed to helm a troubled project, JUMPIN' JACK FLASH, which was already several weeks into pre-production; when the Whoopi Goldberg vehicle did well at the box office upon its release in 1986, Marshall was poised for the sustained industry success that so often eluded other women directors. Her next project, BIG (1988), with Tom Hanks, proved to be a popular comedy about a child who wakes up one morning and finds that he inhabits the body of a thirty-year-old man. The film was well written and, as directed by Marshall, helped revive Tom Hanks's foundering film career. She now had credit for both saving a troubled production and directing a hit movie. Flush with this success, Marshall showed considerable courage with the choice of her next project, a risky switch from comedy to drama that showed a keen judgment about the material. AWAKENINGS (1991), starring Robin Williams and Robert De Niro, was an achingly sad story about a rare neurological disorder, but Marshall managed to give the film an affirmative spirit, and it was a major *succès d'estime*.

Unfortunately, Marshall's string of critical and popular hits was the anomoly for women filmmakers during the eighties, most of whom found themselves marginalized by the industry, despite making, on the whole, interesting and offbeat pictures. After a string of successful independent films in the 1970s, Joan Micklin Silver directed only two features in the eighties (along with two television movies). LOVERBOY (1989) was a flat comedy about a pizza delivery clerk, but CROSSING DELANCEY (1988) was a superb comedy-drama about a young Jewish woman whose grandmother decides to fix her up with an eligible bachelor not quite to her taste.

Amy Heckerling began the eighties with great promise. FAST TIMES AT RIDGEMONT HIGH (1982) was that rare oxymoronic film—an intelligent teen comedy. Chronicling

*Penny Marshall was one of the decade's most successful and enduring women direc-
tors, and the popular success of* BIG, *starring Tom Hanks, helped solidify her career.*

the desires and anxieties of Ridgemont students, whose social lives center around the
local shopping mall, the film helped launch the careers of Sean Penn (as the now-clas-
sic brain-dead surfer dude Spicolli), Phoebe Cates, and the brilliant actor Jennifer Jason
Leigh. Heckerling aimed to approach the requisite nudity of a teen comedy from a
decidedly more female point of view by overturning the movie convention mandating
female nudity but no male nudity. Her resolve to show male nudity, however, drew a
threatened X rating from the MPAA, and as a result she had the lab enlarge the offending shot so the man would be displayed only from the shoulders up. "There was no way
the studio could allow it to be an X, so we had to take the shot and blow it up, so I wound
up having to do exactly what I had always seen in movies—a man's shoulders and a
woman's breasts. I felt bad about that and, in fact, there were reviews that asked how
could I, as a woman, do that."[38]

With the success of FAST TIMES, Heckerling aimed to differentiate herself from the
teen sex comedies that she was now being asked to direct. Unfortunately, her next film,
JOHNNY DANGEROUSLY (1984), was a weak, relatively unfunny gangster comedy starring
Michael Keaton and Joe Piscopo. Feeling that its poor box office and reviews threatened
her career, she rushed into production of NATIONAL LAMPOON'S EUROPEAN VACATION
(1985) without a polished script and then survived the resulting debacle—an unpleasant
production resulting in a bad film—by turning to television work. But at decade's end,
Heckerling returned to features and directed LOOK WHO'S TALKING (1989), a vulgar
comedy with John Travolta about a talking baby. The picture was coarse, with abundant
bathroom humor, but extremely popular, and it renewed Heckerling's standing within the
industry, which had waned since the release of FAST TIMES.

Another filmmaker who sustained an eighties career largely in the subgenre of teen
comedy was Martha Coolidge. She had established a name in feminist circles with a

Amy Heckerling's vivid FAST TIMES AT RIDGEMONT HIGH boasted a deliciously comic performance by Sean Penn.

well-regarded documentary about rape, NOT A PRETTY PICTURE (1975), but her industry films, while concentrating on women's relationships, tended to have a much softer point of view. Coolidge understood that her career in the industry depended on avoiding politically contentious issues. As she acknowledged, "Although my point of view is feminist-influenced, my films aren't political pictures—and certainly Hollywood is not interested in making political pictures. Nor are the studios interested in dealing with an obnoxiously political person. Or anybody who would be abrasive in any way."[39] Coolidge worked more frequently in theatrical features than was the norm for women filmmakers during the period, and her eighties teen comedies comprise VALLEY GIRL (1983),

JOY OF SEX (1984), CITY GIRL (1984), and REAL GENIUS (1985). In the early nineties she broke out of this subgenre with her finest work, to that point, as director, RAMBLIN' ROSE (1991), a gentle drama about a wayward young woman (Laura Dern) who complicates life for a genteel family.

Amy Jones found that exploitation films, rather than teen comedies, provided her with an entry point into the industry. With SLUMBER PARTY MASSACRE (1982) she tried to infuse the conventional slasher film with more a pointedly female perspective, an admittedly difficult task given the requisite formula of male killer and female victims. But she moved out of exploitation pictures with her next film, LOVE LETTERS, a drama in which Jamie Lee Curtis (the queen of slasher pictures) played a young woman intrigued with the tale revealed by her mother's love letters. MAID TO ORDER (1987) was Jones's only other feature of the eighties, a comic fantasy about a rich girl forced to work as a housemaid. Despite the picture's low budget ($4 million), Jones had little control over casting or scoring, and the picture became a programmer, an opportunity to work, rather than a personal project.[40] Jones was much more closely committed to her script for MYSTIC PIZZA (1988), but she was fired from the project by the Goldwyn Company and denied an opportunity to direct it. After MAID TO ORDER, Jones ceased work as a director and began to build a successful career in the nineties as a writer.

Working with exploitation material—drugs, sex, violence, youth—but transforming it into serious and disturbing filmmaking, Penelope Spheeris established a prolific filmmaking career by investigating the anomie and rage within America's teen population. Her best works were two documentaries about punk rock and heavy metal that bookended the decade: THE DECLINE OF WESTERN CIVILIZATION (1981) and THE DECLINE OF WESTERN CIVILIZATION, PART II: THE METAL YEARS (1988). In between, she made a series of fiction films that investigated teen brutality and drug use: SUBURBIA (1983), HOLLYWOOD VICE SQUAD (1986), THE BOYS NEXT DOOR (1986), and DUDES (1987). Spheeris made raw films about ugly realities, and in so doing created trouble for herself from men in the industry who deemed such subjects and styles unsuitable for a woman director: "I believe one reason I have been held at arm's length in the business is that my films have always expressed a certain amount of brutality and anger, and that scares men. They don't want to see women dealing with such emotions."[41] Certainly this was a rough road to follow, both in terms of the films' subject matter and the cool industry reception accorded her work. Despite her ability to maintain a decade-long career making hard films on harsh issues, Spheeris changed her style following DECLINE, PART II. Turning her rapport with youth culture toward comic ends, she found a new level of commercial success with WAYNE'S WORLD (1992), substituting cool irony for the rage hitherto expressed by her film subjects.

Susan Seidelman was a New York University film school graduate whose first feature was made outside the industry as an independent, low-budget production. Shot on the streets of Manhattan, SMITHEREENS (1984) was a comic character study of a drifter who aspires to be a punk rock singer. The film's grit and comic charm attracted the attention of Barbara Boyle, an executive at Orion Pictures who had the authority to green-light low-budget productions. Boyle liked a script Seidelman was pitching about a bored housewife who becomes intrigued with an offbeat character she meets in the personal ads, and her backing enabled Seidelman to turn it into DESPERATELY SEEKING SUSAN (1985), with Madonna and Rosanna Arquette. Though made with the backing of Orion, a mini-major, the picture was shot, and it plays, like an underground film, with a quirky sensibility and loopy narrative that moves in unpredictable directions. Crucially, it got made because the script secured the backing of a female executive. Seidelman had found that male executives had a much cooler reaction to the screenplay. She says it "was the kind of project which a lot of women who were vice-presidents of development had responded to—women tended to like the script. And then they would show it to their male bosses who didn't like it enough to give it the go-ahead."[42]

Unfortunately, Seidelman's next films—MAKING MR. RIGHT (1987), COOKIE (1989), and SHE-DEVIL (1989)—featured increasing budgets and decreasingly favorable critical reactions. SHE-DEVIL, in particular, was widely considered a failure, despite a marvelous performance by Meryl Streep as a comically vengeful wife. A well-mounted BBC production of the Faye Weldon novel was released at the same time, and the feature, with its heavy-handed slapstick, suffered in comparison with the more richly textured BBC miniseries. Seidelman's eighties career is a classic demonstration of the pitfalls of moving from independent filmmaking to industry work. While MAKING MR. RIGHT, COOKIE, and SHE-DEVIL all have excellent qualities, they reflect a more conservative type of filmmaking than what Seidelman had shown in SMITHEREENS and DESPERATELY SEEKING SUSAN. The low economic base of independent film affords considerable aesthetic freedoms to a director (along with technical constraints and a limited audience), while industry employment affords greater technical resources, a larger potential audience, and less aesthetic freedom. It is an insoluable contradiction, and Seidelman is hardly the first filmmaker to discover that the best qualities of her independent work were hard to preserve in her industry-financed projects.

Two other notable filmmakers who worked in features infrequently during the eighties were Randa Haines and Kathryn Bigelow. While compiling extensive television credits as director for "Hill Street Blues" (1981), "Alfred Hitchcock Presents" (1984–84), "Tales from the Crypt" (1989), and the television movie "Something about Amelia" (1984), Haines directed only one feature film. It was, however, one of the decade's prestige pictures, CHILDREN OF A LESSER GOD (1986), focusing on the developing relationship between a teacher (William Hurt) at a school for the deaf and an angry, isolated young deaf woman (Marlee Matlin). Haines elicited exquisite performances from Hurt and Matlin, and although the picture was nominated for Oscars in the categories of best picture, actor, actress (Matlin won here), supporting actress, and screenplay, Haines conspicuously was passed over for a best-director nomination.

Kathryn Bigelow established a strong career in the nineties as a director of stylishly mounted action pictures (BLUE STEEL [1990], POINT BREAK [1991], STRANGE DAYS [1995]). She presaged this in the eighties with THE LOVELESS (1983), about a gang of bikers, and NEAR DARK (1987), a vampire quasi-Western in modern dress about a pack of bloodsuckers roaming the West in a van. Bigelow is a highly articulate filmmaker and a proponent of the view that women directors must not be ghettoized as makers of soft, sensitive films. "Conventionally, hardware pictures, action-oriented, have been male-dominated, and more emotional kind of material has been women's domain. That's breaking down. The notion that there's a woman's aesthetic, a woman's eye, is really debilitating."[43] Bigelow's films are indistinguishable stylistically from male-directed action pictures, and they prove that women can excel as filmmakers in precisely the kinds of material long claimed by men.

Furthermore, the careers of successful female producers demonstrated Bigelow's claim that gender distinctions governing the selection and handling of material were eroding. Debra Hill collaborated as producer with director John Carpenter and on other horror pictures and subsequently added comedy to her producing portfolio: THE FOG

Despite the prestige that accrued to CHILDREN OF A LESSER GOD, *starring Marlee Matlin and William Hurt, its director, Randa Haines, was conspicuously shut out from an Academy Award nomination.*

(1980), HALLOWEEN II (1981), ESCAPE FROM NEW YORK (1981), HALLOWEEN III: SEASON OF THE WITCH (1983), THE DEAD ZONE (1983), CLUE (1985), HEAD OFFICE (1986), ADVENTURES IN BABYSITTING (1987), HEARTBREAK HOTEL (1988), BIG TOP PEE-WEE (1988), and GROSS ANATOMY (1989). Gale Anne Hurd established her producing credentials with expensive, effects-based action films: THE TERMINATOR (1984), ALIENS (1986), ALIEN NATION (1988), BAD DREAMS (1988), and THE ABYSS (1989). Sherry Lansing, who had been head of production at 20th Century–Fox in 1981–82, produced a series of hard-edged dramas: FIRSTBORN (1984), FATAL ATTRACTION (1987), THE ACCUSED (1988), and BLACK RAIN (1989). Kathleen Kennedy maintained an extremely prolific producing career in association with Steven Spielberg. Kennedy's productions included E.T.: THE EXTRA-TERRESTRIAL (1982), GREMLINS (1984), THE GOONIES (1985), BACK TO THE FUTURE (1985), THE COLOR PURPLE (1985), AN AMERICAN TAIL (1986), THE MONEY PIT (1986), EMPIRE OF THE SUN (1987), WHO FRAMED ROGER RABBIT (1988), BACK TO THE FUTURE, PART II (1989), and ALWAYS (1989). In the cases of Kennedy, Lansing, Hill and Hurd, there is little inherent relation between the nature of their pictures and the gender of the producer, and this is true as well for the pictures directed by Penny Marshall, Kathryn Bigelow, and Penelope Spheeris. Bigelow suggested that women "should just be encouraged [by the industry] to work in an as uncompromised a form as possible, be that tougher or softer."[44] To the extent that this began to occur, it was a positive development. The industry began to accommodate the place of women in roles of chief production authority. As this

occurred, though, the industry remained deeply committed to the continuity of its genres and story formulas and, frankly, cared more about these than about the gender of the
people who made the films. The careers of Marshall, Lansing, Hill, Hurd,Kennedy, and
Bigelow demonstrate that by adhering to these traditional formulas and executing them
with great professional skill, women began to secure a place for themselves as filmmakers, where what counted was the quality of the films (normatively defined by the industry), not the gender of the directors or producers.

TIM BURTON   Among other new filmmakers in the 1980s rapidly establishing high-
profile careers was Tim Burton. Trained in animation at the California Institute of Arts,
Burton spent the early eighties at Walt Disney Productions, where he worked as an animator. Given Burton's loopy sensibility and his delight in monsters and eccentric,
twisted characters, Disney was an unlikely employer, and Burton was unhappy inside the
artistic straitjacket of such Disney productions as THE FOX AND THE HOUND (1981). He
found the bland optimism of traditional Disney fare uncomfortably remote from his
interests:

> I was just not Disney material. I just could not draw foxes for the life of me.
> I couldn't do it. I *tried*. I tried, tried. The unholy alliance of animation is: you
> are called upon to be an artist—especially at Disney, where you are per-
> ceived as the artist pure and simple, where your work flows from the artistic
> pencil to the paper, the total artist—but on the other hand, you are called
> upon to be a zombie factory worker. And for me, I could not integrate the
> two.[45]

Despite his frustrations, Burton completed some animated shorts at Disney that
clearly prefigured the styles and subject matter of his subsequent features. VINCENT
(1982) used a German expressionist style (which Burton would employ again to great
effect on BATMAN [1989]) and narration by Vincent Price (who would do a cameo in
EDWARD SCISSORHANDS [1990]) to explore the fantasies of a young, disturbed suburban boy. Anticipating EDWARD SCISSORHANDS, FRANKENWEENIE (1984) visualized the
Frankenstein myth in the suburbs.

Unable to be a Disney team player, Burton left the studio, whereupon he established
a successful feature career making quirky, darkly funny fables replete with eccentric
oddballs and endearing monsters. Burton loved and identified with the monsters that he
had seen in movies and read about in fairy tales because he connected them with the
constricting life of his suburban boyhood, from which he felt outcast and alienated:
"Monster movies are my form of myth, of fairy tale. The purpose of fairy tales for me is
a kind of extreme, symbolic version of life, of what you're going through. In America, in
suburbia, there is no sense of culture, there is no sense of passion. So I think those
served that very specific purpose for me."[46]

Burton's first feature, PEE-WEE'S BIG ADVENTURE (1985), was a funny, inventive
fantasy showcasing actor Paul Reubens' antic, screeching adult-child character, Pee-
Wee Herman, a comic grotesque in the middle of suburbia launched on a wild adventure as he tries to retrieve his stolen bicycle. The picture did fabulous business, placing
in the year's top twenty box-office films. The industry took note and offered him better
budgets. His follow-up picture, BEETLEJUICE (1988), was a dizzying romp through the
afterlife, presided over by Michael Keaton's titular character, a dervish with an unbri-

Paul Reubens as the title character in PEE-WEE'S BIG ADVENTURE, *director Tim Burton's auspicious debut feature.*

dled libido who instructs a pair of ghosts (Alec Baldwin and Geena Davis) on the essentials of effective haunting. Enlivened by Keaton's antics and Burton's boldly eccentric humor (e.g., the afterlife as an overstuffed bureaucracy with case workers and ghosts stacked up in waiting rooms), the picture was one of the year's most popular films.

Burton's affinity for dark-hued fairy tales and his solid box office led Warner Bros. executives to recruit him for BATMAN. Though his films had been solid commercial performers, Burton, at the time, seemed an odd choice to helm a production that had blockbuster potential. According to conventional wisdom, his style was too nontraditional and outré for a mainstream blockbuster. Furthermore, the selection of Burton as director, and Michael Keaton to play Batman offended fans of the comic strip, who dreaded whatever this team was going to concoct. Warners, it appeared, was taking a tremendous risk with these unlikely candidates. But Burton outfoxed all the prognosticators by jettisoning the traditional D.C. Comics rendition for an alternative conception of the character as a dark, tormented knight presiding over a noir world. The film's stunning production design, by Anton Furst, visualized the noir aspects of Gotham City with an oppressive flair and compensated for the film's narrative weaknesses. Burton, Furst, and cinematographer Roger Pratt created a strikingly grim Gotham City, with fascist-style architecture, expressionist shadows, and a black-on-black color palette. Seldom has architecture, conveyed with miniature models and mattes, been employed so flamboyantly as a dominant element of *mise-en-scène* as in Furst's elegantly monstrous designs. It was the most impressive cinematic cityscape since BLADE RUNNER (1982). Alongside that film at the beginning of the decade, BATMAN is a key achievement of eighties production design.

A memorable score by Danny Elfman, in an ongoing partnership with Burton that ranks as one of cinema's best director-composer teams, added punch to the action and gave the film an epic emotional scale. Jack Nicholson's manic star turn as the Joker helped to offset the visual gloom, and Warner Bros. had the biggest hit in its history. BATMAN generated $150 million in domestic rentals for 1989, making it the third biggest picture of the decade.

But Burton's ambivalence about such big-buck filmmaking was quickly apparent. Inevitably tagged for the sequel, Burton made BATMAN RETURNS (1992) even more grotesque and nightmarish a film, with a central character (the Penguin, played by Danny DeVito) of uncommon vulgarity and repugnance. Perhaps because of its darkness and unpalatability, the film performed below Warners' expectations. Disappointed Warners executives farmed the Batman franchise out to a new director and star for its third installment and introduced a revamped style that jettisoned Burton's noirish design in favor of straight action-adventure.

Despite the (for Warners) unacceptable direction in which he had taken BATMAN RETURNS, Burton's sly, twisted humor and affinity for the dark side proved in the eighties to be wholly compatible with funding and distribution from the majors. Burton's popular success enabled him to develop a strikingly original cinematic voice that preferred bold comic fantasies in darkly twisted film worlds. Rather than becoming more cautious with each level of box-office success, however, Burton only grew bolder until he succeeded at subverting the parameters of blockbuster filmmaking with BATMAN RETURNS, a picture that is the antithesis of commercially conservative filmmaking. As he says about his penchant for aesthetic risk, "Those are the only things worth expressing, in some ways: danger, and presenting subversive subjects in a fun way."[47] Herein lies a major distinction between Burton's work and that of David Lynch, the other surrealist of eighties American cinema. In contrast with Lynch's cold gaze, Burton had a warm regard for the loopy characters at the center of his films, and this made his work more endearing and more popular than Lynch's.

JAMES CAMERON   In the 1990s, James Cameron would direct TITANIC (1998), at that time the highest-grossing picture in film history. His work during the 1980s followed a trajectory toward the ever-bigger budgets and increasingly complex effects that came to be associated with his name and that TITANIC epitomized. His work centered in science fiction, and he credited Stanley Kubrick's 2001: A SPACE ODYSSEY (1968) with providing the experience that opened his eyes to film and showed him that cinema could function as art. Honoring the Kubrick influence, he approached science fiction as a serious medium that could reflect upon fundamental issues in human life, rather than as a genre to showcase gadgets and machines and in which people were cardboard cutouts relegated to the background. Accordingly, THE TERMINATOR (1984), ALIENS (1986), and THE ABYSS (1989) place human dramas at the center of their dramatic stages and use these as a basis for exploring issues posed by technology's increasing dominance in the modern world. Cameron's work drew a huge popular response because of his shrewd handling of character and his emphasis on powerful emotional drama, coupled with an extraordinary storytelling skill and impressive visual sense. Cameron confessed to disliking ambiguities in films and remarked that he admires the straight-ahead, no-nonsense narrative style of 1940s Hollywood pictures, and his work, for better and worse, reflected these feelings. The clarity of issue and character in his films is the foundation of their narrative power and humanizes their futuristic settings, while at the same time it tends to limit their artistic resonance.

Cameron started his career doing effects work on low-budget films, including Roger Corman's BATTLE BEYOND THE STARS (1980) and John Carpenter's ESCAPE FROM NEW YORK (1981). When offered his first chance to direct, he took it, although it was a less than auspicious debut: PIRANHA II: THE SPAWNING (1983) was a joint U.S.–Italian production and a sequel to a popular Corman film that had been scripted by John Sayles and directed by Joe Dante. Cameron quarreled with the picture's Italian producer and has said that the film, as released, reflects the producer's editing of the material.[48] While struggling with this project, Cameron wrote the treatment for THE TERMINATOR and, with then-wife Gale Anne Hurd acting as producer, got a production deal from Hemdale.

THE TERMINATOR is a stunning example of action film storytelling, shot and edited to achieve a relentless pace. but, characteristic of Cameron's work, grounding its pyrotechnics in human drama. The film's premise is relatively simple, but in it one sees Cameron reworking some of the themes from his inspirational film, 2001: A SPACE ODYSSEY. These involve the ceding of authority by people to the technological systems they have created and the paradox of intelligent machinery vying with human beings for control over their environment. The film's framing story is set in 2029, a postapocalyptic world run by machines that have triggered a nuclear war to exterminate their human makers. After the war, the surviving humans are herded into extermination camps or used as slaves who load bodies into disposal units that run twenty-four hours a day. Guerrilla war breaks out between the hunter-killer machines and the few surviving humans. The narrative is a time-loop paradox in which a soldier of the future, Kyle (Michael Biehn), is sent back to Los Angeles, circa 1984, to protect Sarah Conner (Linda Hamilton), who will become the mother of the man who leads the guerrillas in their battle against the machines. The machines, for their part, have created a terminator, a cyborg (part man, part machine), and have sent it back through time to hunt and kill Sarah. The film develops as an extended chase with Kyle trying to protect Sarah and to elude or kill the terminator (Arnold Schwarzenegger in the performance that sparked his career). The temporal paradox of the narrative becomes apparent when it is disclosed that the man who sends Kyle into the past is John Conner, Sarah's son, who has been fathered by Kyle during a night of tenderness he shares with Sarah.

The Terminator focuses on the loss of human feeling and identity in a totalitarian world. The bleak future is a nightmare of pain, violence, and death, where the surviving humans have to disconnect themselves from their emotions in order to elude the machines. Looking at Kyle's scars, Sarah murmurs, "So much pain." Kyle replies, "Pain can be controlled. You just disconnect it." Sarah responds, "So you feel nothing?" The terminator represents the ultimate outcome of this deadening of feeling and mechanization of behavior. Like the replicants in Blade Runner and the androids in the Alien films, it is virtually indistinguishable from its human opponents, yet its responses are completely roboticized. Inside, it has a hyper-alloy combat chassis controlled by a microprocessor, while its exterior is covered with living human tissue—flesh, hair, blood—that has been specially grown for the cyborgs. Thus, while the terminator represents the frightening techno-fascism of the future, the tenderness between Sarah and Kyle is the emotional heart of the film and that which the narrative affirms.

At the end of the film, Sarah has become a female warrior, skilled in the techniques of combat and survival, and critics pointed to this unique and new vision of steely feminism. Cameron elaborated on this in his next picture, Aliens, which grounds its drama in Ripley's (Sigourney Weaver) trauma-induced anxieties and the strength of body and will she exhibits to overcome these. Preserved in suspended animation for fifty-seven years following her escape from the Nostromo and its alien visitor (events dramatized in Alien [1979], the first film of the series), Ripley has been drifting through space in her shuttle when the Company (the moniker given to her mysterious corporate employer) rescues her and persuades her to return to LV-426, the planet from which the alien was retrieved. The Company maintains a colony of Terra-formers on LV-426. These seventy families have been working to install an atmosphere processor manufactured by the Company that will generate breathable air on the planet. The Terra-formers have vanished, however, and the Company decides to send Ripley and a squad of Colonial Marines to investigate. The human drama of the film resides in Ripley's need to confront her terror of the planet and its alien inhabitants, and she rises to this challenge when an infant girl, Newt, is discovered in hiding. Ripley becomes her surrogate mother, and in the film's flamboyant climax, she does battle against the alien queen, two ferocious mothers duking it out to protect their progeny. Here, as in The Terminator, Cameron spectacularly transformed the imagery of women in American film by offering lean, grimly determined female warriors outfitted with powerful weaponry. (Terminator 2: Judgment Day [1991] is the climax of this feminist warrior trilogy.) As in his previous film, Cameron surrounded the human drama with a fast-paced, straight-ahead action narrative that swept the viewer along in its forward rush. He was keenly aware of the classic status that Ridley Scott's Alien had achieved and determined to find a different style and sensibility for his picture. Accordingly, rather than replicating the techno-Gothic horror design of Scott's film, he based his sequel on Vietnam and World War II combat movies, ensuring that his production would be clearly differentiated from its predecessor.

James Cameron directs the riveting ALIENS, *which took that series in a new and differ-ent direction from the Ridley Scott original.*

After ALIENS, Cameron embarked on the lengthy production schedules that would become the norm on his next pictures. With its extensive underwater sequences and complex machinery, THE ABYSS (1989) was an extremely difficult, and at times danger-ous, shoot. The film is a white-knuckle ride to the bottom of the ocean, where a salvage crew attempting the retrieval of nuclear weapons from a downed Navy sub encounters a race of alien beings. The storyline is relatively simple and straightforward, but Cameron keeps the tension ratcheted high with several amazing action sequences. Once again, the Kubrick influence works through the material, though this time with dimin-ished success. (The film also reworks material from THE DAY THE EARTH STOOD STILL [1951].) One of the visual highpoints is a scene analogous to the stargate sequence in 2001, as Virgil Brigman (Ed Harris) gets a dazzling tour of the aliens' under-water kingdom. The crux of the film is a utopian wish for world peace, which is achieved through the intervention of the aliens (as in THE DAY THE EARTH STOOD STILL). But Cameron renders their intervention so literally as to dissipate the inherent mystery of their presence and to flatten the film's concluding emotional tone. (These qualities are exacerbated in a longer version of the film that Cameron issued in 1991 for home video.) By contrast, the wisdom of Kubrick's approach in 2001 is evident. By working at a non-verbal level with imagery whose portents elude straightforward interpretation, Kubrick evoked the ineffable with a genuine sense of mystery. Cameron spells everything out for the viewer and for the film's characters, with the result that the narrative resolution becomes trite. He might have trusted that the aesthetic evocation of mystery could be powerful, but this was a filmmaker who disliked ambiguities. THE ABYSS suffers as the result of that preference, despite the undeniable power of the film's riveting narrative. Cameron's fascination with the machinery of cinema and his technological ambitions seemed boundless, but they were checked by an artistic imagination that prized clarity

The difficult filming conditions of THE ABYSS *included the picture's elaborate underwater sets and cramped confines.*

over mystery and straight-ahead storytelling over more nuanced and less tidy narrative designs. In fairness to his work, though, it must be said that this was not a verdict rendered by the popular audience.

JOE DANTE   A witty and clever filmmaker, Joe Dante made the transition from low-budget Roger Corman productions in the 1970s to a career with the majors that was marked, alternately, by success and frustration. With a smart script by John Sayles, Dante's top-of-the-decade horror homage THE HOWLING (1981), his second film as director, was the funniest, most affectionate, and scariest horror movie anyone had seen in years. Full of references to THE WOLF MAN (1941) and big-bad-wolf cartoons, THE HOWLING was sly and self-conscious and grounded Rick Baker's state-of-the-art werewolf transformations in solid story and character. The crisp editing and movie in-jokes would become hallmarks of Dante's work. He had trained as an editor at Corman's New World Pictures from 1974 to 1976, and his love for cinema was based on a voluminous knowledge of old movies. Thus, though Dante's eighties films typically involved a lot of special effects, the films are rarely mechanical, and they have a playful, lively spirit that prevents the effects from dominating the picture.

THE HOWLING did respectable business ($8 million in rentals) for a B movie without a major marketing push, and Dante's evident filmmaking savvy brought him under the Spielberg aegis at this point. (Dante and Robert Zemeckis were the most talented filmmakers that Spielberg mentored during the eighties.) Spielberg liked THE HOWLING and sent Dante the script for what became GREMLINS (1984). Surprised at this sudden missive, Dante thought perhaps Spielberg had mistakenly sent it to the wrong person. But another invitation followed. With Spielberg producing, Dante directed a striking episode of TWILIGHT ZONE: THE MOVIE (1983), Dante's first experience working on a major studio production. "It's a Good Life" portrayed a boy trapped in a nightmarish mental world, unable to turn off the cartoon- and TV-derived images that flood his mind. Shot and edited with manic energy, the episode stood out as the most stylish and striking segment of the film. In it, Dante explored a darker side of the movie mania that he portrayed in more affectionate terms in his later MATINEE (1993).

GREMLINS followed, and its success launched Dante as a specialist in clever, effects-driven comedies. Dante's experiences as a director for the majors, however, were checkered with frustrations and struggle, and the GREMLINS experience presaged these tribulations. (Jim Hillier profiles these problems in detail in *The New Hollywood*.) The film seques from a warm and sentimental opening, depicting a loving family at Christmas, to the evocation of a funny but scary nightmare in which the titular, mischievous, mean-spirited creatures overrun the family's wholesome, picture-postcard community. This latter turn of events provided Dante with lots of opportunity for movie in-jokes (cameos include animator Chuck Jones and Spielberg) and funny Gremlin skits. These contained a fair amount of rather nasty violence (e.g., Gremlins in the blender, Gremlins in the microwave, woosh, splat!) and helped prod the MPAA to revise the PG rating by adding a PG-13 category to designate general-appeal films with harder violence. GREMLINS, though, was essentially a live-action cartoon with all the mayhem and lack of emotional consequence that typically beset cartoon characters. The executives at Warner Bros., the film's distributor, objected to this material and preferred that the film retain the sweetness of its opening sequences, with the darkness of its latter half toned down. They did not like the escalating mayhem the gremlins wreak nor their predominance in the latter half of the picture. Warners objected to the dailies that contained this material and objected again when the picture was assembled in rough cut form. Spielberg, though, interceded on Dante's behalf, and when Warners screened the film at a sneak preview, the audience loved the gremlins' antics and embraced the very things the Warners executives had disliked. These disparate reactions showed Dante how precarious and uncertain a director's position might be in relation to the majors, amid the uncertainties about what an audience wanted and how to shape material accordingly. In this case, the picture vindicated Dante's choices. GREMLINS went on to become an enormous hit, the third biggest box-office film of 1984.

Dante's subsequent films represented less happy collaborations with the majors. EXPLORERS (1985) was planned as a gentle fantasy about three kids who meet an alien, but Dante found his efforts to develop and polish the production stymied by Paramount, which rushed and pushed for an early summer release, leaving Dante less than a year to complete the script, get the sets constructed, and shoot and edit the picture. Moreover, Dante's aliens proved to be unsatisfying for the young audience Paramount wanted to capture and that had been conditioned by Spielberg's science fiction movies to expect emotional fireworks. Knowing humanity only through its television shows, Dante's aliens offer the viewer no epiphanies, no grand emotional payoff, just the stilted and skewed perspectives of TV talk. The picture previewed badly and never found an audience.

Dante's next film was based on a script that he did not originate. INNERSPACE (1987, with Spielberg producing) was an update of FANTASTIC VOYAGE (1966) and starred Dennis Quaid as a Navy pilot shrunken to microscopic size and injected into a man's body. Dante was eager to rebound from the misfire of EXPLORERS, and he crafted a tight, witty, and entertaining film. This time, however, the picture was sabotaged by its marketing. Warner Bros. designed an ad campaign with nondescript art that failed to com-

Dennis Quaid in INNERSPACE, *Joe Dante's playful update of* FANTASTIC VOYAGE.

municate what the film was about or what kind of picture—comedy, thriller—it was. Though his film tested well, Dante again had an expensive picture that lost money and failed to realize its potential. After directing a segment of AMAZON WOMEN ON THE MOON (1987), Dante began to plan for GREMLINS 2, but it would be several years before that production could be completed. To remain active as a director, Dante agreed to direct a Tom Hanks vehicle, THE 'BURBS (1989), and since it was a star vehicle, he had to adapt his style to Hanks's requirements, which at that time entailed broad comedy and slapstick. The film performed reasonably well, but it was a project on which Dante was essentially a director for hire rather than one that he had initiated and helped develop. Dante reversed his career slide with GREMLINS 2: THE NEW BATCH (1990), a sequel that topped the original with wonderful, bizarre gags and a plethora of movie in-jokes.

Dante was one of the happiest talents to have emerged in the 1980s. An intelligent filmmaker, he loved the medium, and his best films balance their special effects with an engagingly absurdist sensibility. His career, though, was a mixture of generally fine filmmaking and the disappointments and compromises wrought by unacceptably tight deadlines, poor marketing, and work-for-hire projects. His tribulations show the difficulties of sustaining a major directing career amid the uncertainties of studio politics and box-office fashions.

LAWRENCE KASDAN   Kasdan excelled as a screenwriter in the early 1980s, and he made the difficult transition to filmmaker with an impressively assured debut. He co-wrote three of the decade's most popular films: THE EMPIRE STRIKES BACK, RAIDERS OF THE LOST ARK, and RETURN OF THE JEDI. These scripts demonstrated a shrewd understanding of the popular audience and his ability to write commercial material, but the resulting films were, in some ways, antithetical to the kind of filmmaking he wished to practice. These are fast, furiously plotted pictures that have effects, not actors, at their center, whereas Kasdan's filmmaking proved to be literate, character-centered, and marked by a methodical, almost contemplative pacing. He characterized RAIDERS as the kind of movie that doesn't really require dialogue, just physical action and movement, whereas his own work as director featured extraordinary dialogue and character-based exposition.

Kasdan intentionally designed his first film as director to be one that was out of step with contemporary filmmaking. BODY HEAT (1981) is an outstanding film noir and a very skillful updating of the genre. Kasdan proudly described the picture as "talk heavy." "I wanted to make a movie that you have to listen to, because I don't think there have been many in America lately and I miss them."[49] Kathleen Turner gave a star-making performance in her role as Matty Walker, a femme fatale seducing and betraying Florida lawyer Ned Racine (William Hurt). Matty's sultry, torpid sexuality conceals a diabolically

William Hurt's impulsive Florida lawyer gets in over his head in BODY HEAT, *an elegant film noir from director Lawrence Kasdan.*

clever mind and a history of lethal manipulation that put her on par with Barbara Stanwyck's Phyllis Dietrichson in DOUBLE INDEMNITY (1944). Modeled on this and other classic noirs, BODY HEAT smartly updates the noir tradition and places it in convincingly contemporary terms. In place of the urban iconography, shadows, and paranoia of classic noir, Kasdan offers a bright, sun-dappled vision of Florida as a swamp of desire and moral turpitude and makes the omnipresent heat an index of the ambition and corruption that destroy Racine. The film's opening scene elegantly conveys Kasdan's narrative gambit with its foreshadowing of doom. Racine stands at his window watching a building burn in the distance, and he tells a nurse, who is one of his casual lovers, "It's the Seawater Inn. My family used to eat dinner there twenty-five years ago. Now somebody's torched it to clear the lot. Probably one of my clients." "It's a shame," she replies, to which Racine murmurs, "My history is burning up out there."

As in this scene, the talk throughout BODY HEAT is sharp and clever, the kind of dialogue a viewer has to listen for. When Ned meets Matty and tries some bad pickup lines on her, she smiles approvingly and says, "You're not too smart. I like that in a man." Late in the film when Racine suspects that Matty is duping him, he tells her, "Keep talking, Matty. Experience has shown that I can be convinced of anything."

Kasdan followed BODY HEAT with THE BIG CHILL (1983), a portrait of disillusioned sixties activists coping with the eighties and feeling that their material successes have compromised their social ideals. The film's political content and its portrait of generational change seemed overly slick and calculated in comparison with John Sayles's low-budget THE RETURN OF THE SECAUCUS SEVEN (1980), also about a group of sixties leftists weathering changed circumstances. Eminently successful in their chosen careers, Kasdan's characters suffer little but an occasional pang of conscience about how their lives have deviated from the ideals of their political youth. But the dialogue was as good as ever, and Kasdan again proved himself an actor's director. In contrast with BODY HEAT's intimate focus on Ned and Matty, THE BIG CHILL was an ensemble piece, and it featured a gallery of strong performances by Glenn Close, Mary Kay Place, JoBeth Williams, William Hurt, Jeff Goldblum, Tom Beringer, and Kevin Kline.

The powerful ensemble effect—that the characters really are intimate friends—is testament to Kasdan's directing skill and to his working methods. Although the film seems very casual in its structure, with loosely connected and seemingly improvised scenes, the script by Kasdan and Barbara Benedek was extremely detailed, and Kasdan was meticulous in his planning. He graphed relations among the scenes and used time charts to place the characters in relation to each other during the forty-eight hours of story time. He insisted on an extended rehearsal period for the cast (rare in filmmaking), during which they evolved back stories for the characters and developed scenes between those written in the script, all to connect the group of friends as tightly as possible. During the fifty-three-day shoot, Kasdan insisted that all the actors remain on location and on the sets, whether they were in the camera frame or not. The latter requirement especially made for arduous conditions (the industry norm excuses performers from being on call for scenes in which they don't appear). But the effect of these methods was electric. Seldom have the intimate bonds between an ensemble of people been evoked so tangibly on screen. This clarity of effect, coupled with the funny dialogue and the evocative performances, helped the film find a sizable audience. Kasdan connected with viewers nostalgic for the sixties, yearning for ideals in the go-go eighties, and in this regard his film was shrewdly pitched at an audience whose demographics corresponded with the film's main characters. Despite the preference of some critics for the Sayles film, THE BIG CHILL found its audience in young professionals who came of age in the sixties as well as those who came later, those who, experiencing the chill, knew the world as a cold place antithetical to their ideals. For such viewers, the film's characters were like old friends, and this rapport lifted the picture to strong box-office success. Some years later, with sixties angst still resonant, Kasdan's film inspired the popular televison series "Thirtysomething."

Kasdan faltered with his next project, SILVERADO (1985), though his considerable skill at handling an ensemble cast was on display again . An affectionate homage to the series Western and one of the few eighties productions in that genre, SILVERADO starred Kevin Kline, Scott Glenn, Danny Glover, and Kevin Costner (whose role had been excised from THE BIG CHILL during post-production) as a band of gunslinger heroes out to save a town from its corrupt sheriff. Unlike his earlier films, SILVERADO was a picture he might have described (had he written the script for another director) as the kind that doesn't need dialogue. Thus, the film did not play to his strengths as director. The pacing is extremely fast, and the editing moves the viewer rapidly to another scene whenever the actors get ready to have a conversation. Action is all in SILVERADO, and as a result, the film is more superficial than THE BIG CHILL.

Kasdan finished the decade, however, with a strong return to form. THE ACCIDENTAL TOURIST (1988) was a remarkably low-key adaptation of Anne Tyler's novel about a couple (William Hurt and Kathleen Turner again) whose marriage falters following the death of their child. The film is exquisitely paced, with Kasdan gradually, slowly peeling away the defenses of Macon Leary (Hurt) to reveal the grief and vulnerability that his repressed demeanor conceals. As with BODY HEAT, Kasdan bases his narrative on a unifying metaphor, here expressed in the title. "The Accidental Tourist" is the name of a series of guides penned by Leary for reluctant travelers, and as he learns anew to risk his emotions amid life's perils, he realizes there is no true safety in being an accidental tourist. Kasdan structures the film around William Hurt's remarkably restrained and subtle performance, one of the very best in eighties cinema. The performance is a treasure, but it's not the kind that wins an Academy Award. Hurt is so self-effacing in the role that he was overlooked by the Academy in its Oscar nominations. (Dustin Hoffman won that year for RAIN MAN, with a more labored, mannered performance as an autistic.) As BODY HEAT did for Kathleen Turner, however, THE ACCIDENTAL TOURIST gave Geena Davis (in a supporting role as the eccentric woman who pulls Macon out of his shell) a big career boost and launched her toward stardom.

Kasdan's work showcased the talents of a fine writer committed to directing his own scripts in pictures that extolled the virtues of a literate cinema based in real human experience and where performance and dialogue worked the medium's magic. These were vital attributes in an era when the industry's big films often chose technical effects over scripting and performance. But they are not attributes that tend to get much attention in the marketplace or by critics. Filmmakers who show off their bag of tricks through flashy editing or swooping camera moves receive the lion's share of attention. "That's the problem with a lot of my movies, I'm afraid. I'm amazed my movies do as well as they do, because I think they're just really out of time, you know, they're not what's going down."[50] Rather than going for the obvious or explicit emotional shadings in a scene or film, Kasdan aimed for subtlety and nuance, and he believed that the best art is often that which conceals the effort that has gone into its design. "Sometimes when you do your best work, it hides itself, it doesn't show itself off. The critical establishment doesn't understand movies at all, so what they respond to is the most flamboyant camera movement, the most flamboyant acting." Kasdan's films could never be accused of flashy style. Along with Woody Allen, Barry Levinson, and John Sayles, though, he created an intelligent body of work that showed the importance of a solid script, and the written and spoken word, for a distinguished film.

BARRY LEVINSON   Writer-director Barry Levinson's first feature, DINER (1982), was the sleeper surprise of that year and boasted a cast of young actors who would soon become much better known: Steve Guttenberg, Daniel Stern, Mickey Rourke, Kevin Bacon, Ellen Barkin, Paul Reiser. Wickedly well written by Levinson and hilarious, DINER portrayed the drifting lives of a group of young men in 1959 Baltimore. The five friends exist in a state of arrested adolescence, having finished high school but anxious and unable to assume adult responsibilities. They hang out at the Fells Point Diner and jaw the nights away, arguing about topics like whether Frank Sinatra or Johnny Mathis is the better singer (the argument being settled when everyone realizes that while Sinatra is good, they make out to Mathis). The overlapping dialogue and fast, bantering conversations became Levinson hallmarks, and the dialogue is as good as it gets in movies. Modell (Paul Reiser) complains, a wonderful non sequitur, "You know what word I'm not comfortable with? 'Nuance.' That's not a real word. Like 'gesture,' 'gesture' is a good word. At least you know where you stand with 'gesture.' But 'nuance', I don't know. Maybe I'm wrong." Two other friends, Fenwick (Kevin Bacon) and Mookie (Mickey Rourke) spy an attractive young woman riding a horse. They're working stiffs, and she's obviously a Baltimore blueblood. They stop their car, and Mookie flirts and asks her name. "Jane Chisholm," she says, "like the Chisholm Trail," and rides off. Mookie asks Fenwick, "What's the Chisholm Trail?" and Fenwick, after a pause, replies, "You ever get the feeling there's something going on we don't know about?"

Other Levinson hallmarks include the Baltimore locale and his eye for period detail. Two of the guys go see a Bergman movie at the now-defunct Five West Theatre, one of Baltimore's venerable art houses. A customer in a television store wants an Emerson TV because they're the best, and he didn't like seeing "Bonanza" in color because the Ponderosa didn't look real. The guys at the diner eat their fries with gravy, not ketchup. They watch WBAL-TV and listen to WCAO radio. Levinson, who grew up in Baltimore in the 1940s, knows this locale and has mined it for his his best and most personal film-making. TIN MEN (1987) is a companion piece to DINER, studying two feuding aluminum siding salesmen in early sixties Baltimore, characters who are wonderfully played by Richard Dreyfuss and Danny DeVito. Less comic and aleatory in structure, more melancholy, AVALON (1990) examines the acculturation of several generations of an immigrant family that settled in Baltimore. Levinson powerfully evokes the estrangement of the youngest generation and ties it to the personal alienation television has fostered. With a running time over two hours, a focus on European immigrants, and a dearth of stars, AVALON was a decidedly uncommercial film. In many ways Levinson's most ambitious and personal film, it historicizes the Baltimore setting by studying its changes over time, whereas DINER and TIN MEN provide snapshots of the locale during one brief period. Together, these films make an impressive trilogy about an American city and its changing subcultures. Levinson also used the Baltimore location for "Homicide," a remarkable network television series on which he served as producer.

Levinson alternated between these small, hometown pictures and larger-budget, more commercial projects: THE NATURAL (1984), with Robert Redford; YOUNG

Diner, where the Baltimore boys gather.

Sherlock Holmes (1985), for executive producer Steven Spielberg; and Rain Man (1988), which earned $86 million in domestic rentals. The latter film, a comedy-drama, studied the bond that develops between a callow young man (Tom Cruise) and the autistic brother (Dustin Hoffman) he did not know he had. Levinson as director solved the structural problems of the Rain Man script that had stymied other directors and kept the project in limbo for a year. Essentially, these problems involved how to handle the brothers' long car ride to Las Vegas, and Levinson, characteristically, approached the driving sequences as a means for developing and deepening the characters and their relationship. While Levinson's role on this picture was as a director for hire, his participation ensured that the project fulfilled its inherent potential and remained an actor-centered piece. (Levinson appears in a cameo role as a psychiatrist near the end of the film.) The success of Rain Man enabled Levinson to make Avalon and seemed to validate his strategy of doing a personal picture followed by one for the box office. The commercial projects are, as expected, more calculated in their appeal, while his Baltimore pictures have been riskier. Levinson's eighties career was exemplary for the skill with which he practiced both commercial and personal filmmaking, two very different modes that ordinarily are hard to reconcile.

Spike Lee Trained in the early 1980s at New York University's film school, Lee is, along with Martin Scorsese, NYU's most famous filmmaker alumnus. Unlike other contemporary filmmakers, though, Lee's films grew from his concerns with real-world racial and social issues. He was less enamored of cinema than a Spielberg or a Joe Dante, and his filmmaking interests flowed from his feelings and concerns about the society in which he lived, particularly its heritage of racial animosity.

Noting this difference between himself and other film school graduates, he said,

> See, I wasn't really raised on movies. I went to see them, but I wasn't like
> Spielberg and the rest of these guys. They wanted to be filmmakers when
> they were still in Pampers. That wasn't my case. And in a lot of ways this
> might be an advantage, because for a lot of these guys, their films are about
> films they've seen. Their films are *about* films.[51]

Lee's NYU thesis film, JOE'S BED-STUY BARBERSHOP: WE CUT HEADS (1982), was
showcased in the 1983 Museum of Modern Art New Directors/New Films series, and
his debut feature, SHE'S GOTTA HAVE IT (1986), was a playful comedy about a sexually
forthright woman and the befuddled men in her life. Lee completed the film for
$114,000 after devoting Herculean efforts to fund-raising, and he benefited as a young
filmmaker trying to break into the industry from the extensive network of independent
film distributors that was flourishing at mid-decade. Filmed in black and white, the picture proved to be very successful, grossing $7.5 million domestically, and it featured the
stylistic traits that would become Lee signatures: radical shifts of tone and form (e.g., the
inclusion of a color musical sequence), Brechtian devices (direct address to the camera
by performers), and a sharp, satirical skewering of racial attitudes.

Best of all for black audiences, they finally had a filmmaker who spoke directly to
them, who understood the subtleties, norms, and humor of black American culture.
Lee's success heralded the rise in the nineties of a new generation of black American
filmmakers (John Singleton, Robert Townsend, the Hughes brothers) and from their
works a film culture that specifically welcomed African Americans to the movies.

After Island Pictures, the independent distributor of SHE'S GOTTA HAVE IT, pulled
out of its deal for Lee's next production, the David Puttnam regime at Columbia agreed
to fund the $6 million SCHOOL DAZE (1988). Puttnam was intent on using Columbia to
advance quality films by alternative filmmakers (see ch. 2), and Lee turned this policy to
his advantage by obtaining production monies and distribution. SCHOOL DAZE was an
edgy, tone-shifting portrait of color issues (e.g., social determinations about who is black
and who isn't) among the students at an all-black college, and it was controversial for
some black viewers because of its airing of class and race issues within the black community. The picture was not a critical success, and it was one of many Puttnam pictures
to lose money for Columbia ($11 million for production and advertising against $6 million in rentals). But it gave Lee access for the first time to an established major.

Lee's next film, DO THE RIGHT THING (1989), proved to be one of his best pictures,
one of the decade's major films, and it brought him to the front rank of contemporary
American filmmakers. In this portrait of a Brooklyn neighborhood on a scorchingly hot
summer day, Lee humanized his theme of racial and ethnic tension with a gallery of
memorable characters, most especially pizzeria owner Sal. As played by Danny Aiello in
a performance that lends much heart and feeling to the film, Sal is an Italian American
who is devoted to the black and Hispanic neighborhood where his business resides and
is proud that this community has eaten his food for many years. Yet Sal is also a racist,
and a confrontation with a black customer (the hulking Radio Raheem, who has refused
to turn down his portable stereo) provokes Sal to express his underlying animosities. The
police arrive and side with Sal, the property owner. Arresting Radio Raheem, they
employ a choke hold that strangles and kills him. (This police choke hold had been
implicated in several real-world deaths, and Lee implicitly referenced these by its inclu-

*Mookie (Spike Lee) and Sal (Danny Aiello) have competing
social visions in* Do the Right Thing.

sion in the film.) Reacting to the police brutality, an angry crowd trashes and burns Sal's
pizzeria in the film's ambiguous climax. Lee's staging of this finale elicited differing reactions from white and black audiences. Mookie, the film's most engaging and likable character and the only black employee who works for Sal, instigates the trashing and burning
of the pizzeria. Lee remarked during the film's release that white viewers asked him why
Mookie threw the trash can through the window of Sal's business. "No black person has
ever asked me, 'Did Mookie do the right thing?' Never. Only white people. White people are like, 'Oh, I like Mookie so much up to that point. He's a nice character. Why'd
he have to throw the garbage can through the window?' Black people, there's no question in their minds why he does that."[52]

Lee concludes the film with quotations from Martin Luther King, Jr., and Malcolm
X expressing their different philosophies regarding pacifism and armed struggle. The
simultaneous opposition of the King and Malcolm quotations intensified the film's ambiguities (what is the right thing?), and these helped spark a national controversy over the
picture and its portrait of race in America. These debates were healthy for the nation
and healthy for cinema. During a year where the big films were such escapist fare as
Batman, Indiana Jones and the Last Crusade, Lethal Weapon 2, and Honey,
I Shrunk the Kids, Do the Right Thing was a powerful reminder that cinema can
also function as a vital and vibrant medium of social discourse. The picture was successful in this regard because of the uncommon richness of its portrait of racial and ethnic tension. Amid the black, Hispanic, white, and Korean characters who express the

racial polarities of contemporary American society, Sal is a fascinating and emotionally affecting character, who embodies the dilemmas of the present, and Lee and Aiello develop the character with exceptional nuance. Exemplifyng these nuances is Sal's resonse to a black patron's objection that there are no faces of famous black celebrities among the photos of prominent Italian Americans that adorn the walls of the pizzeria. Black people eat in here, the patron says, so black people should be pictured on the walls. Sal replies that it's his pizzeria, and he'll chose who goes on the walls, and if the patron opens his own business he'll have the same privilege. Lee endorsed and agreed with Sal's defense of his entreprenureal privileges. Sal's stance helped Lee develop one of the film's subthemes, which was about the need for black-owned businesses and the connection those enterprises would forge between economic development and degrees of social freedom. For Lee and for the film, Sal embodied both progressive and reactionary attitudes, and this gave the character and the film an aesthetic and social complexity that made its art and its politics especially memorable.

DO THE RIGHT THING positioned Lee at decade's end for a major career in the nineties. His subsequent work in that decade fulfilled the promise this picture had suggested. MO' BETTER BLUES (1990), JUNGLE FEVER (1991), MALCOLM X (1992), GET ON THE BUS (1996), and THREE LITTLE GIRLS (1997) sustained the edgy dialogue about race in America, and the often confrontational aesthetic style, that DO THE RIGHT THING had so memorably brokered.

OLIVER STONE   In the 1980s, Oliver Stone brought left-leaning politics back to the American cinema, although to call his work leftist is to minimize its ambiguities and its internal contradictions. Stone studied film at New York University after serving in the army in Vietnam, and he directed his first feature in 1974 (SEIZURE). His second film as director, THE HAND (1981), was an unremarkable horror picture. In the late seventies and early eighties, Stone penned several notorious scripts (MIDNIGHT EXPRESS, SCARFACE, YEAR OF THE DRAGON) that earned him a trash-peddling reputation, but the depth of his socio-political conviction was soon apparent.

His third film, SALVADOR (1986), established his as a powerful directorial voice in American cinema and the only major filmmaker to create popular films that criticized U.S. foreign and domestic policy. Based on the experiences of journalist Richard Boyle (memorably played by James Woods), SALVADOR chronicles the bloody civil war in El Salvador and condemns the United States for its support of that country's savage and corrupt government. Shot and edited with ferocious intensity, the film searingly depicts the corruption and brutality of the Salvadoran regime and its bloodthirsty security forces. Stone unflinchingly shows graphic atrocities, including the bodies of death squad victims and the rape and murder of American church women, but this was too much for his distributor. Orion withdrew from its distribution deal because it believed the film was too violent.

Stone excised the most extreme violence and instances of sexual depravity, and he shortened the picture's overall length. Working at white-hot speed, fired by his love of filmmaking and passion for this subject, he had filmed more material than he could successfully shape into a two-hour picture. Cutting the film for content and length made the narrative more jagged than it ought to have been, but the film retained its power to grip and shock the viewer over the injustices it depicted: "I wound up pulling a lot of the violence out, and that weakened the story. The picture was two hours long and it really should've been two and a half hours. But I knew we couldn't get that version played, so I cut ruthlessly. The final version has been criticized for being choppy, and it is."[53]

James Woods and John Savage take cover in SALVADOR, *Oliver Stone's go-for-broke account of the political repression in El Salvador. In this searing film, Stone found his voice as a director.*

With Orion out as distributor, Stone formed a productive relationship with Hemdale, a prominent independent that had promised to back his long-cherished project for a Vietnam War film. But Hemdale lacked the resources to give SALVADOR a major marketing push. As a result, the film never received the widespread national attention that a theatrical release can generate, and it went quickly to video. Though it is hardly an undiscovered film, it remains less widely known than Stone's subsequent, higher-profile productions, and this is unfortunate. In the intensity of its political vision and its moral involvement with the subject it depicts, and in its hell-bent, go-for-broke style of filmmaking, SALVADOR is one of the decade's most remarkable pictures.

With the completion of SALVADOR, Stone launched the production of his next, and breakthrough, film. PLATOON was a project he had cherished for years, and fittingly, it had a bigger impact and was better received than anything he had previously done. When released in 1987, it was hailed by critics as the most authentic treatment of Vietnam yet filmed, despite Stone's inflection of the material with religious allusions and an overt *bildungsroman* narrative structure. Coming at the end of the Chuck Norris–Sylvester Stallone Vietnam picture cycle, in which they played ridiculously superpowered warriors, Stone's film was more faithful to the physical experience of living and fighting in a jungle environment, and it depicted in powerfully symbolic terms the war's divisive effect on America and its soldiers. The titular platoon is split between the moral examples offered by two sergeants, one savage and brutal, the other idealistic

Sergeant Elias (Willem Dafoe) achieves his Christly apotheosis in Platoon. *This composition became the film's best-known and most enduring image.*

and compassionate. In the narrative savagery wins, but Stone shows in chilling detail the terms of the victory, most famously in a sequence where the Americans torture and slaughter Vietnamese villagers. Few scenes of violence in contemporary cinema have been as disturbing to watch, as morally discomforting, or as closely rooted in harrowing historical experience.

To accentuate the film's authenticity, Stone subjected his cast of actors to an unusual, rigorous pre-production course of training. For two weeks, the actors underwent grueling combat exercises under the instruction of marine officer Dale Dye, marching on full-gear hikes, living in the woods, digging trenches in which they slept, and rapelling down a sixty-five-foot tower. By the end of the second week, the cast was exhausted and weary. They had become existentially one with the characters they'd play. It was a bold move for Stone to do this, but the remarkable results are plainly evident in the film. The actors do not seem to be performing. Instead, they inhabit the characters with absolute authenticity. Stone pointed out, "The idea was to [mess] with their heads so we could get that dog-tired attitude, the anger, the irritation, the casual way of brutality, the casual approach to death. These are all the assets and liabilities of infantrymen."[54]

Released after the first two Rambo movies had caricatured the war with comic book heroics, Platoon's close attention to the physical stresses of living and fighting in the jungle was unprecedented, as was its powerful, if ambiguous, moral vision of the war. The picture exerted a marked influence on subsequent Vietnam War productions, and it won Stone his first best Director Oscar.

Characteristically, Stone moved immediately to his next project. Wall Street (1987) was a trenchant portrait of corporate raiders and the culture of greed that sustained them. Filmed with his customary visual gusto, the picture featured lots of camera movement to suggest the prowling sharks of this predatory environment. As with his two previous films, Stone once again had taken a difficult issue and transformed it into powerful filmmaking. Stone wrote for the film's villain, millionaire raider Gordon Gekko (Michael Douglas), one of the decade's memorable speeches, the "greed is good" monologue in which Gekko justifies his ruthless financial behavior. Stone was disappointed by the mixed reviews the picture received, but he quickly commenced another production, TALK RADIO (1988), about the anomie and rage that pervades modern culture. Adapted from Eric Bogosian's stage play and starring Bogosian as an abrasive talk show host, Stone's film is aggressively cinematic, filled with elaborate camera moves, tight cutting and a sustained tension that leads inevitably to a violent climax. For all of its technical polish, the picture was a fast project made while he was prepping BORN ON THE FOURTH OF JULY (1989), a long-delayed, much cherished project about Ron Kovic, a gung-ho marine crippled by a battlefield wound in Vietnam.

This picture won Stone his second best-director Oscar and gave actor Tom Cruise the role of his life. Stone was notorious for challenging his actors, sometimes roughly, to get beyond their limitations. Cruise was a performer who rarely stretched his gifts, but he was astonishing in the range of emotion that he commands here. He is one with this character, and he has never been better than here (as Michael Douglas has never been better than in WALL STREET). The picture's style is bombastic and operatic, yet Stone captured the idealism of the early sixties and the bitter strife of the war years with his customary intensity. In the nineties he continued to apply this stylistic fervor to political filmmaking with the revisionist pictures JFK (1991), NIXON (1995), and THE DOORS (1991).

Stone was an original and unique American filmmaker, defiantly occupying a cinematic-political territory virtually of his own making. He stood virtually alone as director and artist in an industry where political timidity is the rule for commercial filmmaking. While Stone could sometimes be preachy or heavy-handed about the subjects on which his films were based, his film style was sensual and sense-assaulting. This intensity attracted a large audience, which gave him considerable power in the industry, and he defended his style, pointing out, "The world is spinning much faster than my camera and myself. . . . I think movies have to break through the three dimensions, as close as you can get. I think you go for every . . . thing you can to make it *live*."⁵⁵

THE WORKING DIRECTORS

While many seventies auteurs had a hard time in the eighties, the industry accommodated an influx of new directors (albeit to varying degrees) and provided continued, steady employment for sophisticated filmmakers gifted and skilled at working with the majors. These latter were filmmakers who maintained a consistent and prolific output and sustained distribution deals with the studios despite the industry's turmoil and transformations. Some of these filmmakers were quiet workers, whose films generally did not attract the media attention accorded Spielberg, Lucas, or Zemeckis or the sustained academic attention accorded more cerebral filmmakers. Academics and scholars tended to slight the work of many of these directors (excepting Woody Allen and possibly Sidney Lumet) because their films did not seem intellectually ambitious or cinematically self-conscious or because their merits, based in performance, dialogue, and storytelling skill, seemed overly traditional. But cinema is filled with great films and directors who fall outside established canons of academic respectability. The directors in this category were consistently intelligent filmmakers who worked regularly and reliably and who, unlike the embattled auteurs, sustained good relations with the industry. In this regard, it is not unfair to suggest that their work exemplified some of the best attributes of the American cinema: a remarkable finessing of the tensions between commerce and creative expression, a dependably high level of quality, and a vital connection to a popular audience.

WOODY ALLEN   Woody Allen directed ten features between 1980 and 1989, as well as a segment ("Oedipus Wrecks") of the anthology film NEW YORK STORIES (1989). This extraordinary output, which set Allen apart from his peers, was made possible by Allen's depth of imagination, his special ability to work quickly, and his ongoing relationship with producers Jack Rollins, Charles Joffe, and Robert Greenhut. During the 1970s, Allen worked under contract to United Artists, whose chair, Arthur B. Krim, felt a special fondness and respect for Allen's talent and for his films. The terms of Allen's relationship with UA provided an important foundation for his eighties work. Historically, UA had been dedicated to providing directors with creative freedoms atypical of the majors, but even at UA Allen had special status. His contract called for films budgeted at $2 million, with Allen having total artistic control once UA approved the story, and Allen and his producers received 50 percent of net profits on each production. When other issues not covered by contract came up, such as Allen's opposition to the presentation of his films on airlines or television, Krim reliably supported him and in ways that were not accorded other filmmakers. About this Krim noted, "We can say with total credibility that we do it for Woody because he's special."[56]

In 1978, frictions with UA parent Transamerica led Krim and four of his executives to leave UA and set up their own company, Orion Pictures. UA desperately wanted to keep Allen, but once he had completed the outstanding pictures under his contract, he joined Orion in 1980 out of loyalty to Krim and his executive staff. Again he was accorded total artistic freedom plus 15 percent of gross receipts, split among Allen and his producers. The distinguishing feature of Allen's relationship with Krim and Orion was the mutual respect each accorded the other. Krim was proud of Allen's special talent and his place as an Orion filmmaker. "I feel that because Woody has been with us so long, it is a motivation for other top creative people to come to us."[57] Respecting the needs of his financial backers, Allen resolutely stayed within budget and made good use of their money, never quarreling over story ideas, for example, or over projects that Orion questioned. His imagination was so fertile that he simply returned with another, better idea.

Allen's sharp, polished scripts formed a solid basis for his films, and he developed an approach to shooting—capturing a scene in a single master shot with characters and camera in constant choreographed motion—that protected the dialogue as written. By contrast, the more shots—coverage—into which a scene is broken, the greater an editor's opportunity for reworking the script as filmed. This approach also simplified the editing of his pictures. "I've done an enormous amount of movies in just a few takes. So for some pictures, we, my editor Susan Morse and I, could put the whole picture together in just one week, starting from scratch, because there are just master-shots. Forty master shots and then it's finished."[58]

Furthermore, although this method required an intense and extended planning session between Allen and his cinematographer, it remained an efficient manner of working. Most of a production day would be spent by Allen and the cinematographer in blocking the scene's physical action, camera moves, and lighting design. By late afternoon, when the cast would be called in for shooting, few hours remained in the day, but Allen would then shoot the entire scene in one take, consuming five or six pages of script, which, as he noted, was a very respectable day's work. His method safeguarded the dialogue, gave the actors an extended interval of time (the length of the master shot) in which to play their characters, and facilitated an economical use of production time. It was an ingenious solution to the perennial problem of how to accomplish the most with finite resources.

The diversity of Allen's work demonstrated one of his special features as a filmmaker—his desire to try new subjects and styles, an outgrowth of his special relationship with Orion, which supported this diversity. STARDUST MEMORIES (1980), shot in black and white on high-contrast stock, was a Felliniesque portrait of a disillusioned filmmaker. With luminous cinematography by Gordon Willis, A MIDSUMMER NIGHT'S SEX COMEDY (1982) was a tribute to summer, the country (from staunch urbanite Allen!), and Felix Mendelssohn. It was written and shot around the ongoing production of ZELIG (1983), a black-and-white fake documentary about a human chameleon (a picture whose conception and design prefigures FORREST GUMP [1994]). Also in black and white, BROADWAY DANNY ROSE (1984) was an affectionate homage to vaudeville and the Borscht Belt comedy that Allen practiced in his stand-up days. The melancholy of THE PURPLE ROSE OF CAIRO (1985), about the seductive allure of the movies, was balanced by the sweetness of HANNAH AND HER SISTERS (1986), one of Allen's most popular films and one in which he permitted himself a movie-style happy ending. RADIO

Woody Allen plays an eccentric inventor in A MIDSUMMER NIGHT'S SEX COMEDY, *with luminous cinematography by Gordon Willis.*

Days (1987), a loving, warm tribute to radio in the forties, preceded two psychological dramas, September (1987), which Allen rewrote, recast and refilmed a second time when he judged the first effort to be poor, and Another Woman (1988). Allen ended the decade with Crimes and Misdemeanors (1989), one of his best pictures, about a physician who arranges the murder of his lover and comes to believe there have been no moral or ethical consequences to his act.

Allen's singular ability to work so quickly and so well, backed by the support of Orion, gave him greater creative freedom in the eighties than any other American filmmaker. In this regard alone, Allen was the truest and most successful auteur in eighties American cinema.

Clint Eastwood   Like Woody Allen, Clint Eastwood enjoyed a long-standing relationship, based on mutual respect, fiscal conservatism, and speedy production methods, with a major distributor, in this case, Warner Bros. Eastwood's reputation in the industry for honoring budgets and shooting schedules was peerless and a major source of the confidence that Warner executives placed in him over the years. He was a rare filmmaker who could bring a production in under budget and ahead of schedule. Unlike Allen, though, Eastwood was a major box-office attraction, capable of generating millions of dollars in worldwide rentals. These factors help account for the remarkable freedoms he enjoyed to branch out as a director and actor, trying subjects, styles, and characters not normally associated with his minimalist, tough-guy image. Eastwood served as director and producer, and usually as actor, on the films that he made for his production company, Malpaso Productions, which Warner distributed.

Eastwood carefully alternated his eighties projects between those that featured him in conventional roles associated with his screen persona and ones lying outside its rather rigid boundaries. Thus, as director and star, he followed the sweet, whimsical Bronco Billy (1980) and the tender, melancholy Honkytonk Man (1982), in which he played a country-western singer, with four pictures that cast him in action roles. He appeared as a fighter pilot in Firefox (1982), Dirty Harry Callahan in Sudden Impact (1983), a Western gunfighter in Pale Rider (1985), and a foul-mouthed Marine sergeant in Heartbreak Ridge (1986). He then realized a long-cherished project into which he poured his love of jazz. Bird (1988) was based on the life of sax great Charlie Parker, and Eastwood did not take an acting role in it. He also served as executive producer of another jazz film, the documentary Thelonious Monk: Straight, No Chaser (1989). White Hunter, Black Heart (1990) showed him in an uncharacteristically loquacious role, one based on director John Huston's sojourn in Africa while filming The African Queen (1951). And, as if this output were not enough, at mid-decade he directed an episode of Spielberg's "Amazing Stories" TV series. Furthermore, he acted in a string of pictures on which he did not serve as credited director (although his uncredited influence on the productions was significant): Any Which Way You Can (1980), City Heat (1984), Tightrope (1984), The Dead Pool (1988), and Pink Cadillac (1989).

Eastwood paid a price for his experimental forays into new territory. His box office clout notably diminished during the decade as most of these pictures failed to attract a large audience (excepting the very successful Sudden Impact). But his risk paid off handsomely in the nineties, when his directing career won him new critical and public recognition for Unforgiven (1992) and The Bridges of Madison County (1995). He laid the foundation for this recognition during the eighties when he acted and

Clint Eastwood on the camera crane directing HEARTBREAK RIDGE.

directed at a brisk clip, honing his skills at each and building a substantial body of work that critics eventually noticed both for its unexpected variety and for the iconic power of his star persona. The most notable aspect of Eastwood's directing style was the relaxed and unpretentious tone that he set for cast and crew. It inspired everyone to work as a team and to do so with vigor and efficiency.

Eastwood's relaxed methods had significant implications for his creative approach to cinema. He valued the unpredictable constraints imposed by sets and locations, and while he would plan the work in advance, he also believed that the best effects are often those that arise from unanticipated circumstances. Spontaneity was welcomed, not feared, by Eastwood. He valued the discoveries an actor might make on camera and the benefits that might accrue from a novel way of blocking a scene's action and filming. To provide his camera operator with maximum flexibility in covering a scene's dynamic and sometimes unplanned action, Eastwood frequently used the Steadicam. By stabilizing a handheld camera, the Steadicam enabled his operator to "catch the moment[s]" arising within a scene's dynamics and facilitated rapid and efficient filming.[59] Because he felt it hindered his ability to work efficiently, Eastwood avoided using video assist. He found that people would gather after each take to watch the monitor and volunteer opinions on the effectiveness of the shot, a process that disrupted the flow of each day's work.

About his working methods, he said, "It's much more interesting to me if you're making decisions on the spot. You have to have a plan, but within that plan you adjust to something new as it hits you for the first time. I try to be open to that. The [new possibilities] you find tend to be a little better than you might have expected."[60] Jack Green, a regular Eastwood cinematographer, lit scenes for Eastwood in ways that provided multiple options for blocking and visually designing the action. Green pointed out how Eastwood's preference for looseness and spontaneity affected the lighting design:

> I like to light environments so that Clint has total flexibility. The night before the shoot, he usually indicates how the scene will unfold and where the camera will go, and he's certainly very well-prepared for what he wants to achieve. But Clint dislikes anything that constricts him or puts a preconceived thought into his mind. He wants to be able to walk in and do things that are completely spontaneous.[61]

Eastwood's aesthetic approach was quite dissimilar to George Lucas's fondness for digital methods of production. Lucas defined cinematic artistry as the ability to use digital design to completely overcome the constraints imposed by performers, locations, or external light sources. For Eastwood, creativity lay in working with those constraints and finding freedom within them. One is a technologically based concept of artistry, the other derives excitement from unexpected aspects of the encounters with sets and performers. One seeks control, the other a certain freedom. In these distinctions lie fundamentally different philosophies of cinema and filmmaking. While many applications of cinema technology inclined the medium in its blockbuster phase toward the example and direction offered by Lucas, Eastwood's approach exemplified the crucial countertradition of using the machinery to find the humanly meaningful moments at the center of a film.

SIDNEY LUMET   Lumet's work consistently exhibited the strengths bequeathed him by his training as a director for stage and television. He made films quickly and economically and was exceptionally skilled at working with actors. Lumet worked steadily and reliably throughout the decade, but with his interests in performance and morally ambiguous drama he stood apart from the industry's fascination with blockbusters and effects-driven narratives. Lumet could prepare and execute a production in rapid order, and he typically stayed within a modest budget. These attributes ensured his steady employment. PRINCE OF THE CITY (1981), for example, had over 130 speaking roles and 135 locations, which Lumet coordinated for a quick fifty-two-day shoot. Performers were eager to work with Lumet because he was an outstanding director of actors. Whereas many directors disliked rehearsals or advising actors on how to build their characters, Lumet excelled at both. Paul Newman, for example, gave one of his best performances as a drunken lawyer seeking redemption in Lumet's THE VERDICT (1982), but he was not getting to the guts of the alcoholic character until Lumet offered him some discreetly personal but pointed advice on how to do so.

Lumet gave his skilled performers a cinematic showcase for their abilities; that is, he used the unique tools of cinema to extend and deepen the actor's contribution. In RUNNING ON EMPTY (1988), for example, a film about sixties radicals living underground, Lumet used editing in a judicious way to accentuate the emotional relationships conveyed by his actors. For the tense reunion scene between Annie (Christine Lahti) and the father (Steven Hill) whom she rejected because of her radical politics, Lumet used two cameras so the actors could play the scene without interruption. He placed the cameras to facilitate shot-reverse shot cutting, and in post-production he cut back and

Sidney Lumet directs Paul Newman in THE VERDICT.

forth between the performers, isolating each in his or her own frame, using the cut points to separate visually father from daughter. In a subsequent scene with a very different emotional tone—Annie playing piano with her son, whom she loves but must now leave forever—Lumet used no editing. To capture the intimacy of the moment, he shot the scene in one take, using a discreet framing on the performers' backs as they sit at the piano, and slowly dollied the camera closer. Annie and her son relate to one another in an extended, unbroken visual and dramatic space. Lumet did more than simply film performances. He deepened those performances using the tools of cinema to integrate them into a coherent visual and emotional design.

In the eighties, Lumet returned to the themes of police corruption and the moral ambiguities of law enforcement that he had forcefully explored in 1974's SERPICO. The epic PRINCE OF THE CITY portrayed a corrupt cop desperately seeking redemption by informing on his friends and partners. While the decade's big box-office films typically shunned ambiguity, Lumet loved the mysteries of character and motive in PRINCE ("Its ambiguity on every level was one of the most exciting things about it").[62] He explored these ambiguities through his visual design of the picture, using only wide-angle or telephoto lenses to give the camera a duplicitous relationship with what it filmed. Q&A (1990) offered another dark portrait of corruption and betrayal on an urban police force.

Lumet was one of the few American directors to look at the legacy of leftist politics in American culture and society. DANIEL (1983), which examined the trauma inflicted on children of activist parents (modeled on the Rosenbergs), who were arrested and executed for espionage in the 1950s, effectively and movingly contrasted the major generations of leftist protest in the 1930s and the 1960s. RUNNING ON EMPTY sympathetically portrayed a pair of 1960s radicals on the run from the FBI, living underground, with nowhere to go in the eighties, an era in which sixties ideals seemed eclipsed. Lumet alternated these personal projects with more commercial pictures that, whatever their limitations, were crisply directed: Just Tell Me What You Want (1980), Deathtrap (1982), Garbo Talks (1984), Power (1986), The Morning After (1986), and Family Business (1989).

In an industry where star egos are often as large as their paychecks, Lumet remained humble and realistic about the contribution he made to his films.

> How much in charge am I? *Is the movie* un Film de Sidney Lumet? I'm dependent on weather, budget, what the leading lady had for breakfast, who the leading man is in love with. I'm dependent on the talents and idiosyncrasies, the moods and egos, the politics and personalities, of more than a hundred different people. And that's just in the making of the movie. At this point I won't even begin to discuss the studio, financing, distribution, marketing, and so on.[63]

At the same time, Lumet believed that movies are an art, and this was where his interest in the medium, and his ambitions for it, rested. "The amount of attention paid to movies is directly related to pictures of quality. It's the movies that are works of art that create this interest, even if they're not on the ten-highest grosses list too often."[64] This was Lumet in the eighties—never on the high-gross list, working on smaller budgets, yet making a string of challenging and often quite personal films placed in distribution by the majors.

Sydney Pollack   Sydney Pollack was the best 1980s equivalent of what, in the old days, were the outstanding studio contract directors—Raoul Walsh, Michael Curtiz, William Wellman. Like them, Pollack could handle a variety of stories, themes, and textures, work within budget and with the vagaries of studio politics, and turn out consistently distinguished filmmaking. Like theirs, his films lacked a consistency of style or theme but boasted a skilled, sensitive handling of actors and a knack for effective storytelling. Pollack, in fact, was one of the best popular storytellers among contemporary American directors. Because of his training for the stage and his experience teaching acting classes, he was exceptionally good with actors and gave performance pride of place in his films.

Whereas many contemporary directors avoided rehearsals because they did not enjoy working with actors, Pollack disliked rehearsing for entirely different reasons. The insufficient period (typically under a week) allowed for rehearsal on a film production was counterproductive, he felt, and drained the freshness from a performance, precisely the freshness that he wanted to capture on film. "In a film, I'm always trying to catch a performance before it examines itself so much that it loses its life," he pointed out.

> I find that I get more exciting performances from really gifted actors out of the rush of their own intuitive understanding of the part, usually in the first couple of times that they do it. It has a spontaneity and a freshness and a life that I don't know how to get unless I am able to rehearse for five or six weeks. And I've never been able to get a whole cast together, on a location, for that long prior to filming.[65]

Pollack's eighties productions demonstrated this care with actors and a particular facility for working with stars and helping craft star performances. These are essential attributes of popular filmmaking. ABSENCE OF MALICE (1981) toplined Paul Newman as the innocent victim of a smear article by reporter Sally Field. TOOTSIE (1983) showcased Dustin Hoffman's hilarious performance as an actor impersonating a prim woman to win a key television role. Although Pollack was not noted as a director of comedies—he had specialized in straight dramas—his direction of TOOTSIE showed a real flair for comic timing.

OUT OF AFRICA (1985) teamed Pollack again with actor Robert Redford, with whom he frequently collaborated, in one of the decade's best films, an exquisitely constructed epic narrative about the experiences of writer Isak Dinesan (a luminous Meryl Streep) during her years in Africa managing a coffee plantation. The virtues of OUT OF AFRICA are the old-fashioned ones: a carefully structured script, unhurried pacing with narrative climaxes given proper proportion, and sentiment without sentimentality. Few

Meryl Streep as Karen Blixen in the magisterial OUT OF AFRICA.

contemporary directors could bring off this feat of popular storytelling. Pollack's facility with narrative was closely connected to his respect for the performer. The narrative of OUT OF AFRICA covered a large span of story time, during which Streep's character underwent significant emotional changes. Like virtually all films, this one was shot out of continuity, but Pollack stressed that the shooting continuity had to respect the emotional arc of the characters: "I would never play a critical emotional scene near the end of a story, before we've filmed the necessary early parts. You do film out of continuity, but there are certain things that have to be done. . ... You don't want to start with the end scene, and say, 'Oh, don't worry, just trust me.' That's silliness."[66]

Interestingly, despite his filmmaking savvy, Pollack completely misjudged the picture's chances of popular success. "I liked it personally, but if I'd had to make a bet as to whether or not it was going to be a successful film, and my children's lives depended on my bet, I certainly would have bet that it wasn't going to be. It was three hours long, it was talky, there were no action scenes in it, it was not about young people."[67] The film's surprising box office was augmented by its industry honors. It won Oscars for best picture, director, screenplay, cinematography, and music score.

Pollack's next film was his one misfire of the decade, HAVANA (1990), an expensive production that failed to find an audience. Robert Redford and Lena Olin played lovers whose affair unfolded against the backdrop of the Cuban revolution. Whereas Redford and Streep had a special chemistry that made OUT OF AFRICA work, Redford and Olin failed to connect on screen, and this left a gaping hole where the heart of the picture ought to have been. For his part, Pollack believed it was a well-made film, but, as with his OUT OF AFRICA experience, he admitted that it is difficult to predict a film's level of popular success. Despite HAVANA, his track record was impressive, and the eighties for Pollack were a decade that saw his work earn critical as well as box-office distinction.

INDEPENDENTS AND OUTSIDERS

The expanding video and cable television markets spawned a significant demand for new film product by mid-decade. Because the majors were unable to fund a production increase to meet this demand, independent film faced a propitious opportunity for enlarging its presence in the domestic market. As we have seen in table 2.4, in 1986 and 1987 the number of independent productions set for release by majors and indies exploded from an average of 179 during the previous three years to 295 in 1986 and 267 in 1987. Moreover, independent distribution outside the majors jumped from an average of 132 during the previous three years to 242 in 1986 and 203 in 1987. On the downside, more than a third of independent films failed to secure a release during those years.

By the mid-1980s, independent distributors were helping to fund this production bubble.[68] John Sayles's MATEWAN was cofinanced by Cinecom International. The Coen brothers signed a multipicture contract with Circle Releasing, and Alan Rudolph found a solid backer for his best eighties pictures (CHOOSE ME, TROUBLE IN MIND, THE MODERNS) in Alive Pictures. Oliver Stone's breakthrough films, SALVADOR and PLATOON, were financed by Hemdale (which also distributed SALVADOR). Moreover, another independent, Vestron, Inc., pre-bought the video rights to PLATOON, contributing a vital source of funding.

By decade's end, many of these companies, and others, had folded or were absorbed by parent firms. In 1988–89, Cinecom and Atlantic Releasing were sold, and Film-Dallas, Island Pictures (Alive), and Vestron, which had overextended itself, went under.

The bubble of independent production, so striking a component of the latter 1980s, received considerable buffeting by decade's end with the failure of these sources of financing and distribution. But during this period, a host of uniquely talented American filmmakers took advantage of its opportunities and established solid careers. Several of the filmmakers discussed in this section moved in and out of production and distribution deals with major studios while making resolutely nontraditional films. This phenomenon demonstrates the flexibility of the industry as well as its ability to absorb unconventional talents and niche market products.

JOEL AND ETHAN COEN   The Coen brothers split their filmmaking responsibilities, with Joel directing, Ethan producing, and both taking a writing credit. They established a close relationship with Washington D.C.-based Circle Films. Circle funded and distributed their eighties productions and allowed the Coens to work without interference, once a project had been approved.

With the backing of Circle, the Coens established a strong and prolific career with an eclectic series of films whose style and subject matter were often unpredictable. In the eighties, they completed only two films, but these were bravura showpieces that aggressively announced their talents. Joel Coen studied film at New York University (a school with a number of alums working in the eighties—Martin Scorsese, Jim Jarmusch, Spike Lee), and his direction showed a corresponding cinematic self-consciousness. In BLOOD SIMPLE (1984), for example, the camera tracks down the length of a bar. Its path blocked by a drunken, somnolent customer, the camera tracks up, over, and past this character, and continues on its way. The drunk, of course, was a convenient prop, an excuse for moving the camera in this obstreperous way, which said, in effect, to the viewer, "Are you watching?"

BLOOD SIMPLE was their debut film, and like the first works by many directors, it has a flashy and showy style that indicates its authors are hungry filmmakers ready for attention. A film noir set in Texas, and therefore without the genre's typical urban iconography, BLOOD SIMPLE strongly evokes the greed, treachery, and human debasement that are essential attributes of the noir world. The narrative is relatively simple but has enough twists to keep the first-time viewer guessing about likely outcomes. Marty (Dan Hedaya) owns a bar and suspects that his wife, Abby (Frances McDormand, who became a regular performer in Coen films), has been cheating on him with one of his employees, Ray (John Gertz). Marty hires an impressively sleazy detective (M. Emmet Walsh in a performance of oily perfection and reptilian menace) to investigate. When Marty subsequently asks the detective to kill Abby and Ray, the story slides into a serpentine mode, with cross and doublecross and an escalating body count. The tension is well modulated, and the film climaxes with two memorable set pieces. In one, Ray buries a not-yet-dead Marty in a remote field, piling spades of dirt atop the protesting victim. The other is a vividly bloody showdown between Abby and the detective that provides the film with a wonderful curtain line, uttered by her bemused and dying antagonist.

BLOOD SIMPLE was such a colorfully misanthropic film that the Coens evidently sought to avoid being typecast as crime film directors. Their next film, RAISING ARIZONA (1987), was a loopy comedy about babysnatching. A childless couple, H. I. (Nicolas Cage) and Edwina (Holly Hunter) McDonnough, steal a baby from a wealthy couple who have quintuplets. "Hi" and "Ed" reason that five babies are too many, and that the couple won't miss one if it disappears. Their actions precipitate a wild series of

"Hi" McDonnough (Nicolas Cage) abducts baby Nathan in RAISING ARIZONA.

events involving the quintuplets' parents, a pair of prison escapees (John Goodman and William Forsythe), and Leonard Smalls, a.k.a. "The Lone Biker of the Apocalypse," a flamboyant figure who haunts H.I.'s nightmares and comes to visit him in the flesh. To call RAISING ARIZONA a comedy, however, is misleading. It is neither funny nor witty. It is more tall tale than comedy, a film of outlandish characters and improbable events. In neither this film nor BLOOD SIMPLE, do the characters exhibit complexity or an inner psychic richness. The Coens excelled at taking stock characters and planting them in well-conceived narratives given a striking visual design. These are formalistic movies, and the pleasures they extend derive from their well-crafted designs, rather than from richly modulated drama.

As the decade ended, the Coens were at work on MILLER'S CROSSING (1990), a low-key gangster film distinguished by its dense and complex story line, and they were poised for a prolific outpouring of work, including BARTON FINK (1991), THE HUDSUCKER PROXY (1994), FARGO (1996), and THE BIG LEBOWSKI (1997). They survived the demise of Circle Films and continued to make iconoclastic movies while attracting (in the nineties) distribution deals from the majors. Measured by their output and their creative and business acumen, the Coens were distinguished filmmakers. They showed that independents could forge a highly successful career on the periphery of the industry and that a demonstrable audience niche would produce the funding and distribution to sustain intelligent and eccentric productions.

JIM JARMUSCH   A New York University Film School graduate, Jim Jarmusch was a teaching assistant for famed director Nicholas Ray, and he worked with German filmmaker Wim Wenders on his film about Ray, LIGHTNING OVER WATER (1980). Wenders gave Jarmusch some raw black-and-white film stock, unused by Wenders for the project he was then working on, THE STATE OF THINGS (1982). From this Jarmusch made the first half-hour installment of what eventually became STRANGER THAN PARADISE

(1984). Made for $100,000, Jarmusch's cult hit was a minimalist tale about a New York drifter whose Hungarian cousin visits him unexpectedly. With a third companion they embark for the wintry bleakness of Cleveland and then on to Florida. The narrative, such as it is, was deliberately aimless, the visual style was cool and distancing, and the film's charm resided in its oddball characters and their endearingly dysfunctional relationships with their surroundings. To promote the film, the distributor, Samuel Goldwyn Company, designed a brilliant trailer around Screamin' Jay Hawkins's performance of "I Put a Spell on You," and the film went on to gross $2.5 million. This was a notable success because the film's style is quite restrained, favoring long takes with little movement or action on screen and no use of editing to pump up its rhythms. Jarmusch was surprised at this popular acceptance. "I'm still a little confused by STRANGER's success. I thought that formally and structurally the film would keep audiences at a distance and it would become a cult film in Europe and there'd be little interest in America."[69]

Not only did the film do well commercially, but it was also a major influence on other aspiring young filmmakers, who were impressed with what he had accomplished on so little money. Spike Lee, for example, said, "A great film for me to see was Jim Jarmusch's STRANGER THAN PARADISE. It opened up to me what the possibilities could be. 'Specially since I knew Jim; he was ahead of me in film school. I knew I could do this now."[70]

Jarmusch's next feature, DOWN BY LAW (1986), focused on a trio of odd cellmates (a pimp, a disc jockey, and an Italian immigrant) in a wayward narrative of escape and cultural discovery. Narrative grew even more diffuse in MYSTERY TRAIN (1989), about the chance encounters among characters inhabiting three different stories, linked by the hotel where they stay. The picture was financed by Japan's JVC Entertainment, demonstrating that even independent film might benefit from the emerging global entertainment economy.

Unlike John Sayles, who was a social realist and who therefore made movies that were accessible for a popular audience, Jarmusch practiced a more severe, controlled, and intellectualized style that was not for all tastes. His camerawork was typically spare, and it framed the action at some remove from the characters. This visual distancing helped create the cool tone of his work and prevented the viewer from enjoying an uninhibited emotional access to the characters, as is the norm in mainstream filmmaking. Jarmusch's approach to narrative dissipated the normative pleasures of commercial cinema in other ways as well. From the standpoint of story, not much happens in a Jarmusch film. "Most films aren't demanding of the audiences," he noted. "They don't trust the audience, cutting to a new shot every six or seven seconds." Jarmusch rejected montage and its inherent ability to energize a film's pacing and provide viewers with a continuing visual stimulation and excitement. In this regard, the minimalism of his work had greater affinities with the aesthetic design of such foreign filmmakers as Robert Bresson and Yasujiro Ozu, though Jarmusch's films typically lack the warmth and sentiment of the latter director's work. This austerity has limited the popular appeal of his pictures (especially in comparison with his fellow NYU alum Spike Lee), but Jarmusch's eighties work was a major inspiration and encouragement for other up-and-coming independent filmmakers, and its studied refusal of the normative aesthetic of commercial film showed how varied are the possibilities for creative expression in cinema.

DAVID LYNCH   David Lynch established a unique artistic voice in eighties cinema largely on the strength of one film, BLUE VELVET, released in 1986 to significant critical and popular reception (on the relatively smaller scale accorded an art film). Prior to that, his career had moved in contradictory directions. With an art school background, Lynch spent five years making ERASERHEAD (1976), his first feature, on borrowed money. This nightmarish film about a freakish misfit living in squalor became a popular cult item and positioned him for his next assignment. Mel Brooks invited him to direct THE ELEPHANT MAN (1980), a Brooksfilm production with distribution by Paramount. In comparison with his other work, Lynch softened the ugliness of his imagery and sweetened his outlook for this tale of Victorian sensation John Merrick, horribly disfigured by elephantiasis. In evoking London during the early industrial period, Lynch worked in an essentially realistic mode, unusual for him, though he included notable scenes of hallucinatory imagery loosely correlated with the Elephant Man's subjectivity. The film as a whole, though, lacked the extended surreality of his later films. While well made, it does not have their abrasiveness or Lynch's willingness to indict society as a whole for the squalor he depicts. The deformity of Merrick (well played by John Hurt under pounds of make-up) is not yet the universal human condition that it becomes in BLUE VELVET and WILD AT HEART. The picture generated a respectable $8.5 million in domestic rentals and gave Lynch the career boost he needed to move to his next picture. Unfortunately, it turned out to be one of the 1980s' great messes, DUNE (1984), a $40 million attempt to film Frank Herbert's massive, classic sci-fi novel. The resulting film was unbalanced by its budget and production design and was criticized by Herbert fans and by critics for its overbearing imagery and narrative incoherence.

Thus far, Lynch's eighties career had veered away from the weirdness of ERASERHEAD into mainstream projects, and Lynch now returned to his surrealist roots with BLUE VELVET (1986). Highly praised by critics, the film presented an unusually harsh vision of the world, replete with sexual perversity and sadomasochistic cruelty. Lynch begins by evoking what appears to be a bucolic, small-town community. He shows roses in front of a white picket fence under a postcard sky, a smiling fireman on a passing truck, children crossing the street under the watchful eye of a traffic guard, a man watering his lawn. But all is illusion. In the next moment, the man has a seizure and collapses, and the camera moves from his crumpled body to a subterranean view of the lawn to show the savagery that lies hidden beneath its apparent placidity. Insects prey upon one another in a riotous frenzy.

In the opening moments of the film, Lynch vividly establishes its aesthetic and moral design—the revelation of savagery and depravity beneath the polite surfaces of daily life. Young Jeffrey Beaumont (Kyle MacLachlan) finds a severed ear in the woods and, fascinated by its mystery, searches for answers. His quest involves him in the affairs of a psychopath, Frank Booth (Dennis Hopper), and the woman (Isabella Rossellini) he has forced into a sadomasochistic affair. As Jeffrey pursues the mystery and becomes Booth's prey, Lynch shows the horror that accompanies the cheery facade of Jeffrey's hometown. Dennis Hopper's human monster, Frank Booth, is a vivid personification of evil and perversity and one of the memorable villains in eighties cinema.

It is certainly arguable that Lynch intended the subversion of small-town homilies in the film to serve a political function in Reagan America by implying that the period's ideologies of home, hearth, and family repressed the truth about human affairs. While the evocation of evil in the film is quite powerful, however, Lynch offers nothing to oppose this except Jeffrey's naive and childlike query about why people like Frank Booth exist. Furthermore, when order is restored at film's end, Lynch presents his vision of "normality" in extraordinarily alienated terms, which imply that it has no credibility. Jeffrey's

Dennis Hopper, as Frank Booth, menaces Kyle MacLachlan in Blue Velvet.

trip through hell has not enlightened him or deepened his character. He and everyone in his family remain cheerfully blind. Thus, Blue Velvet is a work of ambiguous merits. It went places that few other widely distributed films of the period dared go, and it offered a pointed rejoinder to the "don't worry, be happy" cultural politics of the era. But Lynch's apparent inability to see anything but ugliness, and to find only evil credible, limited the film's aesthetic and moral resonance. Nevertheless, many critics placed Blue Velvet on their ten-best lists that year.

Lynch's eighties film career now seemed to lack a second act. He extended the ominous, anxiety-laden style of Blue Velvet to network television with the series "Twin Peaks" (1990), which was wildly successful in its first season. His follow-up feature to Blue Velvet was Wild at Heart (1990), a twisted, kinky, lovers-on-the-run road movie that crossed Elvis Presley with The Wizard of Oz (1939) and often seemed, in its insistent fascination with grotesquerie and ugliness, like a retread of Blue Velvet. Even such fine performers as Nicolas Cage and Laura Dern, as the pair of lovers, failed to provide the material with much nuance. When "Twin Peaks" faltered in a subsequent season, its oddness began to look labored and contrived. Lynch's feature film career then stalled in the nineties, the surrealism that seemed so fresh and daring in Blue Velvet becoming stale with repetition. For all of its flaws, Blue Velvent remained one of the most original and talked-about pictures of the decade.

Alan Rudolph In the 1970s, Alan Rudolph was a protégé of Robert Altman, serving as an assistant director on The Long Goodbye (1973), California Split (1974), and Nashville (1975) and coscripting Buffalo Bill and the Indians (1976). Rudolph emerged from Altman's shadow in the later seventies and sustained his own distinctive film career throughout the eighties. The wayward narratives of Rudolph's

Keith Carradine with one of his outlandish hairdos in Alan Rudolph's playful TROUBLE IN MIND.

films and his fondness for ensemble casts were familiar elements of the Altman stylistic. Rudolph found an independent distributor for his most offbeat films in Island Alive.

The box-office failure of REMEMBER MY NAME (1978), distributed by Columbia Pictures (and produced by Altman's Lion's Gate Films), led to the collapse of Rudolph's next project, THE MODERNS, about the American artists' colony in 1920s Paris. Rudolph was compelled to seek out more conventional material, and the early eighties saw him directing ROADIE (1980), a loud comedy built around rock singer Meatloaf; ENDANGERED SPECIES (1982), an environmental thriller for MGM; and SONGWRITER (1984), a limp comedy about country-western singers that starred Willie Nelson and Kris Kristofferson. During this period, he also made a sharp documentary, RETURN ENGAGEMENT (1983), about Timothy Leary and G. Gordon Liddy, who had formed a late, odd career as lecture circuit partners.

Rudolph's distinctive style emerged in mid-decade with the pictures he released through Island Alive (which in 1985 became Island Pictures), a prominent indie distributor. CHOOSE ME (1984), shot in less than a month for $750,000, became one of his biggest successes. CHOOSE ME focused on a group of characters who hang out in a singles bar and listen to the romantic advice of a popular talk show host (Geneviève Bujold). Rudolph's ensemble cast was extremely engaging, and the picture remained one of his most endearing portraits of the vagaries of the heart. TROUBLE IN MIND (1985) was a campy film noir, set in the future in an unnamed Pacific Northwest town, with Kris Kristofferson as a grizzled ex-cop trying to pick up his life after release from prison. The picture boasted a fine, moody Mark Isham score, striking production design that made inventive use of real locations, a series of increasingly outrageous coiffures for actor Keith Carradine, and Divine, the famous transvestite from John Waters's films, as a bald villain. This remarkable combination of elements made for an original, if not always wholly successful, film.

Rudolph next did MADE IN HEAVEN (1987), a conventional love story (despite the oddness of having the lovers literally meet in heaven) for Lorimar. But he returned to Alive Pictures with THE MODERNS (1988), his long-planned project about Americans in Paris, played by the Rudolph stock company, most notably Geneviève Bujold, Keith Carradine, and Geraldine Chaplin. In contrast with the loose, laid-back style and airy substance of CHOOSE ME, THE MODERNS boasted a finely detailed portrait of this chapter in art history and a series of provocative debates, voiced by the characters, about the philosophy of art. This ambitious and well-defined picture was the last that Rudolph released through Island, which folded in 1989.

Despite their generally poor commercial record, Rudolph's films were visually stylish and consistently offered the pleasure of unexpected designs, quirky characters, and an absurdist sense of humor. "I don't do realistic films. I don't even believe they exist," he said.[71] CHOOSE ME and TROUBLE IN MIND are two of the 1980s most unique films, and THE MODERNS looks long and with great fascination at art world aesthetics, a topic and area of interest that demonstrated Rudolph's maverick tastes (relative to the industry). His quintessential distance from mainstream American film was best captured by Robert Altman in THE PLAYER (1992), wherein Rudolph appears (after being mistaken for Martin Scorsese in a gag that acknowledges Rudolph's relative anonymity to the general public) as a screenwriter pitching a new, high-concept action picture. It'll be a cynical political thriller, he promises, but with lots of heart. It will be GHOST meets MANCHURIAN CANDIDATE and, oh yes, it'll star Bruce Willis.

JOHN SAYLES   By virtue of his productivity and increasing critical and popular cachet, John Sayles was the most successful independent filmmaker of the period, and he aimed to maximize the opportunities afforded by his independent status. Except for the ill-fated BABY, IT'S YOU (1983), he resolutely stayed away from the majors, preferring to raise funding himself for his inexpensive films because of the greater creative freedom this gave him. With his first production he carefully positioned himself and defined the kind of filmmaking he wanted to practice. Of this experience, he said, "Most people who are trying to break into movies make a small horror picture. But I may only get to do this one time, and if that's the case, if I'm only going to get one shot, why not make something that I would want to see, that I wouldn't get to see unless I made it myself, or somebody not working in the studio system made it?"[72]

His first feature, RETURN OF THE SECAUCUS SEVEN (1980), was made for $125,000, with Sayles personally committing $60,000 of that total. Though Sayles did not originally plan for the picture to have a theatrical release (he saw it instead as an audition piece), it won the attention and favor of several specialty distributors when it was exhibited at festivals. As a promotional ploy, its distributors, Specialty Films and Libra Films, successfully and shrewdly compared Sayles's thrifty accomplishment to the bloated budget of UA's disastrous HEAVEN'S GATE, released the same year.

The picture makes for an interesting, if not wholly fair, comparison with Lawrence Kasdan's THE BIG CHILL (1983). Both deal with a group of old friends on a holiday weekend who reminisce and compare the different directions their lives have taken. Both sets of characters are former sixties activists who find themselves nostalgic for the ideals and camaraderie of their youth. Kasdan's characters have more upscale occupations and consequently lead more affluent lives, and they are also older than Sayles's group, which is just turning thirty. Sayles's group, in turn, is much less angst-ridden and melancholy over lost opportunities and ideals. Thus, the aim of RETURN OF THE SECAUCUS SEVEN is relatively more modest than THE BIG CHILL, which tries to summarize the predicament of a generation. Sayles's characters do not labor under this symbolism and social import. Kasdan's film has often been criticized for not delving deeper into its characters than it does, but then, neither does Sayles present deeply nuanced character portraits. Both films offer a casual but insightful look at the bonds among these friends, with their social attitudes given only a glancing treatment.

Sayles later would come a long way from the beginner's command of cinema technique that he showed in this film. The camerawork is uninflected, with most shots taken at eye-level positions. The shots are stationary, and the camera almost never moves to reframe the action. Thus, the staging is generally nondynamic, and there is no choreography of action in relation to a fluid camera. The setups are mostly conventional, with scenes covered by a master shot and alternating close-ups. Except for a couple of notable montages (each of which goes on longer than it should), the editing by Sayles is functional and unassertive.

Thus, RETURN OF THE SECAUCUS SEVEN showcases the talents of a novice film-maker who was, at this point in his career, an exquisite writer and a fine director of actors but who had not yet mastered the plastic properties of cinema. The charm of the film lies in the witty writing and the endearing performances of the ensemble cast (prominent members include Maggie Renzi, who would produce a number of Sayles's subsequent films, and David Strathairn, whose versatility Sayles employed in a wide range of roles). From this auspicious debut, Sayles quickly established a productive career as director, writer, and performer while deepening his control of the camera and his understanding of what editing can contribute. He also frequently scripted films for other directors (ALLIGATOR [1980], BATTLE BEYOND THE STARS [1980], THE HOWLING [1981], THE CHALLENGE [1982], ENORMOUS CHANGES AT THE LAST MINUTE [1983], THE CLAN OF THE CAVE BEAR [1986], WILD THING [1987], BREAKING IN [1989]).

As director, Sayles completed six features during the eighties, a remarkable accomplishment for one working outside the industry's major production and distribution venues. LIANNA (1983) compassionately portrayed a woman's estrangement from a boorish husband and realization of her bisexual identity. Sayles's writing was as sensitive and sharp as ever, and he demonstrated his gift for drawing convincing female characters (rarely evident in male filmmakers) and directing women. (One of the most effective scenes in SECAUCUS SEVEN contrasted the women, who were sharing intimate conversation with one another, and the guys, who were off bonding, without words, in a basketball game.) BABY, IT'S YOU dealt with the awkward romance between a middle-class Jewish girl and a working-class Catholic boy in 1960s New Jersey. Working for a major studio, Sayles here strove to make a film with some commercial potential rather than the picture as he had written it. THE BROTHER FROM ANOTHER PLANET (1984), about a black alien visiting Earth who experiences the disparities and tensions between the races, MATEWAN (1987), about an Appalachian coal miner's strike, and EIGHT MEN OUT (1988), about the 1919 Chicago White Sox scandal, showed Sayles's developing mastery of film form and narrative and his willingness to tackle subjects of social significance. As Sayles's command of the medium's properties grew, his emphasis on sharp dialogue and sincere performances remained a characteristic strength of his work. In EIGHT MEN OUT, he vividly characterized the eight members of the Chicago White Sox who were banned from the game for throwing the 1919 World Series, along with a large gallery of supporting players (gamblers, hoods, journalists) that included such historical figures as Charlie Comisky and Ring Lardner (played by Sayles). Though the cast of characters is large, Sayles's dramatic focus remains sharp, with the characters precisely drawn. And his scrappy, thrifty independent filmmaker's sense served him well here. Working on a relatively low budget, he and cinematographer Robert Richardson shrewdly chose their camera positions to cover the baseball action in ways that did not reveal how small were the number of extras peopling the stands. Like MATEWAN, the film is rich in period detail but never loses the human drama, and the story is evocatively capped with an epilogue in 1925 that shows former Sox players Buck Weaver and Shoeless Joe Jackson, ghosts of their former selves, hanging around the bush leagues, unrecognized by the fans and virtually forgotten.

MATEWAN is Sayles's best film of the decade. Based on a miners' strike in Mingo County, West Virginia, in 1920, it vibrantly portrays the struggle of white, black, and

Chris Cooper as a union organizer arrives in the town of MATEWAN *in John Sayles's epic paean to labor rights.*

Italian miners against the exploitative and ruthless business practices of the Stone Mountain Coal Company. The company owns the town of Matewan and, as was customary in the industry at that time, pays its workers in scrip redeemable at the company store. When a union representative, Joe Kenehan (Chris Cooper), arrives in town to organize the striking miners, the company retaliates by hiring black and Italian workers to take their place. Kenehan, though, rallies all of the miners by pointing out that the company has white fighting black, black fighting Italian, and hollow fighting hollow instead of addressing the real struggle, which is between those who work and those who don't. "All we got in common is our misery," he says, "and at least we can share it." The company sends in a pair of hired killers to intimidate Kenehan and the other miners, and when the strikers refuse to back down, a shoot-out ensues between the townspeople and the company goons.

With its large cast and finely textured historical detail, MATEWAN approaches an epic stature and scope, and during the anti-union eighties (President Reagan had fired the nation's striking air traffic controllers in 1981), it voiced a solidly pro-union and worker-centered politics. While showing the complexity of the historical incident, Sayles never lost sight of the basic class and economic conflict at the root of the strike, and seldom has a contemporary American film invested labor with such dignity and heroism. Sayles's choice of Haskell Wexler as cinematographer was a natural one. Wexler was among the industry's finest cinematographers, and he vividly captured the atmosphere of Appalachia. His control of light gave the film a professional patina that Sayles's earlier work had not possessed. Moreover, Wexler's left-wing political sensibility was eminently suited to the project. (Wexler's filmmaking credentials, in this regard, included his work as director or codirector of LATINO [1985], UNDERGROUND [1976], INTRODUCTION TO

THE ENEMY [1974], BRAZIL: A REPORT ON TORTURE [1971], and MEDIUM COOL [1968] and as cinematographer of COMING HOME [1978], BOUND FOR GLORY [1976], and INTERVIEWS WITH MY LAI VETERANS [1970]). Resonant with emotion and drama, MATEWAN is an outstanding example of socially committed filmmaking, in which the human drama and the sociohistorical context are masterfully integrated. Once again, it was Sayles's fine writing and sense of character that provided the solid foundation for this huge film.

Despite the social aspirations a film like MATEWAN possessed, Sayles was unpretentious in his approach to filmmaking. He believed that his function as a director was to offer stories with values, stories that would provide audiences with positive social and cultural experiences. Few industry filmmakers could be said to have such an orientation, nor did the industry encourage such an outlook. Thus, he remained apart from the majors, where the pursuit of high grosses often generated formulaic filmmaking and at times an indifference to the quality of the cultural experience that film can offer. As Sayles described it, "If storytelling has a positive function, it's to put us in touch with other people's lives, to help us connect and draw strength or knowledge from people we'll never meet, to help us see beyond our own experience."[73] This was an honorable mission for cinema to undertake, and Sayles kept its banner high during the decade.

PAUL SCHRADER   Although Paul Schrader sustained distribution deals with the majors (Paramount, Universal, Warner Bros.), his choice of projects was markedly unconventional, and, as a result, he never operated within the hub or heart of the industry. Trained in film school (Columbia and UCLA) and, before that, a graduate of Calvin College, Schrader's films reflected these twin influences. They displayed a marked self-consciousness of form and a concern with spiritual crises and rituals of scarification and spiritual redemption, exemplified in his screen plays for Martin Scorsese's TAXI DRIVER (1976) and his own HARDCORE (1979). The box-office impact of the films he directed was small, but he successfully attracted support from the majors for his offbeat subjects and intensively stylized pictures.

AMERICAN GIGOLO (1980) broke with Hollywood tradition by offering a male character as sex object. Richard Gere is Julian Kay, a male prostitute whose earnings enable him to sustain an aloof and narcissistic life. John Bailey's cinematography and Ferdinando Scarfiotti's production design showcase Julian's seductive persona, with lingering shots of his wardrobe and grooming rituals and the polished circles in which he moves. In designing and filming his apartment, Schrader, Bailey, and Scarfiotti replicated the venetian blind motif that Scarfiotti had created for Bertolucci's THE CONFORMIST (1970), and Schrader had Bailey include a few still-life shots of Julian's pad in the manner of Yasujiro Ozu, another filmmaker Schrader much admired. (More analytic and intellectual than most American directors, Schrader had published a book about the "transcendental style" of Ozu, Robert Bresson, and Carl Dreyer.) The Bresson influence, in turn, is quite strong in the film. Its narrative moves toward a resolution modeled on Bresson's PICKPOCKET (1959), wherein an aloof and disconnected character accepts the love another individual offers him. Julian's emotional isolation is threatened by his involvement with Michelle Stratton (Lauren Hutton), the lonely wife of a politician. Another denizen of Julian's sex world frames him for murder, and while he is incarcerated, Michelle compromises her social standing by supplying Julian with an alibi. Confronted with her love and generosity, he attains a moment of fragile grace, and Schrader ends the film here, in a close-up of Julian's head resting against Michelle's

Julian Kaye attains his moment of grace at the end of AMERICAN GIGOLO, *as Paul Schrader pays homage to Robert Bresson's* PICKPOCKET.

hand. The spiritual grace that Julian achieves, though, is a formalistic one, derived as an homage to Bresson, and not one that emerges organically from the narrative and characterizations. Like Julian, the film is cold and distant, and Schrader wanted, in the final shot, a sudden infusion of emotion that would transform the film's austerity. But as Schrader admitted, it's hard to do Bresson in the American cinema—the moment of transcendence must be predicated on an aesthetic of denial and austerity, "and if you do too much denial then you're out of the commercial cinema. . . . I've mitigated the denial, but then of course the blinding moments don't stand out so much."[74] Schrader's control of the film's visual design (this was his first teaming with Scarfiotti and with Giorgio Moroder, who composed the film's score), the skill with which he uses Gere, and his integration of Bertolucci, Ozu, and Bresson make the picture a fascinating one to watch. And it is one to which he would return—he used the same ending (and repeated the PICKPOCKET motif) at the conclusion of LIGHT SLEEPER (1991).

Schrader had written the script for what became LIGHT OF DAY (1987) but was unable to get this project going, so he next agreed to film a genre picture from a script that he had not originated. CAT PEOPLE (1982) was a triumph of production design, featuring an especially close collaboration between Schrader and Ferdinando Scarfiotti (with Moroder again doing the score) in an update of the 1942 Val Lewton horror classic, with a Calvinist emphasis upon the dangers of sexuality. Irena Gallier (Nastassja Kinski) joins her brother, Paul (Malcolm MacDowell), in New Orleans and learns to her dismay that they are part of an ancient, incestuous race that sacrificed its children to leopards. The souls of the sacrificed grew in the leopards until the animals assumed human form, but those afflicted could mate only with their own siblings. Sex with an outsider would trigger the animal transformation, and the leopard would have to kill again before it could return to human form.

This absurd narrative premise is related by a character in the film. Schrader, however, plays the story line straight, with no humor or irony, and the film never overcomes this premise. His directorial concerns, though, lay elsewhere than the elaboration of this narrative line. The camera movement, lighting, and color are extremely sensual, and they frame the core issue of the film—the terror of sexuality and its animal-like elements—which the horror structure enabled Schrader to pose. Irena struggles with the ghastly knowledge of her family history as she falls in love with Oliver Yates (John Heard), curator of the New Orleans zoo. To make love with Oliver is to risk the animal transformation, but the two of them decide to consummate their attraction, despite its dangers. The major problem with the film is that the sexual metaphor, though potent, loses its poetry by virtue of Schrader's extremely literal treatment. In the Lewton original, all was suggested, hinted, latent. In the remake, the animal is real, the viscera and blood shockingly graphic. As a result, the metaphor never attains the imaginative power that it possesses in the Lewton film. Furthermore, once the metaphor is posed, it receives little elaboration or development. Cat People is an unsuccessful attempt to sexualize and poetically transfigure generic horror material.

By contrast, Schrader's next film is a masterpiece of conceptual precision and aesthetic design. Mishima: A Life in Four Chapters (1985), about Japanese novelist-filmmaker Yukio Mishima, is an extremely stylized meditation on trials of spirit and flesh, with stunning production design by Eiko Ishioka and cinematography by Schrader regular John Bailey. Its audacious visual design, complex narrative structure, and masterful thematic integration made this Schrader's best film of the decade. Mishima was Japan's most celebrated author, whose output included thirty-five plays, twenty-five novels, hundreds of short stories, and several short films. He closely identified with Japan's feudal past, its veneration for the emperor, and the warrior code of the samurai. Haunted by the disparity between word and action, Mishima sought to unite these two modes of being, and as his obsession with Japan's feudal past deepened, he came to feel that death would provide the ultimate union of pen and sword. On 25 November 1970, Mishima and several cadets of his private army seized control of Japan's Eastern Army barracks. Mishima harangued the troops from a balcony, condemning Japan's materialism and spiritual softness and urging them to join him in restoring the old national virtues. Jeered by the soldiers, Mishima retreated from the balcony. Inside a general's office, he performed the warrior's ultimate rite, *seppuku* (ritual suicide), encoded by tradition as an honorable way of concluding one' life.

His drastic action stunned Japan, and it provides the frame and structure for Schrader's kaleidoscopic, time-shifting film. The picture is composed of four sections, the first three of which achieve synthesis in the last: Beauty, Art, Action, and Harmony of Pen and Sword. Mishima's actions on 25 November are intercut through the Beauty, Art, and Action sections and constitute the predominant focus of the concluding episode. The other material includes black-and-white flashbacks to scenes of the writer's youth, adolescence, and adulthood and color footage of floridly rendered visualizations of key Mishima novels: Temple of the Golden Pavilion, Kyoko's House, and Runaway Horses. The presentation of these is overtly theatrical, with minimalist but extremely stylized sets, fly-away flats, and chiaroscuro spotlighting of the key action. Each novel culminates in an act of personal destruction, with the film freezing this action at its onset and as the transition point to the next of the film's four episodes. The

Yukio Mishima (Ken Ogata) achieves the union of pen and sword as his life becomes art in MISHIMA.

result of this careful design is the suggestion that, through his work, Mishima was moving closer to, and preparing himself for, the final, extreme action of 25 November. By juxtaposing this literary material with the biographical passages of Mishima's life, Schrader vividly evokes the psychosexual obsessions and anxieties that fused with ultra-conservative nationalism and produced the writer's veneration for an aesthetic of beauty transfigured in death. Schrader shows Mishima's childhood frailty, the separation from his mother, his homoerotic desires and cult of bodybuilding, and his turn toward a samurai and military ideal of physical hardness and spiritual purity. While he never suggests that an answer can be found in any one of these factors, he shows how inexorably they combined to bring Mishima to the conviction that the ritual of disembowelment and beheading might constitute the supreme expression of his life's ideal and aesthetic. This act of self-destruction would be a grand moment of theater and make the life and the aesthetic as one.

Sustained by a hypnotic score by Philip Glass, MISHIMA is a superbly realized portrait of an enigmatic and paradoxical figure. With its complex temporal structure, it is nearly a non-narrative work. This, and its array of disparate visual styles, give it an "art film" status that places it far outside the normative patterns of American commercial film. More remarkable still, it was shot in Japan and all of the dialogue is in Japanese, except for some occasional English-language narration supplied by actor Roy Scheider. With MISHIMA, Schrader pursued a very personal project (his brother Leonard, a long-time Japanophile, co-wrote the screenplay), gave it a compellingly unorthodox design, and got a distribution deal with Warner Bros. This confluence of factors produced one of the decade's most original and impressive films.

For his next film, LIGHT OF DAY (1987), Schrader abandoned the florid style that he had practiced in the eighties thus far and returned to the low-key naturalism and work-

ing-class focus that he had so memorably evoked in his first film as director, BLUE
COLLAR (1978). As a result of this shift, LIGHT OF DAY has an emotional honesty and
power that the other, more formalistic pictures do not achieve (though Schrader feels
ambivalent about the film's restrained style), and some measure of this was no doubt due
to the personal nature of this project. Schrader remarked that this was a picture about
his mother and his relationship to her.[75] Michael J. Fox and rock singer Joan Jett (a
strong performance in her first film) play siblings trying to make a go of their rock band
amid the economic hard times of Ohio's factory towns. As in BLUE COLLAR, Schrader
portrays the harshness and anxiety of working-class lives made marginal by an economy
that is expanding in other sectors and regions than those the film's characters occupy. In
this regard, LIGHT OF DAY vividly evokes the hard edge of the 1980s economy and the
communities and lives that fared badly during that era's industrial downturn. But the
central focus of the film is a remarkably nuanced family portrait, exploring Joe and
Patti's relationship to each other and to their parents, principally Patti's tangled relations
with her mother. Jeanette (Gena Rowlands, luminous in the role) has been estranged
from daughter Patti, and the film traces their melancholy reconciliation. It occurs as part
of an extraordinarily tender, suspenseful, and moving deathbed scene, one that eschews
melodrama in favor of honest human feeling. Schrader really grew here as a filmmaker,
despite the mixed feelings he has about this picture. His script is solid and finely crafted,
and he grounds the film in writing and performance rather than in the more formalistic
areas of production design and cinematography, as had been his norm. From Michael J.
Fox he evoked a performance of sincerity and depth and one that, in its hardscrabble,
working-class origin, is the antithesis of the upwardly mobile, self-reliant, and comic
personalities that Fox more typically played in the decade's films. With MISHIMA,
LIGHT OF DAY shows a filmmaker of uncommon versatility and range.

Schrader finished the decade with PATTY HEARST (1988), which details the anguish
and psychological torture of the kidnapped heiress, a film that returned to the proto-
typical Schrader focus on spiritual anguish and fleshly ordeal. Schrader aimed here for
an assaultive film style, and the first extended section of the film is confined to Hearst's
narrowed perspective while in captivity. The assaultive style probably foredoomed the
film's chances for commercial success.

In addition to his work as a director, Schrader was prized in the industry as a leading
screenwriter. His eighties scripts included those for AMERICAN GIGOLO, MISHIMA, and
LIGHT OF DAY, as well as two for Martin Scorsese (RAGING BULL [1980] and THE LAST
TEMPTATION OF CHRIST [1988]) and one for Peter Weir (THE MOSQUITO COAST
[1986]). As this range of projects indicates, Schrader was one of the decade's most interesting and intelligent filmmakers. The industry's ability to accommodate his unusual
films says much about the institutional flexibility of the eighties and about the space
open for unconventional filmmakers, partly as a result of the general need for product
in the ancillary markets. These factors bequeathed substantial benefits to eighties cinema, as the range and caliber of filmmaking covered in this chapter demonstrates.

7

Genres and Production Cycles

Contrary to a popular critical perspective that 1980s Hollywood marched in lockstep with the Reagan revolution, film production during the decade exhibited multiple and often contradictory sociopolitical perspectives.[1] Existing in some tension with this social engagement were the era's genre pictures. Genre production was prolific, and many of the period's biggest hits were straight genre pieces.

While genre films can be inflected with social content, what may count for most viewers are the pleasures derived from the repetition of familiar elements of character and story. If a genre persists over decades, it does so because its core elements transcend the issues of a political-social period, even as individual pictures in the genre may be responsive to a specific zeitgeist. HIGH NOON (1952) speaks to the conflicts of the McCarthy period, but its core genre elements gesture beyond this moment. Portions of this film can be illuminated with reference to 1950s political culture, but the genre is not reducible to them, and neither are the building blocks of setting, character, and conflict that make HIGH NOON a Western. Similarly, while E.T. (1982) may indeed manifest certain tropes of the Reagan period, its continued popularity demonstrates that it also speaks beyond these.

The industry's investment in traditional genres, then, should be seen as a measure of institutional stability and the continuity of product lines with built-in audience appeal. This investment often superseded the phenomena of eighties political and social culture, but not always. Many movies in the eighties were creatures of their time, and the period unquestionably influenced filmmakers, though not in any hoary base-superstructure manner. The Reagan years were an intensely ideological period, with a symbolic politics waged in the cultural arena. American film responded to this climate. The movies offered supportive as well as contentious responses, but these did not correlate in any clean way with the period's genres. Significant responses were found not only in cycles of production addressed to topical political and social issues that were salient for the period but also in extremely volatile controversies over the moral content of contemporary film. In this chapter, I first discuss the status of popular genres during the decade and then explore the cycles of topical filmmaking and their connection with the era's defining social issues. In the next chapter, I explore the controversies that centered on issues of movies and morality.

Genres

FANTASY/SCIENCE FICTION

Without question, the decade's most popular genre was science fiction and fantasy, furnishing more blockbusters during the period than any other genre. These included six of the decade's top ten films: THE EMPIRE STRIKES BACK (1980), E.T.: THE EXTRA-TERRESTRIAL (1982), RETURN OF THE JEDI (1983), BACK TO THE FUTURE (1985), WHO FRAMED ROGER RABBIT (1988), and BATMAN (1989). The genre was dominated by the high-tech blockbusters fashioned by George Lucas (who nevertheless had one prominent bomb in HOWARD THE DUCK [1986]) and Steven Spielberg and the horde of sci-fi films that imitated their formulas. The second and third installments of Lucas's STAR WARS epic—EMPIRE and JEDI—premiered in the first half of the decade, and the series influenced scores of lesser films that emphasized space battles, video game aesthetics, and movie serial characters and narratives: BATTLE BEYOND THE STARS (1980), FLASH GORDON (1980), TRON (1982), THE ADVENTURES OF BUCKAROO BANZAI ACROSS THE EIGHTH DIMENSION (1984), THE LAST STARFIGHTER (1984).

Another strain of eighties sci-fi emphasized whimsy and light comedy and, in this regard, was probably influenced by the sentimentally bickering robots R2D2 and C3PO in the Lucas productions, as well as Spielberg's blend of comedy and sentiment in E.T. These films included COCOON (1985), SHORT CIRCUIT (1986), °BATTERIES NOT INCLUDED (1987), COCOON: THE RETURN (1988), MY STEPMOTHER IS AN ALIEN (1988), and HONEY, I SHRUNK THE KIDS (1989). Spielberg's Amblin Productions was responsible for °BATTERIES NOT INCLUDED as well as for the time travel hits BACK TO THE FUTURE (1985) and BACK TO THE FUTURE, PART II (1989).

Beyond the STAR WARS films and the Spielberg orbit, the genre boasted two additional high-profile and very popular franchise series, the SUPERMAN and STAR TREK films. Both series survived ponderous, undistinguished debut films in 1978 and 1979 to flourish in more imaginative subsequent installments. SUPERMAN II (1980) and SUPERMAN III (1983) were directed by Richard Lester, who brought his flair for oddball comedy and self-conscious style to the material, taking it in unexpected and delightful directions. SUPERMAN III, in particular, was that rarity, an eccentric blockbuster. Costarring Richard Pryor, it featured a less-than-virtuous Superman dueling with his darker side. But the picture was regarded as unacceptably deviant, and it marked Lester's last turn at the helm of the series (a similar fate befell Tim Burton after BATMAN RETURNS [1992]). SUPERMAN IV: THE QUEST FOR PEACE (1987) passed to Sidney J. Furie and was a dull, plodding, preachy affair in which the Man of Steel tries to rid the world of nuclear weapons.

The STAR TREK series flew on profitably throughout the eighties and into the nineties and spawned, in turn, several spin-off TV series. In contrast to the high-tech, special effects–driven STAR WARS pictures, the TREK films emulated the original TV series in their emphasis on character and ideas, with effects work relegated to a background element. This design was pitched to the fans of the original shows because these fans had kept the property alive after the TV series was canceled, and their devotion sustained its evolution into a highly successful film series.

STAR TREK II: THE WRATH OF KHAN (1982) brought back a popular villain from the TV show to do battle with the crew of the Enterprise. Khan was played with scene-chewing delight by Ricardo Montalban in a striking, pectoral-baring costume. The tone

Rick Moranis faces his unique comic dilemma in HONEY, I
SHRUNK THE KIDS.

of the film, at once exciting and goofy, was perfectly matched to its television progeni-
tor, and its popular success kickstarted the film series in the eighties. Actor Leonard
Nimoy (who played Spock, everyone's favorite Enterprise crew member) directed the
next two entries, widely regarded as among the best in the franchise: STAR TREK III:
THE SEARCH FOR SPOCK (1984) and STAR TREK IV: THE VOYAGE HOME (1986).
William Shatner (who played Captain Kirk of the Enterprise) took over directing chores
on the next installment, STAR TREK V: THE FINAL FRONTIER (1989), a relatively weaker
entry that lacked the strong narrative drive of previous episodes.

The STAR TREK series counterbalanced the relative anti-intellectualism of the STAR
WARS films by honoring the cerebral components of the genre, which had long enabled
writers and filmmakers to use science fiction as a framework for exploring ideas. This
aspect of the genre, historically important in both literature and cinema, had been diminished in Lucas's effects-driven pictures and in Spielberg's sentimental, family-oriented

productions. Other notable films that used the genre in a more intellectually inclined direction included Ken Russell's ALTERED STATES (1980), in which a scientist (William Hurt in his film debut) conducts mind-altering experiments on himself; Fred Schepisi's ICEMAN (1984), about the culture clash ensuing from the discovery of a Neanderthal man frozen in ice and revived by scientists; 2010 (1984), the long-awaited but rather pedestrian sequel to Kubrick's magesterial 2001: A SPACE ODYSSEY, (1968); and Terry Gilliam's BRAZIL (1985), a futurist rendition of Orwell's *1984* that manages to be both visionary and terrifically bleak. Grim portents were offered in the Mad Max films—THE ROAD WARRIOR (1981) and MAD MAX BEYOND THUNDERDOME (1985)—and in a large cycle of dystopic films that used the genre within a sociopolitical context to warn of an antidemocratic future. I examine this cycle later in the chapter. One prominent film in that cycle—THE TERMINATOR (1984)—launched the career of director James Cameron (discussed in ch. 6). Working in the genre for the rest of the decade, Cameron followed TERMINATOR with ALIENS (1986), the sequel to Ridley Scott's trend-setting ALIEN (1979), and THE ABYSS (1989).

The extraordinary popularity of fantasy and science fiction was a function of the narrative approach exemplified in the Spielberg-Lucas films as well as the industry's innovations in the technology available to filmmakers, primarily in the areas of computer effects and sound. Offering sensual light-and-sound shows anchored to breathless narrative pacing, these pictures were unprecedented in their technical virtuosity and helped transform cinema into an amusement park ride for millions of viewers. The moviegoing public responded enthusiastically. Fantasy and sci-fi had the highest average earnings of top box-office films by genre throughout the decade, with an especially strong showing in the years 1980–85. The industry's research and development of improved sound systems and computerized effects paid big box-office dividends. George Lucas and his engineers at Lucasfilm were instrumental in helping lead this technological makeover.[2]

During the 1980s, digital imaging began to make some inroads, but it did not take off in a big way until the following decade.[3] Soon to become a leading effects house, Pacific Data Images (PDI) was founded in 1980. Its initial clients included television networks, and it designed eye-catching computer logos for "Entertainment Tonight" and ABC sports programming including the 1984 Winter Olympics. By the later eighties and into the nineties, PDI was producing digital effects for the major studios in such high-profile films as CARLITO'S WAY (1993), BATMAN RETURNS (1992), GHOST (1990), NATURAL BORN KILLERS (1994), TRUE LIES (1994), and TERMINATOR 2: JUDGMENT DAY (1991).

Fantasy and sci-fi films showcased the early applications of digital effects, thereby announcing the advent of a new chapter in the capabilities of commercial filmmaking. STAR TREK II: THE WRATH OF KHAN contained a striking sixty-second effects sequence showing the transformation of a dead planet into a lush and living world. Created by Lucasfilm, this minute of color computer graphics included a convincing rendition of fire and three-dimensional geographic features including mountains and oceans. The computer effects were not merely a part of the sequence but in fact were the sequence, and they generated tremendous interest throughout the industry in exploring these new capabilities.

Unfortunately, the next applications were showcased in films that had weak narratives and performed poorly at the box office. Disney's TRON contained over forty minutes of computer animation, much of it composited with live action elements, and THE LAST

Ricardo Montalban's vivid villainy enlivened STAR TREK II:
THE WRATH OF KHAN.

STARFIGHTER featured twenty minutes of computerized space action. The new effects were insufficient to boost the popularity of these pictures. In the meantime, Lucasfilm included short computer-animated sequences in RETURN OF THE JEDI and YOUNG SHERLOCK HOLMES (1985), but it wasn't until Cameron's THE ABYSS that CGI (computer generated images) finally came of age in in the slithery, watery alien designed by Industrial Light and Magic.

The creature had started in the computer as wireframe animation, onto which the animators composited a rippling liquid texture (in a process called texture mapping) and shimmery highlights that gave it a three-dimensional appearance. Furthermore, in a way that dramatically heralded the future, the CGI creature interacted in a convincing and fully dimensional way with the human, live-action elements of the shot. When actress Mary Elizabeth Mastrantonio touches the creature, her finger goes "inside" the alien, glimpsed through its translucent surface, and it, in turn, reacts to her touch, rippling with sensation. The effect is completely credible, even though the alien existed only in computer space and had no live-action correlate in the shot. Here lay the future of

TRON helped inaugurate the era of digital effects in film, although their widespread use by the industry was still a decade away.

digitally based filmmaking: the ability to convincingly integrate the 2D and 3D components of a scene, computer space with live-action space. From this flowed all of the jaw-dropping digital effects of the nineties in pictures like TERMINATOR 2, DEATH BECOMES HER (1992), JURASSIC PARK (1993), and TRUE LIES.

As eighties films began the shift toward digital animation, they also benefited from dramatic improvements in sound. Used on E.T. (1980), POLTERGEIST (1982), and STAR TREK II: THE WRATH OF KHAN (1982), digital audio heralded a revolution in sound production. In contrast to analog methods of sound recording and mixing, digital audio offered a greatly expanded dynamic range and the elimination of background noise and signal degradation caused by the multigenerational pre-dubs commonly used in a sound mix. As a result, digital audio gave sound engineers the ability to manipulate sound elements without signal loss and gave viewers increased separation of sound elements in clean and well-articulated mixes.[4]

The introduction in 1982 of audio CDs in the consumer market helped drive the conversion to digital in film production by accentuating the disparities between film sound (merely adequate) and the much higher quality available to home listeners on their audio systems. Initially during the changeover, film productions used an unsatisfying combination of analog and digital formats because sound editing was still done on mag-striped film and with sound sources archived on magnetic tape.

But the digital storage of sound information was not far off. In 1984, Lucasfilm had a proprietary digital sound workstation (audio signal processor, or ASP) that stored and mixed sound in digital format. For INDIANA JONES AND THE TEMPLE OF DOOM (1984), the ASP workstation created complex background sound effects. For example, when Jones is surrounded by a bevy of arrows flying toward him, ASP electronically extended the arrows' whizzing sounds and added Doppler effects (a means of spatializing sound by altering its pitch). The digital audio project leader at Lucasfilm stressed the efficiency of this new approach as compared to more traditional methods. About the arrow scene in TEMPLE OF DOOM he noted, "It would have taken three people to do this on normal equipment: one to control the tape speed to create the Doppler effect; one to control the left-to-right pan; and one to ride the volume fader. We programmed the controls of the ASP so that these effects could be controlled just by tweaking a knob or two."[5]

As for sound reproduction in the theater, it was multichannel but not digital. Release prints still carried an optical analog sound track on which the sound information was visually encoded. Dolby had introduced a four-channel stereo optical sound system in 1976. This was Dolby Stereo, in which the left and right channels on the stereo track were encoded with four channels of information (left, center, right, and surround). Extraced by a decoder during playback, they helped make the sound field far more spatial and three-dimensional than it had been previously. (For the 70mm format, Dolby had introduced in the 1970s a six-channel system that carried stereo surrounds.) Because the stereo track carried by the film was still an optical one, however, the dynamic range captured by a post-production sound mix was severely limited. When converting the signal from magnetic tape to the optical track during post-production, directors and mixers were invariably disappointed at the loss of sound, compression of dynamic range, and distortion in the upper register that occurred. Low-volume sound effects would vanish into the hiss of the track (a problem that Dolby Noise Reduction worked to minimize). High volume produced a different problem. On optical tracks, the louder the sound, the larger its visual encoding (i.e., the more space it occupies on the track). Since the track space available between frame line and sprocket holes is fixed, volume levels that exhaust this space edge into harsh noise. Thus, though digital techniques were making inroads into post-production, sound playback in theaters was still an analog process.

While Dolby Stereo proliferated in the late 1970s and the 1980s, many theater auditoriums continued to maintain substandard audio equipment, which degraded the benefits that Dolby Stereo brought to film sound. To improve theater sound and complement the advances being made by Dolby Laboratories, George Lucas in 1980 commenced development of a program to specifiy a set of criteria to ensure optimal theater sound. In 1982 Lucasfilm constructed a state-of-the-art post-production facility where the THX system (named after his first feature, THX-1138 [1971]) was developed. Introduced in 1983 and implemented at two theaters presenting RETURN OF THE JEDI, the THX Sound System Program was a set of technical standards for gauging the adequacy of theatrical sound. THX-certified theaters were those that met the specifications (for image was well as sound) of Lucasfilm's engineers and, consequently, were those in which viewers could be assured of hearing the best possible sound. The THX program examined and tested a theater's auditorium for levels of background noise, acoustic isolation, amount of reverberation, the viewing angle of the screen, alignment of the projector and conformation with SMPTE's standard of sixteen footlamberts of light from the screen, and use of equipment on the THX Approved Equipment List. The program assessed a theater's architecture, acoustics, and equipment and would make any necessary custom installations. Exhibition had been the film industry's weak segment for decades. Poor screen illumination and inferior sound reproduction effectively erased the advances made by cinematographers, Eastman Kodak, and Dolby Laboratories in improving the look and sound of contemporary film. The THX certification program addressed this problem and helped raise the industry's and the public's awareness of the factors affecting film presentation in theaters. Theaters that underwent the expense of the THX upgrade could then use their certification as a marketing tool. In 1986, Lucasfilm began research to extend the THX program to home audiovisual equipment, and in 1990 unveiled the Home THX Program for use in calibrating home theater to optimum specifications.

As Lucasfilm's THX program began to upgrade the quality of theatrical presentation, Dolby continued to make improvements on its system. In 1986, Dolby SR (Spectral Recording) offered an improved four-channel optical system with noise reduction that made possible a wider dynamic range and better frequency response. INNERSPACE (1987) and ROBOCOP (1987) were among the first films exhibited in Dolby SR. For the home videotape market, Dolby Surround decoders, debuting in 1982, enabled consumers to play videotapes of Dolby-encoded movies with three-channel reproduction (left, right, and surround), while the subsequent marketing of Dolby Prologic receivers enabled the decoding of center-channel information as well. Thus, sound in cinema and in high-grade home environments had become remarkably dimensional. Whereas earlier generations of film carried only one-channel sound, reproduced from what was effectively a center-channel speaker behind the screen, Dolby's four-channel system created a wide and enveloping sound field with left and right front channels, a center front channel, and a surround channel. The front left, front right, and center channels had been conceived for a representation of sound continuity, so that, as Dolby engineer Robert Warren pointed out, "if a sound moves from left to right, the sound field in front is consistent. You simply observe the motion of it moving; you don't hear it changing color or changing timbre as it shifts."[6] By contrast, the surround channels were reserved for ambient effects and to provide the viewer with an immersive audio experience. As Warren explained, with surround the concept is

> to flood the auditorium with sound from everywhere but the screen, so that you have a very wide natural sound field that really doesn't have any direction or motion to it. Since the surround channel is primarily used for ambiences . . . room tone, and special effects, fly-ins and fly-outs, you don't want the surround channel to detract or to pull your attention away from the story on the screen. . . . Probably the best way to observe sound that's coming from the surround channel is to turn it off. If you can hear the difference, then it's probably loud enough for ambiences and room tones.[7]

Despite the advance that this more spatialized sound field represented, Dolby mixes still had to contend with the inherent limitations of optical sound tracks. This problem did not change until the introduction of Dolby Digital in 1992. The process debuted with BATMAN RETURNS and carried an optical analog sound track as well as a digital one stored between the sprocket holes. It was a 5.1 channel system that configured the surround speakers as rear left and rear right channels and added a separate channel dedicated to bass signals (the .1 channel). With its multitude of discrete channels, Dolby Digital stimulated audio engineers to produce extremely aggressive mixes, with emphatic use of surround channels far beyond the mainly ambient uses that Robert Warren described for Dolby Surround. Since then, competing digital systems have proliferated, such as Sony Dynamic Digital Sound (SDDS) and DTS, which produces sound via CD playback synched with film projection.

In the eighties, digital sound playback in theater auditoriums remained a goal yet to be achieved. The end result of digital audio production techniques was an optical sound track on the release print. As a result, the industry moved slowly to embrace all-digital production practices. For example, the digital editing of an entire sound track did not occur until 1992's LAWNMOWER MAN.[8] Despite the industry's slow adoption of all-digital sound, filmgoers experienced striking improvements in the audio quality of motion pictures and in the expressive sound designs that multichannel encoding and selected digital audio methods made possible. While these changes cut across all genres of film, their effects were most striking in fantasy and science fiction because of sound's ability to heighten the credibility and physicality of visual effects, an important part of such filmmaking. Augmenting its popularity with moviegoers, fantasy and sci-fi functioned as the industry's showcase for the dramatic new advances in electronic effects and audio quality.

COMEDY

Audiences always enjoy laughing, and comedy films performed very strongly in the 1980s, with outstanding box office throughout the decade. Special effects were on display in a few of the biggest pictures (GHOSTBUSTERS [1989], GREMLINS [1984], HONEY, I SHRUNK THE KIDS [1989]). More commonly, though, the era's comedies worked on the basis of situation, performance, and writing, although these varied wildly in their degrees of sophistication. Outstanding writing and refined comic performances helped make these the decade's most distinguished comedies: AIRPLANE (1980), ARTHUR (1981), S.O.B. (1981), MELVIN AND HOWARD (1981), VICTOR/VICTORIA (1982), DINER (1982), MY FAVORITE YEAR (1982), TOOTSIE (1983), PLANES, TRAINS, AND AUTOMOBILES (1987), ROXANNE (1987), MOONSTRUCK (1988), A FISH CALLED WANDA (1988), and THE WAR OF THE ROSES (1989). MELVIN AND HOWARD, DINER, MOONSTRUCK, and ROXANNE are low-key films in which the humor and charm grows organically out of the characters and their situations. Among the finest character-centered comedies were those directed by Blake Edwards, whose prolific output included S.O.B. and VICTOR/VICTORIA as well as THE MAN WHO LOVED WOMEN (1983), MICKI AND MAUDE (1984), A FINE MESS (1985), THAT'S LIFE (1985), and BLIND DATE (1987). Two other directors whose long film careers are identified with sophisticated comedy made their final theatrical films in the eighties: Billy Wilder (BUDDY BUDDY [1982]) and Stanley Donen (BLAME IT ON RIO [1984]).

By contrast with the elegance and sophistication of these productions, many others were more frantic concoctions in which jokes and physical stunts dominated story and character. A string of Burt Reynolds car-crash comedies helped sustain his popularity while eroding his critical reputation: SMOKEY AND THE BANDIT II (1980), THE CANNONBALL RUN (1981), STROKER ACE (1983), and CANNONBALL RUN II (1984). In the latter half of the decade, his career slipped into obscurity, in part because of the fallout from these relentlessly lowbrow pictures. The counterculture comic team of Cheech and Chong starred in CHEECH AND CHONG'S NEXT MOVIE (1980), CHEECH AND CHONG'S NICE DREAMS (1981), STILL SMOKIN' (1983), and CHEECH AND CHONG'S THE CORSICAN BROTHERS (1984). "Saturday Night Live" alumni Chevy Chase, John Belushi, Bill Murray, and Dan Aykroyd made the transition to film with mixed results in CADDYSHACK (1980), STRIPES (1981), CONTINENTAL DIVIDE (1981), NEIGHBORS (1982), NATIONAL LAMPOON'S VACATION (1983), DOCTOR DETROIT (1983), and FLETCH (1985). Though an occasional guest rather than a "Saturday Night Live" regular, Steve Martin sustained the most prolific film career among those comics associated with SNL: THE JERK (1980), DEAD MEN DON'T WEAR PLAID (1982), THE MAN WITH TWO BRAINS (1983), THE LONELY GUY (1984), PLANES, TRAINS AND AUTOMOBILES

Bill Murray and Dan Aykroyd in Ghostbusters. *The film's canny blend of comedy and horror helped make it one of the decade's standout, genre-straddling productions.*

(1987), ROXANNE (1987), and DIRTY ROTTEN SCOUNDRELS (1988). ROXANNE especially is a delight, a sweet romantic fable that Martin, as the film's producer, writer, and star, intelligently modeled on the Edmond Rostand play *Cyrano de Bergerac*.

A huge number of comedies in the 1980s played to the nation's teenage audience, a demographic group courted by the studios because of its voracious moviegoing habits. Amy Heckerling's seminal FAST TIMES AT RIDGEMONT HIGH (1982) captured with great vitality the hormonal obsessions and mall-centered lives of Southern California teens. Sean Penn's wonderful performance as spaced-out, cool-dude Spicolli set the trend for Bill and Ted, Beavis and Butthead, and every other doped-out funster that came after. In the wake of FAST TIMES, teen comedies proliferated: PORKY'S (1982), SPRING BREAK (1983), PORKY'S II: THE NEXT DAY (1983), VALLEY GIRL (1983), REVENGE OF THE NERDS (1984), BACHELOR PARTY (1984), WEIRD SCIENCE (1985), REAL GENIUS (1985), BACK TO SCHOOL (1985), PORKY'S REVENGE (1985). The longest-running adolescent-oriented comedy series was probably the POLICE ACADEMY series. Debuting with POLICE ACADEMY (1984) and starring Steve Guttenberg as the chief oddball of a group of slapstick dolts enrolled as police-in-training, the series eventually ran into the mid-1990s with seven installments. The best of the teen comedies, though, were those made by director and producer John Hughes. With an accent on character unusual for the pictures pitched to the adolescent audience, Hughes' films included SIXTEEN CANDLES (1984), THE BREAKFAST CLUB (1985), PRETTY IN PINK (1986), and FERRIS BUELLER'S DAY OFF (1986).

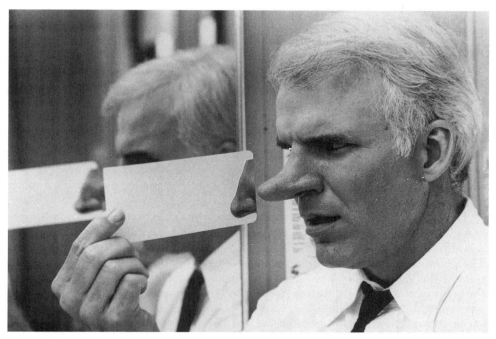

Steve Martin's Roxanne *was an intelligent and winsome updating of* Cyrano de Bergerac.

While often coarse and vulgar, the teen films were undeniably popular and gave the genre much vitality while connecting it to a large and devoted audience. As a whole, though, the genre was extremely healthy and included a large number of well-supported productions. Its outstanding popularity was especially striking in 1981 and 1988, when almost every film in the top ten was a comedy vehicle. In 1981 the seven comedies out of the top ten were Stir Crazy, 9 to 5, Stripes, Any Which Way You Can, Arthur, The Cannonball Run, and Four Seasons. In 1988, the eight comedies among the top ten were Who Framed Roger Rabbit; Coming to America; Good Morning, Vietnam; "Crocodile" Dundee II; Big; Three Men and a Baby; Moonstruck; and Beetlejuice.

The continuing appeal of comedies argues strongly for the presence of genre as an institutionally stabilizing factor and for certain base-level audience desires and motivations relative to the movies, motives that generalize beyond the zeitgeist of a political-social period. With regard to comedy, these motives, in the eighties as in other periods, lay in viewers' seeking enjoyment from light-spirited diversions. The reaffirmation of a viewer's sense of joy and well-being is among the most gratifying and important appeals that the movies possess. This, in fact, is one of the core demands the public makes upon the medium. The industry has always known this and been responsive to it, and it has prospered by generating product to meet the demand. This successful confluence of production and viewer gratification has helped the studios to predict and rationalize their production cycles and has helped sustain the ongoing relationship of the movies with their public. Thus, comedy remained one of the most successful of eighties genres and one of the most important for the industry.

HORROR

Horror also proved to be one of the decade's most important genres, measured in terms of popularity as well as social impact. The decade opened with a huge spike in production (chart 7.1), from thirty-five pictures produced in 1979 to seventy in 1980 and ninety-three in 1981. In 1980–81, top-renting horror films included DRESSED TO KILL, FRIDAY THE 13TH, THE SHINING, THE FOG, PROM NIGHT, GRADUATION DAY, HALLOWEEN II, and MANIAC. This spike in the cycle marked the onset of some notoriously violent pictures and a general degradation of the genre in which horror equated with graphic bloodletting.

The laws of the market quickly asserted themselves. The production boom resulted in a glut of films that could not be distributed to available outlets, precipating a sharp downturn in horror picture starts in 1982 and a 50 percent falloff in rentals by 1983.[9] The genre spiked again in 1986–87, hitting a peak of 105 pictures in 1987. At middecade, the video market was thriving, and many of these pictures were low-budget, throwaway entries aimed at this ancillary. In 1986, for example, one-third of horror films were straight-to-video releases.[10]

The horror genre was responsible for the decade's most gut-wrenching, stomach-churning violence in pictures that amounted to little more than primers on how to slaughter people. In this regard, the genre lost the finely detailed psychological and atmospheric focus of its artistic peak in the thirties and forties in the productions of Universal Pictures and the Val Lewton films at RKO. Contemporary films like SCHIZOID (1980), MANIAC (1980), TERROR TRAIN (1980), HE KNOWS YOU'RE ALONE

CHART 7.1
U.S. Horror Film Production

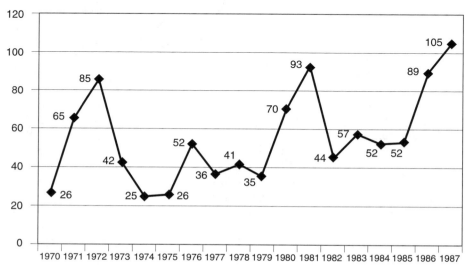

SOURCE: *Variety*, 8 June 1988, p. 24.

(1981), and DRILLER KILLER (1979) ignited controversy and protest for their portraits of slaughter and their sexual politics. In this way, the horror genre helped instigate some of the bitterest of the decade's culture wars focusing on the movies. In the next chapter, I examine these conflicts and the issues animating them.

For a few filmmakers, the genre furnished material for serious and ambitious work. Of only two films that Stanley Kubrick made during the decade, one—THE SHINING (1980)—fell in this genre and was based on a Stephen King novel. While the picture was generally disliked by King fans, Kubrick concentrated on the psychological effects wrought upon a family by the evil and haunted estate of which they are caretakers. The father (Jack Nicholson) undergoes a spectacular mental collapse that leads him to a murderous frenzy directed at his wife and child. While these plot mechanics are in themselves unremarkable, Kubrick gives them vitality through the impressive visual treatment that he accords the hotel. Filming its vast spaces and long corridors with wide-angle lenses and a prowling Steadicam, Kubrick and cinematographer John Alcott imbue the estate with a sinister, lurking presence that, in time assumes tangible form in the various ghosts that materialize to torment the family.

Like all of his pictures, THE SHINING examines the ways that people cede control of their lives to the forces and structures that surround them. Whereas other of his pictures have presented the dilemma in terms of technology (2001: A SPACE ODYSSEY), military and political chains of command (PATHS OF GLORY [1957], DR. STRANGELOVE [1964]), or class-bound social mores (BARRY LYNDON [1975]), THE SHINING invests its *mise-en-scène* in a statement about the power of environment and locale over personality, in this case the environment and locale being construed in terms of the evil and supernatural that are normative for the genre. For popular viewers, though, Kubrick invested the film

While few major filmmakers worked in horror, Stanley Kubrick notably ventured into the genre with THE SHINING.

with too much ambiguity for an era that equated horror with spectacles of slaughter. THE SHINING did not find a large audience, but as an exercise in visual design it is an impressive work.

Another unusual picture, WOLFEN (1981), is one of the decade's most ambitious horror films. Directed by Michael Wadleigh, who resurfaced after more than a decade of obscurity since he directed WOODSTOCK (1970), WOLFEN uses the trappings of horror for mystical and metaphoric ends. A pack of wolflike creatures is terrorizing New York City, attacking a wealthy businessman and prowling Wall Street as well as killing derelicts in the South Bronx. Outfitted with the latest in high-tech weaponry and surveillance equipment, the corporate state sees only political terrorists, a group called Götterdämmerung that uses a wolf's head as its emblem. But a city detective (Albert Finney) learns the truth. The wolfen are spirits from ancient Native American lore come to make war on capitalism, whose predatory ways and despoliation of the environment have invited a counter-response from these ancient predators. The film ends with the wolfen inflicting a spectacular assault on Wall Street and then vanishing back into the city. The film's ecological values and its veneration for the spirituality of cultural outsiders (the Native Americans) give it a distinctly sixties ambience and show that horror can serve quite effectively as a vehicle of social and political criticism. Furthermore, the visual design of WOLFEN features outstanding Steadicam work used in sequences showing, by means of infrared images, the wolfen's perspective as they run and stalk their victims. The moving camerawork in these sequences is as exhilarating and hypnotic as that in THE SHINING.

While Kubrick and Wadleigh had made unusual forays into the genre, David Cronenberg emerged as its most outstanding serious filmmaker. After a series of low-budget pictures—SCANNERS (1981), VIDEODROME (1983)—Cronenberg directed three haunting films that invest their horrors with a strong and detailed psychological foundation. THE DEAD ZONE (1983) remains among the best film treatments of a Stephen King novel. Following a traffic accident, a man (Christopher Walken) develops premonitory powers, able to see a person's fate by touching the person or an article of his or her clothing. The gift, though, becomes a curse. Walken inhabits a dead zone because he sees the boundaries that frame life and death, and this intensifies his feelings of alienation and melancholy. Furthermore, it precipitates an acute moral and spiritual crisis. He meets a politician (Martin Sheen) who, his gift shows him, is a modern Hitler who will plunge the world into nuclear destruction. Knowing what he does, is he then justified in murdering the politician? Throughout the picture, Cronenberg maintains an intensely melancholy tone, avoiding bloody effects and keeping the focus a resolutely psychological one as he probes mysteries of life, death, and destiny.

THE FLY (1986) is one of those rare cases in which the remake surpasses the original film. Cronenberg reworked the 1958 picture of the same title about a man whose scientific experiment goes awry and splices his genes with that of a common housefly. Seth Brundle (Jeff Goldblum) mutates into Brundlefly before the horrified eyes of his girlfriend (Geena Davis). Cronenberg presents the mutation as a powerful metaphor for debilitating diseases like cancer and AIDS that deform their victims with exquisite bodily tortures, and the scene that causes audiences to squirm with the greatest discomfort is also the most moving. His body an oozing mass of tissue that is literally falling apart, Seth turns to his girlfriend in despair, and she embraces him in a powerful statement that her love for him transcends his bodily manifestation. It's a brilliant scene that subjects the

Michael Wadleigh's WOLFEN *was a poetic and metaphoric treatment of ecology issues via the horror film.*

audience to a disturbingly ambivalent experience and, in this, shows that real horror, intelligently used, has a spiritual dimension and purpose that few films ever realize.

DEAD RINGERS (1988) is an ultra-creepy film about twin gynecologists (Jeremy Irons in tour-de-force performances) who share lives, living quarters, patients, and lovers. Cronenberg's focus here is almost entirely suggestive and psychological, with little overt horror. Characteristically, he explores themes of bodily mutilation and mental disintegration, as the doctors' minds and personalities warp in ever more demented and evil directions.

In these three films, Cronenberg eschewed the sadism of the genre to focus on the human terms of horror, and there he found the universal experiences of disease, decay, death, psychological loss, and spiritual suffering. In doing so, his work reconnected the genre with the authentic human tragedies from which the art and aesthetic of horror arise.

Several other front rank directors dabbled in horror during the decade. In CAT PEOPLE (1982), Paul Schrader remade the 1942 Val Lewton classic about a strange young woman with a family curse that causes her to transform into a predatory cat when she is angered or sexually aroused. Lewton's film, like all of his outstanding horror pictures at RKO, emphasized mystery, implication, and atmosphere. By contrast, Schrader played up sex and explicit violence, attributes that overly literalized the ambiguities and narrative mystery of Lewton's original production. Schrader's CAT PEOPLE was memorable mainly because of the outstanding production design by Ferdinando

Scarfiotti, particularly in the film's prelude, which conjures the African plains as if in a fevered dream.

Though he would be known mainly for high-concept action films like TOP GUN (1986), Tony Scott essayed a vampire movie in THE HUNGER (1983). Catherine Deneuve plays the vampire, with David Bowie as her companion, though Scott's emphasis was on visual design, not horror, and in his elegant images he crossed high fashion with punk. Several other directors perceived the affinities between punk culture and vampire lore: Joel Schumacher in THE LOST BOYS (1987) and Kathryn Bigelow in NEAR DARK (1987).

Alan Parker and John Schlesinger made brief forays into demonism and Satan worship in ANGEL HEART (1987) and THE BELIEVERS (1987). In the former, Mickey Rourke is Harry Angel, a private eye hired by a mysterious Louis Cyphre (Robert De Niro) on a missing person case. Cyphre turns out to be the devil, and the story is really about Angel's damnation. While the tale is predictable, Parker's strongly imaged film is among the more striking examples of American Gothic. In THE BELIEVERS, a widower (Martin Sheen) and his son run afoul of a Manhattan relegous cult that practices child sacrifice. Schlesinger crafts a disturbing film, but it is cold and brutal, showing the violent death in the opening scene of Sheen's wife and, at the end, of his child. Horror in the eighties was particularly unsparing of its viewers.

Joseph Ruben's THE STEPFATHER (1986) was an outstanding horror film, as was John McNaughton's HENRY: PORTRAIT OF A SERIAL KILLER (1986, released in 1990). Ruben's film zeroed in on the family and, like much contemporary horror, showed it as a breeding ground for monsters. A seemingly virtuous, clean-living man (Terry O'Quinn), who wants the perfect family, turns out to be a psychopath with a penchant for slaughtering wife and children when they fail to live up to his ideal of perfection. Ruben's taut direction makes this a highly suspenseful picture that critiques the family politics of the political Right by showing the thin line between virtue and aberrant repression.

McNaughton's film is among the most disturbing pictures ever made. With a dispassionate tone and with graphic but controlled violence, it shows and studies the horrendous cruelties of Henry (Michael Rooker), a human monster modeled on Texas serial killer Henry Lee Lucas, who perpetrates a number of torture murders without feeling or remorse. Henry's friend Otis becomes a partner in crime, and Otis is even more disturbing and creepy than Henry, pursuing behaviors—incest, necrophilia—that Henry finds objectionable. Otis's sister is the one character who offers Henry some tenderness and emotional connection, yet these prove to be too disturbing for him. In the final scene he murders her, leaves her dismembered body in a trunk by the roadside, and wanders off, deeper into America, to pursue the killings that alone give his life meaning.

McNaughton avoids the moralizing apparatus that usually accrues to serial killer films—subplots showing police and FBI hunting the killer, victims grieving over their shattered lives, and the conventional narrative suspense that intercutting among this material typically generates. Instead, he makes the viewer dwell exclusively in the emotionally barren mental landscape of Henry, in his isolation and alienation. This is a terrifying place. McNaughton thus invites his viewers to confront the human monster at close range, with no answers provided, no absolution offered, and no release.

Cronenberg's work, WOLFEN, THE SHINING, THE STEPFATHER, and HENRY: PORTRAIT OF A SERIAL KILLER represent the high achievements of horror in the eighties, with the genre being used in a serious way by ambitious filmmakers. Outside these efforts, much of the sheer popular appeal of horror could be found in the numerous series and production cycles that highlighted favorite characters or the work of name directors and authors. Joe Dante's THE HOWLING (1980), an uncommonly smart and witty werewolf movie with a script by John Sayles, revived interest in lycanthropes and touched off a minor run of werewolf pictures. John Landis's AN AMERICAN WEREWOLF IN LONDON (1981) mixed black humor and graphic gore, while TEEN WOLF (1985) played werewolves for laughs and SILVER BULLET (1985) took them more seriously. Subsequent HOWLING movies—the series ran to seven installments and into the mid-nineties—failed to recapture the original's sly humor. Unlike other horror franchises, however, the HOWLING movies happily went in totally unexpected directions, with story settings that included Transylvania and monsters that included Australian marsupial werewolves carrying baby critters in a pouch.

Another large cycle of films clustered about the fiction of author Stephen King: CHRISTINE (1982), CUJO (1983), THE DEAD ZONE (1983), CHILDREN OF THE CORN (1984), and PET SEMATARY (1989). Excepting THE DEAD ZONE, this was an undistinguished group of films that nevertheless demonstrated the cachet of King among fans of the genre. One of the worst horror films of the decade was actually directed by King: MAXIMUM OVERDRIVE (1986), about trucks that come to life and terrorize patrons at a roadside diner.

The combination of graphic gore and humor in AN AMERICAN WEREWOLF IN LONDON proved to be trendsetting. Horror in the eighties often placed ultraviolence and mutilation in a cartoonish context and played them for laughs. Sam Raimi's The EVIL DEAD (1982) and EVIL DEAD II (1987) and Stuart Gordon's RE-ANIMATOR (1985) epitomized these Grand Guignol comedies. Without the ultraviolence, though, horror-comedy could be big box office. Blending these genres to great effect were GHOSTBUSTERS (1984), GREMLINS (1984), and BEETLEJUICE (1988), with THE WITCHES OF EASTWICK (1987) as a relatively less successful example.

While the diversity of these productions shows that horror was a variegated genre, its greatest impact as a pop-cultural phenomenon lay in two extraordinarily popular franchise series, FRIDAY THE 13TH and A NIGHTMARE ON ELM STREET. These films introduced a pair of serial killers who became wildly popular among teenage fans of the genre. FRIDAY THE 13TH (1980), directed by Sean Cunningham, introduced Camp Crystal Lake as the stalking ground of a gruesome killer preying on vacationing teenagers. In the film's twist ending the killer turns out to be a woman (Betsy Palmer) angry over the drowning death of her son, Jason, twenty years before. Blaming camp counselors for his death, she murders out of vengeance. Dozens more teens are butchered in FRIDAY THE 13TH, PART 2 (1981), and Jason Voorhees emerged as the relentless, seemingly indestructable killer whose persona became synonymous with the series. FRIDAY THE 13TH: THE FINAL CHAPTER (1984) was no such thing, and the next episode, FRIDAY THE 13TH, PART V: A NEW BEGINNING (1985) introduced a copycat killer to keep the franchise alive. Jason returned in FRIDAY THE 13TH, PART VI: JASON LIVES (1986) and PART VII: THE NEW BLOOD (1988), while in PART VIII: JASON TAKES MANHATTAN (1989), the locale shifted from Crystal Lake to a cruise ship.

The FRIDAY series was a remorseless presentation of serial killing, made especially disturbing by the almost mystical impenetrability of Jason, his huge, masked presence looming from the shadows and carrying dull-bladed implements of butchery. His impenetrability was emblemized, famously, in the hockey mask that he wore and that came to serve as his face, hard, featureless, inhuman. Like other prominent serial killers in fran-

The hulking Jason Voorhees stalked through the FRIDAY THE *13TH series, dispatching nubile teens with relentless efficiency.*

chise series—Michael Myers in the HALLOWEEN films and "Leatherface" in the TEXAS CHAINSAW MASSACRE pictures—the mask served to obliterate his humanity and to portray him as a being that eludes understanding or categorization.

While Jason's undifferentiated personality makes him the lumpenproletariat of serial killers, Freddy Kreuger established an elegant, witty, even urbane and charming persona in the ELM STREET films: A NIGHTMARE ON ELM STREET (1984), A NIGHTMARE ON ELM STREET, PART 2: FREDDY'S REVENGE (1985), A NIGHTMARE ON ELM STREET 3: DREAM WARRIORS (1987), A NIGHTMARE ON ELM STREET 4: THE DREAM MASTER (1988, directed by Renny Harlin, who went on to establish a solid, commercially successful career outside the genre), and A NIGHTMARE ON ELM STREET: THE DREAM CHILD (1989). The first in the series, directed by Wes Craven, introduced Freddy as a child molester who had been burned alive by outraged parents but whose evil was too powerful for death to hold him in its grip. Freddy returns here and throughout the series, entering the dreams of the Elm Street children to torture them psychologically and then kill them in macabre ways. This is his way of getting revenge on those who burned him.

With some brilliance, Craven introduced dreamscapes as the surreal staging grounds for Freddy's predation, and this enabled the series to play, in elaborate and imaginative ways, with special effects and the magic time-space warp and antirational logic of the dream world. This surrealism is most marked in DREAM WARRIORS, co-written by

Compared with Jason, Freddy Kreuger was more urbane and elegant, though no less sadistic or bloodthirsty.

Craven. This mind-bending surrealism, plus the performance of Robert Englund as Freddy, mugging, joking, and winking at the audience as he slaughters people, gave the series a degree of self-consciousness. By DREAM WARRIORS, the series was elaborating its own formal rules of play and quoting these. The humor and self-consciousness helped give Freddy a degree of popularity among teen viewers that far surpassed that of his main competitors, Jason Voorhees and Michael Myers.

Myers stalked through the HALLOWEEN series, which elaborated a mythology surrounding this character, who had been introduced as the personification of evil in John Carpenter's original film (1978). HALLOWEEN II (1981) resumes the action of its predecessor on the same evening that the original story concluded. Michael continues to stalk Laurie (Jamie Lee Curtis), an intended victim who had eluded him, while being pursued in turn by his nemesis Dr. Sam Loomis (Donald Pleasance). HALLOWEEN III: SEASON OF THE WITCH (1983) was an oddity in that it dropped the storyline of Myers-Laurie-Loomis and focused instead on a crazed toymaker intent on massacring children with booby-trapped Halloween toys. After this misfire, which fans of the series did not support, the francise resumed its familiar format with Loomis chasing Myers in HALLOWEEN 4: THE RETURN OF MICHAEL MYERS (1988) and HALLOWEEN 5 (1989). Carpenter had long since disassociated himself from the series, and as the long hiatus between parts 2 and 4 (which focus on Michael Myers) demonstrates, the series never attained the popularity and fan following that Jason and Freddy Kreuger were inspiring.

The remaining archetypal masked killer in this eighties pantheon was "Leatherface," a hulking, silent butcher with a chain saw, part of a family of cannibals introduced in Tobe Hooper's classic, THE TEXAS CHAINSAW MASSACRE (1974). Given the striking popularity of the decade's other masked killers, Leatherface made an inevitable comeback in

The Texas Chainsaw Massacre 2 (1986). Directed again by Hooper, this installment substituted broad, slapstick comedy for the claustrophobic terror of the original film, and the comic and horror elements failed to integrate with one another. The third entry in the series, Leatherface: Texas Chainsaw Massacre III (1989), followed the story line of the original film closely, but its gore was reduced by prerelease cuts that damaged its narrative integrity. After his memorable and terrifying debut in the 1974 film, Leatherface never again found a suitable vehicle to showcase his demented talents and thus remained a third-string star in the decade's horror pantheon.

Hooper, too, had a fitful career after his 1974 classic. His feature films found little commercial success—The Funhouse (1981), about a group of teens spending the night in a deserted carnival; Lifeforce (1985), a weird picture about outer-space vampires; and Invaders from Mars (1986), a critically reviled remake of the fifties science fiction classic. Hooper also directed for television, most notably "Freddy's Nightmares" (1988), a series inspired by the Elm Street films, and "Tales from the Crypt," an anthology horror series.

Hooper's biggest film of the decade, both in terms of its budget and its popular success, was also a nagging reminder that his career had stalled. Poltergeist (1982) was a solid hit about a family, the Freelings, whose suburban existence is undermined by vengeful ghosts who kidnap their little girl. The picture was produced by Steven Spielberg, and rumors circulated upon its release that Spielberg had taken control of the picture's direction and editing. The film certainly bears many Spielberg hallmarks, from the surburban family milieu and special effects to the reassuring ending. Whatever the truth to these rumors, the film's Spielberg association overshadowed Hooper's role as director in its critical reception. Hooper did continue to work for Spielberg, directing a 1985 episode of Spielberg's TV series "Amazing Stories," but unfortunately his biggest hit of the decade was a picture widely regarded as not his own.

Accentuating the series nature of eighties horror, Poltergeist generated two follow-up pictures, Poltergeist II (1986) and Poltergeist III (1988). More lasting than the impact of the series, though, was the folklore about a curse that sprang up following the deaths of two young actresses who had played members of the Freeling family. Dominique Dunne (who played Dana Freeling) was murdered by an estranged lover during release of the first picture, and before release of the third film, Heather O'Rourke (who played Carol Ann Freeling) died unexpectedly following a surgical procedure. These two events stimulated much discussion of a Poltergeist curse.

Horror in the 1980s, then, was big box office, and it spawned several trendsetting series that added new, archetypal monsters to the genre's pantheon. Horror, though, was not a genre in which many serious filmmakers were content to work. Cronenberg, Wadleigh, Kubrick, Ruben, and McNaughton were visitors to the genre who did not stay long. Craven was highly ambivalent about his own success. He felt it limited his ability to work simply as a filmmaker, unconfined by the constraints of a genre in which he believed he had become imprisoned. Of the Hollywood genres, horror has always enjoyed a somewhat debased prestige. In the eighties, its mutation into ultraviolence enhanced this status and generally kept serious filmmakers away from its terrain.

The Musical

Although the classical Hollywood musical is passé, the genre continued in the 1980s, in productions that showed clearly the crises that beset the form. By mutating for the times, the musical retained some of its old vitality, though these changes robbed the genre of its aesthetic authenticity. The genre's main problem was that it had outlived the cinematic conditions that had given it life and greatness. More than other genres, the musical was an integral part of old Hollywood. The musical was vitally connected with the era when performers, musicians, choreographers, arrangers, and filmmakers like Gene Kelly, Fred Astaire, Vincente Minnelli, Roger Edens, and Hermes Pan were under long-term studio contract and worked full-time turning out a series of uniquely stylized pictures. Musicals flourished because the studios had the extensive rosters of in-house talent requisite for the form.

Producer Arthur Freed at MGM, for example, headed a production unit responsible for that studio's classic productions, including THE WIZARD OF OZ (1939), SINGIN' IN THE RAIN (1952), and AN AMERICAN IN PARIS (1951). THE BAND WAGON (1953), another Freed production, had its musical origins in the Howard Dietz–Arthur Schwartz song catalog and its narrative origins in the personal experiences of its key production personnel, including Fred Astaire and scriptwriters Betty Comden and Adolph Green. In fashioning the story, all contributed anecdotes drawn from their professional lives. The picture's self-conscious integration of narrative and music owes much to the ensemble work of everyone involved, including also the associate producer Roger Edens, director Vincente Minnelli, choreographer Michael Kidd, and musical designer Oliver Smith.[11] This kind of group effort depended on secure, long-term working relationships in which a director like Vincente Minnelli and a performer like Astaire would have the opportunity to explore and elaborate a variety of visual and musical styles over the course of many films and the production staff to support these efforts. It is precisely this condition that was lacking in the transient, piecework relationships that prevailed in 1980s filmmaking. Thus, the musical was affected more deeply than other film genres.

Furthermore, changing audience tastes helped erode the classic movie musical. More than other genres, the musical offered filmmakers opportunities to take cinema in markedly antirealistic and antinarrative directions. During the musical numbers, films opened onto dimensions of total self-consciousness and exquisite stylization. The hypersaturated colors of the "Broadway Melody" number in SINGIN' IN THE RAIN, the abstract set design of "The Girl Hunt" ballet from THE BAND WAGON, or the elaborate homages to impressionist painting in the concluding ballet of AN AMERICAN IN PARIS emphasize artifice and the musical and visual properties of the design so emphatically as to overwhelm narrative and character as the normative focal points of popular film.

This has proven to be problematic for contemporary audiences in several ways. Eighties viewers delighted in artifice and style, but they did so primarily through other genres, like science fiction, where the design elements were subordinated more thoroughly to narrative. The rejection of narrative inherent in every classical musical, where the story line is minimal and functions to serve the production numbers, is a design that contemporary moviegoers found troublesome, if not disturbing. For elaborate exercises in design and style, they turned to the extended effects sequences of action and science fiction films. These films, though, were more plot-driven than the classical musicals, and their effects sequences did not puncture narrative as the musical had done. Contemporary audiences were relatively unforgiving of the narrative transgressions committed by the musical.

Furthermore, the genre's emotional tone helped to seal its doom. Its buoyant optimism and frothy sentimentality struck many contemporary viewers as weirdly naive and difficult to relate to. The idea that a man might be so overcome with happiness at the thought of his beloved that he would sing and dance in the rain seemed preposterous. In contrast with the zest for life displayed by the musical, contemporary viewers found a darker and more cynical outlook in film to be a truer reflection of the world they inhabited. In this sense, serial killers replaced the singing, dancing lovers that the musical offered. The classic Hollywood productions had come to seem disconnected from a more contemporary time and place.

But the musical did not die or vanish. Musicals remained in active production throughout the decade, though they mutated in response to the aforementioned changes in industry and audience. Production was spotty and hardly prolific. Moreover, there were no musical stars, no performers whose star persona was bound to the genre. Certainly there were stars in the decade's musicals, and these included Dolly Parton (THE BEST LITTLE WHOREHOUSE IN TEXAS [1982]), Prince (PURPLE RAIN [1984]), John Travolta (STAYING ALIVE [1983]), Patrick Swayze (DIRTY DANCING [1987]), Neil Diamond (THE JAZZ SINGER [1980]) and Olivia Newton-John (XANADU [1980]). But Parton, Diamond, Prince, and Newton-John had established their star credentials in the recorded-music industry and transferred these to cinema. Gene Kelly did appear in a small role in XANADU, but his presence here was ghostly, a reminder of times past and now lost. There has been no successor to his generation of musical film stars, and eighties productions had to rely on talent developed in other media besides cinema. There is no star of eighties musicals whose song and dance talents were tied specifically to the movies and were a function of cinema. LA BAMBA (1987) and PURPLE RAIN (1984) illustrate the musical talents of the real-life concert performers Ritchie Valens and Prince. And Robert Altman's POPEYE (1980), with its cast of nonmusical performers (Robin Williams, Shelley Duvall) and intentionally sloppy production numbers, showed some contempt for the talent and its showcasing that the genre traditionally exemplified.

The top-earning musicals were either high-concept films, pictures built around popular (nonmusical) stars or singers, or based on a hit stage play or previous popular film. These sources are very different from the genre's earlier predilection for growing a film out of a renowned composer's song catalog (e.g., Gershwin and AN AMERICAN IN PARIS, Irving Berlin and EASTER PARADE [1948], Dietz-Schwartz and THE BAND WAGON). THE BEST LITTLE WHOREHOUSE IN TEXAS (1982) was based on a Broadway hit and did feature the singing talents of Dolly Parton, but it also relied upon the star charisma of nonmusical Burt Reynolds and even built a production number around character actor Charles Durning. The results were uneven at best. Also based on a Broadway hit, ANNIE (1982) toplined dramatic actor Albert Finney and television star Carol Burnett and, strangely enough, was directed by John Huston, a gifted filmmaker but one who never possessed the light and nimble touch of Vincente Minnelli or Stanley Donen, established masters of the genre. Other prominent adaptations of stage productions included A CHORUS LINE (1985) and LITTLE SHOP OF HORRORS (1986). These latter pictures were given a strong marketing push but generated weak box office, in the $10–13 million range.

A second group of musicals was arguably more cinematic, but it took the genre in a new and bogus stylistic direction. This group was composed of the high-concept films, including FLASHDANCE (1983), STAYING ALIVE (1983), FOOTLOOSE (1984), PURPLE RAIN, and DIRTY DANCING (1987). STAYING ALIVE was a sequel to the popular SATURDAY NIGHT FEVER (1977). Again starring John Travolta, whose disco character is now trying to forge a career as a Broadway dancer, the picture was directed, improbably, by Sylvester Stallone, whose film work is more noted for muscles and violence.

Under his aegis, Travolta muscled up, took off his shirt, and flexed his way through an outlandish production number, "Satan's Alley," designed as a musical trip through hell. Indeed, this is where it took the genre. PURPLE RAIN was built around the persona of rock performer Prince, while FLASHDANCE, FOOTLOOSE, and DIRTY DANCING all featured catchy narrative premises: a woman steel welder who's also a sexy dancer, a sexy male dancer who lands in a small, repressive town, and a spoiled girl vacationing in the Catskills who learns about life from a sensual working-class performer.

These pictures collectively debased the filming of dance. Montage editing and a driving musical beat hyped the pace and energy level of the musical sequences, and while this made them cinematic, it also undermined the authenticity of the musical performances. FLASHDANCE, in particular, is an aggressively edited film in which a viewer's sense of Jennifer Beals's musical talents is more a function of cinematography and editing and less a function of the performer's own movements. (Actually, a real dancer doubled for Beals in these sequences, but her performance was still overwhelmed by the editing.) In this regard, the montage style of musical presentation in the high-concept films violated the aesthetic premise that informed the work of the genre's great talents. Fred Astaire and Gene Kelly insisted that their dance numbers be filmed using longer takes and a fluid camera to follow their movements, with minimal editing. Camera positions were full-figure framings to show the dancer's entire body and to respect the integrity of the choreography and its execution by the performer. By contrast, the use of extreme close-ups of face, hands, arms, and feet, in FLASHDANCE and others, is a strategy to create the *impression* of a dance performance, conveyed through the manipulations of cinema, rather than the presentation of an actual performance. Thus, while this style is exciting and cinematic, it is a fradulent way of rendering the dancer's art. But the montage aesthetic was a response to the genre's crisis, namely, the dearth of cinema-specific musical talent, and was perhaps an effort to disguise that lack.

This problem notwithstanding, FLASHDANCE was a seminal film of the 1980s. It mixed music with quick editing to perfect one of the decade's first rock video movies. In these terms, it was tremendously influential and tremendously lucrative for Paramount, a phenomenon that I discussed in chapter 3. In the wake of FLASHDANCE, the cross-marketing of movies and popular music formats (album, singles, rock videos) became an essential prop of eighties movie distribution. Thus, though the genre was far from its glory days and was bereft of genre-specific talent, at their most influential the movie musicals showed the studios where the decade's pot of gold lay and how to reach into it. Eighties musicals, then, will be remembered for their marketing innovations, not their art.

THE WESTERN

The Western was the most miserably performing genre of the decade. While the genre's box office had fallen in the 1970s, it still saw fairly robust production and some outstanding achievements (MCCABE AND MRS. MILLER [1971], ULZANA'S RAID [1972], PAT GARRETT AND BILLY THE KID [1973]). In the 1980s, though, the production of Western features fell dramatically, and the genre saw few outstanding films that are likely to have enduring value. When the decade began, studio executives already considered the genre to be a risky venture in which to place production capital, and, as if to confirm this perception, four prominent Westerns were visible failures in 1980. These films were widely regarded by the industry as tests of the genre's viability, and their fate was interpreted as evidence of an exhausted market.

The four films in question were BRONCO BILLY, THE LONG RIDERS, TOM HORN, and HEAVEN'S GATE. The latter picture has already been discussed in chapter 1. Partly because of the box-office credentials of actor-director Clint Eastwood, Warner Bros. had positioned BRONCO BILLY as a major, hoped-for summer hit. In retrospect, however, it is easy to see that the studio's hopes were unrealistic, regardless of the picture's status as a Western (even that was problematic, as the picture is set in the modern era). Eastwood's film is a very slight confection, delicate in spirit and whimsical in its charms. None of these attributes were likely to ignite the box office. Eastwood plays a failed shoe salesman who turns to promoting a Wild West show peopled by oddballs and eccentrics and pitched to wholesome family entertainment and all the "little pards" who idolize cowboys.

In this regard, Eastwood was returning, in a historical and cultural sense, to the genre's broadest basis of support among a juvenile audience. The only problem was that this juvenile audience, which had thrived on B Westerns and TV shows from the 1930s through the early 1960s, had by the 1980s grown tired of Westerns and moved on to space adventures with their more exotic weaponry and snappier pace. Thus, BRONCO BILLY was a film curiously out of time and without a real audience to which it could connect, a problem compounded by the film's genre-bending proclivities. It blends the Western with the screwball comedy, pairing Billy (Eastwood) with a ditzy heiress on the run (Sondra Locke) in the manner of a Frank Capra Depression-era comedy. Furthermore, Eastwood's role, and the laid-back, genial spirit of the film, were too far removed from the hard, violent action that the popular audience wanted and expected of an Eastwood picture. Despite a last-minute change of advertising, BRONCO BILLY generated a lackluster $14 million in rentals, dashing Warner Bros.' hope that it would be a major summer release.

Walter Hill's THE LONG RIDERS is among the few distinguished Westerns of the decade, but shows the characteristics of his work, problems that have limited the commercial impact of his career and that certainly constrained the performance of this film. Hill was primarily a stylist and an extraordinary choreographer of physical action. He tended to eschew the exploration of character and emotion, preferring instead a kind of mythic abstractness for his characters (seen most intensively in THE DRIVER [1978] and THE WARRIORS [1979]). As a result, his pictures are good looking and impressively staged but dramatically thin, a problem that besets THE LONG RIDERS. Hill the stylist is very much on display here. The most memorable aspect of the picture is its casting. Hill chose real-life brothers to play the outlaw siblings who compose the Jesse James–Cole Younger gang: David, Keith, and Robert Carradine as Cole, Jim, and Bob Younger; Stacy and James Keach as Frank and Jesse James; Dennis and Randy Quaid as Ed and Clell Miller; and Christopher and Nicholas Guest as Charlie and Bob Ford. In addition to this remarkable casting, Hill's stylization finds full flourish in his staging of the disastrous Northfield, Minnesota, raid in which the gang was decimated. Hill uses slow motion and squibs to capture the horror of this bloody massacre and innovates by using sound to herald in slowed time the approach of screaming bullets before they strike their hapless victims. Despite this bravura set piece and Hill's evident passion for the rituals of the genre, audiences remained uninterested in the picture. It returned only $6 million in rentals that year for Paramount.

Performing even more dismally, with $4 million in rentals, was Steve McQueen's TOM HORN. Of the Westerns that failed commercially in 1980, TOM HORN suffered the unkindest fate. Its release was virtually straight to video, where it has remained in limbo ever since. Relatively unknown to viewers, it is one of the most beautifully autumnal Westerns of recent decades and is the genre's finest achievement of the eighties. This said, however, the reasons for its present obscurity are evident. It has an art house simplicity and purity of design and an absolutely sad and depressing ending that grants the viewer no emotional respite or sense of victory. An "end of the West" picture, it relates the tale of Horn's final years, when he drifted into Wyoming territory and agreed to work for the region's big cattle ranchers ridding the ranges of rustlers. Horn is framed for a murder he never committed and hung, and the film moves relentlessly toward this downbeat conclusion (one the distributor and most viewers plainly would not like). Steve McQueen produced the picture, and it was a very personal project for him, an evident labor of love, despite his physical illness, which is plainly manifest before the camera. (He completed only one more film, THE HUNTER [1980], before dying of cancer.) His performance is masterfully controlled, at once violent and delicate, and it conveys a depth of feeling for the West that is both moving and beautiful and absolutely essential to a great Western. To showcase this performance, the film offers a poetic presentation of the frontier, plains, and mountains as the basis of Horn's life and ethic of individual freedom. With superb widescreen cinematography by John Alonzo, the picture needs to be seen on the large screen and translates poorly to television and home video. Thus, it suffered a doubly unkind fate. Its membership in a declining genre hurt its reception, and its relegation to home video doom damaged its lovely and calculated visual design. Given its unkind fate, TOM HORN is one of the decade's film casualties.

Steve McQueen's autumnal TOM HORN *was the most distinguished Western of the 1980s.*

The other films that approached the genre seriously were mostly low-key, and often low-budget, productions. Independent filmmaker Robert Young's THE BALLAD OF GREGORIO CORTEZ (1981) was a restrained and documentary-like account of a famous Texas manhunt during which a young Mexican, Cortez (Edward James Olmos), who has accidently killed a sheriff, eludes a huge posse for weeks. A production of public television's American Playhouse, the film saw limited theatrical distribution. Mellow and affectionate in its depiction of the end of the West, Phillip Borsos's THE GRAY FOX (1982) starred veteran character actor Richard Farnsworth as Bill Miner, a notorious stagecoach robber who is jailed for thirty years, after which he emerges into a new, modern century and promptly turns his talents to robbing trains. Australian director Fred Schepisi's BARBAROSA (1982) examined the birth of myth and legend through the life and adventures of the titular character (played by Willie Nelson), a wandering outlaw on the Texas-Mexico border. Nelson is marvelous in the role, and Schepisi spins the film like a shaggy-dog story, taking the character past the point of death and into the realm of folklore.

A sure sign of the genre's faltering appeal was the abundance of comical and juvenile Westerns. THE LEGEND OF THE LONE RANGER (1981) resurrected the popular children's hero from radio and television but seemed unable to deal with the character except as a campy figure, lacking the sincerity of his radio and television incarnations, which compelled belief in his virtuous nature. Zorro, another popular character of Western lore, became a figure of camp in ZORRO THE GAY BLADE (1981). Starring George Hamilton (who also produced), it was intended as a follow-up to Hamilton's successful send-up of Dracula movies, LOVE AT FIRST BITE (1979), but it lacked that picture's charm. Paul Bartel's LUST IN THE DUST (1985) parodied hunt-for-gold Westerns and starred Divine, the transvestite actor associated with John Waters's films. Singing cowboy movies got an affectionate send-up in RUSTLER'S RHAPSODY (1985), starring Tom Berenger, and even country singers Roy Clark and Mel Tillis found themselves in the midst of a comic Western in UPHILL ALL THE WAY (1986).

The best of the comic Westerns was John Landis's THREE AMIGOS! (1986), starring Steve Martin, Chevy Chase, and Martin Short as unemployed singing-cowboy movie actors. They go to Mexico for a command performance but instead become involved in an adventure helping a village get rid of its bandit leader. The story inevitably references such Americans-in-Mexico classics as THE MAGNIFICENT SEVEN (1960) and THE WILD BUNCH (1969). Augmenting the WILD BUNCH connection, Alphonso Arau, a prominent villain in that film, played the chief baddie here.

Two prominent Westerns pitched to juvenile audiences were SILVERADO (1986) and YOUNG GUNS (1988). The first, directed by Lawrence Kasdan, was a big-budget effort to revive the rollicking spirit of the old series Westerns, much as Kasdan had done with the old movie serials in his script for RAIDERS OF THE LOST ARK. Four adventurers (Kevin Kline, Scott Glenn, Kevin Costner, Danny Glover) team up to rid a town of a corrupt sheriff. The pacing that Kasdan sets is so brisk and fast as to be constraining. Whenever the action begins to slow or a character to grow reflective, the film cuts nervously to some new scene or plot development. The result is a lively but superficial film. YOUNG GUNS, dubbed at the time the first "Brat Pack" Western, starred Emilio Estevez as Billy the Kid and Lou Diamond Phillips, Kiefer Sutherland, Dermot Mulroney, and Charlie Sheen as members of his outlaw gang. Each was a popular star who had made his name in adolescent-themed productions. Shot and edited with MTV rhythms and featuring a rock music score, the picture undeniably reinvigorated the genre for younger viewers, even if its noise and preening adolescence seemed vulgar to older viewers.

Amid these parodies and juvenilia, Clint Eastwood's PALE RIDER, released at mid-decade, was clearly the most ambitious effort to work honorably in the genre and take seriously its mythic underpinnings. Furthermore, because it was Eastwood's first real period Western since 1976's THE OUTLAW JOSEY WALES, the picture's release generated much anticipation. Unfortunately, PALE RIDER was disappointingly derivative. Perhaps seeking to give his picture a classical structure, Eastwood modeled the film upon George Stevens's SHANE (1953), with Eastwood's mysterious gunman as the Shane figure who saves a mining community from the rapacious businessman who wants to control it. Stevens's film was highly self-conscious in its exploration of the genre's mythology. His treatment had been exhaustive and has been criticized (though not by this author) for being too elaborate and deliberate in its deployment of the genre's symbolism. Given this situation, Eastwood's reworking of the material did not extend it or invest it with greater resonance. Thus, PALE RIDER seemed decidedly unoriginal, a surprising fate considering Eastwood's otherwise visionary use of the genre (HIGH PLAINS DRIFTER [1973], THE OUTLAW JOSEY WALES, and UNFORGIVEN [1992]). If even Eastwood faltered in the eighties in his efforts to make a Western, what future did the genre have?

With its aesthetic possibilities seemingly dimmed, the genre failed to make much of an effect at the nation's box office. THE LEGEND OF THE LONE RANGER was a commercial failure in 1981, earning a paltry $7 million in rentals. Two years later, THE GRAY

Patterned on SHANE, *Clint Eastwood's* PALE RIDER *was the most ambitious of the decade's Westerns.*

Fox fell short of $2 million in rentals, and THE MAN FROM SNOWY RIVER's $9 million rentals were earned in 1982 by an Australian film that performed fairly well (for an import) in U.S. distribution. Eastwood's PALE RIDER ($21 million in rentals) generated the genre's biggest box office of the decade, despite its testimony to the Western's anachronistic, bygone status. SILVERADO (1985, $16 million), THREE AMIGOS! (1986, $18 million), and YOUNG GUNS (1988, $19 million) failed to create much excitement.

The Western had seemingly lost its cultural force. While good Westerns would continue to be made (TV's "Lonesome Dove," Eastwood's subsequent UNFORGIVEN), the prolific production rate that characterized the genre in earlier times was over. The eighties were a terrible decade for fans of the genre.

Cycles of Topical Production

The salient social and cultural issues of the 1980s surfaced in films outside the familiar frameworks afforded by genre. Cycles of film coalesced about diverse issues, including the Midwest farm crisis that triggered a rash of small-farm foreclosures (PLACES IN THE HEART [1984], COUNTRY [1984], THE RIVER [1984]); international terrorism (NIGHTHAWKS [1981], THE LITTLE DRUMMER GIRL [1984], HALF MOON STREET [1986], DIE HARD [1988]); U.S.-USSR espionage and cultural relations (MOSCOW ON THE HUDSON [1984], SPIES LIKE US [1985], WHITE NIGHTS [1985], THE FALCON AND THE SNOWMAN [1985], RUSSKIES [1987], THE FOURTH PROTOCOL [1987], NO WAY OUT [1987], LITTLE NIKITA [1988], THE PACKAGE [1989]); chasing wealth in a go-go economy (RISKY BUSINESS [1983], TRADING PLACES [1983], BREWSTER'S MILLIONS [1985], THE SECRET OF MY SUCCESS [1987], WALL STREET [1987]); yuppie love (KEY EXCHANGE [1985], ST. ELMO'S FIRE [1985], ABOUT LAST NIGHT [1986]); the uncertain legacy of the political Left in American society (RETURN OF THE SECAUCUS SEVEN [1980], THE BIG CHILL [1985], DANIEL [1983], RUNNING ON EMPTY [1988]); and the social fragmentation and anomie afflicting diverse groups and breeding alienation, bitterness, and rage (RIVER'S EDGE [1986], TALK RADIO [1988], COLORS [1988]).

Throughout the 1980s, despite the economic dominance of the fantasy blockbusters and the industry's continued investment in traditional genres, a significant set of American films adopted a topical focus by engaging the issues of their day. In this way, they became part of the period's ideological ferment. Indeed, it would be more surprising had Hollywood film not responded and embodied some of the anxieties and controversies of that politically self-conscious period. Ronald Reagan's election to the presidency was presented by his campaign managers and by media analysts as a political revolution (even though his "mandate" consisted of just 29 percent of the eligible electorate's vote), as a decisive political shift in the culture that signaled a major realignment of political forces and a revision of the role and administration of government. Consistent with this perception and mission, Reagan's administration was, in its first term, an activist one, cutting taxes, curtailing social services, deregulating business, and promoting the view that less government was better government and presiding over a transfer of wealth during which the personal income of the poorest one-fifth of the population decreased by 10 percent while the income of the wealthiest one-fifth increased by 16 percent.[12]

Moreover, as a result of the tax cuts enacted by the Reagan administration and continued high levels of government spending, the U.S. deficit exploded, more than doubling to soar beyond $200 billion.[13] Responses by affected groups to these developments were predictably intense, heightening the political tensions of the period. To promote its policies and in its discussions of domestic and foreign issues, the administration elaborated a set of political themes that achieved prominence during the era. These included the omnipresent danger of terrorism, the Soviet Union as an evil empire engaged in relentless territorial expansion, and governmental bureaucracy as a threat to individual economic and political freedom.

Many of these themes found their way into Hollywood film, but they were often garbled in the process of transposition or even openly contested. While American film in the 1980s was responsive to the Reagan years, it was not a product of those years in any simple or reactive way. In fact, a major feature of the period's production is what I will call its ideological conglomeration. This is an important characteristic of sociopolitical expression in the American cinema, and it is motivated by the industry's practical business incentives.

Given their high production costs, American films need to attract as many viewers as they can, and the broad-based appeals they offer are often incompatible with strict ideological or political coherence. This is why the tradition of "message" filmmaking in the American industry is so minimal and toothless. To maximize its commercial (audience) base, Hollywood film operates through a process of conglomeration, mixing a variety of sometimes disparate ideological appeals into an ambiguous whole. American film foregrounds narrative and character emotions, and while those narratives may manifest on occasion a political view, more often this is a matter of metaphor and implication. To be overtly political except in the most general terms (e.g., affirming patriotism or family) is to risk loss of market share. Thus, Hollywood has mostly regarded political filmmaking as being incompatible with box-office success, except in times of exigent circumstance, such as World War II. But here is a paradox. Box-office success requires a degree of topicality. Filmmaking that is vital, vibrant, and connected with the concerns people feel in their lives offers a powerful incentive for going to the movies. In many cases, the industry resolves this paradox by designing films so that their sociopolitical dimensions are matters of implication, material forming the background of a narrative, and conglomerated values. This process is a basic mechanism for linking film to a multitextured society from which viewers and profits alike come.

Accordingly, American film production manifests numerous interesting contradictions. Gulf and Western Industries, through its subsidiary Paramount Pictures, distributed Bernardo Bertolucci's Marxist epic 1900 (1977) as well as REDS (1981), Warren Beatty's homage to American communist John Reed. Corporate capitalism was savaged (in fantasy) in BLADE RUNNER (1982) and ROBOCOP (1987) at the same time that it promoted its wares through numerous marketing tie-ins to popular pictures. While eighties film conformed to the underlying characteristic of ideological conglomeration, some production cycles addressed the period's topical issues in an unusually direct manner, some even adopting an explicitly partisan focus. The period's films thus manifested an interesting tension between these modes of address, making the period a significant one for the history of American social filmmaking.

Among the most striking of the period's topical film cycles were those celebrating a new cold war, those portraying the revolutions in Central and South America and the Vietnam War, and those using science fiction to imaginatively recast contemporary economic problems in darkly futurist terms.

New Cold War Films

Compared to the 1970s, the Reagan years were associated with significant changes in U.S. foreign policy and the U.S. role in global affairs. Some Hollywood films of the period participated in these changes by emulating the White House's rhetoric and geopolitical analysis. As the 1970s ended, many neoconservatives believed that the United States had lost international standing in world affairs and was a declining military power, hobbled by an excessive concern for human rights during the Carter years. If it was U.S. military power that had maintained peace since World War II (according to this view), many on the Right felt that policies of détente and human rights were now assisting Moscow's global strategic ambitions by preventing the United States from properly defending its authoritarian Third World friends.

For the political Right, U.S. military weakness led to the "loss" of Nicaragua and Iran and had emboldened the Soviets to invade Afghanistan in 1979. Moreover, the failed rescue of American hostages in Iran, and the daily taunts of their captors, seemed to reveal America as a hobbled giant, scarred by the Vietnam trauma and no longer willing or capable of using its military. Meanwhile, the Soviet Union allegedly was advancing its geopolitical interests by fomenting unrest in Central America and the Carribean basin. To correct this perceived imbalance in global military power, the Right argued for a resurgence of American military force. Robert Tucker's important *Foreign Affairs* article of 1980 expounded the concept of a resurgent America.[14]

U.S. defense spending would have to be increased as an investment in peace while social spending would be slashed. President Reagan justified these policies by citing the Soviet threat. He claimed the Soviets were conducting "the greatest military build-up in the history of man."[15] Faced with this provocation, Reagan argued, the U.S. must respond with the military readiness and will to counter Soviet moves in the Third World wherever they appeared. As a result of this rhetoric and these suggested policies, the era saw an efflorescence of the traditional anticommunism of American politics. In the political culture of the period, the Soviet Union was demonized, portrayed as an outlaw nation and as the locus of evil in the modern world. President Reagan, for example, described the Soviet Union as "a society which wantonly disregards individual rights and the value of human life and seeks constantly to expand and dominate other nations."[16] In accord with its perceptions and as the eighties began, the administration waged a new cold war against the Soviets, conducted through political discourse and, more concretely, through clandestine operations (e.g., support for anti-Marxist forces in Nicaragua, Guatemala, and El Salvador).

A prominent cycle of new cold war films participated in this demonization of the Soviets. Red Dawn (1984), Rocky IV (1985), Invasion USA (1985), Top Gun (1986), The Delta Force (1986), Heartbreak Ridge (1986), Iron Eagle (1986), Iron Eagle II (1988) and Rambo III (1988) enact ideological dramas in which Soviet depredations arouse the slumbering American giant. Many of these films are explicit agitprop. Rambo III pits Stallone's superhuman warrior against the Soviet invaders in Afghanistan and is dedicated, in the final credits, to "the people of Afghanistan." The film's imagery celebrates American strength and power. Rambo shoots Soviet helicopters out of the sky with explosive arrows. He drives a tank straight into an oncoming helicopter and survives the explosions.

Rambo is such a supremely powerful (and superhuman) warrior that he became a charged national emblem in the era's cultural discourse, a creature of mythology and

Rambo, the Ur-image of resurgent America.

symbolism embodying the resolve and strength of no single person but of an entire nation. Thus, President Reagan invoked his name and example when making threats against real Middle Eastern hostage takers. The images of Rambo living as a pacifist among Buddhist monks at the film's beginning are satirical jabs at the U.S. posture of international disengagement during the Carter years. (Another popular rescue-the-hostages drama, THE DELTA FORCE, opened with the failure of President Carter's military mission to rescue the Iranian hostages and then linked this to U.S. failure in Vietnam. Both are ignomies that the film's narrative fantasy is designed to overcome.)

When Col. Trautman (Richard Crenna) finds Rambo in the monastery, he tries to persuade Rambo to accompany him to Afghanistan to aid the resistance. Trautman tells Rambo that his presence will make a difference. Rambo asks, skeptically, "Not like last time?," meaning Vietnam, which he believes was a war the United States did not wish to win or try to win. Trautman reassures him that things will be different and tells Rambo that he has to come "full circle," that he'll always be emotionally crippled until he recognizes that he is a warrior, a full-blooded combat soldier. Trautman's advice was the directive for the country offered by the political Right, which viewed the legacy of Vietnam and the Carter years as a wrong-headed reluctance to use military power.

As a charged national symbol, rampaging through Southeast Asia (RAMBO: FIRST BLOOD, PART II) and Afghanistan (RAMBO III), Rambo enacts his country's symbolic transformation in the Reagan years from disengagement and false consciousness to the triumphant application of military force. That this was an ideological transformation is demonstrated by a vivid disparity between the Reagan and Bush administrations. Despite the bellicosity of its political rhetoric, the Reagan administration launched no major military ventures. Its support for the Contra war against Nicaragua was a secret, black-bag operation. By contrast, in the first three years of the Bush presidency, the United States launched two military offensives, in Panama and Iraq. Rambo, therefore, was a projection of the political imagination rather than a correlate with real military ventures.

Like the Rambo pictures, other films in the cycle worked as explicit agitprop for a renewal of America's warrior spirit. RED DAWN, portraying a Soviet invasion of America, is a primer on Soviet hostility and the means of waging guerilla resistance. A daring band of high school students takes up arms against the invaders, and the generational symbolism was potent. While the focus on adolescents was partly a marketing ploy to attract the crucial young audience for motion pictures, it also enabled writer and director John Milius to make a political statement about differing administrations. It is the youth of today in the film—that is, of the Reagan years—that has the fortitude necessary to take up arms against oppression. At the end of the film, the young heroes are commemorated as great American patriots, alongside Teddy Roosevelt and the Rough Riders.

Another group of Soviet-sponsored invaders wreaks havoc on America in INVASION USA. The invaders are composed of blacks, Latins, and Asians, a catalog of groups excluded from the New Right's America, and they proceed to blow up churches, shopping malls, and families at home celebrating Christmas. Standing against this terrorist army is the national security infrastructure—the FBI, CIA, army, and police—and the film's hero, Hunter (Chuck Norris), a frontier cowboy who personifies America's mythology (out of the Western) of regenerate violence.

ROCKY IV opens with a graphic showing a boxing glove emblazoned with the American flag and one with the hammer and sickle crashing against each other and exploding. The film pits Rocky against a robotic Soviet boxer named Drago, each character functioning as an explicit political emblem. Before he can fight his Soviet opponent, Rocky has to overcome his weakened state, as the country must do relative to the post-Vietnam years. The film opens to find him absorbed in material comforts, his body gone soft, and with no interest in squaring off against Drago. But once Drago brutally beats Rocky's friend to death, America's hero goes back into training and pursues victory. Rocky's conversion from passivity to intervention is emblematic of the major discourse of this production cycle. These often-polemical films explicitly advocate the themes of Reagan-era foreign policy: the lamentable weakness of the United States, the viciousness of the Soviet Union and its allies, and the need for a resurgent American military and a Pax Americana.

Most of the films in this cycle are action narratives, many depict invasion-and-rescue scenarios (powerful American warriors defending the heartland against Soviet invaders or rescuing victims of the Soviets), and many display great anxieties over the fate of fathers or father figures who, in RED DAWN, IRON EAGLE, TOP GUN, and RAMBO III, are threatened with capture and torture or whose authority is jeopardized because questions surround their honor. The heroes of TOP GUN and IRON EAGLE are tormented by the questions of honor that surround their father's behavior, and Rambo has to rescue Trautman, his surrogate father, when Trautman is captured by the Soviets in Afghanistan. The narratives collectively vindicate the honor of the father or father figure as a means of encoding and resolving the crisis of national authority to which the period's militarism was a response.

Furthermore, the prominence of the action-adventure format in the new cold war cycle is most important. The predictability of cold war thought—its rigidity, reductive-

High school guerrilla fighters defend America against its Soviet invaders in John Milius's RED DAWN.

ness, and patterned nature—facilitated its representation by action-adventure narratives. Because the ideology and the action narratives employ a repertoire of conventionalized expectations (rooted in their shared Manichean schema of good and evil), they bonded with each other as content and form. The vigilante, superhero narratives of action and violence provided a formal structure capable of absorbing the incipient violence and paranoia of cold war ideology. In this way, the cold war discourse became part of the structured rules governing the narrative operations of these films. Content and ideology, form and function became as one. Rambo, Hunter, and the other righteous heroes of the cycle emerged as sleek, powerful emblems of the political imagination. These invasion-and-rescue films structurally integrated political and narrative meaning in a fluid, sometimes seamless way. As such, they are extraordinarily successful examples of popular political filmmaking.

They are not, however, without their interesting contradictions. John Milius's RED DAWN aims to celebrate American guerrilla fighters seeking to overturn the Soviet dictatorship of America, and it cannot disengage itself from the Marxian tradition that promotes resistance and revolution. Thus, interesting ambiguities creep into its paranoid vision, most notably in the film's sympathetic characterization of a Cuban military officer who helps administer the occupation of America. Because the officer is a committed Marxist and a skilled guerrilla fighter, he becomes increasingly sympathetic to the film's heroes, the high school kids fighting the Soviet invaders. The Cuban officer feels empathy for these American commandos waging war against a corrupt regime supported, like Batista's was in Cuba, by an outside power. Thus, RED DAWN finds itself acknowledging that the United States and the Soviet Union share a common historical

heritage of violent revolution and that this heritage might afford the basis of a cooperative relationship.

RAMBO III analogizes the Soviet invasion of Afghanistan with the American presence
in Vietnam, thereby undercutting its cold war politics. Rambo's friend and mentor, Col.
Trautman, is captured and tortured by the Soviets. Defiantly, he tells them,

> You know there won't be a victory. Every day your war machines lose ground
> to a group of poorly armed, poorly equipped freedom fighters. The fact is
> that you underestimated your competition. If you'd studied your history,
> you'd know these people have never given up to anyone. They'd rather die
> than be slaves to an invading army. You can't defeat a people like that. We
> tried. We already had our Vietnam. Now you're gonna have yours.

This speech is a remarkable example of ideological conglomeration. It conjoins a leftist analysis of the U.S. role in Vietnam (envisioning the United States as an invader trying to crush an indigenous people's desire for freedom) with cold war perceptions of
Soviet expansionism and the need for U.S. force to stop it. The cold war components of
Trautman's speech use then-current terminology and thereby connect with domestic
political agendas. "Freedom fighters" was the name given to the Nicaraguan Contras by
the Reagan administration. The speech portrays the United States as both a Third World
aggressor and a committed defender of Third World freedom and democracy. The ideological mishmash that results holds appeals for diverging political segments of the audience, as the imperatives of blockbuster economics reorganize the politics of the film.

Toward the end of the decade, world events swept past the paranoia of these films
and the new cold war to which they belonged. The Soviet empire began to collapse, and
the satellite nations of Eastern Europe became independent. These transformations
registered in the new cold war cycle. At its conclusion, ROCKY IV acknowledges the
possibility of Soviet-American peace and cooperation. Rocky appeals to the Soviet
audience in the name of brotherhood, freedom, and independence. They stand and
give thunderous cheers to his ideals and are even joined by Soviet leaders. In IRON
EAGLE II (1988), a joint U.S.-Soviet military force battles a renegade Middle Eastern
nation, and the film ends with an appeal for both nations to overcome their hostilities.
In a similar fashion, RED HEAT (1988), about an American cop and a Soviet policeman
tracking a criminal wanted by both countries, envisioned and advocated a warmer U.S.-
USSR relationship.

The new cold war films thus began to dissipate by decade's end. In part, this was a
response to the changing conditions in Eastern Europe (the loosening of Soviet control),
but it was also a sign that the film cycle itself had grown exhausted from repetition.
From a narrative standpoint, it never had anywhere to go beyond the repetition of familiar and increasingly predictable scenarios of invasion, subversion, and rescue. The cycle
and its sometimes strident politics wore out. Nevertheless, these new cold war productions constitute one of the most significant film cycles of the decade. The ideological
explicitness of these films, their simplistic conflicts of good and evil and open political
advocacy, tie them more closely to characteristics of propaganda than Hollywood generally has permitted in the past, except for the red-scare films of the HUAC period. The
anti-Soviet politics of the Reagan years produced two major ideological tracts—RED
DAWN and ROCKY IV—and the other rescue and invasion films helped intensify and
extend the nation's cold war culture.

As the emissary of America, Rocky rouses the Soviets to the American way in ROCKY IV.

Cold war, by definition, is the extension of military conflict to the realm of culture, where artworks substitute for battlefield engagements. These films thus helped acclimate their audiences to the prospect of unending geopolitical strife between rival empires. They helped create and sustain in their viewers a psychology of threat, of encirclement, of narrowed social and political discourse requisite for a heavily militarized society. Given the apocalyptic leanings of the films, one may rejoice that the political culture that nourished them eventually relaxed and abated. But they stand as a striking signpost of the decade's fundamental political anxieties.

POLITICAL REBELLION AND REBEL FILMMAKING

One of the great idées fixes of the Reagan administration was a corollary of the new cold war, and it helped inspire a provocative and unique film cycle (as well as, unfortunately, a great deal of real-world suffering). This was the belief that the Soviet Union was consolidating control over Central America and might use this territory as a staging ground for an attack on the United States. President Reagan told a joint session of Congress in 1983, "The national security of all the Americas is at stake in Central America. If we cannot defend ourselves there, we cannot expect to prevail elsewhere. Our credibility would collapse, our alliances would crumble, and the safety of our homeland would be put in jeopardy."[17]

In so speaking, President Reagan tied the new cold war to the one begun under President Truman and viewed it as a continuation of the former. He cited the Truman Doctrine in a 1983 speech before Congress on the threat posed to the United States by the revolutionary government in Nicaragua (which the administration considered a Soviet proxy). Remarking that Truman's words pledging defense of "free peoples who are resisting attempted subjugation by armed minorities or by outside pressures" were as relevant in 1983 as in 1947, Reagan outlined a scenario in which creeping Soviet total-itarianism threatened the northern hemisphere and demanded a vigorous U.S. response. To justify Truman's pledge to intervene against the Left in Greece, Dean Acheson in 1949 had employed the "rotten apple" theory of Communist subversion: "Like apples in a barrel infected by one rotten one, the corruption of Greece would infect Iran and all to the East. It would also carry infection to Africa through Asia Minor and Egypt, and to Europe through Italy and France."[18] President Reagan replicated the geopolitical logic of Acheson's scenario. Explaining why the "loss" of Nicaragua was so threatening to world peace, Reagan said, "Using Nicaragua as a base, the Soviets and Cubans can become the dominant power in the crucial corridor between North and South America. Established there, they will be in a position to threaten the Panama Canal, interdict our vital Caribbean sea lanes and, ultimately, move against Mexico."[19]

The events that triggered the administration's obsession with Central America as a Soviet proxy were a series of leftist governments assuming power in a region that the United States had always regarded as its backyard, where it claimed the prerogative of deciding which governments stayed in place and which did not. In 1979, Maurice Bishop's socialist New Jewel Movement overthrew the government of Eric Gairy in Grenada, which was backed by the United States and Great Britain. Also in 1979, and regarded as a more significant threat, the Sandinista National Liberation Front toppled the corrupt Somoza dynasty that had ruled Nicaragua since it was installed by the U.S. Marines in 1933. A strong guerilla army confronted the Guatemalan government, and the Farabundo Martí National Liberation Front posed a credible military and political challenge to El Salvador's rulers.

Egregiously bad social and economic conditions motivated the popular rebellions in Guatemala, Nicaragua, and El Salvador. Huge concentrations of wealth and land in the hands of a few, alongside massive poverty, disfigured these societies. In Guatemala dur-ing the 1970s, for example, the top quarter of the population earned 67 percent of the nation's wealth while the bottom quarter earned only 7 percent.[20] Ninety percent of the rural work force owned no land. In El Salvador, conditions were worse. Two percent of the population owned 60 percent of the land and earned one-third of the nation's income.[21] In 1975, more than 45 percent of the rural population was estimated to be unemployed.[22] Despite these glaring socioeconomic problems, the administration chose to see Soviet meddling as the cause of the regional conflicts.

In Guatemala and El Salvador, the governments were run by or were closely allied with the military, which received large amounts of U.S. aid and training. The military and the Salvadoran and Guatemalan governments used this aid to conduct internal repression, subjecting dissidents, priests, teachers, and other citizens to a slaughter that was especially bloody in the early 1980s. In its 1984 report on El Salvador, Amnesty International protested "the continued involvement of all branches of the security and military forces in a systematic and widespread program of torture, mutilation, 'disap-pearance,' and the individual and mass extrajudicial execution of men, women and chil-dren from all sectors of Salvadoran society."[23] The group reached similar conclusions regarding Guatemala. Meanwhile, the United States funded the regimes and trained many of the officers implicated in these acts.

The fires of revolution in Central America burned brightly enough that a remarkable cycle of film production coalesced around these issues. Whereas the RED DAWN–RAMBO III cycle explicitly manifested the era's cold war ideologies, the Latin America films broke with the assumptions of Washington foreign policy and offered sympathetic portraits of the regional uprisings. In place of the political paranoia of the new cold war cycle, the Latin America films largely defended the regional rebellions. The collective focus of MISSING (1982), UNDER FIRE (1983), EL NORTE (1984), LATINO (1985), SALVADOR (1986), and ROMERO (1989) is a hemispheric one as these films dramatize events in Chile, Nicaragua, Guatemala, and El Salvador. Furthermore, while the conflicts the films portray make for highly charged drama, consistent with popular cinema, these pictures are inclined toward the interventionist aesthetics and politics of a committed, partisan cinema whose sympathies are with the political Left.

The unusual attributes of this cycle are partly due to its conditions of production. While MISSING and UNDER FIRE are major studio films, the others are independent productions. SALVADOR was financed and distributed by Hemdale. ROMERO was financed by a number of Catholic organizations, and EL NORTE was directed by independent filmmaker Gregory Nava with distribution by Island Alive. LATINO was made on a shoestring budget by cinematographer and engaged leftist Haskell Wexler. Operating outside the mechanisms of studio funding and distribution, this film cycle broke with the predominant assumptions of cold war thought and the strictures governing the political expressions deemed appropriate in a Hollywood film. By doing so, these films demonstrated how nontraditional mechanisms of funding and distribution can facilitate the expression of alternative sociopolitical views.

EL NORTE is the least partisan film in the cycle. It tells a story about two Guatemalan teenagers fleeing the poverty and repression of their country. They make an arduous journey north to the United States, which they believe will provide them with freedom and abundance. Policies of cultural segregation confine them to a Spanish section of Los

In EL NORTE, Enrique and Rosa make an arduous journey from Guatemala to the United States, where they face lives of continuing hardship.

Angeles, where a succession of menial jobs and further impoverishment becomes their future. Compared to the other films in the cycle, EL NORTE is less directly concerned with the strife in Latin America. Its characters seek to avoid this strife in their journey to the United States, and the specifics of the Guatemalan political situation fall outside the film's narrative trajectory. But the economic oppression and military persecution in Guatemala provide the motivation for the story, and the film's harsh exposé of the hardships suffered by refugees from the conflict, and the closed opportunities available to them in the United States, place *El Norte* in the politically critical company of the other films in the cycle.

As a studio picture (distributed by Orion) with big stars (Nick Nolte and Gene Hackman), UNDER FIRE has the most conventional and formulaic structure of this group of films. It is a journalistic version of love in the tropics, dealing with the romantic triangle among three U.S. reporters (Nolte, Joanna Cassidy, and Hackman) covering the uprising in Nicaragua in 1979. As such, romance and action are foreground elements in the narrative, but the film's political sympathies are clearly stated. The story studies the conversion of reporters Nolte and Cassidy from detached (i.e., objective) journalists to partisans of the revolution who fake a news photo to aid the rebellion. The film ends with the triumph of the Sandinistas and the American reporters' assertion that they'd do it all again (i.e., fake the photo to aid the cause) if they had to.

Despite the formulaic romance of the story and its straightforward emphasis on action, UNDER FIRE offers an important sequence that deconstructs the film's melodrama. The National Guard murder reporter Hackman, and Claire (Joanna Cassidy) breaks down when she sees news footage of the execution. The camera moves in close to capture her sadness, and the music swells to wrap viewer and character in its emotional embrace. But the scene's proferring of sweet pathos is abruptly interrupted. A Nicaraguan nurse glances at her skeptically and points out that thousands of Nicaraguans have died fighting the Somoza dynasty. "Maybe we should have killed an American journalist fifty years ago," she says, meaning that maybe now North Americans will care about what is happening here. Stung by these words, Claire stops weeping, and the scene ends. The historical perspective supplied by the nurse neutralizes the melodramatic pleasures toward which the scene had been building. One American's death, after all, pales beside the deaths of so many Nicaraguans. Hollywood films rarely question the melodramatic discourse they offer. UNDER FIRE not only does this but places it in the service of political analysis.

LATINO offers another perspective on the conflict in Nicaragua but one that is less successful as political cinema. The story deals with two Hispanic Green Berets who clandestinely train the Contra forces in Nicaragua as part of a CIA-funded army. One of the officers comes to question his mission and its political objectives, and at the end he is captured by Nicaraguans defending their farm co-op against Contra attacks. Unfortunately the film's dialogue often sounds like political sloganeering, and the narrative moves clumsily to make its political points. As a result, the political perspectives become heavy-handed and preach to the already converted rather than communicate in the visceral and popular manner of the new cold war films.

Like UNDER FIRE but with a more sustained political vision, MISSING employs the conventions of Hollywood cinema (an emotionally charged narrative and stars Jack Lemmon and Sissy Spacek) to construct a powerful portrait of the 1973 military coup in Chile that, with U.S. support, overthrew the elected government of socialist president Salvador Allende. Unlike the dramas about the reclamation of a father's honor in the

American journalists Nick Nolte and Joanna Cassidy meet the Nicaraguan guerrillas in UNDER FIRE.

new cold war films, MISSING presents a tale of the sacrifice of a son by a complacent father, Ed Horman (Jack Lemmon), who has castigated his son's political affiliation with the Chilean poor and, too late, learns the sobering truth about U.S. complicity in the coup. Horman's transformation from a naive and complacent American to one whose ideological blinkers have been painfully torn off is the film's central and most powerful political device. Beyond this, the film vividly portrays the ferocity of the military coup, accompanied by book burnings and the abduction and murder of civilians, and director Constantin Costa-Gavras creates resonant images that work as political metaphors. During the coup, for example, a crowd of Chilean bourgeoisie interrupt their party to applaud the troops marching below their window. The soldiers, in turn, salute the bourgeoisie in a series of shots that explicate the class allegiances driving the coup.

The conflicts in El Salvador were portrayed with much emotional force in two disparate films, ROMERO and SALVADOR. The former film dramatizes the life of the Salvadoran archbishop Oscar Romero (portrayed by Raul Julia) from his appointment in 1977 to his 1980 assassination, concentrating on his growing commitment to the poor and to a belief in the legitimacy of open insurrection against the government. Toward the end of his life, Romero declared, "These are insurrectional times. The morality of the church permits insurrection when all other paths have been exhausted."[24] Through its compassionate portrayal of Romero's political radicalization, the film shows the conditions that helped generate "liberation theology," a clergy in support of the poor and oppressed, motivated by outrage over the scale of the oppression in Guatemala and El Salvador and from a conviction that the Bible contains a social and political message that is revolutionary in its implications as it councils clergy to stand with the poor and dispossessed.

A young American witnesses the onset of the military coup in MISSING *and is subsequently detained, tortured and "disappeared."*

Like SALVADOR, ROMERO structures its narrative with reference to especially egregious real-life outrages, such as the murder of Father Rutilio Grande, who was assassinated in 1977 while on his way to mass. The army then occupied the town, conducted house-to-house searches, and beat the occupants. The assasination of Grande marked a new and darker chapter in Salvadoran politics, in which priests were targeted by the army and death squads. (Romero was another victim of this campaign.) In the film, after Grande's assassination, the army occupies the church, and Romero returns to it to retrieve the Eucharist. An American soldier blocks his way and machine-guns the altar in a shocking display of sacrilege and political contempt. Through this character, the film acknowledges, obliquely, the American role in the conflict, the side the United States had chosen, and the conflict with the U.S. government that Romero's evolving politics would precipitate.

The film, however, remains ambivalent about the extent of Romero's conversion to liberation theology. Late in the film, in a scene that complicates his stance, he accuses a priest, allied with the guerrillas, of losing God and waging class warfare just like the rich. But despite its uneasiness over Romero's politics, the film eloquently portrays the suffering of the archbishop and his country. At the climax, as Romero pleads during mass for the military to lay down its arms and stop the slaughter, his words are intercut with photographs of real death squad victims, their mutilations offering eloquent testimony for his plea. And in the final shot of the film, stirred by Romero's prophecy that he will arise in the Salvadoran people and that their suffering will lead to El Salvador's liberation, a crowd of urban poor rises, walks toward the camera, and engulfs it.

SALVADOR, directed by Oliver Stone, portrays the most notorious acts of terror and violence during 1980–81 in El Salvador (these included the rape and murder of a group of American church women and the assassination of Archbishop Romero). Like MISSING and its portrait of the U.S. role in Chile, SALVADOR explicitly fixes blame for the disintegration of Salvadoran civil society on U.S. support for a repressive military regime. The film dramatizes the impact of Ronald Reagan's presidential victory on the political process in El Salvador, particularly the ultra-Right's belief that terror and violence against the Left would be accepted by Washington. The film shows death squads riding through the streets, firing their guns into the air, as radios announce Reagan's presidential victory. The film contextualizes President Reagan's cold war rhetoric in terms of its human cost in a sequence that intercuts the president on television warning about the Communist march through Central America and into the United States with shots of hospitalized children who were wounded by the Salvadoran military. The film also implies that the Reagan administration signaled El Salvador's right wing that death squad activities would be tolerated in the name of anticommunism. Furthermore, in a practice unusual for the American cinema, Stone identifies left-wing political organizations by name (e.g., the FMLN and the Democratic Revolutionary Front).

In the film's most politically pointed scene, the protagonist, Richard Boyle (James Woods), denounces U.S. intervention. Boyle tells a U.S. colonel and a State Department analyst, "You haven't presented one shred of proof to the American public that this is anything but a legitimate peasant revolution." He charges that the death squads are the brainchild of the CIA. "You let them shut down the universities, wipe out the best minds in the country. You let them kill whoever they want, let them wipe out the Catholic Church, and all because they're not Communists." This sequence contains the most explicit denunciations of U.S. foreign policy ever offered by an American film, and they came from the battle zone, at a time when the events and anguish the film depicts were still ongoing.

Raul Julia as the martyred Salvadoran archbishop in ROMERO.

Despite the film's partisan objections to U.S. intervention, though, SALVADOR shows some ambivalence in its regard for the guerrillas. During the picture's climax, Boyle sees them commiting battlefield executions, and he condemns them for being as brutal as the ultra-Right. This ambivalence toward the political Left is an enduring feature of American cinema, and the other films in this cycle have difficulty, as well, engaging the Left as a viable alternative in the region. MISSING fails to identify the Allende government by name or even the country where the events in the film occur. The guerrillas in ROMERO and UNDER FIRE remain a nebulous presence, vaguely defined as to policies and goals. The political Left has traditionally eluded the representational conventions of the American cinema, and it should not be surprising that the same problem recurs in this cycle of films, despite its inclination toward engagement with the cause of the region's poor.

Despite this tendency, the cycle clearly positioned itself outside the framework of cold war politics that regarded the problems in Latin America as a local manifestation of the global struggle between the United States and the Soviet Union. Despite the ambivalence about revolution that is an indelible part of U.S. culture and that many of these films share, this small group of oppositional works engaged the controversies of their historical moment and tried to envision an alternative and more humane political future. The Reagan administration's account of Communist subversion and falling dominoes maintained the claims of empire, based in traditional attitudes regarding Central America as the backyard, or property, of the United States. By suggesting that the roots of insurrection lay in indigenous, oppressive socio-economic conditions, rather than in a power projection by Moscow, these films challenged imperial prerogatives by endorsing regional claims to free government and an end to dictatorship and the misery it helped create.

Given the predominance of cold war thought in the 1980s, it should come as no surprise that at least one prominent Hollywood film placed the Latin America conflicts in a cold war package. PREDATOR (1988), an Arnold Schwarzenegger action vehicle, offered a strikingly literal manifestation of cold war anxieties, albeit transposed into science fiction terms. In the film's story, consistent with new cold war narrative scenarios of invasion and rescue, the CIA recruits a team of commandos to go into an unnamed Central American country where guerilla fighters are holding American hostages. Once there, however, the commandos find that an alien warrior is hunting them. Central America, it seems, really is in the grip of an alien subversive presence! At the climax, a nuclear explosion saves the region from the alien invader. The fantasy of the narrative offered a solution to the region's problems that otherwise could not be articulated in real-world discourse.

But fantasy might offer other solutions as well. Just as the region's problems could be given a cold war twist with PREDATOR, they might also be played for laughs. Paul Mazursky's MOON OVER PARADOR (1988) is a comedy about dictatorship and repression in the mythical country of Parador. At the end, under a new populist government, the CIA, the aristocracy, and the guerrillas join hands and live in harmony and peace. PREDATOR and MOON OVER PARADOR, though, are clearly outliers of the Latin America film cycle, the core politics of which were outside mainstream discourse and opposed to Washington's line on the region's disorders.

Compared with the new cold war films, the Latin America pictures had negligible box-office effect. This was certainly a function of their limited, often independent distribution. But it was also due to the cycle's inability to fuse genre and ideology in the

The turmoil in Central America got a cold war sci-fi twist in
PREDATOR.

powerful manner achieved by the new cold war films. Reinforcing dominant ideologies may always hold greater profit potential. TOP GUN earned $82 million in rentals for Paramount in 1986. ROCKY IV earned $76 million, RAMBO III $28 million, and RED DAWN $17 million, whereas MISSING, the top earner in the Latin America cycle, returned only $8 million in rentals. Based on these box-office returns, the cold war fantasies seemed to have had greater resonance for the moviegoing public during the eighties than the Latin America cycle. The cold war films more successfully fused their politics with popular genre elements. On the other hand, the small group of films about Latin America earnestly tried to understand and portray the regional conditions breeding insurrection and thereby expose North American viewers to alternative accounts of the region's turmoil, envisioning hope for a better future. These films offered a persuasive and powerful counterforce to the cold war drift of American political culture in the eighties and the right-wing politics of the Sylvester Stallone–Chuck Norris action epics. As such, their redemptive and humanistic value was an essential part of eighties cinema.

THE VIETNAM WAR CYCLE

During the 1980s, the Vietnam War finally received the extensive screen treatment that had been so conspicuously lacking in the 1960s and 1970s, when Hollywood preferred to ignore the issue, believing it to be too controversial and therefore bad box office. THE BOYS IN COMPANY C, GO TELL THE SPARTANS, THE DEER HUNTER, COMING HOME, and APOCALYPSE NOW in 1978–79 marked the beginning of a sustained wave of production that swept across much of the 1980s. The latter three pictures were major studio productions, with big-name stars, and were supported with aggressive marketing campaigns. They therefore had great visibility.

Furthermore, when THE DEER HUNTER won five Academy Awards, including best picture and director, the Hollywood industry signaled officially that its long-standing ban on Vietnam War films had ended. (Throughout the seventies, however, Vietnam had figured indirectly in American films, most unfortunately in the tiresome stereotype of the psycho killer who is a Vietnam vet in pictures like THE VISITORS [1972], TAXI DRIVER [1976], ROLLING THUNDER [1977], and THE EXTERMINATOR [1980].)[25] Hollywood's willingness to support major productions about the war (i.e., those that treated the war explicitly and not as a background element) was partly a function of the passage of time having made the subject more approachable than in the contentious years of the war itself. But the passage of too much time might also be a problem. American ground troops withdrew from Vietnam in 1973, and if American cinema was ever to make films about that war, time was slipping away. Box-office interest in the subject depended on timely treatments.

But there is a more significant reason for the cycle than time having making the subject safer. Hollywood took up the Vietnam War because it still reverberated throughout American society and culture. It remained resonant and powerful as a traumatic national experience and because American culture had never achieved a consensus about the war or about the U.S. defeat. Was it a good war? Was it necessary? Why had the United States lost? These questions transfixed the nation in the eighties, making the aftershocks of Vietnam major forces in the era's political culture. Commentators across the political spectrum agreed that the politics of resurgent America were an effort to overcome the lingering effects of the Vietnam defeat.[26] The war created a breach in the U.S. empire, and the terrible social conflicts of the Vietnam years had inhibited subsequent projections of U.S. power. The specter of Vietnam, for example, haunted U.S. responses to the conflicts in Central America. In the early 1980s, when a U.S. invasion seemed a real possibility, Nicaragua and El Salvador were often described as the new Vietnam and Central America a new quagmire for the country. Rather than risk this, the administration decided to intervene surreptitiously, by means of clandestine CIA support for the Contras and the provision of funding and training for government security forces in El Salvador.

Hollywood turned to Vietnam in the 1980s, then, because the issue remained a provocative one and because the politics of the period were compelling an examination of this legacy so that it might, at last, be exorcised. As a result, American film helped lead a national dialogue about the war and provided the images and narratives that would, for young viewers, count as persuasive evidence about the war and as a history of it. In doing so, American film forged a powerful relationship with a popular audience around this subject. Unfortunately, American film has tended to work better as myth than as history, and Hollywood's Vietnam productions were no exception. They treated the war through symbol, metaphor, and allegory and failed to portray some of its crucial historical elements. They offered vivid and cathartic imagery but unreliable history.

The Vietnam productions fell into two categories, roughly separated at mid-decade. During the first half of the 1980s, the problem of Americans missing in action furnished the basis for what regrettably became an increasingly cartoonish series of action-adventure films starring, most notably, Chuck Norris and Sylvester Stallone. Productions in this category included UNCOMMON VALOR (1983) (much less cartoonish than its successors), the low-budget P.O.W.: THE ESCAPE (1986), the Chuck Norris series beginning in 1984 with MISSING IN ACTION, continuing with MISSING IN ACTION 2: THE BEGINNING (1985), and concluding with BRADDOCK: MISSING IN ACTION III (1988), and the ideological and stylistic climax of the cycle, RAMBO: FIRST BLOOD, PART II (1984), Sylvester Stallone's sequel to FIRST BLOOD (1982), the picture that introduced his John Rambo character.

The problem of Americans missing in action and the humanitarian issues surrounding their identification and return were urgently compelling ones; they had remained one of the war's lingering and unresolved dilemmas and were among its bitterest legacies. Compared with the war's other politically divisive issues, though, the MIA question was one about which consensus was easier. It was therefore a relatively safer topic for film production than other aspects of the war would be. Considering this, then, it is remarkable how quickly the MIA films degenerated into comic book fantasy, becoming in the Stallone and Norris vehicles celebratory bloodfests about the exploits of superhuman American warriors. Stallone's Rambo and Norris's Braddock characters return to Vietnam in the postwar period to search for American MIAs, and they reengage the enemy, winning a series of spectacular skirmishes that carried redemptive value for America and worked as symbolic victories and as negations of the national defeat that had proven to be so haunting. It is significant that the narratives of the Rambo and Braddock movies are set after 1973, when real historical events cannot contest the substitute symbolic victories of the stories.

The climax of the MIA cycle is Rambo, a film whose hero is so outsized, so overcharged, and so unstoppable that his victory against the Vietnamese was never in question, as assured, according to the argument constructed by the film's ideological narrative, as U.S. victory should have been, had the country wanted to win. As the pure distillation of U.S. martial prowess, Rambo gets to rewrite history by beating the foe his country could not. Before going into action, Rambo asks Colonel Trautman, "Do we get to win this time?" Rambo wins by beating the Vietnamese at their own game. He uses the jungle as cover, striking his enemies suddenly and then disappearing, fighting with primitive weapons, a knife and bow, instead of high-tech gear. In the film's most extravagant reinvention, as a superb guerilla fighter, Rambo (in fantasy) becomes the Vietnamese (in history). As one scholar of the Vietnam War films has noted, "To 'win' the war we are symbolically re-fighting on the screen, to reverse the verdict of history, we must be transformed into our enemies (who won in the 'real' world), while they are transformed into us."[27]

This transformation occurs in the Chuck Norris and Sylvester Stallone films through an inversion of the military dynamics of the war. The films depict American warriors who are masters of guerilla tactics and jungle combat. By contrast, the Vietnamese blunder through the brush and are hampered by its confines. Furthermore, in Rambo, the Vietnamese are pictured as being confined to a fixed position in a fortress. In actuality, it was the North Vietnamese Army (NVA) and the National Liberation Front of South Vietnam (NLF), America's opponents, who were the masters of guerilla combat, effectively employing hit-and-run tactics that badgered and frustrated U.S. forces. Mobility is a cardinal principle of guerilla warfare, where stratagems are based on flexibility, on the surprise and suddenness of attacking and retreating.[28] The NVA and NLF positioned battalions in remote areas and then enticed Americans into those areas, where they could be attacked at will. Countrywide, guerilla activities tied down and harassed American forces.[29] As a result, the NVA and NLF were able to force American troops into a reactive defense role and permitted the Vietnamese to attack at their own discretion. By choosing when to fight, the NVA and NLF were able to control the size of their losses. In contrast to these stratagems, American forces practiced counterinsurgency methods designed to sever the connection between the guerrillas and their base of popular support. These methods had two components. One, search and destroy, involved trying to take the war to the enemy by destroying his means of support among the people and off the land, while the other, pacification, involved trying to win the hearts and minds of the Vietnamese.[30] In neither case were the Americans adapting to the jungle and building strategies that made effective use of it.

The Rambo and Braddock films, however, proffered a historical fantasy in which the wily American guerilla fights circles around the befuddled Vietnamese. This scenario offered an elaborate denial of America's defeat in that war and altered the terms of the American presence in the jungles of Southeast Asia. Rambo's guerilla tactics symbolically transform the American military from a counterinsurgency force to a revolutionary one (e.g., by waging guerilla war against occupying powers, the Soviets and the NVA, as depicted in the film), permitting American culture to imaginatively reclaim its revolutionary heritage. But it was the problematic relationship of this heritage to America's role in Vietnam that was among the most explosive issues of the war. The Stallone and Norris films, though, were not about to reexamine the war's tortuous complexities and do them justice. Instead, the films offered fantasies calculated to appeal to the politics of resurgent America.

In the Rambo dramas, Stallone's emotionally bruised veteran longs for love and acceptance by his countrymen, yet the films' insistence on his blood-crazed warrior impulses denotes a degree of ambivalence toward this character. The ambivalence is strongest in FIRST BLOOD, the film that introduced the character. There, Rambo is clearly a psychopath. He responds to police harassment by escaping to the woods of the Pacific Northwest, setting traps that wound and mutilate his police pursuers, then returns to town to blow up a gas station and a hardware store and to machine-gun the local sheriff. A psychopath gunning down local police does not make a fit hero for a movie series, so subsequent films relocated Rambo far from U.S. soil and turned him loose on America's enemies, the Soviets and the Vietnamese.

Rambo's ongoing bloodthirst, then, links him to those loners, crazies, and vigilantes that made up Hollywood's unfortunate portrait of Vietnam veterans in 1970s films. But public attitudes toward Vietnam veterans had been shifting, moving toward a recognition that they deserved honor and acceptance. The Vietnam Veterans Memorial, for example, was dedicated in Washington, D.C., in 1982 and symbolized the change in public opinion. Inevitably, Hollywood responded to this shift, and beginning in 1986, films dispensed with the Rambo paradigm. The picture that initiated this change was Oliver Stone's PLATOON (1986). Stone's film about a platoon split between the examples offered by its two sergeants, one saintly, the other savage, had enormous impact on viewers and other filmmakers by virtue of its close attention to the physical experience of living and fighting in a jungle environment and by virtue of its refusal of comic book superheroics. Stone had served in Vietnam, and he had long wanted to make a picture that would show the onerous conditions of that war and the bravery of American soldiers.

But he also knew the savagery of the war and its terrible effects on the country. As a result, he avoided a simplistic celebration of American courage and fortitude (the Rambo films had already done this) and created a film, instead, that examined ideals *and* their corruption, nobility and heroism *and* cruelty. (In this context, it is striking that Stone assented to the Chrysler Corp. ad carried by PLATOON on home video. In the ad, Chrysler's Lee Iacocca recuperates Vietnam as a war like all other wars the United States has fought and proclaims that Vietnam exemplified the true spirit of America, which is to go to war when called. This principle, in fact, was among the most hotly contested issues of the war. About agreeing to the ad, Stone subsequently remarked, "I shouldn't have done that.")[31] The resulting work was exceptionally powerful, corrosive even, but its great popular success demonstrated that the moviegoing public wanted honest, if difficult, treatments of the war.

Oliver Stone's PLATOON *altered the terms by which Hollywood depicted the Vietnam War.*

To achieve his multifaceted portrait, Stone used a *bildungsroman* narrative about the moral education of a naive new recruit, Taylor (Charlie Sheen), whose admiration and loyalties are torn between two surrogate fathers, Sergeant Elias (Willem Dafoe) and Sergeant Barnes (Tom Berringer). Elias embodies the humane impulses that Stone locates in the American soldiers, while Barnes represents the savage and debasing aspects of war. In the film's symbolic parable, Barnes kills Elias, implying that in Vietnam ideals were sacrificed to savagery, yet it is Elias's example that is the enduring one and that the film affirms. Through his narrative structure, Stone presents Vietnam as a singularly American experience. Rendering it through the prism of metaphor and allegory, he represents it as a struggle between good and evil, waged within the American heart and soul. In his closing reflection, Taylor concludes, "I think now, looking back, we did not fight the enemy. We fought ourselves, and the enemy was in us." While this made for powerful filmmaking, it remained a solipsistic point of view, however, excluding the Vietnamese from the war and most of its historical context. But in fairness to the film, these were not its intentions.

PLATOON announced the new direction for Vietnam productions. Instead of offering falsely inflated heroics, PLATOON and its successors, HAMBURGER HILL (1987), 84 CHARLIE MOPIC (1989), THE HANOI HILTON (1987), and GARDENS OF STONE (1987), eulogized the American presence in Vietnam. They found American heroism in the ability of its soldiers to endure suffering and privations while participating in a venture whose purpose and ideals few felt good about. Productions during the second half of the decade thereby helped rehabilitate the screen image of the Vietnam soldier and veteran, an image that had been badly tarnished during the seventies and early eighties. This revised focus should be counted as a major achievement of American film during the

latter eighties, especially as these affirmative and elegiac portraits achieved such resonance for many who served in Vietnam. Offsetting these more affirmative portraits were
continuing meditations upon the darkness, corruption, and brutality of the war in FULL
METAL JACKET (1987), OFF LIMITS (1988), and CASUALTIES OF WAR (1989).

Just as the war generated split and contending interpretations of its history and
seemed to resist historical closure, American film never succeeded in fully coming to
terms with it. This was probably more a problem of political culture than of cinema, but
eighties Vietnam films are instructive in this regard. They collectively sought and
employed metaphor, symbolism, and mythology, rather than historical perspective, in an
effort to grasp the war's significance and convey it to audiences. APOCALYPSE NOW,
PLATOON, FULL METAL JACKET, CASUALTIES OF WAR, and BORN ON THE FOURTH OF
JULY (1989) employed metaphors of bodily and spiritual corruption and symbolic dual-
ities of decency and savagery contending for the American heart as narrative modes for
understanding the war. This spiritual and metaphysical focus coexisted with an emphasis on the immediate, physical experiences of soldiers in the jungle (84 CHARLIE
MOPIC, HAMBURGER HILL, PLATOON).

These emphases made for good poetry and powerful filmmaking, but their philosophical and symbolic designs omitted key aspects of the war that are decisive for its
comprehension. Despite the Pentagon's extensive intelligence on the NVA and NLF
that clarified their administrative structure and operational methods, the Vietnamese
enemy has typically appeared in the films as a shadowy figure darting through the jungle. The Pentagon knew the enemy well and had gathered a great deal of data about the
forces the United States was fighting. But Hollywood's films imply otherwise. There, the
enemy is portrayed in the vaguest of terms. In doing so, these films break with a long-
standing tradition in Hollywood war movies of portraying enemies in vivid and detailed
ways. Only one film of the eighties—GOOD MORNING, VIETNAM (1987),—sufficiently

HAMBURGER HILL showed unstintingly the carnage of the war on both sides.

individualized a Vietnamese guerrilla fighter as to allow him to state cogently his reasons for battling the Americans. This is an interesting bias when one considers the plethora of World War II films that permit the Nazis to state their cause and that, on occasion, even draw individual characters as tragic and sympathetic figures.

The United States was in Vietnam ostensibly to assist the government of South Vietnam and its army in fighting the North. However, portraits of the South Vietnamese regime and the political forces with which the United States allied itself are almost totally lacking in eighties films. In them, as in Hollywood Westerns, American soldiers fight alone against a lurking enemy. The roots of the war lay in the immediate years following World War II and the U.S. decision to support the French in an effort to retain Vietnam as a colony, but virtually all eighties productions are set in the late 1960s, a time of high drama but one that does not clarify the reasons for the war. This restrictive time period enables filmmakers to provide little more than a snapshot of a much broader event.

In addition, the bombing campaign against North Vietnam and its ferocity were among the most controversial facets of the war, but the air war has remained relatively unexamined on film, with the occasional exception in pictures like FLIGHT OF THE INTRUDER (1991) and BAT 21 (1988). Furthermore, when Hollywood films acknowledge domestic opposition to the war, it tends to be presented as protest in the streets. The protagonist in GARDENS OF STONE, for example, punches out an obnoxious antiwar liberal who is an obvious agitator. By 1970, though, most Americans wanted the United States out of Vietnam, a position that was coupled with dislike for antiwar protestors.[32] Thus, at that time many Americans were against the war even as they disliked public protest. For the films, then, to equate antiwar opposition with street protest is to minimize the unpopularity of the war and the extent of domestic opposition to it.

Because the foregoing elements are missing from most eighties Vietnam films, the cycle offers young viewers (who get their history from movies and television) an extremely vivid but incomplete portrait of the war. Without knowing the enemy and the conflict's history, the war cannot be understood. With their laudable intentions, the Vietnam films constructed a cultural discourse on the war that has substituted in cinema for its painful history. The films removed from the war some of its most important social, historical, and political factors. In their place, they present the war as a bleak, existential landscape of violence and death, resistant to comprehension and devoid of larger meanings except those of American courage and fortitude. This focus lent itself especially well to the overtly philosophical and symbolic design of THE DEER HUNTER, APOCALYPSE NOW, BORN ON THE FOURTH OF JULY, CASUALTIES OF WAR, PLATOON, and FULL METAL JACKET. A complementary focus, tied to the presentation of Southeast Asia as an existential arena containing a bloody conflict without apparent meaning, was the celebration of brotherhood, camaraderie, and honor among the ground troops in 84 CHARLIE MOPIC, HAMBURGER HILL, GARDENS OF STONE, and PLATOON.

The American experience in Vietnam has come to be seen on film as a journey into the heart of darkness, into an irrational region of savagery that defies explanation. This, of course, is a political position and argument, and it tends to insulate the war from close scrutiny for a popular audience. Francis Ford Coppola was more prescient than he may have known when he and his screenwriters transposed Joseph Conrad's metaphor to the Vietnam War, for in one way or another American films of the 1980s remained trapped within the terms of that metaphor.

Born on the Fourth of July symbolized the war's trauma to America through the bodily damage afflicting its central character, Ron Kovic.

Dystopian Science Fiction

While the productions of George Lucas and Steven Spielberg and the Star Trek series accounted for the top science fiction hits of the decade, a darker cycle of pessimistic sci-fi productions extrapolated from ongoing socioeconomic problems of eighties American society and projected these into a grim and dystopian future. In the guise of science fiction, American film pictured pessimistic visions of contemporary society and its ailing economy, visions that were stark antitheses to the emotional cheeriness and social optimism of the Lucas-Spielberg pictures.

While Ronald Reagan proclaimed the virtues of unfettered capitalism and the need for increased defense spending and reduced social services, these dystopian thrillers portrayed possible outcomes of such policies several generations hence. The future world they conjured was nonapocalyptic; that is, it represented no radical, violent break with the present but rather an extension. (Thus, The Terminator [1984], which pictures a postapocalyptic society, does not fit with this cycle.) Environmental pollution, urban decay and overcrowding, drugs, violent crime, homelessness and unemployment, media manipulation and domination of political discourse, corporate concentration and the irresponsible pursuit of profit, alliances between corporate and state power—these modern conditions, projected into the future, linked the worlds of the dystopian sci-fi cycle with recognizable elements of contemporary society. The dystopian thrillers threw up a disturbing mirror image of contemporary U.S. culture and warned, through the imaginative mediations of fantasy, "Look at what you could become."

The dystopian cycle spanned the entire decade and included ALIEN (1979) and its sequel ALIENS (1986), ESCAPE FROM NEW YORK (1981), OUTLAND (1981), BLADE RUNNER (1982), THE RUNNING MAN (1987), ROBOCOP (1987) and its sequel ROBOCOP 2 (1990), and TOTAL RECALL (1990). Described by one critic as "new bad future films," the pictures presented striking visions of "the present caught in the future."[33] In every case, the portrait was an unflattering one and stressed chronic conditions of political and economic injustice. In ESCAPE FROM NEW YORK, Manhattan has been turned into a giant prison colony for political prisoners and criminals, run by a quasi-fascist police state. In OUTLAND, BLADE RUNNER, the two ALIEN films, and TOTAL RECALL, ruthless corporations, allied with the state, engage in interplantary imperialism and readily sacrifice human victims in their quest for new markets and weapons. In THE RUNNING MAN, ROBOCOP, and TOTAL RECALL, the mass media manufacture counterfeit realities that undermine reliable perceptions of self and society.

Running through most of these films, and arising as a response to the commerce and corruption they depict, is a crisis of self and psyche. The worlds depicted here are filled with ersatz realities, created by the media or the corporate state and confusing the boundaries between real and not real. "More human than human" is the slogan of BLADE RUNNER's Tyrell Corp., which manufactures synthetic humans, called replicants. Murphy, the robotized cop in ROBOCOP, is tormented by vestigial memories of his human life and family. In TOTAL RECALL, customers contract with Rekall, Inc., for memory implants that simulate exciting and enjoyable vacations. Rekall advertises, "You can buy the memory of your ideal vacation cheaper, safer, and better than the real thing." When Quaid (Arnold Schwarzenegger) buys an implant, he is plunged into a

One of the most influential films of the decade, BLADE RUNNER vividly defined the parameters of the dystopian sci-fi cycle.

nightmare world in which he can no longer distinguish between real events and those occurring only in his mind.

Thus, in ROBOCOP, TOTAL RECALL, and BLADE RUNNER, psychic crisis accompanies, and is engendered by, the pathologies of state and economy. In this connection, it is notable that director Ridley Scott added extra footage to the director's cut of BLADE RUNNER, released on home video in the 1990s, that made the character of Deckard, the protagonist, more ambiguous and raised an unanswered question about whether he is a human or a replicant. (Both BLADE RUNNER and TOTAL RECALL are based on the fiction of Philip K. Dick, whose concerns about the mechanization of human identity and the production of machines that seem more real than their inventors are core anxieties of the dystopian cycle.)

BLADE RUNNER, an enormously influential film in the cycle, boasted a brilliant production design by Laurence J. Paull and Syd Mead that established an enduring *mise-en-scène* for the new bad future films: a megalopolis of high-tech grandeur perched atop decaying architectural forms, choked by a multicultural mass of overpopulated urban poor. The dissolution of geographical, architectural, and cultural boundaries, visualized by the *mise-en-scène* in the visual and acoustic flux of its dense cityscape, evokes a postmodern landscape. It is a world whose epistemological boundaries have collapsed and is awash in a sea of simulacra and pseudorealities ("more human than human"). Syd Mead described the mixture of opulence and decay in BLADE RUNNER's futurist city as

> a rather depressing "alley" environment which is a negative caricature of the normal city street. The result: a maze of mechanical detail overlaid onto barely recognizable architecture producing an encrusted combination of style which we humorously labeled "retro-deco." . . . Everything had to have a patina of grime and soot over a makeshift high-tech feeling."[34]

BLADE RUNNER's city envisions the internationalization of capital linked with a crumbling infrastructure. Various languages and cultures coexist among the multicultural populace while hovercars and electronic billboards advertise consumer goods and the pleasures to be found in the off-world colonies. Drawing the connections between the film's *mise-en-scène* and contemporary eighties society, Giuliana Bruno stressed, "The link betwen postmodernism and late capitalism is highlighted in the film's representation of post-industrial decay. The future does not realize an idealized, aseptic technological order, but is seen simply as the development of the present state of the city and of the social order of late capitalism."[35]

In their narratives of commerce gone mad and rampant, in which both the psyche and the outer environment have been transformed into commodities, the dystopian films collectively envisioned a widening gulf between rich and poor, the operation of social services by for-profit corporations, and the extension of market values across the entire spectrum of society and human relations. ROBOCOP was especially relentless and savage in its satire of these conditions. In its future society, the private business sector has been completely deregulated and now runs Detroit, with the Omni Consumer Products corporation funding the police department and the military. OCP markets ED-209, an enforcement robot programmed for urban pacification. "We practically are the military," OCP's chief remarks, alluding to the alliance of industry and coercive force that has made the film's Detroit into a new center of fascism. The public's attention is diverted from this unholy alliance by the media's infotainment programming, that is, entertainment masquerading as news. A series of "Media Breaks" punctuate the film's narrative with stories satirizing government doublespeak (a presidential press conference aboard "the Star Wars Orbiting Peace Platform") and for-profit health care (corporate ads for the Family Heart Center).

The images and narratives of the dystopian cycle mimicked the eighties environment of curtailed social services and privatization of the public sector. The 1980s have been called, in popular parlance, "the decade of greed," and the dystopian films, depicting multinational and interplanetary corporate empires coexisting with a decaying infrastructure, offered striking visualizations of this spirit. More often than not, these films portrayed the United States as a kind of Third World country, ruled by its business sector, with the bulk of its citizens impoverished, imprisoned, or under state surveillance. In ESCAPE FROM NEW YORK and THE RUNNING MAN, society operates a vast penal network, and in BLADE RUNNER and TOTAL RECALL penal and labor colonies have been extended "off-world." Such conditions extinguish freedom, and here lie the darkest implications of the dystopian cycle. No functioning democracy is depicted in these films. Social disintegration and chaos have destroyed the foundations for effective political participation in public life. With social decay everywhere, state power concentrated among a corrupt few, and no political alternatives available, the future as depicted here becomes a frightening, authoritarian nightmare in which political freedom and its necessary economic foundation have been destroyed.

The dystopian films thus sounded a warning about, and registered a deep unease over, the economic and social policies of the 1980s, but their political content was conjoined with the conventions of action thrillers and (in ROBOCOP and TOTAL RECALL

ROBOCOP lampooned the social politics of eighties America, using science fiction to comment on economic and cultural pathologies.

especially) flamboyantly graphic violence. This was an uneasy mixture, and the claims for spectacle and excitement that it encouraged a popular audience to make sometimes obfuscated the films' political elements. This problem is clearest in ROBOCOP, which offered a sharp satire about the social Darwinism of the Reagan era's unfettered capitalism. (A man-on-the-street interviewee tells the Media Break crew, "It's a free society, except there ain't nothing free. There's no guarantees, you know. You're on your own. It's the law of the jungle." A prominent member of a powerful crime ring remarks, "No better way to steal money than free enterprise.") The film's satire was conjoined with action set pieces and explicitly detailed violence in ways that probably overwhelmed the satire for many viewers.

While the new cold war films inflected the conventions of action-adventure with right-wing political perspectives, the dystopian thrillers inflected them with left-leaning ones. As a whole, the cycle sustains a critique and a portrait of capitalism run amok. The efflorescence of the dystopian cycle indicated that, despite the Reagan administration's promise of a new "Morning in America," the nation was fissured with deep anxieties about its future and an ongoing suspicion that the eighties economy was tragically unfair. The future these films conjured contained many attributes of their era, but hope for a better tomorrow was not among them.

These production cycles demonstrate that American film took a variety of positions in regard to the decade's political issues. The new cold war films hued closely to the administration's line on foreign policy issues involving the Soviet Union, although, as discussed, a number of the films showed significant ideological contradictions. The cycle dealing with unrest in Central America was consistently skeptical and critical about the Reagan Administration's claims about a power projection by Moscow in America's backyard. Of all these production cycles, the Vietnam War films showed the greatest ambivalence about the claims of empire and America's role in world affairs, and this perception was consistent with the legacy that the war had left the nation. Dystopian science fiction blended its social critique with the commercial appeals of spectacle, special effects, and violence. These qualities mitigated but did not neutralize the cycle's economic critique of eighties America.

The richness of Hollywood's output in the eighties is evident in this heterodox mix of styles, subjects, and ideological appeals. Analyses of American film are ill served by efforts to reduce its heterodoxy to one, or a few, schemata that claim to explain all. Although the Reagan Presidency excelled at ideological production, Hollywood film was neither monodimensional nor coterminous with the politics of those years. This is a heartening fact because it establishes an important foundation for the artistic role that film may play, giving form to the issues and contradictions of those moments in time that imbricate filmmaker and viewers alike.

8

Movies and Morality

The social and political dimension of eighties filmmaking had two components. The first, examined in chapter 7, involved the production of topical films that responded to key issues on the period's public agenda. From the new cold war and Vietnam to the symbolic transformations of dystopian science fiction, eighties filmmakers responded to their period with passion and imagination.

Their period also responded to them, with skirmishes and outright wars over the moral content of American film. While controversies about the appropriate content of motion pictures and their potential social effects are as old as the medium, the 1980s were a peak period for such activity. Arguments roiled within and outside the industry over portrayals of violence, sexuality, and religion; the horror genre; the burgeoning adult videotape industry, and such prominent studio pictures as CRUISING (1980), DRESSED TO KILL (1980), and THE LAST TEMPTATION OF CHRIST (1988).

These debates involved groups on both the political Right and Left and therefore do not easily reduce to a single agenda. They were, however, part of a major development during the Reagan years: the rise of a symbolic politics, that is, the waging of political conflicts on cultural terrain. As Charles Lyons has noted, "Debates over film censorship from 1980 to 1992 reflected a culture in conflict over sex, race, family values, and homosexuality. They also demonstrated that political struggles were being fought in a cultural arena."[1] The rise of a symbolic cultural politics was connected to the era's general ideological ferment. Of special significance in this regard were the activities of the New Right and its success in capitalizing on divisive ideological appeals in the wake of the collapse and general discrediting of liberalism. The New Right was an especially activist segment of the American electorate in the 1980s, successful at mobilizing its constituencies and with political ambitions, as John Dolan of the National Conservative Political Action Committee put it, "to take control of the culture."[2]

An important caveat needs to be stressed here. The political Right, and conservatism in general, is not to be confused with the New Right. American conservatism was a heterodox coalition, including an old guard of traditional conservatives (e.g., William Buckley) who had been around for years and had watched their fortunes grow and decline but mostly lie fallow since the 1964 Goldwater defeat. It also comprised a neoconservative wing of converted former liberals who enthusiastically embraced their new political identity.[3] And it comprised as well the more extreme New Right coalition. This was a diffuse network of single-issue groups focused on (and generally opposing) such topics as busing, abortion, gun control, gay and women's rights, and school prayer (the New Right favored the latter). Direct-mail guru Richard Viguerie was a key player facilitating the growth of the New Right, using direct-mail campaigns to rouse opinion on hot-button issues. The extremism of the New Right made it both visible and troublesome for the Reagan administration. Many of these groups were too rabid to be permitted to have a close identification with the administration, but much of the impression that the country had swung to the Right during the 1980s was due to the high visibility of such groups and causes as Anita Bryant's crusade against gay rights, Phyllis Schafley's anti-ERA Eagle Forum, and Jerry Falwell's Moral Majority.

The growth of political action groups and their efforts to reach narrow segments of the electorate over highly emotional issues was a key factor in the rise of the era's symbolic politics. Such divisive issues as abortion, school prayer, pornography, and gay rights furnished effective bases around which to mobilize resources and constituents. Viguerie noted, "We never really won until we began stressing issues like busing, abortion, school prayer, and gun control. We talked about the sanctity of free enterprise, about the Communist onslaught until we were blue in the face."[4] Effective methods for generating funds lay in making appeals to anger, fear, and hostility connected to symbolic issues perceived as threats to traditional family life. John Dolan admitted that the shriller the appeal, the more anger a direct mailing elicited, the easier it was to get money.[5] A politics of cultural symbolism held special appeal for groups who felt marginalized by the movement and direction of society, disenfranchised and alienated by their perception that the predominant social values are inimical to their own. James McEvoy points out that "symbolic politics are the politics of groups that enjoy relatively greater representation than newly challenging groups but which are somewhat marginal with respect to their relations with the dominant segments of the society."[6] Thus, New Right political activity during the 1980s expressed anxieties over the state of American culture and society, anxieties rooted in the perception of a growing adversarial culture whose constituents—radical students, women's libbers, gays, bohemian artists and intellectuals— were seen as threats to their own values and preferred norms of social authority.

The dominant symbolic motifs of the Reagan period portrayed a society under threat. America and the family were besieged by resurgent forces of chaos and disorder: communism, gay and women's rights, school busing, abortion. Twentieth-century America had gone astray, had been misled by the hitherto-prevailing liberal culture with its permissive and overly tolerant attitudes. Internationally, concern for human rights and a reluctance to use military force were aiding the Soviets' plans for world conquest. Domestically, society had lost its spiritual bearings, and homosexuality, abortion, and pornography threatened the body politic. President Reagan observed that "modern-day secularism [was] discarding the tried and time-tested values upon which our very civilization is based."[7] All were threats to the nostalgic vision the administration offered of an America of small government, small business, and local communities organized around family and church. The Reagan "revolution" thus was an attempt to turn back the clock to a more pristine America, to a time when traditional authority was not challenged by oppositional racial, sexual, political, or economic interests. Stimulated by the bellicose rhetoric of the New Right, groups on the political Left, ranging from the women's movement to gay rights activists, joined in the era's divisive interpetations of cultural products and agendas for society. Hollywood films became a flashpoint in these battles, which targeted movie content while projecting more substantial and broader visions of what an appropriate American society should look like.

The struggles over movie censorship in the 1980s were stoked by a climate in which ideological battle lines were quickly drawn in culture and the arts. Though the reassertion of a more conservative national politics atop the corpse of liberalism helped fire the cultural battles of the period, and though the New Right's voice was among the most strident in this dialogue, groups of other political persuasions joined in the fray, at times to promote their own agendas, at times to respond to policy initiatives or campaigns that they deemed hostile to their interests. Efforts to adjudicate the terms of cinematic representation focused on disputed forms of visual symbolism and their potential social effects. Because a mix of groups from the Right and the Left entered the fray over movie content, this ideological range vividly demonstrated the volatility of the era's political symbolism and the extent to which the culture had become politicized and polarized. The issues that emerged in the debates over movie censorship do not reduce to a convenient ideological grouping. Instead, they were diverse (and divisive). Their volatility and persistence through the decade showed that the anxieties and hostilities that surround symbolic politics, once roused, are not easily extinguished. Indeed, the fracturing and splintering of American culture into divided, hostile encampments, so visible throughout the 1980s persists into the present era. In this sense, the battles that I now discuss, and the charged, antagonistic social atmosphere of which they were part, helped initiate a process of social disintegration that may be irreversible.

The Ratings Flap over CRUISING

In early 1980, the nation's gay community mobilized to protest images of homosexuality in three new releases, CRUISING, WINDOWS, and AMERICAN GIGOLO. These protests, and the general controversy centered on CRUISING, precipitated a crisis in the industry over the validity of its movie ratings code. Hollywood films had a long tradition of depicting gay sexuality as renegade and perverted, but in the 1980s the gay community had attained a degree of cultural visibility and political muscle that it had not previously possessed. It now exercised that muscle over these productions, which it deemed to contain unacceptably salacious and insulting depictions of homosexuality. CRUISING, the most notorious of these pictures, luridly depicted gay sadomasochistic subcultures. WINDOWS offered a homicidal lesbian, and AMERICAN GIGOLO depicted a (heterosexual) male prostitute against a backdrop of tawdry hetero- and homosexuality.

Of these pictures, CRUISING was the most inflammatory, triggered the angriest community outbursts, and had the strongest social impact. Protests over this film were the opening act in a decade-long controversy over sex and violence in the movies, particularly in films where the sex and violence were conjoined with each other. Arguments over sexual violence in the movies, in society, and in potential connections between the two would focus on CRUISING, the *Penthouse* production of CALIGULA (1980), Brian De Palma's DRESSED TO KILL (1980) and BODY DOUBLE (1984), the burgeoning cycle of violent horror films, and the expanding markets for video pornography. The cumulative effect of these productions, and the battles that surrounded them, helped feed public perceptions that the film industry was out of touch with grassroots America and was peddling lewd material to make a buck.

Furthermore, the sex-violence controversies revived long-standing concerns over the usefulness of the MPAA's single-letter ratings codes and eventually forced a revision of those codes. (In contrast with the imagery of CRUISING and WINDOWS, it should be

CRUISING's depiction of a gay underworld elicited widespread protest. A New York cop (Al Pacino) dons the attire and tries to pass as gay.

noted that other Hollywood films of the period showed a new sensitivity and openness toward gay sexuality. MAKING LOVE [1980], which contained a then-daring on-screen kiss between two men, PERSONAL BEST [1982], DEATHTRAP [1982], PARTNERS [1982], and VICTOR/VICTORIA [1982] were compassionate and matter-of-fact about their gay characters. Hollywood, though, had not embraced gay sexuality, and the industry remained timid and cautious in its treatments of the issue, as the exclusion of the gay subplots from THE COLOR PURPLE [1986] and FRIED GREEN TOMATOES [1989] demonstrated.)

CRUISING offered perhaps the decade's ugliest and most unpleasant depiction of sexual extremism. Al Pacino plays a New York cop, Steve Burns, trying to catch a predator who is killing and mutilating gay men who frequent sadomasochistic clubs. Posing as a gay man, the cop goes undercover to infiltrate the somewhat secretive world of S&M fetishists. He studies the signals and codes practiced by initiates in this community, and he hangs out in the clubs the victims attended. During these visits, he begins to make some personal discoveries about his own sexuality that disturb him and cause problems in the relationship with his girlfriend. Burns becomes less sure of his own heterosexuality as the persona he has adopted in the clubs assumes an increasingly dominant place in his psyche. As the film progresses, the narrative becomes increasingly incoherent, but it suggests that Burns not only bears a physical likeness to the killer but may even be the killer. The denouement is confusing, and it is difficult to ascertain Burns's level of responsibility for the serial killings. But, however poorly plotted the film is, its lurid story line suggests that gay sexuality is part of a milieu of violence, exploitation, and perversity. CRUISING's fascination with the S&M world goes beyond curiosity and becomes obsessively prurient. Burns's sojourns through the leather-and-chains domain provides the film with ample opportunities to take a leering look at exotic sexual practices. During the sequences in the S&M clubs, director William Friedkin fills his shots with shadowy figures groping and contorting in implied forms of extravagant sexual behavior. These lurid depictions are calculated to play to a straight audience's prejudices and to evoke from such viewers a punitive emotional response toward the characters. In this way, the film seems to imply that the killer's victims got what they deserved for their sexual transgressions and that, if Burns were the killer, his rage stemmed from self-loathing over his own sexual appetites.

The gay community was outraged by these depictions, and activists picketed the film during production and again during the picture's release, outside theaters in New York and San Francisco. Gay leaders denounced the film and asked why Friedkin felt compelled to make such a picture. The mayor of San Francisco requested that distributor United Artists reimburse the city $130,000 to cover the cost of providing police protection around a downtown theater on opening night. In the event, no violence occurred, but the mayor's request showed the level of concern felt by city officials and the level of animosity the film had aroused in the gay community. But reaction and antipathy toward this picture extended beyond the confines of this community. CRUISING created problems for the industry in its relations with the public at large and with exhibitors. Beyond the explicit and nasty violence depicted in the killer's attacks on gays, the film's fascination with tabooed sexual practices, and the prurient attention it gave these, caused many within and outside the industry to openly question the validity of the picture's R rating. *Variety* raised this issue in its review of the film: "To put it bluntly, if an R allows the showing of one man greasing his fist followed by the rising ecstasy and pain of a second

CRUISING *depicts gay sexuality as furtive, secretive, and dark.*

man held in chains by others, then there's only one close-up left for the X."[8]

Exhibitors were particularly uneasy about showing the film in their theaters, and some of the nation's biggest chains openly broke with the MPAA over its designation of CRUISING as an R-rated picture. These exhibitors publicly declared that the picture should have been an X by virtue of its explicit, unsavory sex and violence. This rebellion precipitated a showdown with the MPAA over the integrity of its ratings system. General Cinema Corp., the nation's biggest theater chain, booked CRUISING into thirty-three of its theaters on a blind-bid basis (committing to show the picture in advance of seeing it). When they finally saw CRUISING four months later, just before its national release, GCC executives were appalled and flatly refused to show the picture in any of their theaters, citing a policy against booking X-rated films. "We stand by our original opinion that CRUISING was mis-rated, deserves an X and therefore won't play our houses as a matter of policy," GCC noted.[9]

The GCC decision undercut the economic stability of the industry, as that stability rested on cooperative relations between the major studios and exhibitors. GCC had in essence revoked an MPAA rating and asserted its own authority to determine a more appropriate designation for CRUISING, invoking corporate policy over the disposition of X-rated pictures. For the MPAA and its head, Jack Valenti, GCC's actions threatened the validity of the whole ratings enterprise, which, lacking the force of law, depended on mutual cooperation and observance of the codes by all sectors of the movie industry. If MPAA ratings could be so questioned, then the agency's protective authority would be weakened. The organization operated as a buffer, shielding the majors from outside efforts to regulate its products and lobbying Washington to promote issues and bills favorable to the business. If the ratings system were undermined or its authority impeded, as it had been by the GCC decision, the industry could be more vulnerable to charges from outside groups that its films were unwholesome, unhealthy, or otherwise deserving of censure. To some extent, this is what occurred in the next few years, as attacks on the industry mounted and the MPAA scrambled to rebut the attacks and, in some instances, agreed to changes that it had earlier refused to carry out.

The MPAA's problems over CRUISING worsened. A second major theater chain openly contested the picture's rating. United Artists Theater Circuit worried about the community criticism that it might arouse if it showed the film. UATC feared that this criticism might come from a multitude of sources, gay groups as well as more conservative critics angered by the film's relatively explicit depictions of sexuality. Unlike GCC, UATC did not cancel its bookings of the film, but it did assert its belief that the film was really an X-rated picture being marketed by its distributor as an R. UATC posted signs at all of its theaters showing CRUISING that advised moviegoers, "In the opinion of management this picture should be rated X. No one under 18 will be admitted."[10] UATC, therefore, would exhibit the film as if it were X-rated, enforcing the admissions restrictions appropriate for X-rated pictures. In addition to the responses of these chains, a San Diego exhibitor, the College Theatre, filed a civil suit in federal court charging that the filmmakers, production company (Lorimar), distributor (United Artists), and the MPAA's Classification and Rating Administration had misrepresented the nature of the film by virtue of its R rating.

In light of the heat the picture and the ratings flap generated, the MPAA responded slowly to the widespread criticism directed its way. After the picture's first-run release had ended, the MPAA ordered that all outstanding prints of the film be withdrawn from circulation. These would be replaced with a new, revised version of the film after the

MPAA had reexamined it and certified that it was, in fact, an R-rated picture. The MPAA's failure to intervene until the first-run release had concluded is significant. To do otherwise, to withdraw the film from initial release, would damage the picture's earnings potential beyond the harm the controversy had already inflicted. That the MPAA acted conservatively, rather than in a proactive manner, is an important point in light of the degree to which public confidence in the industry fell during the decade. The industry's slow response was one of many factors that influenced public perception that Hollywood was out of touch with average America, that the industry was peddling sex and violence for profit, and that its regulatory agencies were toothless.

After the print recall, the history of the ratings dispute becomes tortuous and subject to contradictory accounts by the involved parties. In a maneuver that was perhaps intended to deflect criticism of lax MPAA ratings, the board stipulated that the film's original R designation was granted on condition that the filmmakers delete material from two scenes. The MPAA claimed, though, that the requested changes had not been made. In effect, the MPAA said that the picture they designated as an R and the version that went into national release were not the same, hence the directive that existing prints be recalled and swapped with the revised version that incorporated the requisite cuts. It is difficult to see what difference these alterations would have made because they were cosmetic rather than substantive. The changes involved using a longer editing transition out of a murder scene to soften its brutality and a masked frame bar in another scene to conceal some implied sexual activity in one of the S&M bars. These minimal changes are typical of the compromises that filmmakers negotiate with the MPAA. The problem in every case involves the practical necessity of specifying thresholds for the different rating categories. At what point does an R become an X? How many offending frames must be removed to reduce an X to an R?

In their cut of a picture initially submitted for a rating, filmmakers routinely include more sex and violence than they in fact want the picture to have. Thus, in the negotiations that follow, filmmakers have wiggle room, an ability to make trims requested by the MPAA that do not result in a substantially different film from what was intended. This strategem requires that the MPAA specify exactly what shots, editing devices, or frames must be deleted to move the film from one ratings category to another. In practice, it often comes down to an offending shot or image whose excision or alteration everyone agrees will mark the difference between R and X. A major problem with this approach is that it trivializes the distinctions between ratings categories. In other words, it fails to address such intangibles as the overall spirit of a work. This eludes negotiation. Certainly, the spirit of CRUISING is unrelievedly nasty and ugly, and a few shot trims cannot address this ugliness or ameliorate it. It was this spirit, as much as the content of any individual shot or scene, that outraged the gay groups that picketed the film. But the MPAA could operate only in terms of the negotiating points that define its prerelease transactions with filmmakers, who are under contract to deliver a cut of a film that will satisfy the rating that the distributor has agreed the picture will carry. Achieving the rating means that everyone involved must agree on the designated trims.

Thus, in defending its rating of CRUISING, the MPAA cited failure by the filmmakers to make the cuts required to earn the R rating. This line of argument contained an implicit defense of the integrity of the picture's original rating (and of the ratings system as a whole). Jack Valenti suggested that Friedkin's failure to make the trims specified by the MPAA was an honest mistake, an oversight, but Friedkin and the film's producer, Jerry Weintraub, claimed they had made all the cuts the MPAA originally required before the picture went into national release.[11] The net result of this confusing turn of events and these competing claims was that the MPAA could publicly distance itself from the version of CRUISING that had aroused such ire upon its national release.

However, there was also a new problem. The MPAA's position that the film had not been properly edited to qualify for its R rating seemed to acknowledge that the first version of CRUISING was what its detractors had claimed all along, an X-rated picture. To be sure, Jack Valenti denied that it was, and he claimed that the ratings system was stronger than ever. He maintained that the controversy proved the board was responsive to the public and was capable of taking action to enforce its stipulations about what cuts were required for a particular ratings designation. But the MPAA was on losing ground here, as subsequent events would confirm. It had effectively admitted that an X-rated film went into national release with an R rating.

Sex and Violence Continued: The Case of CALIGULA

While CRUISING was in release, eliciting angry controversy over its R rating and its depictions of outré sexuality, *Penthouse* publisher Bob Guccione was pushing CALIGULA, a hardcore sex- and violence-spattered portrait of ancient Rome. Guccione's *Penthouse*-financed production was distributed by Analysis Film Releasing on a four-wall basis, whereby the distributor rented a theater rather than leasing a print to an exhibitor. This distribution strategy was canny. Guccione and Analysis targeted art cinemas, and by four-walling these prestigious houses, they kept the film out of the grind houses that catered to the sex trade, effectively avoiding the pornography exhibition circuit. Thus, CALIGULA would be screened in theaters that specialized in foreign and art films and thereby retain its aura as a prestige (i.e., expensively budgeted) sex film (though there was far more violence than sex in the picture), untainted by an association with porno houses. Guccione was targeting a more upscale audience, and he was on the cusp of a wave of mass-marketed pornography that was about to break nationwide, courtesy of the video revolution. CALIGULA heralded the big marketing push that sex films would soon enjoy in the middle and late 1980s. Thus, the battles over CALIGULA were harbingers of a brewing storm over sex films, and, in tandem with CRUISING, Guccione's picture roused the specter for many social watchdog groups of an immoral media industry thrusting its products on an unwilling public.

From the start, and as Guccione expected and indeed wanted, CALIGULA was engulfed by protest over its salacious content and by legal challenges from groups seeking to have it declared an obscenity. The antipornography organization Morality in Media unsuccessfully tried to sue federal officials for failing to declare the film obscene after it was seized by U.S. Customs in 1979 when Guccione brought the film into the country. Morality in Media's legal effort was assisted by a Memphis attorney who had prosecuted DEEP THROAT cases in Tennessee, and the objective was to have the film destroyed after it was judged obscene.

Morality in Media lost its challenge in February 1980, but Guccione anticipated further efforts and was willing to commit sizable resources to the film's legal defense. He had plenty of opportunities. On 17 June 1980, when the film was playing nationally in forty theaters, CALIGULA was banned in Boston, and police seized prints of the picture. Guccione responded, "We always felt that somewhere down the line we would have to mount a massive legal defense of the film to clear up any doubts about its non-obscen-

Malcolm MacDowell portrays the Emperor Caligula in the luridly violent Penthouse *production.*

ity. Boston is giving us that opportunity."[12] Guccione's willingness to spend money defending the film, of course, was not solely a function of First Amendment principles. The legal challenges and moral controversies generated by the film provided excellent marketing opportunities, what Guccione termed "the kind of coverage money can never buy."[13]

Penthouse won its Boston case. On 1 August, a Boston municipal court ruled that CALIGULA was not obscene by virtue of passing the *Miller* test. A legal finding of obscenity had to use the guidelines established by the Supreme Court's 1973 *Miller* ruling. To be judged obscene under *Miller*, a work must fail a tripartite test. It must (1) lack serious literary, artistic, political, or scientific value; (2) contain patently offensive depictions of sexual acts; and (3) appeal on the whole to a prurient interest (with prurience assessed by "the average person, applying contemporary community standards"). If a work failed to meet any one of these standards, then it could not be found legally obscene. The *Miller* test, as it was interpreted in the early 1980s, made obscenity convictions difficult to obtain. The standards to be applied under Miller contained multiple exclusionary conditions. A book or film might portray graphic sexual activity, deemed of prurient appeal, offensive to some or all viewers, but might still be salvageable by virtue of its literary, political, or scientific value. Pornographers in the late 1970s and early 1980s gleefully lampooned the notion of redeeming value in the *Miller* test. While it offered them protection, they found it an irresistible target for satire. Sex films of those years periodically interrupted the hormonal activities so that a character might briefly expound on world political issues. Then, having gotten the redeeming social value out of the way, the sexual carousing could begin again.

The Boston judge decided that, while the film contained offensive depictions of sex, appealed to prurient interests, and lacked artistic and scientific value, its depiction of ancient Rome contained political values that enabled it to pass the *Miller* test.[14] According to the judge, the film's depiction of corruption in ancient Rome dramatized the political theme that "absolute power corrupts absolutely." CALIGULA thus escaped an obscenity finding based on *Miller*'s provision for political content. But there was yet another problem faced by local prosecutors who attempted to suppress the film from regional exhibition. In its depictions of Roman decadence, Guccione's film was preponderantly violent rather than sexual, and *Miller* said nothing about violence as a basis for obscenity prosecution. Obscenity was a matter of sex, not violence, a factor noted by a Madison, Wisconsin, district attorney in his decision to decline a local antiporn crusader's request that CALIGULA be prosecuted. "I note particularly in this regard that the most offensive portions of the film are those explicitly depicting violent, and not sexual, conduct, which is not in any way prohibited by the criminal law."[15] Guccione acknowledged that the film was preponderantly violent and that its violence tended to counteract and contradict the prurient appeal of the few sex scenes. "I maintain the film is actually anti-erotic . . . in every one of its scenes you'll find a mixture of gore or violence or some other rather ugly things."[16]

Penthouse did not win an unbroken string of legal victories in its efforts to distribute CALIGULA. Faced with a civil suit in Fairlawn, Ohio, seeking to prevent the film's exhibition on the grounds that it would be a "public nuisance," *Penthouse* withdrew the film from exhibition there rather than go to trial. The alliance of forces behind the Ohio complaint was symptomatic of the cultural politics of the early 1980s. The complaint was organized and prepared by Citizens for Decency through Law, a private watchdog group ready to mobilize against films it deemed immoral. The CDL attorney advised the city against trying to prosecute *Penthouse* criminally (i.e., for obscenity), recommended a civil proceeding instead because it would be quicker and would not run up against the *Miller* test, and offered to represent Fairlawn in the case. With *Penthouse* pulling the film, CDL effectively won its case without having to go to trial. The *Penthouse* attorney viewed the Fairlawn events as symptoms of the new cultural alignments represented, and reinforced, by Ronald Reagan's presidential victory: "Apparently, these extremists have interpreted a change by administration to mean a clarion call for a mandate to shackle the public's mind again."[17]

Despite its major victories in Boston and New York, *Penthouse* also moved more cautiously when packaging the film for video distribution in the Western Hemisphere. So that the picture might gain clearance by some of the region's more conservative regimes, *Penthouse* arranged with Vestron Video to release a softer, R-rated version of the picture rather the X-rated version distributed to theaters.

The legal challenges that surrounded the release of CALIGULA demonstrated two factors of increasing importance as the decade progressed. First, grassroots opposition to works deemed pornographic was substantial; in the years to come, the antipornography movement would grow in scope and power. Many groups such as the CDL and Morality in Media would organize efforts to suppress sex films and to alter what they regarded as Hollywood's propensity to manufacture immoral pictures. These efforts helped intensify the culture wars of the period. Second, the *Miller* test as traditionally interpreted did not give prosecutors or antiporn forces an especially effective weapon to use in going after the distribution of sex books or films. As a result, antiporn groups sought greater legal power and won it, and *Miller* itself was reconsidered in new strategies of prosecution. I will turn to these developments later in this chapter.

The Pornography of Horror

CALIGULA was an independent production financed and distributed outside the Hollywood system. As such and unlike CRUISING, it drew little fire directly at the Hollywood industry. By contrast, Brian De Palma's DRESSED TO KILL, also a 1980 release, and BODY DOUBLE (1984), revived long-standing feminist criticisms of sexual violence in the media, aroused calls that pornography was seeping into mainstream movies, and once more showed Hollywood for its cultural critics as an industry manufacturing decadent products that conjoined sex and violence.

The De Palma films were big-budget, prestige examples of a general shift toward explicit gore throughout the horror genre. In the 1980s horror mutated into an especially vicious brand of filmmaking that offered viewers unsparingly graphic violence. As noted in chapter 7, the horror genre saw a spike in production during 1980–81 (ninety-three pictures in 1980 alone). In 1980, horror and science fiction films accounted for nearly 40 percent of domestic film rentals.[18] The horror films included a large number of blood-spattered slaughter fests like BLOOD BEACH, MANIAC, and PROM NIGHT. The "slasher films" took over the genre as horror became synonymous with narratives about serial killers slaughtering promiscuous teenagers. The killings were rendered in lurid detail and with imaginative glee by an emerging new group of effects artists. These included Tom Savini (DAWN OF THE DEAD [1978], MANIAC [1980], FRIDAY THE 13TH [1980], EYES OF A STRANGER [1981]), Rick Baker (THE FUNHOUSE [1981], THE THING [1982]), and Rob Bottin (THE HOWLING [1981], THE THING). Not all of the pictures on which they worked were slasher films, but they all showcased the splatter effects that prosthetics and latex had brought to cinema.

It was the slasher films, though, that aroused the greatest outcry, both within and without the industry. The imagery of impaled, broken, and mutilated bodies seemed to demonstrate a rampant sadism in popular culture, promulgated by filmmakers and elicited with force in audiences who thrilled to each new audacious screen killing. Faced with the profusion of such bloodfests at the international film markets in 1980, distributors and studio sales reps expressed revulsion at the products and dismay at the decay and decadence of a once artful genre. "All they want is blood pouring off the screen. I question the mental balance of the people making and buying this stuff," noted one Carolco executive.[19] Imagery of victims dismembered by spikes, axes, chain saws, and power drills or run through meat grinders evoked a swift and stern backlash from the critical community and from feminist scholars who pointed out that a basic slasher film premise was a male killer stalking and slaughtering a bevy of young and attractive female victims.

Particularly troubling was a stylistic feature that quickly became cliché—the use of a subjective camera to represent the killer's point of view as he stalked his victims. This optical device appeared in Michael Powell's PEEPING TOM (1960) and in Hitchcock's PSYCHO (1960) before John Carpenter elaborated it throughout HALLOWEEN (1978) and established its effectiveness in the slasher cycle (for which HALLOWEEN was the

With raised knife, a demon prepares to finish off its teen victim in Sam Raimi's EVIL DEAD, *one of the bloodiest of the decade's gorefests.*

key filmic model). The extended subjective camerawork made the viewer share the killer's visual perspective during the elaborate stalking scenes that preceded the killings. The camerawork seemed to invite viewers to accompany the killers and to participate in their rituals. Many critics found this, and the genre as a whole, to be morally objectionable and to appeal to pruriently sadistic impulses. Prominent film reviewers Gene Siskel and Roger Ebert used their newspaper columns and weekly public TV review show to attack the proliferation of slasher films. Calling the films "gruesome and despicable," they argued that the pictures expressed a hatred of women and were a kind of backlash against women's liberation, offering stories that suggested that women should stay in their places or be cruelly killed. Ebert noted his personal discomfort watching the films in public with an audience. "Audiences are cheering the killers on. It's a scary experience."[20]

Following Ebert and Siskel, the *Chicago Tribune* in 1980 attacked the film industry, challenging the MPAA to give the slasher pictures an X rating. As in the controversies that surrounded CRUISING, the horror films were regarded as having been improperly rated. The *Tribune* pointed to the double standard about sex and violence that prevailed in the policy of the MPAA's Classification and Ratings Administration (CARA): "X ratings are generally reserved for movies with explicit, anatomical sex. Lacking that, all kinds of bloody cruelty and sadism can be shown in a movie that is classified as R."Agreeing with Siskel and Ebert about the antifemale attitude of the pictures, the *Tribune* continued, "The public would not tolerate this kind of eye-ball gouging sadism if it were directed against animals instead of women. But in these new films, the fact that the horror is inflicted on women appears to be the very point."[21]

As a result of the sustained outcry and protest surrounding the slasher films, major distributors curtailed press screenings for the pictures, and many national publications stopped reviewing them. By 1983, the market glut that had prevailed over the past two years resulted in a 50 percent drop in horror production and a 50 percent falloff in rentals.[22] The decline in rentals also reflected the shift from theatrical to a straight-to-video release for many of the low-budget pictures. This trend continued, as did the manufacture of slasher pictures despite the social criticism they engendered. Of the eighty-nine horror pictures produced in 1986, one-third went straight to video.[23] Thus, video proved to be an amenable forum for the distribution of stigmatized cultural products. In the latter 1980s the blood epics, like sex films, shifted to video and the private home as the preferred site for consumption. The resulting decentralization of consumption, as compared with theatrical viewing, assisted in the distribution of renegade material. The huge shelves of gory horror titles in video stores (including those that, like Blockbuster, will not stock sex films) demonstrates the continued viability of splatter films. Moreover, the popular fascination with their serial-killer heroes that so alarmed critics in the early 1980s has continued to thrive, as the Web pages devoted in cyberspace to Jason, Freddy Krueger, and other filmic butchers demonstrate today.

Brian De Palma's DRESSED TO KILL and BODY DOUBLE epitomized for many feminists the violent misogyny that seemed to proliferate throughout eighties horror. In contrast to low-budget quickies like MANIAC, De Palma's films gained high visibility from major studio advertising campaigns, and DRESSED TO KILL did very respectable box office in 1980. It focused on a cross-dressing psychiatrist (played by Michael Caine) who commits a series of razor murders, most prominently a brutal slashing attack on a woman, Kate Miller (played by Angie Dickinson), in an elevator. This killing was modeled on the shower murder of Marion Crane in Hitchcock's PSYCHO, as much of De Palma's work patterned itself on Hitchcock films. Yet whereas the sequence in PSYCHO is clinical and dispassionate (and terrifies because of this), the attack in the elevator is more graphic, more prolonged, and more attentive to the anxiety and struggles of the victim to survive. Of key importance, the graphic violence is visited upon a character whose intimate sexual desires and responses the viewer has witnessed. Marion Crane, too, was conducting an adulterous affair in PSYCHO, but the film's action begins after her lunchtime tryst with Sam Loomis has ended. By contrast, DRESSED TO KILL opens with a sensuous, sexual episode with Kate in the shower, and the scene's relative explicitness invites the (male) viewer to enjoy the voyeuristic pleasures that it offers. After evoking Kate's sensuality, the narrative then punishes her for this. She learns that her lover may have given her a sexually transmitted disease, and subsequently she is attacked in the elevator. The escalating severity of her punishments follows directly upon the expression of her sexual pleasure in the opening scene. Thus, DRESSED TO KILL is more graphically violent and more explicitly sexual than PSYCHO, and it conjoins the violence and the sex more intensively and punitively than had Hitchcock, who, by contrast, merely pointed to both conditions.

More audacious yet in its linking of sex and violence, BODY DOUBLE went beyond the previous film's razor killing to offer the decade's ghastliest sequence of sexual slaughter in a mainstream film. The film's plot was modeled on Hitchcock's REAR WINDOW (1954) and VERTIGO (1958), but it lacks their sophistication and elegance. Jake Scully (Craig Wasson), an unemployed actor in need of a place to stay, meets a fellow actor, Sam, who offers to let Jake tend the apartment of a friend who is out of town. The place is huge, with a wall of windows on one side that looks down on another apartment complex below. Using a telescope, Jake watches an attractive woman, Gloria Revelle, in the other apartment as she does a nightly seminude dance before her window. Like Jeffries in REAR

Gloria Revelle is menaced by the killer in BODY DOUBLE'*s appalling
drill murder scene*

WINDOW, Jake is emotionally drawn to this character, whom he watches with a long-focus
lens, and, like Scotty Ferguson in VERTIGO, he begins to follow her as she journeys about
on her daily routines. Jake grows alarmed when he repeatedly spies another man, apparently an Indian, also following Gloria and grows to feel that this character means her
harm. Indeed, he does, but unknown to Jake, the Indian is really Sam in a mask, and Sam
is really Alex Revelle, Gloria's husband, who is plotting her murder. Alex sets Jake up as
a witness to the murder, a witness who will say that an Indian did the killing.

The murder scene is extremely gruesome and horrific. It begins with Jake watching
Gloria through the telescope when he sees the Indian elsewhere in her apartment, carrying a huge power drill. Alarmed, Jake rushes out, trying to reach Gloria in time to warn
her, but of course, he cannot. As Gloria confronts the Indian in her bedroom, the viewer
realizes with horror that the drill will be the implement of murder. What follows is
drawn out at great and sadistic length, the better to prolong Gloria's torment and the
viewer's shock. The Indian tries several times to impale her, but she manages to wrest
free, though not without being bloodied in the attempt. When, finally, the killing occurs,
De Palma shows Gloria's frenzied face, wide-eyed in terror, as she falls backward to the
floor. The ensuing action is blocked from view by a sofa in the foreground, but the
viewer can see the drill vibrating in the killer's hands as it makes contact, and, in the next
shots from the floor below, the drill end punches through the ceiling, accompanied by a
torrent of blood. De Palma then shows the impaled body.

This appalling sequence has sexualized its violence so that it becomes difficult to find
an acceptably moral point of view on the carnage. As in DRESSED TO KILL, the violence
becomes a punitive response directed at a woman because of her sexuality. Gloria's window dancing establishes her as a sensual and sexually expressive character, and (improbable as this is) she responds erotically to Jake after he retrieves her purse from a thief.
The murder scene occurs in Gloria's bedroom with her partially dressed in a robe and

panties. In their struggles at one point, she and the killer both fall onto the bed. Moreover, while the oversized drill is patently absurd as a murder weapon, it functions quite vividly as a phallic image, and this association is accentuated by De Palma's low-angle camera positions. As a phallic emblem, the drill makes the killing into a kind of perverted sexual act, a veritable rape, which expresses contempt and loathing for the woman and her softness before the steel and rage of the man. The chain saw killing in SCARFACE was a horrendous scene as well, but what differentiates the two is precisely the sexualized aspects of the drill murder. The gangland killing was sadistic but nonsexual; Gloria's death is sexually sadistic. Thus, as a male filmmaker who had choreographed and orchestrated Gloria's end, there was no way for De Palma to evade the charges of feminists that it was a scene redolent of misogyny.

Subsequent narrative events in BODY DOUBLE intensified the film's tawdry aura. To solve the mystery of Gloria's death, Jake enters the world of pornographic filmmaking when he sees a porn actress, Holly Body (Melanie Griffith in an endearing performance), performing the same dance routine as Gloria. While there is no explicit sex associated with these scenes, De Palma's inclusion of the porn industry in the film's narrative seemed gratuitous and without structural foundation or requirement. Moreover, it encouraged the film's critics to tie the misogyny of the drill killing to the pornography sequences as evidence of both De Palma's outlook and the social values embodied by pornography in general. The commingling of graphic violence against women with the narrative setting of pornographic filmmaking epitomized for many of the film's feminist critics their charges that pornography was really an expression of violence against women and that Hollywood was now manufacturing such material.

DRESSED TO KILL and BODY DOUBLE outraged antipornography feminists who were organizing in the early 1980s around the issue of violent pornography. For them, the De Palma films represented the mainstreaming of pornography by the film industry. Janella Miller, for example, an antipornography attorney, wrote that BODY DOUBLE was "the latest movie in the stream of Hollywood offerings in which women are brutally murdered."[24] Their charges were echoed by some nationally prominent film critics. Andrew Sarris called DRESSED TO KILL "soft-core porn and hard-edged horror."[25] Antipornography feminists staged protests in front of theaters showing DRESSED TO KILL in major cities, including New York, San Francisco, Los Angeles, and Boston, and Women against Violence in Pornography and Media (WAVPM) issued a printed statement objecting, "From the insidious combination of violence and sexuality in its promotional material to scene after scene of women raped, killed, or nearly killed, DRESSED TO KILL is a master work of misogyny."[26] The protests, though, seemed to add to the film's box-office appeal, as its revenues continued to rise, and Doreen Leidholdt, of Women against Pornography (WAP), noted that the tactics of protest and demonstration had been counterproductive. "After DRESSED TO KILL, we realized that protesting the eroticizing of violence in Hollywood films was not effective. We had been especially scared about DRESSED TO KILL and wanted to educate the public that these movies were doing exactly what so much of violent pornography is doing."[27] Thereafter, WAP discontinued its practice of mounting protests in front of theaters.

De Palma's own pronouncements about his films helped inflame the atmosphere. After the production of SCARFACE (1983), he baited his critics by announcing, "I'm going to go out and make an X-rated suspense porn picture. . . . They wanna see suspense, they wanna see terror, they wanna see SEX—I'm the person for the job."[28] Though his next film, BODY DOUBLE, carried an R rating, in other respects, mainly its conjoining of violence with the narrative's world of pornographic filmmaking, De Palma seemed to have carried out his threat. In the wake of the critical animus roused by BODY DOUBLE, De Palma defended his right as a filmmaker to shape images and narratives as he saw fit. He claimed that he thought of using the power drill because more ordinary implements of murder had been used in stories so often they were no longer exciting. "I do a lot of murder mysteries; after a while you get tired of the instruments. Agatha Christie must've dealt with this day in and day out. You can use a knife, a rope, but now we have electrical instruments—which are truly terrifying." He noted that while people might discuss the social or political implications of a film, "those making the form should not be bound by these things." He added, "I'd hate to live in a world where art is left in the hands of the political people. I'd leave the country if it came to that—sounds like Russia." He maintained that political control of the arts quickly dissipates them: "In politically restricted societies where politicians control artists, you don't get interesting works of art." Countering the arguments of BODY DOUBLE's critics, De Palma disagreed with the view that watching sex and violence in movies makes some viewers want to go out and imitate what they had seen on screen. People aren't so easily influenced, he maintained: "If you have a misogynist outlook a sexist film could strike a chord in you, but I don't think it engenders sexism. I don't think women are beaten or raped because the rapist has been affected by the entertainment industry. If there were statistics to prove that, they'd be on the front page of every newspaper in the country."[29]

De Palma's attempt to define and stand behind First Amendment rights as a filmmaker was, of course, inadequate to defuse the controversy engulfing his work. It was inadequate partly because of his own inflammatory statements and because of the sensationalism of the films. But it also failed because the issues evoked by his work—the coupling of sex with violence in the media and with expressions of violence against women—transcended their incarnation in a single film or filmmaker. Those issues were now on the cultural agenda of the period. De Palma's work had helped put them there, but they were bigger than he or his films. Moreover, they intersected with the escalating offensive against film pornography, of which De Palma's works were regarded as mainstream variants. Feminist critics, as we have seen, attacked De Palma's films, but they also went after what they regarded as the source fueling Hollywood's recent glamorization of sexual violence.

The Offensive against Pornographic Films

The reaction against De Palma's films was especially heated because a concerted feminist attack on pornography had gathered considerable momentum in the early 1980s. The criticism of De Palma's work was, in significant ways, an offshoot of this more extended and broad-based initiative. Graphic sexual violence in mainstream movies and the increasing prevalence of pornographic materials in society came to be regarded as twin symptoms of one problem, namely, expressions of misogyny in contemporary visual culture. An unusual alliance had emerged between antipornography feminists and right-wing Christian fundamentalists over the perceived threat that pornography posed to women and the family. Groups like WAVPM and WAP organized against pornography and argued that it was a form of violence against women, as some feminist scholars had been suggesting in print since the 1970s. These included Kathleen Barry, Susan

Body Double's setting in the world of pornographic filmmaking added to its controversy.

Brownmiller, Susan Griffin, Laura Lederer, Gloria Steinem, and Andrea Dworkin.[30] These scholars argued that pornographic films, books, and magazines expressed a hatred of women, dehumanizing them as sex objects for the camera and for the male viewer or reader. Understood in these terms, pornography turned women into things and, by doing so, helped sustain a cultural atmosphere engendering misogynistic violence. Extending this analysis of pornography to legal principle, Dworkin and law professor Catharine A. MacKinnon crafted a legal strategy charging that pornography was a civil offense infringing on the rights of women to lead safe, secure lives. This approach became the basis for antiporn ordinances passed in Minneapolis and Indianapolis in 1983.

The Moral Majority supported the efforts of the antiporn feminists, and the Reagan administration backed the antiporn drive, convening an Attorney General's Commission on Pornography, headed by Edwin Meese, that opened hearings in 1985 into the social effects of pornographic films and other media. In 1980, Morality in Media had called for a task force of antiporn prosecutors, and the attorney general's commission aimed to furnish sufficient evidence of social harm to motivate a national crackdown on pornography. Thus, the byzantine cultural politics of the Reagan period produced the unlikely alliance of right-wing fundamentalists and antipornography feminists joined by a national, political, and legal effort to quash adult films, books, and magazines.

Because this seemed an alliance in support of censorship, it split the feminist movement. Prominent feminist scholars criticized the campaign against pornography by pointing out that pornography was not a single entity, but, like sexuality, was complex and differentiated, and they questioned the reflexive equation of porn with violence.[31] Moreover, they suggested that the antiporn movement risked reproducing the dominant gender ideologies that feminism had historically battled. "The anti-pornography movement in a sense restates the main premises of the old gender system: the dominant cultural ideology elaborates the threat of sexual danger, so the anti-pornography movement

The availability of adult titles on home video gave pornography a new level of cultural visibility.

responds by pushing for sexual safety via the control of public expression of male sexuality."[32] Furthermore, feminists outside the antiporn movement regarded its alliance with the political Right as dangerous. Ellen Carol DuBois and Linda Gordon noted that the "feminist attack on pornography and sexual 'perversion' in our time . . . fails to distinguish its politics from a conservative and antifeminist version of social purity, the Moral Majority and 'family protection movement.'"[33] The Christian and political Right was hostile to feminism, so that by joining with it, antiporn feminists risked advancing the cultural agenda of groups whose censorship activities wouldn't stop with pornography. Lawyer Alan Dershowitz noted, "The short-sightedness here is evidenced when you scratch just a bit below the surface of the alliance and discover that the very next group—after pornographers—on the Moral Majority's hit list are feminists."[34]

The unusual grouping of allies notwithstanding, the antipornography alliance achieved significant cultural power and an official governmental backing in the attorney general's commission. The key point for film history is that this offensive against pornography coincided with the entry of adult films into mainstream popular culture. The vehicle for this entry was the videocassette, which brought sex films out of tawdry theaters and into the nation's living rooms and bedrooms. Before this, pornographic films were available in a small number of urban theaters and as 8mm shorts sold in adult bookstores. This, though, was a restrictive set of outlets, and to get these materials a customer had to make a special trip to these locations. By contrast, video outlets nationwide maintained special adult sections of porn videos, making this class of material far more accessible and widely distributed than ever before. Porn films, of course, had already come "aboveground" before the advent of video. In 1972, DEEP THROAT, THE DEVIL AND MISS JONES, and BEHIND THE GREEN DOOR were shrewdly marketed to attract segments of the mainstream audience as well as porn devotees. The widespread publicity these films received was a significant initial step in the expansion of the porn film domain. The era of the porn feature film had begun.

It would be video, though, that reconfigured the porn industry. The shift to video enabled the adult industry to expand its output, reach a bigger slice of audience, and enjoy skyrocketing revenues. These transformations gave porn films an unprecedented cultural visibility in the 1980s and helped to trigger the antiporn backlash. The changeover to video from theatrical distribution of sex films was rapid, and it was assisted by zoning regulations designed to combat pornography. In 1980, the spread of zoning ordinances confining adult theaters to "red light" districts had resulted in the closure of approximately thirty to fifty theaters, and by 1983, though some seven hundred adult theaters continued to operate, videocassettes had begun to bite significantly into their business, which fell by 20 percent after another decrease the year before. While a given adult feature in 1983 might earn, at most, $200,000 from theater distribution (this from distribution of a mere twenty-four prints), video sales could easily net another $50,000.[35]

The move toward made-for-video pornography was therefore inexorable. HIGH SCHOOL MEMORIES (1980), DEBBIE DOES DALLAS (1978), and BABYLON PINK(1979) helped initiate the made-for-video trend, while the adult industry failed to protect its theatrical market by sequencing ancillary releases after theatrical, like the Hollywood industry did. A former president of the Adult Film Association of America noted, "Instead of first liquidating theatrical release, then, in order, videos, videocassette, cable-TV and regular TV, the last not really appropriate, adult films are released day-and-date in theaters and cassettes. . . . This has seriously hurt the theatrical attendance."[36] As attendance fell, some theaters responded by increasing their house nut (the portion of box-office receipts they retained), further eroding industry revenues from the theatrical sector. By 1986, the number of surviving adult theaters was estimated at two hundred and the revenue share from video and cable at 80 percent of the industry's total earnings.[37] Shooting a direct-to-video picture offered extraordinary savings on production expenses, from the $125,000 to $150,000 needed for a ten-day film production to as little as $25,000 for a one-hour video.[38] As we have seen in chart 3.8, 1984 and 1985 were the take-off years for adult video, with huge increases in the number of videos in general release. Revenues from the sale of adult tapes also climbed steadily in these years (chart 3.9). Thus, the years 1984 and 1985, which saw the explosive growth of adult video (and its accompanying cultural presence), correspond as well to the critical period during which the antipornography movement attained visibility and then strategic power with the convening of the Attorney General's Commission on Pornography.

Issuing its report in 1986, the commission concluded that pornography containing violent or degrading behavior was the most prevalent type of material currently available and, furthermore, that violent pornography caused crimes of violence against women.[39] This was a strikingly different conclusion from the one reached earlier by the President's Commission on Obscenity and Pornography, which in 1971 had found no evidence of harmful effects and declined to recommend legal restrictions on adult access to sexually explicit materials. The Meese report's findings and recommendations resulted in the formation of a National Obscenity Enforcement Unit, a team of federal prosecutors to assist local authorities, and a program of stepped-up prosecution of obscenity cases using RICO provisions for the seizure of assets at the time of indictment and the *Miller* decision's provision for violation of local community standards. This was a different and more effective application of *Miller*. Because a plethora of local communities existed nationwide, distributors of adult material, shipping across state lines or exhibiting their wares in different regions, risked incurring obscenity charges based on the stipulation that they were in violation of local community standards. Thus interpreted, obscenity became a highly fluid designation. The same film could be legally obscene in one locale and not in another. Using this approach, the Obscenity Enforcement Unit embarked on a series of sting operations, ordering sex materials from conservative communities and then prosecuting mail order distributors for shipping obscene materials in violation of the local standards.

Using another strategy, the unit brought multiple prosecutions, concurrently or consecutively, against an offender. These originated from different regions of the country and were designed to exhaust or bankrupt the legal defense resources of the targeted business. National distributors of pornography faced a new vulnerability to economic and legal attack and a substantial increase in legal risk incurred by the distribution of sex films and videos. During this renewed offensive against porn, investigations of adult pornography rose from 81 in 1981–85 to 222 in 1987–91.[40] But the industry, as we saw in chapter 3, remained robust through this period. The Reagan administration had won its legal war against pornography, but the traffic continued to flourish.

The efflorescence of the antiporn movement in the early and mid-1980s demonstrated the heat that symbolic cultural politics could generate and the effect on these cultural struggles of the new media of film distribution and their ancillary markets. Videotape did not merely revolutionize adult filmmaking. It transformed porn films from the enterprise of scattered, outlaw producer-filmmakers to an industry (albeit a stigmatized one) of substantial cultural reach (a truism in that in the early years of video rentals, most of a retailer's revenue came from the adult titles in the back room) and with its own festivals, stars, auteur directors, trade shows, and awards ceremonies. The fight over film, and then video, pornography was the decade's most heated, bitter, and fiercely-waged film controversy. It affected the debates over the sexual politics of violent horror films and mainstream Hollywood product (De Palma's work in particular), and it helped erode the cultural capital of Hollywood filmmaking when it assumed explicitly violent or sexual forms. Moreover, the popularity of film and video pornography helped efface the distinctions between images of explicit sexuality in Hollywood film and in graphic porn films, with sex in Hollywood films becoming ever more explicit, direct and sustained. Pictures like BODY HEAT (1981), CRIMES OF PASSION (1984), 9 1/2 WEEKS (1986), and BODY OF EVIDENCE (1993) demonstrate this influence.

Religious Outrage over THE LAST TEMPTATION OF CHRIST

The sex, violence, and pornography controversy raged for more than half of the decade, and while it posed the most extended and powerful challenge to business as usual in the American cinema, it was not the last such significant challenge of the 1980s. Martin Scorsese's THE LAST TEMPTATION OF CHRIST (1988) aroused the enmity of the Christian Right, which aimed a powerful volley of threats and protests at Universal/MCA, the picture's distributor, at Scorsese, and at exhibitors who contemplated booking the film. The picture was based on Níkos Kazantzákis's novel, which explored the human side of Christ, presenting him as subject to doubts, sexual urges, and other human vulnerabilities that constitute his last temptation.

Willem Dafoe plays Jesus in the film, and not only does he give an impassioned performance, but his face, hair, and beard strikingly resemble Christ as he is pictured in contemporary iconography. (Two years earlier, Dafoe had played the Christ-like Elias in PLATOON.) As the film begins, Jesus is tormented by voices and visions that cause him exquisite physical and psychic pain, and he is not sure if they come from God or Satan. In one of the film's fictional embellishments, he works at making crosses for the Romans, who are crucifying Jewish rebels; by doing so he hopes to make God hate him enough to stop the voices in his head. This anguished portrait of a humanly suffering Christ connects him, and the film, to Scorsese's other portraits of such lacerated characters as Travis Bickle and Jake LaMotta. Their psychological suffering and physical punishment achieve such intensity as to imply, and disclose, a spiritual dimension within

Martin Scorsese directs Barbara Hershey, Willem Dafoe, and Harvey Keitel on location for THE LAST TEMPTATION OF CHRIST.

their fleshly and otherwise secular ordeals. This confluence, and contest, of the fleshly and the spiritual is precisely what THE LAST TEMPTATION studies. Considered within the corpus of Scorsese's work, therefore, it is a logical outcome of the director's interest in the spiritual components of worldly existence. Scorsese had again partnered with screenwriter Paul Schrader, who scripted TAXI DRIVER (1976) and RAGING BULL (1980) and whose interest in rituals of physical ordeal and spiritual transcendence is a matter of record.

It would, however, be exactly this focus on the human dimensions of Christ's suffering that generated the critical response from sectors of the Christian community. The film takes Christ quite seriously and deals sincerely with issues of faith and spirituality, and it vividly portrays the celebrated events that transpire along Christ's passage toward the cross: the changing of water into wine, the raising of Lazarus from the dead, the conflict with the moneylenders in the temple. But unlike the tradition established by Hollywood's Bible pictures, the ancient world depicted here is not clean and sanitized. It is hot, dirty, and oppressive, with sand that abrades the skin. The depiction of Mary Magdalene's prostitution shows it as tawdry and unpleasant. It is not something alluded to in a parable but is shown as a physical act and thereby made tangible. Christ is shown as a social revolutionary, opposed to the Roman Empire and cognizant that his Gospel will cause its downfall. These are the political issues that precipitated Rome's response, and the film's depiction of these differentiates it from other Hollywood productions, which do not show the social conditions in which the Christ story is imbricated.

But of all these unorthodox depictions, the most significant for producing the film's controversy is the titular last temptation. As Christ hangs on the cross, Satan comes to him one final time in an effort to dissuade him from completing the sacrifice. Assuming the form of a bucolic child, the Devil pretends to be Christ's guardian angel, and he tempts Jesus' human side into forsaking its divinity. The angelic child removes the nails from Jesus' feet and hands and leads him away from the cross, promising that God has relented and no longer requires his sacrifice. Jesus then embarks upon a life of ordinary human pleasure. He lives as a man, marries, fathers many children (with several women), and grows old. On his deathbed, the disciples visit, and conversing with them, he realizes that without his sacrifice, there is no salvation for any. Moreover, he realizes that his life as a man has been the Devil's seduction, renounces that temptation, and reclaims his place on the cross and with God. The film ends here, with Jesus on the cross, comforted by the knowledge that he has, at last, fulfilled his holy purpose. (Considered in strict narrative terms, the last temptation episode makes little sense. Why, if the Devil is orchestrating this final temptation, would one of the disciples point out to Jesus that the child angel is really Satan? Surely Satan would have arranged events so as to exclude this possibility. It would be more convincing for Christ to make the discovery unaided and unprompted.)

For many Christians, the last temptation was an inflammatory sacrilege because it visualized a Jesus engaged in profane behavior (the sex and the siring of many children) and one who had renounced his Father and who had come to believe that the stories of his death and transfiguration were lies. (Other scenes in the film, as well, were controversial, such as one wherein Jesus watches Mary Magdalene having sex with a procession of customers.) The Jesus depicted here suffers a momentary but telling failure of nerve before the prospect of torturous death, and he willingly embraces his fleshly existence. Making matters worse in this regard, the film opened with a title card acknowledging that it was not based on the Gospels but was a fictional exploration of the conflict between spirit and flesh, and for many this fictional embellishment of the Gospels was tantamount to an attack upon them. But an alternative case can be made that, without temptation, there is no salvation, and that the film aimed to show the magnitude of Christ's sacrifice by exploring the implications and the agonies it posed for his human side.

Scorsese's Catholic heritage prompted him to take this premise quite literally and to make the picture as a portrait of these tensions between Christ's human and divine aspects. Reports of a sacriligious Hollywood film, though, circulated among the Christian Right, which commenced its protests well before the picture was completed and ready for release. In a public statement responding to the film's growing prerelease controversy, Scorsese said, "I believe it is a religious film about suffering and the struggle to find God. It was made with conviction and love and so I believe it is an affirmation of faith, not a denial. Further, I feel strongly that people everywhere will be able to identify with the human side of Jesus as well as his divine side."[41] He closed by asking people not to prejudge the picture before it was released.

Despite Scorsese's plea, reaction to the upcoming release was swift and bitter. Bill Bright, founder of the Campus Crusade for Christ, publicly offered Universal $10 million dollars for the negative and prints of the film so they could be destroyed. The Reverend Donald Wildman, head of the American Family Association, threatened Universal with economic ruin if it released the picture: "AFA will begin a boycott that will bankrupt MCA. You have my word on it."[42] The Reverend Jerry Falwell also threatened a boycott of MCA, and the Reverend R. L. Haymers, whose Fundamentalist Baptist Tabernacle actively demonstrated against the film, seemed to threaten violence, saying "If they're going to leave the sex scene during the dream sequence in, they can probably expect violence."[43] The furor took a nasty anti-Semitic turn. Universal head Sidney Scheinberg and MCA head Lew Wasserman were Jewish. Several activist groups implied that the picture was a Jewish plot to smear Christianity. The Los

Willem Dafoe, as Jesus, spreads the Gospel and elicits both converts and detractors.

Angeles–based Fundamentalist Baptist Tabernacle picketed the studio with signs and banners reading "Wasserman Endangers Israel" and "Wasserman Fans Jew Hatred with 'Temptation.'"[44] Director Franco Zefferelli referred in remarks broadcast on radio to "that Jewish cultural scum of Los Angeles, which is always spoiling for a chance to attack the Christian world."[45]

The protests sought to effect precensorship of the film by persuading exhibitors to refuse bookings and by intimidating Universal from releasing the picture. The MPAA issued a statement condemning censorship and affirming free expession, and the statement was signed on behalf of all the major studios. Prior to undertaking the production, Universal sought, and received, cofinancing from Cineplex Odeon, then the nation's second-biggest theater chain, thereby guaranteeing some playoff sites. Universal head Tom Pollock said that without the participation of Cineplex, the production could not have been approved. "I doubt we would have made the picture if we had not been a partner with Cineplex. . . . The fact that they co-invested in the movie with us assured us of exhibition."[46] The coventure with Cineplex was a wise move because the controversy persuaded several prominent exhibition chains from booking the film. These included General Cinema, Carmike Cinemas, Wometco Theaters, Luxury Theaters, and Edwards Theaters, accounting for more than two thousand screens.

The picture opened 12 August on nine screens, one each in New York; Los Angeles; Toronto; Chicago; Washington, D.C.; San Francisco; Seattle; and Minneapolis. Stimulated by the controversy, public curiosity was strong, and the picture's initial business was robust. The first three days' rental from the nine screens showing the film was $400,000. When the film went into a wider release one week later, however, business began to slacken. By year's end, Universal-Cineplex saw $3.7 million in rental returns, which equaled the picture's $3 million production budget.

The Christian Right had not succeeded in shutting the picture down or in intimidating Universal or the MPAA, which took strong First Amendment stands. But the controversy reinforced the widespread perception of Hollywood among the political Right as a godless industry whose products were corrosive to the spiritual health and values of the nation. The Christian Right, in particular, felt emboldened during the Reagan years to engage in skirmishes over political and artistic issues because President Reagan courted this voter bloc. Speaking at the Annual Convention of the National Association of Evangelicals in 1983, for example, Reagan told his audience that modern secularism was hostile to the fundamental values of civilization.[47] Coming from the president of the United States, this could be construed as an encouragment to police the nation's culture. Cognizant of these political currents and their cultural effects, the film's screenwriter, Paul Schrader, pointed out that Hollywood made a convenient target for political organizing because it was perceived by the Right as a morally corrupt community:

> A lot of the protest about THE LAST TEMPTATION OF CHRIST was really from an anti-intellectual wing of social and political Christianity. It doesn't have much to do with Christianity itself. They preempted the debate for a number of reasons. It didn't even matter whether they had seen the film, that was irrelevant to what was in it for them. They preempted the debate by saying *Hollywood* is seeking to defame our Lord, *we* are seeking to defend our Lord, please send us money, help us in this fight. Well, when couched in those terms, mainstream Christianity has to ally itself with fundamentalism—it's not going to ally itself with Hollywood.[48]

The fallout over THE LAST TEMPTATION OF CHRIST underscored the deepening alienation between Hollywood and large segments of the public, and it was intensified by the fact that the American film tradition was a thoroughly secular one. Outside of Hollywood Bible epics (THE TEN COMMANDMENTS [1956], BEN-HUR [1959]), there is no tradition of religious-themed filmmaking in the American cinema and certainly no exploration of spiritual issues within a religious context. This estrangement in American film from matters of spirit and religion helped make Scorsese's picture more conspicuous than it otherwise would have been. Without counter-examples to prove its good intentions and respect for spiritual issues, Hollywood was forced to rely on a First Amendment defense, which, as far as Christians upset over THE LAST TEMPTATION were concerned, was a lame maneuver. For them, the issue was not whether Universal/MCA had the right to make such a film, but that it would have made *this* film about religion in the absence of others. People are intensely serious about matters of religion and faith. This being so, it is difficult not to sense an element of arrogance in the industry's First Amendment claims. Coupled with its demonstrable lack of interest in religion as a subject for filmmaking, the industry's free speech defense seemed to embody a disregard for the Christian community the film had provoked and little recognition that this might be a legitimately sensitive topic. While it is commendable on principle that the industry took a First Amendment stance, this position hardly addressed the issues and conflicts at hand, and it served to further polarize the sides involved in the dispute. The LAST TEMPTATION fracas illuminated the problems and dangers that can result when a secular industry makes a rare and unconventional foray into religious territory.

The Effect of the Moral Controversies on the MPAA

How did the MPAA, as the film industry's representative, react to the protracted, decade-long period of agitation over the representational content of American film? The MPAA's historic mission had been to serve as a watchdog advancing the industry's interests and protecting it from meddling by outside governmental or public groups. As in the 1930s, when the Production Code Administration was created, the 1980s was a period of great agitation over the moral content of American film. It was therefore a time of potential crisis for the industry during which the buffer function the MPAA would be expected to play would be of vital importance.

The MPAA knew which way the political winds were blowing. It threatened, for example, to give Brian De Palma's DRESSED TO KILL an X rating unless he trimmed some of the film's violence. De Palma protested the cuts (but made them nevertheless), and Jack Valenti situated the conflict over the cuts in DRESSED TO KILL within the reigning sociopolitical context. The country's temperament had shifted. It was now more conservative, Valenti acknowledged, and the MPAA would be responsive to these changes. "The political climate in this country is shifting to the right, and that means more conservative attitudes toward sex and violence. But a lot of creative people are still living in the world of revolution."[49] De Palma charged that the MPAA was taking a tougher line with his film because of the bruising fight it had suffered over CRUISING and the accusations that it had misrated that picture. Doubtless it was, as the agency assumed its traditional role as mediator and buffer between the industry and its public. If it had not done so with CRUISING, it would act preemptively to minimize the bloodshed and nastiness of DRESSED TO KILL. But this film, too, became a flashpoint for criticism and demonstrated, for many of its critics, that the MPAA was still failing to police the industry effectively.

The CRUISING debacle put the MPAA on the defensive regarding the credibility of its ratings system, and the next few years intensified the debate over the usefulness of the CARA ratings. During the big horror film boom of 1980–81, some of the grisliest of the batch (ZOMBIE, MANIAC) were released without ratings because their distributors anticipated that, were the films submitted to CARA, they would receive an X rating (which was by then identified with porn films). Thus, the CARA system was of no help in alerting viewers to the content of these ultraviolent pictures. Furthermore, CARA had long been accused of being more permissive about violence in films than about sex, and in 1981 the National Coalition on Television Violence charged that Hollywood was responsible for unleashing a tidal wave of violent films. An NCTV official raised the (for the industry) dread specter of outside intervention. "Given its history—that the film industry has been allowed to self-regulate and it's failed—I prefer a civilian or government board."[50] The CARA ratings, then, were proving to be an ineffective way of informing the public about potentially objectionable material in films and of shielding viewers from the worst excesses of the resurgence of graphic violence in early eighties horror.

During this period the MPAA also faced an erosion of CARA's authority in terms of the video releases of CARA-rated theatrical films. Through mutual agreement of distributors and exhibitors, the CARA ratings had been implemented successfully in the area of theatrical exhibition, but what now of video, which provided an alternative outlet for distribution? Distributors could forgo theatrical entirely, releasing straight to video. Doing so, they could bypass CARA, and they could even release alternative versions of a film on video. These circumstances threatened the integrity of the ratings system. In 1984, the MPAA filed a trademark infringement suit against the theatrical and home video distributors of I SPIT ON YOUR GRAVE, a low-budget horror film that had been rated X by the MPAA in 1978 under the title DAY OF THE WOMAN. (While the filmmaking is exceptionally crude, the picture is nevertheless noteworthy for the way it reverses the sexual politics of slasher films and other graphically violent thrillers. The killer here is a woman exacting revenge on the gang of men who raped her, and the narrative point of view throughout is aligned with this character and her experiences. Rather than offering a sexually appealing female victim, as in De Palma's films, I SPIT ON YOUR GRAVE has a

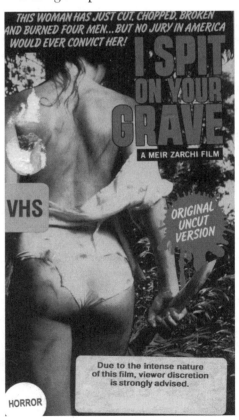

This low-budget horror film prompted a revision of the MPAA's ratings procedures for the theatrical and home video markets.

resourceful female hero and enlists the viewer's approval as she punishes her transgressors.) Cinemagic, the production company, then reedited the picture for theatrical distribution, toning down its violence, and the MPAA revised its initial rating, awarding it an R. The subsequent video release, however, contained the originally deleted seventeen minutes of violent footage (deletions that had shifted the theatrical version from X to R) even though the video, as distributed by Wizard Video, still carried CARA's R rating in its trademark boxed-R format.

The MPAA pointed out that this rating pertained to the revised 1978 cut of the picture, not to what was now being released on video. The MPAA's suit cited "irreparable damage to the MPAA and the credibility of its rating system" through such attempts to circumvent CARA's authority. The MPAA filed its suit in January 1984 and by August had reached agreements with all major video distributors to implement a universal procedure for use of MPAA ratings, which hereafter would designate versions of a film on videotape and disc that are identical to that released in theaters. Agreeing to the uniform policy were CBS/Fox Video, Embassy Home Entertainment, Independent United Distributors, Key Video, MCA Home Video, Media Home Entertainment, MGM/UA Home Video, MTA Home Entertainment, Paramount Home Video, RCA/Columbia Pictures Home Video, Thorn EMI, Vestron Video, Walt Disney Home Video, and Warner Home Video.[51]

With this agreement, the MPAA safeguarded the implementation of the CARA ratings in the ancillary video markets. Those ratings, however, had just undergone a significant alteration. Stung by heated criticism of the PG rating awarded to INDIANA JONES AND THE TEMPLE OF DOOM (1984), which shows a pulsating heart ripped from a man's chest, and by criticism of the violence in GREMLINS (1984, also PG), the MPAA reluctantly agreed to revise its rating categories by adding a new designation, PG-13, that would be an intermediate between PG and R. For years, Jack Valenti had been resisting suggestions that the MPAA revise its categories, but that changed on 27 July 1984 when PG-13 became official. The new category was a direct response to charges that the MPAA was soft on violence and that the violent content of some PG films was inappropriate for children.

PG-13, therefore, designated a film about which "parents are strongly cautioned to give special guidance for attendance of children under 13. Some material may be inappropriate for young children." The U.S. Catholic Conference charged that the new rating would dilute the usefulness of the R—that it would, in effect, label as PG-13 some films that previously would have been R. The boundaries between the ratings categories remained as fluid and problematic as ever, but PG-13 offered a new means for designating product that may have been too soft for an R but inappropriate for young children. Denying that PG-13 would substitute for the old R, Valenti said, "If the violence is real tough, if it is persistent, it still will go into R. What we have now and didn't have before is a way station between R and PG. If there are any doubts about a picture being a little tough for a PG, it will be a PG-13."[52]

Revision of the ratings categories demonstrated the MPAA's flexibility and shrewdness in maneuvering to respond to the tides of public and critical opinion that had been running against its ratings designations since the beginning of the decade. While the MPAA might still take a firm stand in support of First Amendment rights, as it did during the LAST TEMPTATION OF CHRIST fracas, it also worked, in its protective role, to mitigate public fallout over perceived excesses of violence and sex in the industry's products, recognizing, in Valenti's terms, that the national mood and culture had shifted

Controversy over Indiana Jones and the Temple of Doom
helped prod the MPAA to revise its ratings codes.

rightward during the decade. Furthermore, it stayed out of battles it perceived as peripheral to its members' interests. The legislative investigations and prosecutions of the adult film business, for example, drew little MPAA comment and no involvement.

Despite the MPAA's efforts to protect the legitimate film industry, though, by defending and then altering its ratings categories, the long-term consequences of the 1980s battles over movies and morality have been momentous. The double standard over permissible levels of sex and violence in American film still prevails, and the cumulative effect of so many films perceived as inappropriately rated has served to undermine the authority and validity of the CARA system. (An additional symptom of this was the 1990 revision that created an NC-17 designation to substitute for the old X on the theory that it would escape X's stigma and permit serious, nonexploitative adult-themed filmmaking. Almost instantly, though, NC-17 was labeled and rejected by the public and critics as X in a different costume, and the Hollywood majors avoided funding or distributing NC-17 pictures.)

In larger terms, the expansion of graphic sex and violence in eighties cinema helped produce a substantial moral estrangement between the industry and its public that continued and intensified in the 1990s when political struggles and culture wars over the arts reached new levels of acrimony. Summarizing the alienation from Hollywood experienced by what he regarded as a sizable segment of the public, critic Michael Medved wrote, "Few of us view the show business capital as a magical source of uplifting entertainment, romantic aspiration, or even harmless fun. Instead, tens of millions of Americans now see the entertainment industry as an all-powerful enemy, an alien force that assaults our most cherished values and corrupts our children. The dream factory has become the poison factory."[53] Whether or not Medved spoke for as large a public as he claimed, there is no disputing that an imposing community of viewers and citizens had come to find Hollywood a source for many of the nation's most enduring problems afflicting familes and children. While the Hollywood industry had long been subject to such criticism, it was unusually intense in the 1980s. Moreover, the volatility of the moral climate surrounding American film saw no resolution during that decade. Instead, a sustained and unabated period of crisis prevailed, and the Hollywood industry saw its cultural capital substantially eroded. That erosion has not been stopped; it continues into the present period. Thus, as the 1980s closed, the industry confronted its continuing and unresolved economic problems and an accumulating moral tarnish that it was unwilling to address in a substantive way. Neither of those conditions augured well for its future.

9

American Documentary in the 1980s

CARL PLANTINGA

The 1980s brought remarkable developments to documentary filmmaking in the United States. The decade witnessed the emergence of several promising and innovative filmmakers; the bold exploration of new techniques and styles; increased theatrical, video, and television distribution and exhibition; and significant efforts to educate the American public about social and political issues. By the end of the decade, more Americans were viewing documentaries than ever before, and interest in the documentary had reached an intensity not seen since the days of direct cinema and the social and political unrest of the 1960s. Despite consistent problems with funding and distribution, American documentary of the 1980s gathered a momentum that extended into the 1990s.

Before tracing the history of the genre, it is essential to circumscribe the use of the term *documentary*. The films falling under the rubric *nonfiction*—for example, social documentaries, nature, concert, comedy performance, IMAX, instructional, and promotional films—are too diverse to allow for a coherent historical or critical account. Thus I will follow conventional practice in setting aside one particular exemplar of nonfiction—the social documentary of feature length (over fifty minutes)—as my focus. Social documentaries deal with human society, broadly speaking, and range from biographies, autobiographies, and histories to films analyzing current social and cultural phenomena.[1]

This chapter emphasizes three aspects of documentary history in the 1980s: (1) the business of documentary filmmaking (financing, distribution, and exhibition); (2) the cultural functions of documentaries; and (3) developments in the art and technique of documentary filmmaking. Film is essentially a technological medium, and the history of documentary filmmaking technology might also be deemed important. Here, though, I devote little space to developments in technology, because the decade saw comparatively few important changes.

With only minor improvements, 1980s documentary filmmakers used equipment similar to that which sparked the *cinéma vérité* movement in the 1960s: lightweight 16mm motion picture cameras, sound recorders capable of recording synchronized sound, and a range of microphones suitable for varied situations and environments.[2] While *cinéma vérité* purists were dedicated to the use of existing light, the 1980s filmmaker more often used a lighting kit to supply sufficient light for exposure or to "sculpt" the image. Documentary filmmakers in the 1980s also had access to fast color film stocks that enabled color cinematography in low-light conditions. Thus, color was the norm and black-and-white film stock, for decades the hallmark of the documentary film, was rarely used.

The 1980s was the decade of the rapid development of small-format video and cable television. With a few exceptions, however, these affected distribution and exhibition more than the production of feature documentaries, as I describe below. Video enabled all kinds of novel activities, encouraging widespread home videography, the use of video for surveillance, and community-based video activism. Nonetheless, documentary films, whether destined for theatrical distribution or television broadcast, were still shot on film. Video production technology did have at least one use for the documentary filmmaker; it provided an easy and inexpensive means of testing potential interviewees for the camera. By the early 1980s, video was being used as a tool to test and select interviewees, and the practice became commonplace as the decade progressed.[3] In preparation for the filming of COMMON THREADS: STORIES FROM THE QUILT (1989), for example, directors Robert Epstein and Jeffrey Friedman conducted about fifty video interviews to enable them to select five interviews to record on more expensive film stock. Although technological factors such as these were not unimportant, the most significant developments lay in the economics, cultural import, and styles and techniques of American documentary of the 1980s.

The Business of American Documentary

The economics of documentary filmmaking in the 1980s were governed by two major factors. The first—that documentary films were rarely profitable for their makers—was hardly unique to the 1980s, but nonetheless important to an understanding of the genre. Documentary filmmakers were forced to spend a good deal of their time raising funds before production and securing distribution after. As documentary director Jon Else says, "Half the battle in making documentaries is finding subjects which embody an emotionally charged drama, lived by people worth caring about. . . . The other half is finding the money."[4]

Second, the increasing pervasiveness of television and video blurred the distinction between film and television documentaries. Successful theatrical distribution was an outcome few documentary filmmakers counted on and fewer achieved. For many documentaries, the largest audiences were found on public television, and thus many filmmakers turned to the Corporation for Public Broadcasting for financing. Although the commercial television networks tended to avoid feature-length documentaries and typically broadcast only in-house programming anyway, the situation was different with public television. On the various Public Broadcasting System (PBS) stations in the 1980s, serious documentaries were common. The most prestigious regularly scheduled documentary series was "Frontline," but other series such as "Odyssey" and "American Masters" also showed interesting films. Moreover, the Corporation for Public Broadcasting developed various schemes (of questionable success) to fund independent documentary filmmaking, as I describe below. One sign of this blending between film and television documentary was that the Academy of Motion Picture Arts and Sciences began to nominate for best feature documentary programs designed specifically for various PBS television series.[5]

Given the meager financial returns expected by most documentary filmmakers, fundraising and securing distribution were (and still are) an integral aspect of documentary filmmaking. As one observer wrote in the early 1980s, "If you don't think raising money for a documentary film is creative, and if you don't think getting a film circulating safely in the world is creative, you don't understand a massive portion of the documentary filmmaker's craft and art."[6] The cost of an hour-long broadcast-quality film might be $150,000 to $250,000, and given the difficulty in making profits, a documentary filmmaker would most likely be searching for grants and benefactors rather than investors. The four sources of funding were federal and state programs, foundations, corporations, and individuals (supporters, relatives, or friends). Various organizations might grant varied amounts of money, but a filmmaker could usually count on stiff competition for every dollar. For small amounts—up to $25,000—a filmmaker could solicit state and local arts councils, private foundations, church groups, and individual investors. One could also apply to the Independent Film Program of the American Film Institute for such grants. Larger grants were sought from the National Endowment for the Arts, state and local humanities organizations, foreign television systems such as West Germany's ZDF, and the Corporation for Public Broadcasting.[7] The Film Fund, an organization specializing in financing social-issue documentaries, offered some support until its demise in 1986.

For independent documentary filmmakers, the National Endowment for the Humanities was often the most generous source of grant money for "humanities projects in the media." Between 1980 and 1989, annual NEH Media Grants, including grants-in-kind, totaled between $8.6 and $10.6 million, with the exception of 1982 ($5.1 million), when President Ronald Reagan and his budget director, David Stockman, slashed funding for the NEH. Funding levels for media projects rose and fell during the 1980s, but the trend was slightly downward while production costs grew throughout the decade. The biggest funding year was 1980 (at $10.6 million), and by 1989 funding had fallen to $10.3 million.[8] Fiscal year 1980 saw 291 applications and 83 grants awarded. The 1980 awards ranged from $4,000 to $1 million and averaged $114,000. Not all of the NEH Media Grant money went to documentary productions, of course, but also to radio programs, fiction films, and scriptwriting projects.

Some documentary filmmakers were able to fund their projects through one or two major sources, thus cutting the time devoted to fundraising significantly. At NEH, the larger grants typically awarded for documentary projects ranged between $150,000 and $250,000, but only a few filmmakers each year could count on such generous support. Home Box Office funded some excellent documentaries, including Bill Couturie's DEAR AMERICA: LETTERS HOME FROM VIETNAM (1987) and COMMON THREADS: STORIES FROM THE QUILT. Filmmakers occasionally won full support from an arts agency or other institution. An example is Ross Spears's AGEE (1980), which lists the Tennessee Arts Commission as its sole funding source. Ken Burns's popular nine-part documentary THE CIVIL WAR (1989) was financed in large part by General Motors.

Filmmakers were usually forced to seek funds from many different sources, however, and financing involved major work in grant writing and other forms of solicitation. For a typical example, Ken Burns's BROOKLYN BRIDGE (1981), produced before Burns had become a celebrated filmmaker, lists among its funding sources the New York

Council for the Humanities, the National Endowment for the Humanities, the Public Television Stations of New York State, Citibank, Abraham and Strauss, the American Society of Civil Engineers, New York Telephone, Consolidated Edison, and the New York State Council for the Arts. The producer of the PBS civil rights history EYES ON THE PRIZE (1987), Henry Hampton, worked for six years to obtain the $2.5 million required for the first six shows. He eventually gained support from no fewer than forty-four underwriters.[9] Robert Epstein and Richard Schmiechen held fund-raisers and even direct-mail campaigns to complete THE TIMES OF HARVEY MILK (1984), and were certainly not alone in those practices.[10]

The scarcity of funds also put constraints on documentary style and subject matter. Of course, each funding institution provided guidelines for the kind of projects it would fund, and political considerations often played a role in the grant-making process. The National Endowment for the Humanities is a case in point. The NEH Media Grants were for

Candidate Harvey Milk campaigns for the position of San Francisco city supervisor. From THE TIMES OF HARVEY MILK *(1984).*

projects about subjects central to the humanities. The emphasis, therefore, was on solid scholarship and clarity and effectiveness in its presentation—the documentary as a vehicle to treat a subject in the humanities. Such requirements encouraged conservatism in style and technique, and a filmmaker interested in exploring new directions in documentary style had to look elsewhere for funding.

"Acceptable" topics and political perspectives were also prescribed by the NEH and were subject to the vicissitudes of the changing political climate. In the late 1970s and early 1980s, the NEH had funded widely seen progressive documentaries such as THE LIFE AND TIMES OF ROSIE THE RIVETER (Connie Field, 1980), THE GOOD FIGHT (Mary Dore, Noel Buckner, Sam Sills, 1983), and SEEING RED (Jim Klein and Julia Reichert, 1983). The Reagan administration soon decided to define the humanities more narrowly, and the NEH closed its doors to explicitly political documentaries. New guidelines announced in 1984 under William Bennett, NEH chairman since 1981, declared ineligible projects that "advocate a particular program of social action or change."[11] The perception among many filmmakers was that politically or stylistically progressive projects were increasingly unlikely to receive federal funding. Filmmakers making documentaries about Latin America—for example, Deborah Shaffer, Susana

Muñoz, and Glenn Silber—all reported funding prejudices against various projects. As Shaffer said, "Under the Carter administration the funding appointees in federal foundations were interested in topics like labor history. Now it's Great Works of Literature."[12] Susana Muñoz and Lourdes Portillo produced the 1985 film Las Madres: the Mothers of Plaza del Mayo, about Argentinean women who bravely protested the kidnapping and disappearance of their sons and daughters by the military Junta. The film was eventually nominated for an Academy Award, but the filmmakers report that federal moneys from the NEA, NEH, the Corporation for Public Broadcasting, and the federally funded American Film Institute were closed to them. In Muñoz's words, "Obviously, the trend is now toward safe, mild stuff."[13]

Throughout the 1980s, documentary filmmakers turned to public television organizations for funding. For seven years, between 1977 and 1984, independents could apply for money from the Independent Documentary Fund. The fund had been set up by David Loxton, a producer with WNET New York, and it was financed largely by the Ford Foundation and the National Endowment for the Arts. Grants were evaluated by peer paneling, and David Loxton oversaw projects as executive editor. Among the many significant films financed in part or in whole by the fund was the Academy Award–winning The Times of Harvey Milk; Les Blank's film about director Werner Herzog at

During World War II, women worked in heavy industry, doing jobs formerly reserved for men. From Connie Field's The Life and Times of Rosie the Riveter *(1980).*

work, Burden of Dreams (1982); and Errol Morris's look at small-town eccentrics, Vernon, Florida (1980). Although the Independent Documentary Fund was welcomed by filmmakers, it served only a few of them. Moreover, the projects it funded were still overseen by a public television producer (Loxton) and thus, in the opinion of some, were not truly independent.

It is also important to understand the role of the Corporation for Public Broadcasting (CPB) in financing and showing independent documentaries.[14] The function of CPB was in part to fund programming for public television. Although it procured its monies largely from the federal government, it was designed as an independent entity to minimize governmental intrusion into programming decisions. Independent filmmakers argued that CPB should reserve some of its funding for truly independent work by filmmakers wholly outside the public television system. After vigorous lobbying by various coalitions of independent filmmakers, the 1978 congressional bill for public television funding directed the CPB to reserve "a substantial amount" of its programming funds for independent filmmakers, with 1980 given as a deadline for compliance. This provision brought continuous and sometimes rancorous debate among independents, PBS, and CPB about the intent of Congress and the meaning of the word *independent*. It also initiated competition between local public television stations and independent producers for the funds reserved for "independents."

Lewis Freedman, who began as director of the CPB program fund in 1980, was responsible for complying with the congressional mandate to provide "a substantial amount" of funding to independents. Rather than create an independent agency or turn money over to the Independent Documentary Fund, he instead created two ill-fated series, "Matters of Life and Death" and "Crisis to Crisis," designed to showcase independent productions. Whether such programming could justifiably be called independent was doubtful, but it remained a moot question, since both series failed to become a part of the PBS core schedule.[15] Freedman next turned to the "Frontline" documentaries to meet the congressional mandate; "Frontline" executive producer David Fanning had promised to use independent producers for his series. Independents, however, argued that these producers would not be independent but "freelance," since their programs and ideas would be subject to the editorial standards of the series they worked for.

David Hull, who succeeded Freedman as director of the CPB program fund in 1983, created an Open Solicitation Fund of $5 million per year. The funds, however, were open not only to independents but also to PBS stations. Moreover, there was no guarantee that grant winners could show their work on public television. After more intense lobbying by coalitions of independent producers, Congress in 1988 wrote a provision into the public television funding bill directing the CPB to provide $6 million per year for three years to an Independent Production Service. Implementation of the funding was extremely slow, and the first show funded as a result of this mandate did not appear on PBS until the 1992–93 season.

An encouraging development for independent filmmakers was the genesis of a new PBS series, "P.O.V." (the letters of the title denoting "point of view"), which since 1988 has shown ten to twelve independent documentaries per season. Some of the films shown by the series generated controversy at local PBS stations and nationally. The airing of Marlon Riggs's Tongues Untied (1989) caused the most consternation. A funny and angry film about what it is like to be black and gay, Tongues Untied caused North Carolina senator Jesse Helms to argue for funding cuts to the National Endowment for the Arts, which had partially funded the film. Helms, arguing that Riggs's film "blatantly

Marlon Riggs's 1989 film Tongues Untied, *about the experience of black gay men, caused controversy about the public funding of documentaries and art.*

promoted homosexuality as an acceptable lifestyle," used the documentary as a rallying point for the push to purge public television of its "liberal bias."[16]

From its very beginning, PBS had to market P.O.V. carefully, as consisting of films driven by personal visions (points of view) and thus not subject to made-for-television aesthetics or conventional standards of objectivity. Documentaries shown during the first season included Deborah Shaffer's Fire from the Mountain (1987), on Nicaraguan history and politics; Lucy Winer and Paula de Koenigsberg's Rate it X (1986), about sexism in American culture; Las Madres: the Mothers of Plaza del Mayo; The Good Fight, about Americans serving in the Spanish Civil War; and Errol Morris's Gates of Heaven (1978), a brilliant study of two pet cemeteries in California and the people who run them.[17] Through the 1990s, "P.O.V." continued to be the most important television outlet for the screening of independent documentaries. In public television, uncertain and unstable funding discourages the production of creative and risky programming. Scarcity of funding, William Hoynes argues, breeds a "mentality of scarcity and dependence" and a "logic of safety."[18] A result is a rhetoric of objectivity and fairness. "P.O.V.," on the other hand, is clearly identified as a program that transcends such standards. Thus it not only provided an opportunity for independent filmmakers to screen their work for large audiences; it also allowed for some of public television's most innovative and provocative programming.

As mentioned above, few documentaries in the 1980s enjoyed the large sums of money brought by successful theatrical distribution. Despite what *Variety*'s Richard Gold called "the current boomlet in theatrical documentaries" in the mid-1980s, Gold also noted that "the consensus is that documentaries remain the toughest of all sells to exhibitors, draw the smallest advances and return the most marginal profits in the picture business."[19] Of the American nonperformance documentaries of the 1980s, only the wildly successful ROGER AND ME (1989), at $6.7 million, grossed over $5 million in box-office receipts. After ROGER AND ME, the most successful American documentary films were KOYAANISQATSI (1983) at $3.2 million, IMAGINE: JOHN LENNON (1988) at $2.2 million, HELL'S ANGELS FOREVER (1983) at $2 million, STREETWISE (1985) at $1.8 million, and THE THIN BLUE LINE (1988) at $1.2 million.[20] Small as these returns were compared to commercial fiction films, they were nonetheless cause for some optimism.

This may seem a dismal record in comparison with the expectations of mainstream Hollywood, but several observers noted that by the mid to late 1980s, more United States commercial cinemas than ever before were showing documentary films.[21] The breakthrough film was Barbara Kopple's HARLAN COUNTY, U.S.A. (1976), the first independently made social documentary to gain widespread theatrical distribution. Next came THE ATOMIC CAFE, which grossed over $1 million in 1982.[22] As the decade progressed, greater numbers of documentaries were being shown in theaters. For a documentary, a successful theatrical run was not measured with a Hollywood yardstick. Most documentaries were distributed on 16mm rather than the usual 35mm, and since 16mm venues were rare, a $500,000 box-office gross would be considered a major success. Documentaries would typically open in one or two cities, hope for publicity or good reviews, then move out gradually. The Ken Burns film HUEY LONG (1985), for example, received positive reviews, including mention on the PBS review program "Sneak Previews." This enabled the distributor to move the documentary into twenty-four cities, and the film eventually grossed around $600,000.[23] Because advertising budgets were typically minuscule, filmmakers depended on free publicity to get the word out. Publicity came from reviews in the popular media, of course, but also from screenings and awards at major film festivals.

A major coup would be to win a nomination for an Academy Award for best feature documentary. Winning an Oscar was apparently a much-coveted goal, and during the late 1980s and into the 1990s, significant controversy was generated by the Oscars nomination process. To put it bluntly, none of the films most favored by either the critics or the public managed to get nominated for best feature documentary. In 1989, forty-five filmmakers (including Pamela Yates, Spike Lee, and Louis Malle) signed and circulated an "Open Letter to the Film Community" in which they expressed "outrage" that the overwhelming critical and popular success of the year, Michael Moore's ROGER AND ME, was passed up for an Academy Award.[24] It was not simply that Moore's film was ignored, however; resentment had been building for some time. At issue was the method by which films were nominated, the makeup of the nominating committee, charges of conflict of interest, and the perception that the nominating committee had priggish ideas about what constituted a "proper" documentary. This controversy about documentaries and Oscars escalated in the 1990s, when films such as PARIS IS BURNING, 35 UP, HEARTS OF DARKNESS, A BRIEF HISTORY OF TIME, EMPIRE OF THE AIR, BROTHER'S KEEPER, and HOOP DREAMS all failed to win nominations.[25] Prominent film critic Roger Ebert suspected a conspiracy on the part of Hollywood to protect big studio interests, suggesting that "the Academy wishes the documentary makers would drop dead and go away and not take time away from the glamorous promotion of features. This is getting embarrassing."[26]

Lost in all the hoopla was the unfortunate fact that being nominated for an Academy Award, while it might increase visibility for a film, rarely helped much in theatrical distribution. The 1985 Academy Award winner BROKEN RAINBOW deals with the effects of Congress's decision to give to the Hopi tribe some land formerly settled by Navajo Indians and the forced relocation this caused. Filmmakers Victoria Mudd and Maria Florio attribute their limited theatrical success to winning the Oscar. As Florio claimed, "If we'd only gotten the nomination, the film would have been forgotten; it would play Sunday mornings at one L.A. art theater, and that would have been the end of that."[27] Despite Florio's testimony, however, the Oscars usually influenced theatrical distribution very little, and the public seemed to sense the chasm between what they found interesting and what the nominating committees thought were good documentaries. Few of the public's favorites were ever nominated for Academy Awards, and those that were nominated did not fare especially well at the box office.

Documentary filmmakers did not have to rely solely on commercial theatrical distribution for revenue. Some filmmakers, including Mudd and Florio, took distribution into their own hands and organized screenings outside the regular theatrical venues. Filmmakers could tap the market generated by educational institutions and special interest groups. BROKEN RAINBOW showed in theatrical runs in San Francisco, Los Angeles, and Denver. In addition, it was shown by hundreds of private groups who rented a print for $175 or held benefits in which portions of the proceeds would go to the filmmakers and the rest to the Navajo cause.[28] Many documentary filmmakers, realizing where their chief market lay, produced educational study guides to accompany their films on video. When one purchases or rents Meg Switzgable's 1982 IN OUR WATER, a film that well illustrates the kind of roadblocks a citizen encounters when taking on polluting corporations, one also gets a study guide made possible by a grant from J. C. Penney.

Distribution continued to be a major problem for documentary filmmakers, and many were disappointed to find that, after years of work and the production of a worthwhile film, few people took notice. While home video sales became increasingly important as a means of distribution, documentaries often found themselves squeezed out by fiction films and economies of scale. A video copy of FAST TIMES AT RIDGEMONT HIGH (1982) or INDIANA JONES AND THE TEMPLE OF DOOM (1984) could expect massive video sales, and low prices could be set accordingly. Even when a documentary was distributed on video, the distributor could expect comparatively few sales and often set a much higher sales price. Thus many lesser-known documentaries were priced out of the home video market.

Documentaries and American Culture

With a basic understanding of how documentaries were financed and distributed in 1980s America, we now turn to how these films were used in American culture and to what purposes they were put. Given the difficulties of financing and distribution, documentary filmmakers rarely had profits as a primary motivation for making films; typically they were enthusiastic about the craft of filmmaking, fascinated with the subjects of their films, or strongly committed to initiating social change through their work. American documentaries stood at the margins of 1980s mainstream culture but played important roles nonetheless. One role was to present progressive alternatives to mainstream politics and social thought, as I detail below. Another was to offer informative and in-depth films at a time when the television networks increasingly turned to the newsmagazine format and away from in-depth documentaries.

The 1980s saw a continuation of a function that documentaries can perform particularly well, namely, to provide a visual and aural record of and information about a whole range of issues. The kinds of subjects dealt with by filmmakers tended to cluster around common concerns, but were ultimately as diverse as the filmmakers themselves, ranging from female body builders in PUMPING IRON II: THE WOMEN (George Butler, 1985) to the Hell's Angels in HELL'S ANGELS FOREVER (Richard Chase, 1983) to homeless street children in Seattle in STREETWISE (Martin Bell, May Ellen Mark, and Cheryl McCall, 1985). Frederick Wiseman, a well-known American documentary filmmaker since the late 1960s, continued to make direct cinema films about American institutions at the rate of about one film per year. Among these are MODEL (1981), about the fashion industry; DEAF (1986), on the experiences and culture of the deaf; MISSILE (1987), on life at a nuclear missile facility; and NEAR DEATH (1989), about the institutional practices surrounding death and dying. Les Blank produced more of his joyful explorations of the folk cultures of various American ethnic groups with films such as J'AI ÉTÉ AU BAL (I WENT TO THE DANCE) (1989), on the Cajun and Zydeco music of Louisiana, and IN HEAVEN THERE IS NO BEER? (1984), about polka music and dancing. Blank also contributed BURDEN OF DREAMS (1982), a fascinating study of German filmmaker Werner Herzog on location in the jungle to shoot FITZCARRALDO (1982). Other filmmakers and institutions were intent on regional interests. Ross Spears, for example, concentrates on southerners and the South with his 1980 film AGEE and LONG SHADOWS (1987), examining the cultural legacy of the Civil War. Appalshop, a nonprofit folk arts cooperative, continued to make documentaries about Appalachia.

Numerous film biographies offered accounts of the lives of the famous and noteworthy, for example, PAUL ROBESON: TRIBUTE TO AN ARTIST (Saul Turell, 1980), EIGHT MINUTES TO MIDNIGHT: A PORTRAIT OF DR. HELEN CALDICOTT (Mary Benjamin, 1981), PORTRAIT OF MAYA ANGELOU (David Gruber, 1982), BURROUGHS (Howard Brookner, 1983), FREDERICK DOUGLASS: AN AMERICAN LIFE (William Greaves, 1984), GEORGE STEVENS: A FILMMAKER'S JOURNEY (George Stevens, Jr., 1985), THOMAS HART BENTON (Ken Burns, 1988), the excellent film ADAM CLAYTON POWELL (Richard Kilberg and Yvonne Smith, 1989), and SUPER CHIEF: THE LIFE AND LEGACY OF EARL WARREN (Judith Leonard and Bill Jersey, 1989).

American history was a favorite topic. While Ken Burns is best known for his historical series THE CIVIL WAR (1989), he also produced BROOKLYN BRIDGE (1981), THE SHAKERS: HANDS TO WORK, HEARTS TO GOD (1984), HUEY LONG (1985), THE STATUE OF LIBERTY (1985, with Buddy Squires), and THOMAS HART BENTON. Other valuable historical documentaries include the public television films VIETNAM: A TELEVISION HISTORY (1983), EYES ON THE PRIZE: AMERICA'S CIVIL RIGHTS YEARS and EYES ON THE PRIZE II: AMERICA AT THE RACIAL CROSSROADS, 1965–1985 (both Henry Hampton, 1989), THE DAY AFTER TRINITY: ROBERT J. OPPENHEIMER AND THE ATOMIC BOMB (John Else, 1981), and RADIO BIKINI (Robert Stone, 1987). Although the most striking 1980s films about Vietnam were fiction films, documentary filmmakers continued to explore the war and its aftermath. Two notable films include SOLDIERS IN HIDING (Japhet Asher, 1985) and DEAR AMERICA: LETTERS HOME FROM VIETNAM (Bill Couturie, 1987).

The medium of film is well suited to record musical performances because film not only records the sound of the performance but also its visual details. Some 1980s films about music and performers not only recorded the performances but also aquainted us with the musicians and their culture. Among the best of these is FROM MAO TO

Two of the thousands of polka dancers appearing in Les Blank's IN HEAVEN THERE IS NO BEER? *(1984).*

MOZART: ISAAC STERN IN CHINA (Murray Lerner, 1980), which follows Stern's fascinating trip to mainland China to meet with and teach classical musicians there. SAY AMEN, SOMEBODY (George T. Nierenberg, 1984) uses *cinéma vérité* techniques to show us some of the personalities important in African-American gospel music. Penelope Spheeris provides valuable cultural documents with her THE DECLINE OF WESTERN CIVILIZATION (1980), on punk music and culture, and THE DECLINE OF WESTERN CIVILIZATION, PART II: THE METAL YEARS (1988).

While many documentary filmmakers in the 1980s worked within the bounds of mainstream political and social thought, just as many were part of a noticeable progressive movement in social issues and foreign policy. The decade saw a wider diversity of filmmakers who made films about social issues that the mainstream media tended to avoid. There was an explosion of filmmaking by women, ethnic minorities, and gays during the 1980s. In part this was due to a perceived need to deal with pressing issues being ignored in the mainstream media. Filmmaking by women and minorities was also made possible by the fact that financing for documentary films was not governed by the so-called free market but came primarily from government sources (NEH, NEA, CPB, state humanities councils, etc.) bent on granting funds to a diversity of filmmakers.

During the 1980s, many documentary films squarely confronted issues of gender, ethnicity, sexuality, and American foreign and domestic policy, most often from a leftist perspective. Many of these films' makers were educated during the turbulent sixties and now had the maturity and resources to use the film medium for their activism. For example, while the Reagan administration was waging a covert war on the Sandinistas in Nicaragua and supporting military regimes in South and Central America, American documentarists were busily making films explicitly and implicitly critical of American foreign policy. Numerous documentaries appeared in the 1980s dealing with political problems in South America and especially Central America—so many, in fact, that the film journal *Cineaste* was able to offer two separate surveys of films about those regions.[29] Deborah Shaffer, for example, directed several such documentaries in the 1980s, including NICARAGUA: REPORT FROM THE FRONT (1984, with Ana Maria Garcia and Glenn Silber), WITNESS TO WAR: DR. CHARLIE CLEMENTS (1984), FIRE FROM THE MOUNTAIN (1987), and DANCE OF HOPE (1989). DANCE OF HOPE was filmed in Chile near the end of the Pinochet rule; FIRE FROM THE MOUNTAIN is a look at the war in Nicaragua through the eyes of Nicaraguan writer and former guerrilla Omar Cabezas; WITNESS TO WAR, for which Shaffer won an Oscar for best short documentary, tells the story of Dr. Charlie Clements, an Air Force Academy graduate and Vietnam veteran who spends a year in El Salvador with the rebels attending to their medical needs. Also of importance is WHEN THE MOUNTAINS TREMBLE (1982), by Pamela Yates, Tom Sigel, and Peter Kinoy, a film about political oppression in Guatemala and U.S. complicity in supporting a corrupt regime there.

The 1980s also brought films about domestic social movements, most importantly about gender, race, ethnicity, sexual orientation, and homelessness, all calling for equal treatment and the cessation of discrimination and discriminatory practices. Films about gender and women's issues include the well-known THE LIFE AND TIMES OF ROSIE THE RIVETER (Connie Field, 1980), on women working in heavy industry during World War II; SOLDIER GIRLS (Joan Churchill and Nicholas Broomfield, 1981); RATE IT X (Paula de Koenigsberg and Lucy Winer, 1986); and INTERNATIONAL SWEET HEARTS OF RHYTHM (Greta Schiller and Andrea Weiss, 1986).[30] Films also appeared by and about racial and ethnic minorities, including (to name just a few) the work of William Greaves (BOOKER T. WASHINGTON: THE LIFE AND LEGACY [1982], FREDERICK DOUGLASS: AN AMERICAN LIFE [1984], BLACK POWER IN AMERICA: MYTH OR REALITY [1986], and IDA B. WELLS: A PASSION FOR JUSTICE [1989]), Marlon Riggs's ETHNIC NOTIONS (1987) and TONGUES UNTIED (1989), Christine Choy and Renee Tajima's MISSISSIPPI TRIANGLE (1985) and WHO KILLED VINCENT CHIN? (1988), and YO SOY (Jesus Salvador Trevino, 1985).[31]

Many filmmakers worked in the area of homosexual rights and the alarming AIDS epidemic. Two of the best of these films—brilliant documentaries by any standard—are THE TIMES OF HARVEY MILK (Robert Epstein and Richard Schmiechen, 1984) and COMMON THREADS: STORIES FROM THE QUILT (Robert Epstein and Jeffrey Friedman, 1989), both winners of Oscars for best feature documentary in their respective years.[32] Documentarians also confronted entrenched social issues such as homelessness, poverty, unemployment, and the prison system, with films such as DOWN AND OUT IN AMERICA (Joseph Feury and Milton Justice, 1986), PROMISES TO KEEP (Ginny Durrin, 1988), THE BRONX: A CRY FOR HELP (Brent Owens, 1988), LIGHTNING OVER BRADDOCK: A RUSTBOWL FANTASY (Tony Buba, 1988), ROGER AND ME (Michael Moore, 1989), and THROUGH THE WIRE (Nina Rosenblum, 1989). Other films deal with the history of labor and political movements. MILES OF SMILES, YEARS OF STRUGGLE (Jack Santino and Paul Wagner, 1983) tells the history of attempts by black

Pullman train car porters to unionize, and places their efforts in the larger context of the struggle for civil rights. THE GOOD FIGHT (Mary Dore, Noel Buckner, and Sam Sills, 1983) details the efforts of the Abraham Lincoln Battalion as they fought fascism in the Spanish Civil War. Finally, SEEING RED (Jim Klein and Julia Reichert, 1984) interviews onetime members of the American Communist party.

That most documentaries on social issues and foreign policy were both funded by government grants and had a progressive bent was not lost on the Reagan administration, which employed various means to curb such films. While Republican attempts to cut funding to both the NEA and the NEH were intermittently successful, funding levels generally remained constant throughout the 1980s while production costs rose. The struggle against "liberal" filmmaking, however, extended beyond levels of funding to attempts to redirect monies away from certain kinds of projects. As I noted above, the NEH, under director William Bennett, narrowed its definition of the humanities to exclude films that promote social causes. As Bennett said, "If you look at the record, you would form the opinion that the NEH was a national organization for raising social consciousness."[33] For Bennett and the Reagan administration, this was a negative.

One struggle that occupied the last half of the decade had to do with the United States Information Agency (USIA) and American documentaries exported to other countries. It was part of the business of the USIA to grant "education" certificates to documentary films. This enabled distributors to avoid high import taxes in sixty countries under a 1942 international treaty called the Beruit Agreement. During the early 1980s, the USIA under the Reagan administration had begun to deny certificates to certain films that espoused "liberal" political positions. These were films, for example, about Nicaragua (implying that the United States was the aggressor), uranium mining, and the threat of nuclear war.

The Center for Constitutional Rights brought a lawsuit against the USIA in 1985, arguing that such practices were arbitrary and violated the First Amendment to the Constitution. In 1986, a federal judge ruled that the regulations used by the USIA to approve distribution of films abroad were unconstitutional and far too vague. One of these regulations, for example, allowed the agency to deny special export status for films that attempted to "influence opinion, conviction or policy." The USIA responded to this ruling with new regulatory guidelines permitting it to label certain films as "propaganda" and thus deny them duty-free status, and requiring films to acknowledge viewpoints other than their own and represent "difference of opinion or other point of view."[34] In 1988, the Ninth Circuit Court of Appeals struck down these new regulations. Both decisions were seen as a victory for supporters of the First Amendment, denying the government the right to label films as propaganda on the basis of whether they criticize the policies of the current presidential administration.

During the 1980s, then, documentary filmmakers continued to make compelling and informative films about diverse issues. Despite attempts by the Reagan administration to curb the production of films it deemed "liberal" or "left-wing," the 1980s saw an energetic movement to make progressive films about domestic social issues and foreign affairs. Moreover, with the rise of videotape and cable television, more people than ever before were seeing serious documentary films. By the end of the decade the place of documentary film in the mainstream media was expanding on public television. Moreover, by offering an alternative to official politics and mainstream social thought, documentaries played an important social role in 1980s America.

The Art of American Documentary in the 1980s

By the "art" of American documentary I mean basically two things. The first is the craft of making documentary films and developments in the techniques and methods used by documentary filmmakers. The second depends on a conventional understanding of a "work of art" created by an artist. Here the concern is with creative films and emerging documentary filmmakers, especially those who show an interest in expanding the boundaries of conventional documentary styles and going beyond journalistic objectivity.

The documentary legacy of the 1960s, the movement known as direct cinema or *cinéma vérité*, provided a backdrop against which 1980s developments in documentary style can be assessed. *Cinéma vérité* was a style that emerged at the end of the 1950s, with the availability of new technologies. Lightweight cameras and sound equipment enabled the recording of 16mm images and synchronized sound with a crew of two persons moving independently of each other. This new technology allowed for unprecedented spontaneity and freedom in documentary filmmaking and encouraged an aesthetic of "reality." The goal for many became to "capture" reality on film and tape and to allow it to "speak for itself," or to present the material such that viewers are allowed freedom of interpretation. Various techniques that manipulated this pristine image and sound recording—for example, voice-over narration—were seen as authoritarian and artificial.

Cinéma vérité was criticized from the start, but by the 1980s it was clearly seen by many as theoretically misguided and too restrictive for the practicing filmmaker. It was misguided because it exaggerated the ability of the camera to provide an objective record of any scene or event. *Cinéma vérité* films could not escape the manipulation of the real that they so consciously tried to avoid, and the initial enthusiastic pronouncements of early *cinéma vérité* practitioners seem naive in retrospect. On the other hand, *vérité* techniques were restrictive because without voice-over narration, a musical score, and other creative devices, documentaries were unable to explicitly deal with abstract ideas. While *cinéma vérité* techniques were fine for capturing the sights and sounds of an event, they were less able to provide history, context, and analysis. In emphasizing the recording capabilities of the camera, *cinéma vérité* techniques also effaced the filmmaker. One of the most celebrated documentary filmmakers of the 1980s, Errol Morris (GATES OF HEAVEN [1978]; VERNON, FLORIDA [1980], THE THIN BLUE LINE [1988]), professed to admire the films of Frederick Wiseman, the best-known practitioner of *vérité* (although Wiseman rejects the term *cinéma vérité*). Yet Morris practiced a style of filmmaking that couldn't be further from Wiseman's. Morris says he tries to be "as obtrusive as possible" in making his films. "I believe cinéma vérité set back documentary filmmaking twenty or thirty years," he says. "There's no reason why documentaries can't be as personal as fiction filmmaking and bear the imprint of those who made them. Truth isn't guaranteed by style or expression. It isn't guaranteed by anything."[35]

Although Fred Wiseman and a few others continued to make films in the *cinéma vérité* style, the usual documentary in the 1980s differed greatly from that paradigm. The documentary of the 1980s typically incorporated filmed interviews, archival footage, musical scores, and most often a voice-over narrator or narrators to give information and analysis. One film that is conventional in style yet tells a compelling story is Jon Else's THE DAY AFTER TRINITY: ROBERT J. OPPENHEIMER AND THE ATOMIC

Errol Morris, maker of THE THIN BLUE LINE *(1988), flanked by the film's central characters, Randall Dale Adams (left) and David Harris (right).*

BOMB. The film features a deep-voiced (male) voice-over narrator, interviews with former acquaintances and relatives of Oppenheimer, archival materials (photographs, press clippings, and film footage), and appropriate music. Given the degree to which *cinéma vérité* practitioners had opposed voice-over narration, it is a mark of the wholesale rejection of *vérité* methods that voice-overs had become so common in the 1980s. Most often the narrator is impersonal (unidentified), and a male with a stentorian voice. Sometimes major Hollywood stars would lend their voices to a project they believed in. Martin Sheen provided the voice-over for PROMISES TO KEEP, for example, and Dustin Hoffman for COMMON THREADS: STORIES FROM THE QUILT. Many filmmakers tried to avoid "omnipotent" narration by using, as much as possible, recorded voices from existing films, historical television or radio broadcasts, or the voices of those interviewed. FOR ALL MANKIND (Al Reinert and Betsy Broyles Brier, 1989), a poetic film about NASA moon missions, uses only the voices of the astronauts and ground control personnel recorded at the time of their missions. Other documentaries avoided such impersonal narration by choosing narrators who were involved in the subject of the film, and then by clearly identifying the narrator. MILES OF SMILES, YEARS OF STRUGGLE, for example, identifies its voice-over narrator as the one hundred-year-old Rosina Tucker, the wife of a Pullman porter.

While *cinéma vérité* had thought arrangements and reenactments to be dishonest or manipulative, filmmakers in the 1980s were more willing to engage in such practices. In his AGEE, for example, Ross Spears has actors reenact family gatherings on the warm Tennessee nights of James Agee's childhood. In WHEN THE MOUNTAINS TREMBLE, Pamela Yates reenacts a stormy meeting between the elected leader of Guatemala and the U.S. ambassador. The director who most consistently employed scene arrangements and reenactments, however, was Errol Morris, each of whose documentary films takes the practice to new heights. By GATES OF HEAVEN (1978) Morris had developed his conventional techniques for filming interviews with arranged backgrounds, careful lighting, and placement of the camera at a consistent height from the ground and distance from the person being interviewed. In THE THIN BLUE LINE (1988), one of the most celebrated documentaries of the 1980s, Morris reenacts the murder of a policeman, shown over and again from the perspectives of several different witnesses. The recreations do not show what the film takes to be "the truth," but are presented to illustrate the stories of witnesses, most of whom are shown to be unreliable. Thus the recreations contribute to the theme of memory and the difficulty of knowing and reconstructing the past. Morris takes reenactments and arrangements further still in A BRIEF HISTORY OF TIME, where he actually constructed a set to appear as though it were the office of physicist Stephen Hawking. The assumption of documentary filmmakers who explore such techniques is that insight extends beyond surface appearances, and that at times the documentary can communicate such insights more effectively by a direct manipulation of those appearances.

Documentarians of the 1980s found other ways to leave the methodological constrictions of *cinéma vérité* behind. The use of music to express mood and emotion became very common. For example, FOR ALL MANKIND uses "space" music composed by Brian Eno, THE THIN BLUE LINE expresses a sense of mystery and fate through the compositions of Philip Glass, and Bobby McFerrin and Voicestra composed and performed the musical compositions for COMMON THREADS: STORIES FROM THE QUILT. THE ATOMIC CAFE (Kevin Rafferty, Jayne Loader, and Pierce Rafferty, 1982) used archival footage of silly government propaganda and naive period songs (such as "Atomic Cocktail" and "Duck and Cover") to paint an ironic picture of government attempts to soothe the cold war fears of post–World War II America.

Perhaps the most artful visual style is found in the documentaries of fashion photographer Bruce Weber, whose films BROKEN NOSES (1987) and LET'S GET LOST (with Nan Bush, 1988) are both impressionistic personality studies. Although LET'S GET LOST, about jazz trumpeter Chet Baker, is the better-known film (having been nominated for an Academy Award), BROKEN NOSES is at least as compelling, telling the story of the vibrant, good-hearted professional lightweight boxer Andy Minsker and his boxing club for boys in Portland, Oregon. Both films feature Weber's stylized black-and-white cinematography, making use of careful and artful compositions, flash frames and quick fades in and out, a roving camera, expressionistic low-key lighting, and sometimes the use of moving lights and even spotlights. Together with Chet Baker's cool, relaxed jazz scores (on both films), Weber's films conjure up a dreamlike world that takes us far away from the idea of the documentary as a record of objective reality.

A film that gained much attention as a personal documentary is Ross McElwee's SHERMAN'S MARCH (1986), a highly reflexive and intimate film that examines McElwee's travels in the South, ostensibly to follow General Sherman's Civil War march of destruction.[36] The film's subtitle, A MEDITATION ON THE POSSIBILITY OF ROMANTIC LOVE IN THE SOUTH DURING AN ERA OF NUCLEAR WEAPONS PROLIFERATION, gives some idea of other directions in which the film meanders. Ultimately, the film is about Ross McElwee and his romantic interests, and is important for marking the development of personal and idiosyncratic documentary filmmaking. What McElwee rejects is not so much *cinéma vérité* as the conventions of traditional historical or journalistic documentary.

Andy Minsker and his boxing club for boys in Bruce Weber's BROKEN NOSES (1987).

Although the film begins with a conventional off-screen voice-over narration, McElwee soon rejects this approach for a more personal style in which he often films his encounters with others and films himself talking to the camera.

Some filmmakers became highly interested in questions of epistemology and in so doing produced highly unconventional work. Can truth be known and represented in the documentary? If so, what are the best methods of doing so? Jill Godmilow's film FAR FROM POLAND (1984) wonders how to best make a film about the Solidarity movement in Poland after her entry visa had been denied by the Polish consulate. The film becomes a highly reflexive meditation not only on Solidarity but on knowledge and representation, incorporating the questioning of the filmmaker-narrator, voice-overs over black screens, and staged and recreated interviews. Trinh T. Minh-ha is explicit in her rejection of truth and even meaning in representation. Her films, for example, SURNAME VIÊT GIVEN NAME NAM (1989) are highly disruptive in style, refusing the coherence and clarity of more conventional documentary techniques.[37] (Both Godmilow and Minh-ha are treated as experimentalists in ch. 10.)

Michael Moore's ROGER AND ME (1989) was not only the biggest box-office success of any nonperformance documentary in history but also generated the most intense controversy, making the documentary a common subject for discussion. In ROGER AND ME, Michael Moore takes on General Motors and then-CEO Roger Smith. Moore appears in his film as a shaggy citizen of Flint, Michigan, on a righteous quest to show Roger Smith the havoc the CEO caused by closing down factories in Flint and moving the work to Mexico. Initially the film drew attention because it is immensely entertaining, because it skewers Smith and General Motors, and because it fared phenomenally well first at various film festivals and later theatrically (after having been purchased for distribution by Warner Bros.). Michael Moore showed a special talent for self-promotion both within his film and in his public appearances.

Although the automobile industry was naturally critical of Moore and his film from the very beginning, the more intense furor did not develop until Harlan Jacobsen, then editor of *Film Comment*, accused Moore of dishonesty.[38] In an interview and cover story for *Film Comment*, Jacobsen criticizes Moore for representing events out of chronology in ROGER AND ME. For example, Moore makes it appear as though an unemployed auto worker steals the cash register of a pizzeria while President Reagan is visiting, when in fact the register was stolen a few days earlier. Moore also makes it appear as though the massive layoffs in Flint occurred all at once in 1987, when in fact they had been occurring in smaller numbers for many years. In general, Moore rearranges and streamlines

Michael Moore, maker of ROGER AND ME *(1989), poses with Rhoda Britton (the Rabbit Lady) and deputy sheriff Fred Ross.*

his account of the factory shutdowns and Flint's response to create the tidy narrative structure of a Hollywood movie, and in so doing, leaves himself open to charges of deception. Richard Schickel in *Time*, for example, accuses Moore of "imposing" a "fictional design that proves the predetermined point he wants to make."[39] Then came Pauline Kael's withering review in the NEW YORKER. Kael attacked the mocking humor of the film, which holds up various unemployed Flint citizens, such as the "Rabbit Lady," who sells rabbits for "pets or meat," as objects of our ridicule. ROGER AND ME, Kael writes, "made me feel cheap for laughing."[40]

In a sense, the discussion about truth telling and deception sparked by Moore's film is an extension of the characteristic problem for documentary filmmakers in the 1980s and beyond. After rejecting the theoretical assumptions and practical methodology of *cinéma vérité*, filmmakers are left to struggle with an inevitable conflict between the creativity that is an ineluctable aspect of all filmmaking and the need to show and tell the ostensible truth. In response to Michael Moore's manipulations, some critics claimed that he had lied, while others countered that his rearranging was simply an instance of the inevitable manipulations all documentary filmmakers must incorporate into their films. Part of the problem here is that while many filmmakers have rejected the *cinéma vérité* claims about documentary—that it is or should be the unmanipulated record of reality—the public and many critics have not. The more difficult issue, however, and one that will continue to confront documentary filmmakers, is how to distinguish legitimate creative techniques from those that are manipulative and deceptive. No documentary can be a mere objective recording of reality, but that does not rule out the possibility that the art of a film can misrepresent and deceive.[41] Questions about documentary art, then, do not simply concern entertainment or imagination; they are also about how to make claims through the medium of film—compellingly, creatively, and without deceiving the audience.

Conclusion

Despite ongoing problems with financing and distribution, by the end of the 1980s the documentary genre in the United States was doing comparatively well. It was still extremely difficult to secure theatrical distribution, but nonetheless documentary films were being shown theatrically in greater numbers than ever before. Public television was showing and financing more independent documentaries, although spots on "P.O.V.," for example, were given to only ten to twelve independent films per year. For independent documentary filmmakers, the end of the decade promised more opportunities to produce and distribute their work.

One enduring legacy of the 1980s will be the significant trend toward filmmaking by women, members of ethnic and racial minorities, and gays and lesbians, together with the progressive social and political messages that strongly emerged during a decade when mainstream politics was generally thought to be quite conservative. When one looks at who is making documentary films, one can only conclude that the institutions of documentary were open to a wide diversity of people. While filmmakers sometimes claimed that funds were closed to innovative and politically incisive projects, it must also be concluded that the dominant political project of American documentary, if the American political scene be the standard of measure, was decidedly progressive.

The 1980s was also a decade of remarkable stylistic experimentation, and the decade brought the emergence of several filmmakers who saw documentary as an art form or means of personal expression. Filmmakers such as Errol Morris and especially Michael Moore brought a good deal of attention to the documentary and prepared the way for increased coverage in the popular media, rising interest by the public, and more theatrical distribution for documentaries in the 1990s. As filmmakers experimented with personal expression and creative uses of technique, the documentary was increasingly seen not only as a vehicle for information or social activism but as an art form in its own right.

10

Experimental Cinema in the 1980s

SCOTT MACDONALD

All history—including film history—is provisional and under constant revision. But no arena of modern film history provides more of a challenge to the historian than what is most often called *avant-garde film* or *experimental film* (various other terms have been used for various sectors of this immense, other cinema).[1] While we can know how many commercial films are produced during any one calendar year, the personal nature of so many avant-garde films, and the limited distribution and exhibition options for this work, are capable of keeping even some of the most remarkable films outside the general awareness, even of those relatively few who are fascinated with alternative cinema. Further, because so many avant-garde filmmakers are exploring cinema in new, "obscure" ways—that is, because few of these filmmakers feel an economic stake in abiding by any particular set of commercial conventions—even when those of us who *are* interested find our way to these films, we are often confronted by experiences we cannot make head nor tail of, at least at first, and sometimes for years. I have often found myself entirely confused about what a filmmaker is attempting to accomplish, even after multiple viewings of a film; and yet I may remain interested, even confident that at some point I *will* understand. Finally, because so many "avant-garde" films offer explicit or implicit critiques of conventional industrial film and television, and of the conventions and traditions of particular areas of noncommercial film, those of us committed to understanding the varieties of avant-garde practice must also stay reasonably abreast of film production in other areas.

By the 1980s, it was becoming clear that, whatever hopes for a vital, national avant-garde film scene had been nourished first, during the late 1940s through the early 1960s, by the remarkably successful New York film society Cinema 16, and then, during the 1960s and early 1970s, by the emergence of what Jonas Mekas called the new American cinema (and what others called "underground film," "expanded cinema," "abstract film," or "visionary film"), the reality was that the future of avant-garde exhibition and distribution was precarious at best.[2] The demise of such fixtures of the media scene as New York's Collective for Living Cinema in 1984 and the Pasadena Film Forum in 1983 (the

Film Forum relocated to Los Angeles where it struggled until the end of the decade), of Media Study/Buffalo soon after, and then of the San Francisco distributor Serious Business were signs of trouble for alternative media makers and those who admired and used their work. Even the existence of the New York Film-makers' Cooperative, one of the two leading distributors of avant-garde film (Canyon Cinema in San Francisco is the other), seemed precarious: the New York "Coop" could not find a way to update its 1974 catalog until 1989.[3] By the end of the decade virtually no one was sanguine about the future of avant-garde cinema in America.

There were several reasons for this apparent slippage in energy. Most obviously, the public audience willing to pay to have their assumptions about the

Logo from the Collective for Living Cinema in New York.

movies confronted by films that stretched the limits of conventional cinematic terminology and history was disappearing. As early as the mid-1960s, the increasing commercial openness about nudity and eroticism, as well as the violent and bizarre, was luring audiences away from the film societies and the underground screening rooms that, until the 1970s, had been virtually the only exhibitors of such material. The advent of "midnight movies" in particular was simultaneously a triumph for the avant-garde and confirmation of a fundamental split in its audience.[4] If for a time, unusual formal strategies and edgy subject matter had often existed in the same films—in Stan Brakhage's— WINDOW WATER BABY MOVING (1959), for example, and in Bruce Conner's COSMIC RAY (1962), Kenneth Anger's SCORPIO RISING (1963), Andy Warhol's KISS (1963) and CHELSEA GIRLS, (1966), Jack Smith's FLAMING CREATURES (1964), George Kuchar's HOLD ME WHILE I'M NAKED (1966), Carolee Schneemann's FUSES (1967)—the 1970s successes of such filmmakers as John Waters (MULTIPLE MANIACS [1970], PINK FLAMINGOS [1972], FEMALE TROUBLE [1974]) and Paul Morrissey (FLESH [1968], TRASH [1970]), and of THE ROCKY HORROR PICTURE SHOW (Jim Sharman, 1975), ERASERHEAD (David Lynch, 1977), as well as of hardcore pornography and new, more visceral horror films—George Romero's NIGHT OF THE LIVING DEAD (1968), Tobe Hooper's THE TEXAS CHAINSAW MASSACRE (1974)—created a gap between different sectors of what had seemed to be a single audience. While some filmgoers could enjoy the midnight movies, the new horror films, the pornography, *and* the formal experiments of Michael Snow, Hollis Frampton, Ernie Gehr, and Paul Sharits, most could not; many abandoned avant-garde screening rooms and never returned.

There were other distractions as well. The then-new medium of video art was beginning to emerge, demanding the attention and resources of many of the same organizations that were committed to the maintenance of avant-garde cinema.[5] And if at first this emerging video work was less impressive than contemporaneous avant-garde film, the video artists could nevertheless claim that their newer medium was in fact more "avant-garde," at least technologically, than avant-garde film itself. By the 1980s, these two alternative histories often found themselves pitted against one another, despite the many obvious formal and ideological relationships between avant-garde filmmakers and video artists. Some established filmmakers resented the new medium, in much the same way that serious commercial filmmakers have sometimes resented the onslaught of commercial television; and some fought efforts by media artists who made both film and video to have their video work distributed by the same avant-garde film distributors, though Gene Youngblood would argue that the attempts to separate film and video were illogical, since both media were part of the same "cinematic" tradition.[6]

A final major distraction from avant-garde film was less direct. The decision of many academic institutions to develop film studies programs allowed some of those familiar with avant-garde film history to hope that this history would be used, more and more frequently, to critique conventional filmgoing from within the classroom movie theater. For these people, avant-garde film was a tradition that had developed alongside the commercial industry, the way the history of poetry has developed alongside the more fully commercial history of the novel. As film departments expanded, it seemed only fitting that, as in other areas of the arts and humanities, the best work of all kinds would be made part of the curriculum. However, while this curricularization did occur to some degree, the process of using alternative cinema to critique commercial cinema and its audience was, in large measure, sidetracked by the influx of new theoretical approaches from Europe and subsequently other sectors of the world. Applying new anthropological, linguistic, psychological, political, and philosophical insights to the history of commercial cinema became the focus of academic film studies, and the idea of using the movie theater space itself as an arena for doing theoretical work directly—*cinematically*—never fully developed. The result is that, even in the 1990s, the unparalleled pedagogical resources of avant-garde film history have remained underutilized at best.

If the health of avant-garde distribution and exhibition seemed more precarious during the 1980s than it had during the previous three decades, it would be unfair not to recognize that individuals and institutions continued to labor on behalf of the field. In New York City, avant-garde films and filmmakers were presented at the Museum of Modern Art's Cineprobe series (curated by Larry Kardish and Jytte Jensen), at the American Museum of the Moving Image (program director, David Schwartz), at the Whitney Museum of American Art (program director, John Hanhardt), at the Millennium Film Workshop (program director, Howard Guttenplan), at the Donnell branch of the New York Public Library (program director, Marie Nesthus), at Film Forum (program director, Karen Cooper) and at Anthology Film Archives (program directors, Robert Haller and Jonas Mekas), though this particular pillar of the New York avant-garde community at times seemed on the verge of collapse. In the Bay Area, Steve Anker continued his inventive programming at the San Francisco Cinematheque, and the Pacific Film Archive, under the directorship of Edith Kramer, continued to present a wide range of programs in Berkeley (Kathy Geritz was responsible for avant-garde programming). And across the country, a network of screening spaces—Berks Filmmakers in Reading, Pennsylvania (under the directorship of Gary Adlestein and Jerry Orr), the Walker Art Center in Minneapolis (under the directorship of Bruce Jenkins), Cornell Cinema (directed by Richard Herskowitz), the Harvard Film Archive (directed by Vlada Petric), Chicago Filmmakers (screenings programmed by Brenda Webb), among others—maintained some public visibility for alternative cinema. The 1980s also saw the development by John Columbus of the Black Maria Film Festival, a traveling film festival focusing on short films and videos, and the continued success of the Ann Arbor Film Festival, directed by Ruth Bradley until 1984 and subsequently by Vicki Honeyman. Canyon Cinema, under the directorship of Dominic Angerame, seemed as healthy as ever. The Museum of Modern Art's Circulating Film Library, under the directorship of Mary Lea Bank and William Sloan, expanded its collection and, with a new catalog in 1984 and a substantial supplement in 1990, emerged as a major distributor of avant-garde work.

In any case, how one understands the continued, even increased, marginalization of avant-garde cinema (and a variety of factors in addition to those I've described could be cited, even the tendency of music video makers to exploit avant-garde techniques and siphon off a younger audience interested in moving-image experiment), the general weakening of the infrastructure for avant-garde exhibition and distribution was part of a remarkable paradox: despite the increasing tenuousness of the possibilities for *seeing* avant-garde cinema, the actual production of interesting work continued through the 1980s with remarkable consistency. Indeed, on the level of productivity, the 1980s were one of the more impressive decades for the American avant-garde, which has always tended to be a history of individuals finding ways to make work despite limited financial support. The filmmaking achievements of the 1980s can be suggested in a three-part arrangement. First, a good many of those filmmakers who had made significant contributions from the 1940s through the 1970s continued to be productive. In some cases, the 1980s saw a revival of reputations thought to be fading by the mid-1970s, in other instances, the production of impressive films at the ends of careers that were slowly tailing off. Second, several general approaches to filmmaking, none of them entirely new to the avant-garde, became focal points for exploration and resulted in new bodies of work that represented healthy additions, and in some cases correctives, to the history of American avant-garde filmmaking up through the 1970s. And finally, the 1980s saw the maturation of a number of film artists whose best work can rival the most interesting avant-garde cinema from any decade and who can function here as tentative representatives of the complex zeitgeist of the moment.

1. Continuations and Transformations

Among the already established filmmakers for whom the 1980s were a productive decade, the most obvious was Stan Brakhage, whose astonishing output had already become legendary.[7] The Canyon Cinema catalog lists sixty-two Brakhage films completed from 1980 to 1989; and this does not include the twenty-five "Songs" Brakhage transferred from 8mm to 16mm or the new sound version of FLESH OF MORNING, finished in 1986. Brakhage remained not only prolific, but accomplished and inventive. The decade began with THE ROMAN NUMERAL SERIES (actually, parts 1 and 2 of the series were finished in 1979, the remaining seven sections in 1980), nine brief, lovely, evocative lightscapes, each of which combines the texture, color, and quiver of light in somewhat different ways. At times, the imagery seems to hover at the edge of identifiability (the horizontal striping of "VII," e.g., reveals that the imagery originates on a television screen) and in some cases verges on allusion (the mandala shapes in "V" suggest Jim Davis and Jordan Belson); but overall the series of films seems a combination of Brakhage's ongoing fascination with recording and exploring visual realms just at the edge of human consciousness and cinematic possibility, as a means of honoring not just light, but Light as emblem of the spirit.

UNCONSCIOUS LONDON STRATA (1982) is a longer (twenty-two minutes), more elaborate exploration of the concerns evident in THE ROMAN NUMERAL SERIES, though its
visual mysteriousness is more playful. Filmed during Brakhage's first visit to London, the
imagery is a semiabstract history, simultaneously, of this particular visit and of
Brakhage's sense of British history. Within an impressive exploration of color, texture,
and visual rhythm (like SCENES FROM UNDER CHILDHOOD, I [1967] and THE TEXT OF
LIGHT [1974], UNCONSCIOUS LONDON STRATA is a tour de force) the viewer is able to
recognize a variety of London landmarks—the Thames, St. Paul's Cathedral, the Houses
of Parliament—until, in the film's final gesture, we see a brief passage of time-lapsed
imagery of a busy intersection, an emblem of the present moment and of modernity in
general. As is true in a good many of Brakhage's films since the 1960s, a variety of general kinds of imagery are edited into a weave, a skein, that becomes increasingly familiar and at least to some degree readable as the film proceeds. Much the same structure
is evident in the four parts of Brakhage's final major series of the 1980s, VISIONS IN
MEDITATION (the first two sections, #1 and #2: MESA VERDE, were completed in 1989,
#3: PLATO'S CAVE and #4: D. H. LAWRENCE in 1990), which, like UNCONSCIOUS
LONDON STRATA, explores both the "strata" of Brakhage's unconscious and various (in
this case, American) geographies that have fascinated him.

    While the domesticity that by 1960 had come to seem so fundamental in Brakhage's
work remained a crucial dimension of many of his 1980s films, it was a domesticity in
transition: the decade saw the conclusion of Stan and Jane Brakhage's life together and
the beginning of Brakhage's new life with Marilyn Jull—a transition that can be charted
in JANE (1985), THE LOOM (1986), and MARILYN'S WINDOW (1988). Indeed, THE
LOOM in particular seems to represent both the culmination of the complex life Jane and
Stan Brakhage had built together and Brakhage's re-visioning of this life. While THE
LOOM is structurally of a piece with a good many earlier films—as the title implies, it is
a weave of a variety of threads into a visual skein—the imagery itself seems new and distinctive, and brimming with allusions to the history of culture. The focus of THE LOOM
is the animal pen just outside what was the Brakhage home in the mountains above
Boulder, Colorado, where their ducks, chickens, geese, and goats were kept. We see
these animals, and, from time to time their owners, in multilayered compositions distinguished by their flatness. In fact, it is this flatness that causes THE LOOM to be as art-
historically evocative as it is.

    The combination of the length of THE LOOM (fifty minutes) and its relentlessly slow
pace provides a cinematic environment within which Brakhage can allude to the representation of animals in cultural history. Some compositions recall the cave paintings of
southern France and northern Spain; others recall biblical scenes, and especially the tradition of the crèche. At times, Brakhage's compositions suggest medieval tapestries; in
other instances, they evoke Native American petroglyphs (indeed, the overall structure
of THE LOOM is evocative of Navajo rugs). Many particular compositions also suggest
more recent cultural artifacts. One obvious reference is to the American Quaker folk
painter Edward Hicks, especially his *The Peaceable Kingdom* (1843) and *The Cornell
Farm* (1849). Henri Rousseau's jungle fantasies also seem relevant. At times we see into
the pen through the grid of the fence that encloses it and at other times see the animals
moving in front of the fence, making Eadweard Muybridge's animal locomotion photographs a particularly obvious and consistent reference. In his catalogue notes for THE
LOOM, Brakhage himself makes clear his indebtedness to Georges Méliès ("The film is
very inspired by Georges Méliès: the animals exist . . . as on a stage"), whose develop-

ment of superimposition is the source for Brakhage's layering of the imagery in the film.[8] The emphasis on the pen as a frieze is suggestive not only of Méliès, however, but also of other early filmmakers, and of Ken Jacobs, whose TOM, TOM, THE PIPER'S SON explores the dimensions of the friezelike space of the early Biograph version of the nursery rhyme.

But for all Brakhage's visual inventiveness and allusiveness in THE LOOM, the space he explores remains, fundamentally, an *enclosure*, not just literally, but in his use of the film frame; the multiple layers of imagery do not open out but fold in on themselves— a way of suggesting, perhaps, that for all the psychic complexity of the life he and Jane had built together, domesticity had ceased to be a liberation for them. That Stan Brakhage's respect and admiration for Jane Brakhage had not wavered is obvious both in THE LOOM and in JANE; but the freedom of movement evident in MARILYN'S WINDOW, a freedom more in keeping with much of Brakhage's earlier work, suggests that his domestic energies had been relocated, bringing to a close the most elaborately visualized domestic saga in the annals of American cinema.

The 1980s also saw the continuation of one other major strand in the skein of Brakhage's career, as well as the exploration of a new cinematic avenue. Paintings and collage-on-film have always been crucial in Brakhage's work. Indeed, the collage work MOTHLIGHT (1963) remains Brakhage's most frequently rented film; and as recently as October 1997 heard Brakhage claim that of all his filmmaking, painting-on-film is most fundamental to his self-definition as an artist. The 1980s saw the production of a number of paintings-on-film, including CASWALLON TRILOGY (1986) and LOUD VISUAL NOISES (1986), and the collage film, THE GARDEN OF EARTHLY DELIGHTS (1981), a Rocky Mountain version of MOTHLIGHT. As its title suggests, THE GARDEN OF EARTHLY DELIGHTS is an evocation of, and a response to, the Hieronymus Bosch

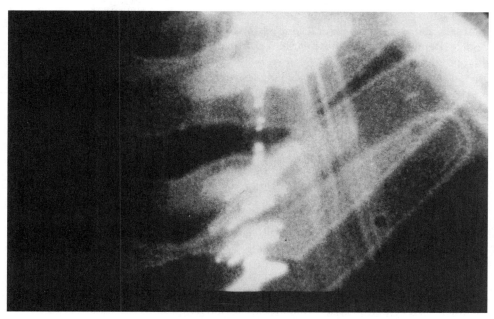

Light reflections in Stan Brakhage's THE ROMAN NUMERAL SERIES #14 *(1981).*

painting. Here the "earthly delights" are not sinful sensual indulgences that must lead, in the end, to punishment; rather, the seeds, leaves, and other bits of vegetation that make up the film reflect Brakhage's delight in the simple beauties of God's Earth, envisioned (as it has so often been in American cultural history) as the original Eden. At the same time, the "garden" is not only Brakhage's Rocky Mountain surround but also the viewers' retinas, where the disparate imagery in the successive frames of THE GARDEN OF EARTHLY DELIGHT combine to form imagery of vegetation that exists nowhere but in the viewers' consciousness. In this use of retinal collage, the film echoes Bosch's depiction of fantastic beings.

Perhaps the most elaborate new direction in the Brakhage films of the 1980s is represented by the re-visioning of the Faust story in FAUSTFILM: AN OPERA: PART I (1987), FAUST'S OTHER: AN IDYLL (1988), FAUST 3: CANDIDA ALBACORE (1988), and FAUST 4 (1989). In collaboration with composer Rick Corrigan and actor and sound editor Joel Haertling, Brakhage dramatizes his version of Faust, using actors and actresses, as well as his own spoken narration. While the films are visually inventive in ways in keeping with Brakhage's career, the new mix of elements creates a set of experiences quite distinct from those familiar to most of Brakhage's audience.

While James Benning seemed to some observers to have peaked in the mid-1970s with his homages to midwestern cityscape and landscape ($8^{1}/_{2}$ x 11 [1974], 11 x 14 [1976], and ONE WAY BOOGIE WOOGIE, [1977]), his most impressive features of the 1980s—AMERICAN DREAMS (1984) and LANDSCAPE SUICIDE (1986)—reveal a significant development of Benning's vision and a very different orientation from Brakhage's to the cinematic surround of the moment. While Brakhage has been relentless in articulating the cinematic vision that came to maturity in the late 1950s and early 1960s, and at least in his own work, ignoring a wide range of developments in avant-garde film (as well as in popular commercial film and documentary), Benning has always been alert to the artistic excitements of the moment and inventive about integrating them into his work. Benning's 1980s features incorporate several of the major trends of American (and international) avant-garde filmmaking of the 1970s, but in a move typical of the later decade, Benning redirects those earlier approaches into new, more ideologically specific directions.

AMERICAN DREAMS reveals considerable indebtedness to the body of work P. Adams Sitney called "structural film," and especially to Michael Snow, George Landow (Owen Land), and Hollis Frampton, whose death from cancer in 1984, at age forty-eight, was one of the crucial events of the 1980s.[9] Like earlier structural films, AMERICAN DREAMS employs a rigorously designed formal structure. Throughout the film's fifty-eight minutes, the viewer's attention is split between the serial presentation of Benning's considerable collection of Hank Aaron memorabilia (baseball cards and the like), each item shown front and back in chronological order; and the handwritten text that scrolls from right to left across the bottom of the image.[10] The use of "I" in this text is at first ambiguous (we assume we're reading Benning's diary), but at the end of AMERICAN DREAMS, Benning reveals, as a kind of punchline, that he has reproduced excerpts from the diary of fellow Milwaukee native Arthur Bremer, who shot George Wallace in Laurel, Maryland, in 1972. On the sound track, Benning regularly intercuts between excerpts from popular songs of the period beginning with Aaron's arrival in the Major Leagues in 1954 until his retirement from baseball in 1976, and excerpts from influential public statements of the period. The two narratives—Aaron's quest of Babe Ruth's record and Bremer's quest to kill a public figure (he stalked Richard Nixon before shooting

Hank Aaron baseball card and excerpt from Arthur Bremer diary, in James Benning's AMERICAN DREAMS *(1984).*

Wallace)—come together at the film's auditory conclusion, when the sound of a gunshot is followed by a broadcast of Aaron's "shot" into the bleachers that surpassed Babe Ruth's home run record.

Benning's decision to focus on two quests—one the positive, the other the negative side of the American Dream—is reflected in his own relentlessly formal design: his film proceeds relentlessly to its final "shot" as well. While early structural film often explored material dimensions of cinema, AMERICAN DREAMS uses an organization typical of structural film to confront the issues of race and gender.[11] Benning's admiration of Aaron's amazing career is implicitly a counterpoint to George Wallace's resistance to racial integration; and all three of the men whose obsessions structure AMERICAN DREAMS—Aaron, Bremer, Benning—deal with life in ways that in the 1980s were coming to seem fundamentally male.

If none of Benning's other films of the 1980s is as rigorously structured as AMERICAN DREAMS, his other features—HIM AND ME (1982), LANDSCAPE SUICIDE, and USED INNOCENCE (1988)—reflect similar redirections of tendencies familiar from the 1970s. Even the fact that all three films are feature-length reflects Benning's implicit concern, shared by other filmmakers of the decade, with his economic future: as the infrastructure of avant-garde exhibition and distribution seemed to weaken, some compromises with the commercial infrastructure seemed increasingly sensible, both to filmmakers who had been or wanted to be identified with the earlier structuralists, and to filmmak-

ers who saw themselves in rebellion against pretensions of formal "purity": Beth B and
Scott B, for example. The "Bs," who made a name for themselves during the mid-1970s
with their narratively oriented, Super 8 "no-wave" or "punk" melodramas, were also
moving toward feature-length, first in later versions of THE OFFENDERS (at first presented serially in rock clubs, then made into a single feature in 1979), and in THE TRAP
DOOR (1980, seventy minutes) and VORTEX (1983, ninety minutes), their final collaborations (while both remained active during the later 1980s, neither made films with the
narrative power or visual interest of the films they made together).

If Benning's features of the 1980s are formally a long way from the New York punk
films of the period, his frequent focus on crime in these films reflects the punk determination to move avant-garde filmmaking away from a focus on "essential" elements of
cinema or on the sensibilities of artist filmmakers toward a full incorporation of nitty-
gritty social realities. LANDSCAPE SUICIDE explores the *place* of two famous crimes: Ed
Gein's murders and grave robbing in rural Plainfield, Wisconsin, and the 1984 "cheer-
leader murder" in Orinda, California, a posh suburb of San Francisco; and USED
INNOCENCE focuses on the career of convicted Wisconsin murderer Lawrencia
Bembenek. Even HIM AND ME, made soon after Benning moved to New York and into
the punk scene, focuses on the sudden, mysterious death of the protagonist's boyfriend
as he sleeps next to her.

On a formal level, Benning's films of the period and the Bs' punk shorts and features
share an increasing commitment to the incorporation not only of sound but also of

Dr. Shrinkelstein (Jack Smith) hypnotizes Jeremy (John Ahearn) in Beth B and Scott
B's "punk film" THE TRAP DOOR.

scripted melodrama that became characteristic of much 1980s work. Early in the decade, an issue of *October* (no. 17, summer 1981) was devoted to what it called "the New Talkies," signaling a compromise position between avant-garde and industry filmmaking that had been inconceivable when synch-sound recording was possible only on industry sound stages, and silence (as in Brakhage's films) or at least non-synch uses of sound were defiant, if economically necessitated, declarations of independence from the commercial.

Most filmmakers who had established their reputations in the 1960s and 1970s were not as prolific as Brakhage, or even Benning. But some made contributions that confirmed the visions established in earlier work. Andrew Noren contributed THE LIGHTED FIELD (1987, discussed later). Jonas Mekas continued to produce new films using material shot during earlier decades. Mekas's HE STANDS IN THE DESERT COUNTING THE SECONDS OF HIS LIFE (filmed in 1969, edited in 1985) is a feature-length series of sketches of the movers and shakers of the sixties art scene, including film artists representative of a wide range of approaches—Hans Richter, Alberto Cavalcanti, Roberto Rossellini, Marcel Hanoun, Peter Kubelka, Ken Jacobs, Kenneth Anger, Willard Van Dyke, Andy Warhol, Yoko Ono—filmed in the lyric, free-form, gestural style Mekas had used in WALDEN (1969).[12] Richard Myers continued to combine formalist invention, personal exploration, and a commitment to his local surround in Kent, Ohio, in JUNGLE GIRL (1984) and MOVING PICTURES (1990). Larry Gottheim continued the inventive explorations of sound and image begun in his ELECTIVE AFFINITIES series in the lovely MNEMOSYNE, MOTHER OF MUSES (1986). Ernie Gehr contributed SIGNAL: GERMANY ON THE AIR (1985), a complex visual-auditory evocation of modern (and Nazi) Berlin. Robert Huot continued to make diary films, though by the 1980s, he had switched from 16mm to Super 8 sound film. Yvonne Rainer also remained active and influential (she is discussed later).

Mary Leed and Jake Leed in Richard Myers's JUNGLE GIRL (1984).

Other filmmakers continued to work in, or near, animation, in ways characteristic of their earlier careers. There were regular contributions by Robert Breer, whose SWISS ARMY KNIFE WITH RATS AND PIGEONS (1981), TRIAL BALLOONS (1982), BANG! (1986), and A FROG ON THE SWING (1989) continued the frame-by-frame explorations of perceptual and intellectual space-time that established his reputation in the 1950s; and by Jordan Belson, who continued to create films that evoke the "inner imagery" he has discovered through meditation and the "outer imagery" he has conjectured on the basis of his interest in macrocosmic terrestrial and extra-terrestrial processes. Belson made a feature film's worth of 35mm imagery for Philip Kaufman's THE RIGHT STUFF (1983), and a series of short 16mm films in the tradition of his influential 1960s films, including SYNCHRONICITY SUITE (1980: PISCES/BLUES, APOLLO'S LYRE, SEAPEACE, ELEUSIS/CROTONS), THE ASTRONAUT'S DREAM (1981), MOONLIGHT (1981), FIREFLIES (1985), and THOUGHTFORMS (1987). Gunvor Nelson explored the "space" between live action and animation in FRAME LINE (1983), LIGHT YEARS (1987), and LIGHT YEARS EXPANDING (1988). And Larry Jordan contributed SOPHIE'S PLACE (1986), a feature-length animation in the tradition of Harry Smith's HEAVEN AND EARTH MAGIC FEATURE (1960), focusing on the figure of St. Sophia—probably the most impressive longer American avant-garde animation of the decade.

The 1980s also served as a transformative moment for some moving-image makers. One type of transformation is evident in the work of J. J. Murphy, who established himself as a major "structural" filmmaker with PRINT GENERATION (1974) and continued to use approaches identified with avant-garde filmmaking through the 1970s; then, having proved he could make contributions to several avant-garde traditions, he decided to prove to himself that he could also make "movies," scripted melodramatic narratives. If none of Murphy's narrative films of the 1980s—THE NIGHT BELONGS TO THE POLICE

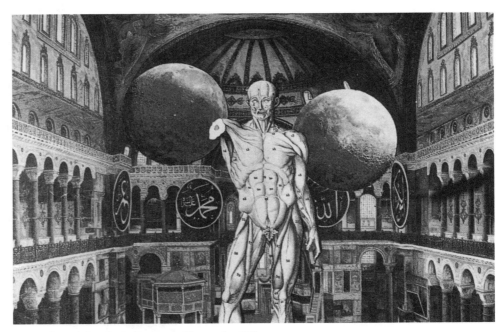

From Larry Jordan's SOPHIE'S PLACE *(1986).*

(1982), TERMINAL DISORDER (1983), FRAME OF MIND (1985)—are as impressive as PRINT GENERATION, Murphy's quest to prove to himself that he could do something other than maintain his reputation as an avant-garde artist was, on a personal level, as "experimental" as the sensibilities of filmmakers whose 1980s films fit more precisely our expectations of avant-garde film and filmmakers.

Another transformation—more of a career "dissolve," perhaps—is evident in George Kuchar's increasing commitment to video. While Kuchar continued to produce the kinds of trashy melodrama that had established his reputation, both on his own (CATTLE MUTILATIONS [1983], THE X PEOPLE [1985]) and in collaboration with his students at the San Francisco Art Institute (BOULEVARD KISHKA [1981], THE ONEERS [1982] CLUB VATICAN [1984], MOTEL CAPRI [1986]), his primary focus was increasingly video. Indeed, by the end of the decade, Video Data Bank was publishing two catalogs: one for Kuchar's work, the other for everyone else.[13] For Kuchar, the economy and flexibility of the camcorder represent less a change in medium than a return to what 8mm filmmaking and subsequently 16mm and Super 8 had offered independent makers: easy access to the regular production of moving-image art. Those who insisted that cinema was intrinsically superior to video had become, as Kuchar said later, exactly what in an earlier decade they had seemed to hate: after all, the commitment of so many in the American avant-garde to small-gauge film production had been seen by earlier critics as a choice of a less sophisticated medium; *real* movies, of course, were made in 35mm or wider gauges.

Indeed, Kuchar's shift to video can be seen here as symbolic of the shift from film to video by a good many fledgling makers of the 1980s and 1990s, whose access to film production is constricted by the realities of economic class, but who have been able to develop careers as a result of the accessibility of video equipment. Since the 1980s, critiques of commercial film and television—especially those motivated by class and ethnicity—are far more likely to be produced in video than in film; video is now what film was, from the days of the socialist collective Nykino in the 1930s through the emergence of Newsreel (and Third World Newsreel) in the 1960s and 1970s: the logical medium for those who are economically disenfranchised but committed to the idea of producing social change through the use of moving-image polemic.[14]

Developing Trends

While particular types of American avant-garde film are parts of international artistic traditions that have been developing for decades, avant-garde cinema in general is nevertheless directly connected to the commercial cinema: without a film industry, the equipment necessary for avant-garde film production and exhibition could not "trickle down" to individuals and small groups making films on tiny budgets; and without the business of 16mm distribution of commercial films to academic and other cultural venues, avant-garde filmmakers for whom 16mm is, by virtue of economic necessity, the "gauge of choice" would quickly find themselves without film-stock. Not only is avant-garde film history attached to the industry by a celluloid umbilical cord, but because most audiences for avant-garde film—and most filmmakers as well—have been trained as viewers by commercial film and television long before they become familiar with alternative cinema, the characteristic tendencies of avant-garde cinema at any one moment, and the experiences of particular films, are most easily understood in terms of how they depart from the commercial mainstream, how they critique the conventional assumptions of popular cinema and television.

During the 1980s, a good many filmmakers and films explicitly or implicitly critiqued the industry in one of two general ways: first, they expanded and deepened the range of "voices" available to filmgoers; second, they concentrated on particular elements of the film experience, exploring them to a degree impractical for commercial filmmakers. The centrifugal tendency is best exemplified by the development of a sophisticated, complex feminist cinema—and in many cases, a lesbian feminist cinema—in which the raw, confrontational tendencies of 1960s and 1970s feminist film became a part of the more-developed visions of women's lives and potentials. The centripetal tendency is evident in the explosion of "recycled cinema," in which moving-image artists often deconstructed particular moments in specific industrial films. While these two tendencies may, at first glance, seem opposed, the "broadening" tendency of feminist film and the "narrowing" tendency of recycled cinema both lead to the same end: a sustained critique of the ideological and formal limitations and compromises of commercial media.

FEMINIST CINEMA

In the United States, the 1980s were a remarkable decade for women filmmakers, not just in the number of films produced and the feminist passion expressed in many of these films, but in their inventiveness, complexity, and subtlety. This impressive productivity was accompanied by a good bit of written theory and criticism;[15] Even in the area of distribution, there was good news for women: during the 1980s, Women Make Movies had considerable success in making available a range of avant-garde film and polemical documentary (and celebrated its twenty-fifth anniversary in 1997).

One of the most-discussed feminist films of the early 1980s was Lizzie Borden's feminist "sci-fi" feature BORN IN FLAMES (1983), in which events from a not-so-distant future are used to comment on the then-current status of women in American society.[16] While it was as full of confrontational passion as any 1970s feminist polemic, its process of production seemed to break new ground. Most avant-garde films are produced by individuals or small groups, but BORN IN FLAMES represented something like a community effort, not simply in the sense that Borden collaborated with other filmmakers to make it, but also in the sense that the film represented a far broader range of women than most films and used the film production process as a means for energizing feminist multiethnic organization. In its formal rawness and its awareness of the nitty-gritty of urban life, BORN IN FLAMES was reminiscent of the Super 8 punk films of Beth B and Scott B and Vivienne Dick; and in the disjunctiveness of its narrative, it recalls many earlier avant-garde films—but in its direct call to action and its determination to bridge ethnic and class distinctions in the name of a revolutionary repositioning of women within American media culture, it felt both fresh and feisty. Borden's other film of the 1980s, WORKING GIRLS (1986), a melodrama about the day-to-day working life of a middle-class prostitute, revealed Borden's determination to become a commercial director. Unlike BORN IN FLAMES, which used nonactors in part as a means for insuring new character-spectator relationships, WORKING GIRLS was scripted and acted by professionals. However, while it is less unconventional and was less celebrated than BORN IN FLAMES, WORKING GIRLS remains a remarkably open film, especially in its matter-of-fact awareness about women's (and men's) bodies and about sexual desire and fetishization; and while it seems less political than its openly revolutionary predecessor, Borden's awareness of and sympathy for

Guerrilla radio broadcast, in Lizzie Borden's BORN IN FLAMES *(1983).*

the interlocking absurdity of women's and men's sexual roles in Western society allows for the development of a progressive cross-gender awareness.

While she had emerged as a filmmaker in the 1970s, Yvonne Rainer's contribution to 1980s avant-garde film and feminist discourse remained substantial. She began the decade with JOURNEYS FROM BERLIN/1971 (1980), her meditation on Berlin as metaphor for the divided psyche of the West and of modern filmmaking of all kinds.[17] Like BORN IN FLAMES, JOURNEYS FROM BERLIN/1971 argues that the struggles of American women for political and economic power were and are part of a thoroughly multiethnic international struggle; and like Borden's film, Rainer's assembles viewpoints from a wide variety of sources; but JOURNEYS FROM BERLIN/1971 is more demanding of the viewer's patience, as a result of Rainer's extremely slow pacing and her decision to force viewers to read about revolutionary action, rather than to watch (however disjunctive) enactments of it. If the revolutionary form of BORN IN FLAMES was a product of the late 1970s and early 1980s, and was quickly left behind as Borden moved in the direction of Hollywood, Rainer's film was in large measure about her own filmmaking practice, not in the sense that hers was a more politically progressive practice than Borden's, but in her recognition that she, like all of us (including Borden), is a divided self, even as a progressive filmmaker: after all, Rainer's critique of conventional cinema and established Western political power and organization was made possible by grants from the very social systems that JOURNEYS FROM BERLIN/1971 critiques.

Rainer's self-awareness was equally evident in THE MAN WHO ENVIED WOMEN (1985), another feature, this one more specifically focused, as the title suggests, on women; and in PRIVILEGE (1990), which focuses on women in a more fully interethnic context and with a growing consciousness of lesbianism as a personal issue (Rainer announced herself a lesbian soon after the film was complete). As the years pass, it is increasingly obvious that Rainer's films are time capsules of the particular moments during which they were shot and edited. While it offers no particular conclusions about, or solutions to, the set of social and aesthetic issues it raises, THE MAN WHO ENVIED WOMEN does provide a clear sense of the issues facing artists during the mid-1980s. The film's personae wrestle with the particular debates at the heart of the film: most obviously, the question of how one's "personal" concerns as artist or academic or as a partner in a relationship relate to political crises in other parts of the world (in particular, Central America) where people less privileged than Rainer and her characters are brutally, systematically murdered. The film dramatizes a variety of forms of social intercourse often relating to this issue: in a classroom, Jack Deller, a cultural theorist, lectures to a class; at a public hearing, members of the lower Manhattan art community and other downtown residents (many of them Hispanic immigrants) debate the merits of the city's providing financial assistance to artists threatened by gentrification; at a party, Deller (played in this instance by William Raymond; in other instances the same character is played by Larry Loonin) discusses the issue of power as it relates to gender with a former lover, Jackie (Jackie Raynal); and in several instances, we see Deller walking to work or eating in a restaurant while we hear brief, often witty interchanges between couples. In some instances, the length and pacing of particular sequences (the lecture, the party discussion) create just the sort of frustration that we often feel when trying to understand complex, difficult, new theoretical positions: as viewers we are annoyed at the characters' "overintellectualization" while recognizing that there is no easy way and little everyday language for dealing with the larger concerns that trouble us all.

At the heart of THE MAN WHO ENVIED WOMEN is a collage (we see it first in Deller's loft, though its location seems to change), which various characters discuss and sometimes rearrange, apparently at Rainer's suggestion (sometimes we hear her voice in the background). The collage includes a small color image of mutilated El Salvadorans (severed heads, tortured bodies); an advertising image for high-quality cigars, the focus of which is a handsome, successful white businessman; a *New York Times* magazine column in which a priest discusses the need for men to be able to express gentler emotions; a male-physician-directed advertisement for menopausal hormone supplements; an article, "How I Was Broken by the KGB"; and two posters: one for BORN IN FLAMES, the other produced by the "Artists' Call" against intervention in Central America. This collage—formally rough, conceptually dense—is Rainer's film in microcosm; and the voices that discuss the troubling continuities and gaps implied by the juxtapositions are a microcosm of the audience for her films. Like JOURNEYS FROM BERLIN/1971, THE MAN WHO ENVIED WOMEN is a metacollage that combines the elements described above with various forms of quotation. The characters often consciously or unconsciously quote writers who were much discussed during the 1980s (Michel Foucault, Fredric Jameson, Julia Kristeva, B. Ruby Rich), and Rainer provides visual quotations from a wide range of films, including UN CHIEN ANDALOU (1929; in this context, Buñuel's slicing of the woman's eye seems quite gender-conventional!), Hollis Frampton's OTHERWISE UNEXPLAINED FIRES (1976; Rainer's film is dedicated "in memoriam" to Frampton, who was a great admirer of Rainer's work), WATERMOTOR (1978, performed by Trisha Brown, filmed by Babette Mangolte), George Romero's NIGHT OF THE LIVING DEAD (1967), WAVELENGTH (1967) by Michael Snow, and several *films noirs*: John Cromwell's DEAD RECKONING (1947), Fritz Lang's CLASH BY NIGHT (1952), Max Ophul's CAUGHT (1949), and Billy Wilder's DOUBLE INDEMNITY

Feminist revolutionary draws a bead on the audience in Borden's BORN IN FLAMES.

(1944).[18] In 1985, THE MAN WHO ENVIED WOMEN was a kind of cul-de-sac, a trap for anyone accustomed to using moviegoing as an escape: one exited the "real world" only to be relocated back into it. Seeing it more than a decade later, we are able to reenter a previous moment and a set of concerns and debates that made way for the moment we find ourselves in.

PRIVILEGE, which was finished in 1990, took as its central foci menopause and race. In her use of an alter ego, African-American Yvonne Washington (Novella Nelson), to confront protagonist Jenny's (Alice Spivak) psychoanalytic explanation of racial difference and the history of black oppression, Rainer dramatizes a much-discussed debate that now seems characteristic of the end of the decade: a debate about the representation of women of color in the primarily white, bourgeois-oriented history of feminist filmmaking and exhibition. Rainer herself (with Bérénice Reynaud) programmed the "Sexism, Colonialism, Misrepresentation" conference, held at the Collective for Living Cinema and the Dia Art Foundation in 1988, a flashpoint for this debate, which centered on the fact that these two (white, "bourgeois") women programmers were attempting to correct a racially exclusionary history, but at venues frequented almost exclusively by whites and devoted to forms of filmmaking that had privileged aesthetics and psychoanalysis and had seemed to undervalue more activist forms of avant-garde filmmaking.[19]

Clearly related to Rainer's approach in THE MAN WHO ENVIED WOMEN and PRIVILEGE was the approach used by Jill Godmilow in FAR FROM POLAND (1984), a feature focusing on her own attempts to come to grips with the development of the Solidarity movement in Poland. Widely known as a documentarian (her ANTONIA: A PORTRAIT OF THE WOMAN had received an Academy Award nomination in 1975),

Jack Deller (William Raymond) and the collage, in Yvonne Rainer's THE MAN WHO ENVIED WOMEN (1985).

Godmilow combined personal address to the camera about her own production process, documentation of her personal life (including her frustrating relationship with a male partner, Mark Magill), a dramatized version of an interview with Polish labor activist, Anna Walentynowicz, and some footage shot by members of Solidarity to explore the relationship between the personal and political, women and men, "near" and "far." Like so much of the feminist cinema of the 1980s, FAR FROM POLAND questions the conventional distinction between avant-garde film and documentary by working at the ambiguous "seam" between these two traditions.

While Borden, Rainer, and Godmilow were lifelong American citizens working "outward" to explore feminism as a multiethnic international issue, the Vietnamese-born American immigrant Trinh T. Minh-ha provided a look at particular traditions within American (and European) culture, informed by her experience as an outsider. Minh-ha's films, and especially REASSEMBLAGE (1982), provided a different kind of ideological flashpoint for the decade.[20] REASSEMBLAGE is a forty-minute montage film that means to deconstruct and "reassemble" our understanding of how peoples from sectors of the world other than white North America and Europe are represented in the history of anthropology and, more specifically, in the history of ethnographic film, which (except for Margaret Mead) remained, as of 1982, as thoroughly white as any arena of cultural production. In REASSEMBLAGE, Minh-ha seemed to break all the "rules" of ethnographic filmmaking; indeed, some historians of ethnographic documentary (and some historians of avant-garde film) argued that she had no idea what she was doing.[21] What she *was* doing was focusing on the day-to-day activities of women from various sectors of Senegal, but without presuming to have any codifiable "knowledge" about Senegal; indeed, she defiantly abjured pretensions to "objectivity" and "detachment." Further,

Minh-ha's camera is consistently hand-held, her image and sound editing consistently abrupt, "awkward," but she was not using this gestural camerawork and disjunctive editing for purposes of personal self-expression, as had become conventional in much avant-garde film as a result of the gestural camera of Marie Menken, Stan Brakhage, and Jonas Mekas in the 1960s. Even her poetically arranged narration (in her Vietnamese-accented English) recalls the voice-of-god narrator of so many documentary films, only to reveal its cultural and masculine bias. Minh-ha made an influential place for herself in 1980s feminist cinema (she is discussed in more detail later) by working in the historical and ideological gap between two major film traditions, both of which had been defined and peopled largely by white European-American men.

Su Friedrich (also discussed in more detail later) has also worked between the histories of avant-garde film and documentary but from a position more in touch and in tune with the history of American avant-garde filmmaking and especially Maya Deren, Stan Brakhage, and Hollis Frampton.[22] Her THE TIES THAT BIND (1984) used a then-unusual mixture of forms not to question how much we can know about cultural history, but to document and explore the ties that bind her own and her mother's

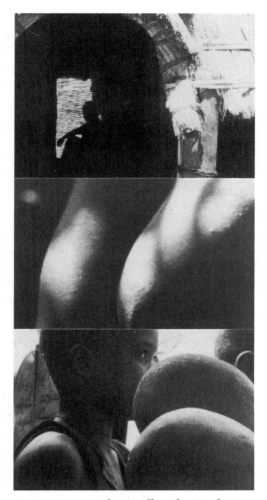

REASSEMBLAGE *photo collage by Trinh T. Minh-ha.*

personal histories to public events past and present. The central thread of THE TIES THAT BIND, an auditory thread, is an interview with Friedrich's mother, Lore Friedrich, about her experiences growing up in an anti-Nazi German household during the 1930s, and during and after World War II, when she married Paul Friedrich (the filmmaker's father) and emigrated to the United States. As we listen to Lore Friedrich's answers to her daughter's questions, which are directly scratched onto the filmstrip, we watch a heavily edited mixture of imagery, some documentary material by Friedrich (Super 8 imagery filmed in Germany; 16mm imagery recorded during a women's demonstration at the Seneca Army Depot in Central New York State; a silent portrait of Lore Friedrich swimming in Lake Michigan and working in an office), much of it found (archival material recorded in Germany during the war; home movies recorded soon after Lore Friedrich's emigration to Chicago; early American archival imagery of a young woman waving an American flag); some of it dramatized for the camera (Friedrich's alter ego taking a bath; hands assembling a plastic model of a traditional Bavarian house). Friedrich's editing of this diverse (all black-and-white) material into a single film provides a cinematic argument for the interconnection between the histories of German Nazism, the American arms buildup of the 1980s, women's struggles for equal employment, and Su Friedrich's personal quest to understand her mother. The hundreds of hours Friedrich labored to develop the intricate set of interconnections between her sound and image tracks result in an overriding formal metaphor for the ties that bind together the past and present, mothers and daughters, and cinematic traditions.

While I cannot here provide a thorough review of significant feminist contributions to 1980s filmmaking or of interesting films in which a feminist awareness is combined with other commitments, a number of other filmmakers must be mentioned. Among the more influential filmmakers of the period was Barbara Hammer, whose energy and persistence were an inspiration to a good many younger (and especially gay) filmmakers: Hammer's ability to get film after film made demonstrated what a radical lesbian filmmaker can accomplish, even in a society willing to provide only limited support; and her engaging public persona enabled her to raise the issue of how a feminist sexual politic might find an appropriately radical form.[23] Other significant 1980s contributors to the increasingly sophisticated representation of women include Abigail Child (MUTINY [1983]; Child is discussed later), Leslie Thornton (ADYNATA [1983]), Michelle Fleming (TROPICAL DEPRESSION [1987], LEFT HANDED MEMORIES [1989], PRIVATE PROPERTY (PUBLIC DOMAIN)[1991]), Zeinabu irene Davis (CYCLES [1989], discussed later), Nina Fonaroff (DEPARTMENT OF THE INTERIOR [1986], A KNOWLEDGE THEY CANNOT LOSE [1989]), and Greta Snider (FUTILITY [1989], BLOOD STORY [1990]).

RECYCLED CINEMA

If a new sensually aware, cinematically refined feminism was the most discussed ideological trend of the 1980s, what has come to be called *recycled cinema* (*found footage film* remains a popular term for it) was the most visible formal tendency of the decade.[24] Recycled cinema has a long history beginning (perhaps) with FALL OF THE ROMANOV DYNASTY (1927) by the Russian filmmaker Esther Shub and in this country with Joseph Cornell's ROSE HOBART (1939) and subsequent films; it was popularized by Bruce Conner in the late 1950s (A MOVIE [1958]) and early 1960s. If the option of recycling cinema was originally, at least in this country, a means for producing films with virtually no capital outlay—both Conner, in A MOVIE, and Raphael Montañez Ortiz in the contemporaneous but comparatively unknown COWBOY AND "INDIAN" FILM (1958) and NEWSREEL (1958) chose the approach because it offered the only entry into filmmaking they could afford—it quickly became a means for dealing with the accumulation of film history itself. And not surprisingly, as each new decade has passed, the option of recycling the ever-increasing cultural archive of film and television imagery (and in doing so, offering various forms of critique of this cultural archive) has seemed more and more attractive, not only because recycling imagery is generally less expensive than shooting new imagery (especially since virtually no avant-garde filmmakers pay for the rights to such material), but because there is an audience for the work that has a sense of the history of the approach.

The reuse of previously recorded film imagery is common in a wide variety of films. Most of the filmmakers discussed as feminists, for example, use earlier footage, either to reassess the cultural past that has done so much to fashion our sense of the genders

Su Friedrich and her mother, Lore Friedrich, during shooting of THE TIES THAT BIND (1984).

or to come to grips with dimensions of their personal pasts. Here, however, I am discussing films or film experiences that are constructed entirely, or almost entirely, from earlier films. While Bruce Conner released only one film during the 1980s, AMERICA IS WAITING (1982), that film and STANDARD GAUGE (1984) by fellow Californian Morgan Fisher can suggest something of the considerable breadth in the ways recycled images were being used by this time. AMERICA IS WAITING is a memorable instance of the method that had characterized Conner's work during the 1960s and 1970s: images from a variety of older films are choreographed to the David Byrne/Brian Eno composition "America Is Waiting." The sound track is used as a continuous thread that provides coherence for Conner's disjunctively edited commentary on American militarism. Over the years, Conner has explored a wide variety of relationships between sound and image: sometimes the juxtaposition between image and sound is ironic; sometimes it enforces parallels. In AMERICA IS WAITING the attitudes implicit in Conner's recycling and in the Byrne/Eno song are roughly parallel, though the specific connections between the two tracks are subtle and complex.

Fisher's STANDARD GAUGE could hardly be less like AMERICA IS WAITING, though Fisher is an admirer of Conner's work and, indeed, makes reference to it in STANDARD GAUGE when he tells the story of how, during some stock-footage work for a commercial feature, he discovered the execution by firing squad "that appears in Bruce Conner's film A MOVIE."[25] But if STANDARD GAUGE can be read in part as Fisher's tribute to Conner, it is a tribute that uses an entirely different approach. As in AMERICA IS WAITING, in Fisher's film we see virtually nothing but found imagery; but while Conner—and most other "cinema recyclers"—present this imagery as it was originally seen (though, of course, within a new editing strategy), Fisher presents his found footage on a rewind as

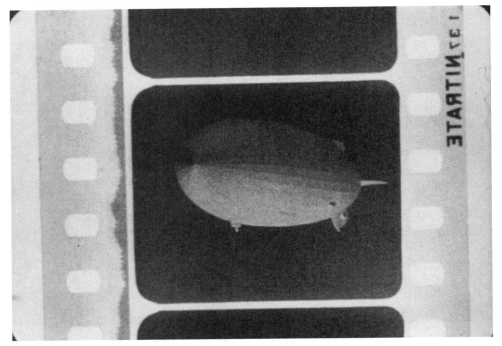

A nitrate-stock filmstrip of the Hindenburg, from Morgan Fisher's STANDARD GAUGE
(1984).

a series of 35mm filmstrips: that is, we see these cinematic memories as celluloid sou-
venirs Fisher has collected over the years; Fisher's sound track is his commentary on the
individual strips of film. While Conner focuses on the way the history of film (the history
of all kinds of film, especially educational films and television commercials) encodes
America's problematic sense of itself, Fisher focuses on the surround of industrial, mass-
market movie-making—on the history of those tens of thousands of marginalized,
unnamed men and women whose labor makes Hollywood possible. It's a history Fisher
has played a part in. Indeed, the strips of imagery he presents during STANDARD GAUGE
were collected during his years of working around the edges of the industry—"edges"
both in a social and industrial sense (Fisher has done stock-footage research, he has been
employed as an editor; friends have worked in the industry) and in the material sense: for
this viewer, the fascination of STANDARD GAUGE is in what Fisher reveals about the various levels of textual and other signification (information directed to labs, editors, and
projectionists) that those of us who have taught film history have always seen, on film
leader and on the edges of the filmstrip, without fully understanding. Ultimately, Fisher's
stance toward the film industry is quite different from Conner's. While Conner's films
reveal the surreality of much of what passes for "normal," Fisher's dramatize his ambivalence about Hollywood: he recognizes that the industry, whatever its failures and limitations, not only makes *all* film history possible, including the very imagery that avant-garde
filmmakers deconstruct and satirize, but that the romance of the movies is what attracts
most avant-garde filmmakers to the field. The filmstrips Fisher presents during
STANDARD GAUGE are relics in the religious sense: shards of an increasingly endangered
history that Fisher both critiques and honors.[26]

Two of the decades most ambitious "recycling" projects are at opposite ends of a somewhat different axis from the one charted by Conner and Fisher. During the 1980s, Ken Jacobs was developing a series of works using what he calls "the Nervous System." Developed during the 1970s, the Nervous System is a pair of interlocking, analytic 16mm projectors that allow Jacobs to superimpose two nearly identical projected film images and, by interrupting the projector beams with one of a number of propeller devices he has devised, to create a range of visual (and with his sound system, auditory) effects.[27]

Nineteen eighty was a watershed year for the Nervous System work, beginning with HELL BREAKS LOOSE (chapter 3 of the series called THE IMPOSSIBLE—a reference in part to the ability to create "impossible" effects with this unusual apparatus), in which Jacobs reexplored the 1905 Biograph film TOM, TOM, THE PIPER'S SON, which had been the focus of his own TOM, TOM, THE PIPER'S SON (1969, revised 1971). HELL BREAKS LOOSE was followed by chapters 4 and 5 of THE IMPOSSIBLE: SCHILLING (1980) and THE WRONG LAUREL (1980); and by XCXHXEXRXRXIXEXSX ("Cherries"—the Xs are a joke on the triple XXX of porn films; 1980), which recycles a bit of French pornography from the 1920s; by KEN JACOBS' THEATER OF UNCONSCIONABLE STUPIDITY PRESENTS CAMERA THRILLS OF THE WAR (1981), THE WHOLE SHEBANG (1982), and MAKING LIGHT OF HISTORY: THE PHILIPPINES ADVENTURE (1983); and at the end of the decade, by TWO WRENCHING DEPARTURES (1989), a tribute to the passing of Jack Smith and Bob Fleischner (two of Jacobs's early collaborators) in which Jacobs recycles

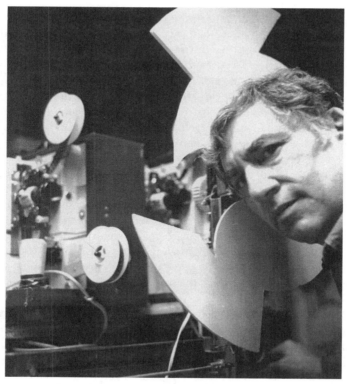

Ken Jacobs with Nervous System apparatus.

bits of his own SATURDAY AFTERNOON BLOOD SACRIFICE (1957) and STAR SPANGLED TO DEATH (1958–60). In some cases, the Nervous System pieces were performed in various versions throughout the decade and into the 1990s.

Jacobs's performances with the Nervous System apparatus are meant to evoke nineteenth-century precinematic magical events, but his use of the apparatus also looks back to a more recent moment in the history of art: Jacobs was trained as a painter (he studied with Hans Hoffmann) and American abstract expressionism remains important to him. For Jacobs, the Nervous System is a cinematic tool with which he can express himself in relation to the celluloid artifacts he collects, abstracting from them a wide range of visual and emotional effects, including (in XCXHXEXRXRXIXEXSX) 3-D and (in TWO WRENCHING DEPARTURES) a sense of human motion that verges on the operatic. He conceives of himself as an "action filmmaker," in the sense that Jackson Pollock was an "action painter"; each Nervous System performance is meant to place the viewer within a perceptual and conceptual environment where a work of art is being created as the audience watches and listens. While Jacobs has strong feelings about many political issues, he is most passionate about the importance of art as a creative space in which the artist expresses the frustrations, the terror, and the ecstasies of particular historical moments. Indeed, Jacobs's loyalty to the idea of art has, in recent years, rendered his work controversial and problematic, especially for those who do not trust this artist's ability to deal with the real issues of his moment in the rarefied ("elitist") space of the avant-garde screening room.[28] But for those less cynical about the implications of art and artist, Jacobs's Nervous System performances are distinctive, memorable excursions that lie somewhere between a visit to a gallery of modern painting and an amusement park ride.

While Jacobs's Nervous System performances are novel cinematic experiences that look backward for their inspiration, Raphael Montañez Ortiz's digital/laser/video works recycle moments from classic film history, using an apparatus that seems the very embodiment of the technological present and future. Having begun his artistic career as a cine-recycler the same year as Bruce Conner, Ortiz explored a variety of performance-oriented, "destructivist" approaches to art making;[29] Then, in the mid-1980s, he developed an apparatus for carefully deconstructing problematic moments from the history of cinema: using laserdisc versions of such films as CITIZEN KANE (1941), KING KONG (1933), GRAND ILLUSION (1937), and BODY AND SOUL (1947), his Apple computer, and a simple sound effects generator, Ortiz began to reorganize passages of film within which various forms of brutality are hidden and the expression of honest sexuality is repressed, and to record the results on video.[30] For Ortiz, his apparatus is a way of defying the tendency of the history of cinema to move relentlessly toward the illusion of resolution and social harmony—a one-way directionality that is encoded within the movie projector, which nearly always moves forward at a predetermined speed toward the production of financial profit. The goal of Ortiz's revisions of classic cinema, and of his use of what he sees as a more fully holistic apparatus for confronting cinema history, is the spiritual serenity that develops through the release of what even the best of conventional cinema represses. As a Puerto Rican–American (with some Native American roots), Ortiz's quest is to reveal how traditional cinema has conspired in the disenfranchisement of many North Americans and to ritually expose repressed elements (in even the best films) that mitigate against a healthy expression of individual psyches and a healthy social diversity—before we carry our damaged spirits into a new millennium.

Between 1985 and 1990, Ortiz produced twenty-five digital/laser/videos, in which he developed the characteristic elements of his approach. In The Kiss (1985), for example,

Ortiz reorganizes a conventional moment from Robert Rossen's BODY AND SOUL, during which the protagonists, a prizefighter (John Garfield) and an artist (Lili Palmer), kiss good-bye after the boxer's visit to the artist's apartment. For Ortiz, this good-bye kiss represented the repression of the obvious sexual attraction of the two characters, a repression demanded not by the characters themselves but by the Hollywood Code. Ortiz's response was to rearrange the frames of the passage and repeat them in a rhythmic manner that releases the erotic repressed by the kiss: the characters seem lost in a wild sexual encounter. In DANCE NO. 1 (1985), Ortiz rearranges the moment from CITIZEN KANE when Kane, Jedediah Leland, and Mr. Bernstein arrive at the *Inquirer* office to take control of the newspaper. For Ortiz, this amusing scene, in which Mr. Carter, the current editor of the paper, must turn over his office to Kane, represses Kane's arrogant, classist demonstration of power—a power he has in no way earned. Ortiz's response is to transform the scene into a dance spectacle, revealing the "dance" elements originally built into this cinematic moment for what they are: a repression of Mr. Carter's public humiliation so that the audience can enjoy Carter's pain without being conscious of Kane's, and their, meanness.

By the 1980s, recycled cinema had become the most pervasive formal trend in avant-garde film. On the one hand, the popularity of the approach may have been a result of a paradox: while reusing imagery produced by the film industry without obtaining permission may have seemed risky, it was a risk without appreciable danger, since no one was ever charged with any crime. Of course, the industry's lack of interest in those pilfering its history in the service of their own careers was a function of the comparatively impoverished state of the avant-garde scene: since no one was making any money, no matter how ingenious and provocative the films were, why would the industry bother to track down those intent on turning industrial products against the industry that produced them? On the other hand, the pervasiveness of recycled cinema was a function of the wealth and diversity of the material available for recycling, which included not only commercial features the industry seemed uninterested in protecting from avant-gardists but also all manner of outdated educational and scientific films, outdated television commercials shot on film, and the huge reservoir of home movie and personal travel material that had been accumulating for generations.

Having experimented with a variety of conceptualist and minimalist approaches in the 1970s, Alan Berliner began to finish noteworthy short films made almost entirely of recycled imagery and sound in the early 1980s, including CITY EDITION (1980), MYTH IN THE ELECTRIC AGE (1981), NATURAL HISTORY (1983), and EVERYWHERE AT ONCE (1985). In each of these films, Berliner, who is something of an obsessive collector of old imagery and sound (he has won Emmies for his sound work for television), would choose a general theme and construct a complex sound-image montage that explored that theme. For example, the theme of CITY EDITION is the newspaper, which Berliner evokes not only by framing the film's elaborate montage within recycled imagery of newspapers being printed, but by juxtaposing images and sounds in a manner that reiterates the bizarre juxtapositions of news stories on any given newspaper page and the overall organizations of material characteristic of newspapers. The staccato energy of Berliner's editing is an avant-garde version of the dramatic energy of Howard Hawks's HIS GIRL FRIDAY (1940). The most notable formal accomplishment of Berliner's early recycled films is his considerable awareness of the myriad possibilities for creating a sense of synchronization between images and sounds that come from very different sectors of the culture and clearly "don't belong" to each other.[31]

If CITY EDITION and EVERYWHERE AT ONCE (discussed briefly later) are Berliner's most successful early contributions to recycled cinema, the hour-long THE FAMILY ALBUM (1986) is his most accomplished film of the 1980s, as well as an obvious premonition of his impressive films of the 1990s: INTIMATE STRANGER (1991) and NOBODY'S BUSINESS (1996). The "theme" of THE FAMILY ALBUM is the tradition of domestic documentation and celebration of family life in 16mm home movies during the past several generations. Structured as a cycle of life, beginning with imagery of babies and moving through various conventional phases of family life up to the funerals of elderly members of families, THE FAMILY ALBUM simultaneously honors the considerable skill and luck of those who have brought cameras into the family circle and provides a bittersweet sense of the American family in the mid-twentieth century—bittersweet because it becomes clear, as the film proceeds, that the essential function of home movie making has been to create happy visual memories of families, regardless of how dysfunctional those families may have been. Indeed, THE FAMILY ALBUM represents a very different relationship between image and sound from that developed in Berliner's earlier recycled films. Here, sound functions as a counterpoint to the film's often exquisite and poignant recycling of family imagery, suggesting a basic pattern in American family life: the relentless performance of continuity and coherence despite the reality of pervasive personal frustration, disappointment, and loss.

During the 1980s, recycled cinema produced a wide range of articulations, too many to detail here. Phil Solomon developed a variety of procedures for chemically treating filmed imagery, producing a series of evocative, exquisitely textured films, including THE SECRET GARDEN (1988), THE EXQUISITE HOUR (1989), and REMAINS TO BE SEEN (1989). Lewis Klahr was combining Super 8 imagery from abbreviated versions of

Family celebration recycled in Alan Berliner's THE FAMILY ALBUM *(1986).*

Bicyclist riding through crystallizing emulsion in Phil Solomon's Remains to
Be Seen *(1989).*

Hollywood features and cartoons to create his Picture Books for Adults (1983–85). Craig
Baldwin was developing his reputation as a "media pirate" in RocketKitKongoKit
(1986), and in the remarkable Tribulation 99: Alien Anomalies under America
(1990), his pseudo-documentary send-up of cold war–era paranoia and propaganda.
Also memorable are Michael Wallen's Decodings (1983), William Farley's Tribute
(1986), and Heather McAdams's Scratchman II (1982). A very different sense of
"found" material was evident in Leslie Thornton's Peggy and Fred in Hell
(Prologue) (1984) and in the Peggy and Fred films that followed. Instead of recycling
actual film material, Thornton recycled the gestures that, as children, we internalize as
a result of our immersion in a thoroughly mediated society. Thornton's work was important for a good many younger filmmakers and is related to the work of Abigail Child (discussed later), whose films often mimic the gestures of commercial *films noirs*. Each of
these filmmakers is worthy of extended analysis and discussion.[32]

The 1980s also saw a developing interest in the global or the transnational, the flip
side of which was an increasing fascination with particular places, conceived either as
geographic regions or as ethnic communities. During a decade that, as a result of the
availability of inexpensive air travel, saw the development of a network of international
film festivals serving a wide range of films, as well as of the Internet and the World Wide
Web, it was perhaps inevitable that avant-garde filmmakers would explore forms of cinema that recognize the increasing internationality of everyday experience, while avoiding (at least to some degree) the commercial trope of the Western adventurer (James
Bond, Indiana Jones) who visits a variety of international locales in the process of maintaining the World-Wide economic and sociopolitical status quo. Of course, like virtually
all trends in alternative cinema, this urge toward the global has roots in earlier decades:
Peter Kubelka's Unsere Afrikareise (1966) is one prototype, Warren Sonbert's The
Carriage Trade (1972), another. In each of these films, the filmmaker's journey—in

Kubelka's case, a particular journey with a group of wealthy Austrians through various African locales to a big-game hunting safari, which Kubelka reveals as the quintessential colonialist activity; in Sonbert's case, an ongoing journey from one continent to another—is presented not as a single, obvious adventure narrative but as a complex montage within which various places and issues intersect. In fact, the reliance on montage in these films is their fundamental metaphor for the world, which is seen not as a set of locations some of which are "naturally" at the service of others, but as a huge interlocking organism in which every place and people coexists with and impinges on all others.

In American avant-garde film, Sonbert was the preeminent "globalist" (he died of AIDS in 1995). THE CARRIAGE TRADE revealed the approach that was to characterize the series of films he finished during the 1980s—A WOMAN'S TOUCH (1983), THE CUP AND THE LIP (1986), HONOR AND OBEY (1988), and FRIENDLY WITNESS (1989)— films that, fittingly, were popular at international film festivals.[33] With the exception of FRIENDLY WITNESS, which was constructed from outtakes from earlier Sonbert films, each of these films was the result of two separate processes. First, Sonbert recorded informal, handheld travel imagery during his journeys (though based in San Francisco, Sonbert was an inveterate global traveler). In many cases, this was conventional travel imagery (images of landmarks, including those that draw tourists), though in other instances the footage was more personal: images of friends and of events interesting or important to Sonbert. Having collected imagery over a period of months, Sonbert would study it carefully, becoming aware of every visual and conceptual nuance of every image he decided to use, and then would construct an immense montage experience in which each image and each intersection of one image with another functions as a nexus of visual and conceptual motifs. In a general sense, the motifs within any particular film address specific issues, though the experience of each film's montage tends to open up a variety of possibilities, rather than to direct the viewer in a particular ideological direction, as do, for example, the montages in the Russian revolutionary films of the 1920s (of which Sonbert was always conscious). Indeed, each of Sonbert's mature films provides a complex meditation on a set of themes that simultaneously expresses Sonbert's concerns while providing viewers with a complex perceptual and conceptual field that the eye and mind can explore, viewing after viewing. While all of Sonbert's films from THE CARRIAGE TRADE through HONOR AND OBEY are silent, in his final film of the 1980s (and in the final film released before his death, SHORT FUSE [1993]) Sonbert returned to sound, developing a complex network of interconnections not only between image and image but also between image and sound.

The energy of Sonbert's films is a function of what at first may seem a paradox between the consistent informality of his handheld imagery and the nearly obsessive awareness evident "underneath" this apparent informality. But in fact, there is no paradox here: each of these two dimensions of Sonbert's films reflects a different aspect of an essentially democratic, egalitarian spirit. On the one hand, the informality of Sonbert's camerawork, along with his willingness to record popular touristic locations and his personal interactions with friends, declares Sonbert's relationship to the tradition of home movies and informal documentations of travel. On the other hand, the complex visual and auditory awareness revealed by a careful exploration of any given passage of the finished films is a way of demonstrating that it is the artist's responsibility to be aware that every place, every moment, all peoples and each person, are deserving of perceptual and conceptual commitment. Indeed, when particular moments in

Middle-Eastern street scene from Warren Sonbert's FRIENDLY WITNESS *(1989).*

Sonbert's films remind us of the militaristic and fascistic elements of one or another of the societies through which Sonbert travels, we understand these elements as an implicit danger to Sonbert's unpretentious social mobility and the personal freedom it represents.

Related approaches to the transnational are evident in Holly Fisher's SOFT SHOE (1987) and in Alan Berliner's aptly titled EVERYWHERE AT ONCE. For SOFT SHOE, Fisher used her considerable dexterity with the optical printer to construct a Muybridge-inspired cine-kaleidoscope of imagery filmed in Romania, Germany, and France, in both rural areas and in cities. Like Sonbert, Fisher films from within everyday events and subsequently formalizes her imagery during the editing and printing process. SOFT SHOE is both a frequently stunning personal evocation of a journey and a premonition of the end of the cold war. In EVERYWHERE AT ONCE, each simple cut from one image to another is capable of moving the viewer either across town or around the world. Of course, since Berliner's films recycle imagery recorded by others and only collected and edited by Berliner, they are more fully postmodern than the Sonbert films, which are records of the filmmaker's personal explorations in the world.

A very different approach to the transnational is evident in two films made outside of what is usually considered avant-garde history: Godfrey Reggio's POWAQQATSI (1987) and Ron Fricke's CHRONOS (1988). Reggio's 35mm feature—the second part of the proposed *qatsi* trilogy (*qatsi* is a Hopi word for life) that had begun with the widely seen KOYAANISQATSI (1984), which was shot by Fricke—was made possible by "angel financing" and, while "presented" by Francis Ford Coppola and George Lucas, has more in common with Sonbert's films and other avant-garde explorations of the transnational than with Hollywood commercial features. POWAQQATSI is a homage primarily to Third World laboring people. Sequences were filmed in multiple locations within Brazil, Egypt, India, Kenya, Nepal, and Peru, as well as in the cities of Hong Kong, Jerusalem, Berlin, and Chartres. While KOYAANISQATSI relies on time-lapse imagery, POWAQQATSI relies on slow motion, which transforms the movements of the working people Reggio films into cine-ballet (both KOYAANISQATSI and POWAQQATSI were made as collaborations with composer Philip Glass).[34] While Reggio's feature, like the Sonbert and Berliner films, seems to take us everywhere at once, Reggio does provide a general organization that suggests the attitudes underlying the project: after a prelude that depicts men carrying dirt out of a huge open mine (Reggio's imagery suggests both the Sisyphus myth and, near the end of the passage, as an exhausted or dead worker is carried up the side of the mine, the Pietá), the film moves from labor within various rural settings to men and women struggling to sustain themselves in crowded cities. The implication seems to be that, as grueling as rural labor is, it allows for the maintenance of more human dignity than life in urban centers. POWAQQATSI concludes with the definition of its title: "*pow waq qat si* (from the Hopi language, *powaq* sorcerer + *qatsi* life) n. an entity, a way of life, that consumes the life forces of other beings in order to further its own life." For Reggio, the sorcerer seems to be no particular political system, but rather the increasing desire to consume in all modern societies.

Compared to the obsessive rigor of Sonbert's films, POWAQQATSI is loosely organized (though the production process necessary to get the film made required considerable organization of hundreds of people in locations across the globe) and underconceptualized: Reggio's imagery is often impressive and moving, though some viewers complain that POWAQQATSI is pretentious kitsch, little more than an extended advertisement that provides no means for digesting the painful realities it exploits. What Reggio and his collaborators *are* able to accomplish, however, is a modern audience-pleasing version of the essential fascination with human movement that inspired Eadweard Muybridge's motion study photographs and the Lumière brothers' earliest photographs-in-motion. Whatever its limitations, POWAQQATSI proves that modern audiences can be enthralled by nonnarrative imagery of the everyday and the exotic, including forms of physical labor the commercial cinema ignores entirely.

When the Reggio/Fricke collaboration that produced KOYAANISQATSI came to an end, Fricke began making his own global cinematic excursions. His CHRONOS (1985) is an IMAX journey to impressive sites in Europe, North Africa, and the United States, filmed in time-lapse and accompanied by music composed by Michael Stearns that seems meant to create the same response to the magnificent diversity of the world that the Philip Glass sound track is meant to provide for POWAQQATSI. Fricke focuses on famous, awe-inspiring locations—the Grand Canyon, the pyramids of Giza, the Acropolis at Athens, the Vatican, Venice, Luxor (Egypt)—and seems uninterested in providing much beyond a generalized sense of awe, though Fricke's subsequent first feature, BARAKA (1993), a global excursion to major spiritual sites, is somewhat more specifically focused.

More intellectually sophisticated explorations of the global are evident in Yvonne Rainer's JOURNEYS FROM BERLIN/1971 and Su Friedrich's THE TIES THAT BIND (both discussed earlier); in Trinh T. Minh-ha's NAKED SPACES: LIVING IS ROUND (1985, discussed later); and in the Peter Watkins megafilm THE JOURNEY (1987), which was produced in fourteen different nations, including the United States, during 1984–85.

Graffiti and child in Iquitos, Peru, from Godfrey Reggio's POWAQQATSI *(1987).*

Watkins, who has conventionally been labeled a documentarian, may seem out of place in this chapter; but he is, and has always been, as much an avant-garde filmmaker as a documentarian: in general, his work has provided ongoing critiques of both the commercial narrative industry and the history of documentary—and this seems particularly true of THE JOURNEY.[35]

THE JOURNEY began as an attempt to mobilize the network of screening venues that had developed for *exhibiting* alternative cinema for the *production* of a globally collaborative film experiment that would critique conventional media systems while modeling more progressive possibilities. The 14 1/2-hour epic was produced by a network of community-based "support groups" that assisted in financing the film, provided their labor during the production, and added their voices to the discussions of such issues as the escalating arms race and world hunger (and the failure of media and educational organizations to deal seriously with such issues), as well as to a series of community psychodramatizations of social crises. These community-based elements were supplemented by the reminiscences of survivors of the World War II bombings of Hiroshima, Nagasaki, and Hamburg; by films, photographs, and other contributions by other (professional and amateur) artists; and by various frequently experimental uses of image, sound, and on-screen text.

The finished film is an immense weave of motifs that is divided into nineteen serially organized episodes that can be programmed individually or in various groupings—or, of course, presented in its entirety. While Watkins's commitment to the family discussions of social issues was considerable—these conversations are left as complete and unedited as Watkins's film technology allowed (Watkins was to calculate later that the average length of a shot in THE JOURNEY was 45.9 seconds)—his overall editing strategy continually shifts viewers from one section of the world to another and in a great many instances

Peter Watkins directing a crowd during the central New York State shooting of THE
JOURNEY *(1987).*

locates viewers in several sectors of the Earth simultaneously: during the title sequence
near the beginning of THE JOURNEY, for example, we see the words "The Journey" in
many different languages scroll through the frame from right to left, while we hear three
different layers of sound, each recorded at a different time and in a different country.

Watkins's combination of respect for individuals (including the "everyday" people the
commercial media tends to ignore or patronize) and his continually expanding global
consciousness—both of which are integrated formally into the texture of THE JOURNEY
(the respect, in Watkins's slow, careful pacing; the global consciousness, in the montage
structure)—provide a double-leveled critique of virtually all contemporary media making, including most avant-garde film, in which formal choices tend to obscure social
problems, if such problems are even suggested, rather than model forms of personal
action, social and political interaction, and cinematic form that might assist in amelio-
rating these problems by reconstituting world political and media organizations. Despite
its considerable achievements, however, THE JOURNEY was not widely seen: its experimental structure kept it out of most theaters and with few exceptions off television; it
seemed too much a documentary for avant-garde screening spaces and was too experimental and unwieldly for most documentary programmers. Watkins hoped that the
global network he developed for producing THE JOURNEY would function as an ongoing political organization that would use the film for progressive action. In the end, however, THE JOURNEY seems to have become, at most, a potential conceptual inspiration
for the transnationally inclined—akin perhaps to the conceptual inspiration the ever-so-
slow Warhol films of the 1960s provided for a generation of avant-garde filmmakers
reacting against media overload.

Representations of Ethnicity

While the increasing accessibility of international travel and the advent of on-line technologies were internationalizing the 1980s, suggesting to filmmakers that on some level we are "everywhere at once," and further, that every domestic political issue is, equally, a transnational issue, other filmmakers were responding to internationalization and postmodernization by focusing on the particulars of place. This interest in place was not new, even for some of the filmmakers who need to be recognized here, but it does seem a dimension of avant-garde film destined for increased recognition, especially because the social force of globalization and its potential for international cultural homogenization are sure to become more powerful in the coming years.

Two different aspects of the idea of place require some comment: "place" as in ethnic community and "place" meaning landscape and cityscape. The 1980s certainly saw an increasing contribution to film history by ethnic communities traditionally marginalized by mainstream cinema: particularly, African-Americans, Asian-Americans, and Hispanics. Not surprisingly, filmmakers coming from these communities (or really these clusters of communities) tended to set their sights on commercial success either as feature directors or as documentarians: while some European-American avant-garde filmmakers may have enjoyed, even fetishized, cultural marginalization (Hollis Frampton once said, "Nothing is more wonderful than to have no one pay the slightest attention to what you are doing; if you're going to grow, you can grow at your own speed"), filmmakers from sectors of society that had had virtually no access to film production, much less to popular audiences, were not likely to hunger for the "advantages" of invisibility.[36]

For African-American filmmakers, and for filmmakers from other ethnically marginalized groups as well, the simple presentation of nonstereotypical characters in narrative melodrama and documentary *was* avant-garde, even if the films were formally conventional. Indeed, most viewers' ease in understanding commercial or semicommercial films with more progressive depictions of ethnicity seemed to make them more fully "avant-garde," at least in a political sense, than what was usually called the film avant-garde. The fact that avant-garde film had never really achieved more than a marginal recognition in the larger culture, even among dedicated moviegoers, rendered its tactics suspect, at best, among those interested in using film to affect the political and cinematic status of marginalized groups. And this was especially true because the "avant-garde" had paid no more attention to the issue of ethnicity than the commercial cinema had. As a result, many filmmakers attempted to move into the neighborhood of conventional cinema, bringing their own ethnic histories and personal challenges with them, rather than to produce radical approaches to cinematic form in an invisible underground.

One flashpoint for ethnically progressive cinema was UCLA, where the desire for alternatives to Hollywood's imaging of ethnic groups produced a spirited group of African-American filmmakers who have come to be known as "the L.A. Rebellion," as well as comparable groups of Asian-American and Chicano filmmakers.[37] Perhaps the most important figures to emerge from the L.A. Rebellion are Charles Burnett and Julie Dash. Burnett, whose thesis film at UCLA was the remarkable KILLER OF SHEEP (1977), was active throughout the 1980s, finishing two films on African-American family life—MY BROTHER'S WEDDING (1983) and TO SLEEP WITH ANGER (1990)—and working on films by others: he was cinematographer for Alile Sharon Larkin's A DIFFERENT IMAGE (1981) and for Billy Woodberry's BLESS THEIR LITTLE HEARTS

(1984) and contributed to many other films.[38] Dash's best-known film of the 1980s was ILLUSIONS (1983), a short narrative about an African-American film executive who is able to pass as white and a young African-American singer who provides the singing voice for a white star. By the end of the 1980s, Dash had finished principal shooting for her first 35mm feature, the period piece DAUGHTERS OF THE DUST (1992).[39] While Dash focused on African-American history, Burnett, Woodberry, and Larkin focused on the day-to-day lives of African-American men and women. This focus on people too "normal" for Hollywood melodrama also characterizes other noteworthy contributions by African-Americans, including Kathleen Collins, whose LOSING GROUND (1982) depicts two young African-American professionals (a college professor and a painter) trying to integrate their creative lives with their personal relationship.

Some films did attempt to incorporate avant-garde tactics into narrative melodrama, presumably on the widely held assumption among avant-gardists that radical film content requires, or at least profits from, radical film form. Three films from 1989 suggest the range of such experiments. While many avant-garde filmmakers of the 1960s through the 1980s returned to the beginnings of cinema (and especially to Eadweard Muybridge's motion photography and the Lumière brothers' single-shot films) for inspiration, Charles Lane returned to the great silent comedy directors and actors, especially Charlie Chaplin, Buster Keaton, and Harry Langdon. Using an approach he had developed in A PLACE IN TIME (1977), Lane directed and starred in SIDEWALK STORIES (1989), a "silent comedy" (the action is accompanied by music, and at the very end by a bit of dialogue) about an underdog sketch artist who takes care of a young child when her father is mugged and murdered. While Chaplin's THE KID (1921) was a mainstream

The Artist (Charles Lane, seated) threatened by a larger competitor, in Lane's
SIDEWALK STORIES (1989).

success, Lane's use of a Chaplinesque approach in an era when synch sound had come to seem inevitable was a radical departure from the mainstream, and apparently as a result, SIDEWALK STORIES found its way to few audiences: indeed, Lane's failure to achieve a popular audience for this lovely, accomplished feature seems one of the remarkable events of the 1980s.

For CYCLES, Zeinabu irene Davis not only used a variety of approaches identified with avant-garde film but also used them in an experimental narrative about a topic normally considered taboo in conventional media, except for purposes of humor: menstruation. Davis's protagonist is waiting the arrival of her period, which she and Davis recognize as a natural and holy cycle that unites her with her ancestors. Ritualistically, she cleans her apartment and her body—the ritual quality of these activities is emphasized by Davis's use of unusual angles and extreme close-ups—then sleeps a dream-filled sleep and awakes to find she has begun to menstruate. The film's mini-events are punctuated with allusions to elements of African diasporic tradition and by comments by a chorus of women whose accents suggest the broad range of diasporic sisterhood.

The most influential 1980s film that uses avant-garde form as a means for exploring ethnicity is Spike Lee's DO THE RIGHT THING (1989), which combines a narrative melodrama about an ethnically diverse group of characters highly unusual in an American commercial film with an overall structure reminiscent of the avant-garde documentary tradition of the "city symphony." Like the European masterworks of the genre—BERLIN: SYMPHONY OF A BIG CITY (Walther Ruttmann, 1927), THE MAN WITH THE MOVIE CAMERA (Dziga Vertov, 1929), NOTHING BUT THE HOURS (Alberto Cavalcanti, 1926)—Lee's film charts the trajectory of a single day in the life of a city. While the European city symphonies focus on the commercial and industrial centers of the capital cities they depict, DO THE RIGHT THING implicitly argues that the real energy of New York (and by implication, any modern city) rests in the ethnic diversity of its neighborhoods, which is most obvious not on a workday but on a summer weekend. Lee's film has generally been understood as an unusual, abrasive commercial narrative; but it is also this nation's most remarkable city symphony (remarkable in part because of its commercial success)—especially in Lee's use of his production process to demonstrate the efficacy of the interethnic collaboration his characters are *not* able to maintain on the hottest day of the summer in a Bedford-Stuyvesant neighborhood in Brooklyn.[40]

Wayne Wang's CHAN IS MISSING (1981) was to Asian-American independent media what KILLER OF SHEEP was to African-American independent media: as Burnett critiques American clichés about ghetto life, Wang's feature critiques the commercial distortions of the Chinese epitomized by Charlie Chan. Wang was an inspiration to the generation of Asian-American filmmakers who came of age in the 1980s. Two noteworthy figures in the emergence of Asian-American cinema are Christine Choy, who arrived in the United States in 1967, became involved with Newsreel in the 1970s, helped to found Third World Newsreel, and developed as a documentarian and polemicist in the 1970s; and Renee Tajima, a native-born Japanese-American who became politically active as an adolescent in Los Angeles and a media activist while at Harvard. Choy was prolific in the 1980s, though her two most impressive films were made as collaborations with others. For MISSISSIPPI TRIANGLE (1984), Choy, Allan Siegel, and Worth Long devised a production process that echoed the ethnic triangularity that was the focus of the film: Choy shot the sections of the film dealing with the Mississippi Delta Chinese-American community, Worth Long shot the sections dealing with African-Americans in

Chinese-African-American Arlee Hen buys groceries from Chinese-American grocer in the Mississippi Delta region, in MISSISSIPPI TRIANGLE (1984), directed by Christine Choy, Allan Siegel, and Worth Long.

the Delta (Charles Burnett, who did contribute to the film, was originally scheduled to film these sections), and Allan Siegel shot the Delta European-Americans.[41] Choy's other major film of the 1980s was a collaboration with Tajima: the two worked together to document the Vincent Chin case (Chin was murdered by Ronald Ebens in Detroit when Ebens mistook Chin for Japanese; the case had become a major focus of the Chinese-American community nationwide), and to use the case as a way of exploring the complexity of American ethnicity. Choy and Tajima continued to work together until 1990. Their final work on American ethnicity, YELLOW TALE BLUES: TWO AMERICAN FAMILIES, explored their own families as two aspects of Asian-American reality: Chinese and Japanese, immigrant and native born.

Roughly parallel developments were taking place within various Hispanic communities, though the immense variety of cultural connections identified by *Hispanic* and the underexploration of Latin American art making by scholars makes generalizations difficult. On the East Coast, Raphael Montañez was making digital/laser/videos. In San Francisco and in El Paso, Texas, Willie Varela (who moved to the Bay Area from West Texas in the early 1980s and returned near the end of the decade) continued to make highly visual explorations of his personal surround in Super 8. And in San Francisco, Susana Muñoz and Lourdes Portillo made LAS MADRES: THE MOTHERS OF PLAZA DEL MAYO (1985) and LA OFRENDA: THE DAYS OF THE DEAD (1988) and worked to develop a network of Chicana and Mexican women filmmakers: a conference she instigated, "Cruzando Fronteras Escuentreo de Mujeres Cineastas y Videoastas Latinas" ("Across the Border: Conference of Latin Film and Video Makers"), was held in November 1990 in Tijuana, Mexico.[42]

A very different approach to dealing with ethnicity—one that, like Do the Right Thing, models a filmmaking practice that crosses ethnic "barriers" while honoring the traditions of ethnic community—is Lynne Sachs's Sermons and Sacred Pictures (1989), which samples and recycles 16mm films (and photography and sound recording) made by the Reverend L. O. Taylor during the late 1930s, 1940s, and 1950s. Taylor, a black Baptist preacher from Memphis, used his filmmaking as a means of confirming the feeling of community among his parishioners; screenings were exciting local events, not only because individuals might see themselves on screen from within the excitement of a community gathering, but because Taylor was a capable filmmaker: his imagery of out-door baptisms, for example, is impressive. For her film, Sachs (who is white) returned to her native Memphis and visited what had been Taylor's parish, interviewing people and filming them at a screening of Taylor's films. Sachs's film invites viewers into the evolution of this community: as we sit in our audience watching excerpts from Taylor's films over the heads of 1987 Memphis Baptists, our level of identification and difference measures the progress we feel we've made, or have failed to make, in coming to terms with the history of ethnicity in America.

Landscape and Cityscape

In exploring film's ability to come to terms with the other sense of American place—the physical "place" of American countryside and American towns and cities—avant-garde filmmakers have taken a wide variety of different tacks. Few filmmakers have dedicated as much time to recording American place as Rudy Burckhardt, who made his first American films in 1937, soon after he emigrated to New York from Switzerland.[43] Burckhardt's most memorable early films are unpretentious New York city symphonies—The Climate of New York (1948), for example, and Under the Brooklyn Bridge (1953)—and his fascination with New York has remained consistent ever since, accounting for such 1980s films as All Major Credit Cards (1982), Central Park in the Dark (1985), and Zipper (1987). All of these films are records of Burckhardt's excursions around New York City and, to a lesser degree, other American locales, including rural Maine, where he has spent time during the summers. Burckhardt's films are strictly observational; we learn little about him, except that he has maintained a commitment to recording New York spaces and faces at street level, in those areas of the city where its diversity and energy seem most apparent: in Cental Park, for example, and on Fourteenth Street. Burckhardt's most elaborate place-oriented film of the 1980s is the compilation piece Around the World in Thirty Years (1983), which includes his interpretations of various places during various decades: Manhattan in 1966; Port-au-Prince, Haiti, in 1976; Naples, Italy, in 1951; Peru in 1975; Tokyo in 1982; and rural Maine in 1981. Close in spirit to Sonbert's transnational montages, Around the World in Thirty Years also reveals the remarkable consistency in Burckhardt's studies of place over the past half-century.

The most impressive place-centered films of the 1980s are probably Nathaniel Dorsky's Hours for Jerome (shot from 1966 to 1970, edited from 1980 to 1982); Peter Hutton's New York Portrait, Part II (1980) and Part III (1990; he had begun his series of New York City Portraits in the 1970s, with New York Near Sleep for Saskia [1972] and New York Portrait, Part I [1977]) and his homage to Hudson River School painter Thomas Cole, Landscape (for Manon) (1987); and Andrew Noren's The Lighted Field (1987). Dorsky and Hutton are discussed later. Noren, who established himself as a major figure, especially in what came to be called "diary film," in the 1960s, continued to refine his dexterity with the 16mm camera during the 1970s in the series of films he calls THE ADVENTURES OF THE EXQUISITE CORPSE. In 1987 he completed the fifth part of the series, THE LIGHTED FIELD. THE LIGHTED FIELD is a sixty-one-minute, black-and-white, silent exploration of Noren's domestic environment in New Jersey and of various sectors of Manhattan, where Noren works as a news archivist for Sherman Grinberg (THE LIGHTED FIELD includes some imagery from the archive that Noren rescued from decay).[44] For Noren, the camera is analogous to a musical instrument; with it he can "play" light and shadow with remarkable subtlety and ingenuity, sometimes recording exquisite domestic moments—portraits of his spouse, his children, pets, the backyard—at others using single-framing to rocket viewers along New York streets or creating dizzying kaleidoscopic experiences by turning the camera over and over. All in all, THE LIGHTED FIELD is a kind of high-energy prayer of thanksgiving that embodies Noren's painstaking observation of the everyday visual worlds he moves through, condensing endless hours of attention into a film experience of remarkable density and power.

Also noteworthy for their depictions of place are Michael Rudnick's lovely, good-humored time-lapse portrait of San Francisco, PANORAMA (1982); KOYANNISQATSI, the feature directed by Godfrey Reggio and shot by Ron Fricke, which begins with spectacular images of Monument Valley and other natural wonders of the American Southwest, and then uses time-lapse to explore American cities, especially Los Angeles and New York; and Peter von Ziegesar's time-lapse portrait of Manhattan, CONCERN FOR THE CITY (1986).

Other filmmakers have attempted to produce what might be called filmic essays on place. Distinguished instances include Babette Mangolte's THE SKY ON LOCATION

Storm in the Catskills in Peter Hutton's LANDSCAPE (FOR MANON) (1987).

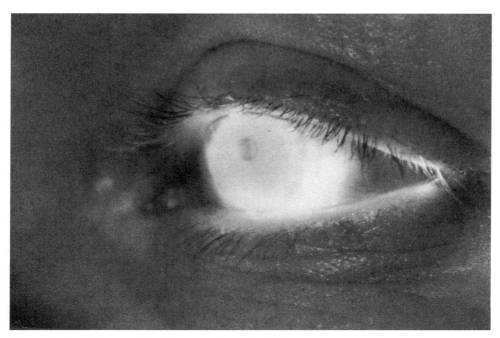

From Andrew Noren's THE LIGHTED FIELD *(1987).*

(1983) and Marjorie Keller's THE ANSWERING FURROW (1985). Mangolte's feature is an exploration of the American West. Made at a moment when beautiful images of landscape seemed at best old-fashioned and at worst outré, at least for an independent woman filmmaker, THE SKY ON LOCATION seems increasingly prescient of the developing interest in place as a nexus of geography and history that, in the 1990s, is fueling the fields of American studies and environmental studies. By the time she made THE SKY ON LOCATION, Mangolte had established herself as a talented cinematographer with her contributions to a series of landmark feminist films of the 1970s and early 1980s: Yvonne Rainer's LIVES OF PERFORMERS (1972) and FILM ABOUT A WOMAN WHO . . . (1974), Chantal Akerman's JEANNE DIELMAN, 23 QUAI DU COMMERCE, 1080 BRUXELLES (1983), and Sally Potter's THE GOLD DIGGERS (1983).[45] Nowhere are her abilities as cinematographer more evident, however, than in THE SKY ON LOCATION, a visual record of a series of automobile trips Mangolte took through the Far West during 1980–81 (Mangolte estimates that she and her assistant drove twenty-thousand miles), arranged roughly into a seasonal cycle. Inspired by *Nature and Culture*, Barbara Novak's landmark study of nineteenth-century American landscape painting, Mangolte attempts to convey something of what seeing the remarkable vistas of the West must have felt like to the first generations of European-American explorers.[46] While her visuals pay homage to pristine Western landscapes, her experimental sound track provides a context that problematizes the beauty of the spaces she films. Mangolte uses three narrators. She herself comments on her experiences (in her French-accented English); two other narrators— a woman, Honora Ferguson, and a man, Bruce Boston—provide historical and theoretical observations. By interweaving her stunning imagery and her own personal, engaged responses to the landscapes with Ferguson's and Boston's rather detached comments (they were recorded in a studio space in New York), Mangolte communicates that mixture of awe and cynicism that inevitably characterizes our modern sense of the West: a remarkably beautiful place with a history of now-embarrassing moral and political compromises and environmental atrocities.

While Mangolte's focus is on classic American landscape, the focus of Marjorie Keller's THE ANSWERING FURROW (1985) is the relationship of her father's gardening and the classic Roman idea of the pastoral, as represented in particular by Virgil's *Georgics*. Divided into a series of four "georgics," THE ANSWERING FURROW begins with imagery of Keller's father's newly planted garden in spring (she images the filmstrip as a furrow). "Georgic II" provides a classic context for this activity with imagery recorded during trips to France, Italy, and Greece: gardening is seen as a spiritual activity that unites ancients and moderns, fathers and daughters. "Georgic III" depicts "the old man in autumn," seeing to the maintenance of his garden. And in the brief "Georgic IV" we see Keller herself at season's end, preparing the compost for future gardens. Subtle and evocative, THE ANSWERING FURROW is both informal (in Keller's use of handheld camera and in her acceptance of imagery that by conventional standards seems underlit or overexposed) and rigorously conceived as a filmic statement on the sources of her own art making. The film is now rendered all the more poignant by Keller's sudden death in 1994, a significant loss to the field: Keller was not only a productive filmmaker but also an editor (of the journal *Motion Picture*), a writer (her *The Untutored Eye: Childhood in the Films of Cocteau, Cornell, and Brakhage* was published by Associated University Presses in 1986), and a teacher and programmer.

A final and particularly elaborate instance of the 1980s tendency to study American place—finished, interestingly, the same year as Spike Lee's great city symphony—is

From Babette Mangolte's THE SKY ON LOCATION (1983).

WATER AND POWER (1989) by Pat O'Neill, who established himself as a master of the optical printer in the 1970s in a series of surreal tours-de-force. At fifty-seven minutes, WATER AND POWER was O'Neill's magnum opus (to that date); its focus, Los Angeles and the rural Owens Valley landscape that was drained by the city's on-going development.[47] As in his earlier films, in WATER AND POWER O'Neill creates a series of surreal tableaux: in this case, color imagery of Los Angeles and environs, filmed in time-lapse, is combined with time-lapsed, black-and-white imagery of men and women performing a variety of activities—climbing a ladder, strumming a guitar—reminiscent of Eadweard Muybridge's motion studies and Étienne-Jules Marey's chronophotographs, and with imagery and sound from a variety of big-budget and independent movies and television shows. WATER AND POWER, which has much in common both philosophically and technically with Reggio's KOYAANISQATSI, simultaneously evokes the city symphony form and critiques the most fundamental convention of the form: the assumption that the urban can be separated from the rural. In WATER AND POWER, O'Neill often layers imagery of urban Los Angeles with imagery recorded in the Owens Valley, suggesting what is particularly obvious in Southern California: that the urban and the rural are two parts of a single reality, and that, in this particular case, the life of Los Angeles captured in O'Neill's high-energy compositions is developed at the cost of what, for American nature writer Mary Austin (*The Land of Little Rain*, 1903), was one of American's most beautiful regions.

From Pat O'Neill's WATER AND POWER *(1989).*

Some Noteworthy Careers

While particular trends seem to characterize particular moments in the history of art and literature, any given era is also memorable because of the maturation of individual careers and the appearance of particular works, whether these careers and works exemplify the characteristic trends or not. In the history of American fiction, the 1930s can be characterized as the decade during which the economic ravages of the Great Depression instigated direct tough-guy approaches to storytelling and style, many of them affirmations of Marxist-inspired forms of social organization; and yet the most distinguished career to emerge from that decade is surely William Faulkner's. For this commentator, the 1980s are memorable, not simply because of the several trends I've discussed, but also because the decade saw the emergence of a variety of noteworthy careers. For purposes of this chapter, I have chosen to focus on Abigail Child, Nathaniel Dorsky, Su Friedrich, Peter Hutton, Elias Merhige, Anne Charlotte Robertson, Peter Rose, and Trinh T. Minh-ha. Of course, I am under no illusion that these are the only careers worth discussing at length. The eight brief discussions are presented alphabetically.

Abigail Child

During any productive moment of film history, our awareness of particular contributions is likely to include not only filmmakers and films we have explored in some detail but also those we are still coming to grips with. And especially in the history of avant-garde film, the speed with which we come to understand what a filmmaker is doing, fully enough to articulate this understanding in words, has virtually no relationship to the quality of the work. Indeed, some of the more interesting films of any given period may seem at first quite opaque. Given the range of demands on our attention, even those of us committed to an exploration of avant-garde film may avoid writing about particular films that provide special challenges. One obvious instance is Ken Jacobs's Nervous System pieces, each of which exists only during Jacobs's performance of it and changes during every performance: how can one take useful notes on such evanescent work, much less write with any precision about it? Even when films exist as prints, certain qualities may tend to defy precise analysis. Abigail Child's staccato montages of the 1980s are a particularly obvious instance. Child edits sound and image so densely that, even though her films are not terribly long, a scholar interested in pursuing a thorough analysis is likely to be dumbfounded, at least at first. For me, Child's work poses one of the challenges of the moment. I do not feel I have come to understand her films, but I feel compelled to do so—though it is already clear to me that the process will take longer to accomplish than time for this chapter allows.

Most of Child's 1980s films are sections of a metafilm she calls Is This What You Were Born For? The eight sections of this piece were not completed in the order of their final numbering, which has itself evolved: the series includes Prefaces (1981; part 1), Mutiny (1983; part 3), Covert Action (1984; part 5), Perils (1986; part 6), Mayhem (1987; part 7), Both 2 (1988; part 4), Both 1 (1989; part 2), and Mercy (1989; part 8). While the connections between some parts are relatively clear—Perils and Mayhem use the same actors and characters, and much the same sense of design— other connections are not at all obvious, though throughout this body of work Child's particular approach to editing sound and image is consistent and distinctive. In each film, Child combines a wide range of materials (usually both found footage and imagery she shoots herself) so that we are fully aware of the precision of her editing, especially her coordination of sound and image and her construction of continuing visual and auditory motion from bits of originally unrelated movements. The result is an exquisite jaggedness, a coherent cacophony.

Each of the films in IS THIS WHAT YOU WERE BORN FOR? stakes out a specific territory that Child explores using a motif structure. MUTINY, for example, is a kind of documentary mosaic of women's activities in which the activities of young suburban women (imagery Child originally recorded for a more conventional documentary) are juxtaposed with images of experimental performance art in downtown Manhattan (performers include a street musician who makes scratch music with a violin and a woman who makes bizarre sounds with her mouth), as well as with women debating issues and a found-footage performance by a Latin singer. Child's barrage editing—her mutiny against easy coherence—creates a sense of the ethnic diversity and artistic energy of the downtown scene and, in particular, a sense of women mutinying against culturally mainstream definitions of femininity. COVERT ACTION relies more fully on found-footage material to explore the idea of representing the couple—man and woman, woman and woman, child and child—within a period of intense debate about the politics of the body. MAYHEM uses a more equal mixture of enacted fiction and found footage to evoke the tradition of *film noir*, especially the genre's mystery and sexuality and its formal reliance on chiaroscuro.

NATHANIEL DORSKY

The long history of avant-garde filmmaking is made up of many kinds of careers. In some cases, filmmakers have seen themselves on the cutting edge of new, progressive attitudes, and their films as models of progressive filmmaking practice: Su Friedrich and Trinh T. Minh-ha are noteworthy 1980s instances. In other cases, filmmakers have understood their work as functioning outside the particular sociopolitical developments of the moment, a personal spiritual quest leading them through the essences of cinema toward a heightened awareness. Nathaniel Dorsky is such a filmmaker. Dorsky established himself in the 1960s with a trilogy of short films depicting his emergence from adolescence (INGREEN, 1964; A FALL TRIP HOME, 1964; SUMMERWIND, 1965), and then seemed almost to disappear until the 1980s—though he was shooting material for films that wouldn't be completed until later and working on films by other filmmakers (for example, he edited three of Ralph Steiner's "Joy of Seeing" films: A LOOK AT LAUNDRY [1971], BEYOND NIAGARA [1973]; and LOOK PARK [1974]). In terms of completed films, the 1980s were Dorsky's most productive period to date. The decade began with his editing one of American avant-garde cinema's preeminent homages to temperate-zone seasonality, HOURS FOR JEROME (the imagery was shot from 1966 to 1970, edited from 1980 to 1982, and culminated with two remarkable explorations of cinematic texture: PNEUMA [1983] and ALAYA [1987]).

HOURS FOR JEROME refers to the medieval BOOK OF HOURS, the medieval prayer book that was produced in many versions throughout Europe from the mid-thirteenth to the mid-sixteenth centuries. Each version of THE BOOK OF HOURS included a set of prayers and other information useful for Roman Catholics and extensive "illumination"—paintings representing important scenes from the history of Christianity. Saint Jerome was sometimes a subject of these paintings, though the literal Jerome in HOURS

FOR JEROME is Jerome Hiler, Dorsky's partner and personal "saint" since the 1960s. HOURS FOR JEROME is a silent, fifty-minute depiction of the seasonal cycle as Dorsky experienced it in New York City and in rural northern New Jersey, beginning in spring and ending in winter (HOURS FOR JEROME divides into two parts: part 1 covers spring and summer, part 2, fall and winter). Dorsky uses a range of techniques—time lapse, slow motion, color and black and white, long continuous shots, heavily edited montages—to create consistently stunning imagery that asks that the viewers respect the everyday realities of life and the visual subtleties of cinematic art by developing their sensitivity to nuances of color, chiaroscuro, and rhythm.

PNEUMA and ALAYA explore texture itself, as seen in two different forms. For PNEUMA, Dorsky processed a variety of out-of-date, discontinued film stocks without exposing the film, and subsequently chose from the results (in some instances, rephotographing them). In the finished film, we experience a wide range of cinematic textures. Each film stock reveals a different density of grain and a different range of color. At times, the textures create three-dimensional illusions; at other times, they draw attention to the filmstrip moving through the projector. ALAYA creates a related range of effects using sand: sometimes we see, or seem to see, vast desertscapes, and sometimes the film frame marks off a simple, flat, textured space. Often the granularity of the sand merges with the grain of the emulsion, blurring the distinction between what is represented and the process of representation.

Both films posit a viewer willing to enjoy the act of seeing itself, though, as Dorsky's titles suggest, this act of perception means to move the viewer through the material to something beyond: *pneuma* means soul or divine inspiration; *alaya* is a Sanskrit word

Grains of sand in extreme close-up, from Nathaniel Dorsky's ALAYA (1987).

that means "accumulation," though in Buddhist thought it suggests the primordial individuality that underlies our social context, or, as Dorsky put it to me in conversation, "If you considered yourself A MOVIE projector, *alaya* would be the projector bulb."[48] While some viewers may see Dorsky's work as a throwback to the 1960s and early 1970s and the era of formalist "art for art's sake" filmmaking, PNEUMA and ALAYA are as fully a response to postmodern American culture as the most virulent anticapitalist polemic. By asking viewers not just to consume endless representations of "reality," but to meditate on the essence, the "soul," of cinematic representation, Dorsky transforms the textures of film stock and of sand into emblems of the spirit: he breathes life into the "dust" of cinema. Like so much of the formalist avant-garde, Dorsky's filmmaking is ultimately an elegy to a disappearing medium—an elegy that, at least for a moment, means to transcend the physical limitations of the medium and, by implication, of human life itself.

SU FRIEDRICH

Su Friedrich's first films were made in the late 1970s and were much influenced by what British filmmaker and theoretician Laura Mulvey has called "scorched earth" feminist filmmaking: that is, filmmaking that found unacceptable any capitulation to the history of commercial film and television's exploitation of women's bodies and sexuality for the pleasure of male-centered audiences.[49] But by the time she made GENTLY DOWN THE STREAM (1981), Friedrich had begun to move away from the scorched earth approach. In GENTLY DOWN THE STREAM and even more fully in the three longer films she produced during the decade—THE TIES THAT BIND, DAMNED IF YOU DON'T (1987), and SINK OR SWIM (1990)—Friedrich found ways of providing a variety of forms of pleasure, including sensual pleasure, without compromising her feminist and lesbian politics. The results went well beyond the production of her own memorable films: in the 1990s, it is commonplace to see films by emerging film and videomakers that seem inspired by Friedrich's work.

While the generally grim mood of GENTLY DOWN THE STREAM is much of a piece with the despair and anger evident in Friedrich's "scorched earth" films, SCAR TISSUE (1979) and COOL HANDS, WARM HEART (1979), it is a remarkably energetic film because of its unusual combination of means. Having documented her dreams in a dream journal for several years, Friedrich decided to use the most interesting and provocative as a script for a film—in this case, "script" in the literal sense. Having edited the dreams

Successive images from Su Friedrich's GENTLY DOWN THE STREAM *(1981).*

into condensed poetic form, she scratched them, word by word, onto the filmstrip, so that viewers must reconstruct the syntax of these dreams as they watch and, by doing so, are "sutured" into the film. These often-startling texts (e.g., "I/make/a/second/vagina/beside/ my/first/one/I/look/in/surprise/Which/is/the/original?") are the visual and psychic foreground of GENTLY DOWN THE STREAM, while the photographed visuals—imagery of a woman swimming in an indoor pool and working out on a rowing machine, of Madonnas in Catholic churches—provide implicit context and metaphor.[50] While on the one hand, the jittery scratched texts and the background imagery seem, by conventional standards, informal and unprofessional, Friedrich's obvious care with the timing of her visual texts and with the interplay of text and image makes clear her commitment to the film and to the viewer and dramatizes her determination to construct an energetic experience out of the shards of a troubled period of her life, characterized in particular by her attempt to integrate her Roman Catholic upbringing and her lesbianism.

Friedrich's seemingly eclectic combination of influences in GENTLY DOWN THE STREAM—a no-nonsense radical feminism obvious in her selection of dreams and an approach to visual text that, in this case, is virtually an homage to the hand-scratched titles and signatures in Stan Brakhage's films—became the distinguishing dimension of her 1980s films, though in each film the particulars of Friedrich's syntheses were different. The combination of past and present, visual text and tape-recorded interview, dramatized imagery and found footage, in THE TIES THAT BIND was discussed earlier in this chapter; but the combination of elements in DAMNED IF YOU DON'T was equally inventive and, in some senses, even more cinematically radical. DAMNED IF YOU DON'T is simultaneously a dramatized narrative that evokes the tradition of "trance film," delineated by P. Adams Sitney in *Visionary Film*, and a documentary.[51] In the narrative sequences, one woman, an artist (Ela Troyano), is attracted to another, a nun (Peggy Healey), and pursues her until in the film's final scene we see them making love in the artist's apartment. In the documentary sequences, Friedrich records imagery of nuns and interviews a friend who recalls her conjectures about and desires for some of the sisters who taught her in Catholic school. While there is no scratched text in the film, other forms of text supplement the narrative and documentary elements: these include a reading of excerpts from Judith C. Brown's *Immodest Acts: The Life of a Lesbian Nun in Renaissance Italy* and a narrated deconstruction of the Michael Powell/Emeric Pressburger feature BLACK NARCISSUS (1947), which the artist-protagonist of the film watches on television (Friedrich films excerpts of BLACK NARCISSUS off a television set, carefully incorporating the interference bars into her editing rhythm). These varied sources of story and information are supplemented by sensuous imagery—by the time of DAMNED IF YOU DON'T, Friedrich had refined her ability to work with the subtleties of chiaroscuro—of swans, snakes, and white whales.

As was true in THE TIES THAT BIND, Friedrich uses her skill as editor to interweave the film's diverse strands into a thoroughly coherent fabric, which goes further than either telling an interesting story or documenting the sexual ambiguities around life as a nun: when the artist undresses the nun at the conclusion of DAMNED IF YOU DON'T, their coming together suggests a synthesis of the sensual and the spiritual that answers both the "scorched earth" feminists of the 1970s and those in the tradition of avantgarde film who have been suspicious of the use of cinema to engage political issues. For Friedrich, women (and especially lesbians) are damned by society if they openly express their sensual selves, but are equally damned if they suppress this crucial emotional reality. Since they are "damned if they do, damned if they don't," there is no point in avoiding the sensual, either in our lives, or in filmmaking. In BLACK NARCISSUS (and in DAMNED IF YOU DON'T), Mr. Dean, the male protagonist, sings, defiantly, "No, I cannot be a nun, since I am so fond of pleasure," a line we also hear Friedrich herself sing during her film. As filmmaker Friedrich cannot be a "nun": she cannot refuse either the pleasure of narrative, or the fascination of exploring forbidden topics, or the formal excitements of precise editing and chiaroscuro. DAMNED IF YOU DON'T is a 1980s declaration that while it is important to deconstruct film's past—both the past of the commercial industry and the pasts of alternative forms of cinema—it is even more important to use the many accomplishments of cinema's complex history in new formal and ideological syntheses that can sing the ongoing potential of film to instigate a more progressive and more sensual future.

SINK OR SWIM, the last Friedrich film made during the 1980s, confirms many of the tendencies evident in THE TIES THAT BIND and DAMNED IF YOU DON'T; indeed, it can easily be seen as a companion piece to her film about her mother. SINK OR SWIM is the story of the breakup of her parents' marriage and the effect of their divorce on Friedrich and her siblings. Arranged as a series of stories narrated by a young girl (Jessica Lynn), with visual titles arranged in reverse alphabetical order ("Zygote," "Y chromosome," "X chromosome," "Witness," "Virgin," "Utopia" . . .)—a reference to her father, anthropologist and linguist Paul Friedrich—Friedrich's film takes viewers from the innocent obliviousness of childhood to her mature acceptance of her personal history as an adult. As in GENTLY DOWN THE STREAM, the (in this case, spoken) text of the stories is the film's foreground; the photographed imagery provides context and metaphor. As is true in THE TIES THAT BIND and DAMNED IF YOU DON'T, the film's visuals reveal a wide range of sources—material shot by Friedrich herself is combined with home movies (both of her and her sister as children, and of her father's generation as children) and with other recycled material—all edited together so as to interconnect with the narration (and other sounds) in a wide range of obvious and subtle ways. The more formal, alphabetical organization of SINK OF SWIM can be read not only as Su Friedrich's response to her physical father but also as a simultaneous homage and response to structural film, as epitomized by "father" Hollis Frampton's ZORNS LEMMA (1970). While Frampton's film charts the stages we go through in coming to understand the world around us, Friedrich's film critiques Frampton's apparent assumption that the process of coming to understand is genderless: for Friedrich, maturation was full of both gender-neutral intellectual challenges and the psychic shocks caused by her father's dealing with his daughter in gender-problematic ways that were often typical of men of his generation. As is true in all of Friedrich's longer films of the decade, the filmmaker's precise, subtle editing in SINK OR SWIM—of both disparate visuals and of generally nonsynched visuals and sounds—models the construction of an adult personality (and a progressive film practice) by means of the synthesizing of differences and oppositions into an overriding coherence.

PETER HUTTON

By the 1980s, Peter Hutton had developed a distinctive visual aesthetic (all his films are silent) that suggests a return to the origins of cinema. In general, each Hutton film presents a series of individual images, collected over a considerable time and presented one by one, often separated by moments of black leader. The energy of the imagery and of the finished films is a function of Hutton's serene pace and his mastery of subtleties of composition and especially chiaroscuro (all Hutton's films to date are black and white). Like a number of filmmakers who began making films in the late 1960s and early 1970s, Hutton sees himself in the tradition of the Lumière brothers, whose one-shot-equals-one-film approach represented a simplicity and a directness that seemed the diametric opposite of the media overload propagated, increasingly, by commercial television in the 1960s and by a commercial film industry trying desperately to compete with its younger electronic sibling. If this view of the Lumières as noncommercial artists now seems naive, the irony is that Hutton's films have become—at least within the still economically marginal world of avant-garde exhibition—among the most popular of avant-garde films: current audiences seem to find in these films precisely what Hutton hopes they'll find.[52]

Unlike most filmmakers who have celebrated urban spaces, Hutton's focus in his portraits of New York—and the same is true in his depictions of Budapest and of Moscow and Leningrad (LENIN PORTRAIT, 1983)—is not the city's high-energy modernity but its moments of quiet and the subtle visual mysteries that are visible only to those who venture onto the streets during "off hours." Even when Hutton does focus on moments when large numbers of people are present, he tends to see these events from a distance that recognizes their energy for those involved but suggests an almost spiritual detachment. In NEW YORK PORTRAIT, PART II, for example, Hutton includes imagery of New York harbor shot during the Bicentennial celebration (imagery of fireboats with hoses arcing water, of crowds of people watching, of dirigibles flying overhead) yet the resulting film experience feels virtually the opposite of the original event because of Hutton's use of long-shot, which reduces the boats, dirigibles, and crowds to exquisite miniatures. NEW YORK PORTRAIT, PART II ends with a sequence of shots of a downpour in Manhattan, filmed from an apartment window several stories up. In the final shot (it's thirty-seven seconds long), a man wades out into a flooded intersection and clears the street grate; as the water drains from the intersection, light hits the ripples in such a way that the image becomes a mandala, quite close in its effect to the meditative animations of the Whitney brothers and Jordan Belson.

While Hutton's films are conscious evocations of early cinema, they are also full of allusions to several histories of the representation of rural and urban spaces. The New York portraits are often reminiscent of the history of photography and of particular images by Eugene Atget, Paul Strand, Charles Sheeler, and Alfred Stieglitz. On the other hand, Hutton's "landscape film" LANDSCAPE (FOR MANON) , the first of what has become a series of films documenting the Hudson River Valley, is an evocation of Thomas Cole's paintings of the Catskill Mountains, not only in the sense that the images in LANDSCAPE (FOR MANON) document some of the exact spaces Cole painted but also in its implicit attitude toward nature. While Frederic Church and other painters inspired by Cole tended to emphasize the exciting potential of American landscape for economic development, Cole's paintings are implicitly warnings: they reveal Cole's concern that the on-going exploitation of American "wilderness" threatens the distinctiveness of America itself.[53] Cole tended to paint mountain landscapes the way they *should* look, the way they did look before development had transformed them. Similarly, LANDSCAPE (FOR MANON) tends to create the illusion of pristine nature, and its arrangement of images implies a Cole-esque "backward look." While Hutton's editing is always quietly paced, the trajectory of his editing in this film reverses a conventional tendency of modern film and television editing. During LANDSCAPE (FOR MANON) , Hutton's editing begins serenely and then *slows down*—some of the shots near the middle of the film are

Glowing tree in Peter Hutton's LANDSCAPE (FOR MANON) *(1987).*

nearly a minute long. Near the conclusion of the film the pace speeds up to the original serene pacing. Hutton asks of film viewers that they forgo their expectations of excitement and romance and enjoy the gradual evolutions of individual images. Hutton's films are a form of visual training that offers "new" options: the pleasures of visual subtlety, of taking time to see.

ELIAS MERHIGE

In *The American Cinema: Directors and Directions, 1929-1968* (New York: Dutton, 1968), a book that had considerable influence on those of us who were to become the academic film "establishment" of the 1980s, Andrew Sarris devised a series of imprecise but valuable categories for sorting out the auteurist dimensions of American directorial careers. Of these categories, the one that lists the largest number of directors is "Oddities, One-Shots, and Newcomers" (included are such diverse directors as Lindsay Anderson, John Cassavetes, Francis Ford Coppola, Roger Corman, Mike Nichols, and Peter Watkins). Certainly, a similar category is useful for avant-garde film, which some consider nothing *but* a collection of oddities; but even within the diverse and often bizarre world of alternative cinema, there are particular works that seem to come out of nowhere and to fit no comfortable historical niche. A perfect instance is Elias Merhige's feature BEGOTTEN (1989), which premiered in New York, garnered a good bit of attention, and then did not find a distributor until the mid-1990s.[54]

BEGOTTEN does have precedents—Merhige claims Georges Franju's SANG DE BÊTES (BLOOD OF THE BEASTS, 1949) and Stan Brakhage's THE ACT OF SEEING WITH ONE'S OWN EYES (1971) as inspirations—yet the particular mixture of elements in

BEGOTTEN feels virtually unprecedented.[55] The film hovers between allegory and abstraction. Its narrative line, which is always at the edge of perceptibility, begins with God killing himself as he gives birth to Mother Nature, who is subsequently raped by a group of hooded beings; she survives the rape and struggles through a barren landscape, until near the end of the film we see farmers growing strange crops. God's suicide and the rape of nature are both visceral and ambiguous, largely because of Merhige's impressive exploration of texture and chiaroscuro: indeed, the film's gritty textures provide a second visceral dimension, one that demonstrates a level of commitment to the project on Merhige's part that reflects nature's tortuous journey through the bleak landscape.

If the film's plot line roughly suggests a central trajectory of Western cultural history during the past few centuries, the look of the imagery suggests the deeper and earlier roots of all "civilized" cultural enterprise. Indeed, for Merhige the film is meant to work as a kind of cinematic Rorschach test that can tease the repressed dimensions of conventional filmgoing back into consciousness. Fundamentally, BEGOTTEN is a memorable and suggestive, if peculiar, film *experience* (in the sense that Ken Jacobs's Nervous System pieces are experiences). Whether it will remain not only an "oddity" but a "one-shot," or whether it is simply the first important evidence of a "newcomer" (Merhige spent the 1990s attempting to develop projects in Hollywood), remains to be seen.

ANNE CHARLOTTE ROBERTSON

While the overt intimacy of what came to be called "diary film" seems more characteristic of late 1960s and 1970s avant-garde cinema, the diaristic urge was the source of one of the most unusual film projects of the 1980s: Anne Robertson's DIARY and the various excerpts she has distributed under separate titles. Working consistently in Super 8, Robertson had made several films in the late 1970s, before beginning the diary on 3 November 1981—"which, it turns out, is Saul Levine's birthday. Sort of a psychic tribute there. He was one of the people who encouraged me to continue making films."[56] Having begun filming her experience and recording sound on tape, Robertson became relentless in her quest to represent her life on film. By 1990, when I interviewed her, the DIARY had grown well beyond twenty-four hours (the real length of the DIARY at any given moment is difficult to determine, since Robertson's ever-growing magnum opus is sometimes revised; for example, when she began to have doubts about her inclusion of nude footage of herself, she revised portions of the DIARY by removing this imagery). The length of the DIARY, of course, insures that it is rarely screened in total, and by the 1990s, Robertson began to transfer sections of the film to video for more convenient distribution and exhibition. But from time to time, exhibitors have had the courage to offer more extended access to the DIARY. In 1988, for example, David Schwartz arranged for Robertson to present the complete diary at the American Museum of Moving Image, as part of his admirably inclusive "Independent America: New Film, 1978–1988." Robertson's diary was presented in a small screening room, decorated by Robertson herself (she included furniture, pictures, keepsakes from her home bedroom in Framingham, Massachusetts), where, for eight days spread over two October weekends, she lived during the hours the museum was open and presented reels of the DIARY as home movies, accompanied by taped sound and in-person narration.

The DIARY itself is at times amusing, at times grim, sometimes visually unexceptional, sometimes startling and exquisite, as, for example, when her time-lapsing causes her to seem like a frenzied spirit within her everyday surround. The emotional trajectory of the DIARY is determined in large measure by the ebb and flow of bipolar syndrome, with which Robertson wrestles. Alternately lucid and delusional, Robertson uses filmmaking as a way of maintaining psychic coherence and contact with the world. In his film WALDEN (1969), Jonas Mekas claims, "I make home movies, therefore I live," and while this claim is certainly important to Mekas's sense of himself, it fits Robertson's project more precisely (as Mekas has recently told Robertson).[57] The endless strip of Super 8 film on which Robertson's physical and psychic movements are recorded is Robertson's lifeline. Indeed, making particular films has, according to Robertson, been her means of taking control of serious psychic disorders: her making SUICIDE (1979) silenced internal voices that for three years had tried to convince her to kill herself, and her depiction of herself as the ultimate consumer in MAGAZINE MOUTH (1983) allowed her to take control of her binging.

Within the DIARY, Robertson deals with a wide variety of topics, many of which seem representative of the 1980s. Her battles with her weight—in some passages of the film we see her obsessively measuring her weight gains and losses—reflect the paradoxical American obsessions with overconsumption and correct physical appearance. Her longing for romance (which sometimes takes the form of an obsession with Tom Baker, who played Dr. Who on the television series of the same name), is both typical and, in its endless frustration, poignant. And her battle with the drugs pervasive in American daily life (coffee, cigarettes) and with those her doctors prescribe as a means of controlling her psychic disturbances (drugs that sometimes render her unable to make film) reflect the paradox of the pervasiveness of mind-altering substances in a society that is obsessed with the idea that drugs are evil. In the end, however, it is the combination of Robertson's relentless openness about her life, in all its limitations and frustrations and psychic fragility, and her considerable gifts for making visually arresting imagery that render her DIARY so compelling. Having fought both her own demons and the limited opportunities for small-gauge exhibition, however, the 1990s find Robertson facing a new, poignant reality: just as her films are becoming more widely recognized, Kodak has announced that the availability of Super 8 film is coming to an end.

PETER ROSE

The 1980s saw the normalization of film studies in colleges and universities across the country, along with a developing fascination with new theoretical approaches to film history and practice. This academicizing of cinema was in many ways good news, especially for those with a serious interest in studying film history and current practice; but it was a mixed blessing for avant-garde cinema. Since a good many academic cinephiles had come to film from literary studies and had brought with them a dedication to communicating about cinema in writing, those avant-gardists who saw their own filmmaking as a theoretical enterprise and who saw the theater space as the medium for communicating with film viewers about fundamental theoretical issues suddenly seemed marginal to film history in a new way. Of course, avant-garde film has always been economically marginal; but now even the most astute filmmakers often found their work ignored by academics, whose interest in theory usually tended to return them to the commercial cinema with new tools for exploring the conventions of entertainment. Even the most theoretically interesting avant-garde films were widely ignored, and as a result, the always fragile economics of avant-garde filmmaking seemed as precarious as ever.

The new excitement about film studies in the academy produced a flood of theoretically inspired books and essays. On the one hand, the function of this writing was to illuminate the history of motion pictures, but within the academic structure itself there was also a need to demonstrate to more established academic fields (fields, after all, fighting for the same financial resources as film studies was fighting for) that studying cinema was indeed a serious intellectual pursuit. In a good many cases, this need tended to produce a serious-sounding prose that was virtually indecipherable to anyone not intimately engaged in film studies. For some, this limiting of communication may have seemed an unfortunate but inevitable result of trying to be precise about a complex social phenomenon: those of us who have not studied economics or quantum physics are usually mystified by the discourses within these fields.

For some avant-garde filmmakers, however, the advent of professional film studies, and the frequently obscurantist prose that seemed to come with it, represented a troubling gap between filmmakers, now positioned as intellectual naifs in need of theoretical analysis, and academic sophisticates. For mediamaker, Peter Rose, this increasingly obvious pattern became a subject for film (and video and multimedia performance). Like many avant-garde film- and videomakers, Rose had long been interested in using visual text as part of cinematic experience. But few filmmakers have been as ingenious with text as Rose, first in a portion of his THE MAN WHO COULD NOT SEE FAR ENOUGH (1981), where a self-reflexive text, superimposed over imagery of a landscape filmed from a moving car, initiates a highly formal personal reminiscence; and subsequently in the remarkable "Introduction to *Pleasures of the Text*" (*Pleasures of the Text* is a multimedia performance work), in which Rose presents a lecture about language that becomes increasingly obscure, the more precise he tries to be, until the lecture degenerates into indecipherable gibberish. An early version of this send-up of theoretically inspired academic prose appeared in the *Downtown Review*, a short-lived publication by and for the New York avant-garde film community; later versions were performed by Rose, who also recorded the piece on video, and on audiotape for *Spiral*, another valuable but short-lived publication, edited by Terry Cannon in Los Angeles.

Pleasures of the Text also included Rose's most elaborate filmic exploration of language, SECONDARY CURRENTS (1983), which uses no conventional photographic imagery at all, but combines a complex visual text presented in white against a black background and a sound track to explore several major dimensions of film history's use of text.[58] The earliest section of SECONDARY CURRENTS is an amusing excursion into the tradition of subtitling. Rose's subtitles propose to translate the nonsense language we hear him speaking on the sound track; during the opening section of the film, Rose's nonsense narration sounds like an amalgam of the languages American filmgoers of the 1960s were hearing, as "foreign film" arrived in the United States. Rose's burlesque recalls American viewers' experiences hearing Swedish, Japanese, and Italian and confronting the frustrating reality that what we heard was not adequately represented by the subtitles: in one instance Rose "translates" an extended passage of narration as a single word.

A second area Rose explores is the relationship between the "space" of the narration and the spaces of the film frame and the theater. At one point, the "narrator" leaves the microphone he's speaking into and talks himself out of the room into a natural setting (the subtitles continue to translate his commentary) and then, after a moment when the "narrator" is "beyond the film," inaudible, and therefore untranslatable, he returns to the mike, bumping into things on his trip back through the room. During the final section of SECONDARY CURRENTS, two other textual issues are explored. As in

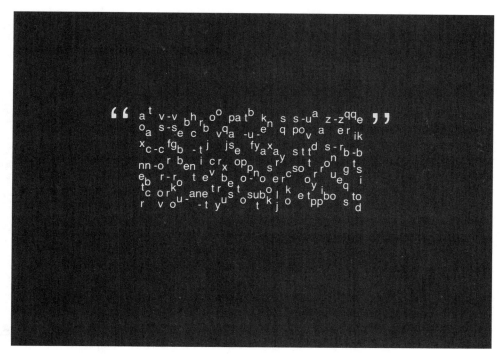

Visual language going berserk in Peter Rose's SECONDARY CURRENTS *(1983).*

"Introduction," Rose burlesques the increasing complexity of academic writing about film: "an unrepentant dilution of constructed meaning whose meandering lucubrations foretold the essential entropy of euphostolic processes and peregrinations"; and as in "Introduction," Rose's translated commentary becomes increasingly indecipherable, especially because the extended sentences must be presented only a phrase at a time in the subtitles. The viewer quickly loses the ability to apprehend the text, and by the end of the film, Rose's narration and its visual correlative have degenerated into a set of incoherent sounds and graphic signs that match the state of the viewer's noncomprehension.

The entropy of the "narration" is visualized in a culmination of Rose's exploration of cinematic text as image. All through SECONDARY CURRENTS, Rose plays with the viewer's assumptions about how subtitles will be organized. At first, he presents the "translations" across the bottom of the image in conventional subtitle form. But as the text continues, he varies the format, sometimes arranging several lines one above the other in formations very unusual for subtitling. As the viewer's ability to apprehend the text dissipates near the end of the film, the text moves out from the bottom, ultimately covering the entire frame with increasingly dense graphic signs that, finally are animated in various kinds of motion. This proliferation of signs across the space of the frame culminates when the letters and numbers so completely cover the space that they become a moving field within which a series of much larger words are formed: "I FEAR/I DISSOLVE/MY VOICE/EXPLODING/MEANING." The sound of an explosion, juxtaposed with a dark, empty screen, follows.

What happens during the final moments of the film varies depending on the version Rose is showing. The most elaborate of the several versions concludes with the viewer's becoming aware of a text written on the celluloid strip. This text cannot be read during projection; it signifies only that a text is available should the viewer have access to the actual film, as opposed to the theatrical projection of it. This final text plays with the viewer's assumptions about the relationship of various kinds of text and the end of a movie: at some screenings of conventional films we experience various levels of ending, each signaled by a different form of text. The rolling credits may conclude the viewer's experience of film-as-perspectival-illusion, but—especially at 16mm screenings—this ending is often followed by the end leaders (with various kinds of language printed or written on them) that signal the conclusion of the film's material journey through the projector. Normally, the viewer's awareness of end-of-film leader is a function of the somewhat less rigorous expectations of 16mm projectionists (we rarely see leader at professional screenings of 35mm films). But Rose provides a reward for those viewers energetic enough to wonder if the text they see on the leader merely encodes the standard information common on film leader or adds to a film that has continually surprised our expectations—one final text: "I sense a luminous transparency, a limitless linear aperture of indecipherable articulate intelligence—I sense arising, a silent perpendicular emissary unfolding from the invisible. It is becoming vast, provotic, spectral. All is clear now!!!" And when we've read this last text on the filmstrip, we realize it describes precisely the experience that led us to examine the intriguing marks on the strip of (clear) celluloid.

The final text of SECONDARY CURRENTS foreshadows SPIRIT MATTERS (1984), an extended exploration of the potentials and implications of writing directly on the celluloid strip. Other investigations of language, spoken as well as visual, followed, including the videos DIGITAL SPEECH (1984), BABEL (1987), and GENESIS (1988).

TRINH T. MINH-HA

Trinh T. Minh-ha's major films of the 1980s—REASSEMBLAGE (discussed earlier), NAKED SPACES: LIVING IS ROUND (1985), and SURNAME VIÊT GIVEN NAME NAM (1989)—like Friedrich's films of the same period, reveal a filmmaker working "between" conventional film categories, though the particular approaches explored by Minh-ha were quite different from Friedrich's approaches—and more controversial, as well. This difference was a function of Minh-ha's background as a Vietnamese who grew up in Vietnam and subsequently lived in France, Senegal, and the United States. Coming from a cultural heritage quite distant from those that have produced the film industry and the traditional critiques of it, Minh-ha never seems to have felt any particular obligation to replicate, or even respect, Western categories or approaches to cinema. REASSEMBLAGE is neither a conventional documentary (since it does not pretend to present information about its subject) nor an avant-garde film of any recognizable form, though Minh-ha's gestural camerawork and abrupt editing seems as close to avant-garde filmmaking as to any other major cinematic tradition. Indeed, as her title suggests, REASSEMBLAGE means to reassemble conventional cinematic categories.

Minh-ha's first feature, NAKED SPACES: LIVING IS ROUND, is also an amalgam of traditional approaches, though a different amalgam from the one evident in REASSEMBLAGE. NAKED SPACES: LIVING IS ROUND is a study of dwellings in a particular region, and it is a transnational travel film: Minh-ha shot imagery in various sections of Senegal, Mauritania, Togo, Mali, Burkina Faso, and Benin. And yet it conforms to neither of these categories. Ethnographic filmmakers complained that Minh-ha's "poetic license" with imagery and sound created unacceptable representational inaccuracies: we may be looking at dwellings from one region while we hear sounds from another region. And if NAKED SPACES is a travel film, it is hardly the personal record of a journey that we usually expect from the form: like Babette Mangolte's THE SKY ON LOCATION (see discussion earlier), NAKED SPACES is narrated by three narrators, each of whom seems to have a somewhat different sense of history and geography. While she herself is one of these narrators, Minh-ha does not privilege her recollections, but implicitly recognizes that whatever we come to understand about a culture is a combination of our personal experiences and what others, from this culture and from other cultures, have helped us to understand or misunderstand about it. While NAKED SPACES is a visually beautiful film about a fascinating topic, Minh-ha's style mitigates against an easy gaze at the exotic spaces she films. As in REASSEMBLAGE, she edits abruptly, often in the middle of gestures. Her consistently unsmooth camera movements are less expressive of her personal reactions to the people and places she sees than of her desire to interrupt the tradition of documentary (initiated by Robert Flaherty) of allowing us easy, sensual enjoyment of the "exotic."

With SURNAME VIÊT GIVEN NAME NAM (1989), Minh-ha appeared to return to her Vietnamese roots, but this movement into her personal ethnic heritage was simultaneously an expansion into the more diverse sense of contemporary geography and culture that she had developed through working and traveling in Europe, Africa, and North America. Of course, Minh-ha's awareness of the importance of her Vietnamese heritage is evident throughout her filmmaking, even in her African films. Her decision to narrate

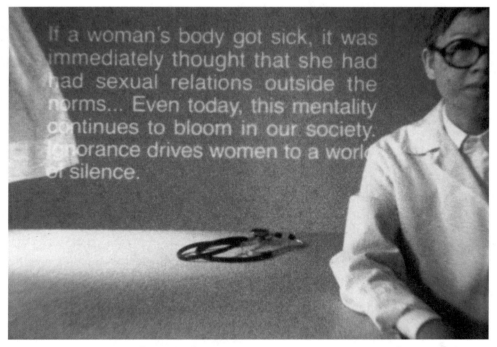

Vietnamese-American playing a doctor in Communist Vietnam in Trinh T. Minh-ha's SURNAME VIÊT GIVEN NAME NAM *(1989).*

REASSEMBLAGE in her own Vietnamese-accented English, and to include herself as one of the three narrators in NAKED SPACES, is evidence of her concern that we not forget that these depictions of African cultures are not presented from an exclusively Western—or African—point of view. At the same time, however, the fact that she speaks in a Vietnamese-accented *English* makes consistently clear that her sense of her own ethnicity is conditioned by her experiences as a transnational citizen of the world.

In NAKED SPACES, Minh-ha provides visual correlatives to this simultaneous sense of the ethnic and the transnational: those moments in rural Senegalese dwellings, seemingly quite far from urban centers where European and North American influences on indigenous African cultures are more obvious, when our seeing a blue plastic bucket or a yellow plastic tub forces us to consider that the ethnic "purity" that is often implicit in our concept of "the indigenous" is as fully an illusion as Hollywood's assumption that certain forms of film entertainment are accessible to "everyone." What we define as "indigenous" may be a complex interaction of particular, native cultural groups that, given our cultural and historical distance, we cannot perceive. And even if we were to imagine a cultural group that has had no contact whatsoever with any other cultural group throughout its entire history, this group could be conceived only in contradistinction to other, different cultural groups, and could conceive itself only by defining cultural distinctions within the group.

In SURNAME VIÊT, the impossibility of the pure indigenous is less the issue, however, than the remarkable complexity of the transnational. Even Minh-ha's title suggests this complexity. Minh-ha's family (and family name, Trinh) may be indigenous to the region of Southeast Asia we call Vietnam, but the French spelling of the "surname" VIÊT reminds us of the long-term French involvement in this part of the world and its inevitable effect on a Vietnamese sense of history and culture, an effect made even more complex and mysterious by the subsequent arrival of the American military, who gave the region the nickname "Nam."

In SURNAME VIÊT GIVEN NAME NAM, our interest in the exotic—hearing women discuss the experience of living in postwar Communist Vietnam—allows us to believe what the film's various Vietnamese spokeswomen tell us. We may wonder that Minh-ha was able to return to Communist Vietnam and get access to these women, several of whom offer telling critiques of life under communist rule, but their extremely accented English (so accented that Minh-ha superimposes textual translations of their comments over the imagery of the women speaking) tends to convince us of the reality of what we think we see. Since we virtually always understand everything everyone in a commercial film or television show says, we may assume that our language difficulties in SURNAME VIÊT result from Minh-ha's inability to find women who speak better English and that, therefore, we are seeing candidly filmed reality. During the second half of the film, however, we discover that these spokeswomen are dramatized by Vietnamese-American women, who themselves have been "translated" from Vietnam to the United States; and we have the opportunity to realize the superficiality of our original assumptions and the dangers of the pervasive media training that teaches us to expect easy translations of difficult cultural issues.[59]

Appendix 1

TABLES AND CHARTS

Listing is in order of their appearance in the text.

Chapter 1

Chapter 2

Chapter 3

Appendix 2

TOP BOX-OFFICE FILMS
OF THE 1980s

These were the decade's big money-earners, measured in terms of the revenues ("rentals") returned to the distributor. Rental figures are distinct from box-office grosses (the total revenues generated at the box office, which are split, according to terms that may vary from film to film, between the distributor, exhibitors, and other claimants). Rentals provide a better indication of a film's earning potential for its production firm and distributor because they omit the revenues taken by exhibitors.

Figures are taken from *Variety*'s annual box-office reports. An asterisk denotes films released late (October–December) the previous year. In 1985, *Variety* altered its policy regarding the reporting of rentals from late-in-the-year releases. Thus, "continuing" denotes films released late the previous year but whose rentals for the current year only are reported. All rental figures in the chart are in millions.

1980

1.	THE EMPIRE STRIKES BACK	$120	6.	COAL MINER'S DAUGHTER	35
2.	KRAMER VS. KRAMER°	60.5	7.	PRIVATE BENJAMIN	33.5
3.	THE JERK°	43	8.	THE BLUES BROTHERS	31
4.	AIRPLANE	38	9.	THE ELECTRIC HORSEMAN°	30.9
5.	SMOKEY AND THE BANDIT	37.6	10.	THE SHINING	30.2

1981

1.	RAIDERS OF THE LOST ARK	$90.4	6.	ANY WHICH WAY YOU CAN°	39.5
2.	SUPERMAN II	64	7.	ARTHUR	37
3.	STIR CRAZY°	58.4	8.	THE CANNONBALL RUN	35.4
4.	9 TO 5°	57.8	9.	FOUR SEASONS	26.8
5.	STRIPES	39.5	10.	FOR YOUR EYES ONLY	25.4

1982

1.	E.T.: THE EXTRA-TERRESTRIAL	$187	7.	STAR TREK II: THE WRATH OF KHAN	
2.	ROCKY III	63.4		40	
3.	ON GOLDEN POND°	63	8.	POLTERGEIST	36
4.	PORKY'S	53.5	9.	ANNIE	35
5.	AN OFFICER AND A GENTLEMAN	52	10.	CHARIOTS OF FIRE°	27.6
6.	THE BEST LITTLE WHOREHOUSE IN TEXAS	48			

1983

1.	RETURN OF THE JEDI	$165.5
2.	TOOTSIE°	94.6
3.	TRADING PLACES	40.6
4.	WARGAMES	36.6
5.	SUPERMAN III	36.4
6.	FLASHDANCE	36.2
7.	STAYING ALIVE	33.6
8.	OCTOPUSSY	33.2
9.	MR. MOM	31.5
10.	48 HRS.°	30.3

1984

1.	GHOSTBUSTERS	$127
2.	INDIANA JONES AND THE TEMPLE OF DOOM	109
3.	GREMLINS	78.5
4.	BEVERLY HILLS COP	58
5.	TERMS OF ENDEARMENT°	50.3
6.	THE KARATE KID	41.7
7.	STAR TREK III: THE SEARCH FOR SPOCK	39
8.	POLICE ACADEMY	38.5
9.	ROMANCING THE STONE	36
10.	SUDDEN IMPACT°	34.6

1985

1.	BACK TO THE FUTURE	$ 94
2.	RAMBO: FIRST BLOOD, PART II	80
3.	ROCKY IV	65
4.	BEVERLY HILLS COP (continuing)	50
5.	COCOON	40
6.	THE GOONIES	29.9
7.	WITNESS	28
8.	POLICE ACADEMY 2	27.2
9.	NATIONAL LAMPOON'S EUROPEAN VACATION	25.6
10.	A VIEW TO A KILL	25.2

1986

1.	TOP GUN	$ 82
2.	THE KARATE KID, PART II	56.9
3.	"CROCODILE" DUNDEE	51
4.	STAR TREK IV: THE VOYAGE HOME	45
5.	ALIENS	42.5
6.	THE COLOR PURPLE (continuing)	41.9
7.	BACK TO SCHOOL	41.7
8.	THE GOLDEN CHILD	33
9.	RUTHLESS PEOPLE	31
10.	OUT OF AFRICA (continuing)	30

1987

1.	BEVERLY HILLS COP II	$ 80.8
2.	PLATOON (continuing)	66.7
3.	FATAL ATTRACTION	60
4.	THREE MEN AND A BABY	45
5.	THE UNTOUCHABLES	36.8
6.	THE WITCHES OF EASTWICK	31.8
7.	PREDATOR	31
8.	DRAGNET	30.1
9.	THE SECRET OF MY SUCCESS	29.5
10.	LETHAL WEAPON	29.5

1988

1.	WHO FRAMED ROGER RABBIT	$ 78
2.	COMING TO AMERICA	65
3.	GOOD MORNING, VIETNAM	58.1
4.	"CROCODILE" DUNDEE II	57.3
5.	BIG	50.8
6.	THREE MEN AND A BABY (continuing)	36.3
7.	DIE HARD	35
8.	COCKTAIL	35
9.	MOONSTRUCK	34.4
10.	BEETLEJUICE	33.3

1989

1.	BATMAN	$150.5
2.	INDIANA JONES AND THE LAST CRUSADE	115.5
3.	LETHAL WEAPON 2	79.5
4.	HONEY, I SHRUNK THE KIDS	71
5.	RAIN MAN (continuing)	65
6.	BACK TO THE FUTURE, PART II	63
7.	GHOSTBUSTERS II	61.6
8.	LOOK WHO'S TALKING	55
9.	PARENTHOOD	48.6
10.	DEAD POETS SOCIETY	47.6

Appendix 3

MAJOR ACADEMY AWARDS, 1980–1989

1980

Picture: ORDINARY PEOPLE (Paramount)
Director: Robert Redford, ORDINARY PEOPLE
Actress: Sissy Spacek, COAL MINER'S DAUGHTER
Actor: Robert De Niro, RAGING BULL
Supporting Actress: Mary Steenburgen, MELVIN AND HOWARD
Supporting Actor: Timothy Hutton, ORDINARY PEOPLE
Cinematography: Geoffrey Unsworth, Chislain Cloquet, TESS
Editing: Thelma Schoonmaker, RAGING BULL
Sound: Bill Varney, Steve Maslow, Gregg Landaker, Peter Sutton, THE EMPIRE
    STRIKES BACK
Art Direction–Set Decoration: Pierre Guffroy, Jack Stevens, TESS
Adapted Screenplay: Alvin Sargent, ORDINARY PEOPLE
Original Screenplay: Bo Goldman, MELVIN AND HOWARD
Music Score: Michael Gore, FAME

1981

Picture: CHARIOTS OF FIRE (Ladd/Warner)
Director: Warren Beatty, REDS
Actress: Katharine Hepburn, ON GOLDEN POND
Actor: Henry Fonda, ON GOLDEN POND
Supporting Actress: Maureen Stapleton, REDS
Supporting Actor: John Gielgud, ARTHUR
Cinematography: Vittorio Storaro, REDS
Editing: Michael Kah, RAIDERS OF THE LOST ARK
Sound: Bill Varney, Steve Maslow, Gregg Landaker, Roy Charman, RAIDERS OF
    THE LOST ARK
Art Direction–Set Decoration: Norman Reynolds, Leslie Dilley, Michael Ford,
    RAIDERS OF THE LOST ARK
Adapted Screenplay: Ernest Thompson, ON GOLDEN POND
Original Screenplay: Colin Welland, CHARIOTS OF FIRE
Music Score: Vangelis, CHARIOTS OF FIRE

449

1982

Picture: GANDHI (Columbia)
Director: Richard Attenborough, GANDHI
Actress: Meryl Streep, SOPHIE'S CHOICE
Actor: Ben Kingsley, GANDHI
Supporting Actress: Jessica Lange, TOOTSIE
Supporting Actor: Louis Gossett, Jr., AN OFFICER AND A GENTLEMAN
Cinematography: Billy Williams, Ronnie Taylor, GANDHI
Editing: John Bloom, GANDHI
Sound: Robert Knudson, Robert J. Glass, Don Digirolama, Gene S. Cantamessa,
    E.T.: THE EXTRA-TERRESTRIAL
Art Direction–Set Decoration: Stuart Craig, Robert W. Laing, Michael Seirton,
    GANDHI
Adapted Screenplay: Constantin Costa-Gavras, Donald Steward, MISSING
Original Screenplay: John Briley, GANDHI
Music Score: John Williams, E.T.: THE EXTRA-TERRESTRIAL

1983

Picture: TERMS OF ENDEARMENT (Paramount)
Director: James L. Brooks, TERMS OF ENDEARMENT
Actress: Shirley MacLaine, TERMS OF ENDEARMENT
Actor: Robert Duvall, TENDER MERCIES
Supporting Actress: Linda Hunt, THE YEAR OF LIVING DANGEROUSLY
Supporting Actor: Jack Nicholson, TERMS OF ENDEARMENT
Cinematography: Sven Nykvist, FANNY AND ALEXANDER
Editing: Glenn Farr, Lisa Fruchtman, Stephen A. Rotter, Douglas Steward, Tom
    Rolf, THE RIGHT STUFF
Sound: Mark Berger, Tom Scott, Randy Thom, David MacMillan, THE RIGHT
    STUFF
Art Direction–Set Decoration: Anna Asp, Susanne Lingheim, FANNY AND
    ALEXANDER
Adapted Screenplay: James L. Brooks, TERMS OF ENDEARMENT
Original Screenplay: Horton Foote, TENDER MERCIES
Music Score: Bill Conti, THE RIGHT STUFF

1984

Picture: AMADEUS (Orion)
Director: Milos Forman, AMADEUS
Actress: Sally Field, PLACES IN THE HEART
Actor: F. Murray Abraham, AMADEUS
Supporting Actress: Peggy Ashcroft, A PASSAGE TO INDIA
Supporting Actor: Haing S. Ngor, THE KILLING FIELDS
Cinematography: Chris Menges, THE KILLING FIELDS
Editing: Jim Clark, THE KILLING FIELDS
Sound: Mark Berger, Tom Scott, Todd Boekelheide, Christopher Newman,
    AMADEUS

Art Direction–Set Decoration: Patrizia Von Brandenstein, Karel Cerny, AMADEUS
Adapted Screenplay: Peter Shaffer, AMADEUS
Original Screenplay: Robert Benton, PLACES IN THE HEART
Music Score: Maurice Jarre, A PASSAGE TO INDIA

1985

Picture: OUT OF AFRICA (Universal)
Director: Sydney Pollack, OUT OF AFRICA
Actress: Geraldine Page, THE TRIP TO BOUNTIFUL
Actor: William Hurt, KISS OF THE SPIDER WOMAN
Supporting Actress: Anjelica Huston, PRIZZI'S HONOR
Supporting Actor: Don Ameche, COCOON
Cinematography: David Watkin, OUT OF AFRICA
Editing: Thom Noble, WITNESS
Sound: Chris Jenkins, Gary Alexander, Larry Stensvold, Peter Handford, OUT OF
    AFRICA
Art Direction–Set Decoration: Stephen Grimes, Josie MacAvin, OUT OF AFRICA
Adapted Screenplay: Kurt Luedtke, OUT OF AFRICA
Original Screenplay: William Kelley, Pamela Wallace, Earl W. Wallace, WITNESS
Music Score: John Barry, OUT OF AFRICA

1986

Picture: PLATOON (Orion)
Director: Oliver Stone, PLATOON
Actress: Marlee Matlin, CHILDREN OF A LESSER GOD
Actor: Paul Newman, THE COLOR OF MONEY
Supporting Actress: Dianne Wiest, HANNAH AND HER SISTERS
Supporting Actor: Michael Caine, HANNAH AND HER SISTERS
Cinematography: Chris Menges, THE MISSION
Editing: Claire Simpson, PLATOON
Sound: John K. Wilkinson, Richard D. Rogers, Bud Grenzbach, Simon Kaye,
    PLATOON
Art Direction–Set Decoration: Giannni Quaranta, Brian Ackland-Snow, Brian
    Savegar, Elio Altramura, A ROOM WITH A VIEW
Adapted Screenplay: Ruth Prawer Jhabvala, A ROOM WITH A VIEW
Original Screenplay: Woody Allen, HANNAH AND HER SISTERS
Music Score: Herbie Hancock, ROUND MIDNIGHT

1987

Picture: THE LAST EMPEROR (Columbia)
Director: Bernardo Bertolucci, THE LAST EMPEROR
Actress: Cher, MOONSTRUCK
Actor: Michael Douglas, WALL STREET
Supporting Actress: Olympia Dukakis, MOONSTRUCK
Supporting Actor: Sean Connery, THE UNTOUCHABLES
Cinematography: Vittorio Storaro, THE LAST EMPEROR

Editing: Gabriella Cristiani, THE LAST EMPEROR
Sound: Bill Rowe, Ivan Sharrock, THE LAST EMPEROR
Art Direction–Set Decoration: Ferdinando Scarfiotti, Bruno Cesari, Osvaldo Desideri, THE LAST EMPEROR
Adapted Screenplay: Mark Peploe, Bernardo Bertolucci, THE LAST EMPEROR
Original Screenplay: John Patrick Shanley, MOONSTRUCK
Music Score: Ryuichi Sakamoto, David Byrne, Cong Su, THE LAST EMPEROR

1988

Picture: RAIN MAN (MGM/UA)
Director: Barry Levinson, RAIN MAN
Actress: Jodie Foster, THE ACCUSED
Actor: Dustin Hoffman, RAIN MAN
Supporting Actress: Geena Davis, THE ACCIDENTAL TOURIST
Supporting Actor: Kevin Kline, A FISH CALLED WANDA
Cinematography: Peter Biziou, MISSISSIPPI BURNING
Editing: Arthur Schmidt, WHO FRAMED ROGER RABBIT
Sound: Les Fresholtz, Richard Alexander, Vern Poore, Willie D. Burton, BIRD
Art Direction–Set Decoration: Stuart Craig, Gerard James, DANGEROUS LIAISONS
Adapted Screenplay: Christopher Hampton, DANGEROUS LIAISONS
Original Screenplay: Ronald Bass, Barry Morrow, RAIN MAN
Music Score: Dave Grusin, THE MILAGRO BEANFIELD WAR

1989

Picture: DRIVING MISS DAISY (Warner)
Director: Oliver Stone, BORN ON THE FOURTH OF JULY
Actress: Jessica Tandy, DRIVING MISS DAISY
Actor: Daniel Day-Lewis, MY LEFT FOOT
Supporting Actress: Brenda Fricker, MY LEFT FOOT
Supporting Actor: Denzel Washington, GLORY
Cinematography: Freddie Francis, GLORY
Editing: David Brenner, Joe Hutshing, BORN ON THE FOURTH OF JULY
Sound: Donald O. Mitchell, Gregg Rudloff, Elliot Tyson, Russell Williams II, GLORY
Art Direction–Set Decoration: Anton Furst, Peter Young, BATMAN
Adapted Screenplay: Alfred Uhry, DRIVING MISS DAISY
Original Screenplay: Tom Schulman, DEAD POETS SOCIETY
Music Score: Alan Menken, THE LITTLE MERMAID

Appendix 4

THE NATIONAL FILM REGISTRY

In 1988 Congress passed the National Film Preservation Act, which authorized the Library of Congress to designate twenty-five films each year as national treasures. The films would be preserved and housed at the library. Electronic copies of the films released in video or television markets would carry a disclaimer informing the viewer if the copy had been colorized, cropped, or subject to other alteration of the original artwork. The first twenty-five titles were announced in 1989.

THE BEST YEARS OF OUR LIVES (1946)
CASABLANCA (1942)
CITIZEN KANE (1941)
THE CROWD (1928)
DR. STRANGELOVE (1964)
THE GENERAL (1927)
GONE WITH THE WIND (1939)
THE GRAPES OF WRATH (1940)
HIGH NOON (1952)
INTOLERANCE (1916)
THE LEARNING TREE (1969)
THE MALTESE FALCON (1941)
MR. SMITH GOES TO WASHINGTON (1939)
MODERN TIMES (1936)
NANOOK OF THE NORTH (1922)
ON THE WATERFRONT (1954)
THE SEARCHERS (1956)
SINGIN' IN THE RAIN (1952)
SNOW WHITE AND THE SEVEN DWARFS (1937)
SOME LIKE IT HOT (1959)
STAR WARS (1977)
SUNRISE (1927)
SUNSET BLVD. (1950)
VERTIGO (1958)
THE WIZARD OF OZ (1939)

Notes

INTRODUCTION

1. Rita Koselka, "Mergermania in Medialand," *Forbes*, 23 October 1995, p. 254.
2. Dan Moreau, "Memo to Michael Eisner: Viacom Beat You to the Finish," *Kiplinger's Personal Finance Magazine*, October 1995, p. 38.
3. George Garneau, "Disney Enters News Business," *Editor and Publisher*, 5 August 1995, p. 5.
4. John M. Higgins, "Cable, the Value-Added Medium," *Broadcasting and Cable*, 12 May 1997, p. 90.
5. Koselka, "Mergermania in Medialand," p. 254.
6. Andy Marx, "Hollywood Studios: Kings of Content," *InterActive Week*, 10 October 1994, p. 30.
7. Peter Biskind, "Blockbuster: The Last Crusade," in *Seeing through Movies*, ed. Mark Crispin Miller (New York: Pantheon, 1990), p. 137.
8. William Palmer, *The Films of the Eighties* (Carbondale: Southern Illinois University Press, 1993), p. 12.
9. I cover this in detail in Stephen Prince, *Savage Cinema: Sam Peckinpah and the Rise of Ultraviolent Movies* (Austin: University of Texas Press, 1998), pp. 12–27.
10. *Mass Media Hearings*, vol. 9A: *A Report to the National Commission on the Causes and Prevention of Violence* (Washington, D.C.: U.S. Government Printing Office), p. 193.
11. Peter Wood, "How a Film Changes from an 'X' to an 'R,'" *New York Times*, 20 July 1980, section C.
12. Leonard Klady, "Budgets in the Hot Zone: The Sum Also Rises," *Variety*, 16–22 March 1998, p. 1.
13. Harold L. Vogel, *Entertainment Industry Economics*, 2d ed. (New York: Cambridge University Press, 1990), pp. 46, 51.
14. Stratford Sherman, "Why Disney Had to Buy ABC," *Fortune*, 4 September 1995, p. 80.
15. Koselka, "Mergermania in Medialand," p. 254

CHAPTER 1. THE INDUSTRY AT THE DAWN OF THE DECADE

1. *Variety*, 13 January 1982, p. 1; 12 January 1983, p. 7; 11 January 1984, p. 7; 8 January 1986, p. 7.
2. *Variety*, 2 December 1981, p. 5.
3. Twentieth Century–Fox, *Annual Report*, p.7.
4. Ibid.
5. Ibid.
6. Columbia Pictures Industries, Inc., Form 10-K, 1980, p. 8.
7. This and other information on WCI from Warner Communications, Inc., Form 10-K, 1980.
8. Ibid.
9. Ibid.
10. All information on MCA, Inc., is taken from MCA, Inc., Forms 10-K, 1981, 1983.
11. *Variety*, 19 January 1983, p. 131.
12. Gulf and Western, Form 10-K, 1980, p. 4.
13. MGM, Form 10-K, 1979, p. 1.
14. MGM, Form 10-K, 1981, p. 2.
15. Ibid., Notes to Financial Statements: United Artists Acquisition.

16. Ibid., Five Year Summary of Operations and Selected Financial Data.
17. Walt Disney Co., Form 10-K, 1980, p. 20.
18. Walt Disney Co., Forms 10-K, 1983, 1985.
19. *Variety*, 2 December 1981, p. 5.
20. WCI, Form 10-K, 1981.
21. "The Fed's Plan for Economic Recovery," *Business Week*, 13 December 1982, p. 92; Walter Heller, "A 'Yes But' Economy in 1980," *Wall Street Journal*, 23 January 1980.
22. "Why Consumers Won't Spend," *Business Week*, 4 October 1982, p. 40; "Fortune Forecast," *Fortune*, 14 June 1982, p. 59.
23. *Variety*, 16 January 1980, pp. 5, 36.
24. Ibid.
25. *The International Motion Picture Almanac for 1983* (New York: Quigley, 1983), p. 33A.
26. MPAA data contained in MPAA, *1996 U.S. Economic Review*, p. 8.
27. Twentieth Century–Fox, *Annual Report*, 1980.
28. WCI, Form 10-K, 1980, p. 28.
29. *Variety*, 30 December 1981, pp. 3, 24.
30. *Variety*, 22 December 1982, p. 3.
31. Harold L. Vogel, *Entertainment Industry Economics*, 2d ed. (New York: Cambridge University Press, 1990), p. 87.
32. WCI, Form 10-K, 1981, p. 7.
33. *Variety*, 3 January 1980, p. 80.
34. *Variety*, 24 December 1980, p. 5.
35. *Variety*, 14 January 1983, p. 46.
36. Ibid.
37. *Variety*, 1 April 1981, p. 3.
38. "How TV Is Revolutionizing Hollywood," *Business Week*, 21 February 1983, p. 89.
39. Robert Lindsey, "HBO: Home Box Office Moves In on Hollywood," *New York*, 12 June 1983, p. 67.
40. Ibid, p. 35.
41. Ibid, p. 32.
42. Jan Mayer, "Hard Bargainer," *Wall Street Journal*, 15 August 1983, p. 8.
43. Ibid., p. 1.
44. Vogel, *Entertainment Industry Economics*, p. 68.
45. Tony Schwartz, "Hollywood Debates HBO Role in Film Financing," *New York Times*, 7 January 1982, p. D1.
46. Lindsay, "HBO," p. 33.
47. Ibid.
48. Tony Schwartz, "U.S. Says Five Companies Broke Law in Plan to Limit Movies on Pay TV," *New York Times*, 5 August 1980, p. D15.
49. Ibid.
50. "Getty's Pay-TV Venture Is Sued by Justice Unit," *Wall Street Journal*, 5 August 1980, p. 5.
51. Tony Schwartz, "New Pay TV Network," *New York Times*, 19 May 1980, p. D10.
52. Stephen Stansweet, "As New Movie Studio Starts Work, It Seeks Credibility, Tries to Break Hollywood Mold," *Wall St. Journal*, 23 May 1983, p. 37.
53. A. D. Murphy, "Warners Tops in '85 Domestic Rentals," *Variety*, 8 January 1986, p. 73.
54. *Variety*, 14 November 1984, pp. 3, 38.
55. *Variety*, 21 September 1983, p. 3.
56. Steven Bach, *Final Cut: Dreams and Disaster in the Making of Heaven's Gate* (New York: Morrow, 1985), pp. 372, 400. Bach is the source for most of the discussion that follows.
57. Ibid., p. 122.
58. Ibid., p. 206.
59. Ibid., p. 208.
60. Ibid., pp. 231, 239, 251, 282.
61. Ibid., p. 252.
62. Canby quoted in ibid., p. 363.
63. Geri, "Heaven's Gate," *Variety*, 26 November 1980, p. 14.
64. "1980–83 Big Buck Scorecard," *Variety*, 11 January, 1984, p. 10.

65. "UA Domestic Rentals Off 32%," *Variety*, 24 September 1980, p. 3.
66. Transamerica Corp., Form 10-K, 1980, p. 22.
67. Transamerica Corp., Form 10-K, 1981.
68. Frank Rosenfelt, "MGM in Big Expansion for '8os," *Variety*, 9 January 1980, p. 9.
69. Hy Hollinger, "Production Control Changes Marked 1981," *Variety*, 13 January 1982, p. 1.
70. See "Spreading Risks: Q&A on New Methods of Feature Film Financing," *Variety*, 8 January 1986, pp. 28, 96.
71. Tom Girard, "How HBO, CBS, Col Tri-Star Deal Works," *Variety*, 14 November 1984, p. 38.
72. Lawrence Cohn, "Hollywood Goes on a Spending Spree," *Variety*, 1 September 1982, p. 5.
73. Lawrence Cohn, "Domestic Recoup Rare on Mega-Buck Pic Rentals," *Variety*, 12 January 1983, p. 7.
74. Lawrence Cohn, "Megabuck Pix Increased Ratios," *Variety*, pp. 10, 82.

CHAPTER 2. MERGER MANIA

1. Coca-Cola Co., Form 10-K, 1982, p. 5.
2. Richard W. Stevenson, "In Hollywood, Big Just Gets Bigger," *New York Times*, 14 October 1990.
3. Jim Robbins, "Theater Building Zooms," *Variety*, 11 January 1984, p. 17.
4. Martin Sikora, "The M&A Bonanza of the '8os . . . And Its Legacy," *Mergers and Acquisitions* 24, no. 5 (March/April 1990): 90.
5. Ibid., p. 91.
6. Murdoch quoted in Wolfgang J. Koschnick, "I Can Think of More Important Things Than Being Loved by Everybody," *Forbes*, 27 November 1989, p. 102.
7. Brenton Schlender, "Restless Wildcat," *Wall Street Journal*, 23 February 1981, p. 1.
8. "Diversification Blues," *Mergers and Acquisitions* 21, no. 6 (May/June, 1987): 13–14.
9. "Latest 10-Q on 20th-Fox," *Variety*, 2 September 1981, p. 7.
10. "The Shifting Fortunes of Marvin Davis," *Business Week*, 8 April 1989, p. 36.
11. Thomas C. Hayes, "Murdoch Will Buy Out Davis' Holdings in Fox," *New York Times*, 24 September 1985, p. D1.
12. Ibid.
13. "Warner Buys Out Murdoch For $172-Mil," *Variety*, 21 March 1984, p. 1.
14. "50 Largest Foreign Acquisitions in the U.S., 1980–89," *Mergers and Acquisitions* 24 (March/April 1990): 113.
15. News Corp. Ltd., Form 10-K, 1986, pp. 6–7.
16. "Murdoch's Profits Bolstered by TV, 20th Ancillaries," *Variety*, 12 November 1986, pp. 3, 33.
17. Koschnick, "I Can Think," p. 104.
18. Coca-Cola Co., "The Strategy for the 1980s," Form 10-K, 1982, p. 2.
19. Myron Magnet, "Coke Tries Selling Movies Like Soda Pop," *Fortune*, 26 December 1983, pp. 119–120.
20. Coca-Cola Co., letter to shareholders, Form 10-K, 1982, p. 6.
21. David Fox, "Coke Holds Fiscal Court on Colpix Turf," *Variety*, 24 November 1982, p. 3.
22. Coca-Cola Co., letter, p. 7.
23. Harold L. Vogel, *Entertainment Industry Economics*, 2d ed. (New York: Cambridge University Press, 1990), p. 70.
24. Ibid.
25. Magnet, "Coke Tries Selling," pp. 122, 124.
26. Coca-Cola Co., Form 10-K, 1983.
27. See Justin Wyatt, *High Concept: Movies and Marketing in Hollywood* (Austin: University of Texas Press, 1994), p. 86.
28. Charles Kipps, *Out of Focus: Power, Pride, and Prejudice: David Puttnam in Hollywood* (New York: Morrow, 1989), pp. 190, 200.
29. Charles Kipps, "The Rise and Fall of the Coca-Cola Kid," *Variety*, 18 May 1988, p. 7.
30. Ibid.
31. Kipps, *Out of Focus*, p. 157.
32. Kipps, "Rise and Fall," p. 7.
33. Ibid., p. 30; Kipps, *Out of Focus*, p. 298.
34. Lawrence Cohn, "High Cost Pics Largely on the Money in '88," *Variety*, 11–17 January 1989, p. 30.
35. Coca-Cola Co., Form 10-K, 1989.

36. Sony Corp., *Annual Report*, 1991.
37. "50 Largest Foreign Acquisitions," p. 113; "An Allure for Foreign Buyers," *Mergers and Acquisitions* 22, no. 6 (May/June 1988): 12.
38. For details of the settlement, see Laura Landro, "Sony, Warner Settle Dispute over Producers," *Wall Street Journal*, 17 November 1989, p. 1.
39. Sony Corp., *Annual Report*, 1991; Sony Corp., Form 10-K, 1991.
40. Gulf and Western, "Gulf and Western in the '80s," Form 10-K, 1982, p. 10.
41. "G&W Revamp Places Diller at Head of Leisure Group, Plus Par," *Variety*, 16 March 1983, p. 5.
42. "Gulf and Western to Sell Florida, Dominican Sugar Operations," *Variety*, 20 June 1984, p. 3.
43. Gulf and Western, Form 10-K, 1985, p. 3.
44. Richard Gold, "G&W Pares Down to Media Only: Possibilities Abound," *Variety*, 12–18 April 1989, p. 4.
45. "Diversification Blues," p. 13.
46. Richard Gold, "Warners, G&W Succeed By Doin' What Comes Naturally," *Variety*, 6 April 1988, p. 7.
47. Seideman, "It's the Game," p. 41.
48. WCI, letter to shareholders, Form 10-K, 1981, p. 6.
49. Tony Seideman, "It's the Game, Not the Name, That Ultimately Sells Vidiots," *Variety*, 15 December 1982, p. 41; "Games Plunge WCI Quarter & Next Few Stanzas Downward," *Variety*, 23 February 1982, pp. 4, 27; "Atari Plunges WCI into $19-Mil Loss in 1st '83 Quarter, *Variety*, 27 April 1983, p. 4; Mark B. Silverman, "Awash in $879-Mil Sea of Red Ink, Warner Dumps Atari," *Variety*, 4 July 1984, p. 40.
50. Richard Gold, "New Warner Credit Accord Explored," *Variety*, 19 December 1984, p. 91.
51. For details, see Bill Sapaorito, "A Legal Victory for the Long Term," *Fortune*, 14 August 1989, pp. 56–59.
52. Ibid.
53. Richard Gold, "No Bigness Like Show Bigness," *Variety*, 14–20 June 1989, p. 6.
54. Benjamin J. Stein, "It's about Time," *Barron's*, 17 July 1989, p. 13.
55. Richard Gold, "Par's Block Looks Like a Bust as Court Backs Time Director's Stand," *Variety*, 19–25 July 1989, p. 1.
56. All three quotations are from Richard Gold, "Time's Move of the Year," *Variety*, 8–14 March 1989, pp. 1, 3.
57. Time-Warner, Inc., Form 10-K, 1989.
58. Time-Warner, Inc., "Globalization," Form 10-K, 1989, pp. 1, 3, 14.
59. "Top Countries for U.S. Acquisitions Overseas, 1980–1989," *Mergers and Acquisitions* (March/April 1990): 112.
60. Paramount Communications, Inc., Form 10-K, 1989, p. F-6.
61. Matsushita Electric Industrial Co., Ltd., Annual Reports, 1990, 1991, p. 6.
62. MCA, Inc., Form 10-K, 1989, p. 2.
63. Laura Landro and Richard Turner, "Matsushita Explores Purchase of MCA," *Wall Street Journal*, 25 September 1990, p. B1.
64. *Variety*, 20 January 1988, p. 38.
65. Stratford P. Sherman, "Ted Turner: Back from the Brink," *Fortune*, 7 July 1986, p. 28.
66. Sharon Walsh, "Milken to Pay U.S. $47 Million to Settle Charge of Violating Ban," *Washington Post*, 27 February 1998, p. G1.
67. See Jane Galbraith, "MGM/UA, Turner Shareholders Okay Merger; Expect Coin Soon," *Variety*, 5 March 1986, p. 3.
68. Jane Galbraith, "Turner Keeps Pics, Drops Rest of MGM," *Variety*, 11 June 1986, p. 3.
69. See Alex Ben Block, "Mamma from Turner," *Forbes*, 18 May 1987, pp. 126–28.
70. Pathé Communications Corp., Form 10-K, pp. 8–9.
71. For an account of the takeover attempts, see John Taylor, *Storming the Magic Kingdom: Wall Street, the Raiders, and the Battle for Disney* (New York: Knopf, 1987).
72. Walt Disney Co., Form 10-K, p. 20.
73. Walt Disney Co., Form 10-K, 1984, p. 2.
74. Walt Disney Co., Form 10-K, 1985, 1986.
75. "The Teachings of Chairman Jeff," *Variety*, 4 February 1991, p. 24.
76. Jim Robbins, "Theater Building Zooms," *Variety*, 11 January, 1984, p. 17.

77. Thomas Guback, "The Evolution of the Motion Picture Theater Business in the 1980s," *Journal of Communication* 37, no. 2 (spring 1987): 70.

78. Ibid.

79. Sid Adilman, "The Man behind the Multiplex, and Complex," *Variety*, 26 April–2 May 1989, p. 50.

80. Guback, "Evolution," pp. 68–69.

81. Douglas Gomery profiles Cineplex's history in "Building a Movie Theater Giant: The Rise of Cineplex Odeon," in *Hollywood in the Age of Television*, ed. Tino Balio (Cambridge, Mass: Unwin Hyman, 1990), pp. 377–91. See also the special issue on Cineplex in *Variety*, 28 April–2 May 1989.

82. "When Opportunity Knocks, Open the Door," *Variety*, 26 April–2 May 1989, pp. 54, 64.

83. MPAA, *1996 U.S. Economic Review*, p. 3.

84. "When Opportunity Knocks," p. 64.

85. Gomery, "Building a Movie Theater Giant," p. 381.

86. Deirdre McMurdy, "Fade to Black," *Macleans*, 17 June 1991, p. 41.

87. For discussions of the case, see Gerald F. Phillips, "The Recent Acquisition of Theatre Circuits by Major Distributors," *Entertainment and Sports Lawyer* 5, no. 3. (winter 1987): pp. 1–2, 10–23; Michael Conant, "The Paramount Decrees Reconsidered," *The American Film Industry*, rev. ed., ed. Tino Balio (Madison: University of Wisconsin Press, 1985), pp. 537–73.

88. These percentages were suggested minimums by Warner Bros. in its bid letter to exhibitors for BATMAN (1989). See D. Barry Reardon, "The Studio Distributor," in *The Movie Business Book*, ed. Jason Squires (New York: Fireside, 1992), p. 315.

89. AMC Entertainment, Inc., *Annual Report*, 1986.

90. Will Tusher, "Distribution's Theater Buys Near Peak," *Variety*, 7 January 1987, p. 3.

91. Jim Robbins, "July Lets Warner Return G&W but Involves Consent Decrees," *Variety*, 14–20 December 1988, p. 3.

92. "High Court Upholds Fox Conviction for Block Booking," *Variety*, 10 January 1990, p. 7.

93. Peter Bart, "What Hollywood Isn't Telling MCA's New Owners," *Variety*, 3 December 1990, p. 8.

CHAPTER 3. THE BRAVE NEW ANCILLARY WORLD

1. Gulf and Western, "Leisure Time Revenues," Form 10-K, 1981, p. 6.

2. For discussions of the industry's market research practices, see Susan Obmer, "Measuring Desire, George Gallup and the Origins of Market Research in Hollywood," Ph.D. Dissertation, New York University, 1997; and Justin Wyatt, *High Concept: Movies and Marketing in Hollywood* (Austin: University of Texas Press, 1994), pp. 155–61.

3. D. Barry Reardon, "The Studio Distributor," in *The Movie Business Book*, ed. Jason Squires (New York: Fireside, 1992), pp. 312, 313.

4. John Dempsey, "MGM/UA Building Barter Film Web," *Variety*, 25 July 1984, p. 1.

5. John Dempsey, "Top Pics Pull Huge Syndie Coin," *Variety*, 4 February 1987, pp. 1, 150.

6. "How TV is Revolutionizing Hollywood," *Business Week*, 21 February 1983, p. 80.

7. *1991 International Television and Video Almanac* (New York: Quigley, 1992), p. 607.

8. Morry Roth, "Teens Leaving Theaters for Homevid," *Variety*, 26 February 1986, p. 3; Will Tusher, "Col Survey Shows Vid Rentals Far Outdistancing Admissions," *Variety*, 21 May 1986, pp. 3, 44

9. *1989 International Television and Video Almanac* (New York: Quigley, 1990), pp. 393, 394.

10. Ibid., p. 391; Al Stewart, "Homevid: Child of the '80s Seeks Continued Growth in the '90s," *Variety*, 24 January 1990, p. 153.

11. Charles Kipps, "Wall St. Plugs in VCR Potential," *Variety*, 23 September 1987, p. 118.

12. *1990 International Television and Video Almanac* (New York: Quigley, 1991), p. 625.

13. Kipps, "Wall St.," p. 118.

14. "FBI Exposes Porno and Piracy Affinity," *Variety*, 20 February 1980, p. 7.

15. "FBI Nails Video Pirates," *Variety*, 18 March 1981, p. 277.

16. *1991 International Television and Video Almanac*, p. 604.

17. Will Tusher, "U.S. Losses to Global Piracy Fell 25% in '89, per Valenti," *Variety*, 10 January 1990, p. 13.

18. "How TV Is Revolutionizing Hollywood," p. 81.

19. Quoted in Janet Wasko, *Hollywood in the Information Age* (Austin: University of Texas Press, 1995), p. 128.

20. Jim Harwood, "Federal Court Nixes In-Home Videotaping: Sony Plans Appeal," *Variety*, 21 October 1981, p. 96.

21. Paul Harris, "Supreme Court O.K.'s Home Taping," *Variety*, 18 January 1984, pp. 109, 1.

22. James Lardner, *Fast Forward: Hollywood, the Japanese, and the Onslaught of the VCR*, (New York: Norton, 1987), p. 323.

23. Walt Disney Productions, Form 10-K, 1982, p. 25.

24. Twentieth Century–Fox, Form 10-K, 1980, p. 7.

25. Marie Gelman, "Majors Increase Home Vid Titles 854% in 16 mos.," *Variety*, 5 March 1980, p. 1.

26. Richard B. Childs, "Home Video," in *The Movie Business Book*, ed. Jason Squires (New York: Fireside, 1992), pp. 335–36.

27. Steve Knoll, "Warners Revises Rental Policy," *Variety*, 11 November 1981, p. 1.

28. Tony Seideman, "'Raiders' Setting Sales Marks: Par Claims 500,000 En Route," *Variety*, 23 November 1983, p. 27.

29. Tom Bierbaum, "Paramount's 'Gun' Soars to Revenue/Sales Marks," *Variety*, 25 March 1987, p. 41.

30. Kipps, "Wall St.," p. 1.

31. MCA, Inc., letter to shareholders, "Five Year Financial Highlights," Form 10-K, 1989, p. 6.

32. David Robert Cellitti, "The World on a Silver Platter," *Widescreen Review*, Laser Magic 1998 Issue, p. 27; for a review of the various disc technologies, see "The Video Disc System: A Technical Report by the SMPTE Study Group on Video Disc Recording," *SMPTE Journal* 91, no. 2 (February 1982): 180–85.

33. John Mabey, "Video Disc Basics," *American Cinematographer* 66, no. 3 (March 1985): 89.

34. Steve Schifrin quoted in Mike Jay, "Electronic Editing of Film for Motion Pictures," *American Cinematographer* 62, no. 3 (March 1981): 257.

35. Some aesthetic effects of the video assist are discussed by Jean-Pierre Geuens, "Through the Looking Glasses: From the Camera Obscura to Video Assist," *Film Quarterly* 49, no. 3 (summer 1996): 16–26.

36. Ric Gentry, "Clint Eastwood: An Interview," *Post Script* 17, no. 3 (summer 1998): 13–14.

37. Charles Harpole, letter to Stephen Prince, 18 December 1998.

38. Bob Fisher, "The Emerging New Film/Video Interface," *American Cinematographer* 62, no. 6 (June 1981): 570–73, 615–18.

39. See Thomas Brown, "The Electronic Camera Experiment," *American Cinematographer* 63, no. 1 (January 1982): 28–29, 76–79, 100, and "Coppola's Electronic Cinema System," *American Cinematographer* 63, no. 8 (August 1982): 777–81.

40. Walter Murch, *In the Blink of an Eye: A Perspective on Film Editing* (Los Angeles: Silman-James Press, 1995), p. 77.

41. Several systems are profiled in "Video Assisted Film Editing," *American Cinematographer* 63, no. 3 (March 1982): 297–308.

42. D. M. James Compton and Dimitri S. Dimitri, "Implementation of Time Code Using Datakode Magnetic Control Surface Film," *SMPTE Journal* 95 (July 1986): 727–32.

43. Bob Lasiewics, "Computers in the Editing Room," *American Cinematographer* 66, no. 6 (June 1985): 93.

44. See Michael J. Stanton, "Ediflex, an Electronic Editing System," *American Cinematographer* 68, no. 7, (July 1987): 101–8.

45. Murch, *In the Blink of an Eye*, pp. 98–99.

46. "Top Video Rentals 1989," *Variety*, 24 January 1990, p. 153.

47. *1991 International Television and Video Almanac*, p. 605.

48. Ira Deutcbman, "Independent Distribution and Marketing," in *The Movie Business Book*, ed. Jason E. Squire (New York: Fireside, 1992), p. 322.

49. "Major Distribs Picking Up More Indie Productions," *Variety*, 24 February 1988, p. 66.

50. Sam L. Grogg, "Venture Capital Strategy and FilmDallas," in *The Movie Business Book*, ed. Jason E. Squire (New York: Fireside, 1992), p. 151.

51. Grogg has outlined the fiscal operation of FilmDallas in "Venture Capital Strategy and FilmDallas," pp. 150–58.

52. Ibid.
53. Lawrence Cohn, "Ancillary Market Saves Indies," *Variety*, 24 February 1988, p. 295.
54. Al Stewart, "Smut Out of Rut, Defying Its Foes," *Variety*, 17 January 1990, p. 36.
55. Robert Eberwein, "The Erotic Thriller," *Post Script* 17, no. 3 (summer 1998): 25–33.
56. The vice president and general manager of Key Video, a division of CBS/FOX Video, explains the company's efforts to secure first-generation film materials for home video transfers in Herb Fischer, "Saving Classics on Tape," *American Cinematographer* 66, no. 9 (September 1985): 81–83.
57. See Frank Reinking, "Film to Tape Mysteries Unraveled," *American Cinematographer* 70, no. 9 (September 1989): 73–80.
58. Charles Shiro Tashiro, "Videophilia: What Happens When You Wait for It on Video," *Film Quarterly* 45, no. 1 (fall 1991): 8.
59. Dominic J. Case, "Telecine-Compatible Prints," *SMPTE Journal* 98, no. 6 (June 1989): 453.
60. Tashiro, "Videophilia," p. 14.
61. Ibid.
62. Tashiro (ibid.) provides some illustrations that demonstrate this.
63. All three quotations in Harlan Jacobson, "Old Pix Don't Die, They Fade Away," *Variety*, 9 July 1980, p. 28.
64. For a profile of Tech IB, see Richard W. Haines, *Technicolor Movies: The History of Dye Transfer Printing* (Jefferson, N.C.: McFarland, 1993)
65. See K. J. Carl et al., "Eastman Color Print Film 5384," *SMPTE Journal* 91, no. 12 (December 1982): 1161–70; John Waner, "Report on the New Eastman Color Print Film," *American Cinematographer* 65, no. 4 (April 1982): 391–92.
66. For a discussion of the issues surrounding color fading and the industry's response, see Richard Patterson, "The Preservation of Color Films, Part I," *American Cinematographer* 62, no. 7 (July 1981): 694–96, 714–20; Richard Patterson, "The Preservation of Color Films, Part II," *American Cinematographer* 62, no. 8 (August 1981): 792–822.
67. Tony Seidman, "Homevid Aids Cinema B.O. for Two Pics," *Variety*, 26 October 1983, p. 1; Tom Bierbaum, "Paramount Expects B.O. Boost with Re-Release of 'Footloose' Same Day Cassette Hits Market," *Variety*, 1 August 1984, p. 22.
68. Richard Gold, "H'wood Majors Spinoff Videos from Youth Pix," *Variety*, 22 February 1984, p. 108.
69. Richard Gold, "'Flashdance' Film, LP Feeding Off Each Other," *Variety*, 11 May 1983, p. 3.
70. Gold, "H'wood Majors Spinoff Videos," p. 108.
71. Details of this relationship are outlined by Richard Gold, "Studios and Labels Pan Soundtrack Gold," *Variety*, 18 April 1984, p. 216.
72. Gold, "H'wood Majors Spinoff Videos," p. 108.
73. Richard Gold, "'Purple Rain' Sells Rock at Box Office," *Variety*, 1 August 1984, p. 5.
74. Wyatt, *High Concept*, pp. 50–51.
75. David Breskin, *Filmmakers in Conversation* (Boston: Faber and Faber, 1992), p. 357.
76. Walter Benjamin, *Illuminations*, ed. Hannah Arendt (New York: Schocken Books, 1978), p. 224.
77. John G. Fisher, "Screen and Tube Financing in the Inflated Years Ahead," *Variety*, 9 January 1980, p. 80.
78. Richard Gold, "High Hopes For 'Gremlins' Merchandise," *Variety*, 27 June 1984, p. 5.
79. Ruth A. Inglis, "Self-Regulation in Operation," in *The American Film Industry*, rev. ed., ed. Tino Balio, (Madison: University of Wisconsin Press, 1985), pp. 377–400.
80. Dan Gilroy, "Product Placement in Pics Helps Hedge Costs Majors and Indies," *Variety*, 19 February 1986, p. 399.
81. "Product Pluggola Padding Pic Producers' Budgets," *Variety*, 9 May 1990, p. 22.
82. Ibid.
83. Gilroy, "Product Placement," p. 399.
84. "No Toys in Tokyo Puts 'Turtles' in the Soup," *Variety*, 15 April 1991, pp. 1, 227.
85. Richard Gold, "High Hopes," p. 32.
86. "Turtles, 'Toons and Toys 'R' In," *Variety*, 18 April 1990, p. 8.
87. Warner Communications, Inc., *Annual Report*, 1982.
88. Time–Warner, "Globalization," Form 10-K, 1990, p. 7.
89. "Fewer Big-Budget Films Made It Pay," *Variety*, 8 January 1986, p. 96.

90. Ibid.
91. Harold L. Vogel, *Entertainment Industry Economics*, 2d ed. (New York: Cambridge University Press, 1990), p. 50.

CHAPTER 4. INDEPENDENTS, PACKAGING, AND INFLATIONARY PRESSURE IN 1980S HOLLYWOOD

1. Matt Rothman, "Carolco, Kassar Rise from Redivvied Ashes," *Variety*, 4 January 1993, p. 81.
2. David Kissinger, "Judgment Day for Carolco," *Variety*, 9 December 1991, p. 1.
3. Tom Turgend, "Hungarian-Born Producer Becomes Hollywood Legend," *Northern California Jewish Bulletin*, 22 December 1995: PG.
4. Joshua Hammer, "Total Free Fall," *Newsweek*, 9 March 1992, p. 50.
5. I am listing Vajna and Kassar as associate producers of VICTORY, although their actual production credit is more ambiguous. The end credits list VICTORY as "a co-production of the Victory company and Tom Stern in association with Andy Vajna and Mario Kassar."
6. Ellen Farley, "The U.S. Has Surrendered—Now RAMBO Is Taking the World by Storm," *Business Week*, 26 August 1985, p. 109.
7. Ibid.
8. Richard Gold, "Tri-Star, Carolco Execs Insist RAMBO III Won't Die at B.O." *Variety*, 22 June 1988, p. 24.
9. Richard Zoglin, "An Outbreak of Rambomania," *Time*, 24 June 1985, p. 72.
10. The film grossed $107.9 million in the first forty days of release, leaving competition such as THE GOONIES, FLETCH, and PALE RIDER far behind.
11. "Carolco May Whip Out RAMBO III For Film's Guarantors at Market," *Variety*, 24 February 1988, p. 15.
12. David Puttnam and Neil Watson, *Movies and Money* (New York: Knopf, 1998), p. 225.
13. Alex Ben Block, "Is There Life beyond Rambo?" *Forbes*, 1 June 1987, p. 92.
14. Gold, "Tri-Star, Carolco," p. 4.
15. Ronald Grover, "Now Carolco Needs Fresh Blood, Part II," *Business Week*, 30 May 1988, p. 80.
16. Ronald Grover, "Carolco May Be Headed for a Quick Dissolve," *Business Week*, 6 July 1992, p. 40.
17. Richard Natale, "Live Wire May Spark Carolcoy, " *Variety*, 15 July 1991, p. 60.
18. Hammer, "Total Free Fall," *Newsweek*, 9 March 1992, p. 51.
19. Peter Bart, "Carolco Culture Shock," *Variety*, 26 August 1991, p. 24.
20. Hammer, "Total Free Fall," *Newsweek*, 9 March 1992, p. 51.
21. Lisa Gubernick, "Whose Money Is It, Anyway?" *Forbes*, 12 November 1990, p. 305.
22. Hammer, "Total Free Fall," p. 52.
23. "The Teachings of Chairman Jeff," *Variety*, 4 February 1991, p. 24; Peter Bart, "Times Have Changed, but the Rhetoric Lingers On," *Variety*, 4 February 1991, p. 5.
24. Claudia Eller and Don Groves, "Carolco Prexy Defends Its Talent Megadeals," *Variety*, 29 October 1990, p. 10.
25. "Hasta la Vista, Babies," *Economist*, 13 July 1991, p. 68.
26. Paul Noglows, "Terminated Deal Trips Carolco," *Variety*, 9 December 1991, p. 90.
27. Hammer, "Total Free Fall," *Newsweek*, 9 March 1992, p. 52.
28. Suzan Ayscough, "Steep Deal for Carolco 'Cliff,'" *Variety*, 17 May 1993, p. 120.
29. James Bates and Judy Brennan, "Carolco May Be Close to Restructuring," *Los Angeles Times*, 14 February 1995, p. D4.
30. Judy Brennan, "Red Ink on the Starboard Bow," *Los Angeles Times*, 20 August 1995, Calendar, p. 26.
31. James Bates, "Fox Will Buy Most Assets of Ailing Carolco," *Los Angeles Times*, 11 November 1995, Business, p. 1.
32. James Bates, "Ex-Carolco Chief Goes to Paramount," *Los Angeles Times*, 4 January 1996, Business, p. 2.
33. Lawrence Cohn, "Stars' Rocketing Salaries Keep Pushing Envelope," *Variety*, 24 September 1990, p. 3.
34. Geraldine Fabrikant, "The Hole in Hollywood's Pocket," *New York Times*, 10 December 1990, p. C1.
35. Ibid.
36. Statistics from the *International Motion Picture Almanac* (New York: Quigley, 1989–91).

37. For discussions of the possible effect of video and cable on independent film at the time of the entry of the new technologies, see Alexander Auerbach, "Pay Cable Helps Theatre Boxoffice, Market Study Shows," *Boxoffice*, July 1983, pp. 20–21; Gail Bronson, "Videotapes Give Hollywood a Second Shot at Success," *US News & World Reports*, 4 March 1985, p. 73; Hank Werba, "The Image of Cinema in the '80s," *Variety*, 13 June 1979, pp. 7–8; Lawrence Cohn, "Indie Filmmakers Advised to Regard Pay-TV as a Funding Tap," *Variety*, 17 June 1981, p. 6. For a review of the actual effect of both on the motion picture industry, see Barry R. Litman, *The Motion Picture Mega-Industry* (Boston: Allyn and Bacon, 1998), pp. 74–96, and Janet Wasko, *Hollywood in the Information Age* (Austin: University of Texas Press), 1995, pp. 71–185.

38. Financier John Pierson explains the influence of the video market on independent film of the mid-1980s in *Spike, Mike, Slackers, and Dykes: A Guided Tour across a Decade of American Independent Cinema* (New York: Hyperion Books, 1995), pp. 24–30. He characterizes the results of expected video revenues as spotty, citing the disappointing video release of Jim Jarmusch's STRANGER THAN PARADISE (1984).

39. "Golan-Globus Buy of Cannon to Launch US Prod-Distrib: Sell 10-Point Insurance Plan," *Variety*, 23 May 1979, p. 3.

40. Barry Rehfeld, "Cannon Fathers," *Film Comment*, December 1983, p. 23.

41. Lisa Gubernick, "Cannon Rises Again," *Forbes*, 25 July 1988, p. 43. For a description of the distribution deal between Cannon Films and MGM/UA, see Peter Bart, *Fade Out: The Calamitous Final Days of MGM* (New York: Morrow, 1990), p. 214.

42. Film critic David Denby lists Cannon Films as one of the saviors of American film for their ability to support "artistically ambitious directors"; see his article "Can the Movies Be Saved?" *New York*, 21 July 1986, pp. 24–35.

43. Robert Friedman, "Will Cannon Boom or Bust?" *American Film*, July/August 1986, p. 53.

44. Gubernick, "Cannon Rises Again," p. 43.

45. Peter Newcomb, "Covering Their Bets," *Forbes*, 26 December 1988, p. 10.

46. Will Tusher, "'I Never Had, Nor Expect a Film at or under Budget': De Laurentiis," *Variety*, 3 January 1979, p. 64.

47. William K. Knoedelseder, Jr., "De Laurentiis: Producer's Picture Darkens," *Los Angeles Times*, 30 August 1987, part IV, p. 1.

48. None of these 1986 films managed to amass even $10 million box-office gross domestically: BLUE VELVET grossed $7.144 million in 1986 and $1.406 million in 1987; MANHUNTER, $8.555 million; MAXIMUM OVERDRIVE, $7.188 million; TRANSFORMERS, $5.706 million; MY LITTLE PONY, $5.684 million; and KING KONG LIVES, $4.305 million. Data on theatrical gross comes from Art Murphy's *Boxoffice Register*.

49. As evidence of De Laurentiis's marketing exaggeration, consider the ad line for his 1976 remake of KING KONG (1933): "The most exciting original motion picture event of all time."

50. "Appealing to Gross Greed," *Time*, 1 June 1987, p. 55.

51. Barron quoted in Knoedelseder, "De Laurentiis," p. 2.

52. Jane Lieberman, "Ventura, TWE in Bids for De Laurentiis," *Variety*, 23 November 1988, p. 3.

53. Jane Lieberman, "De Laurentiis Entertainment Group Board, Creditors Approve Buy by Carolco," *Variety*, 26 April 1989, p. 12.

54. Karen Cook, "The Little Studio That Could," *Premiere*, March 1988, p. 17.

55. Kerry Hanson, "A Sad Story," *Forbes*, 14 May 1990, p. 10.

56. "A Jungle War over the PLATOON Video," *Newsweek*, 23 November 1987, p. 56.

57. William Harris, "Lights, Camera, Lawyers!" *Forbes*, 10 August 1987, p. 33.

58. EARTH GIRLS ARE EASY failed miserably in its commercial run domestically, grossing only $3.916 million, thought it has gained cult status since its release in 1989, as evidenced by the large number of personal web pages that list EARTH GIRLS ARE EASY as a favorite movie.

59. For a review of the marketing and distribution decisions behind the film, consult Michael Wiese, "DIRTY DANCING: A Case Study" in *Film and Video Marketing* (Stoneham, Mass.: Butterworth, 1989), pp. 119–218.

60. Paul Grein, "DIRTY DANCING Steps around Competition" *Los Angeles Times*, 11 November 1987, part VI, p. 1.

61. Cook, "Little Studio That Could," p. 17.

62. Al Stewart, "Vestron, Saying Nixed Loan Triggered Woes, Sues Bank," *Variety*, 23 August 1989, p. 59.

63. "Vestron Deal Is Negotiated," *New York Times*, 1 November 1990, p. D5.
64. Producer Julia Phillips recounts several depressing anecdotes about the failure of Quigley and other Vestron executives to guide her film THE BEAT (1988) into the marketplace; see Phillips's autobiography, *You'll Never Eat Lunch in this Town Again* (New York: Random House, 1991), pp. 473–81, 503–4, 508.
65. Robert Rehme, "Indies Must Map Out Strategies to Fit Changing Domestic Market," *Variety*, 20 January 1988, pp. 8, 87.
66. Jim Hillier and Aaron Lipstadt, "The Economics of Independence: Roger Corman and New World Pictures, 1970–80" *Movie* 31/32 (1986), pp. 43–53.
67. Ronald Grover, "High Drama from the Folks Who Brought You GODZILLA 85," *Business Week*, 7 September 1987, p. 30.
68. New World was able to compete with more established television suppliers through stringent cost cutting in production; see Ronald Grover, "Getting Rich on TV's New Austerity," *Business Week*, 6 April 1987, pp. 109–14.
69. Greg Crister, "Tough New World," *Channels*, March 1987, pp. 20–26.
70. "Another Toymaker May Be in Play," *Business Week*, 21 September 1987, p. 108.
71. Joseph McBride, "Rehme Says He May Add to His Duties under New World–Pathé Link-Up," *Variety*, 15 March 1989, p. 24.
72. For an analysis of the methods employed by Miramax Films and New Line Cinema, see Justin Wyatt, "The Formation of the Major Independent: Miramax, New Line, and the New Hollywood," in *Contemporary Hollywood Cinema*, ed. Steve Neale and Murray Smith (London: Routledge, 1998), pp. 74–90.
73. Michael Fleming, "Miramax, Riding 'Sex' Wave, Storms on to the '90s," *Variety*, 31 January 1990, p. 9.
74. Lisa Gubernick, "We Don't Want to Be Walt Disney," *Forbes*, 16 October 1989, pp. 109–10.
75. Anne Thompson, "Will Success Spoil the Weinstein Brothers?" *Film Comment*, July/August 1989, pp. 72–76.
76. For a history of New Line's development, consult the following: "New Line Focuses Product on Three Specialized Areas," *Independent Film Journal*, 10 July 1974, p. 21; "Fiscally Fortified, New Line Accents Production and Pickups," *Variety*, 14 October 1981, p. 12; Maitland McDonagh, "New Line Cinema Sets Out to Achieve Market Identity," *Film Journal*, March 1984, pp. 12 ff.; Lisa Gubernick, "It's Great for a Date," *Forbes*, 6 February 1989, pp. 110–14; Lisa Coleman, "Picking Your Targets," *Forbes*, 21 January 1991, p. 72; Josh Young, "New Line Cinema: It Was a Very Good Year," *New York Times*, 18 September 1994, pp. H13, 20.
77. Lawrence Cohn, "Domestic Market for Indie Pix Soft," *Variety*, 22 February 1989, p. 22.
78. Lawrence Cohn, "Ancillary Market Saves Indies," *Variety* 24 February 1988, p. 295.
79. Tino Balio, "Adjusting to the New Global Economy," in *Film Policy: International, National, and Regional Perspectives*, ed. Albert Moran (London: Routledge, 1996), p. 27.
80. Nancy Griffin and Kim Masters, *Hit and Run: How Jon Peters and Peter Guber Took Sony for a Ride in Hollywood*. (New York: Simon & Schuster, 1996).
81. John Rossant, "Puzzle in Movieland: The Case of the Mystery Moguls," *Business Week*, 13 March 1989, p. 80.

CHAPTER 5. THE TALENT OLIGOPOLY

1. Lisa Gubernick, "Living Off the Past," *Forbes*, 12 June 1989, p. 54.
2. Quoted in Mark Litwak, *Reel Power: The Struggle for Influence and Success in the New Hollywood* (New York: Morrow, 1986), p. 155.
3. Ibid., p. 156.
4. Suzanna Andrews, "The Hollywood Deal Game," *Institutional Investor* 25, no. 13 (November 1991): 69.
5. Quoted in Joseph McBride, ed., *Filmmakers on Filmmaking*, vol. 1 (Los Angeles: Tarcher, 1983), p. 174.
6. Quoted in Janice Castro, "Pocketful of Stars: Michael Ovitz and His Cadre of Agents Are Hollywood's New Power Brokers," *Time*, 13 February 1989, p. 59.
7. Litwak, *Reel Power*, p. 55.
8. "A Star Is Bought," *Economist*, 23 December 1989, p. 16.
9. Frank Rose, *The Agency: William Morris and the Hidden History of Show Business* (New York: HarperCollins, 1995), p. 439.

10. Litwak, *Reel Power*, p. 42.
11. Gubernick, "Living Off the Past," p. 48.
12. Lisa Gubernick, "Backs to the Future," *Forbes*, 15 April 1991, p. 10.
13. Rose, *The Agency*, p. 372.
14. Ibid, p. 369.
15. Robert Slater, *Ovitz: The Inside Story of Hollywood's Most Controversial Power Broker* (New York: McGraw-Hill, 1997), p. 91. Much of the ensuing discussion of CAA derives from this source. Slater spoke directly with Ovitz and with leading industry figures about CAA. While the resulting portrait is perhaps overly flattering of CAA, the book's interviews and for-the-record commentary by industry figures are invaluable.
16. Ibid., p. 95.
17. Ibid., p. 97.
18. Ibid., pp. 106, 107.
19. Ibid., p. 168.
20. Castro, "Pocketful of Stars," p. 58.
21. Slater, *Ovitz*, p. 134.
22. Litwak, *Reel Power*, p. 44.
23. Slater, *Ovitz*, p. 108.
24. Castro, "Pocketful of Stars," p. 59.
25. Litwak, *Reel Power*, p. 29.
26. Slater, *Ovitz*, p. 211.
27. Ibid., p. 178.
28. Laura Landro and Richard Turner, "Matsushita Explores Purchases of MCA," *Wall Street Journal*, 25 September 1990, p. B1.
29. Andrews, "Hollywood Deal Game," p. 76.
30. Lisa Gubernick, "Know Thy Limitations," *Forbes*, 20 January 1992, p. 52.
31. "Par Gives Eddie Murphy a New 5-Pic Pact, More Coin and Control," *Variety*, 2 September 1987, p. 6.
32. Dana Wechsler, "Profits? What Profits?," *Forbes*, 19 February 1990, p. 38.
33. Linda Rapattoni, "Wm. Morris Seeks to Quash Another Par Subpoena," *Variety*, 16 September 1991, p. 21; Rose, *The Agency*, p. 460.
34. Connie Danese, "SAG Conference Addresses (and Denounces) Female Struggles in Films and TV," *Back Stage*, 17 August 1990, p. 3.
35. Ibid.
36. James McBride, "Eddie Murphy Comes Clean," *People Weekly*, 8 August 1988, p. 79.

CHAPTER 6. THE FILMMAKERS

1. For an amusing account of the foibles and frustrations of Hollywood screenwriting, see *Monster* (New York: Random House, 1997), author John Gregory Dunne's account of the eight years required for his (and wife Joan Didiori's) script, based on newscaster Jessica Savitch's life, to reach the screen in mutated form as UP CLOSE AND PERSONAL, a Robert Redford-Michelle Pfeiffer vehicle.
2. Charles Champlin illustrates this by profiling the film's story sessions during pre-production. See Champlin, *George Lucas: The Creative Impulse*. New York: Harry N. Abrams, Inc., 1992, pp. 79–83.
3. Ann Thompson, "George Lucas," PREMIERE 12, no. 9 (May 1999): 68.
4. Ibid., p. 70.
5. Ibid., p. 74.
6. Champlin discusses Lucas's role in connection with these and other films in *George Lucas: The Creative Impulse*, pp. 24–167.
7. Ralph Guggenheim, Rob Lay, and Andy Cohen, "The History, Design, and Architecture of Editdroid," *SMPTE Journal* 94, no. 1 (January 1985): 158; Jeffrey Borish, James A. Moorer, and Peter Nye, "SoundDroid: A New System for Electronic Post-Production of Sound," *SMPTE Journal* 95, no. 5 (May 1986): 567–71.
8. David R. Schwind, "Acoustical Design for the Technical Building at Skywalker Ranch, Part 1: Sound Isolation and Room Acoustics" and Thomas A. Schindler, "Acoustical Design for the Technical Building at Skywalker Ranch, Part 2: Mechanical and Electrical Acoustic Noise Control," *SMPTE Journal* 98, no. 2 (February 1989): 100–112.

9. Ron Magid, "George Lucas: Past, Present, and Future," *American Cinematographer* 78, no. 2 (February 1997): 49.

10. Ibid., p. 52.

11. David Ansen and Peter McAlevery, "The Producer Is King Again," *Newsweek*, 20 May 1985, p. 84.

12. "An Interview with Paramount's Top Guns," *Los Angeles Times*, Calendar section, 18 March 1990.

13. Dunne, *Monster*, p. 75.

14. "An Interview."

15. Barry Koitnow, "A Supersleuth Returns to Beverly Hills," *Orange County Register*, 24 May 1987.

16. Jack Barth, "John Hughes: On Geeks Baring Gifts," *Film Comment*, June 1984, p. 46.

17. Ibid.

18. Cited in Stephen Farber and Marc Green, *Outrageous Conduct: Art, Ego, and the Twilight Zone Case* (New York: Arbor House, 1988), p. 54.

19. Cited with italics in ibid., p. 62.

20. Ibid., p. 13.

21. Quoted in Nancy Griffin and Kim Masters, *Hit and Run: How Jon Peters and Peter Guber Took Sony for a Ride in Hollywood* (New York: Simon and Schuster, 1996), p. 85.

22. Ibid., p. 127.

23. Ibid., p. 162.

24. The film's innovative techniques and production methods are profiled in George Turner, "Who Framed Roger Rabbit?" and George Turner "Cartoons Come to Life in *Roger*," *American Cinematography* 69, no. 7 (July 1988): 44–51, 54–60.

25. Ted Elrick, "Fires . . . Floods . . . Riots . . . Earthquakes . . . John Carpenter," *DGA Magazine*, http://www.dga.org/magazine/interviews/dga_interviews.htm.

26. Ibid.

27. Ibid.

28. Robert Lindsey, "Francis Coppola: Promises to Keep," *New York Times Magazine*, 24 July 1988, p. 27.

29. Quoted in Julie Salomon, *The Devil's Candy: The Bonfire of the Vanities Goes Hollywood* (Boston: Houghton Mifflin, 1991), p. 29.

30. Gary Crowdus and Richard Porton, "The Importance of a Singular, Guiding Vision: An Interview with Arthur Penn," *Cineaste* (spring 1993), p. 14.

31. Robert Seidman and Nicholas Leiber, "Making Peace with the 60s," *American Film*, December 1981, p. 67.

32. Crowdus and Poton, "Importance," p. 16.

33. Mary Pat Kelly, *Martin Scorsese: A Journey* (New York: Thunder's Mouth Press, 1991), p. 160.

34. Ibid., p. 150.

35. Ibid., p. 183.

36. Ibid., p. 195.

37. Jim Hillier, *The New Hollywood* (New York: Continuum, 1994), p. 127. Hillier's book provides an excellent portrait of these filmmakers and has been an important source for my discussion.

38. Ibid., pp. 133–34.

39. Ibid., p. 130.

40. Ibid., p. 83.

41. Ibid., p. 135.

42. Ibid., p. 122.

43. Ibid., p. 127.

44. Ibid.

45. David Breskin, *Inner Views: Filmmakers in Conversation* (Winchester, Mass.: Faber and Faber, 1992), p. 335.

46. Ibid., p. 332.

47. Ibid., p. 346–47.

48. Michael Singer, *A Cut Above: Fifty Film Directors Talk about Their Craft* (Los Angeles: Lone Eagle, 1998), p. 30.

49. "Dialogue on Film: Lawrence Kasdan," *American Film* (April 1982), p. 10.

50. Carole Zucker, *Figures of Light: Actors and Directors Illuminate the Art of Film Acting* (New York: Plenum Press, 1995), p. 297.

51. Breskin, *Inner Views*, p. 179.

52. Ibid., p. 169.

53. James Riordan, *Stone* (New York: Hyperion, 1995), p. 172.
54. Ibid., p. 196.
55. Breskin, *Inner Views*, p. 135.
56. Eric Lax, *Woody Allen: A Biography* (New York: Knopf, 1991), p. 266.
57. Ibid., p. 267.
58. Stig Bjorkman, *Woody Allen on Woody Allen* (New York: Grove Press, 1993), p. 79
59. Ric Gentry, "Clint Eastwoood: An Interview," *Post Script* 17, no. 3 (summer 1998), p. 13.
60. Ric Gentry, "Foul Play in High Places," *American Cinematographer* 78, no. 2 (February 1997): 74.
61. Ibid.
62. Sidney Lumet, *Making Movies* (New York: Knopf, 1995), pp. 54–55.
63. Ibid., p. 17.
64. Ibid., p. 218.
65. Zucker, *Figures of Light*, p. 227.
66. Ibid., p. 228.
67. Ibid., p. 238.
68. A good review of this period can be found in David Rosen with Peter Hamilton, *Off-Hollywood: The Making and Marketing of Independent Films* (New York: Grove Weidenfeld, 1990), pp. 259–87.
69. *American Cinematographer* 66, no. 3 (March 1985): 47.
70. Breskin, *Inner Views*, p. 179.
71. David Rensin, "The Man Who Would Be Difficult," *American Film*, March 1986, p. 53.
72. "Dialogue in Film: John Sayles," *American Film*, May 1986, p. 14.
73. *International Dictionary of Films and Filmmakers: Directors*, 2d ed., ed. Nicolas Thomas. (Chicago: St. James Press, 1991), p. 741.
74. Kevin Jackson, ed., *Schrader on Schrader and Other Writings* (Boston: Faber and Faber, 1990), p. 29.
75. Ibid., p. 185.

CHAPTER 7. GENRES AND PRODUCTION CYCLES

1. As an example of the critical norm, see Andrew Britton, "Blissing Out: The Politics of Reaganite Entertainment," *Movie*, no. 30/31 (1986): 1–42.
2. A profile of this early work can be found in "Computer Research and Development at Lucasfilm," *American Cinematographer* 63, no. 8 (August 1982): 773–75.
3. Christopher W. Baker covers these early applications in *How Did They Do It? Computer Illusion in Film and TV* (Indianapolis: Alpha Books, 1994), pp. 3–13.
4. See, for example, Ed Schilling, "Digital Sound for Film and Video," *American Cinematographer* 65, no. 11 (December 1984): 101–6.
5. Ibid., p. 106.
6. Robert Warren quoted in Vincent LoBrutto, *Sound-on-Film: Interviews with Creators of Film Sound* (Westport, Conn.: Praeger, 1994), p. 133.
7. Ibid., p. 134.
8. Sound designer Frank Serafine makes this claim in ibid., p. 225.
9. Lawrence Cohn, "Horrid Year for Horror Pix at the B.O.," Sound-On-Film: Interviews with Creators of Film Sound (Praeger, 1993), *Variety*, 25 January 1984, p. 3.
10. Lawrence Cohn, "Filmers Resort to Old Scare Tactics," *Variety*, 8 June 1988, p. 1.
11. For the film's production history see Hugh Fordin, *The World of Entertainment!: The Freed Unit at MGM* (New York: Doubleday, 1975), pp. 397–419.
12. "Background Material and Data on Programs within the Jurisdiction of the Committee on Ways and Means," quoted in "Richest Got Richer and Poorest Poorer in 1979-87," *New York Times*, 23 March 1989, pp. A1, A24.
13. Clay Chandler, "After Decades of Deficits, a U.S. Budget Surplus Looms," *Washington Post*, 1 February 1998, pp. A1, A14.
14. Robert W. Tucker, "The Purposes of American Power," Foreign Affairs 59, no. 2 (winter 1980/81): 241–74. Tucker urged caution in implementing such a policy.
15. Ronald Reagan, inauguration address, 21 January 1985, in *Vital Speeches of the Day* 51, no. 8 (1985): 288.

16. Ronald Reagan, address to the nation on the downing of a Korean airliner by the Soviets, 5 September 1983, in *Vital Speeches of the Day* 49, no. 24 (1983): 739.

17. Ronald Reagan, congressional address on Central America, 27 April 1983, in Ronald Reagan, *Speaking My Mind* (New York: Simon and Schuster, 1989), pp. 152–53.

18. Dean Acheson, *Present at the Creation* (New York: Norton, 1969), p. 219.

19. Ronald Reagan, address to the nation on aiding the Contras, 16 March 1986, in *Vital Speeches of the Day* 52, no. 13 (1986): 386.

20. Statistics compiled by the World Bank, quoted in Edelberto Torres-Rivas, "Guatemala: Crisis and Political Violence," *NACLA Report on the Americas* 14, no. 1 (January–February 1980),: 17, 20.

21. Robert Armstrong and Janet Shenk, "El Salvador: A Revolution Brews," *NACLA Report on the Americas* 14, no. 4 (July–August 1980), p. 3.

22. Jenny Pearce, *Under the Eagle* (Boston: South End Press, 1982), p. 210.

23. *Amnesty International Report 1984* (London: Amnesty International, 1984), p. 148.

24. Romero quoted in Robert Armstrong and Janet Shenk, "El Salvador: Why Revolution?," *NACLA Report on the Americas* 14, no. 2 (March–April 1980): 24.

25. A comprehensive list of fiction and documentary feature films produced from 1948 to 1988 and dealing with Vietnam and the French-American wars can be found in Linda Dittmar and Gene Michaud, eds., *From Hanoi to Hollywood: The Vietnam War in American Film* (Rutgers, N.J.: Rutgers University Press, 1990), pp. 350–72.

26. For views from the political left and right, see Noam Chomsky, *Towards a New Cold War* (New York: Pantheon, 1982) and Richard H. Schultz, Jr., and Alan Ned Sabrosky, "Policy and Strategy for the 1980s: Preparing for Low Intensity Conflicts," in *Lessons from an Unconventional War: Reassessing U.S. Strategies for Future Conflicts,* ed. Richard A. Hunt and Richard H. Schultz, Jr. (New York: Pergamon Press, 1982).

27. Louis J. Kern, "MIAs, Myth, and Macho Magic: Post-Apocalyptic Cinematic Visions of Vietnam," in *Search and Clear: Critical Responses to Selected Literature and Films of the Vietnam War,* ed. William J. Searle (Bowling Green, Ohio: Bowling Green State University Popular Press, 1988), p. 48.

28. The chief military strategist for North Vietnam explains the principles of guerilla war in Russell Stetler, ed., *The Military Art of People's War: Selected Writings of General Vo Nguyen Giap* (New York: Monthly Review Press, 1971).

29. The concept of strategic mobility is defined and discussed in *The Pentagon Papers*, vol. 4 (Boston: Beacon Press, n.d.), p. 305.

30. Contradictions between these two components are discussed in Richard A. Hunt, "Strategies at War: Pacification and Attrition in Vietnam," in Hunt and Schultz, *Lessons from an Unconventional War,* pp. 23–47.

31. David Breskin, *Inner Views: Filmmakers in Conversation* (Winchester, Mass: Faber and Faber, 1992), p. 138.

32. Gallup Poll results quoted in Charles DeBenedetti, with Charles Chatfield, *An American Ordeal: The Anti-War Movement of the Vietnam Era* (Syracuse, N.Y.: Syracuse University Press, 1990), p. 271.

33. Fred Glass, "Totally Recalling Arnold: Sex and Violence in the New Bad Future," *Film Quarterly* 44, no. 1 (fall 1990): 2–13. Patricia S. Warrick used the latter phrase to describe the sci-fi fiction of Philip K. Dick, from whose work BLADE RUNNER and TOTAL RECALL were adapted. Patricia S. Warrick, *Mind in Motion: The Fiction of Philip K. Dick* (Carbondale: Southern Illinois University Press, 1987), p. 2.

34. Mead's commentary on the design of the megalopolis may be found on the Criterion laserdisc of BLADE RUNNER.

35. Giuliana Bruno, "Ramble City: Postmodernism and BLADE RUNNER," *October* 41 (summer 1987): 63.

CHAPTER 8. MOVIES AND MORALITY

1. Charles Lyons, "The Paradox of Protest," in Francis G. Couvares, *Movie Censorship and American Culture* (Washington, D.C.: Smithsonian Institution Press, 1996), p. 309.

2. Quoted in Alan Crawford, *Thunder on the Right* (New York: Pantheon, 1980), p. 41.

3. Peter Steinfels examines this group in *The Neo-Conservatives* (New York: Simon and Schuster, 1979).

4. Quoted in Mike Davis, "The New Right's Road to Power," New Left Review 128 (July–August, 1981): 39.

5. Crawford, *Thunder on the Right*, p. 51.

6. James McEvoy III, *Radicals or Conservatives? The Contemporary American Right* (Chicago: Rand McNally, 1971), p. 151.

7. Ronald Reagan, remarks at the Annual Convention of the National Association of Evangelicals, 8 March 1983, reprinted in Reagan, *Speaking My Mind*, (New York: Simon and Schuster, 1989) p. 178.

8. "Cruising," *Variety*, 13 February 1980, p. 16.

9. "2d Look Nix by GCC: 'Cruising' an X Pic," *Variety*, 13 February 1980, p. 5.

10. "UATC Posts Warning at Windows: 'Cruising' is X Film in R Clothing," *Variety*, 20 February 1980, p. 5.

11. "Did 'Cruising' Respect Rulings?," *Variety*, 25 June 1980, p. 4.

12. Stephen Klain, "'Caligula' Banned in Boston," *Variety*, 25 June 1980, p. 3.

13. Ibid., p. 39.

14. "Boston Court Rules 'Caligula' Is Not Obscene on Political Merits," *Variety*, 6 August 1980, p. 6.

15 "'Caligula' Is Upheld, Beating Wisk-Ruling," *Variety*, 18 June 1980, p. 6.

16. Klain, "'Caligula' Banned in Boston," p. 39.

17. "'Caligula' Pulls Out of Ohio Site; Credit Watchdog Tactics," *Variety*, 19 November 1980, p. 28.

18. Lawrence Cohn, "Horror, Sci-Fi Pix Earn 37% of Rentals," *Variety*, 19 November 1980, p. 3.

19. Roger Watkins, "'Demented Revenge' Hits World Screens," *Variety*, 29 October 1980, p. 3.

20. "Chi Tribune Blasts Gory 'X-Films in R-rated Clothing,'" *Variety*, 12 November 1980, p. 6.

21. Ibid, pp. 6, 30.

22. Lawrence Cohn, "Incredible Shrinking Horror Market?," *Variety*, 16 February 1983, p. 7; Lawrence Cohn, "Horrid Year for Horror at the B.O.," *Variety*, 25 January 1984, p. 3.

23. Lawrence Cohn, "Filmers Resort to Old Scare Tactics," *Variety*, 8 June 1988, p. 1.

24. "Pornography: Love or Death?," *Film Comment* 20 (November–December 1984): 40.

25. Andrew Sarris, "Dreck to Kill," *Village Voice*, 17–23 September 1980, p. 44.

26. Quoted in Charles Lyons, *The New Censors: Movies and the Culture Wars* (Philadelphia: Temple University Press, 1997), p. 77.

27. Ibid., p. 79.

28. Quoted in Julie Salomon, *The Devil's Candy: The Bonfire of the Vanities Goes Hollywood* (Boston: Houghton Mifflin, 1991), p. 29.

29. Marcia Pally, "'Double' Trouble," *Film Comment* 20 (September–October 1984): 14.

30. See Kathleen Barry, *Female Sexual Slavery* (New York: Discus Books, 1981); Susan Brownmiller, *Against Our Will: Men, Women, and Rape* (New York: Bantam Books, 1976); Andrea Dworkin, *Woman Hating* (New York: Dutton, 1974) and *Pornography: Men Possessing Women* (New York: Perigee Books, 1981); Susan Griffin, *Pornography and Silence* (New York: Harper and Row, 1981), Laura Lederer, ed., *Take Back the Night: Women on Pornography* (New York: Morrow, 1980); Gloria Steinem, "Erotica and Pornography: A Clear and Present Difference," *Ms.*, November 1978, pp. 53–54, 75.

31. See, for example, Susan Barrowclough, "Not a Love Story," *Screen* 23 (1982): 26–36; Alice Echols, "The Taming of the Id: Feminist Sexual Politics, 1968–83," in Carole S. Vance, ed., *Pleasure and Danger: Exploring Female Sexuality* (Boston: Routledge and Kegan Paul, 1984); Halen Hazen, *Endless Rupture* (New York: Scribners, 1983); Vance, *Pleasure and Danger*.

32. Carole S. Vance, "Pleasure and Danger: Toward a Politics of Sexuality," in Vance, *Pleasure and Danger*, p. 6.

33. Ellen Carol DuBois and Linda Gordon, "Seeking Ecstasy on the Battlefield: Danger and Pleasure in Nineteenth-Century Feminist Sexual Thought," in Vance, *Pleasure and Danger*, p. 43.

34. "Pornography: Love or Death?," p. 33.

35. Will Tusher, "Sex out of Theaters, into Homes," *Variety*, 7 January 1981, p. 7; Lawrence Cohn, "Pix Less Able, but Porn Is Stable," *Variety*, 16 November 1983, p. 1.

36. Ibid., p. 28.

37. Michael Silverman, "X-Rated HV Suppliers Stay Blue, but over Competition, not Meese," *Variety*, 3 September 1986, p. 117.

38. Cohn, "Pix Less Able," p. 28.

39. *Attorney General's Commission on Pornography, Final Report* (Washington, D.C.: U.S. Government Printing Office, 1986), pp. 322–35.

40. William E. Brigman, "Politics and the Pornography Wars," *Wide Angle* 19, no. 3 (July 1997): 163.

41. Amy Dawes, "Christian Groups Blast Universal over 'Christ' Pic," *Variety*, 20 July 1988, p. 8.
42. "Scorsese Pic Center of Holy War," *Variety*, 27 July 1988, p. 26.
43. Ibid.
44. "Christian Groups Blast Universal," p. 8.
45. "Clergy Nail 'Christ' and Universal," *Variety*, 10 August 1988, p. 18.
46. Mary Pat Kelly, *Martin Scorsese: A Journey* (New York: Thunder's Mouth Press, 1991), p. 202.
47. His remarks to this audience are reprinted in Reagan, *Speaking My Mind*, p. 178.
48. Kelly, *Martin Scorsese: A Journey*, p. 236.
49. Peter Wood, "How a Film Changes from an 'X' to an 'R,'" *New York Times*, 20 July 1980, sec. C.
50. Tom Bierbaum, "TV Watchdogs Growl at Films, Seek to Replace MPAA Ratings," *Variety*, 12 August 1981, p. 84.
51. "Video Distribs, MPAA Shake on Cassette Ratings," *Variety*, 15 August 1984, p. 94.
52. Will Tusher, "New PG-13 Rating Instituted By MPAA; Will Cover Some Pix That Would've Been R-Rated," *Variety*, 14 July 1984, p. 30.
53. Michael Medved, *Hollywood vs. America: Popular Culture and the War on Traditional Values* (New York: HarperCollins, 1992), p. 3.

CHAPTER 9. AMERICAN DOCUMENTARY IN THE 1980S

1. The term *social documentary* is an imprecise designation, and films are included and excluded from the category in sometimes arbitrary ways. For example, rock documentaries are often excluded from serious consideration as social documentaries despite the social importance of their subject matter.
2. Some scholars prefer to distinguish *cinéma vérité* from direct cinema. While both movements used the same kind of equipment and believed in a special capacity of the technology to present truth, they differed in some respects. The term *cinéma vérité* is sometimes reserved for the French movement that incorporated reflexive techniques into its documentary filmmaking. The paradigm film is *Chronique d'un été* (Jean Rouch and Edgar Morin, 1960). Direct cinema is thought to be an American movement that eschewed most reflexive techniques. For the purposes of this essay, I will refer to both kinds of filmmaking with the more popular term *cinéma vérité*.
3. Barbara Zheutlin, coordinator, "The Art and Politics of the Documentary: A Symposium," *Cineaste* 11, no. 3 (1981): 13.
4. Ibid. Else is the director of, among other films, THE DAY AFTER TRINITY: ROBERT J. OPPENHEIMER AND THE ATOMIC BOMB (1981).
5. Examples nominated for Academy Awards include BEN'S MILL (1982), made for the PBS series "Odyssey," and BRIDGE TO FREEDOM, 1965 (1987), an episode of the civil rights series EYES ON THE PRIZE: AMERICA'S CIVIL RIGHTS YEARS. The Academy Award winner THE TEN-YEAR LUNCH: THE WIT AND LEGEND OF THE ALGONQUIN ROUND TABLE (1987) was produced for the PBS series "American Masters."
6. Bruce Jackson, *Get the Money and Shoot: The DRI Guide to Funding Documentary Films* (Buffalo, N.Y.: Documentary Research, 1981), p. 4.
7. Ellin Stein, "Leaner Times for Documentarians," *New York Times*, 10 June 1984, sec. 2.
8. See the National Endowment for the Humanities annual reports, 1980–89.
9. James Day, *The Vanishing Vision: The Inside Story of Public Television* (Berkeley and Los Angeles University of California Press, 1995), p. 315.
10. "THE TIMES OF HARVEY MILK: An Interview with Robert Epstein," *Cineaste* 14, no. 3 (1986): 26–27.
11. Stein, "Leaner Times."
12. "US Documentary: The Chill Wind of Reaganomics," *Sight and Sound* 56, no. 2 (spring 1987): 78.
13. "LAS MADRES DE LA PLAZA DE MAYO: An Interview with Susana Muñoz and Lourdes Portillo," *Cineaste* 15, no. 1 (1986): 24.
14. For a more complete account of the relationship between independent production and public television from the 1970s through the early 1990s, see Day, *Vanishing Vision*, pp. 314–30.
15. For a fuller account, see Jan Krawitz, "The Independent Documentary Film: Prospects for Survival," *Journal of Film and Video* 38 (winter 1986): 49–53.
16. Day, *Vanishing Vision*, p. 326.

17. For an account of the first season of "P.O.V., "see Katherine Dieckmann, "Pointy Heads," *Village Voice*, 19 July 1988, pp. 47–48.
18. William Hoynes, *Public Television for Sale: Media, the Market, and the Public Sphere* (Boulder, Colo.: Westview Press, 1994), 94.
19. *Variety*, 12 March 1986, p. 7.
20. *Variety*, 25 February 1991, pp. 5–6. These figures are through 1990. Comedy performance films and rock documentaries tended to be much more successful in theatrical distribution. Of the rock documentaries, for example, U2: RATTLE AND HUM (1988) grossed $8.5 million, and STOP MAKING SENSE (1984) $7 million. EDDIE MURPHY RAW (1987), a comedy performance film, grossed $50 million.
21. This trend toward theatrical distribution continued and strengthened in the 1990s for films such as HEARTS OF DARKNESS, BERKELEY IN THE SIXTIES, PARIS IS BURNING, TRUTH OR DARE, HOOP DREAMS, BROTHER'S KEEPER, AND WHEN WE WERE KINGS.
22. Harmetz, Aljean, "Nonfiction is Surging in Movies," *New York Times*, 17 April 1986, p. C 21.
23. Gold, in *Variety*, 12 March 1986, p. 22.
24. See Glen Collins, "Film Makers Protest to Academy," New York Times, 24 February 1990, p. L13.
25. See Charles Fleming, "Oscar Mocks Boffo Docs," *Variety*, 2 March 1992, pp. 1, 75.
26. "The Oscars' Neglect," *New York Times*, 31 March 1993, p. A22.
27. "BROKEN RAINBOW: An Interview with Victoria Mudd and Maria Florio," *Cineaste* 15, no. 2 (1986): 34–36.
28. Harmetz, "Nonfiction," p. C21.
29. Dennis West, "Revolution in Central America: A Survey of Recent Documentaries," *Cineaste* 12, no. 1 (1982): 18–23, and "Revolution in Central America: A Survey of New Documentaries," *Cineaste* 14, no. 3 (1986): 14–21.
30. For a more comprehensive list of films by and about women in the 1970s and 1980s, see Richard M. Barsam, *Nonfiction Film: A Critical History*, rev. ed. (Bloomington: Indiana University Press, 1992), pp. 361–66.
31. See Adam Knee and Charles Musser, "William Greaves, Documentary Film-making, and the African-American Experience," *Film Quarterly* 45, no. 3 (Spring 1992): 13–25.
32. For a list of films by and about lesbians and gays, see Barsam, *Nonfiction Film*, pp. 366–70.
33. *New York Times*, 10 June 1984, sec. 2.
34. *Variety*, 25 November 1987, p. 35.
35. Bates, Peter. "Truth Not Guaranteed: An Interview with Errol Morris," *Cineaste* 17, no. 1 (1989): 17.
36. A more recent McElwee film is SOMETHING TO DO WITH THE WALL (1990), which introduces us to various West Berliners and others before, during, and after the fall of the Berlin Wall.
37. See her "The Totalizing Quest of Meaning," in *Theorizing Documentary*, ed. Michael Renov (New York: Routledge, 1993), pp. 90–107.
38. "Michael and Me," *Film Comment*, November–December 1989, pp. 16–26.
39. Richard Schickel, "Imposing on Reality," *Time*, 8 January 1990, p. 77.
40. Pauline Kael, "The Current Cinema," *New Yorker*, 8 January 1990, p. 91.
41. For a discussion of the theory of *Nonfiction Film* in relation to these issues, see my *Rhetoric and Representation in Nonfiction Film* (Cambridge: Cambridge University Press, 1997) and "Moving Pictures and the Rhetoric of Nonfiction," in *Post-Theory: Reconstructing Film Studies*, ed. David Bordwell and Noël Carroll (Madison: University of Wisconsin Press, 1996), pp. 307–24.

CHAPTER 10. EXPERIMENTAL CINEMA IN THE 1980S

1. The use of *avant-garde* to designate this arena of cinema has often seemed problematic to film historians. Originally, the term suggested that the filmmakers it designated were leading the way toward a new, more sophisticated cinema; but by the early 1970s, the term's militaristic implications seemed out of synch with the antimilitarist, antinationalist tendencies of many "avant-garde" filmmakers.

   For me, the problem with the term is its suggestion that "avant-garde filmmakers" are out in front of commercial filmmaking (and even of documentary). While it is certainly true that commercial filmmakers have frequently used approaches originated by avant-garde filmmakers, both in feature films and in advertising, it is also true that avant-gardists have borrowed relentlessly from the industry. Indeed, in the 1980s, the pervasiveness of "recycled cinema" (see my discussion of this tendency) is the most obvious evidence that the avant-garde is increasingly dependent on the industry product. But more fundamentally, the cinematic apparatus itself is a product of commercial filmmaking; and all smaller-gauge filmmaking, and all uses of 35mm for noncommercial films, are "trickle down" benefits of the industry's success.

The term *experimental film* has also seemed problematic to many filmmakers working outside the industry: the suggestion seems to be that their films are experiments, rather than finished works of art.

In my writing and teaching, I have tended to use *critical cinema* to suggest all forms of cinema that can be understood as providing critiques of commercial cinema, especially for those whose understanding of film history has been created and nurtured by the industry. For most viewers, exposure to an avant-garde film immediately creates the question, "Is *this* a movie?!"—a question that necessitates some thought about what a movie is and can be: that is, a critique of conventional assumptions about cinema. Obviously, the term *critical cinema* has its own problems.

2. For an overview of Cinema 16's contributions to the American independent film scene, see my *Cinema 16: Documents toward a History of the Film Society*, two double issues of *Wide Angle* 19, nos. 1, 2 (January 1997, April 1997). If Cinema 16 became the model for a national network of film societies, Art in Cinema, the series of exhibition programs established by Richard Foster and Frank Stauffacher, was an inspiration for Vogel and was probably the first set of programs—at least in the United States—to demonstrate that, taken together, the various forms of avant-garde filmmaking (in Europe and in North America) form a reasonably coherent alternative film history.

    Key works in the early history of critical and theoretical writing about avant-garde film include Parker Tyler, *Underground Film: A Critical History* (New York: Evergreen, 1969); Gene Youngblood, *Expanded Cinema* (New York: Dutton, 1970); Jonas Mekas, *Movie Journal: The Rise of the New American Cinema, 1959–1971* (New York: Collier, 1972); David Curtis, *Experimental Cinema* (New York: Delta, 1971); P. Adams Sitney, *Visionary Film* (New York: Oxford University Press, 1974); Amos Vogel, *Film as a Subversive Art* (New York: Random House, 1974); and Malcolm LeGrice, *Abstract Film and Beyond* (Cambridge: MIT Press, 1977).

    The 1980s saw a variety of new critical approaches to avant-garde cinema. Early in the decade, Arden Press in Denver proposed a series of books that would reconnoiter recent developments in the field on an annual basis, but the series ended after only two volumes: Jonathan Rosenbaum's *Film: The Front Line/1983* and David Ehrenstein's *Film: The Front Line/1984*. Rosenbaum, in collaboration with J. Hoberman, also surveyed the midnight-movie phenomenon in *Midnight Movies* (New York: Harper and Row, 1983). The Austrian film journal *Blimp* offered an overview of 1980s American avant-garde filmmaking, including essays by Tom Gunning, David Sterritt, Steve Anker, in its no. 20 (summer 1992) issue.

    More theoretically ambitious books on particular aspects of avant-garde history began to appear later in the decade, including Maureen Turim's *Abstraction in Avant-Garde Film* (Ann Arbor, Mich.: UMI Press, 1985); David James's *Allegories of Cinema: American Film in the Sixties* (Princeton, N.J.: Princeton University Press, 1989); Peter Gidal's *Materialist Film* (London: Routledge, 1989); and *Questions of Third Cinema*, ed. Jim Pines and Paul Willeman (London: British Film Institute, 1989). My own *A Critical Cinema* (Berkeley and Los Angeles: University of California Press, 1988) was the first of what has become a series of volumes of interviews with independent filmmakers, which proposes to provide an oral history of alternative cinema since World War II. Subsequent volumes—*A Critical Cinema 2, A Critical Cinema 3*—were published by California in 1992 and 1998.

    Probably the most energized critical and theoretical territory explored during the 1980s was the relationship of new feminist thinking and the avant-garde: see note 17 for a listing of important contributions to this discourse.

3. The long-awaited revision of the 1975 Film-makers' Cooperative catalog finally appeared in 1989, largely as a result of the efforts of filmmaker Su Friedrich. While Canyon Cinema (2325 Third St., Suite 338, San Francisco, CA 94107) and the Film-makers' Cooperative (175 Lexington Ave., New York, NY 10016) remained the leading distributors of American avant-garde film, the Museum of Modern Art Circulating Film Program (11 W. 53d St., New York, NY 10019) continued to buy and distribute some of the same films available through the two cooperatives, as well as others not available at the Film-makers' Cooperative or at Canyon Cinema.

Film-makers' Cooperative, Canyon Cinema, and the Museum of Modern Art were and are "passive distributors": that is, they offer a catalog of films and videos for rent but do not actively market their titles. Other distributors specialized in the somewhat more active promotion and distribution of particular kinds of alternative cinema, especially films with feminist and multicultural agendas. Most notable among these smaller distributors are Women Make Movies (225 Lafayette St., Suite 207, New York, NY 10012); California Newsreel (149 Ninth St., San Francisco, CA 94103); and Third World Newsreel (335 38th St., 5th Floor, New York, NY 10018).

4. The most useful history of the "midnight movie" phenomenon is Hoberman and Rosenbaum, *Midnight Movies.*

5. Useful background on the early history of video art is available in Gregory Battcock, ed., *New Artists Video* (New York: Dutton, 1978); Doug Hall and Sally Jo Fifer, eds., *Illuminating Video* (New York: Aperture, 1990); and Deirdre Boyle, *Guerilla Television Revisited* (New York: Oxford University Press, 1998).

6. Perhaps the best known of these debates took place at Canyon Cinema at the end of the decade and in the early 1990s. According to Dominic Angerame, longtime director of Canyon Cinema, the debate was not so much about the importance of video, which few doubted, but the likelihood that this organization's commitment to 16mm avant-garde cinema could only be endangered by a flood of new video work demanding the time and energy of a small, already overworked and underpaid staff. In the end, the Canyon board decided to handle videos made by filmmaker members of Canyon and to hope that moving-image artists dedicated primarily to video would found their own cooperative organizations. I spoke to Angerame on the phone on 16 June 1998.

In his overview of Bill Viola's videowork—"Metaphysical Structuralism: The Videotapes of Bill Viola," *Millennium Film Journal*, nos. 20–21 (fall/winter 1988–89): 81–114—Gene Youngblood argues that "cinema" is "the art of organizing a stream of audiovisual events in time" (p. 83), and that film and video are merely two media "through which we can practice cinema . . . just as there are many instruments through which we practice music." Youngblood convincingly locates Viola's videos within the larger history of structural cinema that includes Michael Snow, Ernie Gehr, and Hollis Frampton.

7. Brakhage has always been a prolific lecturer, letter writer, and essayist, as well as a prolific film-maker. A selection of his collected writings—letters, essays, conversations—was edited by Robert A. Haller: *Brakhage Scrapbook: Collected Writings, 1964–1980* (New Paltz, N.Y.: Docementext, 1982). A series of essays on avant-garde filmmakers Jerome Hill, Marie Menken, Sidney Peterson, James Broughton, Maya Deren, Christopher MacLaine, Bruce Conner, and Ken Jacobs—*Film at Wit's End: Eight Avant-Garde Filmmakers* (New Paltz, N.Y.: Documentext)—appeared in 1989. *I . . . Sleeping (Being a Dream Journal and Parenthetical Explication)*, Brakhage's notes on his dreams from February to May 1975, was published in 1988 by Island Cinema Resources on Staten Island, N.Y., and the Visual Studies Workshop in Rochester, N.Y.

8. See *Canyon Cinema Film/Video Catalog 7* (1992), p. 56.

9. See Sitney, *Visionary Film*, ch. 12, for his exploration of "structural film." Portraits of Frampton, Landow, Yvonne Rainer, and Michael Snow are included in Benning's GRAND OPERA of 1978, and Benning's digital work of 1985, PASCAL'S LEMMA, seems an obvious homage to Frampton's ZORN'S LEMMA (1971).

10. AMERICAN DREAMS is arranged into annual segments: the Aaron items, an excerpt from an influential speech and, later, from a popular song of the era correspond to the relevant years. And at the end of each year, Benning indicates the total number of homeruns Aaron had hit to that point in his career.

11. In 1975, the Anthology Film Archives selection committee (James Broughton, Ken Kelman, Peter Kubelka, Jonas Mekas, and P. Adam Sitney) published their canon of "the essential works of the art of the cinema," setting off a sustained debate about what "essential" means in the history of film and who should define it. See Sitney, ed., *The Essential Cinema: Essays on the Films in the Collection of Anthology Film Archives* (New York: Anthology Film Archives and NYU, 1975).

12. Mekas's career received received valuable documentation through the good work of David James, who edited *To Free the Cinema: Jonas Mekas and the New York Underground* (Princeton, N.J.: Princeton Unversity Press, 1992). *To Free the Cinema* includes twenty-four essays by filmmakers and scholars—including Scott Nygren's "Film Writing and the Figure of Death: HE STANDS IN A DESERT COUNTING THE SECONDS OF HIS LIFE" (pp. 241–54)—as well as "Autobiographical Notes," "Showcases I Ran in the Sixties," and a filmography and bibliography by Mekas himself.

13. Video Data Bank, School of Art Institute of Chicago, 112 S. Michigan Ave., Suite 312, Chicago, IL 60603.

14. For a history of Nykino and related developments, see William Alexander, *Film on the Left: American Documentary Film from 1931 to 1942* (Princeton, N.J.: Princeton University Press, 1981). For information on Newsreel, see Michael Renov, "Newsreel, Old and New: Towards a Historical Profile," *Film Quarterly* 51, no. 1 (fall 1987): 20–23.

15. Significant 1980s contributions to the literary discourse about avant-garde cine-feminism include E. Ann Kaplan, *Women and Film: Both Sides of the Camera* (New York: Methuen, 1983); Kaja Silverman, *The Acoustic Mirror: The Female Voice in Psychoanalysis and Cinema* (Bloomington: Indiana University Press, 1988); Lucy Fischer, *Shot/Countershot: Film Tradition and Women's Cinema* (Princeton, N.J.: Princeton University Press, 1989); Laura Mulvey, *Visual and Other Pleasures* (Bloomington: Indiana University Press, 1989); Patricia Mellencamp, *Indiscretions: Avant-Garde Film, Video, and Feminism* (Bloomington: Indiana University Press, 1990); Lauren Rabinowitz, *Points of Resistance: Women, Power, and Politics in the New York Avant-garde Cinema, 1943-1974* (Urbana: University of Illinois Press, 1991); *Issues in Feminist Film Criticism*, ed. Patricia Erens (Bloomington: Indiana University Press, 1990); and the journal *Camera Obscura*.

16. See David Ehrenstein's discussion of *Born in Flames* in *Film: The Frontline/1989*, pp. 114–19. I interviewed Borden about her films for *A Critical Cinema 2*, pp. 249–64.

17. The scripts of Rainer's films of the 1980s are included in *The Films of Yvonne Rainer* (Bloomington: Indiana University Press, 1989). The script of PRIVILEGE is included in Scott MacDonald, ed., *Screen Writings: Scripts and Texts by Independent Filmmakers* (Berkeley and Los Angeles: University of California Press, 1995), pp. 270–331.

18. See Frampton's comments on Rainer in MacDonald, *A Critical Cinema*, pp. 74–75.

19. For information on this debate see Coco Fusco's "Fantasies of Oppositionality," *Afterimage* 16, no. 5 (December 1988); and *Screen* 29, no. 4 (autumn 1988). The program of "Sexism, Colonialism, Misrepresentation" and related papers were published in *Motion Picture* 3, nos. 3–4 (summer/autumn 1990).

20. Trinh T. Minh-ha is an influential essayist as well as an inventive filmmaker. Her collection of essays *Women, Native, Other: Writing Postcoloniality and Feminism* (Bloomington: Indiana University Press) appeared in 1989; a second collection, *When the Moon Waxes Red: Representation, Gender, and Cultural Politics* (New York: Routledge) in 1991. *Framer Framed* (New York: Routledge, 1992) collects the scripts for REASSEMBLAGE, NAKED SPACES: LIVING IS ROUND, AND SURNAME VIÊT GIVEN NAME NAM and nine interviews.

21. A representative response to REASSEMBLAGE occurred at the 1983 Flaherty Film Seminar. This discussion is reproduced in Erik Barnouw and Patricia R. Zimmermann, eds., *The Flaherty: Four Decades in the Cause of Independent Cinema*, a special *Wide Angle* monograph, vol. 17, nos. 1–4 (1995): 108–14.

22. Of course, history moves backward as well as forward. In 1995, Jan-Christopher Horak's *Lovers of Cinema: The First American Film Avant-Garde, 1919–1945* (Madison: University of Wisconsin Press) was to argue against the tendency to see Maya Deren as the originator of American avant-garde filmmaking. In Horak's view, and it is a view I share, the American avant-garde was underway by the 1920s.

23. Hammer organized a discussion of this issue in conjunction with the Second New York Lesbian and Gay Experimental Film Festival. Hammer and four other filmmakers—Su Friedrich, Tom Chomont, Abigail Child, and Jim Hubbard—presented papers at a panel: the papers were reprinted in "Radical Form/Radical Content," *Millennium*, no. 22 (1989): 117–35.

24. To date, the leading scholar of recycled cinema is William C. Wees. See his *Recycled Images* (New York: Anthology Film Archives, 1993). See also the special issue of *Blimp* (Austria), no. 16 (spring 1991), devoted to "Found Footage Film" (it includes essays by Yann Beauvais, Sharon Sandusky, Anthony Reveaux, Carl I. Belz, Dietmar Brehm, and Peter Tscherkassky); and Cecilia Hausheer and Christoph Settele, eds., *Found Footage Film* (Lucern, Switzerland; Viper, 1992), a book that grew out of a retrospective of recycled cinema presented in Lucern (included are essays by Yann Beauvais, Peter Tscherkassky, William Wees, James Peterson, and Willem de Greef, and brief statements by twenty-one filmmakers, including Americans Craig Baldwin, Abigail Child, Bruce Conner, William Farley, Barbara Hammer, Standish D. Lawder, Keith Sanborn, Philip Solomon, Chick Strand, and Leslie Thornton.)

25. The text of Fisher's STANDARD GAUGE is available in MacDonald, *Screen Writings*, pp. 175–89.

26. While commercial film had bounced back from the threat of imminent demise in the late 1960s, much of the past of Hollywood and of other commercial cinemas around the world seemed to Fisher to be disappearing. For example, STANDARD GAUGE mourns the sale of the Technicolor process of IB (imbibition) printing to the People's Republic of China in 1975.

27. The most extensive source of information on Jacobs's career is the catalog, edited by David Schwartz, for his retrospective of Jacobs's work in 1989: *Films That Tell Time: A Ken Jacobs Retrospective* (New York: American Museum of the Moving Image, 1989). The catalog includes Tom Gunning's "Films That Tell Time: Paradoxes of the Cinema of Ken Jacobs," an interview with Jacobs by Gunning and Schwartz, and selected writings by Jacobs. See also my interviews with Jacobs in *A Critical Cinema 3*, pp. 150, 158–65, 363–96.

28. Of the Nervous System pieces, XCXHXEXRXRXIXEXSX has been the most controversial. See Laura Marx, "Here's Gazing at You," *Independent* 16, no. 2 (March 1993): 26–31, and the interviews mentioned in note 26.

29. The best source of information about Ortiz's performance career is Kristine Stiles, ed., *Raphael Montañez Ortiz: Years of the Warrior, 1960/Years of the Psyche, 1988*, a catalogue for a retrospective of Ortiz's work at El Museo del Barrio 26 March–22 May 1988. The catalogue includes an annotated listing of writings by and about Ortiz, including his many Destructionist manifestos. See also my interview with Ortiz in *A Critical Cinema 3*, pp. 324–46.

30. For a more complete discussion of Ortiz's digital/laser/videos see Scott MacDonald, "Media Destructionism: The Digital/Laser/Videos of Raphael Montañez Ortiz," in Ana M. Lopez and Chon A. Noriega, *The Ethnic Eye: Latino Media Arts* (Minneapolis: University of Minnesota Press, 1996), pp. 183–207.

31. The most obvious sources here are Peter Kubelka's *Unsere Afrikareise* ("Our Trip to Africa," 1967) and Larry Gottheim's early experimentation with sound in *Mouches Volantes* (1976)—both Kubelka and Gottheim were forces at the State University of New York at Binghamton when Berliner studied there in the 1970s.

32. Little in the way of extended discussion of the filmmakers listed in these past two paragraphs is available so far. See Tom Gunning's comments on Solomon and Thornton in "New Horizons: Journeys, Documents, Myths, and Counter Myths," *Blimp* (Austria), no. 20 (summer 1992): 4–15; David Sterritt's comments on Baldwin in "Avant-Garde Film: Recent Trends and Key Works," in the same issue of *Blimp*, pp. 16–25; and William Wees's overview of recycled cinema in *Recycled Images*, which also includes "excerpts from conversations" with Craig Baldwin and Leslie Thornton. See also Lewis Klahr's "Why I Did It," in Albert Kilchesty, ed., *Big as Life: An American History of 8mm Films*, the catalogue for an extensive show of 8mm and Super 8 films, curated by Steve Anker and Jytte Jensen, pp. 74–76.

33. Sonbert's approach is discussed in Scott MacDonald, *Avant-Garde Film/Motion Studies* (Cambridge/New York: Cambridge University Press, 1993), pp. 127–36.

34. For Reggio's comments on this collaboration, see MacDonald, *A Critical Cinema 2*, pp. 397–98.

35. For information about the production of The Journey, see Ken Nolley, ed., *The Journey: A Film in the Global Interest* (Willamette Journal of the Liberal Arts, supplemental series 5); and MacDonald, *Avant-Garde Film/Motion Studies*, pp. 169–88.

36. Frampton in MacDonald, *A Critical Cinema*, p. 61.

37. The L.A. Rebellion is discussed by Ntongela Masilela in "The Los Angeles School of Black Filmmakers," in Manthia Diawara, ed., *Black American Cinema* (New York: Routledge, 1993), pp. 107–17.

38. The scripts of KILLER OF SHEEP, ILLUSIONS, A DIFFERENT IMAGE, Charles Lane's SIDEWALK STORIES, and Kathleen Collins's LOSING GROUND are included in Phyllis Rauch Klotman, *Screenplays of the African American Experience* (Bloomington: Indiana University Press, 1991).

39. The production process and the thinking behind DAUGHTERS OF THE DUST are discussed by Dash in *Daughters of the Dust: The Making of an African American Woman's Film* (New York: New Press, 1992), which also includes the screenplay.

40. I detail this argument in "The New York City Symphony: From Rudy Burckhardt to Spike Lee," *Film Quarterly* 51, no. 2 (winter 1998): 2–20.

41. See my interview with Christine Choy in MacDonald, *A Critical Cinema 3*, pp. 196–212, 217. Renee Tajima sketches the early development of her work and Visual Communications, the Asian-American media group that formed at UCLA, in that same interview, pp. 212–17.

42. For a history of chicano and chicana cinema, see Chon Noriega, "Between a Weapon and a Formula: Chicano Cinema and Its Contexts," In Noriega, ed., *Chicanos and Film: Essays on Representation and Resistance* (New York: Garland; 1992), pp. 159–88. See also Ana M. Lopez and Chon Noriega, eds., *The Ethnic Eye: Latino Media Arts* (Minneapolis: University of Minnesota Press, 1996).

43. Burckhardt's career as filmmaker and photographer is reviewed in *Talking Pictures: The Photography of Rudy Burckhardt* (Cambridge, Mass: Zoland Books, 1994) by Burckhardt and Simon Pettet.

44. Noren discusses his career and *The Lighted Field* in MacDonald, *A Critical Cinema 2*, pp. 175–205.

45. Mangolte discusses her career in MacDonald, *A Critical Cinema*, pp. 279–96, and in *Camera Obscura*, nos. 3–4 (summer 1979): 198–210. See also my discussion of *The Sky on Location* in "Re-envisioning the American West," *American Studies* 39, no. 1 (spring 1998): 116–21.

46. Mangolte's final credits include the following statement: "The filmmaker wishes to acknowledge her indebtedness to Barbara Novak's remarkable book, *Nature and Culture* [*Nature and Culture: American Landscape and Painting, 1825–1875* (New York: Oxford University Press,1980)] "

47. David James interviewed O'Neill in *Millennium*, nos. 30–31 (fall 1997): 118–31.

48. Dorsky said this to me in a telephone conversation in spring 1998.

49. See Mulvey's comments in MacDonald, *A Critical Cinema 2*, p. 334.

50. The scripts for Friedrich's GENTLY DOWN THE STREAM and SINK OR SWIM are included in MacDonald, *Screen Writings*, pp. 225–58. Friedrich discusses her career in *A Critical Cinema 2*, pp. 283–318.

51. See Chapters 1 to 5 of Sitney's Visionary Film.

52. See the interview with Hutton in MacDonald, *A Critical Cinema 3*, pp. 241–52.

53. For a recent discussion of Thomas Cole's politics, see Angela Miller, *The Empire of the Eye: Landscape Representation and American Cultural Politics, 1825–1875* (Ithaca: Cornell University Press, 1993), ch. 1.

54. BEGOTTEN was released on video by World Artists Home Video, P.O. Box 36788, Los Angeles, CA 90036-0788 (800-821-1205).

55. See Merhige's comments in MacDonald, *A Critical Cinema 3*, p. 292.

56. See Robertson's comments in MacDonald, *A Critical Cinema 2*, pp. 207–8.

57. According to Robertson, in a conversation with the author in 1997.

58. The texts of Rose's "Introduction to *Pleasures of the Text*" and SECONDARY CURRENTS are included in MacDonald, *Screen Writings*, pp. 156–74.

59. Minh-ha discusses her mixture of real and fabricated interviews in her "'Why a Fish Pond?' Fiction at the Heart of Documentation" (interview by Laleen Jayamane and Anne Rutherford), in *Framer Framed*, pp. 163–68.

Bibliography

"A Star is Bought," *The Economist*, 23 December 1989, Entertainment Industry Survey, 15–16.

Acheson, Dean. *Present at the Creation*. New York: Norton, 1969.

Adilman, Sid. "The Man Behind the Multiplex, and Complex," *Variety*, 26 April–2 May 1989, 50, 84.

Adilman, Sid, Richard Gold, Jim Robbins, and Will Tusher. "When Opportunity Knocks, Open the Door," *Variety*, 26 April-2 May 1989, 54-64.

Alexander, Garth. "No Toys in Tokyo Puts 'Turtles' in the Soup," *Variety*, 15 April 1991, 1, 227.

Alexander, William. *Film on the Left: American Documentary Film from 1931 to 1942*. Princeton, NJ: Princeton University Press, 1981.

Amnesty International Report 1984. London: Amnesty International Publications, 1984.

"An Allure for Foreign Buyers," *Mergers and Acquisitions* 22, no. 6 (May/June 1988): 12.

Andrews, Suzanna. "The Hollywood Deal Game," *Institutional Investor* 25, no. 13 (November 1991): 69–82.

"Another Toymaker May Be in Play," *Business Week*, 21 September 1987, 108.

Ansen, David and Peter McAlevery. "The Producer is King Again," *Newsweek*, 20 May 1985, 84–89.

"Appealing to Gross Greed," *Time* 1 June 1987, p. 55.

Armstrong, Robert and Janet Shenk. "El Salvador-A Revolution Brews," *NACLA Report on the Americas* 14, no. 4 (July–August 1980) 2–36.

"Art and Politics of the Documentary: A Symposium," *Cineaste* 11, no. 3 (1981): 12-21.

"Atari Plunges WCI Into $19-Mil Loss in 1st '83 Quarter," *Variety*, 27 April, 1983, 4, 44.

Attorney General's Commission on Pornography, Final Report, Washington, D.C.: U.S. Government Printing Office, 1986.

Auerbach, Alexander. "Pay Cable Helps Theatre Boxoffice, Market Study Shows," *Boxoffice* July 1983, pp. 20–21.

Ayscough, Suzan. "Steep Deal for Carolco 'Cliff'," *Variety* 17 May, 1993, 1, 120.

Bach, Steven. *Final Cut: Dreams and Disaster in the Making of Heaven's Gate*. New York: Morrow, 1985.

"Background Material and Data on Programs Within the Jurisdiction of the Committee on Ways and Means," quoted in "Richest Got Richer and Poorest Poorer in 1979–87," *New York Times*, 23 March 1989, A1, A24.

Baker, Christopher W. *How Did They Do It? Computer Illusion in Film and TV*. Indianapolis, IN: Alpha Books, 1994.

Balio, Balio. "Adjusting to the New Global Economy," *Film Policy: International, National and Regional Perspectives*. Ed. Albert Moran. London: Routledge, 1996, pp. 23–38.

Balio, Tino, ed., *The American Film Industry*, rev. ed. Madison: University of Wisconsin Press, 1985.

Barsam, Richard M. *Nonfiction Film: A Critical History*, rev. ed. Bloomington: Indiana University Press, 1992.

Bart, Peter. "What Hollywood Isn't Telling MCA's New Owners," *Variety*, 3 December 1990, 1, 8.

———. "Carolco Culture Shock," *Variety*, 26 August 1991, 7, 24.

———. "Times Have Changed, But the Rhetoric Lingers On," *Variety*, 4 February 1991, 5, 24.

———. *Fade Out: The Calamitous Final Days of MGM*. New York: William Morrow, 1990.

Barth, Jack. "John Hughes: On Geeks Baring Gifts," *Film Comment*, June 1984, p. 46.

Bates, James and Judy Brennan. "Carolco May Be Close to Restructuring," *Los Angeles Times*, 14 February 1995, D4.

Bates, James. "Fox Will Buy Most Assets of Ailing Carolco," *Los Angeles Times*, 11 November 1995, Business, D1.

————. "Ex-Carolco Chief Goes to Paramount" *Los Angeles Times*, 4 January 1996, Business, D2.

Bates, Peter. "Truth not Guaranteed: An Interview with Errol Morris," *Cineaste* 17, no. 1 (1989): 16-17.

Battcock, Gregory, ed. *New Artists Video*. New York: Dutton, 1978.

Benjamin, Walter. *Illuminations*. Hannah Arendt ed. New York: Schocken Books, 1978.

Bierbaum, Tom. "Paramount's 'Gun' Soars to Revenue/Sales Marks," *Variety*, 25 March 1987, pp. 41-42.

————. "Paramount Expects B.O. Boost with Re-Release of *Footloose* Same Day Cassette Hits Market," *Variety*, 1 August 1984, 1, 22.

————. "TV Watchdogs Growl At Films, Seek to Replace MPAA Ratings," *Variety*, 12 August 1981, 1, 84.

Block, Alex Ben, "Mamma from Turner," *Forbes*, 18 May 1987, 126–128.

————. "Is There Life Beyond Rambo?" *Forbes*, 1 June 1987, 88-92.

Bob Lasiewics. "Computers in the Editing Room," *American Cinematographer* 66, no. 6 (June, 1985): 94-98.

Borish, Jeffrey, James A. Moorer, and Peter Nye. "SoundDroid: A New System for Electronic Post-Production of Sound," *SMPTE Journal* 95:5 (May 1986): 567–71.

"Boston Court Rules 'Caligula' Is Not Obscene on Political Merits," *Variety*, 6 August 1980, 6, 37.

Boyle, Dierdre. *Guerilla Television Revisited*. New York: Oxford, 1998.

Brennan, Judy. "Red Ink on the Starboard Bow," *Los Angeles Times*, 20 August 1995: Calendar, 26.

Breskin, David. *Inner Views: Filmmakers in Conversation*. Winchester, MA: Faber and Faber, 1992.

Brigman, William E. "Politics and the Pornography Wars," *Wide Angle* 19, no. 3 (July 1997): 149–170.

Britton, Andrew. "Blissing Out: The Politics of Reaganite Entertainment," *Movie*, no. 30/31, 1-42.

"*Broken Rainbow*: An Interview with Victoria Mudd and Maria Florio." *Cineaste* 15, no. 2 (1986): 34–36.

Bronson, Gail. "Videotapes Give Hollywood a Second Shot at Success," *US News & World Report*, 4 March 1985, 73.

Brown, Thomas. "The Electronic Camera Experiment," *American Cinematographer* 63, no. 1 (January, 1982): 28–29, 76–79, 100.

Bruno, Giuliana. "Ramble City: Postmodernism and *Blade Runner*," *October* 41 (Summer, 1987): 61–74.

Bugbee, Victoria. "Stranger Than Paradise." *American Cinematographer* 67, no. 3 (March 1985): 46–55.

Burckhardt, Rudy and Simon Pettet. *Talking Pictures: The Photography of Rudy Burckhardt*. Cambridge, MA: Zoland Books, 1994.

"'Caligula' is Upheld, Beating Wisc.-Ruling," *Variety*, 18 June 1980, 6.

"'Caligula' Pulls Out of Ohio Site; Credit Watchdog Tactics," *Variety*, 19 November 1980, 3, 28.

Carl, K. J. Carl et al. "Eastman Color Print Film 5384," *SMPTE Journal* 91, no. 12 (December, 1982): 1161–1170.

"Carolco May Whip Out Rambo III For Film's Guarantors at Market," *Variety*, 24 February 1988, pp. 15, 418.

Case, Dominic J. "Telecine-Compatible Prints," *SMPTE Journal* 98, no. 6 (June 1989): 451–454.

Castro, Janice, "Pocketful of Stars: Michael Ovitz and His Cadre of Agents are Hollywood's New Power Brokers," *Time*, 13 February 1989, 58–59.

Cellitti, David Robert. "The World on a Silver Platter," *Widescreen Review*, Laser Magic 1998 Issue, pp. 14–48.

Chandler, Clay. "After Decades of Deficits, a U.S. Budget Surplus Looms," *Washington Post*, 1 February 1998, A1, A14.

"Chi Tribune Blasts Gory 'X-Films in R-rated Clothing," *Variety*, 12 November 1980, 6, 30.

Childs, Richard B. "Home Video," in *The Movie Business Book*, ed. Jason Squires. New York: Fireside, 1992, pp. 329–37.

Chomsky, Noam. *Towards a New Cold War*. New York: Pantheon, 1982.

"Clergy Nail 'Christ' and Universal," *Variety*, 10 August 1988, 1, 18.

Cohn, Lawrence. "Ancillary Market Saves Indies," *Variety*, 24 February 1988, 1, 295.

————. "Average Pic Cost Now $9,750,000," *Variety*, 30 December 1981, 3, 24.

————. "Domestic Market for Indie Pix Soft," *Variety*, 22 February 1989, 22.

————. "Domestic Recoup Rare on Mega-Buck Pic Rentals," *Variety*, 12 January 1983, 7, 40.

————. "Filmers Resort to Old Scare Tactics," *Variety*, 8 June 1988, 1, 24.

————. "High cost pics largely on the money in '88," *Variety*, 11-17 January 1989, 30.

————. "Hollywood Goes on a Spending Spree," *Variety*, 1 September 1982, 5, 39.

————. "Horrid Year for Horror at the B.O.," *Variety*, 25 January 1984, 3, 36.

————. "Horror, Sci-Fi Pix Earn 37% of Rentals," *Variety*, 19 November 1980, 5, 32.

————. "Incredible Shrinking Horror Market?," *Variety*, 16 February 1983, 7, 24.

————. "Indie Filmmakers Advised to Regard Pay-TV as a Funding Tap," *Variety*, 17 June 1981, 6, 29.

————. "Megabuck Pix Increased Ratios," *Variety*, 11 January 1984, 10, 82.

————. "Majors' Rentals Rise, Neg Costs Soar," *Variety*, 22 December 1982, 3, 25.

————. "Owner Switcheroos Marked Pic Year: B.O. Declines 7% From '84," *Variety*, 8 January 1986, 7, 78–82, 90.

————. "Pix Less Able, But Porn is Stable," *Variety*, 16 November 1983, 1, 28.

————. "Stars' Rocketing Salaries Keep Pushing Envelope," *Variety*,24 September 1990, 3, 108.

Coleman, Lisa. "Picking Your Targets," *Forbes*, 21 January 1991, 72.

Compton, D.M. James and Dimitri S. Dimitri. "Implementation of Time Code Using Datakode Magnetic Control Surface Film," *SMPTE Journal* 95 (July 1986): 727–732.

"Computer Research and Development at Lucasfilm," *American Cinematographer* 63, no. 8 (August, 1982): 773–75.

Conant, Michael. "The Paramount Decrees Reconsidered," in Tino Balio, ed. *The American Film Industry*, rev. ed. Madison: University of Wisconsin Press, 1985, pp. 537–73.

Cook, Karen. "The Little Studio That Could," *Premiere*, March 1988, 17–18.

"Coppola's Electronic Cinema System," *American Cinematographer* 63, no. 8: 777–81.

Couvares, Francis G. *Movie Censorship and American Culture*. Washington, D.C.: Smithsonian Institution Press, 1996.

Crawford, Alan. *Thunder on the Right*. New York: Pantheon, 1980.

Crister, Greg. "Tough New World," *Channels*, March 1987, 20–26.

Crowdus, Gary and Richard Porton, "The Importance of a Singular, Guiding Vision: An Interview with Arthur Penn," *Cineaste*, (Spring, 1993): 4–16.

Cruising film review, *Variety*, 13 February 1980, 16.

Danese, Connie. "A SAG Conference Addresses (and Denounces) Female Struggles in Films and TV," *Back Stage*, 17 August 1990, 3–4.

Davis, Mike. "The New Right's Road to Power," *New Left Review*, 128 (July–August, 1981): 28–49.

Dawes, Amy. "Christian Groups Blast Universal Over 'Christ' Pic," *Variety*, 20 July 1988, 1, 8.

Day, James. *The Vanishing Vision: The Inside Story of Public Television*. Berkeley: University of California Presss, 1995.

DeBenedetti, Charles. *An American Ordeal: The Anti-War Movement of the Vietnam Era*, Charles Chatfield, assisting author. Syracuse, NY: Syracuse University Press, 1990.

Dempsey, John. "MGM/UA Building Barter Film Web," *Variety*, 25 July 1984, 1, 82.

————. "Top Pics Pull Huge Syndie Coin," *Variety*, 4 February 1987, 1, 150.

Denby, David. "Can the Movies Be Saved?" *New York Magazine*, 21 July 1986: 24–35.

Deutchman, Ira. "Independent Distribution and Marketing" in *The Movie Business Book*, edited by Jason E. Squire. New York: Fireside, 1992, pp. 320–27.

"Dialogue on Film: John Sayles," *American Film*, (May, 1986):13–15.

"Dialogue on Film: Lawrence Kasdan," *American Film* (April 1982): 10–13, 28–31.

"Did 'Cruising' Respect Rulings?," *Variety*, 25 June 1980, 4, 37.

Dittmar, Linda and Gene Michaud, eds. *From Hanoi to Hollywood: The Vietnam War in American Film*. Rutgers, NJ: Rutgers University Press, 1990.

"Diversification Blues," *Mergers and Acquisitions*, 21, no. 6 (May/June, 1987): 13–14.

Dutka, Elaine. "An Interview with Paramount's Top Guns," *Los Angeles Times*, Calendar Section, 18 March 1990, 45–46, 83–84.

Eberwein, Robert. "The Erotic Thriller," *Post Script* 17, no. 3 (Summer, 1998): 25–33.

Eller, Claudia and Don Groves. "Carolco Prexy Defends It Talent Megadeals," *Variety*, 29 October 1990, 3, 10.

Elrick, Ted. "Fires . . . Floods . . . Riots . . . Earthquakes . . . John Carpenter," *DGA Magazine*, http://www.dga.org/magazine/interviews/dga_interviews.htm.

Fabrikant, Geraldine, William Glasgall, Elizabeth Ames, and James R. Norman. "The Shifting Fortunes of Marvin Davis," *Business Week*, 8 April 1989, 36.

Fabrikant, Geraldine. "The Hole in Hollywood's Pocket," *New York Times*, 10 December 1990, C1, C4.

Farber, Stephen and Marc Green. *Outrageous Conduct: Art, Ego, and The Twilight Zone Case*. New York: Arbor House, 1988.

Farley, Ellen. "The U.S. Has Surrendered-Now *Rambo* Is Taking the World by Storm," *Business Week*, 26 August 1985, 109.

"FBI Exposes Porno and Piracy Affinity," *Variety*, 20 February 1980, 7.

"FBI Nails Video Pirates," *Variety*, 18 March 1981, 277.

"Fed's Plan for Economic Recovery," *Business Week*, 13 December 1982, 90–98.

"Fewer Big-Budget Films Made It Pay," *Variety*, 8 January 1986, 9, 96.

"Fiscally Fortified, New Line Accents Production & Pickups," *Variety*, 14 October 1981, 12.

Fischer, Herb. "Saving Classics on Tape," *American Cinematographer* 66, no. 9 (September, 1985): 81–83.

Fisher, Bob. "The Emerging New Film/Video Interface," *American Cinematographer* 62, no. 6 (June, 1981): 570–618.

Fisher, John G. "Screen and Tube Financing in the Inflated Years Ahead," *Variety*, 9 January 1980, 20.

Fleming, Michael. "Product Pluggola Padding Pic Producers' Budgets," *Variety*, 9 May 1990, 1, 22, 24, 91.

———. "Turtles, 'Toons and Toys 'R' In," *Variety*, 18 April 1990, 1, 8.

———. "Miramax, Riding 'Sex' Wave, Storms on to the '90s," *Variety*, 31 January 1990, 9, 16.

"50 Largest Foreign Acquisitions in the U.S. 1980–89," *Mergers and Acquisitions* (March/April 1990): 113.

Fordin, Hugh. *The World of Entertainment!: The Freed Unit at MGM*. New York: Doubleday, 1975.

Form 10-K, AMC Entertainment, Inc., 1986.

Form 10-K, Columbia Pictures Industries, 1980

Form 10-K, Gulf and Western Industries, 1982, 1985

Form 10-K, Matsushita Electrical Industrial Co., Ltd., 1990, 1991.

Form 10-K, MCA, Inc., 1981, 1983, 1989

Form 10-K, MGM, 1979, 1981

Form 10-K, Paramount Communications, Inc., 1989

Form 10-K, Pathe Communications Corp., 1989

Form 10-K, Sony Corp., 1991

Form 10-K, The Coca-Cola Co., 1982, 1983, 1989

Form 10-K, The News Corp. Ltd., 1986

Form 10-K, The Walt Disney Company, 1980, 1982, 1983, 1984, 1985, 1986

Form 10-K, Time-Warner, 1989, 1990.

Form 10-K, Transamerica Corp., 1980, 1981

Form 10-K, Twentieth Century-Fox, 1980

Form 10-K, Warner Communications Co., 1980, 1981, 1982

"Fortune Forecast: A Toehold on Recovery," *Fortune*, 14 June 1982, 59.

Fox, David. "Coke Holds Fiscal Court on Colpix Turf," *Variety*, 24 November 1982, 3, 28.

Frank Rosenfelt. "MGM In Big Expansion for '80s," *Variety*, 9 January 1980, 9.

Friedman, Robert. "Will Cannon Boom or Bust?" *American Film* July/August 1986: 53–59.

"G&W Revamp Places Diller at Head of Leisure Group, Plus Par," *Variety*, 16 March 1983, 5, 26.

Galbraith, Jane. "MGM/UA, Turner Shareholders Okay Merger; Expect Coin Soon," *Variety*, 5 March 1986, 3–34.

———. "Turner Keeps Pics, Drops Rest of MGM," *Variety*, 11 June 1986, 3, 32.

"Games Plunge WCI Quarter & Next Few Stanzas Downward," *Variety*, 23 February 1982, 4, 27.

Gelman, Morrie. "Majors Increase Home Vid Titles 854% in 16 Mos.," *Variety*, 5 March 1980, 1, 94.

Gentry, Ric. "Clint Eastwood: An Interview," *Post Script* 17, no. 3 (Summer 1998): 3–24.

———. "Foul Play in High Places," *American Cinematographer* 78, no. 2 (February 1997): 72–80.

Geri. "Heaven's Gate," *Variety*, 26 November 1980, 14.

"Getty's Pay-TV Venture is Sued By Justice Unit," *Wall Street Journal*, 5 August 1980, 5.

Gidal, Peter. Materialist Film. New York: Routledge, 1989.

Gilroy, Dan. "Product Placement In Pics Helps Hedge Costs Majors and Indies," *Variety*, 19 February 1986, 6, 399.

Girard, Tom. "How HBO, CBS, Col Tri-Star Deal Works," *Variety*, 14 November 1984, 3, 38.

———. "Justice Dept. Greenlights Tri-Star," *Variety*, 21 September 1983, 3, 39.

Glass, Fred. "Totally Recalling Arnold: Sex and Violence in the New Bad Future," *Film Quarterly* 44, no. 1 (Fall 1990): 2–13.

"Golan-Globus Buy of Cannon To Launch US Prod-Distrib; Sell 10-Point Insurance Plan," *Variety*, 23 May 1979, 3, 45.

Gold, Richard. "G&W Pares Down to Media Only; Possibilities Abound," *Variety*, 12–18 April 1989, 1, 4.

———. "High Hopes For 'Gremlins' Merchandise," *Variety*, 27 June 1984, 5, 32.

———. "H'wood Majors Spinoff Videos From Youth Pix," *Variety*, 22 February 1984, 1, 108.

———. "No Bigness Like Show Bigness," *Variety*, 14–20 June 1989, 1, 6-7.

———. "Par's block looks like a bust as court backs Time director's stand," *Variety*, 19-25 July 1989, 1, 6–7.

———. "'Purple Rain' Sells Rock at Box Office," *Variety*, 1 August 1 1984, 5, 29.

———. "Studios and Labels Pan Soundtrack Gold," *Variety*, 18 April 1984, 5, 216.

———. "Time's Move of the Year," *Variety*, 8-14 March 1989, 1, 3.

———. "Warners, G&W Succeed By Doin' What Comes Naturally," *Variety*, 6 April 1988, 7.

———. "'Flashdance' Film, LP Feeding Off Each Other," *Variety*, 11 May 1983, 3, 46.

———. "New Warner Credit Accord Explored," *Variety*, 19 December 1984, 3, 91.

———. "Tri-Star, Carolco Execs Insist Rambo III Won't Die at B.O." *Variety*, 22 June 1988, 4, 24.

Gomery, Douglas. "Building a Movie Theater Giant: The Rise of Cineplex Odeon," in Tim Balio ed. *Hollywood in the Age of Television*. Cambridge, Mass: Unwin Hyman, 1990, pp. 377–91.

Grein, Paul. "Dirty Dancing Steps Around Competition," *Los Angeles Times*, 11 November 1987: Part VI, 1,6.

Griffin, Nancy and Kim Masters. *Hit & Run: How Jon Peters and Peter Guber Took Sony for a Ride in Hollywood*. New York: Simon & Schuster, 1996.

Grogg, Sam L. "Venture Capital Strategy and FilmDallas," in *The Movie Business Book*, ed. Jason E. Squire. New York: Fireside, 1992, 150–58.

Grover, Ronald. "Carolco May Be Headed for a Quick Dissolve," *Business Week*, 6 July 1992, 40.

———. "Getting Rich on TV's New Austerity," *Business Week*, 6 April 1987, 109–14.

———. "High Drama from the Folks Who Brought You *Godzilla 85*," *Business Week*, 7 September 1987, 30.

———. "Now Carolco Needs Fresh Blood, Part II," *Business Week*, 30 May 1988, 80.

Guback, Thomas, "The Evolution of the Motion Picture Theater Business in the 1980s," *Journal of Communication* 37, no. 2 (Spring 1987): 60–77.

Gubernick, Lisa. "Backs to the Future," *Forbes*, 15 April 1991, 10.

———. "Cannon Rises Again," *Forbes*, 25 July 1988, 43–44.

———. "Know Thy Limitations," *Forbes*, 20 January 1992, 51–53.

———. "It's Great for a Date," *Forbes*, 6 February 1989, 110–14.

———. "Living Off the Past," *Forbes*, 12 June 1989, 48–55.

———. "We Don't Want to be Walt Disney," *Forbes*, 16 October 1989, 109–10.

Guens, Jean-Pierre. "Through the Looking Glasses: From the Camera Obscura to Video Assist," *Film Quarterly* 49:3 (Summer 1996): 16–26.

Guggenheim, Ralph, Rob Lay, and Andy Cohen. "The History, Design, and Architecture of Editdroid," *SMPTE Journal* (January 1985): 158.

"Gulf and Western to Sell Florida, Dominican Sugar Operations," *Variety*, 20 June 1984, 3, 30.

Haines, Richard W. *Technicolor Movies: The History of Dye Transfer Printing*. Jefferson, NC: McFarland, 1993.

Hall, Doug and Sally Jo Fifer, eds. *Illuminating Video*. New York: Aperture, 1990.

Haller, Robert A. *Brakhage Scrapbok: Collected Writings 1964-1980*. New Paltz, NY: Documentext, 1982.

Hammer, Josua. "Total Free Fall," *Newsweek*, 9 March 1992, 50–55.

Hanson, Kerry. "A Sad Story," *Forbes*, 14 May 1990, 10.

Harris, William. "Lights, Camera, Lawyers!" *Forbes*, 10 August 1987, 33.

Harwood, Jim. "Federal Court Nixes In-Home Videotaping; Sony Plans Appeal," *Variety*, 21 October 1981, 96.

———. "Stanfill and Valenti Discuss Tomorrows," *Variety*, 24 December 1980, 5, 31.

"Hasta la Vista, Babies . . . ," *Economist*, 13 July 1991: 68.

Hausheer, Cecilia and Christoph Settele, eds. *Found Footage Film*. Lucern, Switzerland: Viper, 1992.

Hayes, Thomas C. "Murdoch Will Buy Out Davis' Holdings in Fox," *New York Times*, 24 September 1985, 1.

Heller, Walter. "A 'Yes But' Economy in 1980," *Wall Street Journal*, 23 January 1980, 22.

"High Court Upholds Fox Conviction for Block Booking," *Variety*, 10 January 1990, 7.

Hillier, Jim and Aaron Lipstadt. "The Economics of Independence: Roger Corman and New World Pictures, 1970–80," *Movie* 31/32 (1986): 43–53.

Hillier, Jim. *The New Hollywood*. New York: Continuum, 1994.

Hollinger, Hy. "Film 'Survival Years' Lie Ahead," *Variety*, 14 January 1981, 11, 46.

———. "Production Control Changes Marked 1981," *Variety*, 13 January 1982, 7, 50.

Horak, Jan-Christopher. *Lovers of Cinema: The First American Film Avant-Garde, 1919–1945*. Madison: University of Wisconsin Press, 1995.

"How TV is Revolutionizing Hollywood," *Business Week*, 21 February 1983, 78–89.

Hoynes, William. *Public Television for Sale: Media, the Market, and the Public Sphere*. Boulder, CO: Westview Press, 1994.

Hunt, Richard A. "Strategies at War: Pacification and Attrition in Vietnam," in Richard A. Hunt and Richard H. Schultz, Jr., eds. *Lessons from an Unconventional War: Reassessing U.S. Strategies for Future Conflicts*. New York: Pergamon Press, 1982, pp. 23–47.

Inglis, Ruth A. "Self-Regulation in Operation," in *The American Film Industry*, ed. Tino Balio, rev. ed. Madison: University of Wisconsin Press, 1985, pp. 377–400.

International Motion Picture Almanac for 1983. New York: Quigley Publishing Co., 1983.

Jackson, Kevin, ed. *Schrader on Schrader & Other Writings*. Boston: Faber and Faber, 1990.

Jacobson, Harlen. "Old Pix Don't Die, They Fade Away," *Variety*, 9 July 1980, 1, 28–29.

James, David. *Allegories of Cinema: American Film in the Sixties*. Princeton, NJ: Princeton University Press, 1989.

———. *To Free the Cinema: Jonas Mekas and the New York Underground*. Princeton, NJ: Princeton University Press, 1992.

Jay, Mike. "Electronic Editing of Film for Motion Pictures," *American Cinematographer* 62, no.3 (March, 1981): 256–57.

"Jungle War Over the Platoon Video," *Newsweek*, 23 November 1987, 56.

Kelly, Mary Pat. *Martin Scorsese: A Journey*. New York: Thunder's Mouth Press, 1991.

Kern, Louis J. "MIAs, Myth and Macho Magic: Post-Apocalyptic Cinematic Visions of Vietnam," in *Search and Clear: Critical Responses to Selected Literature and Films of the Vietnam War*, ed. William J. Searle. Bowling Green, OH: Bowling Green State University Popular Press, 1988.

Kipps, Charles. "The Rise and Fall of the Coca-Cola Kid," *Variety*, 18 May 1988, 7–9, 30.

———. "Wall St. Plugs in VCR Potential," *Variety*, 23 September 1987, 118.

———. *Out of Focus: Power, Pride, and Prejudice - David Puttnam in Hollywood*. New York: William Morrow, 1989.

Kissinger, David. "Judgment Day for Carolco," *Variety*, 9 December 1991, 1, 93.

Klain, Stephen. "'Caligula' Banned in Boston," *Variety*, 25 June 1980, 3, 39.

———. "New Film Vex: Raw Stock and Print Costs," *Variety*, 16 January 1980, 5, 36.

———. "Paramount's All-Rights Software Focus," *Variety*, 1 April 1981, 3, 38.

Knee, Adam and Charles Musser. "William Greaves, Documentary Film-making and the African-American Experience," *Film Quarterly* 45, no. 3 (Spring 1992): 13–25.

Knoedelseder, William K., Jr. "De Laurentiis: Producer's Picture Darkens," *Los Angeles Times*, 30 August 1987: Part IV, 1–2.

Knoll, Steve. "Warners Revises Homevid Policy," *Variety*, 11 November 1981, 1, 81.

Koltnow, Barry. "A Supersleuth Returns to Beverly Hills," *The Orange County Register*, 24 May 1987, H1.

Koschnick, Wolfgang J. "'I Can Think of More Important Things Than Being Loved by Everybody'," *Forbes*, 27 November 1989, 98–104.

Krawitz, Jan. "The Independent Documentary Film: Prospects for Survival," *Journal of Film and Video* 38 (Winter 1986): 49–53.

Landro, Laura. "Sony, Warner Settle Dispute Over Producers," *Wall Street Journal*, 17 November 1989, 1.

Landro, Laura and Richard Turner. "Matsushita Explores Purchase of MCA," *Wall Street Journal*, 25 September 1990, B1, B10.

Lardner, James. *Fast Forward: Hollywood, the Japanese and the Onslaught of the VCR*. New York: Norton, 1987.

"Las Madres de la Plaze de Mayo: An Interview with Susana Munoz and Lourdes Portillo," *Cineaste* 15, no. 1 (1986): 22–25.

"Latest 10-Q on 20th-Fox," *Variety*, 2 September 1981, 7, 23.

Lax, Eric. *Woody Allen: A Biography*. New York: Knopf, 1991.

Lewis, Jon. *Whom God Wishes to Destroy . . . :Francis Coppola and the New Hollywood*. Durham: Duke University Press, 1995.

Lieberman, Jane. "De Laurentiis Entertainment Group Board, Creditors Approve Buy by Carolco," *Variety*, 26 April 1989, 12, 30.

———. "Ventura, TWE in Bids for De Laurentiis," *Variety*, 23 November 1988, 3, 22.

Lindsey, Robert. "Francis Coppola: Promises to Keep," *New York Times Magazine*, 24 July 1988, 22–27.

———. "HBO: Home Box Office Moves in on Hollywood," *New York Magazine*, 12 June 1983, 31–38, 66–71.

Littman, Barry R. *The Motion Picture Mega-Industry*. Boston: Allyn and Bacon, 1998.

Litwak, Mark. *Reel Power: The Struggle for Influence and Success in the New Hollywood*. New York: William Morrow, 1986.

LoBrutto, Vincent. *Sound-on-Film: Interviews with Creators of Film Sound*. Westport, CT: Praeger, 1994.

Lumet, Sidney. *Making Movies*. New York: Knopf, 1995.

Lyons, Charles. *The New Censors: Movies and the Culture Wars*. Philadelphia: Temple University Press, 1997.

———. "The Paradox of Protest" in Francis G. Couvares, *Movie Censorship and American Culture*. Washington, D.C.: Smithsonian Institution Press, 1996, pp. 277–318.

Mabey, John. "Video Disc Basics," *American Cinematographer* 66, no. 3 (March 1985): 89–91.

MacDonald, Scott, ed. *Screen Writings: Scripts and Texts by Independent Filmmakers*. Berkeley: University of California Press, 1995.

MacDonald, Scott. "Cinema 16: Documents Toward a History of the Film Society." *Wide Angle* 19, nos. 1 & 2 (January 1997; April 1997).

———. "Media Destructionism: The Digital/Laser/Videos of Raphael Montanez Ortiz." In *The Ethnic Eye*, ed. Ana M. Lopez and Chon A. Noriega. Minneapolis: University of Minnesota Press, 1996, pp. 183–207.

———. *A Critical Cinema*. Berkeley: University of California Press, 1988.

———. *A Critical Cinema 2*. Berkeley: University of California Press, 1992.

———. *A Critical Cinema 3*. Berkeley: University of California Press, 1998.

———. *Avant-Garde Film/Motion Studies*. Cambridge: Cambridge University Press, 1993.

Magid, Ron. "George Lucas: Past, Present, and Future," *American Cinematographer* (February 1997): 48–54.

Magnet, Myron. "Coke Tries Selling Movies Like Soda Pop," *Fortune*, 26 December 1983, 119–26.

"Major Distribs Picking Up More Indie Productions," *Variety*, 24 February 1988, 66.

Mayer, Jane. "Hard Bargainer," The Wall Street Journal, 15 August 1983, p. 1, 8.

McBride, James. "Eddie Murphy Comes Clean," *People Weekly*, 8 August 1988, 76–81.

McBride, Joseph, ed. *Filmmakers on Filmmaking, Volume One*. Los Angeles: J.P. Tarcher, Inc., 1983.

———. "Rehme Says He May Add to His Duties Under New World-Pathe Link-Up," *Variety*, 15 March 1989, 24.

McDonagh, Maitland. "New Line Cinema Sets Out to Achieve Market Identity," *The Film Journal* March 1984: 12, 68.

McEvoy, James III. *Radicals or Conservatives? The Contemporary American Right*. Chicago: Rand McNally, 1971.

McMurdy, Deirdre. "Fade to Black," *Macleans*, 17 June 1991, 40–41.

Medved, Michael. *Hollywood vs. America: Popular Culture and the War on Traditional Values*. New York: HarperCollins, 1992.

Mellencamp, Patricia. *Indiscretions: Avant-Garde Film, Video and Feminism*. Bloomington: Indiana University Press, 1990.

Moran, Albert, ed. *Film Policy: International, National and Regional Perspectives*. London: Routledge, 1996.

MPAA 1996 U.S. Economic Review. Encino, CA: Motion Picture Association of America, 1997.

Murch, Walter. *In the Blink of an Eye: A Perspective on Film Editing*. Los Angeles, CA: Silman-James Press, 1995.

"Murdoch's Profits Bolstered by TV, 20th Ancillaries," *Variety*, 12 November 1986, 3, 33.

Murphy, A.D. "'82 Film B.O. Up 16% to $3.449-Bil Record," *Variety*, 12 January 1983, 7, 23.

———. "$3.7-Billion Record for 1983 Boxoffice," *Variety*, 11 January 1984, 7, 48.

———. "Universal's 1982 Market Share Record," *Variety*, 19 January 1983, 1, 131.

———. "Warners Tops in '85 Domestic Rentals," *Variety*, 8 January 1986, 13, 73.

———. "Week-By-Week Cumulative Tix Sales Parallel Over 20 Years," *Variety*, 2 December 1981, 5, 21.

Natale, Richard. "Live Wire May Spark Carolco," *Variety*, 15 July 1991, 1, 60.

Neale, Steve and Murray Smith, eds. *Contemporary Hollywood Cinema*. London: Routledge, 1998.

"New Line Focuses Product on Three Specialized Areas," *The Independent Film Journal* 10 July 1974, 21.

Newcomb, Peter. "Covering Their Bets," *Forbes*, 26 December 1988, 10.

"1980-83 Big Buck Scorecard," *Variety*, 11 January 1984, 10, 50.

1989 International Television and Video Almanac. New York: Quigley Publishing Co., Inc., 1990.

1990 International Television and Video Almanac. New York: Quigley Publishing Co., Inc., 1991.

1991 International Television and Video Almanac. New York: Quigley Publishing Co., Inc., 1992.

Noglows, Paul. "Terminated Deal Trips Carolco," *Variety*, 9 December 1991, 89-90.

Noriega, Chon. *Chicanos and Film: Essays on Representation and Resistance*. New York: Garland, 1992.

"North American Theatrical Film Rental Market Shares," *Variety*, 20 January 1988, 38.

Novak, Barbara. *Nature and Culture: American Landscape and Painting, 1925–1875*. New York: Oxford, 1980.

Ohmer, Susan. *Measuring Desire: George Gallup and the Origins of Market Research in Hollywood*. Ph.D. Dissertation, New York University, 1997.

Pally, Marcia. Double-Trouble, *Film Comment*, 20 (September–October 1984): 12–17.

Par Gives Eddie Murphy A New 5-Pic Pact, More Coin and Control," *Variety*, 2 September 1987, 6, 38.

Patterson, Richard, "The Preservation of Color Films, Part I," *American Cinematographer* 62, no. 7 (July 1981):. 694–96, 714–20.

Patterson, Richard. "The Preservation of Color Films, Part II," *American Cinematographer* 62, no. 8 (August 1981): 792–822.

Paul Harris. "Supreme Court O.K.'s Home Taping," *Variety*, 18 January 1984, 1, 109.

Paulson, C. Robert and Michael J. Doyle. "The Video Disk System: A Technical Report by the SMPTE Study Group on Video Disc Recording," *SMPTE Journal* 91:2 (February, 1982): 180–85.

Pearce, Jenny. *Under the Eagle*. Boston: South End Press, 1982.

Pentagon Papers, vol. 4. Boston: Beacon Press.

Phillips, Gerald F. "The Recent Acquisition of Theatre Circuits by Major Distributors," *The Entertainment and Sports Lawyer* 5, no. 3. (Winter, 1987): 1–2, 10–23.

Phillips, Julia. *You'll Never Eat Lunch in this Town Again*. New York: Random House, 1991.

Pierson, John. *Spike, Mike, Slackers & Dykes: A Guided Tour across a Decade of American Independent Cinema*. New York: Hyperion Books, 1995.

Plantinga, Carl. "Moving Pictures and the Rhetoric of Nonfiction." In *Post-Theory: Reconstructing Film Studies*, eds. David Bordwell and Noel Carroll. Madison: University of Wisconsin Press, 1996, 307–24.

———. *Rhetoric and Representation in Nonfiction Film*. Cambridge: Cambridge University Press, 1997.

"Pornography: Love or Death?," *Film Comment* 20 (November-December 1984): 30–49.

Puttnam, David and Neil Watson. *Movies and Money*. New York: Alfred A. Knopf, 1998.

Rabinowitz, Lauren. *Points of Resistance: Women, Power and Politics in the New York Avant-Garde Cinema, 1943–1974*. Chicago: University of Illinois Press, 1991.

Rapattoni, Linda, "Wm. Morris Seeks to Quash Another Par Subpoena," *Variety*, 16 September 1991, 21.

Reagan, Ronald. Address to the nation on aiding the Contras, 16 March 1986, *in Vital Speeches of the Day* 52, no. 13: 386–89.

———. Address to the nation on the downing of a Korean airliner by the Soviets, September 5, 1983, in *Vital Speeches of the Day* 49, no. 24: 738–40.

———. Inauguration Address, 21 January 1985, in *Vital Speeches of the Day* 51, no. 8: 226–28.

————. *Speaking My Mind.* New York: Simon and Schuster, 1989.

Reardon, Barry. "The Studio Distributor," in Jason E. Squire, ed. *The Movie Business Book*, second ed. New York: Fireside, 1992, pp. 310–19.

Rehfeld, Barry. "Cannon Fathers," *Film Comment* December 1983: 20–24.

Rehme, Robert. "Indies Must Map Out Strategies To Fit Changing Domestic Market," *Variety*, 20 January 1988, 8, 87.

Reinking, Frank. "Film to Tape Mysteries Unraveled," *American Cinematographer* 70, no. 9 (September, 1989): 73–80.

Renov, Michael. "Newsreel: Old and New-Towards a Historical Profile," *Film Quarterly* 51, no. 1 (Fall 1987): 20–23.

————. *Theorizing Documentary.* New York: Routledge, 1993.

Rensin, David. "The Man Who Would Be Different," *American Film* (March, 1986): 52–54.

Riordan, James. *Stone.* New York: Hyperion, 1995.

Robbins, Jim. "July Lets Warner Return G&W but Involves Consent Decrees," *Variety*, 14–20 December 1988, 3.

————. "Theater Building Zooms," *Variety*, 11 January 1984, 17, 38.

Robert Armstrong and Janet Shenk. "El Salvador-Why Revolution?," *NACLA Report on the Americas* 14, no. 2 (March-April 1980): 3–35.

Rose, Frank. *The Agency: William Morris and the Hidden History of Show Businesss.* New York: HarperCollins, 1995.

Rosen, David with Peter Hamilton. *Off-Hollywood: The Making and Marketing of Independent Films.* New York: Grove Weidenfeld, 1990.

Rossant, John. "Puzzle in Movieland: The Case of the Mystery Moguls," *Business Week*, 13 March 1989, 80.

Roth, Morry. "Teens Leaving Theaters for Homevid," *Variety*, 26 February 1986, 3, 34.

Rothman, Matt. "Carolco, Kassar Rise from Redivvied Ashes," *Variety*, 4 January 1993, 81–82.

Salomon, Julie. *The Devil's Candy: The Bonfire of the Vanities Goes Hollywood.* Boston: Houghton Mifflin, 1991.

Sapaorito, Bill. "A Legal Victory for the Long Term," *Fortune*, 14 August 1989, 56–59.

Sarris, Andrew. "Dreck to Kill," *Village Voice*, 17-23 September 1980, 44.

————. "The Independent Cinema," in *The New American Cinema*, ed. Gregory Battcock. New York: Dutton, 1967, pp. 51–57.

Schilling, Ed. "Digital Sound for Film and Video," *American Cinematographer* 65, no. 11 (December, 1984): 101–06.

Schindler, Thomas A. "Acoustical Design for the Technical Building at Skywalker Ranch. Part 2: Mechanical and Electrical Acoustic Noise Control," *SMPTE Journal* 98:2 (February 1989): 106–12.

Schlender, Brenton. "Restless Wildcat: Marvin Davis's Offer to Buy Fox Film Fits Maverick Driller's Style," *Wall Street Journal*, 23 February 1981, 1, 25.

Schultz, Richard H., Jr. and Alan Ned Sabrosky. "Policy and Strategy for the 1980s: Preparing for Low Intensity Conflicts," in *Lessons from an Unconventional War: Reassessing U.S. Strategies for Future Conflicts*, ed. Richard A. Hunt and Richard H. Schultz, Jr. New York: Pergamon Press, 1982.

Schwartz, Tony. "Hollywood Debates HBO Role in Film Financing," *New York Times*, 7 January 1982, D1.

————. "U.S. Says Five Companies Broke Law in Plan to Limit Movies on Pay TV," *New York Times*, 5 August 1980, A1, D15.

Schwind, David R. "Acoustical Design for the Technical Building at Skywalker Ranch. Part 1: Sound Isolation and Room Acoustics," *SMPTE Journal* 98:2 (February 1989): 100–105.

"Scorsese Pic Center of Holy War," *Variety*, 27 July 1988, 3, 26.

"2d Look Nix by GCC: 'Cruising' an X Pic," *Variety*, 13 February 1980, 5, 219.

Seidman, Robert and Nicholas Leiber. "Making Peace with the 60s," *American Film* (December, 1981): 67–71.

Seidman, Tony. "Homevid Aids Cinema B.O. For Two Pics," *Variety*, 26 October 1983, 1, 396.

————. "It's the Game, Not the Name, That Ultimately Sells Vidiots," *Variety*, 15 December 1982, 41–42.

————. "'Raiders' Setting Sales Marks; Par Claims 500,000 En Route," *Variety*, 23 November 1983, 27.

Sherman, Stratford P. "Ted Turner: Back From the Brink," *Fortune*, 7 July 1986, 25–31.

Sikora, Martin. "The M&A Bonanza of the '80s . . . And Its Legacy," *Mergers and Acquisitions* 24, no. 5 (March/April 1990): 90–95.

Silverman, Mark B. "Awash in $879-Mil Sea of Red Ink, Warner Dumps Atari," *Variety*, 4 July 1984, 40.

Silverman, Michael. "X-Rated HV Suppliers Stay Blue, But Over Competition, Not Meese," *Variety*, 3 September 1986, 117, 120.

Silverman, Syd. "Show Biz: Never the Same Again," *Variety*, 13 January 1982, 1, 70–78.

Singer, Michael. *A Cut Above: 50 Film Directors Talk About Their Craft*. Los Angeles: Lone Eagle Publishing Co., 1998.

Sitney, P. Adam. *The Essential Cinema: Essays on the Films in the Collection of Anthology Film Archives*. New York: Anthology Film Archives and New York University, 1975.

Slater, Robert, *Ovitz: The Inside Story of Hollywood's Most Controversial Power Broker*. New York: McGraw-Hill, 1997.

"Spreading Risks: Q&A on New Methods of Feature Film Financing," *Variety*, 8 January 1986, 28, 96, 100,

Squire, Jason E., ed. *The Movie Business Book*. second ed. New York: Fireside, 1992.

Stansweet, Stephen J. "As New Movie Studio Starts Work, It Seeks Credibility, Tries to Break Hollywood Mold," *Wall Street Journal*, 23 May 1983, 37.

Stanton, Michael J. "Ediflex, an Electronic Editing System," *American Cinematographer* 68, no. 7: 101–08.

Stein, Benjamin J. "It's About Time," *Barron's*, 17 July 1989, 13, 34.

Steinfels, Peter. *The Neo-Conservatives*. New York: Simon and Schuster, 1979.

Stetler, Russell ed. *The Military Art of People's War: Selected Writings of General Vo Nguyen Giap*. New York: Monthly Review Press, 1971.

Stevenson, Richard W. "In Hollywood, Big Just Gets Bigger, *New York Times*, 14 October 1990, section 3, p. 12.

Stewart, Al. "Homevid: Child of the '80s Seeks Continued Growth in the '90s," *Variety*, 24 January 1990, 153.

———. "Smut Out of Rut, Defying Its Foes," *Variety*, 17 January 1990, 1, 35–36.

———. "Vestron, Saying Nixed Loan Triggered Woes, Sues Bank," *Variety*, 23 August 1989, 59.

Tashiro, Charles Shiro. "Videophilia: What Happens When You Wait for It on Video," *Film Quarterly* 45(1) (Fall, 1991): 7–17.

Taylor, John. *Storming the Magic Kingdom: Wall Street, the Raiders and the Battle for Disney*. New York: Knopf, 1987.

"The Teachings of Chairman Jeff," *Variety*, 4 February 1991, 5, 24, 26.

Thompson, Ann. "George Lucas," *Premiere*, 12, no. 9 (May 1999): 68–77.

———. "Will Success Spoil the Weinstein Brothers?," *Film Comment* July/August 1989: 72–76.

"The Times of Harvey Milk: An Interview with Robert Epstein." *Cineaste* 14, no. 3 (1980): 26–27.

"Top Countries for U.S. Acquisitions Overseas 1980-1989," *Mergers and Acquisitions* (March/April 1990): 112.

"Top Video Rentals 1989," *Variety*, 24 January 1990, 153.

Torres-Rivas, Edelberto. "Guatemala-Crisis and Political Violence," *NACLA Report on the Americas* 14, no. 1 (January-February 1980): 16–27.

Tucker, Robert W. "The Purposes of American Power," *Foreign Affairs* 59, no. 2 (Winter 1980/81): 241–74.

Turgend, Tom. "Hungarian-Born Producer Becomes Hollywood Legend," *Northern California Jewish Bulletin* 22 December 1995: PG.

Turim, Maureen. *Abstraction in Avant-Garde Film*. Ann Arbor: UMI Press, 1985.

Tusher, Will. "Col Survey Shows Vid Rentals Far Outdistancing Admissions," *Variety*, 21 May 1986, 3, 44.

———. "Distribution's Theater Buys Near Peak," *Variety*, 7 January 1987, 3, 24.

———. "'I Never Had, Nor Expect a Film at Or Under Budget': De Laurentiis," *Variety*, 3 January 1979, 64.

———. "New PG-13 Rating Instituted By MPAA; Will Cover Some Pix That Would've Been R-Rated," *Variety*, 14 July 1984, 3, 30.

———."Sex Out of Theaters, Into Homes," *Variety*, 7 January 1981, 7, 21.

———. "U.S. Losses to Global Piracy Fell 25% in '89, per Valenti," *Variety*, 10 January 1990, 13, 21.

"U.S. Documentary: The Chill Wind of Reagonomics," *Sight and Sound* 56, no. 2 (Spring 1987): 78.

"UA Domestic Rentals Off 32%," *Variety*, 24 September 1980, 3, 6.

"UATC Posts Warning at Windows: 'Cruising' is X Film in R Clothing," *Variety*, 20 February 1980, 5.

"Vestron Deal Is Negotiated," *New York Times*, 1 November 1990, D5.

"Video Assisted Film Editing," *American Cinematographer* 63, no. 3: 297–308.

"Video Distribs, MPAA Shake on Cassette Ratings," *Variety*, 15 August 1984, 1, 94.

Vogel, Harold L. *Entertainment Industry Economics*. New York: Cambridge University Press, 1990, 87.

Walsh, Sharon. "Milken to Pay U.S. $47 Million to Settle Charge of Violating Ban," *Washington Post*, 27 February 1998, G1.

Waner, John. "Report on the New Eastman Color Print Film," *American Cinematographer* 65, no. 4 (April 1982): 391–92.

"Warner Buys Out Murdoch For $172-Mil," *Variety*, 21 March 1984, 1, 150.

Warrick, Patricia S. *Mind in Motion: The Fiction of Philip K. Dick*. Carbondale: Southern Illinois University Press, 1987.

Wasko, Janet. *Hollywood in the Information Age*. Austin: University of Texas Press, 1995.

Watkins, Roger."'Demented Revenge' Hits World Screens," *Variety*, 29 October 1980, 3, 33.

Wechsler, Dana. "Profits? What Profits?," *Forbes*, 19 February 1990, 38–40.

Wees, William C. *Recycled Images*. New York: Anthology Film Archives, 1993.

Werba, Hank. "The Image of Cinema in the '80s," *Variety*, 13 June 1979, 7, 32.

West, Dennis. "Revolution in Central America: A Survey of Recent Documentaries," *Cineaste* 12, no. 1 (1982): 18–23.

———. "Revolution in Central America: A Survey of Recent Documentaries." *Cineaste* 14, no. 3 (1986): 14–21.

"Why Consumers Won't Spend," *Business Week*, 4 October 1982, 40–42.

Wiese, Michael. "Dirty Dancing: A Case Study," *Film & Video Marketing*. Stoneham, MA: Butterworth Publishing, 1989, 119–218.

Wood, Peter. "'Dressed to Kill'-How a Film Changes from an 'X' to an 'R'," *New York Times*, 20 July 1980, C13, 19.

Wyatt, Justin. "The Formation of the Major Independent: Miramax, New Line and the New Hollywood," *Contemporary Hollywood Cinema*, eds. Steve Neale and Murray Smith. London: Routledge, 1998, 74–90.

———. *High Concept: Movies and Marketing in Hollywood*. Austin: University of Texas Press, 1994.

Young, Josh. "New Line Cinema: It Was a Very Good Year," *New York Times*, 18 September 1994, H13, 20–21.

Youngblood, Gene. "Metaphysical Structuralism: The Videotapes of Bill Viola," *Millennium Film Journal* no. 20-21 (Fall/Winter 1988-89): 81–114.

Zoglin, Richard. "An Outbreak of Rambomania," *Time*, 24 June 1985, 72–73.

Zucker, Carole. *Figures of Light: Actors and Directors Illuminate the Art of Film Acting*. New York: Plenum Press, 1995.

Picture Sources

Anthology Film Archives: 391, 400

James Benning: 397

Alan Berliner: 414

Beth B and Scott B: 398

Les Blank —Flower Films: 380

Lizzie Borden: 403, 405

Christine Choy: 424

Cineplex Odeon, 86–87

Sylvia de Swaan: 420

Nathaniel Dorsky: 432

Morgan Fisher: 410

Su Friedrich: 409, 433

Peter Hutton: 426, 437

Ken Jacobs: 411

Charles Lane: 422

Babette Mangolte: 428

Trinh T. Minh-ha: 407, 443

Movie Star News: 201

Museum of Modern Art/Film Stills Archive: 105, 207 (bottom), 317, 319, 321, 323, 325, 326, 327, 333, 334, 336, 337, 339, 373, 374, 376, 384, 386, 387

Richard Myers: 399

Andrew Noren: 427

Pat O'Neill: 429

Jerry Ohlinger's Movie Material Store, Inc.: 4, 6, 8, 12, 13, 16, 27, 28, 30, 32, 34, 36, 38, 43, 53, 56, 57, 76, 78, 91, 93, 106, 112, 113, 116, 119, 120, 134, 135, 137, 146, 151, 152, 153, 155, 157, 165, 167, 169, 171, 173, 174, 176, 177, 178, 180, 181, 184, 185, 188, 189, 194, 195, 203, 211, 212, 215, 219, 223, 225, 227, 229, 231, 234, 236, 239, 240, 243, 245, 249, 250, 252, 253, 257, 259, 261, 267, 269, 271, 274, 277, 281, 283, 285, 289, 291, 292, 296, 297, 299, 301, 304, 305, 311, 313, 344, 345, 349, 361, 363, 368

Photofest 55, 62, 72, 77, 77, 83, 100, 109, 205, 207 (top), 209, 216, 218

Yvonne Rainer: 406

Godfrey Reggio: 419

Remember When, Dallas, Texas: 146, 151, 152, 153, 155, 157

Peter Rose: 441

Phil Solomon: 415

Warren Sonbert: 417

William C. Wees: 395

General Index

Italic numerals signify illustrations.

Index of Films

Italic numerals indicate illustrations.

NOTTINGHAM UNIVERSITY LIBRARY